Be™

DEVELOPER'S
GUIDE

DEVELOPER'S GUIDE

The Be Development Team

O'REILLY™

Cambridge · Köln · Paris · Sebastopol · Tokyo

Be™ Developer's Guide

Published by O'Reilly & Associates, Inc., 101 Morris Street, Sebastopol, CA 95472.

Be, Inc.
800 El Camino Real
Suite 300
Menlo Park, CA 94025
http://www.be.com

ISBN: 1-56592-287-5

Table of Contents

If you use a computer everyday, chances are good that your hardware is no more than five years old. And if you actually *like* computers, it's more likely that you own a box that's less than two years old. How old is your operating system? Updates help, certainly, but how old is the *core* software technology behind your "Version X" or "UltraLimp '96" OS?

In the last five years, the computer hardware industry has undergone drastic changes. CPU speeds and disk capacities have shot through the roof while the price per MegaHertz and Gigabyte has fallen dramatically. Computers now boast two, four, even eight CPUs on a single motherboard. The major OS vendors try to keep up with this change, but they have other concerns, such as maintaining backwards compatibility and supporting their loyal following. They can't make the clean break with the past that new hardware demands.

The BeOS is a fresh start. Be likes hardware—the faster the better. If you've seen it running, then you know what a computer can do when the dead weight is removed.

But the BeOS isn't just about speed. It's also about the things that a modern OS should give you automatically, with no outboard equipment, and without having to reboot your computer every time you make a change. Like networking, true parallel processing, real-time response in the user interface, recognition of standard data formats. Intelligent design that recognizes and knows how to use the capacities of the hardware to its fullest: That's the reason for the BeOS.

About the Be Books

There are two books that make up the Be developer's reference bible. Together, they contain descriptions of every C++ class, every function, every constant that the BeOS defines, and let you know how and when to use them. If you want to design an application that will run on the BeOS, you'll need these books.

The first book, the *Be Developer's Guide*, describes the foundation "kits" in the OS; these are the kits that every developer will need to understand:

- *The Application Kit.* This is the kit that gets you started.
- *The Storage Kit.* An interface to the file system.
- *The Interface Kit.* Windows, views, buttons, controls—everything you need to design a graphic user interface.
- *The Kernel Kit.* Access to the lowest programmable level of the BeOS.
- *The Support Kit.* A catchall for common functionality and definitions.

Be Advanced Topics—the "geek" book—is about special topics. There you'll find the kits that don't pertain to every application. But most developers will need to know at least a little bit about some of them:

- *The Media Kit.* Real-time processing of audio and video data.
- *The Midi Kit.* MIDI data generation and processing, including the Headspace® General MIDI synthesizer.
- *The Game Kit.* Lets your game take over the machine.
- *The OpenGL Kit.* An implementation of the OpenGL® 3D graphics interface.
- *The Network Kit.* An interface to the network and mail.
- *The Device Kit.* Lets you create your own device drivers.

Support Information

Be provides as much information as possible about the BeOS via the Web and other electronic means. Our belief is that if you can get help yourself, even in the middle of the night, you'll feel better about your experience with the BeOS.

For basic customer and technical support, visit the Support section of the Be web site at *http://www.be.com/support/index.html*.

Support offers a wealth of Frequently Asked Questions (FAQs), software updates, and user and technical manuals, including links to the latest version of this Developer's Guide, in both on-line and downloadable formats. You can also find information about Be's electronic mailing lists, and on-going information about the BeOS, at the following sites:

Be FAQs: *http://www.be.com/support/qandas/index.html*

BeOS Updates: *http://www.be.com/support/updates/index.html*

Be Documentation: *http://www.be.com/documentation/index.html*

Be Internet Mailing Lists: *http://www.be.com/aboutbe/mailinglists.html*

Also available on our web site is an Assistance Request form, to use when you cannot find the information you need on the web site, and want to request help from our Customer Technical Support group: *http://www.be.com/support/assist/custsupport.html*.

If you cannot submit a help request via a web form, send e-mail to one of our support addresses. Please help us help you by including as much information about the problem as possible, such as *the* configuration of your system, what you were doing, what happened, what you expected to have happen and why, and anything else about your configuration or problem that you think we should know.

Here is a list of Be's support addresses and their uses.

For BeOS users in the Americas or Pacific Rim:

- *custsupport@be.com* — for questions regarding set up, installation, configuration and compatibility of the BeOS, or other technical questions that are not about programming or coding.

- *custservices@be.com* — for assistance with obtaining any of our products or for questions about your BeOS subscription.

For BeOS users in Europe:

- *custsupport@beeurope.com* — for questions regarding set up, installation, configuration and compatibility of the BeOS, or other technical questions that are not about programming or coding.

- *custservices@beeurope.com* — for assistance with obtaining any of our products or for questions about your BeOS subscription.

By using the Web as your first stop for support information, you help yourself and us. You will likely find the answer yourself more quickly than we can get it to you, and we can conserve our resources to help you more quickly on those occasions when you need more in-depth assistance.

If web searching and e-mail don't do the trick and you would rather talk to a human, you can call us. We're available Monday through Friday, between 6 AM and 6 PM (Pacific time) for people in the Western hemisphere and 8 AM to 6 PM GMT for those of you in the Eastern Hemisphere. Be's support phone numbers can be found (you guessed it) on our web site at *http://www.be.com/support/index.html*.

CHAPTER ONE

Introduction

Introduction

The Be operating system (BeOS™) is designed to take advantage of modern computer hardware, particularly machines with more than one CPU. The BeOS offers:

- Preemptive multithreading (true "multitasking")
- Protected address spaces
- Virtual memory
- An attributed file system
- Dynamically loaded device drivers
- Interapplication messaging
- Built-in networking
- Real-time streaming of audio and video data
- Shared, dynamically linked libraries
- An object-oriented programming environment

The BeOS is designed for efficient multithreading from top to bottom. For example, the application framework creates a separate thread for each window. On systems with more than one processor, the kernel automatically splits assignments between the CPUs and gives priority to threads that need uninterrupted attention.

The application programming interface (API) is designed to make the features of the BeOS easy to use. Written in C++, it includes numerous class definitions from which you can take much of the framework for your application.

Software Overview

The BeOS software lies in three layers:

- A microkernel that works directly with the hardware and device drivers.

- Servers that attend to the needs of running applications. The servers take over much of the low-level work that would normally have to be done by each application.

- Dynamically linked libraries that provide an interface to the servers and the Be software that you use to build your applications.

Applications are built on top of these layers, as illustrated below:

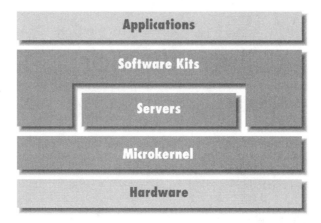

The API for all system software is organized into several "kits." Each kit has a distinct domain—there's a kit that contains the fundamental software for creating and running an application, a kit for putting together a user interface, one for accessing the file system, another for networking, and so on.

Servers

Servers are separate processes that run in the background and carry out basic tasks for client applications. They typically serve any number of running applications at the same time.

If you look inside the */boot/beos/system/servers* directory, you'll see a number of servers listed. The one that you should know about is the Application Server.

The *Application Server* handles most of the low-level user interface work: It creates and manages windows on the screen, renders images, and monitors what the user is doing with the keyboard and mouse. It's the application's conduit for both drawing output and event input.

An application connects itself to the server when it constructs a BApplication object (as defined in the Application Kit). This should be one of the first things that every application does. Every BWindow object (defined in the Interface Kit) also makes a connection to the Application Server when it's constructed. Each window runs independently of other windows—in its own thread and with its own connection to the server.

Kits

The Be software kits are written in C++ and make significant use of class definitions (the two notable exceptions are the Kernel Kit and Network Kit, which are primarily straight C). Some of the kits are important to all applications, others are used only by applications that are concerned with specific topics. Most applications will need to open files and put windows on-screen, for example; fewer will want to process audio data.

The kits are summarized below:

- The **Application Kit** identifies your application as a distinct entity, lets your application communicate with other applications, and defines a messaging service that the system uses to notify your application of user events (mouse down, key up, and so on).

  The Application Kit's principal class is BApplication. Virtually every application must have one (and only one) BApplication object to act as its global representative. Begin with this kit before programming with any of the others.

- The **Storage Kit** is an interface to the file system. The BeOS recognizes more than one file system architecture. These architectures are abstracted by the kernel so that each distinct architecture "looks" the same to the Storage Kit. Some architectures are more powerful than others, but the fundamental concept of hierarchically organized files and directories is enforced at the kernel level.

- The **Interface Kit** is used to build and run a graphical and interactive user interface. It structures the tasks of drawing in windows and handling the messages that report user actions (like clicks and keystrokes). Its BWindow class encapsulates an interface to windows. Its BView class embodies a complete graphics environment for drawing.

  Each window is represented by a separate BWindow object and is served by a separate thread. A BWindow has a hierarchy of associated BView objects; each BView draws one portion of what's displayed in the window and responds to user actions prompted by the display. The Interface Kit defines a number of specific BViews, such as BListView, BButton, BScrollBar, and BTextView—as well as various supporting classes, such as BRegion, BBitmap, and BPicture.

  Every application that puts a window on-screen will need to make use of this kit.

- The **Kernel Kit** defines a C interface for creating, coordinating, and communicating between threads. It also defines a system of memory management, letting you share memory between application and lock chunks of memory into RAM. Applications that rely on the higher-level kits may not need to use much of this kit.

- The **Media Kit** defines an architecture for processing audio and video data. It gives applications the ability to generate, examine, manipulate, and realize (or "render") medium-specific data in real time. Applications can, for example, synchronize the transmission of data to different media devices, so they can easily incorporate and coordinate audio and video output.

- The **Midi Kit** lets you generate and process music data in MIDI (Musical Instrument Digital Interface) format. The Kit includes a General MIDI synthesizer designed by the folks at Headspace®, Incorporated (*http://www.headspace.com*).

- The **OpenGL Kit** is an implementation of the OpenGL® 3D graphics interface.

- The **Device Kit** defines the API for creating loadable device drivers. Drivers for graphics cards run as extensions of the Application Server; printer drivers run in the Print Server. All other drivers are loaded by the kernel.

- The **Game Kit** consists of a single class—BWindowScreen—that gives an application direct access to the graphics card driver for the screen. Designed for the needs of game makers, BWindowScreen can be used by any application— even the ones that don't let you shoot at aliens.

- The **Network Kit** contains C functions that let you identify remote machines that are connected to the network and communicate with those machines through the TCP and UDP message protocols. This kit also contains API (including the BMailMessage class) that lets applications talk to the Be mail daemon and send and receive SMTP and POP mail messages.

- The **Support Kit** is a collection of various defined types, error codes, and other facilities that support Be application development and the work of the other kits. It includes basic type definitions, the BList class for organizing ordered collections of data, and a system for archiving objects and reconstructing them from their archives.

Libraries

The Be software is organized into a set of dynamically linked libraries (DLLs). Code from the library is not compiled into your application. Instead, the library is resident on the user's machine and your application links to it when it's launched.

The libraries are found in */boot/beos/system/lib*; dynamic libraries are identified by a ".so" suffix:

Library	Contents
libroot.so	Provides access to the kernel; all applications must link with this library.
libbe.so	Contains the Application, Interface, and Support Kits, as well as most of the Storage Kit. All applications should link with this one, too.
libGL.so	The OpenGL Kit.
libdevice.so	The Device Kit.
libgame.so	The Game Kit.
libmedia.so	The Media Kit.
libmidi.so	The Midi Kit.
libmail.so	The library for applications that want to use the mail portions of the Network Kit.
libnet.so	The rest of the Network Kit.
libnetdev.so	The library for developing a Network Server add-on.
libtracker.so	Contains parts of the Tracker application that can be used by other applications. Currently, the library contains the code for the BFilePanel class (the API is defined by the Storage Kit).

Conventions

This section looks at some of the conventions that the BeOS and this book follow. It includes:

Documentation conventions
The way we've put this book together—how classes are described and how font typefaces are used.

Naming conventions
Our standards for the API.

Programming conventions
The conventions for allocating and freeing memory, for creating objects, and more.

Documentation Conventions

Class Descriptions

Since most Be software is organized into classes, much of the documentation you'll be reading in this book will be about classes and their member functions. Each class description is divided into the following sections:

Overview

An introductory description of the class.

Data Members

A list of the public and protected data members declared by the class, if there are any. If this section is missing, the class declares only private data members, or doesn't declare any data members at all.

Hook Functions

A list of the virtual functions that you're invited (or expected) to override in a derived class. Hook functions are called automatically by the system at critical junctures; they "hook" application-specific code into the generic workings of the kit.

Hook functions are listed in this section only for the class that first declares them. If class *A* declares a hook function and its derived class, *B*, implements it, the function will be described as a "Member Function" for both classes, but will be listed as a hook function only for class *A*.

Constructor and Destructor

The class constructor and destructor. Only documented constructors produce valid members of a class. Don't rely on default constructors.

Static Functions

The static functions that are declared for the class. Static functions don't operate on a particular object, but serve a class-wide purpose. Often they return an instance of the class or set a state shared by all instances.

Member Functions

A full description of all public and protected member functions, including hook functions—but not static functions and the constructor and destructor, which are described in their own sections. The functions are alphabetized.

Operators

A description of any operators that are overloaded to handle the class type.

If a section isn't relevant for a particular class—if the class doesn't define any hook functions or overload any operators, for example—that section is omitted.

Rely only on the documented API. You may occasionally find a public function declared in a header file but not documented in the class description. The reason it's not documented is probably because it's not supported and not safe; don't use it.

Typography

API elements are presented in a distinct font—for example, `system_time()`, `be_app`, and `B_STRING_TYPE`. The only exceptions are class names, which appear in the same font as surrounding text—for example, BFile and BOutlineListView.

Where it presents the syntax of a function or data structure, the book gives each part of the definition its own font style. For example:

---

virtual status_t **Invoke**(BMessage **message* = NULL)

typedef char **font_family**[B_FONT_FAMILY_LENGTH + 1]

Four different fonts are used:

- The API element being defined is bold—for example, **Invoke()** and **font_family**.
- The names of other API elements that enter into the definition (such as default arguments) are in a non-bold version of the API font—for example, NULL and B_FONT_FAMILY_LENGTH.
- The names of parameters are italic—for example, *message*.
- Data types are in plain (roman) text—status_t, BMessage, and char in the examples above—as are other keywords like typedef and virtual.

Naming Conventions

All our class names begin with the prefix "B". The rest of the name is in mixed case; for example:

BTextView

BFile

BDACStream

BMessageQueue

BScrollBar

BList

The simplest thing you can do to prevent namespace collisions is to refrain from putting the "B" prefix on class names you invent.

Other names associated with a class—the names of data members and member functions—are also in mixed case. The names of member functions begin with an uppercase letter—for example, `AddResource()` and `UpdateIfNeeded()`. The names of data members begin with a lowercase letter (`what` and `bottom`). Member names are in a protected namespace and won't clash with the names you assign in your own code; they therefore don't have—or need—a "B" prefix.

All other names in the Be API are single case—either all uppercase or all lowercase—and use underbars to mark where separate words are joined into a single name.

The names of constants are all uppercase and begin with the prefix "B_". For example:

```
B_LONG_TYPE
B_OP_OVER
B_PULSE
```

The only exceptions are common constants not specific to the Be operating system. For example:

```
true
false
NULL
```

All other names—global variables, macros, nonmember functions, members of structures, and defined types—are all lowercase. Global variables generally begin with "be_",

```
be_app
be_roster
be_clipboard
```

but other names lack a prefix. They're distinguished only by being lowercase. For example:

```
rgb_color
system_time()
app_info
```

To summarize:

Category	Prefix	Spelling
Class names	B	Mixed case
Member functions	*none*	Mixed case, beginning with an uppercase letter
Data members	*none*	Mixed case, beginning with a lowercase letter
Constants	B_	All uppercase
Global variables	be_	All lowercase
Everything else	*none*	All lowercase

Occasionally, private names are visible in public header files. These names are marked with prefixed underbars, and often postfixed ones as well—for example, `_pthread_` and `_remove_volume_()`. Don't rely on these names in the code you write. They're neither documented nor supported, and may change or disappear in the next release.

An underbar prefix is also used for kit-internal names that may intrude on an application's namespace, even though they don't show up in a header file. For example, the kits use some behind-the-scenes threads and give them names like "_pulse_task_" and they may put kit-internal data in public messages under names like "_button_". If you were to assign the same names to your threads and data entries, they might conflict with kit code. Since you can't anticipate every name used internally by the kits, it's best to avoid all names that begin in underbars.

Programming Conventions

The software kits were designed with some conventions in mind. Knowing a few of them will help you write efficient code and avoid pitfalls. The conventions for MIME types, memory allocation, and object creation are described below.

MIME Types

To type data, files, applications, protocols, and just about anything else that needs to be identified at run time, the BeOS adopts—and extends—the MIME (Multipurpose Internet Mail Extensions) media types. This single system is used throughout the operating system.

A MIME media type is a string in the following form:

supertype/subtype

The top-level *supertype* name designates a general category of data—such as text or image data—and the *subtype* names a specific format of that general type. For example, "image/jpeg" indicates image data in JPEG format and "text/plain" is plain, unadorned text.

The MIME standard defines seven top-level *supertype* categories. They are:

"text"
  Data formats that encode characters; "plain" and "enriched" are common subtypes.

"image"
  Data formats that capture pictures that can be produced on a display device like a monitor or printer; "jpeg" and "gif" are two of the subtypes.

"audio"
> Data that can produce sounds through an audio output device, like a speaker or a telephone; "basic" is a recognized subtype.

"video"
> Formats that capture moving images; "mpeg" is one subtype.

"application"
> Executable data.

"multipart"
> Multiple-format data.

"message"
> This is used to indicate that the data is an e-mail message.

In the BeOS, every application is identified by a type string in the "application" category. For example, "application/x-vnd.Be-simpleclock" identifies the Clock application and "application/x-vnd.Be-STEE" identifies StyledEdit. This MIME type name serves as the application's *signature*.

Be defines an additional supertype:

"suite"
> Identifiers for groups of message protocols.

Although the set of type categories is limited, experimental and private subtypes can be freely formed. However, they should be marked with an initial uppercase or lowercase "x", as in the signature examples above.

Responsibility for Allocated Memory

The general rule is that whoever allocates memory is responsible for freeing it:

- If your application allocates memory, it should free it.

- If a kit allocates memory and passes your application a pointer to it, the kit retains responsibility for freeing it.

For example, a `Text()` function like this one,

```
char *text = someObject->Text();
```

returns a pointer to a string of characters residing in memory that belongs to the object that allocated it. The object is responsible for freeing the string.

The data that's passed back to you by pointer isn't guaranteed to be valid forever. In general, you should copy pointed-to data if you want it to stick around.

In contrast, a `GetText()` function would copy the string into memory that your application provides:

```
char *text = (char *)malloc(someObject->TextLength() + 1);
someObject->GetText(text);
```

Your application is responsible for the copy.

In some cases, you're asked to allocate an object that kit functions fill in with data:

```
BPicture *picture = new BPicture;
someViewObject->BeginPicture(picture);
. . .
someViewObject->EndPicture();
```

Again, you're responsible for freeing the object.

Assigned Responsibility

The principle of you-allocate-it-you-free-it is modified in cases where one object is assigned to another. For example, in the Interface Kit, you can make one BView object the child of another BView:

```
myView->AddChild(anotherView);
```

The parent BView takes responsibility for its child; when the parent is deleted, it will make sure that its children are also deleted. Similarly, a BMenu object in the Interface Kit takes responsibility for its BMenuItems.

Exceptions

Sometimes a BeOS class is in a better position to allocate memory than the application. An example is the `FindResource()` function in the BResources class of the Storage Kit. This function allocates memory on the caller's behalf and copies resource data to it; it then passes responsibility for the memory to the caller:

```
size_t length;
void *res = resObj.FindResource(B_RAW_TYPE, "name", &length);
```

The BResources object allocates the memory in this case because it knows better than the caller how much resource data there is and, therefore, how much memory to allocate.

Exceptions like this are rare and are clearly stated in the documentation.

Object Allocation

All objects can be dynamically allocated (using the **new** operator). Most, but not all, can also be statically allocated (put on the stack). In general, you should statically allocate objects whenever you can. However, some objects may not work correctly unless they're allocated in dynamic memory. The general rules are:

- If you assign one object to another (as, for example, a child BView in the Interface Kit is assigned to its parent BView or a BMessage is assigned to a BInvoker), you should dynamically allocate the assigned object.

    This is because there may be circumstances that would cause the other object to free the object you assigned it. For example, a parent BView deletes its children when it is itself deleted. In the Be software kits, all such deletions are done with the `delete` operator. Therefore, the original allocation should always be done with `new`.

- If an object controls a thread, it must be dynamically allocated. This applies to all BLooper objects, including the BApplication object (in the Application Kit) and all BWindows and BAlerts (in the Interface Kit).

CHAPTER TWO

The Application Kit

Application Inheritance Hierarchy

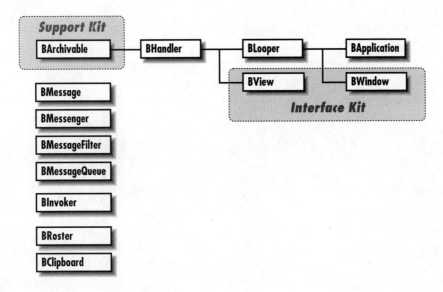

The Application Kit

The Application Kit is the starting point for all applications. Its classes establish an application as an identifiable entity—one that can cooperate and communicate with other applications (including the Tracker). It lays a foundation for the other kits. Before designing and building your application, you should become comfortably familiar with this basic kit.

There are four parts to the Application Kit:

- *Messaging*. The kit sets up a mechanism through which an application can easily make itself multithreaded and a messaging service that permits the threads to talk to each other. This service can deliver messages within your own application, or from one application to another—it's used for both inter- and intra-application communication. It's also used by the BeOS to deliver user event messages (key clicks, mouse moves) to your application.

- *The BApplication class*. Every application must have a single instance of the BApplication class—or of a class derived from BApplication. Your app's BApplication object establishes a connection to the Application Server. The server is a background process that takes over many of the fundamental tasks common to all applications: It renders images in windows, controls the cursor, and keeps track of system resources.

  The BApplication object also runs the application's main message loop, where it receives messages that concern the application as a whole. Externally, this object represents the application to other applications; internally, it's the center where applicationwide services and global information can be found. Because of its pivotal role, it's assigned to a global variable, **be_app**, to make it easily accessible.

  Other kits—the Interface Kit in particular—won't work until a BApplication object has been constructed.

- *The BRoster class.* The BRoster object keeps track of all running applications. It can identify applications, launch them, and provide the information needed to set up communications with them.

- *The BClipboard class.* The BClipboard object provides an interface to the clipboard where cut and copied data can be stored, and from which it can be pasted.

The messaging framework is described in the next section, followed by a discussion of scripting. The classes follow in alphabetical order.

Messaging

The Application Kit provides a high-level messaging service built on top of the kernel's system of ports, threads, and semaphores. The service lets you:

- Put together parcels of structured information that can be sent from one thread to another. The parcels are BMessage objects.

- Deliver messages to a destination. This is the job of a BMessenger object—although local messages can be "posted" directly, without the aid of a messenger. BMessengers represent remote destinations and can be used instead of pointers to keep track of local objects.

- Process messages as they arrive. This task is entrusted to BLooper objects. A BLooper sits on top of a thread in which it runs a message loop, getting messages and dispatching them one at a time.

- Define your own message-handling code. A BLooper dispatches an arriving message by calling a "hook" function of a BHandler object. Each application can implement these functions as it sees fit.

The following sections examine the messaging system components.

Messages

BMessage objects are parcels of information that can be transferred between threads. The message source constructs a BMessage object, adds whatever information it wants to it, and then passes the parcel to a function that delivers it to a destination.

A BMessage can hold structured data of any type or amount. When you add data to a message, you assign it a name and a type code. If more than one piece of information is added under the same name, the BMessage sets up an array of data for that name. The name (along with an optional index into the array) is then used to retrieve the data.

For example, this code adds a floating-point number to a BMessage under the name "pi",

```
BMessage *msg = new BMessage;
float pi = 3.1416;
msg->AddData("pi", B_FLOAT_TYPE, &pi, sizeof(float));
```

and this code locates it:

```
float *pi;
ssize_t numBytes;
msg->FindData("pi", B_FLOAT_TYPE, &pi, &numBytes);
```

A number of specialized functions simplify the code for specific data types. Adding and finding pi would most typically look like this:

```
BMessage *msg = new BMessage;
msg->AddFloat("pi", 3.1416);

float pi;
msg->FindFloat("pi", &pi);
```

Command Constant

In addition to named data, a BMessage object also has a public data member, called what, that says what the message is about. The constant may:

- Convey a request of some kind (such as SORT_ITEMS or BEGIN_ANIMATION).
- Announce an event (such as LIMIT_EXCEEDED or B_WINDOW_RESIZED).
- Label the information that's being passed (such as PATIENT_INFO or NEW_COLOR).

Not all messages have data fields, but all should have a command constant. A constant like RECEIPT_ACKNOWLEDGED or CANCEL may be enough to convey a complete message.

The BeOS defines command constants for a number of standard messages—such as B_REPLY, B_KEY_DOWN, and B_RESET_STATUS_BAR. They're discussed where the topics they relate to come up in this manual and are summarized in Appendix A, *Message Protocols*.

By convention, the constant alone is sufficient to identify a message. It's assumed that all messages with the same constant are used for the same purpose and contain the same kinds of data.

Type Codes

Data added to a BMessage is associated with a name and stored with two relevant pieces of information:

- The number of bytes in the data
- A type code indicating what kind of data it is

The Support Kit defines a number of codes for common data types, including these:

Type	Meaning
B_CHAR_TYPE	A single character
B_INT32_TYPE	A 32-bit integer (int32, uint32, vint32, or vuint32)
B_FLOAT_TYPE	A float
B_SIZE_T_TYPE	A size_t value
B_MESSENGER_TYPE	A BMessenger object
B_RECT_TYPE	A BRect object
B_RGB_COLOR_TYPE	An rgb_color structure
B_STRING_TYPE	A null-terminated character string
B_COLOR_8_BIT_TYPE	Raw bitmap data in the B_COLOR_8_BIT color space

In addition, B_MIME_TYPE indicates that the name of the data item is a MIME-like string that conveys the true type of the data. The full list of types can be found under "Type Codes" in Chapter 6, *The Support Kit*.

You can add data to a message even if its type isn't on the list. A BMessage will accept any kind of data; you must simply invent your own codes for unlisted types.

Message Protocols

Both the source and the destination of a message must agree upon its format—the what constant and the names and types of data fields. They must also agree on details of the exchange—when the message can be sent, whether it requires a response, what the format of the reply should be, what it means if an expected data item is omitted, and so on.

None of this is a problem for messages that are used only within an application; the application developer can keep track of the details. However, protocols must be published for messages that communicate between applications. You're urged to publish the specifications for all messages your application is willing to accept from outside sources and for all those that it can package for delivery to other applications. The more that message protocols are shared, the easier it is for applications to cooperate with each other and take advantage of each other's special features.

The software kits define protocols for a number of messages. They're discussed in Appendix A, *Message Protocols*.

Extensions

It's important that the message constants and type codes you define not be confused with those already defined by the BeOS, or those that the BeOS might define in the future. For this reason, we've adopted a strict convention for assigning values to all Be-defined constants. The value assigned will always be formed by combining four characters into a multicharacter constant, with the characters limited to uppercase letters and the underbar. For example, `B_KEY_DOWN` and `B_VALUE_CHANGED` are defined as follows:

```
enum {
    . . .
    B_KEY_DOWN = '_KYD',
    B_VALUE_CHANGED = '_VCH',
    . . .
};
```

And `B_DOUBLE_TYPE` and `B_POINTER_TYPE` are defined as follows:

```
enum {
    . . .
    B_DOUBLE_TYPE = 'DBLE',
    B_POINTER_TYPE  = 'PNTR',
    . . .
};
```

Use a different convention to define your own constants (or you'll risk having your message misinterpreted). Include some lowercase letters, numerals, or symbols (other than the underbar) in your multicharacter constants, or assign numeric values that can't be confused with the value of four concatenated characters. For example, you might safely define constants like these:

```
#define PRIVATE_TYPE    0x1f3d
#define OWN_TYPE        'Rcrd'
```

Message Ownership

Typically, when an application creates an object, it retains responsibility for it; it's up to the application to free the objects it allocates when they're no longer needed. BMessage objects are no exception to this rule. Passing a message to the messaging mechanism doesn't relieve you of responsibility for it. The system makes a copy so you can delete the object immediately if you have no further use for it.

Similarly, when the system delivers a BMessage to you, it retains ownership of the object and will eventually delete it—after you're finished responding to it. A message receiver can assert responsibility for a message—essentially replacing the system as its owner—by detaching it from the message loop (with BLooper's `DetachCurrentMessage()` function).

Message Loops

In the Be model, messages are delivered to threads running *message loops*. Arriving messages are first placed in a queue. They're then taken from the queue one at a time and dispatched to an object that can respond. When the response is finished, the thread deletes the message and takes the next one from the queue—or, if the queue is empty, waits until another message arrives.

The message loop therefore dominates the thread. The thread does nothing but get messages and respond to them; it's driven by message input.

BLooper objects set up these message loops. A BLooper spawns a thread and sets the loop in motion. Posting a message to the BLooper delivers it to the thread (places it in the queue). The BLooper removes messages from the queue and dispatches them to BHandler objects. BHandlers are the objects ultimately responsible for received messages. Everything that the thread does begins with a BHandler's response to a message.

Two hook functions come into play in this process—one defined in the BLooper class and one declared by BHandler:

- BLooper's `DispatchMessage()` function is called to pass responsibility for a message to a BHandler object. It's fully implemented by BLooper (and kit classes derived from BLooper) and is only rarely overridden by applications.

- `MessageReceived()` is the BHandler function that `DispatchMessage()` calls by default. It's up to applications to implement this function to handle expected messages. For example:

```
void MyHandler::MessageReceived(BMessage *message)
{
    switch ( message->what ) {
    case COME_HERE:
        . . .
        break;
    case GO_THERE:
        . . .
        break;
    default:
        baseClass::MessageReceived(message);
        break;
    }
}
```

There's a close relationship between the BLooper role of running a message loop and the BHandler role of responding to messages. The BLooper class inherits from BHandler, so the same object can fill both roles. The BLooper is the default handler for the messages it receives.

While a thread is responding to a message, it keeps the BLooper that dispatched the message locked. The thread locks the BLooper before calling `DispatchMessage()` and unlocks it after `DispatchMessage()` returns.

Handler Associations

To be notified of an arriving message, a BHandler must "belong" to the BLooper; it must have been added to the BLooper's list of eligible handlers. The list can contain any number of objects, but at any given time a BHandler can belong to only one BLooper.

Handlers that belong to the same BLooper can be chained in a linked list. If an object can't respond to a message, the system passes the message to its next handler.

BLooper's `AddHandler()` function sets up the looper-handler association; BHandler's `SetNextHandler()` sets the handler-handler link.

Message Filters

You can arrange to have a filtering function examine an incoming message before the BLooper dispatches it—before `DispatchMessage()` and the target BHandler's hook function are called. The filter can set up conditions for handling the message, change the target handler, or even prevent the message from being dispatched and respond to it directly.

The filtering function is associated with a BMessageFilter object, which holds the criteria for when the filter should apply. If a BMessageFilter is attached to a BHandler (`AddFilter()`), it filters only messages destined for that BHandler. If it's attached as a common filter to a BLooper object (`AddCommonFilter()`), it can filter any message that the BLooper dispatches, no matter what the handler. (In addition to the list of common filters, a BLooper can, like other BHandlers, maintain a list of filters specific to its role as a target handler.)

System Messages

Special dispatching is provided for a subset of messages defined by the system. These *system messages* are dispatched not by calling `MessageReceived()`, but by calling a BHandler hook function specific to the message.

System messages generally originate from within the Be operating system (from servers, the kits, or the Tracker). They notify applications of external events, usually something the user has done—moved the mouse, pressed a key, resized a window, selected a document to open, or some other action of a similar sort. The command constant of the message names the event—for example, B_KEY_DOWN, B_SCREEN_CHANGED, or B_REFS_RECEIVED—and the message may carry data describing the event. The receiver is free to respond to the message (or not) in any way that's appropriate.

A few system messages name an action the receiver is expected to take, such as B_ZOOM or B_MINIMIZE. The message tells the receiver what must be done. Even these messages are prompted by an event of some kind—such as the user clicking the zoom button in a window tab.

System messages have a fixed format. The names and types of data fields are always the same for each kind of message. For example, the system message that reports a user keystroke on the keyboard—a "key-down" event—has B_KEY_DOWN as the command constant, a "when" field for the time of the event, a "key" field for the key that was hit, a "modifiers" field for the modifier keys that were down at the time, and so on.

Although the set of system-defined messages is small, they're the most frequent messages for most applications. For example, when the user types a sentence, the application receives a series of B_KEY_DOWN messages, one for each keystroke.

Specialized BLoopers

System messages aren't delivered to just any BLooper object. The software kits derive specialized classes from BLooper to give significant entities in the application their own threads and message loops. These are the objects that receive system messages and define how they're dispatched. Each message is matched to the specific kind of BLooper that's concerned with the particular event it reports or the particular instruction it delivers.

More specifically, both the BApplication class in this kit and the BWindow class in the Interface Kit derive from BLooper:

• The BApplication object runs a message loop in the main thread and receives messages that concern the application as a whole—such as requests to quit the application or to open a document.

• Each BWindow object runs in its own thread and receives messages that report activity in the user interface—including notifications that the user typed a particular character on the keyboard, moved the cursor on-screen, or pressed a mouse button. Every window that the user sees is represented by a separate BWindow object.

Each of these classes is concerned with only a subset of system messages—BApplication with *application messages* (discussed on page 41) and BWindow objects with *interface messages* (discussed in Chapter 4, *The Interface Kit*). In addition, the generic BLooper class defines a B_QUIT_REQUESTED message that's common to both groups. Each class arranges for special handling of the system messages it's concerned with.

Message-Specific Dispatching

Every system message is dispatched by calling a specific virtual "hook" function, one that's matched to the message. For example, when the Application Server sends a B_KEY_DOWN message to the window where the user is typing, the BWindow determines which object is responsible for displaying typed characters and calls that object's KeyDown() virtual function. Similarly, a message that reports a user request for basic information about the application is dispatched by calling the BApplication object's AboutRequested() function. Messages that report the movement of the cursor are dispatched by calling MouseMoved(), those that report a change in the screen configuration by calling ScreenChanged(), and so on.

These hook functions are declared in classes derived from BHandler and are often recognizable by their names. Hook functions fall into three groups:

- Those that are left to the application to implement. These functions are named for what they announce—for what led to the function call rather than for what the function might be implemented to do. KeyDown() is an example.

- Those that have a default implementation to cover the common case. Like those in the first group, these functions also are named for the occurrence that prompted the function call. ScreenChanged() is an example.

- Those that are fully implemented to perform a particular task. These are functions that you can call, but they're also hooks that are called for you. Like most ordinary functions, they're named for what they do—like Zoom()—not for what led to the function call.

The hook functions that are matched to system messages can fall into any of these three categories. Since most system messages report events, they mostly fall into the first two categories. The function is named for the message, and the message for the event it reports.

However, if a system message delivers an instruction for the application to do something in particular, its hook function falls into the third group. The function is fully implemented in system software, but can be overridden by the application. The function is named for what it does, and the message is named for the function.

Picking a Handler and a Hook Function

A BLooper picks a BHandler for a system message based on what the message is. For example, a BWindow calls upon the object that displays the current selection to handle a B_KEY_DOWN message. It asks the object in charge of the area where the user clicked to handle a B_MOUSE_DOWN message. And it handles messages that affect the window as a whole—such as B_WINDOW_RESIZED—itself.

The BLooper identifies system messages by their command constants alone (their **what** data members). If a message is received and its command constant matches the constant for a system message, the BLooper will dispatch it by calling the message-specific hook function—regardless what data field the message may have.

If the constant doesn't match a system message that the BLooper knows about, the message is dispatched by calling `MessageReceived()`. `MessageReceived()` is, therefore, reserved for application-defined messages. It's typically implemented to distribute the responsibility for received messages to other functions. That's something that's already taken care of for system messages, since each of them is mapped to its own function.

Application-Defined Messages

Although the system creates and delivers most messages, an application can create messages of its own and have them delivered to a chosen destination. There are three ways to initiate a message:

- Messages can be *posted* to a thread of the same application.
- They can be *sent* to a thread anywhere, generally one in a remote application.
- They can be dragged and *dropped*.

Posted Messages

Messages are posted by calling a BLooper's `PostMessage()` function. For example:

```
BMessage message(FORGET_ABOUT_IT);
myLooper->PostMessage(&message, targetHandler);
```

This hands the message to the BLooper so that it can be dispatched in sequence along with other messages the thread receives. Posting depends on the message source knowing the address of the destination BLooper; it therefore works only for application-internal messages.

Target Handlers

As the example above shows, it's possible to name a target BHandler when posting a message. The only requirement is that the BHandler must belong to the BLooper; it must have been added to the BLooper's list of eligible handlers.

The target is respected when the message is dispatched; the dispatcher always calls a hook function belonging to the designated BHandler. If the message matches one that the system defines and the target BHandler is the kind of object that's expected to handle that type of message, the dispatcher will call the target's message-specific hook function. However, if the designated target isn't the handler of design for the message, the BLooper will call its `MessageReceived()` function.

For example, if a `B_KEY_DOWN` message is posted to a BWindow object and a BView is named as the target, the BWindow will dispatch the message by calling the BView's `KeyDown()` function. However, if the BWindow itself is named as the target, it will dispatch the message by calling its own `MessageReceived()` function. BView objects are expected to handle keyboard messages; BWindows are not.

Preferred Handlers

A BLooper can also keep track of a *preferred handler* for the messages it receives. When the target handler is a `NULL` pointer,

```
BMessage message(FORGET_ABOUT_IT);
myLooper->PostMessage(&message, NULL);
```

the BLooper resorts to its preferred handler.

This feature allows messages to be targeted dynamically. The BLooper can change the object it considers its preferred handler to fit the exigencies of the moment. For example, a BWindow makes sure that whatever object is the current focus of the user's actions is its preferred handler. Thus, `PostMessage()` calls that don't name another handler will always affect the current focus.

Sent Messages

Messages can be posted only within an application—where the thread that calls `PostMessage()` and the thread that responds to the message are in the same team and may even be the same thread.

To send a message to another application, it's necessary to first set up a BMessenger object as a local representative of the remote destination. BMessengers can be constructed in two ways:

- By naming a particular instance of a running application. The BRoster object can provide signatures and team identifiers for all running applications.

- By naming a particular BHandler or BLooper object in your own application.

The first method constructs a BMessenger that can send messages to the main thread of the remote application, where they'll be received and handled by its BApplication object.

The second method constructs a BMessenger that's targeted to a BLooper and BHandler (including, possibly, the BLooper's preferred handler) in your own application. However, you can place the BMessenger in a message and send it to a remote application. That application can then employ the BMessenger to target messages to your objects.

Thus, a BMessenger can be seen as a local identifier for a remote BLooper/BHandler pair. Calling the object's `SendMessage()` function delivers the message to the remote destination. BMessengers can also send messages to local destinations. However, it's generally simpler to post a local message than to send it—although the results are the same and posting a message isn't any more efficient than sending it.

Dropped Messages

Through a service of the Interface Kit, users can drag messages from a source location and drop them on a chosen destination, perhaps in another application. The source application puts the message together and hands it over to the Application Server, which tracks where the user drags it. The drag-and-drop session is initiated by BView's `DragMessage()` function. For example:

```
BMessage message(COLOR);
message.AddData("color", B_RGB_COLOR_TYPE, &theColor, sizeof(rgb_color));
myView->DragMessage(&message, aBitmap, offsetsIntoTheBitmap);
```

When the user drops the message inside a window somewhere, the server delivers it to the BWindow object and targets it to the BView (a kind of BHandler) that's in charge of the portion of the window where the message was dropped. The message is placed in the BWindow's queue and is dispatched like all other messages. In contrast to messages that are posted or sent in application code, only the user determines the destination of a dragged message.

A message receiver can discover whether and where a message was dropped by calling the BMessage object's `WasDropped()` and `DropPoint()` functions.

See "Responding to the User" in Chapter 4, *The Interface Kit*, for details on how to initiate a drag-and-drop session.

Two-Way Communication

A delivered BMessage carries a return address with it. The message receiver can reply to the message by calling the BMessage's `SendReply()` function. Replies can be synchronous or asynchronous.

Synchronous Replies

A message sender can ask for a synchronous reply when calling the sending function. For example:

```
BMessage reply;
myMessenger.SendMessage(&message, &reply);
if ( reply.what != B_NO_REPLY ) {
    . . .
}
```

In this case, `SendMessage()` waits for the reply; it doesn't return until one is received. (In case the message receiver refuses to cooperate, a default reply is sent when the original message is deleted.)

A message receiver can discover whether the sender is waiting for a synchronous reply by calling the BMessage's `IsSourceWaiting()` function.

Asynchronous Replies

A message sender can provide for an asynchronous reply by designating a BHandler object for the return message. For example:

```
myMessenger.SendMessage(&message, replyHandler);
```

In this case, the sending function doesn't wait for the reply; the reply message will be directed to the named BHandler. An asynchronous reply is always possible. If a BHandler isn't designated for it, the BApplication object will act as the default handler.

You can also name a target BHandler for an asynchronous reply to posted and dragged messages:

```
myLooper->PostMessage(&message, NULL, replyHandler);

myView->DragMessage(&message, aBitmap, offsets, replyHander);
```

Replies to Replies

BMessage's `SendReply()` function has the same syntax as `SendMessage()`, so it's possible to ask for a synchronous reply to a message that is itself a reply,

```
BMessage message(READY);
BMessage reply;
theMessage->SendReply(&message, &reply);
if ( reply->what != B_NO_REPLY ) {
    . . .
}
```

or to designate a BHandler for an asynchronous reply to the reply:

```
theMessage->SendReply(&message, someHandler);
```

In this way, two applications can maintain an ongoing exchange of messages.

Publishing Message Protocols

The messaging system is most interesting—and most useful—when data types are shared by a variety of applications. Shared types open avenues for applications to cooperate with each other. You are therefore encouraged to publish the data types that your application defines and can accept in a BMessage, along with their assigned type codes.

Contact Be (*devsupport@be.com*) to register any types you intend to publish, so that you can be sure to choose a code that hasn't already been adopted by another developer.

If your application can respond to certain kinds of remote messages, you should publish the message protocol—the constant that should initialize the `what` data member of the BMessage, the names of expected data fields, the types of data they contain, the number of data items allowed in each field, and so on. If your application sends replies to these messages, you should publish the reply protocols as well.

Scripting

Scripting is a way of using messages to control an application. The control is exercised through BHandler objects, since they're the objects that respond to messages.

Any message, especially any message delivered from a remote source, can be considered a scripting message, since it tells the application that receives it what to do. However, a "script" usually is thought of as a series of instructions (or in this case, messages) that put an application through its paces. Therefore, the scripting system must build on the bare messaging framework discussed in the previous section to make applications more vulnerable to outside control.

To aid scripting, the BeOS includes the following features:

• A set of messages that target self-declared properties of objects.

• A way of specifying which particular instance of a property a message targets.

• A method of resolving specifiers to find the object that should handle a message.

• The ability for an object to advertise the set (or *suite*) of messages it can handle and specifiers it can resolve.

The following sections explain how these features complement each other and together define a scripting system.

Messages, Properties, and Specifiers

To open objects to external control, the scripting system defines a small set of messages that target object properties. There are four such messages:

• `B_CREATE_PROPERTY` creates a new instance of the property
• `B_DELETE_PROPERTY` destroys an instance of the property
• `B_SET_PROPERTY` sets the value of (an instance of) the property
• `B_GET_PROPERTY` gets the value of (an instance of) the property

These messages are not system messages; they're dispatched by calling `MessageReceived()`.

The messages are generic; none of them is specific to a particular property or BHandler. However, almost anything associated with an object can be conceived as a property of the object—its current state, another object it knows about, a service it provides, and so on. Therefore, these messages can potentially put an object under almost total control. For example, a simple on-screen gadget, like an on-off switch, could treat its label, size, location, current setting, enabled state, the window it's in, and what it turns on and off as properties. An object representing a modem might regard its data rate, current connection, readiness to send or receive, and even the data it transmits as properties.

Treating an attribute of an object as a property doesn't mean that the object must be implemented any differently; it means only that the object's message-handling code will recognize messages that name the property.

The messages listed above have meaning only to the extent that BHandlers provide code that responds to them for particular properties. It's up to each class derived from BHandler to decide which messages its objects will respond to and for which properties. For example, an on-off switch might honor both `B_GET_PROPERTY` and `B_SET_PROPERTY` messages for its current setting, but would probably not allow a `B_SET_PROPERTY` message to change the window it's in. A BHandler is as scriptable as you decide to make it.

Object Properties

A property is a value with a name. The name is a character string and is specific to an object's class. For example, a BaggyPants class might recognize properties such as "Waist", "Leg", "Zipped", and "Pocket". The data type of the property and the set of permissible values depend on the property. For example, the "Waist" property might take `int32` measurements between 10 and 42 as values and "Zipped" could be either `true` or `false`.

In some cases, a property might be represented by another object. For example, "Pocket" could designate an object, possibly one with its own set of properties.

An object might also have more than one representative of a property. Although a BaggyPants object would have just one "Waist", it probably would have a pair of "Leg" values and likely more than one "Pocket". A property name can cover a set of data elements, provided the elements are all of the same type.

Therefore, a scripting message must not only name a particular property, it must also specify a particular instance of the property—which "Leg" or "Pocket" is targeted by a `B_SET_PROPERTY` message, for example. This is the task of a *specifier* that's added to each message.

Specifiers

A specifier has two jobs: It must name a property, and it must pick out a particular instance of the property. It therefore needs a structure that can combine various pieces of arbitrary information. Since this is exactly what BMessage objects are designed to do, a specifier takes the form of a BMessage inside another BMessage. The scripting BMessage holds its specifier BMessages in a named data array, just as it holds other data. However, because specifiers are a special breed with a peculiar role to play, they're added to the scripting message by a special function, AddSpecifier()—not by the functions that would normally be called to add one message to another. AddSpecifier() places the specifiers in a data field named "specifiers" and can often construct the specifier BMessage from information it's passed.

A specifier message has two required elements:

- It records the property name in a field named "property".

- Its **what** data member is a constant that indicates how to find a particular instance of the property—a particular "Leg" or "Pocket" belonging to the BaggyPants object, for example.

There are six standard specifier constants:

- B_INDEX_SPECIFIER. The specifier message has a field named "index" with an index to particular instance of the property. For example, if a BaggyPants object keeps its "Pocket" objects in a list, the index would pick an object from the list.

- B_REVERSE_INDEX_SPECIFIER. The index counts forward from the end of the list.

- B_RANGE_SPECIFIER. In addition to an "index" field, the specifier message has a field named "range" that counts a range of items beginning at the index.

- B_REVERSE_RANGE_SPECIFIER. The "index" counts from the end of the list forward. Depending on the kind of data and the message protocol, the "range" may extend toward the front of the list from the index or toward the end of the list. In other words, the index works in reverse, the range may or may not.

- B_NAME_SPECIFIER. The specifier message has a "name" field with the name of a particular instance of the property. For example, "right" and "left" could name different "Leg" values of the BaggyPants object.

- B_DIRECT_SPECIFIER. The property name is sufficient specification by itself, usually because there's just one instance of the property. For example, "Zipped" or "Waist" could directly specify particular data of the BaggyPants object. If there's more than one value for the property, a B_DIRECT_SPECIFIER would specify them all (both "Leg" values, for example).

Applications can define other types of specifiers. The two required elements are a "property" field with the name of the property and a **what** constant that doesn't clash with those listed above (or with any that may be added in future releases). To prevent clashes, Be will never define specifier constants with values greater than B_SPECIFIERS_END. Define your own constants as increments from that value.

The Specifier Stack

A BMessage can contain more than one specifier. Suppose, for example, that a record is kept of what's in each "Pocket" of the BaggyPants object. (It doesn't matter whether the record is kept by the BaggyPants object or by a separate Pocket object.) If this is treated as a "Contents" property, a B_GET_PROPERTY message assigned to a BaggyPants object could ask for the first five items in the left hip pocket. It would need two specifiers: The one at index 0 would be for the "Contents" property and the one at index 1 would be for the "Pocket" property:

Specifier at index 0:

> Property name: "Contents"
> Specifier: B_RANGE_SPECIFIER
> Specifier fields: "index" = 0, "range" = 5

Specifier at index 1:

> Property name: "Pocket"
> Specifier: B_NAME_SPECIFIER
> Specifier fields: "name" = "left hip"

If we imagine a Wardrobe class with a "Pants" property, we can extend the example so that a message directed to a Wardrobe object can ask, "Get the first 5 items in the left hip pocket of the pair of pants that were worn yesterday." It would need an additional specifier something like this:

Specifier at index 2:

> Property name: "Pants"
> Specifier: B_REVERSE_INDEX_SPECIFIER
> Specifier fields: "index" = 1

In more practical terms, a message sent to a BApplication object can use specifiers to target properties of a view. For example, it could ask, "Get the enclosing rectangle for the BView named "George" in the application's fifth window." The only limits on the number of specifiers are those imposed by the imagination and the application's architecture.

Clearly, the specifiers are ordered. The order of evaluation is the reverse of the order in which `AddSpecifier()` adds them to the "specifiers" array. The specifier with the highest index must be evaluated first. After each specifier is evaluated, it's popped from the stack so the one with the next highest index can be evaluated, and so on until none remain.

The specifier that must be evaluated next is the *current specifier*; `GetCurrentSpecifier()` opens that specifier in the BMessage and reveals its contents.

Resolving Specifiers

The presence of a specifier in a BMessage always raises a doubt about the designated handler for the message. That's because the specifier might specify another BHandler. Suppose, for example, that the BaggyPants and Pocket classes both derive from BHandler and that Pocket objects respond to `REMOVE_HAND` messages. A `REMOVE_HAND` message could be targeted to a BaggyPants object, but with a specifier naming one of its "Pocket" values. It would then be up to the BaggyPants object to make sure the message was redirected to the specified Pocket object. That object would respond to the message just like any other `REMOVE_HAND` message, without regard to the specifier.

To settle the question of which object should ultimately handle a message with specifiers, the message is passed to the target BHandler's `ResolveSpecifier()` hook function before being dispatched. Derived classes implement `ResolveSpecifier()` to examine the message and (at least) the current specifier to determine which BHandler should be the message target—or should be given a chance to resolve the next specifier. For example, the BaggyPants version of `ResolveSpecifier()` would resolve specifiers for its "Pocket" property by finding the specified Pocket object and making it the new target of the message.

`ResolveSpecifier()` is called once for each proposed target—as long as the message has unevaluated specifiers. For example, the Wardrobe object that gets the message illustrated in the previous section ("Get the first 5 items in the left hip pocket of the pants worn yesterday") would resolve the "pants worn yesterday" specifier and designate the BaggyPants object as the new target. The BaggyPants object would then resolve the "left hip pocket" specifier and name the appropriate Pocket object as the target. That object would recognize that it could respond to a "get the first 5 items" message and designate itself as the target, ending the series of `ResolveSpecifier()` calls.

Specifier Roles

From these examples, it's apparent that specifiers play at least two roles:

- They're an integral part of the content of a message that targets a particular property of an object (a B_GET_PROPERTY message, for example).

- They also help direct a message to the object that knows how to respond. Specifiers can be nothing more than a way of picking the object that should be responsible for the message. The message doesn't have to be one that targets an object property.

For both cases, BHandler classes must provide ResolveSpecifier() functions that evaluate the specifiers. For the first case, they must also implement a MessageReceived() function that responds to the message.

Unresolved Specifiers

If a specifier is malformed—for example, if it contains an out-of-range index—ResolveSpecifier() can prevent the message from being handled (simply by returning NULL). In that case, no further attempt is made to resolve specifiers and the message is not dispatched. (To explain what has happened, ResolveSpecifier() should send an error message in reply.)

If ResolveSpecifier() doesn't recognize the current specifier, it calls the inherited version of the function to give its base class a chance. If the specifier can't be resolved by any class, it should reach the BHandler version of ResolveSpecifier() (through successive calls to the inherited function). If the BHandler class also can't resolve the specifier, it presumes that the message can't be handled. It prevents the message from being dispatched and arranges for a B_MESSAGE_NOT_UNDERSTOOD reply.

Message Protocols

The specifier is just one part of the protocol for a scripting message. For example, a B_SET_PROPERTY message must contain a new value for the property being set and a B_GET_PROPERTY message anticipates a message in reply with the requested information.

Detailed protocols will be worked out as the scripting system is used and extended. For now, follow these limited guidelines:

- A B_SET_PROPERTY message has a field named "data" with the new data values that should be set. If a range of values is specified, the "data" array must cover the range. It might contain a single item—for example, a single string for a range of text—or it might have one item in the array for each value in the range.

- Every scripting message should receive a reply. The reply message has a data field named "error" with an error code indicating the success or failure of the scripting request—such as, B_OK or B_BAD_SCRIPT_SYNTAX. If no other constant is appropriate, the what data member of the reply should be the default B_REPLY.

- For a successful B_GET_PROPERTY message, the reply message has a field named "result" with the requested data. If a range of values are requested, the "result" array must cover the range with a single item (such as a string) or with a separate item for each value in the range.

The scripting system takes care of some replies. If a specifier isn't recognized, it will fall through to the BHandler version of ResolveSpecifier(), which sends a B_MESSAGE_NOT_UNDERSTOOD reply. If the specifiers can be resolved but the message isn't recognized, it falls through to the BHandler version of MessageReceived(), which also sends a B_MESSAGE_NOT_UNDERSTOOD reply.

Suites

To make scripting work, BHandler classes need to advertise—in documentation and at run time—the specifiers they can resolve and the messages they can respond to. If an object's scripting capabilities aren't documented, no one will know to use them. Moreover, unless it's possible to match those capabilities with an actual object at run time, the scripting enterprise will remain static and subject to guesswork.

To facilitate the exchange of information at run time, a class can group the specifiers and messages it understands into one or more sets—or *suites*—and assign each one a name. A suite name has the form of a MIME-like identifier with "suite" as the type and a specific name as the subtype. For example, "suite/vnd.Be-view" is the name of a set of scripting messages and specifiers that a BView object in the Interface Kit understands. Once a suite is named and documented, other classes may choose to support it with their own implementations.

At run time, you can query an object for the suites it supports by sending it a B_GET_SUPPORTED_SUITES message. In return, you can expect a B_REPLY message with an "error" field containing an error code. If the code is B_OK, the message should also have a field named "suites" with the names of all suites the target object understands.

To make this query work, scriptable BHandler classes implement a GetSupportedSuites() function that adds one or more suite names to the reply message. (Despite the fact that the message and the function have matching names, B_GET_SUPPORTED_SUITES is not a system message.)

A suite can include any type of message. It's not limited to messages with specifiers or those that target object properties. (However, all the suites currently defined in the BeOS are restricted to B_SET_PROPERTY and B_GET_PROPERTY messages. This will change in future releases.)

The Universal Suite

The implementations of ResolveSpecifier() and MessageReceived() in the BHandler class are inherited by all derived classes—as long as they call the inherited versions of these functions in their own implementations. Therefore, the BHandler class is able to impart a minimal, but important, set of scripting capabilities to every message-handling object, no matter what its class. These capabilities constitute a universal suite shared by all objects that respond to messages. Because it's universal, the suite doesn't need a name.

However, it does require some explanation. Any BHandler can respond to:

- A B_GET_PROPERTY message with a B_DIRECT_SPECIFIER specifier for the "Messenger" property. In its reply, the BHandler provides a BMessenger object that can send messages directly to the BHandler. Thus, you can use an array of specifiers to locate a particular BHandler—such as the third button in an alert panel of a particular application—and then communicate directly with that object through the BMessenger it provides.

- A B_GET_PROPERTY message with a B_DIRECT_SPECIFIER specifier for the "InternalName" property. The BHandler returns its name in the reply message.

- A B_GET_SUPPORTED_SUITES message. This message and the reply were discussed on the preceding pages.

Documentation

A suite name means nothing without some documentation detailing what specifiers and messages the suite includes and the protocols for using them. Since a suite can be implemented by more than one class, suites could reasonably be documented in a separate section apart from any particular class. However, for the current release, all suites the BeOS defines are supported by only one class. Also, some classes have scripting capabilities but don't give them suite names. Therefore, in this book, the class descriptions for scriptable BHandler objects have a "Scripting Support" section in the class overview with information about the scripting capabilities of the class. The BHandler and BApplication classes in this kit have "Scripting Support" descriptions. In the Interface Kit, the BWindow, BView, BTextView, BControl, and BTextControl classes have them.

BApplication

Derived from: public BLooper

Declared in: be/app/Application.h

Library: libbe.so

Overview

The BApplication class defines an object that represents and serves the entire application. Every Be application must have one (and only one) BApplication object. It's usually the first object the application constructs and the last one it deletes.

The BApplication object has these primary responsibilities:

- *It makes a connection to the Application Server.* Any application that puts a window on-screen or relies on other system services needs this connection. It's made automatically when the BApplication object is constructed.

- *It runs the application's main message loop.* The BApplication object is a kind of BLooper, but instead of spawning an independent thread, it runs a message loop in the application's main thread (the thread that the `main()` function executes in). This loop receives and processes messages that affect the entire application, including the initial messages received from remote applications. It gets several messages from the Tracker (such as reports of what documents to open). Any application that's known to the Tracker or that cooperates with other applications needs a main message loop.

- *It's the home for applicationwide elements of the user interface.* For example, it's expected to put a panel on-screen with information about the application for the user, it keeps a list of the application's windows, and it also lets you set, hide, and show the application's cursor. The ability to define the look of the cursor is provided by BApplication's `SetCursor()` function.

The user interface centers mainly on windows and is defined in the Interface Kit. The BApplication object merely contains the elements that are common to all windows and specific to the application.

Derived Classes

BApplication typically serves as the base class for a derived class that specializes it and extends it in ways that are appropriate for a particular application. It declares (and inherits declarations for) a number of hook functions that you can implement in a derived class to augment and fine-tune what it does.

For example, your application might implement a `RefsReceived()` function to open a document and display it in a window or a `ReadyToRun()` function to finish initializing the application after it has been launched and has started to receive messages. These two functions, like a handful of others, are called in response to system messages that have applicationwide import. All of these messages and the hook functions that respond to them are discussed in the next section.

If you expect your application to get messages from remote sources, or its main thread to get messages from other threads in the application, you should also implement a `MessageReceived()` function to sort through them as they arrive.

A derived class is also a good place to record the global properties of your application and to define functions that give other objects access to those properties.

Application Messages

The BApplication object runs the main message loop where it receives *application messages*—system messages that are not the province of any particular window, but concern the application as a whole. For these messages, the BApplication object acts as both looper (receiving and dispatching the message) and handler (responding to the message).

All seven application messages report events. Two of them notify the application of a change in its status:

- The B_READY_TO_RUN message reports that the application has finished launching and configuring itself.

- The B_APP_ACTIVATED message is delivered when the application becomes the active application—the one that the user is currently engaged with—and when it relinquishes that status to another application.

Two of the messages are requests that the application typically makes of itself:

- A B_QUIT_REQUESTED message is taken by the BApplication object to be a request to shut the entire application down, not just one thread. An application that has a user interface usually interprets some user action (such as clicking a Quit menu item) as a request to quit and, in response, posts a B_QUIT_REQUESTED message to the BApplication object. An application that's the servant of other applications may get the request from a remote source.

- A B_ABOUT_REQUESTED message requests information about the application, usually through an About... menu item. The application should set up this item to deliver a B_ABOUT_REQUESTED message to the BApplication object. In response, the BApplication object should display a window with general information about the application.

Other application messages report information from remote sources:

- The B_ARGV_RECEIVED message is delivered either on-launch or after-launch when the application receives strings of characters the user typed on the command line, or when it's launched by another application and is passed a similar array of character strings.

- The B_REFS_RECEIVED message passes the application one or more references to entries (files or directories) in the file system. Typically, this means the user has chosen some files to open—by picking them in the file panel, double-clicking a document icon in a Tracker window, or dragging the icon and dropping it on the application icon.

The system is the source of one repeated message:

- Periodic B_PULSE messages are posted at regularly spaced intervals. They can be used to arrange repeated actions when precise timing is not critical.

All application messages are received by the BApplication object in the main thread. The object dispatches them all to itself; it doesn't delegate them to any other handler. The following chart lists the hook functions that are called to initiate the application's response to system messages and the base class where each function is declared:

Message type	Hook function	Class
B_READY_TO_RUN	ReadyToRun()	BApplication
B_APP_ACTIVATED	AppActivated()	BApplication
B_QUIT_REQUESTED	QuitRequested()	BLooper
B_ABOUT_REQUESTED	AboutRequested()	BApplication
B_ARGV_RECEIVED	ArgvReceived()	BApplication
B_REFS_RECEIVED	RefsReceived()	BApplication
B_PULSE	Pulse()	BApplication

QuitRequested() is first declared in the BLooper class. BApplication reinterprets it—and reimplements it—to mean a request to quit the whole application, not just one of its threads.

Only three application messages—B_APP_ACTIVATED, B_ARGV_RECEIVED, and B_REFS_RECEIVED—contain any data; the rest are empty. See "Application Messages" in Appendix A, *Message Protocols*, for details on the content of these messages.

Constructing the Object and Running the Message Loop

The BApplication object must be constructed before the application can begin running or put a user interface on-screen. Other objects in other kits depend on the BApplication object and its connection to the Application Server. In particular, you can't construct BWindow objects in the Interface Kit until the BApplication object is in place.

Simply constructing the BApplication object forms the connection to the server. The connection is severed when you quit the application and delete the object.

be_app

The BApplication constructor assigns the new object to a global variable, be_app. This assignment is made automatically—you don't have to create the variable or set its value yourself. be_app is declared in *Application.h* and can be used throughout the code you write (or, more accurately, all code that directly or indirectly includes *Application.h*).

The be_app variable is typed as a pointer to an instance of the BApplication class. If you use a derived class instead—as most applications do—you have to cast the be_app variable when you call a function that's implemented by the derived class.

```
((MyApplication *)be_app)->DoSomethingSpecial();
```

Casting isn't required to call functions defined in the BApplication class (or in the BHandler and BLooper classes it inherits from), nor is it required for virtual functions defined in a derived class but declared by BApplication (or by the classes it inherits from).

main()

Because of its pivotal role, the BApplication object is one of the first objects, if not the very first object, the application creates. It's typically created in the main() function. The job of main() is to set up the application and turn over its operation to the various message loops run by particular objects, including the main message loop run by the BApplication object.

After constructing the BApplication object (and the other objects that your application initially needs), you tell it to begin running the message loop by calling its Run() function. Like the Run() function defined in the BLooper class, BApplication's Run() initiates a message loop and begins processing messages. However, unlike the BLooper function, it doesn't spawn a thread; rather, it takes over the main thread. Because it runs the loop in the same thread in which it was called, Run() doesn't return until the application is told to quit.

At its simplest, the main() function of a Be application would look something like this:

```
#include <Application.h>

main()
{
    . . .
    new BApplication("application/x-vnd.ORA-app5");
    . . .
    be_app->Run();
    delete be_app;
}
```

The string passed to the constructor ("application/x-vnd.ORA-app5") sets the application's signature. This is just a precautionary measure. It's more common (and much better) to set the signature at compile time as an attribute and resource. If there is a compile-time signature, it's used and the one passed to the constructor is ignored.

The main() function shown above doesn't allow for the usual command-line arguments, *argc* and *argv*. It would be possible to have main() parse the *argv* array, but these arguments are also packaged in a B_ARGV_RECEIVED message that the application gets immediately after Run() is called. Instead of handling them within main(), applications generally implement an ArgvReceived() function to do the job. This function can also handle command-line arguments that are passed to the application after it has been launched; it can be called at any time while the application is running.

Configuration Messages Received on Launch

When an application is launched, it may be passed messages that affect how it configures itself. These are the first messages that the BApplication object receives after Run() is called.

For example, when the user double-clicks a document icon to launch an application, the Tracker passes the application a B_REFS_RECEIVED message with information about the document. When launched from the command line, the application gets a B_ARGV_RECEIVED message listing the command-line arguments. When launched by the BRoster object, it might receive an arbitrary set of configuration messages.

After all the messages passed on-launch have been received and responded to, the application gets a B_READY_TO_RUN message and its ReadyToRun() hook function is called. This is the appropriate place to finish initializing the application before it begins running in earnest. It's the application's last chance to present the user with its initial user interface. For example, if a document has not already been opened in response to an on-launch B_REFS_RECEIVED message, ReadyToRun() could be implemented to place a window with an empty document on-screen.

ReadyToRun() is always called to mark the transition from the initial period when the application is being launched to the period when it's up and running—even if it's launched without any configuration messages. The IsLaunching() function can let you know which period the application is in.

Quitting

The main message loop terminates and Run() returns when Quit() is called. Because Run() doesn't spawn a thread, Quit() merely breaks the loop; it doesn't kill the thread or destroy the object (unlike BLooper's version of the function).

Quit() is usually called indirectly, as a byproduct of a B_QUIT_REQUESTED message posted to the BApplication object. The application is notified of the message through a QuitRequested() function call; it calls Quit() if QuitRequested() returns true.

When Run() returns, the application is well down the path of terminating itself. main() simply deletes be_app, cleans up anything else that might need attention, and exits.

Aborted Run

Applications with restricted launch behavior (B_EXCLUSIVE_LAUNCH and B_SINGLE_LAUNCH) may be launched anyway in violation of those restrictions. When this happens, the Run() function returns abruptly without processing any messages and the application quits as it normally does when Run() returns. Messages that carried on-launch information for the aborted application are redirected to the instance of the application that's already running.

Applications should be prepared for their main() functions to be executed in this abortive manner and guard against any undesired consequences.

Locking

You sometimes have to coordinate access to the BApplication object, since a single object serves the entire application and different parts of the application (windows, in particular) will be running in other threads. Locking ensures that one thread won't change the state of the application while another thread is changing the same aspect (or even just trying to examine it).

The BApplication object is locked automatically while the main thread is responding to a message, but it may have to be explicitly locked at other times.

This class inherits the locking mechanism—the Lock(), Unlock(), and other functions—from BLooper. See that class for details.

Scripting Support

The BApplication object can handle the following scripting request:

Property name: "Name" for the name of the application
Specifiers: B_DIRECT_SPECIFIER
Messages: B_GET_PROPERTY only
Data type: A null-terminated string (char *)

It also resolves the following specifiers by forwarding the message to the specified BWindow object:

Property name: "Window" for a BWindow object belonging to the application
Specifiers: B_INDEX_SPECIFIER and B_REVERSE_INDEX_SPECIFIER

The BeOS doesn't bless these rather limited abilities with a suite name.

See the "Scripting" section of this chapter for more information.

Hook Functions

AboutRequested()

Can be implemented to present the user with a window containing information about the application.

AppActivated()

Can be implemented to do whatever is necessary when the application becomes the active application, or when it loses that status.

ArgvReceived()

Can be implemented to parse the array of command-line arguments (or a similar array of argument strings).

Pulse()

Can be implemented to do something over and over again. `Pulse()` is called repeatedly at roughly regular intervals in the absence of any other activity in the main thread.

ReadyToRun()

Can be implemented to set up the application's running environment. This function is called after all messages the application receives on-launch have been responded to.

RefsReceived()

Can be implemented to respond to a message that contains references to files and directories. Typically, the references are to documents that the application is being asked to open.

Constructor and Destructor

BApplication()

BApplication(const char *signature*)
BApplication(BMessage *archive*)

Establishes a connection to the Application Server, assigns *signature* as the application identifier if one hasn't already been set, and initializes the applicationwide variable be_app to point to the new object.

The *signature* that's passed becomes the application identifier only if a signature hasn't been set as a resource or file-system attribute. It's preferable to assign the signature at compile time, since that enables the system to associate the signature with the application even when it's not running.

Every application must have one and only one BApplication object, typically an instance of a derived class. It's usually the first object that the application creates.

Like other BHandlers, the BApplication object is archivable and can be reconstructed from a BMessage *archive*.

~BApplication()

virtual ~**BApplication**(void)

Closes the application's windows, if it has any, without giving them a chance to disagree, kills the window threads, frees the BWindow objects and the BViews they contain, and severs the application's connection to the Application Server.

You can delete the BApplication object only after Run() has exited the main message loop. In the normal course of events, all the application's windows will already have been closed and freed by then.

See also: the BWindow class in the Interface Kit, QuitRequested()

Static Functions

Instantiate()

static BApplication ***Instantiate**(BMessage *archive*)

Returns a new BApplication object, allocated by new and created with the version of the constructor that takes a BMessage *archive*.

See also: BArchivable::Instantiate(), instantiate_object(), Archive()

Member Functions

AboutRequested()

virtual void **AboutRequested**(void)

Implemented by derived classes to put a window on-screen that provides the user with information about the application. The window typically displays copyright data, the version number, license restrictions, the names of the application's authors, a simple description of what the application is for, and similar information.

This function is called when the user operates an About... menu item and a B_ABOUT_REQUESTED message is delivered to the BApplication object as a result.

To set up the menu item, assign it a model message with B_ABOUT_REQUESTED as the command constant and the BApplication object as the target, as follows:

```
BMenuItem *item;
item = new BMenuItem("About application name" B_UTF8_ELLIPSIS,
                        new BMessage(B_ABOUT_REQUESTED));
item->SetTarget(be_app);
menu->AddItem(item);
```

See also: the BMenu class in the Interface Kit

AppActivated()

virtual void **AppActivated**(bool *active*)

Implemented by derived classes to take note when the application becomes—or ceases to be—the active application. The application has just attained that status if the *active* flag is true, and just lost it if the flag is false. The active application is the one that owns the current active window.

This function is called only when the change in active application is a consequence of a window being activated. It will be called when an application is launched (provided that the application puts a window on-screen). However, it's always called after ReadyToRun(), not before.

See also: BWindow::WindowActivated() in the Interface Kit, "B_APP_ACTIVATED" in Appendix A, *Message Protocols*

Archive()

virtual status_t **Archive**(BMessage **archive*, bool *deep* = true) const

Calls the inherited version of Archive(), then adds the application signature to the BMessage *archive*.

See also: BArchivable::Archive(), Instantiate() static function

ArgvReceived()

virtual void **ArgvReceived**(int32 *argc*, char ****argv*)

Implemented by derived classes to respond to a `B_ARGV_RECEIVED` message that passes the application an array of argument strings, typically arguments typed on the command line. *argv* is a pointer to the strings and *argc* is the number of strings in the array. These parameters are identical to those traditionally associated with the `main()` function.

When an application is launched from the command line, the command-line arguments are both passed to `main()` and packaged in a `B_ARGV_RECEIVED` message that's sent to the application on-launch (before `ReadyToRun()` is called). When BRoster's `Launch()` function is passed *argc* and *argv* parameters, they're similarly bundled in an on-launch message.

An application might also get `B_ARGV_RECEIVED` messages after it's launched. For example, imagine a graphics program called "Splotch" that can handle multiple documents and is therefore restricted so that it can't be launched more than once (it's a `B_SINGLE_LAUNCH` or a `B_EXCLUSIVE_LAUNCH` application). If the user types:

```
$ Splotch myArtwork
```

in a shell, it launches the application and passes it an on-launch `B_ARGV_RECEIVED` message with the strings "Splotch" and "myArtwork". Then, if the user types:

```
$ Splotch yourArtwork
```

the running application is again informed with a `B_ARGV_RECEIVED` message. In both cases, the BApplication object dispatches the message by calling this function.

To open either of the artwork files, the Splotch application will need to translate the document pathname into a file reference. It can do this most easily by calling `get_ref_for_path()`, defined in the Storage Kit.

See also: `RefsReceived()`, "B_ARGV_RECEIVED" in Appendix A, *Message Protocols*

CountWindows()

int32 **CountWindows**(void) const

Returns the number of windows belonging to the application. The count includes only windows that the application explicitly created. It omits, for example, the private windows used by BBitmap objects.

See also: the BWindow class in the Interface Kit

DispatchMessage()

virtual void **DispatchMessage**(BMessage **message*, BHandler **target*)

Augments the BLooper function to dispatch system messages by calling a specific hook function. The set of system messages that the BApplication object receives and the hook functions that it calls to respond to them are listed under "Application Messages" in the overview.

Other messages—those defined by the application rather than the Application Kit—are forwarded to the *target* BHandler's `MessageReceived()` function. Note that the *target* is ignored for most system messages.

`DispatchMessage()` locks the BApplication object and keeps it locked until the main thread has finished responding to the message.

See also: `BLooper::DispatchMessage()`, `BHandler::MessageReceived()`

GetAppInfo()

status_t **GetAppInfo**(app_info *theInfo*) const

Writes information about the application into the `app_info` structure referred to by *theInfo*. The structure contains the application signature, the identifier for its main thread, a reference to its executable file in the file system, and other information.

This function is the equivalent to the identically named BRoster function—or, more accurately, to BRoster's `GetRunningAppInfo()`—except that it provides information only about the current application. The following code:

```
app_info info;
if ( be_app->GetAppInfo(&info) == B_OK )
    . . .
```

is a shorthand for:

```
app_info info;
if ( be_roster->GetRunningAppInfo(be_app->Team(), &info) == B_OK )
    . . .
```

`GetAppInfo()` returns `B_OK` if successful, and an error code if not.

See the BRoster function for the error codes and for a description of the information contained in an `app_info` structure.

See also: `BRoster::GetAppInfo()`

HideCursor(), ShowCursor(), ObscureCursor()

void **HideCursor**(void)

void **ShowCursor**(void)

void **ObscureCursor**(void)

HideCursor() removes the cursor from the screen. ShowCursor() restores it. ObscureCursor() hides it temporarily, until the user moves the mouse.

See also: SetCursor(), IsCursorHidden()

IsCursorHidden()

bool **IsCursorHidden**(void) const

Returns true if the cursor is hidden (but not obscured), and false if not.

See also: HideCursor()

IsLaunching()

bool **IsLaunching**(void) const

Returns true if the application is in the process of launching—of getting itself ready to run—and false once the ReadyToRun() function has been called.

IsLaunching() can be called while responding to a message to find out whether the message was received on-launch (to help the application configure itself) or after-launch as an ordinary message.

See also: ReadyToRun()

MessageReceived()

virtual void **MessageReceived**(BMessage **message*)

Augments the BHandler version of MessageReceived() to handle scripting requests delivered to the BApplication object.

See also: BHandler::MessageReceived()

ObscureCursor()   *see* HideCursor()

Pulse()

virtual void **Pulse**(void)

Implemented by derived classes to do something at regular intervals. Pulse() is called regularly as the result of B_PULSE messages, as long as no other messages are pending. By default, pulsing is disabled—the pulse rate is set to 0—but you can enable it by calling the SetPulseRate() function to set an actual rate.

You can implement Pulse() to do whatever you want. However, pulse events aren't accurate enough for actions that require precise timing.

The default version of this function is empty.

See also: BWindow::Pulse() in the Interface Kit, SetPulseRate()

Quit()

virtual void **Quit**(void)

Kills the application by terminating the message loop and causing Run() to return. You rarely call this function directly; it's called for you when the application receives a B_QUIT_REQUESTED message and QuitRequested() returns true to allow the application to shut down.

BApplication's Quit() differs from the BLooper function it overrides in four important respects:

- It doesn't kill the thread. It merely causes the message loop to exit after it finishes with the current message.

- It therefore always returns, even when called from within the main thread.

- It returns immediately. It doesn't wait for the message loop to exit.

- It doesn't delete the object. It's up to you to delete it after Run() returns. (However, for some reason, Quit() *does* delete the BApplication object if it's called when no message loop is running.)

Before shutting down, the BApplication object responds to every message it received prior to the Quit() call.

See also: BLooper::Quit(), QuitRequested()

QuitRequested()

virtual bool **QuitRequested**(void)

Overrides the BLooper function to decide whether the application should really quit when requested to do so.

BApplication's implementation of this function tries to get the permission of the application's windows before agreeing to quit. It works its way through the list of BWindow objects that belong to the application and forwards the QuitRequested() call to each one. If a BWindow agrees to quit (its QuitRequested() function returns true), the BWindow version of Quit() is called to destroy the window. If the window refuses to quit (its QuitRequested() function returns false), the attempt to destroy the window fails and no other windows are asked to quit.

If it's successful in terminating all the application's windows (or if the application didn't have any windows to begin with), this function returns **true** to indicate that the application may quit; if not, it returns **false**.

An application can replace this window-by-window test of whether the application should quit, or augment it by adding a more global test. It might, for example, put a modal window on-screen that gives the user the opportunity to save documents, terminate on-going operations, or cancel the quit request.

This hook function is called for you when the main thread receives a **B_QUIT_REQUESTED** message; you never call it yourself. However, you *do* have to post the **B_QUIT_REQUESTED** message. Typically, the application's main menu has an item labeled "Quit." When the user invokes the item, it should post a **B_QUIT_REQUESTED** message directly to the BApplication object.

See also: BLooper::QuitRequested(), Quit()

ReadyToRun()

> virtual void **ReadyToRun**(void)

Implemented by derived classes to complete the initialization of the application. This is a hook function that's called after all messages that the application receives on-launch have been handled. It's called in response to a **B_READY_TO_RUN** message that's posted immediately after the last on-launch message. If the application isn't launched with any messages, **B_READY_TO_RUN** is the first message it receives.

This function is the application's last opportunity to put its initial user interface on-screen. If the application hasn't yet displayed a window to the user (for example, if it hasn't opened a document in response to an on-launch **B_REFS_RECEIVED** or **B_ARGV_RECEIVED** message), it should do so in ReadyToRun().

The default version of ReadyToRun() is empty.

See also: Run(), IsLaunching()

RefsReceived()

> virtual void **RefsReceived**(BMessage *message)

Implemented by derived classes to do something with file system entries that have been referred to the application in a *message*. The message has **B_REFS_RECEIVED** as its what data member and a single data field named "refs" that contains one or more entry_ref (**B_REF_TYPE**) items.

Typically, the entry refs are for documents that the application is requested to open. For example, when the user double-clicks a document icon in a Tracker window, the

Tracker sends a B_REFS_RECEIVED message to the application that owns the document. The BApplication object dispatches the message by passing it to this function.

There are a number of things you can do with the entry_ref taken from the message. For example, you might create a BEntry object for it and inquire whether it refers to a file:

```
BEntry entry(&ref);
if ( entry.IsFile() )
    . . .
```

If you're sure it's a file reference, you might create a BFile object and open it. For example:

```
void MyApplication::RefsReceived(BMessage *message)
{
    uint32 type;
    int32 count;
    entry_ref ref;
    . . .
    message->GetInfo("refs", &type, &count);
    if ( type != B_REF_TYPE )
        return;
    for ( long i = --count; i >= 0; i-- ) {
        if ( message->FindRef("refs", i, &ref) == B_OK ) {
            BFile file;
            if ( file.SetTo(&ref, B_READ_WRITE) == B_OK )
                . . .
        }
    }
    . . .
}
```

REFS_RECEIVED messages can be received both on-launch (while the application is configuring itself) or after-launch (as ordinary messages received while the application is running).

See also: the BEntry class in the Storage Kit, ArgvReceived(), ReadyToRun(), IsLaunching(), "B_REFS_RECEIVED" in Appendix A, *Message Protocols*

ResolveSpecifier()

virtual BHandler *ResolveSpecifier(BMessage *message*, int32 *index*,
                    BMessage *specifier*, int32 *command*, const char *property*)

Resolves specifiers for the "Name" and "Window" properties. See "Scripting Support" in the class overview and the "Scripting" section of this chapter for more information.

See also: BHandler::ResolveSpecifier()

Run()

virtual thread_id **Run**(void)

Runs a message loop in the application's main thread. This function must be called from main() to start the application running. The loop is terminated and Run() returns when Quit() is called, or (potentially) when a B_QUIT_REQUESTED message is received. It returns the identifier for the main thread (not that it's of much use once the application has stopped running).

This function overrides BLooper's Run() function. Unlike that function, it doesn't spawn a thread for the message loop or return immediately.

See also: BLooper::Run(), ReadyToRun(), QuitRequested()

SetCursor()

void **SetCursor**(const void *cursor)

Sets the cursor image to the bitmap specified in *cursor*. Each application has control over its own cursor and can set and reset it as often as necessary. The cursor on-screen will have the shape specified in *cursor* as long as the application remains the active application. If it loses that status and then regains it, its current cursor is automatically restored.

The first four bytes of *cursor* data is a preamble that gives information about the image, as follows:

- The first byte sets the size of the cursor image. The cursor bitmap is a square, and this byte states the number of pixels on one side. Currently, only 16-pixel-by-16-pixel images are acceptable.

- The second byte specifies the depth of the cursor image, in bits per pixel. Currently, only monochrome one-bit-per-pixel images are acceptable.

- The third and fourth bytes set the *hot spot*, the pixel within the cursor image that's used to report the cursor's location. For example, if the cursor is located over a button on-screen so that the hot spot is within the button rectangle, the cursor is said to point to the button. However, if the hot spot lies outside the button rectangle, even if most of the cursor image is within the rectangle, the cursor doesn't point to the button.

  To locate the hot spot, assume that the pixel in the upper left corner of the cursor image is at (0, 0). Identify the vertical *y* coordinate first, then the horizontal *x* coordinate. For example, a hot spot 5 pixels to the right of the upper left corner and 8 pixels down—at (5, 8)—would be specified as "8, 5."

Image data follows these four bytes. Pixel values are specified from left to right in rows starting at the top of the image and working downward. First comes data specifying the color value of each pixel in the image. In a one-bit-per-pixel image, 1 means black and 0 means white.

Following the color data is a mask that indicates which pixels in the image square are transparent and which are opaque. Transparent pixels are marked 0; they let whatever is underneath that part of the cursor bitmap show through. Opaque pixels are marked 1.

The Application Kit defines two standard cursor images. Each is represented by a constant that you can pass to `SetCursor()`:

B_HAND_CURSOR	The hand image that's seen when the computer is first turned on. This is the default cursor.
B_I_BEAM_CURSOR	The standard I-beam image for selecting text.

See also: `HideCursor()`

SetPulseRate()

void **SetPulseRate**(bigtime_t *microseconds*)

Sets how often `Pulse()` is called (how often `B_PULSE` messages are posted). The interval set should be a multiple of 100,000 microseconds (0.1 second); differences less than 100,000 microseconds will not be noticeable. A finer granularity can't be guaranteed.

The default pulse rate is 0, which disables the pulsing mechanism. Setting a different rate enables it.

See also: `Pulse()`

ShowCursor()   *see HideCursor()*

WindowAt()

BWindow ***WindowAt**(int32 *index*) const

Returns the BWindow object recorded in the list of the application's windows at *index*, or NULL if *index* is out of range. Indices begin at 0 and there are no gaps in the list. Windows aren't listed in any particular order (such as the order they appear on-screen), so the value of *index* has no ulterior meaning. The window list excludes the private windows used by BBitmaps and other objects, but it doesn't distinguish main windows that display documents from palettes, panels, and other supporting windows.

This function can be used to iterate through the window list:

```
BWindow *window;
int32 i = 0;

while ( window = be_app->WindowAt(i++) ) {
    if ( window->Lock() ) {
        . . .
        window->Unlock();
    }
}
```

This works as long as windows aren't being created or deleted while the list *index* is being incremented. Locking the BApplication object doesn't lock the window list.

It's best for an application to maintain its own window list, one that arranges windows in a logical order and can be locked while it's being read.

See also: `CountWindows()`

BClipboard

Derived from: *none*

Declared in: be/app/Clipboard.h

Library: libbe.so

Overview

A clipboard is a shared repository for data—a vehicle for transferring data between applications or between different parts of the same application. An application adds some amount of data to the clipboard, then some other application (or the same application) retrieves (or "finds") that data. This mechanism permits, most notably, the ability to cut, copy, and paste data items. For example, the BTextView class, in the Interface Kit, responds to B_CUT, B_COPY, and B_PASTE messages by adding data to and retrieving it from the system clipboard.

A BClipboard object represents a clipboard and is the programming interface to the clipboard service. If you provide a unique name when constructing a BClipboard object, a new clipboard with that name is created for you. If you provide the name of an existing clipboard, the new object will be an additional interface to that clipboard.

However, for most uses, you don't need a clipboard that's your own creation, but rather one that's common to all applications. The BeOS creates just such a clipboard—named "system"—when you boot the machine. Then, when each application starts up, it's automatically given a BClipboard object for the common clipboard. The object is assigned to a global variable, be_clipboard. The be_clipboard variables in all applications refer (ultimately) to the same system clipboard.

The system be_clipboard object is the one that you should use for all normal cut, copy, and paste operations. An application-created clipboard might be used for more limited data sharing. For example, you can construct a BClipboard with a private name, add data to it, and pass the name to another application. That application can use the name to construct its own BClipboard interface to the clipboard you created.

The Data Container

A clipboard uses a BMessage to hold its data. The BClipboard object hands you the BMessage in response to a Data() request. Once you have the BMessage container, you can add data to it or find what's already there by calling standard BMessage functions. You can ignore the what data member of the BMessage, or you can use it to indicate something about what the clipboard contains.

There are few established conventions for arranging data in the clipboard, other than those that the BMessage class imposes. The BeOS follows this rule: If the what data member of the container BMessage is B_SIMPLE_DATA, the clipboard is understood to hold just one item of data, though it may hold it in more than one data format. For example, a B_SIMPLE_DATA clipboard might contain some copied text in three formats—in a format native to the application that put the text in the clipboard, in a rich but possibly less informative standard format such as HTML or RTF, and as a simple ASCII string. Each format is a separately-named data field in the BMessage.

The retrieving application can choose the format that's most appropriate for the impending paste operation, generally the richest format that it can deal with. It might care what the names of the data fields are, or it might look only at the data types. If the type is B_MIME_TYPE, the name is a MIME string that encodes the true data type. The BTextView object accepts B_MIME_TYPE data with the name "text/plain".

Using the Clipboard

You must bracket all interactions with a BClipboard object with calls to Lock() and Unlock(). This prevents other applications (or other threads of the same application) from accessing the clipboard while you're using it. Conversely, if some other application (or another thread in your application) holds the lock to the clipboard when you call Lock(), your thread will block until the current lock holder calls Unlock()—in other words, Lock() will always succeed, even if it has to wait forever to do so. Currently, there's no way to tell if the clipboard is already locked, nor can you specify a time limit beyond which you won't wait for the lock.

When putting data in the clipboard, interactions should also be bracketed by calls to Clear() and Commit(). Clearing the clipboard removes all data that it currently holds. The Commit() function tells the clipboard that you're serious about the additions you've made. If you don't commit your additions, they'll be lost.

The following code fragment demonstrates the expected sequence of function calls:

```
if ( be_clipboard->Lock() ) {
    be_clipboard->Clear();
    BMessage *clipper = be_clipboard->Data();
    . . .
    clipper->AddString("text", theData);
    . . .
    be_clipboard->Commit();
    be_clipboard->Unlock();
}
```

When retrieving data from the clipboard, it's necessary to lock and unlock the BClipboard object, but not to clear it (which would remove the data before you could look at it) or commit changes. For example:

```
if ( be_clipboard->Lock() ) {
    BMessage *clipper = be_clipboard->Data();
    . . .
    if ( clipper->FindString("text", &theText) == B_OK ) {
        . . .
    }
    . . .
    be_clipboard->Unlock();
}
```

Once the BClipboard is locked, it's possible to both retrieve and add data during the same session, but such a pursuit doesn't correspond to traditional manipulations.

Constructor and Destructor

BClipboard()

> **BClipboard**(const char *name*, bool *transient* = false)

Creates a new BClipboard object for the *name* clipboard. If there's no clipboard with that name or *name* is NULL, one is created. Otherwise, the new object is an interface to the clipboard previously created, by any application, with *name*.

The *transient* flag tells the clipboard service whether to save the clipboard when the system shuts down. If saved, the data in the clipboard will be available again when the user next turns the computer on. If not, the data is lost.

See also: Name()

~BClipboard()

virtual ~BClipboard(void)

Deletes all memory allocated by the BClipboard, including the container BMessage and the data it holds.

Member Functions

Clear()

status_t Clear(void)

Erases all items that are currently on the clipboard. Normally, you call Clear() just after locking the clipboard and just before getting the data container with the intention of adding new data to it. This function returns B_ERROR if the BClipboard isn't locked, and B_OK otherwise.

See also: Commit()

Commit()

status_t Commit(void)

Forces the clipboard to notice the items you added. Additions to the clipboard are lost unless followed by a call to Commit(). The call to Commit() must precede the call to Unlock(). If the BClipboard isn't locked, this function fails and returns B_ERROR. If successful, it returns B_OK.

See also: Clear()

Data()

BMessage *Data(void) const

Returns the BMessage object that holds clipboard data, or NULL if the BClipboard isn't locked. The returned object belongs to the system; you should not free it, assign it to another object, or arrange for it to be delivered as an ordinary message.

See also: the BMessage class

DataSource()

BMessenger DataSource(void) const

Returns a BMessenger object for the application that last committed data to the clipboard. The BMessenger targets that application's BApplication object.

See also: the BMessenger class

Lock(), Unlock()

bool **Lock**(void)

void **Unlock**(void)

These functions lock and unlock the clipboard. Locking the clipboard gives a thread exclusive permission to invoke the other BClipboard functions. If some other thread already has the clipboard locked when your thread calls `Lock()`, your thread will wait until the lock-holding thread calls `Unlock()`. Your thread should also invoke `Unlock()` when it's done manipulating the clipboard.

`Lock()` should invariably be successful and return `true`.

See also: `BLooper::Lock()`

Name()

const char ***Name**(void) const

Returns the name of the clipboard. The returned string belongs to the BClipboard object.

BHandler

Derived from: public BArchivable

Declared in: be/app/Handler.h

Library: libbe.so

Overview

BHandlers are the objects that respond to messages received in message loops. The class declares a hook function—`MessageReceived()`—that derived classes must implement to handle expected messages. BLooper's `DispatchMessage()` function calls `MessageReceived()` to pass incoming messages from the BLooper to the BHandler.

All messages are entrusted to BHandler objects—even system messages, which are dispatched by calling a message-specific function, not `MessageReceived()`. These specific functions are declared in classes derived from BHandler—especially BWindow and BView in the Interface Kit and BLooper and BApplication in this kit. For example, the BApplication class declares a `ReadyToRun()` function to respond to `B_READY_TO_RUN` messages, and the BView class declares a `KeyDown()` function to respond to `B_KEY_DOWN` messages.

All messages that aren't matched to a specific hook function—messages defined by applications rather than the kits—are dispatched by calling `MessageReceived()`.

Associations

To be eligible to get messages from a BLooper, a BHandler must be in the BLooper's circle of handlers. At any given time, a BHandler can belong to only one BLooper. BLooper's `AddHandler()` function is the agent for forming looper-handler associations; a BHandler's `Looper()` function identifies the BLooper it's currently associated with.

BHandlers that belong to the same BLooper can be chained together in a linked list. The default behavior for `MessageReceived()` is simply to pass the message to the next handler in the chain. However, system messages are not passed from handler to handler.

When a BHandler is assigned to a BLooper, the BLooper becomes its default next handler. That assignment can be changed by `SetNextHandler()`.

Targets

You can designate a target BHandler for most messages. The designation is made when calling BLooper's `PostMessage()` function or when constructing the BMessenger object that will send the message. Messages that a user drags and drops are targeted to the object (a BView) that controls the part of the window where the message was dropped. The messaging mechanism eventually passes the target BHandler to `DispatchMessage()`, so that the message can be delivered to its designated destination.

Filtering

Messages can be filtered before they're dispatched—that is, you can define a function that will look at the message before the target BHandler's hook function is called. The filter function is associated with a BMessageFilter object, which records the criteria for calling the function.

Filters that should apply only to messages targeted to a particular BHandler are assigned to the BHandler by `SetFilterList()` or `AddFilter()`. Filters that might apply to any message a BLooper dispatches, regardless of its target, are assigned by the parallel BLooper functions, `SetCommonFilterList()` and `AddCommon-Filter()`. See those functions and the BMessageFilter class for details.

Scripting Support

All BHandler objects respond to the following scripting messages:

Property name: Messenger" for a BMessenger object that targets the BHandler
Specifiers: `B_DIRECT_SPECIFIER`

Messages: B_GET_PROPERTY only

Data type: A BMessenger object (B_MESSENGER_TYPE)

Property name: "InternalName" for the name of the BHandler

Specifiers: B_DIRECT_SPECIFIER

Messages: B_GET_PROPERTY only

Data type: A null-terminated character string (B_STRING_TYPE)

Since any object that can respond to any message at all can respond to these requests, there's no need for a suite name; it's the universal suite.

See the "Scripting" section of this chapter for more information.

Hook Functions

MessageReceived()
Implemented to handle received messages.

Constructor and Destructor

BHandler()

BHandler(const char *name* = NULL)
BHandler(BMessage *archive*)

Initializes the BHandler by assigning it a *name* and registering it with the messaging system. Because BHandlers are archivable objects, they can also be reconstructed from a BMessage *archive*.

~BHandler()

virtual ~BHandler(void)

Removes the BHandler's registration, frees the memory allocated for its name, and gets rid of any BMessageFilters assigned to the BHandler and the BList object that holds them.

Static Functions

Instantiate()

static BHandler *Instantiate(BMessage *archive*)

Returns a new BHandler object, allocated by **new** and created with the version of the constructor that takes a BMessage *archive*. However, if the archive doesn't contain data for a BHandler of some kind, this function returns **NULL**.

See also: BArchivable::Instantiate(), instantiate_object(), Archive()

Member Functions

AddFilter()   *see SetFilterList()*

Archive()

virtual status_t **Archive**(BMessage **archive*, bool *deep* = true) const

Archives the BHandler by writing its name, if any, to the BMessage *archive*.

See also: BArchivable::Archive(), Instantiate() static function

FilterList()   *see SetFilterList()*

GetSupportedSuites()

virtual status_t **GetSupportedSuites**(BMessage **message*)

Implemented by derived classes to report the suites of messages and specifiers they understand. This function is called in response to a B_GET_SUPPORTED_SUITES BMessage delivered to the BHandler.

A suite is identified by a MIME subtype for the type *suite*. For example, a BView object identifies the set of messages it can handle by "suite/vnd.Be-view" and a BControl identifies its set by "suite/vnd.Be-control".

The *message* that's passed as an argument will eventually be sent as a reply to the B_GET_SUPPORTED_SUITES request. Each derived class should place the names of all suites it implements in the message, then pass the message to its base class. The suite names should be placed in a data field named "suites" as B_STRING_TYPE items. For example:

```
status_t MyHandler::GetSupportedSuites(BMessage *message)
{
    status_t err;
    err = message->AddString("suites", "suite/vnd.Me-my_handler");
    if ( err )
        return err;
    return baseClass::GetSupportedSuites(message);
}
```

The return value is added to the message as a `B_INT32_TYPE` value in a field named "error". BHandler's version of the function simply returns `B_OK`.

Looper()

BLooper ***Looper**(void) const

Returns the BLooper object that the BHandler is associated with, or `NULL` if it's not associated with any BLooper. A BHandler must be associated with a BLooper before the BLooper can call upon it to handle messages it dispatches. (However, strictly speaking, this restriction is imposed when the message is posted or when the BMessenger that will send it is constructed, rather than when it's dispatched.)

BLooper objects are automatically associated with themselves; they can act as handlers only for messages that they receive in their own message loops. All other BHandlers must be explicitly tied to a particular BLooper by calling that BLooper's `AddHandler()` function. A BHandler can be associated with only one BLooper at a time.

In the Interface Kit, when a BView is added to a window's view hierarchy, it's also added as a BHandler to the BWindow object.

See also: `BLooper::AddHandler()`, `BLooper::PostMessage()`, the BMessenger constructor

MessageReceived()

virtual void **MessageReceived**(BMessage *_message_)

Implemented by derived classes to respond to messages that are dispatched to the BHandler. The default (BHandler) implementation of this function responds only to scripting requests. It passes all other messages to the next handler by calling that object's version of `MessageReceived()`.

You must implement `MessageReceived()` to handle the variety of messages that might be dispatched to the BHandler. It can distinguish between messages by the value recorded in the `what` data member of the BMessage object. For example:

```
void MyHandler::MessageReceived(BMessage *message)
{
    switch ( message->what ) {
    case COMMAND_ONE:
        . . .
        break;
    case COMMAND_TWO:
        . . .
        break;
```

```
    case COMMAND_THREE:
        . . .
        break;
    default:
        baseClass::MessageReceived(message);
        break;
    . . .
    }
}
```

When defining a version of `MessageReceived()`, you must incorporate the inherited version as well, as shown in the example above. This ensures that:

- Any messages handled by base versions of the function are not overlooked.

- The message is passed to the BHandler's next handler if your version of the function and the inherited versions don't recognize it.

- The scripting system (for all BHandlers) and keyboard navigation (for BView objects) will continue to work. The `MessageReceived()` functions defined in kit classes sometimes include code that helps run these systems.

If the message comes to the end of the line—if it's not recognized and there is no next handler—the BHandler version of this function sends a **B_MESSAGE_ NOT_UNDERSTOOD** reply to notify the message source.

See also: `SetNextHandler()`, `BLooper::PostMessage()`, `BLooper::DispatchMessage()`, `GetSupportedSuites()`

NextHandler()   *see SetNextHandler()*

ResolveSpecifier()

> virtual BHandler ***ResolveSpecifier**(BMessage **message*, int32 *index*,
> BMessage **specifier*, int32 *what*, const char **property*)

Implemented by derived classes to determine the proper handler for a BMessage that has specifiers. The message is targeted to the BHandler, but the specifiers may indicate that it should be assigned to another object. It's the job of `ResolveSpecifier()` to examine at least one specifier, more if necessary, and return the object that should handle the message or look at the next specifier. This function is called before the message is dispatched and before any filtering functions are called.

The BMessage that is about to be dispatched is passed to `ResolveSpecifier()` as the first argument, *message*. The next two arguments detail the specifier that is next in line to be resolved (the current specifier)—*index* is its position in the "specifiers" field in the BMessage and *specifier* is the specifier message itself. The final two arguments extract information from the specifier—*what* is its **what** data member and *property* is the property name in the *specifier* message.

The *what* argument will let you know whether you need to look inside the *specifier* for more information and what information to look for. For example, if *what* is **B_NAME_SPECIFIER**, the specifier BMessage should have a name in a field called "name". If it's **B_RANGE_SPECIFIER**, it should have "index" and "range" fields. See **AddSpecifier()** in the BMessage class for a discussion of specifier contents.

ResolveSpecifier() has four options:

- If the *property* picks out a BHandler object that belongs to another BLooper, it should send or post the message to that BLooper and return **NULL**. The message will be handled in the message loop of the other BLooper; it won't be further processed in this one. For example, a BHandler that kept a list of proxies might use code like the following:

```
if ( (strcmp(property, "Proxy") == 0)
            && (what == B_INDEX_SPECIFIER) ) {
    int32 i;
    if ( specifier->FindInt32("index", &i) == B_OK ) {
        MyProxy *proxy = (MyProxy *)proxyList->ItemAt(i);
        if ( proxy ) {
            message->PopSpecifier();
            if ( proxy->Looper() != Looper() ) {
                proxy->Looper()->PostMessage(message, proxy);
                return NULL;
            }
        }
        . . .
    }
    . . .
}
```

Since this function resolved the specifier at *index*, it calls **PopSpecifier()** to decrement the index before forwarding the message. Otherwise, the next handler would try to resolve the same specifier.

- If the *property* picks out another BHandler object belonging to the same BLooper, it can return that BHandler. For example:

```
if ( proxy ) {
    message->PopSpecifier();
    if ( proxy->Looper() != Looper() ) {
        proxy->Looper()->PostMessage(message, proxy);
        return NULL;
    }
    else {
        return proxy;
    }
}
```

This, in effect, puts the returned object in the BHandler's place as the designated handler for the message. The BLooper will give the returned handler a chance to respond to the message or resolve the next specifier.

Again, `PopSpecifier()` should be called so that an attempt isn't made to resolve the same specifier twice.

- If it can resolve all remaining specifiers and recognizes the message as one that the BHandler itself can handle, it should return the BHandler (`this`). For example:

```
if ( (strcmp(property, "Value") == 0)
            && (message->what == B_GET_PROPERTY) )
    return this;
```

This confirms the BHandler as the message target. `ResolveSpecifier()` won't be called again, so it's not necessary to call `PopSpecifier()` before returning.

- If it doesn't recognize the property or can't resolve the specifier, it should call the inherited version of `ResolveSpecifier()` and return what it returns. For example:

```
return baseClass:ResolveSpecifier(message, index,
                                  specifier, what, property);
```

The BApplication object takes the first path when it resolves a specifier for a "Window" property; it sends the message to the specified BWindow and returns `NULL`. A BWindow follows the second path when it resolves a specifier for a "View" property; it returns the specified BView. Thus, a message initially targeted to the BApplication object can find its way to a BView.

BHandler's version of `ResolveSpecifier()` recognizes a `B_GET_PROPERTY` *message* with a direct *specifier* requesting a "Messenger" for the BHandler or the BHandler's "InternalName" (the same name that its `Name()` function returns). In both cases, it assigns the BHandler (`this`) as the object responsible for the message.

For all other specifiers and messages, it sends a `B_MESSAGE_NOT_UNDERSTOOD` reply and returns `NULL`. The reply message has an "error" field with `B_SCRIPT_SYNTAX` as the error and a "message" field with a longer textual explanation of the error.

See also: `BMessage::AddSpecifier()`, `BMessage::GetCurrentSpecifier()`

SetFilterList(), FilterList(), AddFilter(), RemoveFilter()

virtual void **SetFilterList**(BList *list*)

BList ***FilterList**(void) const

virtual void **AddFilter**(BMessageFilter *filter*)

virtual bool **RemoveFilter**(BMessageFilter *filter*)

These functions manage a list of BMessageFilter objects associated with the BHandler.

`SetFilterList()` assigns the BHandler a new *list* of filters; the list must contain pointers to instances of the BMessageFilter class or to instances of classes that derive from BMessageFilter. The new list replaces any list of filters previously assigned. All objects in the previous list are deleted, as is the BList that contains them. If *list* is `NULL`, the current list is removed without a replacement. `FilterList()` returns the current list of filters.

`AddFilter()` adds a *filter* to the end of the BHandler's list of filters. It creates the BList object if it doesn't already exist. By default, BHandlers don't maintain a BList of filters until one is assigned or the first BMessageFilter is added. `RemoveFilter()` removes a *filter* from the list without deleting it. It returns `true` if successful, and `false` if it can't find the specified filter in the list (or the list doesn't exist). It leaves the BList in place even after removing the last filter.

For `SetFilterList()`, `AddFilter()`, and `RemoveFilter()` to work, the BHandler must be assigned to a BLooper object and the BLooper must be locked.

See also: `BLooper::SetCommonFilterList()`, `BLooper::Lock()`, the BMessageFilter class

SetName(), Name()

> void **SetName**(const char *string*)

> const char ***Name**(void) const

These functions set and return the name that identifies the BHandler. The name is originally set by the constructor. `SetName()` assigns the BHandler a new name, and `Name()` returns the current name. The string returned by `Name()` belongs to the BHandler object; it shouldn't be altered or freed.

See also: the BHandler constructor, `BView::FindView()` in the Interface Kit

SetNextHandler(), NextHandler()

> void **SetNextHandler**(BHandler *handler*)

> BHandler ***NextHandler**(void) const

These functions set and return the BHandler object that's linked to this BHandler. By default, the `MessageReceived()` function passes any messages that a BHandler can't understand to its next handler.

When a BHandler object is added to a BLooper (by BLooper's `AddHandler()` function), the BLooper becomes its next handler by default. BLoopers don't have a next handler.

However, when a BView object is added to a view hierarchy (by `AddChild()`), the Interface Kit assigns the BView's parent as its next handler—unless the parent is the window's top view, in which case the BWindow object becomes its next handler. The handler chain for BViews is therefore BView to BView, up the view hierarchy, to the BWindow object.

`SetNextHandler()` can alter any of these default assignments. For it to work, the BHandler must belong to a BLooper object, its prospective next *handler* must belong to the same BLooper, and the BLooper must be locked.

See also: `MessageReceived()`, `BLooper::AddHandler()`

BInvoker

Derived from:	*none*
Declared in:	be/app/Invoker.h
Library:	libbe.so

Overview

A BInvoker is a simple object that can be "invoked" to send a message to a target destination. That's all it can do. It records the message and keeps track of the destination where it should be delivered. When its `Invoke()` function is called, it sends the message to the target.

A BInvoker instance can be used as an independent object, likely in the service of a more fully functional object of some kind. The class can also be used as a base for more interesting derived classes. Most typically, however, the BInvoker protocol is added, through multiple inheritance, to classes that primarily derive from other, richer base classes. For example, the BControl and BListView classes in the Interface Kit derive from BInvoker as well as, principally, from BView. BMenuItem derives from both BArchivable and BInvoker.

Constructor and Destructor

BInvoker()

BInvoker(BMessage *message,
                    const BHandler *handler, const BLooper *looper = NULL)
BInvoker(BMessage *message, BMessenger messenger)
BInvoker(void)

Initializes the BInvoker with a *message* and sets the target where the message is to be sent when `Invoke()` is called. The target can be set as a local BHandler object, as the preferred handler of a local BLooper, or with a BMessenger object. A BMessenger can target either local or remote objects. The *handler, looper,* and *messenger* arguments passed to the constructor work precisely like identical arguments passed to `SetTarget()`. See that function for a full description of how to set the BInvoker's target.

A BInvoker doesn't have a default message or target. If a target isn't specified when constructing the object, `SetTarget()` must be called to set it. If a message isn't set, `SetMessage()` can be called to set it. However, you can also pass the BMessage to `Invoke()` each time you call it.

See also: `SetTarget()`, `SetMessage()`, `Invoke()`

~BInvoker()

  virtual **~BInvoker**(void)

Frees the BMessage object.

Member Functions

Command()   *see SetMessage()*

HandlerForReply()   *see SetHandlerForReply()*

Invoke()

  virtual status_t **Invoke**(BMessage **message* = NULL)

Sends the *message* passed as an argument—or, if the *message* argument is NULL, the message last assigned by `SetMessage()`—to the designated target. The message is sent asynchronously with no time limit (an infinite timeout).

`Invoke()` is not called for you in BInvoker code; it's designed to be called in derived or client classes when the conditions are met for taking the action encapsulated in the message. For example, a BButton object (defined in the Interface Kit) calls `Invoke()` from its `MouseDown()` and `KeyDown()` functions when the button is clicked or operated from the keyboard. It's up to each derived class to define what events trigger the call to `Invoke()`—what activity constitutes "invoking" the object.

If variable information needs to be added to the message each time it's sent—for example, the current time—it's possible to treat the message assigned to the BInvoker as a model or template for the message that actually gets sent. In this case, you need to get the message from the BInvoker, copy it, add the necessary data to the copy, and pass the copy to `Invoke()`. For example, this code adds the current time:

```
BMessage copy(theInvoker->Message());
copy.AddInt64("when", system_time());
theInvoker->Invoke(&copy);
```

`Invoke()` fails and returns `B_BAD_VALUE` if a BMessage hasn't been assigned to the object and the *message* argument is `NULL`. Otherwise, it returns any errors encountered when sending the message. These are the same errors returned by BMessenger's `SendMessage()` function; they include `B_BAD_PORT_ID` if a target destination hasn't yet been set for the BInvoker or the one that was set has become invalid. If successful in sending the message, `Invoke()` returns `B_OK`.

See also: `SetTarget()`, `SetMessage()`

IsTargetLocal()   *see SetTarget()*

Message()   *see SetMessage()*

Messenger()   *see SetTarget()*

SetHandlerForReply(), HandlerForReply()

> virtual status_t **SetHandlerForReply**(BHandler *replyHandler*)

> BHandler *__HandlerForReply__(void) const

These functions set and return the BHandler object that will be responsible for handling replies to all messages the BInvoker sends. When `Invoke()` is called, the *replyHandler* is passed to the BMessenger's `SendMessage()` function, as follows:

```
theMessenger->SendMessage(message, replyHandler);
```

By default, the handler for replies is `NULL`, which means that all replies will be directed to the BApplication object.

`SetHandlerForReply()` always returns `B_OK`.

See also: `BMessenger::SendMessage()`

SetMessage(), Message(), Command()

> virtual status_t **SetMessage**(BMessage *message*)

> BMessage *__Message__(void) const

> uint32 **Command**(void) const

SetMessage() assigns a *message* to the BInvoker, deleting any message previously assigned. The *message* is not copied; this function transfers ownership of the BMessage object to the BInvoker. The BInvoker will free the object when it's replaced by another message or when the BInvoker is itself freed. Passing a NULL *message* frees the current BMessage object without replacing it.

Message() returns a pointer to the BInvoker's message, and Command() returns its what data member. If a message has not been assigned to the BInvoker, both functions return NULL. (Note that Command() will also return 0 if that happens to be the command constant of the message.)

The message passed to SetMessage() and returned by Message() belongs to the BInvoker object; you can modify it, but you shouldn't assign it to another object or delete it (except by passing NULL to SetMessage()).

SetMessage() always returns B_OK.

See also: Invoke()

SetTarget(), Target(), IsTargetLocal(), Messenger()

virtual status_t **SetTarget**(const BHandler **handler*, const BLooper **looper* = NULL)
virtual status_t **SetTarget**(BMessenger *messenger*)

BHandler ****Target**(BLooper **looper = NULL) const

BMessenger **Messenger**(void) const

bool **IsTargetLocal**(void) const

These functions set the BInvoker's target—the destination of the messages it sends—and return information about the current target.

SetTarget() sets the target to a particular BHandler object, or to the preferred handler of a particular BLooper. It can be passed either a pointer to a BHandler *handler* or a NULL *handler* and a pointer to a BLooper *looper*; it's never necessary to specify both the *handler* and the *looper*, for these reasons:

- If you pass SetTarget() a valid target *handler*, the BInvoker will send messages to the BLooper associated with the *handler* so that the BLooper will dispatch them to that BHandler object. The target *handler* must be a BHandler that's known to a BLooper—that is, it must either be a BLooper itself or have been explicitly added to a BLooper's list of eligible handlers.

  To identify the BLooper where messages should be delivered, SetTarget() calls the *handler*'s Looper() function. Therefore, it's not necessary to also pass SetTarget() a *looper* argument (other than the default NULL). If a BLooper is specified, it must match the object that Looper() returns for the *handler*.

- If you pass `SetTarget()` a NULL *handler* but a valid *looper*, the target will be the BLooper's preferred handler. This permits the targeting decision to be made dynamically. When the BInvoker sends a message to the BLooper, the BLooper will dispatch it to whatever object happens to be its preferred handler at the time.

  For example, the preferred handler of a BWindow object (in the Interface Kit) is the current focus view. Therefore, by passing a NULL *handler* and a BWindow *looper* to `SetTarget()`,

  ```
  theInvoker->SetTarget(NULL, someWindow);
  ```

  the BInvoker can be targeted to whatever BView happens to be in focus when the BWindow receives the message. This is useful for actions that affect the current selection.

- For obvious reasons, the *handler* and *looper* can't both be NULL.

Instead of a BHandler or BLooper, you can set the target as a BMessenger object. The *messenger* will send messages to the BHandler and BLooper specified when it was constructed. The arguments passed to the BMessenger constructor parallel the *handler* and *looper* arguments passed to `SetTarget()`. See the BMessenger class for details.

`Target()` returns the current target BHandler and, if a *looper* argument is provided, fills in a pointer to the target BLooper that will receive the messages `Invoke()` sends. If the target BHandler is the preferred handler of the BLooper, `Target()` returns NULL. It also returns NULL if a target hasn't been set yet.

`Target()` provides the target BHandler and BLooper whether they were set directly, indirectly (where one of the objects is inferred from the other), or through a BMessenger object. However, it can only identify objects that are local to the application. If the BMessenger has a remote target, `Target()` returns NULL and sets the pointer referred to by *looper* to NULL, as it would if a target wasn't set. `IsTargetLocal()` can distinguish these cases; it returns true if the BInvoker and its target are in the same application, and false if they're not.

`Messenger()` returns the BMessenger object the BInvoker uses to send its messages. This may be the *messenger* passed to `SetTarget()` or an object the BInvoker constructs for itself. If a target hasn't been set yet, the returned BMessenger will be invalid.

When successful, `SetTarget()` returns B_OK. It fails and returns B_BAD_VALUE if the proposed target *handler* isn't associated with a BLooper. It also fails if a *handler* and a specific *looper* are both named but the *handler* is associated with some other BLooper object. In this case, it returns B_MISMATCHED_VALUES to indicate that there's a conflict between the two arguments. `SetTarget()` doesn't detect invalid BLoopers and BMessengers.

Target() *see SetTarget()*

BLooper

Derived from: public BHandler

Declared in: be/app/Looper.h

Library: libbe.so

Overview

A BLooper object runs a message loop in a thread that it spawns for that purpose. It's a simple way to create a thread with a message interface.

Various classes in the Be software kits derive from BLooper in order to associate threads with significant entities in the application and to set up message loops with special handling for system messages. In the Application Kit, the BApplication object runs a message loop in the application's main thread. (Unlike other BLoopers, the BApplication object doesn't spawn a separate thread, but takes over the thread in which the application was launched.) In the Interface Kit, each BWindow object runs a loop to handle messages that report activity in the user interface.

Running the Loop

Constructing a BLooper object gets it ready to work, but doesn't actually begin the message loop. Its Run() function must be called to spawn the thread and initiate the loop. Some derived classes may choose to call Run() within the class constructor,

```
MyLooper::MyLooper(const char *name, long priority)
        : BLooper(name, priority)
{
    . . .
    Run();
}
```

so that simply constructing the object yields a fully functioning message loop. Other classes may need to keep object initialization separate from loop initiation. (The BApplication and BWindow classes maintain this separation. An application must explicitly call Run() after constructing the BApplication object; a BWindow calls Run() for you just before putting the window on-screen for the first time.)

Receiving and Dispatching Messages

You can deliver messages to a BLooper's thread by posting them directly (calling its PostMessage() function) or by sending them through a proxy object (calling a

BMessenger's `SendMessage()` function or the `SendReply()` function of a BMessage object). In addition, drag-and-drop operations deliver messages to the threads of the destination windows.

No matter how they get there, all messages are delivered to a port owned by the BLooper object. The BLooper transfers arriving messages from the port to a queue (a BMessageQueue object) as soon as it can. The port doesn't offer much flexibility as a data container and its capacity is fixed (typically 100 slots); the queue is more flexible and has unlimited capacity.

The BLooper takes messages from the queue one at a time, in the order that they arrive, and calls `DispatchMessage()` for each one. `DispatchMessage()` hands the message to a BHandler object; the BHandler kicks off the thread's specific response to the message.

Posting or sending a message to a thread initiates activity within that thread, beginning with the `DispatchMessage()` function. Since `DispatchMessage()` immediately transfers responsibility for incoming messages to BHandler objects, BHandlers determine what happens in the BLooper's thread. Everything that the thread does, it does through BHandlers responding to messages. The BLooper merely runs the posting and dispatching mechanism.

The BLooper object is locked when `DispatchMessage()` is called; it stays locked until the thread has finished responding to the message.

Targeted and Preferred Handlers

When a message is posted or sent to a thread, a target BHandler can be named for it. The target is specified when `PostMessage()` is called or when the BMessenger proxy that will send the message is constructed. Messages that aren't targeted to a specific object are entrusted to the BLooper's *preferred handler*—the object that was last set as the default handler for the thread. The preferred handler can change from time to time depending on circumstances. (For example, a BWindow sets its preferred handler to match its current focus view.)

Because the BLooper class inherits from BHandler, a BLooper can be named as the target for messages it dispatches; a BLooper object can play both roles—the dispatcher role of running the message loop and the handler role of responding to messages. In fact, a BLooper is its own default preferred handler (technically, it's the handler of choice when there's no specific target and the preferred handler is `NULL`, but it amounts to the same thing).

For it to successfully handle messages you define, you must derive a class from BLooper and implement a `MessageReceived()` function that can respond to the messages it dispatches to itself. However, the BLooper class can also be used without change, as it's defined in the kit—as long as all messages are targeted to another handler, or another object is designated as its preferred handler.

Eligible Handlers

A BLooper keeps a list of the BHandler objects that are eligible for the messages it dispatches. `AddHandler()` places a BHandler in the list, and `RemoveHandler()` removes it. (The BLooper is an automatic member of the list; it cannot be removed from its own list or added to the list of another BLooper.)

A BHandler can be associated with only one BLooper at a time; it can't get messages dispatched by any BLooper except the one it's currently affiliated with. However, this eligibility constraint is imposed not by `DispatchMessage()`, but by the BMessenger constructor when a target BHandler is named for the messages it will send and by `PostMessage()` when a BHandler is proposed as the target of a message posted to the BLooper.

The BLooper reveals the membership of its handlers list through its `HandlerAt()` function. A BHandler's `Looper()` function reveals which BLooper it currently belongs to.

Hook Functions

`DispatchMessage()`
Passes incoming messages to a BHandler; can be overridden to change the way certain messages or classes of messages are dispatched.

`QuitRequested()`
Can be implemented to decide whether a request to terminate the message loop and destroy the BLooper should be honored or not.

Constructor and Destructor

BLooper()

BLooper(const char *name* = NULL,
            int32 *priority* = B_NORMAL_PRIORITY,
            int32 *portCapacity* = B_LOOPER_PORT_DEFAULT_CAPACITY)
BLooper(BMessage *archive*)

Assigns the BLooper object a *name* and sets up the port at which it will receive messages and the message queue where messages will reside until they're dispatched. However, you must call `Run()` to spawn the thread that the BLooper will oversee; the constructor doesn't do it. `Run()` creates the thread at the specified *priority* level and begins the message loop.

The *priority* determines how much attention the thread will receive from the scheduler and, consequently, how much CPU time it will get relative to other threads. It's best to choose one of the discrete priority levels defined in *kernel/OS.h*; intermediate priorities are possible but not recommended. The defined priorities, from lowest to highest, are:

B_LOW_PRIORITY	For threads running in the background that shouldn't interrupt other threads.
B_NORMAL_PRIORITY	For all ordinary threads, including the main thread.
B_DISPLAY_PRIORITY	For threads associated with objects in the user interface, including window threads.
B_URGENT_DISPLAY_PRIORITY	For interface threads that deserve more attention than ordinary windows.
B_REAL_TIME_DISPLAY_PRIORITY	For threads that animate the on-screen display.
B_URGENT_PRIORITY	For threads performing time-critical computations.
B_REAL_TIME_PRIORITY	For threads controlling real-time processes that need unfettered access to the CPUs.

Some derived classes may want to call Run() in the constructor, so that the object is set in motion at the time it's created.

A BLooper is constructed in a locked state and must be locked when Run() is called. Run() unlocks the BLooper to begin message processing, but locks it again for each dispatched message.

BLooper objects should always be dynamically allocated (with **new**), never statically allocated on the stack.

See also: Run(), BHandler::SetName()

~BLooper()

virtual ~BLooper(void)

Gets rid of the BLooper's port and all its contents, frees the message queue and all pending messages, stops the message loop, and destroys the thread in which it ran. BHandlers that have been added to the BLooper are not deleted, but BMessageFilter objects added as common filters are, as is the BList object that contains them.

With the exception of the BApplication object, BLoopers should be destroyed by calling the Quit() function (or QuitRequested()), not by using the **delete** operator.

See also: Quit()

Static Functions

Instantiate()

> static BLooper ***Instantiate**(BMessage *archive*)

Returns a new BLooper object, allocated by new and created with the version of the constructor that takes a BMessage *archive*. However, if the *archive* message doesn't contain data for a BLooper object, this function returns NULL.

See also: BArchivable::Instantiate(), instantiate_object(), Archive()

LooperForThread()

> static BLooper ***LooperForThread**(thread_id *thread*)

Returns the BLooper object that runs a message loop in the specified *thread*, or NULL if the thread doesn't belong to a BLooper.

This function is useful in lower-level code to find whether the code is executing in a BLooper's thread and might possibly, therefore, be tying up the message loop and interfering with the responsiveness of the BLooper. For example:

```
BLooper *looper;
if ( looper = LooperForThread(find_thread(NULL) )
    . . .
```

Member Functions

AddCommonFilter()   *see SetCommonFilterList()*

AddHandler(), RemoveHandler(), HandlerAt(), CountHandlers(), IndexOf()

> void **AddHandler**(BHandler *handler*)
>
> bool **RemoveHandler**(BHandler *handler*)
>
> BHandler ***HandlerAt**(int32 *index*) const
>
> int32 **CountHandlers**(void) const
>
> int32 **IndexOf**(BHandler *handler*) const

AddHandler() adds *handler* to the BLooper's list of BHandler objects, and RemoveHandler() removes it. Only BHandlers that have been added to the list are eligible to respond to the messages the BLooper dispatches. (However, this constraint is imposed not by DispatchMessage(), but by PostMessage() and the BMessenger constructor.)

`AddHandler()` fails if the *handler* already belongs to a BLooper; a BHandler can belong to no more than one BLooper at a time. It can change its affiliation from time to time, but must be removed from one BLooper before it can be added to another. `RemoveHandler()` returns `true` if it succeeds in removing the BHandler from the BLooper, and `false` if not or if the *handler* doesn't belong to the BLooper in the first place.

`AddHandler()` also calls the *handler*'s `SetNextHandler()` function to assign it the BLooper as its default next handler. `RemoveHandler()` calls the same function to set the *handler*'s next handler to `NULL`.

`HandlerAt()` returns the BHandler object currently located at *index* in the BLooper's list of eligible handlers, or `NULL` if the index is out of range. Indices begin at 0 and there are no gaps in the list. `CountHandlers()` returns the number of objects currently in the list; the count should always be at least 1, since the list automatically includes the BLooper itself. `IndexOf()` returns the index of the specified *handler*, or `B_ERROR` if that object isn't in the list.

For any of these functions to work, the BLooper must be locked.

See also: `BHandler::Looper()`, `BHandler::SetNextHandler()`, `PostMessage()`, the BMessenger class

Archive()

   virtual status_t **Archive**(BMessage **archive*, bool *deep* = true) const

Archives the BLooper by recording the priority of its thread and the capacity of its port in the BMessage *archive* passed as an argument.

See also: `BArchivable::Archive()`, `Instantiate()` static function

CommonFilterList()   *see SetCommonFilterList()*

CountHandlers()   *see AddHandler()*

CurrentMessage()

   BMessage ****CurrentMessage**(void) const

Returns a pointer to the message that the BLooper's thread is currently processing, or `NULL` if it's currently between messages.

You won't always need this function, since the current message is also passed as an argument to BHandler's `MessageReceived()` hook function. However, the hook functions that respond to system messages (such as `MouseDown()` and

`ScreenChanged()`) are typically passed only part of the information contained in the current BMessage, not the entire object. In such a case, you will have to call `CurrentMessage()` to get complete information about the instruction or event the BMessage object reports.

For example, a `KeyDown()` function (declared in the BView class of the Interface Kit) might check whether the Control key was pressed at the time of the key-down event as follows:

```
void MyView::KeyDown(const char *bytes, int32 numBytes)
{
    BMessage *message = Window()->CurrentMessage();
    if ( message->FindLong("modifiers") & B_CONTROL_KEY ) {
        . . .
    }
    . . .
}
```

See also: `BHandler::MessageReceived()`, `DetachCurrentMessage()`

DetachCurrentMessage()

BMessage ***DetachCurrentMessage**(void)

Detaches the current message (the message the BLooper's thread is currently processing) from the message loop and returns it, or returns `NULL` if the BLooper is between messages. Detaching the message means that:

- It will no longer be the current message. `CurrentMessage()` (and this function) will return `NULL` until the thread gets another message from the queue.

- The thread won't automatically delete the message when the message cycle ends and it's ready to get the next message. It becomes the caller's responsibility to delete the message later (or to post it once more so that it will again be subject to automatic deletion).

Since the message won't be deleted automatically, you have time to reply to it later. However, if the thread that initiated the message is blocked waiting for a reply, you should send one (or get rid of the BMessage) without much delay. If a reply hasn't already been sent by the time the message is deleted, the BMessage destructor sends back a default `B_NO_REPLY` message to indicate that a real reply won't be forthcoming. But if the message isn't deleted and a reply isn't sent, the initiating thread may continue to block. (BMessage's `IsSourceWaiting()` function will let you know whether the message source is waiting for a reply.)

Detaching a message is useful only when you want to stretch out your response to it beyond the end of the message cycle, perhaps passing responsibility for it to another thread while the BLooper's thread continues to get and respond to other messages.

See also: `BHandler::MessageReceived()`, `BMessage::WasDelivered()`, `CurrentMessage()`

DispatchMessage()

> virtual void **DispatchMessage**(BMessage *message*, BHandler *target*)

Dispatches messages as they're received by the BLooper's thread. Precisely how they're dispatched depends on the *message* and the designated *target* BHandler. The BWindow and BApplication classes that derive from BLooper implement their own versions of this function to provide for special dispatching of system messages. Each class defines its own set of such messages.

The *target* may be the BHandler object that was named when the *message* was posted, the handler that was specified when the BMessenger was constructed, the current preferred handler, the handler that was designated as the target for a reply message, or (for a BWindow) the BView where the *message* was dropped. It might be the BLooper itself, acting as a specific target or in its capacity as the default preferred handler. For system messages the target may be `NULL`; if so, the dispatcher must figure out a target for the message based on the contents of the BMessage object.

`DispatchMessage()` is the first stop in the message-handling mechanism. The BLooper's thread calls it automatically as it reads messages from the queue—you never call it yourself.

BLooper's version of `DispatchMessage()` dispatches `B_QUIT_REQUESTED` messages by calling its own `QuitRequested()` function, but only if the message is targeted to the BLooper itself. All other messages are forwarded to the *target*'s `MessageReceived()` function. The BApplication and BWindow classes add other kinds of message-specific dispatching.

You can override this function to dispatch the messages that your own application defines or recognizes. Of course, you can also just wait for these messages to fall through to `MessageReceived()`—the choice is yours. If you do override `DispatchMessage()`, you should:

- Call the base class version of the function *after* you've handled your own messages.
- Exclude all messages that you've handled yourself from the base version call.

For example:

```
void MyLooper::DispatchMessage(BMessage *msg, BHandler *target)
{
    switch ( msg->what ) {
    case MY_MESSAGE1:
        . . .
        break;
```

```
    case MY_MESSAGE2:
        . . .
        break;
    default:
        baseClass::DispatchMessage(msg, target);
        break;
    }
}
```

Don't delete the messages you handle when you're through with them; they're deleted for you.

The system locks the BLooper before calling `DispatchMessage()` and keeps it locked for the duration of the thread's response to the message (until `DispatchMessage()` returns).

See also: the BMessage class, `BHandler::MessageReceived()`, `QuitRequested()`

HandlerAt()   *see AddHandler()*

IndexOf(*see AddHandler()*

IsLocked()   *see LockingThread()*

Lock(), LockWithTimeout(), Unlock()

bool **Lock**(void)

status_t **LockWithTimeout**(bigtime_t *timeout*)

void **Unlock**(void)

These functions provide a mechanism for locking data associated with the BLooper, so that a thread can't alter the data while another thread is in the middle of doing something that depends on it. Only one thread can have the BLooper locked at any given time. `Lock()` blocks until it can lock the object, then returns `true`. If the calling thread already has the object locked, it returns `true` immediately. If another thread has the BLooper locked, it waits until that thread releases the lock and it can acquire it; it then returns `true`. It returns `false` only if the BLooper can't be locked at all—for example, if it was destroyed by another thread.

`LockWithTimeout()` is an alternative to `Lock()` that permits you to limit how long it should block waiting for the lock. The *timeout* is specified in microseconds. If it can't acquire the lock before the time limit expires, it returns `B_TIMED_OUT`. If the *timeout* is 0, it doesn't block but returns immediately with or without the lock. If the *timeout* is `B_INFINITE_TIMEOUT`, it blocks without limit, just as `Lock()` does.

If it locks the BLooper (or if the calling thread already has it locked), LockWithTimeout() returns B_OK. In addition to B_TIMED_OUT, it may also return B_BAD_VALUE if the BLooper has been deleted, is invalid, or was improperly allocated. Each of these failures would cause Lock() to return false.

Note that if Lock() returns 0 (false), it has failed to lock the BLooper, but if LockWithTimeout() returns 0 (B_OK), it has succeeded.

Unlock() releases the lock previously obtained by Lock() or LockWithTimeout(). Only the locking thread should call Unlock(). This is the natural result if it's called in the same section of code to balance a previous Lock() or LockWithTimeout() call, as follows:

```
if ( myLooper->Lock() ) {
    myLooper->DoSomethingCritical();
    . . .
    myLooper->Unlock();
}
```

Calls to Lock() (or LockWithTimeout()) and Unlock() can be nested. For example, the function that's called within the brace of the lock in the example above can itself call Lock() and Unlock():

```
status_t MyLooperClass::DoSomethingCritical(void)
{
    if ( Lock() ) {
        . . .
        Unlock();
        return B_OK;
    }
    return B_ERROR;
}
```

If the locking functions are called more than once from the same thread, it will take an equal number of Unlock() calls from that thread to unlock the BLooper. Only when Unlock() has released the lock at the base level will another thread be permitted to lock the BLooper.

Locking is the basic mechanism for operating safely in a multithreaded environment. It's especially important for the kit classes derived from BLooper—BApplication and BWindow.

However, it's generally not necessary to lock a BLooper when calling functions defined in the class itself or in a derived class. The BLooper is locked for you when:

- It's constructed; Run() unlocks it.
- It dispatches a message; it remains locked until the response to the message is complete.

Moreover, BApplication and BWindow functions are implemented to call Lock() and Unlock() when necessary. Functions you define in classes derived from BLooper (or from BApplication and BWindow) should also call `Lock()` (or `LockWithTimeout()`) and `Unlock()`. In addition, you should employ the locking mechanism when calling functions of a class that's closely associated with a BLooper—for example, when calling functions of a BView that's attached to a BWindow.

Although locking is important and useful, you shouldn't be too cavalier about it. While you hold a BLooper's lock, no other thread can acquire it. If another thread calls a function that tries to lock, the thread will hang until you unlock. Each thread should hold the lock as briefly as possible.

See also: `LockingThread()`, `BMessenger::LockTarget()`, the BLocker class in the Support Kit

LockingThread(), IsLocked(), CountLocks(), CountLockRequests(), Sem()

thread_id **LockingThread**(void) const

bool **IsLocked**(void) const

int32 **CountLocks**(void) const

int32 **CountLockRequests**(void) const

sem_id **Sem**(void) const

These functions may be useful while debugging a BLooper.

`LockingThread()` returns the thread that currently has the BLooper locked, or –1 if the BLooper isn't locked.

`IsLocked()` returns `true` if the calling thread currently has the BLooper locked (if it's the locking thread) and `false` if not (if some other thread is the locking thread or the BLooper isn't locked).

`CountLocks()` returns the number of times the locking thread has locked the BLooper—the number of `Lock()` (or `LockWithTimeout()`) calls that have not yet been balanced by matching `Unlock()` calls.

`CountLockRequests()` returns the number of threads currently trying to lock the BLooper. The count includes the thread that currently has the lock plus all threads currently waiting to acquire it.

`Sem()` returns the `sem_id` for the semaphore that the BLooper uses to implement the locking mechanism.

See also: `Lock()`

MessageReceived()

virtual void **MessageReceived**(BMessage *_message_)

Simply calls the inherited function. For the current release, the BLooper implementation of this function does nothing of importance.

See also: `BHandler::MessageReceived()`

MessageQueue()

BMessageQueue ***MessageQueue**(void) const

Returns the queue that holds messages delivered to the BLooper's thread. You rarely need to examine the message queue directly; it's made available so you can cheat fate by looking ahead.

See also: the BMessageQueue class

PostMessage()

status_t **PostMessage**(BMessage *_message_,
                        BHandler *_handler_,
                        BHandler *_replyHandler_ = NULL)
status_t **PostMessage**(uint32 _command_,
                        BHandler *_handler_,
                        BHandler *_replyHandler_ = NULL)
status_t **PostMessage**(BMessage *_message_)
status_t **PostMessage**(uint32 _command_)

Delivers a _message_ to the BLooper, just as constructing a BMessenger and calling `SendMessage()` would.

If a target _handler_ object is named for the message, it will be passed as the designated handler to `DispatchMessage()`. `DispatchMessage()` will, in turn, call an appropriate function of the _handler_ to respond to the message. However, if the target BHandler isn't associated with the BLooper (if the _handler_'s `Looper()` function returns NULL or some other BLooper object), the posting fails. A BHandler must be associated with a BLooper before it can be the target for dispatched messages; it can't get messages from any other BLooper except the one to which it belongs. For example, BViews in the Interface Kit can receive messages only from the BWindows to which they're attached.

If the _handler_ is NULL, the designated handler will be the BLooper's preferred handler at the time `DispatchMessage()` is called.

For the versions of `PostMessage()` that take a single argument and don't allow you to designate a handler, the handler will be the BLooper object. These shorthand functions may not be supported in the future. It's better programming practice to name the BLooper explicitly as the target *handler*.

Replies to the posted message will be delivered to the *replyHandler* BHandler. Like the target *handler*, this object must belong to a BLooper (not necessarily this BLooper) or be a BLooper itself. If a *replyHandler* isn't specified, replies will be delivered to the BApplication object.

The caller retains ownership of the posted message; it's safe to delete it when `PostMessage()` returns.

If a *command* is passed rather than a message, `PostMessage()` creates a BMessage object, initializes its `what` data member to *command*, and posts it. This simply saves you the step of constructing a BMessage when it won't contain any data. For example, this code

```
myWindow->PostMessage(command, handler);
```

is equivalent to:

```
BMessage message(command);
myWindow->PostMessage(&message, handler);
```

`PostMessage()` returns `B_OK` if successful, `B_MISMATCHED_VALUES` if the posting fails because the proposed target BHandler doesn't belong to the BLooper, and `B_ERROR`, `B_BAD_PORT_ID`, or some other error if it fails because the BLooper is invalid or corrupted.

See also: `BHandler::Looper()`, `DispatchMessage()`

PreferredHandler()   *see SetPreferredHandler()*

Quit()

virtual void **Quit**(void)

Closes down the BLooper, if it's locked. This function fails if the BLooper isn't locked.

If `Run()` hasn't been called yet, `Quit()` just deletes the BLooper object. But if `Run()` has been called, it exits the message loop, frees the message queue, kills the thread, and then deletes the BLooper object.

When `Quit()` is called from the BLooper's thread, all this happens immediately. Any pending messages are ignored and destroyed. Because the thread dies, `Quit()` doesn't return.

However, when called from another thread, `Quit()` waits until all previously posted messages (all messages already in the queue) work their way through the message loop and are handled. It then destroys the BLooper and returns only after the loop, queue, thread, and object no longer exist.

`Quit()` therefore terminates the BLooper synchronously; when it returns, you know that everything has been destroyed. To quit the BLooper asynchronously, you can post a `B_QUIT_REQUESTED` message to the thread (that is, a BMessage with `B_QUIT_REQUESTED` as its `what` data member). `PostMessage()` places the message in the queue and returns immediately.

When it gets a `B_QUIT_REQUESTED` message, the BLooper calls the `Quit-Requested()` virtual function. If `QuitRequested()` returns `true`, as it does by default, it then calls `Quit()`.

See also: `QuitRequested()`

QuitRequested()

   virtual bool **QuitRequested**(void)

Implemented by derived classes to determine whether the BLooper should quit when requested to do so. The BLooper calls this function to respond to `B_QUIT_REQUESTED` messages. If it returns `true`, the BLooper calls `Quit()` to exit the message loop, kill the thread, and delete itself. If it returns `false`, the request is denied and no further action is taken.

BLooper's default implementation of `QuitRequested()` always returns `true`.

A request to quit that's delivered to the BApplication object is, in fact, a request to quit the entire application, not just one thread. BApplication therefore overrides `QuitRequested()` to pass the request on to each window thread before shutting down.

For BWindow objects in the Interface Kit, a request to quit might come from the user clicking the window's close button (a quit-requested event for the window), from the user's decision to quit the application (a quit-requested event for the application), from a Close menu item, or from some other occurrence that forces the window to close.

Classes derived from BWindow typically implement `QuitRequested()` to give the user a chance to save documents before the window is destroyed, or to cancel the request.

If a BWindow represents the last window the application has open (or the last one that gives the user access to menus and the ability to continue doing work), closing the window is tantamount to quitting the application. In this case,

QuitRequested() should make sure the application quits by passing the request along to the BApplication object. For example:

```
bool MyWindow::QuitRequested()
{
    . . .
    if ( myDocuments <= 1 )
        be_app->PostMessage(B_QUIT_REQUESTED, be_app);
    return true;
}
```

After asking the application to quit, QuitRequested() returns true to immediately dispose of the window. If it returns false, BApplication's version of the function will again request the window to quit.

If you call QuitRequested() from your own code, be sure to also provide the code that calls Quit():

```
if ( myLooper->QuitRequested() )
    myLooper->Quit();
```

See also: BApplication::QuitRequested(), Quit()

RemoveCommonFilter() *see SetCommonFilterList()*

Run()

   virtual thread_id **Run**(void)

Spawns a thread at the priority level that was specified when the BLooper was constructed and begins running a message loop in that thread. If successful, this function returns the thread identifier. If unsuccessful, it returns B_NO_MORE_THREADS or B_NO_MEMORY to indicate why.

Run() expects the BLooper to be locked when it's called—and to be locked just once. Since a BLooper is locked on construction, you should not lock it again before calling Run(). Run() will unlock the BLooper, but make sure that it's locked while the thread responds to each dispatched message.

A BLooper can be run only once. If called a second time, Run() returns B_ERROR, but doesn't disrupt the message loop already running. (Currently, it drops into the debugger so you can correct the error.)

The message loop is terminated when Quit() is called, or (potentially) when a B_QUIT_REQUESTED message is received. This also kills the thread and deletes the BLooper object.

See also: the BLooper constructor, the BApplication class, Quit()

SetCommonFilterList(), CommonFilterList(), AddCommonFilter(), RemoveCommonFilter()

virtual void **SetCommonFilterList**(BList *list*)

BList ***CommonFilterList**(void) const

virtual void **AddCommonFilter**(BMessageFilter *filter*)

virtual void **RemoveCommonFilter**(BMessageFilter *filter*)

These functions manage a list of filters that can apply to any message the BLooper receives, regardless of its target BHandler. They complement a similar set of functions defined in the BHandler class. When a filter is associated with a BHandler, it applies only to messages targeted to that BHandler. When it's associated with a BLooper as a common filter, it applies to all messages that the BLooper dispatches, regardless of the target.

In addition to the list of common filters, a BLooper can maintain a filter list in its role as a BHandler. These filters apply only if the BLooper is the target of the message (see `SetFilterList()` in the BHandler class).

`SetCommonFilterList()` assigns the BLooper a new *list* of common filters; the list must contain pointers to instances of the BMessageFilter class or instances of classes that derive from BMessageFilter. The new list replaces any list of common filters previously assigned. All objects in the previous list are deleted, as is the BList itself. If *list* is NULL, the current list is removed without a replacement. `CommonFilterList()` returns the current list of common filters.

`AddCommonFilter()` adds a *filter* to the end of the list of common filters. It creates the BList object if it doesn't already exist. By default, BLoopers don't keep a BList of common filters until one is assigned or `AddCommonFilter()` is called for the first time. `RemoveCommonFilter()` removes a *filter* from the list without freeing it. It returns true if successful, and false if it can't find the specified filter in the list (or the list doesn't exist). It leaves the BList in place even after removing the last filter.

For `SetCommonFilterList()`, `AddCommonFilter()`, and `RemoveCommonFilter()` to work, the BLooper must be loked.

See also: `BHandler::SetFilterList()`, `Lock()`, the BMessageFilter class

SetPreferredHandler(), PreferredHandler()

void **SetPreferredHandler**(void) const

BHandler ***PreferredHandler**(BHandler *handler*)

These functions set and return the BLooper's preferred handler—the BHandler object that should handle messages not specifically targeted to another BHandler.

To designate the current preferred handler—whatever object that may be—as the target of a message, pass `NULL` for the target handler to `PostMessage()` or to the BMessenger constructor.

Posting or sending messages to the preferred handler can be useful. For example, in the Interface Kit, BWindow objects name the current focus view as the preferred handler. This makes it possible for other objects—such as BMenuItems and BButtons—to target messages to the BView that's currently in focus, without knowing what view that might be. For example, by posting its messages to the window's preferred handler, a Cut menu item can make sure that it always acts on whatever view contains the current selection. See Chapter 4, *The Interface Kit*, for information on windows, views, and the role of the focus view.

By default, BLoopers don't have a preferred handler; until one is set, `PreferredHandler()` returns `NULL`. Note however, that messages targeted to the preferred handler are dispatched to the BLooper whenever the preferred handler is `NULL`. In other words, the BLooper acts as default preferred handler, even though the default is formally `NULL`.

See also: `BControl::SetTarget()` and `BMenuItem::SetTarget()` in the Interface Kit, `PostMessage()`

Thread(), Team()

> thread_id **Thread**(void) const

> team_id **Team**(void) const

These functions identify the thread that runs the message loop and the team to which it belongs. `Thread()` returns `B_ERROR` if `Run()` hasn't yet been called to spawn the thread and begin the loop. `Team()` always returns the application's `team_id`.

Unlock()   *see Lock()*

BMessage

Derived from: *none*

Declared in: be/app/Message.h

Library: libbe.so

Overview

A BMessage bundles information so that it can be conveyed from one application to another, one thread of execution to another, or even one object to another. Servers use BMessage objects to notify applications about events. An application can use them to communicate with other applications or to initiate activity in a different thread of the same application. In the Interface Kit, BMessages package information that the user can drag from one location on-screen and drop on another. Behind the scenes in the Storage Kit, they convey queries and hand back requested information.

A BMessage is simply a container. The class defines functions that let you put information into a message, determine what kinds of information are present in a message that's been delivered to you, and get the information out. It also has a function that lets you reply to a message once it's received. But it doesn't have functions that can make the initial delivery. For that it depends on the help of other classes in the Application Kit, particularly BLooper and BMessenger. See the "Messaging" section near the beginning of this chapter for an overview of the messaging mechanism and how BMessage objects work with these other classes.

As a data container, a BMessage can be used for purposes other than sending a message. The operating system assigns them at least three other roles:

- They contain the data that's copied to the clipboard.
- They serve as object archives.
- They record document-specific settings for a print job.

The clipboard is represented by the BClipboard class, documented in this chapter. Archiving and the BArchivable class are described in the Support Kit. Print settings are outlined for the BPrintJob class, in the Interface Kit.

The BMessage class defines five sets of functions:

- The primary set deals with the contents of the message. `AddData()` puts data in a message, `ReplaceData()` replaces it with something else, `MakeEmpty()` and `RemoveName()` remove data previously added, `GetInfo()` gets information about the data the message contains, and `FindData()` retrieves it.

  Most of these functions have specialized versions that are optimized to handle a particular type of data—for example, `AddRect()` adds a BRect object, `AddRef()` adds an `entry_ref` structure complete with the string the structure refers to, and `AddMessage()` adds one BMessage to another.

- A smaller set of functions reports on the status of a received message. For example, `IsSourceWaiting()` tells whether the message sender is waiting for a reply, `WasDropped()` says whether it was dragged and dropped, and `DropPoint()` says where it was dropped.

- A few functions, such as `AddSpecifier()` and `PopSpecifier()`, help with the scripting system.

- `SendReply()` can send a reply to a received message. It works just like `SendMessage()` in the BMessenger class, except that it can't initiate the first message in an exchange and it marks the reply message as a reply.

- Finally, `Flatten()` writes the contents of a message as a flat stream of bytes so the message can be stored on disk or manipulated simply as raw data rather than as an object. `Unflatten()` reconstructs the BMessage from its flattened state.

When data is added to a BMessage, it's associated with a name, a number of bytes, and a type code. The name can be anything you choose, and the number of bytes must be accurate. The type code should permit the message receiver to identify the type of data in the message, so it must be defined as part of a protocol that the sender and receiver both understand. A number of codes for common types are defined in the Support Kit; see "Type Codes" in Chapter 6, *The Support Kit.*

Data Members

uint32 **what**

> A coded constant that captures what the message is about. For example, a message that's delivered to report a mouse-down event will have `B_MOUSE_DOWN` as its **what** data member. An application that requests information from another application might put a `TRANSMIT_DATA` or `SEND_INFO` command in the **what** field. A message that's posted as the result of the user clicking a Cancel button might simply have `CANCEL` as the **what** data member and include no other information.

Constructor and Destructor

BMessage()

> **BMessage**(uint32 *command*)
> **BMessage**(BMessage **message*)
> **BMessage**(const BMessage &*message*)
> **BMessage**(void)

Assigns *command* as the new BMessage object's **what** data member, and ensures that the object otherwise starts out empty. Given the definition of a message constant such as,

```
#define RECEIPT_ACKNOWLEDGED  0x80
```

a complete message can be created as simply as this:

```
BMessage msg(RECEIPT_ACKNOWLEDGED);
```

As a public data member, **what** can also be set explicitly. The following two lines of code are equivalent to the one above:

```
BMessage msg;
msg.what = RECEIPT_ACKNOWLEDGED;
```

Other information can be added to the message by calling **AddData()** or a kindred function.

A BMessage can also be constructed as a copy of another *message*, or assigned from another message:

```
BMessage *differentMsg = new BMessage(QUIT_THAT);
msg = *differentMsg;
```

It's necessary to copy any messages you receive that you want to keep, since the thread that receives the message automatically deletes it before getting the next message. (More typically, you'd copy any data you want to save from the message, but not the BMessage itself.)

As an alternative to copying a received message, you can sometimes detach it from the message loop so that it won't be deleted (see **DetachCurrentMessage()** in the BLooper class).

BMessage objects can be either dynamically allocated with the **new** operator or statically allocated, as shown in the examples above.

When posting or sending a message, or when initiating a drag-and-drop operation, you retain ownership of the BMessage and are responsible for being sure it's destroyed. Stack allocation is therefore often adequate. However, when assigning a BMessage to another object (such as a BInvoker), ownership is transferred with it. Since the object must continue to live after the assigning function returns, dynamic allocation is usually required.

See also: BLooper::DetachCurrentMessage()

~BMessage()

   virtual **~BMessage**(void)

Frees all memory allocated to hold message data. If the message sender is expecting a reply but hasn't received one, a default reply (with **B_NO_REPLY** as the **what** data member) is sent before the message is destroyed.

The system retains ownership of the messages it delivers to you. Each message loop routinely deletes delivered BMessages after the application is finished responding to them.

Member Functions

AddData(), AddBool(), AddInt8(), AddInt16(), AddInt32(), AddInt64(), AddFloat(), AddDouble(), AddString(), AddPoint(), AddRect(), AddRef(), AddMessage(), AddMessenger(), AddPointer(), AddFlat()

> status_t **AddData**(const char *name*, type_code *type*,
>   const void *data*,
>   ssize_t *numBytes*,
>   bool *fixedSize* = true,
>   int32 *numItems* = 1)

> status_t **AddBool**(const char *name*, bool *aBool*)

> status_t **AddInt8**(const char *name*, int8 *anInt8*)

> status_t **AddInt16**(const char *name*, int16 *anInt16*)

> status_t **AddInt32**(const char *name*, int32 *anInt32*)

> status_t **AddInt64**(const char *name*, int64 *anInt64*)

> status_t **AddFloat**(const char *name*, float *aFloat*)

> status_t **AddDouble**(const char *name*, double *aDouble*)

> status_t **AddString**(const char *name*, const char *string*)

> status_t **AddPoint**(const char *name*, BPoint *point*)

> status_t **AddRect**(const char *name*, BRect *rect*)

> status_t **AddRef**(const char *name*, const entry_ref *ref*)

> status_t **AddMessage**(const char *name*, const BMessage *message*)

> status_t **AddMessenger**(const char *name*, BMessenger *messenger*)

> status_t **AddPointer**(const char *name*, const void *pointer*)

> status_t **AddFlat**(const char *name*, BFlattenable *object*, int32 *numItems* = 1)

These functions put data in the BMessage. `AddData()` copies *numBytes* of *data* into the object, and assigns the data a *name* and a *type* code. It copies whatever the *data* pointer points to. For example, if you want to add a string of characters to the message, *data* should be the string pointer (char *). If you want to add only the string pointer, not the characters themselves, *data* should be a pointer to the pointer (char **). The assigned *type* must be a specific data type; it should not be B_ANY_TYPE.

Most of the other functions—AddBool(), AddFloat(), AddRect(), and so on—are specialized and simplified variants of AddData(). They each add a particular type of data to the message, ensure its integrity, and register it under the appropriate type code, as tabulated below:

Function	Adds type	Assigns type code
AddBool()	a bool	B_BOOL_TYPE
AddInt8()	an int8 or uint8	B_INT8_TYPE
AddInt16()	an int16 or uint16	B_INT16_TYPE
AddInt32()	an int32 or uint32	B_INT32_TYPE
AddInt64()	an int64 or uint64	B_INT64_TYPE
AddFloat()	a float	B_FLOAT_TYPE
AddDouble()	a double	B_DOUBLE_TYPE
AddString()	a character string	B_STRING_TYPE
AddPoint()	a BPoint object	B_POINT_TYPE
AddRect()	a BRect object	B_RECT_TYPE
AddRef()	an entry_ref	B_REF_TYPE
AddMessage()	a BMessage object	B_MESSAGE_TYPE
AddMessenger()	a BMessenger object	B_MESSENGER_TYPE
AddPointer()	a pointer to anything	B_POINTER_TYPE

Each of these type-specific functions calculates the number of bytes in the data they add. AddString(), like AddData(), takes a pointer to the data it adds. The *string* must be null-terminated; the null character is counted and copied into the message. Similarly, AddRef() adds the pointed to entry_ref structure to the message (and the variable-length name that's one of the elements of the structure); AddMessage() adds one BMessage to another.

The other functions are simply passed the data directly. For example, AddInt32() takes an int32 or uint32 and AddMessenger() takes a BMessenger object, whereas AddData() would be passed a pointer to an int32 and a pointer to a BMessenger. AddPointer() adds only the pointer it's passed, not the data it points to. To accomplish the same thing, AddData() would take a pointer to the pointer. (The pointer will be valid only locally; it won't be useful to a remote destination.)

AddFlat() flattens an *object* (by calling its Flatten() function) and adds the flat data to the message. It calls the object's TypeCode() function to learn the type code it should associate with the data. FindFlat() will reverse this process and restore the object to its unflat form. The BFlattenable protocol is documented in the Support Kit.

Names of data can be arbitrarily assigned, but a name can't be more than 255 characters long.

If more than one item of data is added under the same name, the BMessage creates an array of data for that name. Each successive call appends another data element to the end of the array. For example, the following code creates an array named "primes" with 37 stored at index 0, 223 stored at index 1, and 1,049 stored at index 2.

```
BMessage *msg = new BMessage(NUMBERS);
int32 x = 37;
int32 y = 223;
int32 z = 1049;

msg->AddInt32("primes", x);
msg->AddFloat("pi", 3.1416);
msg->AddInt32("primes", y);
msg->AddData("primes", B_INT32_TYPE, &z, sizeof(int32));
```

Note that entering other data between some of the elements of an array—in this case, "pi"—doesn't increment the array index.

All elements in a named array must be of the same type; it's an error to try to mix types under the same name.

When you call AddData() to place the first item in an array under a new name, you can provide it with two arguments, *fixedSize* and *numItems*, that will improve the object's efficiency when it adds subsequent items to the array. If the *fixedSize* flag is true, each item in the array must have the same number of bytes; if the flag is false, items can vary in size. For example, all items in an array of integers will be the same size, but the items in an array of strings are likely to have differing lengths. AddData() takes the *numItems* argument as a hint, an indication of how many items will be added to the array. It can more economically allocate memory for the items if it can anticipate how many there will be.

When adding subsequent items to the array, AddData() ignores the *fixedSize* and *numItems* arguments; they're relevant only when the array is first established. You can call AddData() with these arguments to provide the necessary hints when setting up the array, then call other functions to add more items.

You can also provide a *numItems* hint to AddFlat() when you call it to set up a new array. AddFlat() calls the object's IsFixedSize() function to discover whether all items in the array will be the same size.

These functions return B_ERROR if the data is too massive to be added to the message, B_BAD_TYPE if the data can't be added to an existing array because it's the wrong type, B_NO_MEMORY if the BMessage can't get enough memory to hold the data, and B_BAD_VALUE if the proposed *name* for the data is longer than 255 bytes. If all goes well, they return B_OK.

There's no limit on the number of named fields a message can contain or on the size of a field's data. However, since the search is linear, combing through a very long list of names to find a particular piece of data may be inefficient. Also, because of the amount of data that must be moved, an extremely large message (over 100,000 bytes, say) can slow the delivery mechanism. It's sometimes better to put some of the information in a common location (a file, a private clipboard, a shared area of memory) and just refer to it in the message. Sometimes later messages can be used to arrange for the transfer of data if the message receiver requires it.

See also: FindData(), GetInfo()

AddSpecifier()

> status_t **AddSpecifier**(const BMessage *message*)
>
> status_t **AddSpecifier**(const char *property*)
>
> status_t **AddSpecifier**(const char *property*, int32 *index*)
>
> status_t **AddSpecifier**(const char *property*, int32 *index*, int32 *range*)
>
> status_t **AddSpecifier**(const char *property*, const char *name*)

Adds an item to a data field named "specifiers" in the BMessage. The item is itself a message, but one with a special role in the scripting system: It names a property of an object and specifies how to pick out a particular instance of the property.

To identify the property, the specifier *message* has a B_STRING_TYPE field named "property" containing the property name. To identify which instance of the property is of interest, it has a what data member that indicates a method for locating the instance. The method may be supported by additional data fields.

The BeOS defines the following types of specifiers (what data members):

B_INDEX_SPECIFIER	The specifier message has a B_INT32_TYPE field named "index" with the index of a particular instance of the property. Indices begin at 0.
B_REVERSE_INDEX_SPECIFIER	The "index" in the specifier message counts from the end toward the beginning of the list.
B_RANGE_SPECIFIER	The specifier message has an "index" field plus another B_INT32_TYPE field named "range"; it specifies a total count of "range" data items beginning with the item at "index".

B_REVERSE_RANGE_SPECIFIER	The "index" and "range" count from the end of the data toward the beginning. For some types of data, especially text, the range may not work in reverse even though the index does.
B_NAME_SPECIFIER	The specifier message has a B_STRING_ENTRY called "name" with the name of a particular instance of the property.
B_DIRECT_SPECIFIER	The data in question is adequately identified by the property name alone. In other words, the target object has either just one instance of the property or all instances are specified.

Other kinds of specifiers are also possible. So that the ones you define aren't confused with those the BeOS defines (or might define in the future), they should be assigned values greater than B_SPECIFIERS_END. For example:

```
#define VALUE_SPECIFIER B_SPECIFIERS_END + 1
```

You can construct the specifier BMessage yourself and add it by calling the version of AddSpecifier() that takes a *message* argument. Or, for some of the specifiers listed above, you can have AddSpecifier() construct it:

- If you pass a *property* name to AddSpecifier(), and no other arguments, it adds a B_DIRECT_SPECIFIER specifier to the BMessage.

- If you pass a *property* name and an *index*, it adds a B_INDEX_SPECIFIER specifier.

- If you also pass a *range*, it adds a B_RANGE_SPECIFIER specifier.

- If you pass a *name*, it adds a B_NAME_SPECIFIER specifier.

To be recognized as a specifier, a BMessage must be added by calling AddSpecifier(). Constructing a specifier BMessage and calling AddMessage() or AddData() won't work.

If a BMessage has specifiers, the "specifiers" name should not be used for any other data (another type of BMessage, for example). If it doesn't have specifiers, the name is free to be used for any type of data.

AddSpecifier() returns B_OK if it's able to add the specifier to the BMessage and an error code, generally only B_NO_MEMORY to indicate that it has run out of memory, if not.

See also: GetCurrentSpecifier(), HasSpecifiers()

CountNames()

int32 **CountNames**(type_code *type*) const

Returns the number of named data fields in the BMessage that store data of the specified *type*. An array of information held under a single name counts as one field; each name is counted only once, no matter how many data items are stored under that name.

If *type* is B_ANY_TYPE, this function counts all named fields. If *type* is a specific type, it counts only fields that store data registered as that type.

See also: GetInfo()

DropPoint()   *see WasDropped()*

FindData(), FindBool(), FintInt8(), FindInt16(), FindInt32(), FindInt64(), FindFloat(), FindDouble(), FindString(), FindPoint(), FindRect(), FindRef(), FindMessage(), FindMessenger(), FindPointer(), FindFlat()

```
status_t FindData(const char *name,
                  type_code type,
                  int32 index,
                  const void **data,
                  ssize_t *numBytes) const
status_t FindData(const char *name,
                  type_code type,
                  const void **data,
                  ssize_t *numBytes) const

status_t FindBool(const char *name,
                  int32 index,
                  bool *aBool) const
status_t FindBool(const char *name, bool *aBool) const
bool FindBool(const char *name, int32 index = 0) const

status_t FindInt8(const char *name,
                  int32 index,
                  int8 *anInt8) const
status_t FindInt8(const char *name,
                  int8 *anInt8) const

status_t FindInt16(const char *name,
                   int32 index,
                   int16 *anInt16) const
status_t FindInt16(const char *name, int16 *anInt16) const
```

int16 **FindInt16**(const char *_name_, int32 _index_ = 0) const

status_t **FindInt32**(const char *_name_,
           int32 _index_,
           int32 *_anInt32_) const
status_t **FindInt32**(const char *_name_, int32 *_anInt32_) const
int32 **FindInt32**(const char *_name_, int32 _index_ = 0) const

status_t **FindInt64**(const char *_name_,
           int32 _index_,
           int64 *_anInt64_) const
status_t **FindInt64**(const char *_name_, int64 *_anInt64_) const

status_t **FindFloat**(const char *_name_,
           int32 _index_,
           float *_aFloat_) const
status_t **FindFloat**(const char *_name_, float *_aFloat_) const
float **FindFloat**(const char *_name_, int32 _index_ = 0) const

status_t **FindDouble**(const char *_name_,
           int32 _index_,
           double *_aDouble_) const
status_t **FindDouble**(const char *_name_, double *_aDouble_) const
double **FindDouble**(const char *_name_, int32 _index_ = 0) const

status_t **FindString**(const char *_name_,
           int32 _index_,
           const char **_string_) const
status_t **FindString**(const char *_name_, const char **_string_) const
const char ***FindString**(const char *_name_, int32 _index_ = 0) const

status_t **FindPoint**(const char *_name_,
           int32 _index_,
           BPoint *_point_) const
status_t **FindPoint**(const char *_name_, BPoint *_point_) const
BPoint **FindPoint**(const char *_name_, int32 _index_ = 0) const

int32 **FindRect**(const char *_name_,
           int32 _index_,
           BRect *_rect_) const
int32 **FindRect**(const char *_name_, BRect *_rect_) const
BRect **FindRect**(const char *_name_, int32 _index_ = 0) const

status_t **FindRef**(const char *_name_,
           int32 _index_,
           entry_ref *_ref_) const

status_t **FindRef**(const char *_name_, entry_ref *_ref_) const

status_t **FindMessage**(const char *_name_,
                    int32 _index_,
                    BMessage *_message_) const
status_t **FindMessage**(const char *_name_, BMessage *_message_) const

status_t **FindMessenger**(const char *_name_,
                    int32 _index_,
                    BMessenger *_messenger_) const
status_t **FindMessenger**(const char *_name_, BMessenger *_messenger_) const

status_t **FindPointer**(const char *_name_,
                    int32 _index_,
                    void **_pointer_) const
status_t **FindPointer**(const char *_name_, void **_pointer_) const

status_t **FindFlat**(const char *_name_,
                    int32 _index_,
                    BFlattenable *_object_) const
status_t **FindFlat**(const char *_name_, BFlattenable *_object_) const

These functions retrieve data from the BMessage. Each looks for data stored under the specified _name_. If more than one data item has the same name, an _index_ can be provided to tell the function which item in the _name_ array it should find. Indices begin at 0. If an index isn't provided, the function will find the first, or only, item in the array.

FindData() places a pointer to the requested data item in the variable referred to by _data_ and records the size of the item (the number of bytes it takes up) in the variable referred to by _numBytes_. It asks for data of a specified _type_. If the _type_ is B_ANY_TYPE, it provides a pointer to the data no matter what type it actually is. But if _type_ is a specific data type, it provides the pointer only if the _name_ field holds data of that particular type.

It's important to keep in mind that FindData() only gives you a pointer to the data, never the data itself. If the data _is_ a pointer—for example, a pointer to an object—it provides a pointer to the pointer. The variable that's assigned the returned pointer must be doubly indirect. For example:

```
MyClass **object;
ssize_t numBytes;
if ( !msg->FindData("name", B_POINTER_TYPE, &object, &numBytes) )
    (*object)->GetSomeInformation();
    . . .
}
```

The other functions are specialized versions of `FindData()`. They match the corresponding `Add...()` functions and search for named data of a particular type, as described below:

Function	Finds data	Registered as type
FindBool()	a bool	B_BOOL_TYPE
FindInt8()	an int8 or uint8	B_INT8_TYPE
FindInt16()	an int16 or uint16	B_INT16_TYPE
FindInt32()	an int32 or uint32	B_INT32_TYPE
FindInt64()	an int64 or uint64	B_INT64_TYPE
FindFloat()	a float	B_FLOAT_TYPE
FindDouble)	a double	B_DOUBLE_TYPE
FindString()	a character string	B_STRING_TYPE
FindPoint()	a BPoint object	B_POINT_TYPE
FindRect()	a BRect object	B_RECT_TYPE
FindRef()	an entry_ref	B_REF_TYPE
FindMessage()	a BMessage object	B_MESSAGE_TYPE
FindMessenger()	a BMessenger object	B_MESSENGER_TYPE
FindPointer()	a pointer to anything	B_POINTER_TYPE

`FindString()` works like `FindData()`; it places a pointer to the string in the variable that its *string* argument refers to. You have to copy the characters yourself.

The other type-specific functions retrieve the requested data item from the message by copying it to the variable referred to by the last argument; you get the data, not just a pointer to it. For example, `FindMessenger()` assigns the BMessenger it finds in the message to the *messenger* object, whereas `FindData()` would provide only a pointer to a BMessenger. `FindPointer()` puts the found pointer in the void* variable that *pointer* refers to; `FindData()`, as illustrated above, would provide a pointer to the pointer. (If the message was delivered from a remote source, pointers retrieved from the message won't be valid.)

`FindRef()` retrieves an `entry_ref` structure; the data that's used to reconstitute the structure may have been added as an `entry_ref` (through `AddRef()`), or as a flattened BPath object (`AddFlat()`).

`FindFlat()` assigns the object stored in the BMessage to the *object* passed as an argument—it calls the *object*'s `Unflatten()` function and passes it the flat data from the message—provided that the two objects have compatible types. The argument *object*'s `AllowsTypeCode()` function must return `true` when tested with the type code stored in the message; if not, `FindFlat()` fails and returns `B_BAD_VALUE`.

If these functions can't find any data associated with *name*, they return a B_NAME_NOT_FOUND error. If they can't find *name* data of the requested *type* (or the type the function returns), they return B_BAD_TYPE. If the *index* is out of range, they return B_BAD_INDEX. You can rely on the values they retrieve only if they return B_OK and the data was correctly recorded when it was added to the message.

When they fail, FindData() and FindString() provide NULL pointers. FindRect() hands you an invalid rectangle and FindMessenger() an invalid BMessenger. Most of the other functions set the data values to 0, which may be indistinguishable from valid values.

Finding a data item doesn't remove it from the BMessage.

(Several functions, such as FindRect() and FindInt32(), have versions that return the found value directly. These versions don't report errors and may not be supported in the future.)

See also: GetInfo(), AddData()

Flatten(), Unflatten(), FlattenedSize()

> status_t **Flatten**(BDataIO **object*, ssize_t **numBytes* = NULL) const
> status_t **Flatten**(char **address*, ssize_t *numBytes* = NULL) const

> status_t **Unflatten**(BDataIO **object*)
> status_t **Unflatten**(const char **address*)

> ssize_t **FlattenedSize**(void) const

These functions write the BMessage and the data it contains to a "flat" (untyped) buffer of bytes, and reconstruct a BMessage object from such a buffer.

If passed a BDataIO *object* (including a BFile), Flatten() calls the object's Write() function to write the message data. If passed the *address* of a buffer, it begins writing at the start of the buffer. FlattenedSize() returns the number of bytes you must provide in the buffer to hold the flattened object. Flatten() places the number of bytes actually written in the variable that its *numBytes* argument refers to.

Unflatten() empties the BMessage of any information it may happen to contain, then initializes the object from data read from the buffer. If passed a BDataIO *object*, it calls the object's Read() function to read the message data. If passed a buffer *address*, it begins reading at the start of the buffer. It's up to the caller to make sure that Unflatten() reads data that Flatten() wrote and that pointers are positioned correctly.

Flatten() returns any errors encountered when writing the data, or B_OK if there is no error.

If it doesn't recognize the data in the buffer as being a flattened object or there's a failure in reading the data, Unflatten() returns B_BAD_VALUE. If it doesn't have adequate memory to recreate the whole message, it returns B_NO_MEMORY. Otherwise, it returns B_OK.

See also: the BDataIO class in the Support Kit

GetCurrentSpecifier(), PopSpecifier()

status_t **GetCurrentSpecifier**(int32 *index,*
> BMessage *specifier* = NULL,
> int32 *what* = NULL,
> const char **property* = NULL) const

status_t **PopSpecifier**(void)

GetCurrentSpecifier() unpacks the current specifier in the BMessage, the one at the top of the specifier stack; PopSpecifier() changes the notion of which specifier is current, by popping the current one from the stack.

These functions aid in implementing a class-specific version of BHandler's ResolveSpecifier() function—the first gets the specifier that needs to be resolved, and the second pops it from the stack after it is resolved. You can also call them to examine relevant specifiers when handling a message that targets an object property (such as B_GET_PROPERTY or B_DESTROY_PROPERTY).

A scripting BMessage keeps specifiers in a data array named "specifiers"; each specifier is itself a BMessage, but one with a special structure and purpose in the scripting system. See the "Scripting" section near the beginning of this chapter for an overview of the system and the place of specifiers in it.

The specifiers in a message are ordered and, until PopSpecifier() is called, the one that was added last—the one with the greatest index—is the current specifier. PopSpecifier() merely decrements the index that picks the current specifier; it doesn't delete anything from the BMessage.

GetCurrentSpecifier() puts the index of the current specifier in the variable that its first argument, *index,* refers to. If other arguments are provided, it makes the *specifier* BMessage a copy of the current specifier. It also extracts two pieces of information from the *specifier.* It places the **what** data member of the specifier in the *what* variable and a pointer to the property name in the *property* variable. These last two output arguments won't be valid if the *specifier* argument is NULL.

Both functions fail if the BMessage doesn't contain specifiers. In addition, GetCurrentSpecifier() fails if it can't find data in the BMessage for its *specifier* and *property* arguments, and PopSpecifier() fails if the BMessage isn't one that has been delivered to you after being processed through a message loop. When it fails, `GetCurrentSpecifier()` returns `B_BAD_SCRIPT_SYNTAX`, but `PopSpecifier()` returns `B_BAD_VALUE`. On success, both functions return `B_OK`.

See also: `AddSpecifier()`, `HasSpecifier()`, `BHandler::ResolveSpecifier()`

GetInfo()

status_t **GetInfo**(const char **name*,
             type_code **typeFound*,
             int32 **countFound* = NULL) const
status_t **GetInfo**(type_code *type*, int32 *index*,
             char **nameFound,
             type_code **typeFound*,
             int32 **countFound* = NULL) const

Provides information about the data fields stored in the BMessage.

When passed a *name* that matches a name within the BMessage, `GetInfo()` places the type code for data stored under that name in the variable referred to by *typeFound* and writes the number of data items with that name into the variable referred to by *countFound*. It then returns `B_OK`. If it can't find a *name* field within the BMessage, it sets the *countFound* variable to 0, and returns `B_NAME_NOT_FOUND` (without modifying the *typeFound* variable).

When passed a *type* and an *index*, `GetInfo()` looks only at fields that store data of the requested type and provides information about the field at the requested index. Indices begin at 0 and are type specific. For example, if the requested *type* is `B_DOUBLE_TYPE` and the BMessage contains a total of three named fields that store `double` data, the first field would be at *index* 0, the second at 1, and the third at 2— no matter what other types of data actually separate them in the BMessage, and no matter how many data items each field contains. (Note that the index in this case ranges over fields, each with a different name, not over the data items within a particular named field.) If the requested type is `B_ANY_TYPE`, this function looks at all fields and gets information about the one at *index* whatever its type.

If successful in finding data of the *type* requested at *index*, `GetInfo()` returns `B_OK` and provides information about the data through the last three arguments:

- It places a pointer to the name of the data field in the variable referred to by *nameFound*.

- It puts the code for the type of data the field contains in the variable referred to by *typeFound*. This will be the same as the *type* requested, unless the requested type is `B_ANY_TYPE`, in which case *typeFound* will be the actual type stored under the name.

- It records the number of data items stored within the field in the variable referred to by *countFound*.

If `GetInfo()` can't find data of the requested *type* at *index*, it sets the *countFound* variable to 0, and returns `B_BAD_TYPE`. If the index is out of range, it returns `B_BAD_INDEX`.

This version of `GetInfo()` can be used to iterate through all the BMessage's data. For example:

```
char   *name;
uint32  type;
int32   count;

for ( int32 i = 0;
      msg->GetInfo(B_ANY_TYPE, i, &name, &type, &count);
      i++ ) {
      . . .
}
```

If the index is incremented from 0 in this way, all data of the requested type will have been read when `GetInfo()` returns `false`. If the requested type is `B_ANY_TYPE`, as shown above, it will reveal the name and type of every field in the BMessage.

See also: `HasData()`, `AddData()`, `FindData()`

HasData(), HasBool(), HasInt8(), HasInt16(), HasInt32(), HasInt64(), HasFloat(), HasDouble(), HasString(), HasPoint(), HasRect(), HasRef(), HasMessage(), HasMessenger(), HasPointer()

bool **HasData**(const char *name*, type_code *type*, int32 *index* = 0) const

bool **HasBool**(const char *name*, int32 *index* = 0) const

bool **HasInt8**(const char *name*, int32 *index* = 0) const

bool **HasInt16**(const char *name*, int32 *index* = 0) const

bool **HasInt32**(const char *name*, int32 *index* = 0) const

bool **HasInt64**(const char *name*, int32 *index* = 0) const

bool **HasFloat**(const char *name*, int32 *index* = 0) const

bool **HasDouble**(const char *name*, int32 *index* = 0) const

bool **HasString**(const char *name*, int32 *index* = 0) const

bool **HasPoint**(const char *name*, int32 *index* = 0) const bool **HasRect**(const char *name*, int32 *index* = 0) const

bool **HasRef**(const char *name*, int32 *index* = 0) const

bool **HasMessage**(const char *name*, int32 *index* = 0) const

bool **HasMessenger**(const char *name*, int32 *index* = 0) const

bool **HasPointer**(const char *name*, int32 *index* = 0) const

These functions test whether the BMessage contains data of a given name and type. They're generally less useful than the corresponding Find...() functions. If the message contains the data you're looking for, you probably will want to call Find...() to get it. Since the Find...() functions return errors if the message doesn't have data of the requested name and type, it's more efficient to just call Find...() and not bother with Has...(). At any rate, here's how these functions work:

If *type* is B_ANY_TYPE and no *index* is provided, HasData() returns true if the BMessage stores any data at all under the specified *name*, regardless of its type, and false if the name passed doesn't match any within the object.

If *type* is a particular type code, HasData() returns true only if the BMessage has a *name* field that stores data of that type. If the *type* and *name* don't match, it returns false.

If an *index* is supplied, HasData() returns true only if the BMessage has a *name* field that stores a data item of the specified *type* at that particular *index*. If the index is out of range, it returns false.

The other functions—HasBool(), HasFloat(), HasPoint(), and so on—are specialized versions of HasData(). They test for a particular type of data stored under the specified *name*.

See also: GetInfo()

HasSpecifiers()

bool **HasSpecifiers**(void) const

Returns true if the BMessage has specifiers added by an AddSpecifier() function, and false if not.

See also: AddSpecifier(), GetCurrentSpecifier()

IsEmpty()   *see MakeEmpty()*

IsReply()   *see WasDelivered()*

IsSourceRemote()   *see WasDelivered()*

IsSourceWaiting()   *see WasDelivered()*

IsSystem()

> bool **IsSystem**(void) const

Returns `true` if the `what` data member of the BMessage object identifies it as a system-defined message, and `false` if not.

MakeEmpty(), IsEmpty()

> status_t **MakeEmpty**(void)

> bool **IsEmpty**(void) const

`MakeEmpty()` removes and frees all data that has been added to the BMessage, without altering the `what` constant. It returns `B_OK`, unless the message can't be altered (as it can't if it's being dragged), in which case it returns `B_ERROR`.

`IsEmpty()` returns `true` if the BMessage has no data (whether or not it was emptied by `MakeEmpty()`), and `false` if it has some.

See also: `RemoveName()`

Previous()   *see WasDelivered()*

PrintToStream()

> void **PrintToStream**(void) const

Prints information about the BMessage to the standard output stream (`stdout`). Each field of named data is reported in the following format,

`#entry name, type = type, count = count`

where *name* is the name that the data is registered under, *type* is the constant that indicates what type of data it is, and *count* is the number of data items in the named array.

RemoveName(), RemoveData()

> status_t **RemoveName**(const char *name*)

> status_t **RemoveData**(const char *name*, int32 *index* = 0)

`RemoveName()` removes all data entered in the BMessage under *name* and the name itself. `RemoveData()` removes the single item of data at *index* in the *name* array. If the array has just one data item, it removes the array and name just as `RemoveName()` would.

Both functions free the memory that was allocated to hold the data, and return `B_OK` when successful. However, if there's no data in the BMessage under *name*, they return a `B_NAME_NOT_FOUND` error. If message data can be read but can't be changed (as it can't for a message that's being dragged), they both return `B_ERROR`. If the *index* is out of range, `RemoveData()` returns `B_BAD_INDEX` (the index is too high) or `B_BAD_VALUE` (the value passed is a negative number).

See also: `MakeEmpty()`

ReplaceData(), ReplaceBool(), ReplaceInt8(), ReplaceInt16(), ReplaceInt32(), ReplaceInt64(), ReplaceFloat(), ReplaceDouble(), ReplaceString(), ReplacePoint(), ReplaceRect(), ReplaceRef(), ReplaceMessage(), ReplaceMessenger(), ReplacePointer(), ReplaceFlat()

status_t **ReplaceData**(const char *name*,
                 type_code *type*,
                 const void **data*,
                 ssize_t *numBytes*)

status_t **ReplaceData**(const char *name*,
                 type_code *type*,
                 int32 *index*,
                 const void **data*,
                 ssize_t *numBytes*)

status_t **ReplaceBool**(const char *name*, bool *aBool*)
status_t **ReplaceBool**(const char *name*,
                 int32 *index*,
                 bool *aBool*)

status_t **ReplaceInt8**(const char *name*, int8 *anInt8*)
status_t **ReplaceInt8**(const char *name*,
                 int32 *index*,
                 int8 *anInt8*)

status_t **ReplaceInt16**(const char *name*, int16 *anInt16*)

status_t **ReplaceInt16**(const char *_name_,
         int32 _index_,
         int16 _anInt16_)

status_t **ReplaceInt32**(const char *_name_, long _anInt32_)
status_t **ReplaceInt32**(const char *_name_,
         int32 _index_,
         int32 _anInt32_)

status_t **ReplaceInt64**(const char *_name_, int64 _anInt64_)
status_t **ReplaceInt64**(const char *_name_,
         int32 _index_,
         int64 _anInt64_)

status_t **ReplaceFloat**(const char *_name_, float _aFloat_)
status_t **ReplaceFloat**(const char *_name_,
         int32 _index_,
         float _aFloat_)

status_t **ReplaceDouble**(const char *_name_, double _aDouble_)
status_t **ReplaceDouble**(const char *_name_,
         int32 _index_,
         double _aDouble_)

status_t **ReplaceString**(const char *_name_, const char *_string_)
status_t **ReplaceString**(const char *_name_,
         int32 _index_,
         const char *_string_)

status_t **ReplacePoint**(const char *_name_, BPoint _point_)
status_t **ReplacePoint**(const char *_name_,
         int32 _index_,
         BPoint _point_)

status_t **ReplaceRect**(const char *_name_, BRect _rect_)
status_t **ReplaceRect**(const char *_name_,
         int32 _index_,
         BRect _rect_)

status_t **ReplaceRef**(const char *_name_, entry_ref *_ref_)
status_t **ReplaceRef**(const char *_name_,
         int32 _index_,
         entry_ref *_ref_)

status_t **ReplaceMessage**(const char *_name_, BMessage *_message_)

status_t **ReplaceMessage**(const char *name,
                               int32 *index*,
                               BMessage *message)

status_t **ReplaceMessenger**(const char *name, BMessenger *messenger*)
status_t **ReplaceMessenger**(const char *name,
                               int32 *index*,
                               BMessenger *messenger*)

status_t **ReplacePointer**(const char *name, const void *pointer)
status_t **ReplacePointer**(const char *name,
                               int32 *index*,
                               const void *pointer)

status_t **ReplaceFlat**(const char *name, BFlattenable *object)
status_t **ReplaceFlat**(const char *name,
                               int32 *index*,
                               BFlattenable *object)

These functions replace a data item in the *name* field with another item passed as an argument. If an *index* is provided, they replace the item in the *name* array at that index; if an *index* isn't mentioned, they replace the first (or only) item stored under *name*. If an *index* is provided but it's out of range, the replacement fails.

`ReplaceData()` replaces an item in the *name* field with *numBytes* of *data*, but only if the *type* code that's specified for the data matches the type of data that's already stored in the field. The *type* must be specific; it can't be `B_ANY_TYPE`.

`ReplaceFlat()` replaces a flattened object with another *object*, provided that the type reported by the argument *object* (by its `TypeCode()` function) matches the type recorded for the item in the message. If not, it returns `B_BAD_VALUE`.

The other functions are simplified versions of `ReplaceData()`. They each handle the specific type of data declared for their last arguments. They succeed if this type matches the type of data already in the *name* field, and fail if it does not. The new data is added precisely as the counterpart `Add...()` function would add it.

If successful, all these functions return `B_OK`. If unsuccessful, they return an error code—`B_ERROR` if the message is read-only (as it is while the message is being dragged), `B_BAD_INDEX` if the *index* is out of range, `B_NAME_NOT_FOUND` if the *name* field doesn't exist, or `B_BAD_TYPE` if the field doesn't contain data of the specified type.

See also: `AddData()`

ReturnAddress()

BMessenger **ReturnAddress**(void)

Returns a BMessenger object that can be used to reply to the BMessage. Calling the BMessenger's `SendMessage()` function is equivalent to calling `SendReply()`, except that the return message won't be marked as a reply. If a reply isn't allowed (if the BMessage wasn't delivered), the returned BMessenger will be invalid.

If you want to use the `ReturnAddress()` BMessenger to send a synchronous reply, you must do so before the BMessage is deleted and a default reply is sent.

See also: `SendReply()`, `WasDelivered()`

SendReply()

status_t **SendReply**(BMessage *message,
      BMessage *reply,
      bigtime_t sendTimeout = B_INFINITE_TIMEOUT,
      bigtime_t replyTimeout = B_INFINITE_TIMEOUT)
status_t **SendReply**(BMessage *message,
      BHandler *replyHandler = NULL,
      bigtime_t sendTimeout = B_INFINITE_TIMEOUT)
status_t **SendReply**(uint32 command, BMessage *reply)
status_t **SendReply**(uint32 command, BHandler *replyHandler = NULL)

Sends a reply *message* back to the sender of the BMessage (in the case of a synchronous reply) or to a target BHandler (in the case of an asynchronous reply). Whether the reply is synchronous or asynchronous depends on how the BMessage that's sending the reply was itself sent:

- The reply is delivered synchronously if the message sender is waiting for one to arrive. The function that sent the BMessage doesn't return until it receives the reply (or a timeout expires). If an expected reply has not been sent by the time the BMessage object is deleted, a default `B_NO_REPLY` message is returned to the sender. If a reply is sent after the sender gave up waiting for it to arrive, the reply *message* disappears into the bowels of the system.

- The reply is delivered asynchronously if the message sender isn't waiting for a reply. In this case, the sending function designates a target BHandler and BLooper for any replies that might be sent, then returns immediately after putting the BMessage in the pipeline. Posted messages and messages that are dragged and dropped are also eligible for asynchronous replies.

`SendReply()` works only for BMessage objects that have been processed through a message loop and delivered to you. The caller retains ownership of the reply *message* passed to `SendReply()`; it can be deleted (or left to die on the stack) after the function returns.

`SendReply()` sends a message—a reply message, to be sure, but a message nonetheless. It behaves exactly like the other message-sending function, BMessenger's `SendMessage()`:

- By passing it a *reply* argument, you can ask for a synchronous reply to the reply message it sends. It won't return until it receives the reply.

- By supplying a *replyHandler* argument, you can arrange for an expected asynchronous reply. If a specific target isn't specified, the BApplication object will handle the reply if one is sent.

By default, `SendReply()` doesn't return until the reply message is delivered (placed in the BLooper's port queue). It's possible, in some circumstances, for the receiving port queue to be full, in which case `SendReply()` will block until a slot becomes free. However, you can limit how long `SendReply()` will wait to deliver the message before it gives up and returns. The *sendTimeout* argument is the number of microseconds you give the function to do its work. If the time limit is exceeded, the function fails and returns an error (`B_TIMED_OUT`).

When asking for a synchronous reply, separate *sendTimeout* and *replyTimeout* limits can be set for sending the message and receiving the reply. There is no time limit if a timeout value is set to `B_INFINITE_TIMEOUT`—as it is by default. The function won't block at all if the timeout is set to 0.

If a *command* is passed rather than a *message*, `SendReply()` constructs the reply BMessage, initializes its **what** data member with the *command* constant, and sends it just like any other reply. The *command* versions of this function have infinite timeouts; they block until the message is delivered and, if requested, a synchronous reply is received.

This function returns `B_OK` if the reply is successfully sent. If there's a problem in sending the message, it returns the same sort of error code as BMessenger's `SendMessage()`. It may also report a reply-specific problem. The more informative return values are as follows:

Error code	Is returned when
B_BAD_REPLY	Attempting to reply to a message that hasn't been delivered yet.
B_DUPLICATE_REPLY	Sending a reply after one has already been sent and delivered.
B_BAD_THREAD_ID	Sending a reply to a destination thread that no longer exists.
B_BAD_PORT_ID	Sending a reply to a BLooper and port that no longer exist.
B_TIMED_OUT	Taking longer than the specified time limit to deliver a reply message or to receive a synchronous reply to the reply.

If you want to delay sending a reply and keep the BMessage object beyond the time it's scheduled to be deleted, you may be able to detach it from the message loop. See `DetachCurrentMessage()` in the BLooper class.

See also: `BMessenger::SendMessage()`, `BLooper::DetachCurrentMessage()`, `Error`, `ReturnAddress()`

Unflatten()   *see Flatten()*

WasDelivered(), IsSourceRemote(), IsSourceWaiting(), IsReply(), Previous()

bool **WasDelivered**(void) const

bool **IsSourceRemote**(void) const

bool **IsSourceWaiting**(void) const

bool **IsReply**(void) const

const BMessage ***Previous**(void) const

These functions can help if you're engaged in an exchange of messages or managing an ongoing communication.

`WasDelivered()` indicates whether it's possible to send a reply to a message. It returns `true` for a BMessage that was posted, sent, or dropped—that is, one that has been processed through a message loop—and `false` for a message that has not yet been delivered by any means.

`IsSourceRemote()` returns `true` if the message had its source in another application, and `false` if the source is local or the message hasn't been delivered yet.

`IsSourceWaiting()` returns `true` if the message source is waiting for a synchronous reply, and `false` if not. The source thread can request and wait for a reply when calling either BMessenger's `SendMessage()` or BMessage's `SendReply()` function.

`IsReply()` returns `true` if the BMessage is a reply to a previous message (if it was sent by the `SendReply()` function), and `false` if not.

`Previous()` returns the previous message—the message to which the current BMessage is a reply. It works only for a BMessage that's received as an asynchronous reply to a previous message. A synchronous reply is received in the context of the previous message, so it's not necessary to call a function to get it. But when an asynchronous reply is received, the context of the original message is lost; this function can provide it. Previous() returns NULL if the BMessage isn't an asynchronous reply to another message.

See also: BMessenger::SendMessage(), SendReply(), ReturnAddress()

WasDropped(), DropPoint()

bool **WasDropped**(void) const

BPoint **DropPoint**(BPoint *offset* = NULL) const

WasDropped() returns true if the user delivered the BMessage by dragging and dropping it, and false if the message was posted or sent in application code or if it hasn't yet been delivered at all.

DropPoint() reports the point where the cursor was located when the message was dropped (when the user released the mouse button). It directly returns the point in the screen coordinate system and, if an *offset* argument is provided, returns it by reference in coordinates based on the image or rectangle the user dragged. The *offset* assumes a coordinate system with (0.0, 0.0) at the left top corner of the dragged rectangle or image.

Since any value can be a valid coordinate, DropPoint() produces reliable results only if WasDropped() returns true.

See also: BView::DragMessage()

Operators

= (assignment)

BMessage &**operator** =(const BMessage&)

Assigns one BMessage object to another. After the assignment, the two objects are duplicates of each other without shared data.

new

void ***operator new**(size_t *numBytes*)

Allocates memory for a BMessage object, or takes the memory from a previously allocated cache. The caching mechanism is an efficient way of managing memory for objects that are created frequently and used for short periods of time, as BMessages typically are.

delete

void **operator delete**(void *memory*, size_t *numBytes*)

Frees memory allocated by the BMessage version of **new**, which may mean restoring the memory to the cache.

BMessageFilter

Derived from: *none*

Declared in: be/app/MessageFilter.h

Library: libbe.so

Overview

A BMessageFilter holds a function that can look at incoming messages before they're dispatched to their designated handlers. The object keeps the conditions that must be met for the function to be called. The function can do what it likes with the message—it can take care of global matters before the handler-specific response to the message begins; it can modify the target handler for the message; or it can even handle the message itself and prevent it from being dispatched.

You can implement the filtering function either as a member function in a class derived from BMessageFilter or as a nonmember function that you assign to BMessageFilter instances when you construct them. For a member function, you override the `Filter()` hook function that BMessageFilter declares. For a nonmember function, you define a function of type `filter_hook` and pass a pointer to it to the BMessageFilter constructor. The nonmember function doesn't require you to derive a class from BMessageFilter, but it puts the function you implement in the global namespace.

If a `filter_hook` function is assigned to a BMessageFilter object, the system prefers it to the `Filter()` member function; it will not call the member function.

After construction, a BMessageFilter is attached to a message loop by assigning it either to a BHandler object or to a BLooper:

- If assigned to a BHandler object, the filter will apply only to messages targeted to that BHandler. See `SetFilterList()` and `AddFilter()` in the BHandler class.

- If assigned to a BLooper object as a common filter, it can apply to any message the BLooper dispatches regardless of the target handler. See `SetCommonFilterList()` and `AddCommonFilter()` in the BLooper class. (A BLooper can also be assigned specific filters in its role as a BHandler.)

All applicable filters in both categories are applied to a message before the message is dispatched to the target BHandler (before `DispatchMessage()` is called). Common filters apply before handler-specific filters.

The BMessageFilter belongs to the BHandler or BLooper to which it's assigned and should not be deleted in application code unless you first remove it from its owner. It will be deleted when the BHandler or BLooper is destroyed or when a set of replacement filters is assigned.

A BMessageFilter object should be assigned to only one BHandler or BLooper. To use the same filter in a variety of circumstances, simply copy the BMessageFilter object and assign a different instance to each BHandler or BLooper. It's a light object that can easily be duplicated without much overhead.

See also: BHandler::SetFilterList(), BLooper::SetCommonFilterList()

Hook Functions

`Filter()`
  Implemented by derived classes to respond to an incoming message before the message is dispatched to a target BHandler.

Constructor and Destructor

BMessageFilter()

BMessageFilter(message_delivery *delivery*,
              message_source *source*,
              uint32 *command*,
              filter_hook *filter* = NULL)
BMessageFilter(message_delivery *delivery*,
              message_source *source*,
              filter_hook *filter* = NULL)
BMessageFilter(uint32 *command*,
              filter_hook *filter* = NULL)
BMessageFilter(const BMessageFilter &*object*)
BMessageFilter(const BMessageFilter *object*)

Initializes the BMessageFilter object so that its `Filter()` function—or the *filter* hook function passed as an argument—will be called for every incoming message that meets the specified *delivery*, *source*, and *command* criteria.

The first argument, *delivery*, is a constant that specifies how the message must arrive:

• `B_DROPPED_DELIVERY`. Only messages that were dragged and dropped should be filtered.

- B_PROGRAMMED_DELIVERY. Only messages that were posted or sent in application code (by calling PostMessage() or a Send...() function) should be filtered.

- B_ANY_DELIVERY. All messages, no matter how they were delivered, should be filtered.

If a *delivery* method isn't specified, B_ANY_DELIVERY is assumed.

The second argument, *source*, specifies where the message must originate:

- B_LOCAL_SOURCE. Only messages that originate locally, from within the same team as the receiving thread, should be filtered.

- B_REMOTE_SOURCE. Only messages that are delivered from a remote source should be filtered.

- B_ANY_SOURCE. All messages, no matter what their source, should be filtered.

If a message *source* isn't specified, B_ANY_SOURCE is assumed.

The third argument, *command*, limits the filter to a particular type of message. Only messages that have what data members matching the specified *command* constant will be filtered. If a *command* isn't specified, the command constant won't be a criterion in selecting which messages to filter; any message that meets the other criteria will be filtered, no matter what its what data member may be.

The filtering criteria are conjunctive; for the filter function to be called, an arriving message must meet all the criteria specified.

A *filter* function passed as an argument must be of the type filter_hook. This type is defined as follows

> filter_result (***filter_hook**)(BMessage **message*,
>   BHandler ***target*,
>   BMessageFilter **messageFilter*)

The return type of the function and its first two arguments are the same as for the member Filter() function. The third argument gives the filter_hook access to the same information as Filter(). For example, the member function can discover which BLooper is dispatching the message by calling another member function, Looper():

```
filter_result MyFilter::Filter(BMessage *message, BHandler **target)
{
    . . .
    BLooper *theLooper = Looper();
    . . .
}
```

The `filter_hook` can call the same function through its *messageFilter* pointer:

```
filter_result filter(BMessage *message, BHandler **target
                        BMessageFilter *messageFilter)
{
    . . .
    BLooper *theLooper = messageFilter->Looper();
    . . .
}
```

For more information, refer to the description of the member `Filter()` function.

See also: `Filter()`

~BMessageFilter()

virtual ~BMessageFilter(void)

Does nothing.

Member Functions

Command(), FiltersAnyCommand()

uint32 **Command**(void) const

bool **FiltersAnyCommand**(void) const

`Command()` returns the command constant (the `what` data member) that an arriving message must match for the filter to apply. `FiltersAnyCommand()` returns `true` if the filter applies to messages regardless of their `what` data members, and `false` if it's limited to a certain type of message.

Because all command constants are valid, including negative numbers and 0, `Command()` returns a reliable result only if `FiltersAnyCommand()` returns `false`.

See also: the BMessageFilter constructor, the BMessage class

Filter()

virtual filter_result **Filter**(BMessage *message*, BHandler **target*)

Implemented by derived classes to examine an arriving message just before it's dispatched. The *message* is passed as the first argument; the second argument indirectly points to the *target* BHandler object that's slated to respond to the message.

You can implement this function to do anything you please with the *message*, including replace the designated *target* with another BHandler object. For example:

```
filter_result MyFilter::Filter(BMessage *message, BHandler **target)
{
    . . .
    if ( *target->IsIndisposed() )
        *target = *target->FindReplacement();
    . . .
    return B_DISPATCH_MESSAGE;
}
```

The replacement target must be associated with the same BLooper as the original target. If the new target has filters that apply to the *message*, those filtering functions will be called before the message is dispatched.

This function returns a constant that instructs the BLooper whether or not to dispatch the message as planned:

- B_DISPATCH_MESSAGE. Go ahead and dispatch the message.
- B_SKIP_MESSAGE. Stop. Don't dispatch the message and don't filter it any further; this function took care of handling it.

The default version of this function does nothing but return B_DISPATCH_MESSAGE.

If a filter_hook function was assigned to the BMessageFilter object when it was constructed, it will be called instead of Filter().

See also: the BMessageFilter constructor

FiltersAnyCommand()   *see Command()*

Looper()

> BLooper *Looper(void) const

Returns the BLooper object that dispatches the messages that the BMessageFilter filters, or NULL if the BMessageFilter hasn't yet been assigned to a BHandler or BLooper.

MessageDelivery(), MessageSource()

> message_delivery MessageDelivery(void) const
>
> message_source MessageSource(void) const

These functions return constants, set when the BMessageFilter object was constructed, that describe the categories of messages that can be filtered. MessageDelivery() returns a constant that specifies how the message must be

delivered (B_DROPPED_DELIVERY, B_PROGRAMMED_DELIVERY, or B_ANY_
DELIVERY). MessageSource() returns how the source of the message is
constrained (B_LOCAL_SOURCE, B_REMOTE_SOURCE, or B_ANY_SOURCE).

See also: the BMessageFilter constructor

Operators

= (assignment)

BMessageFilter &operator=(const BMessageFilter&)

Assigns one BMessageFilter object to another so that both objects are independent
copies of each other. After the assignment, both objects share the same filtering
function and record the same calling criteria.

BMessageQueue

Derived from: *none*

Declared in: be/app/MessageQueue.h

Library: libbe.so

Class Description

A BMessageQueue maintains a queue where arriving messages (BMessage objects)
are temporarily stored as they wait to be dispatched. Every BLooper object uses a
BMessageQueue to manage the flow of incoming messages; all messages delivered to
the BLooper's thread are placed in the queue. The BLooper removes the oldest
message from the queue, passes it to a BHandler, waits for the thread to finish its
response, deletes the message, then returns to the queue to get the next message.

For the most part, applications can ignore the queue—that is, they can treat it as an
implementation detail. Messages are delivered to a BLooper by calling its
PostMessage() function, by constructing a BMessenger object and calling
SendMessage(), or through a drag-and-drop operation. Each method of delivery
puts the message in a port owned by the BLooper and then in the queue.

A BLooper calls upon a BHandler's MessageReceived() function—and other,
message-specific hook functions—to handle the messages it takes from the queue.
Applications can simply implement the functions that are called to respond to
received messages and not bother about the mechanics of the message loop, port,
and queue.

However, if necessary, you can manipulate the queue directly, or perhaps just look ahead to see what messages are coming. The BLooper has a `MessageQueue()` function that returns its BMessageQueue object.

See also: the BMessage class, `BLooper::MessageQueue()`

Constructor and Destructor

BMessageQueue()

BMessageQueue(void)

Ensures that the queue starts out empty. Messages are placed in the queue by calling `AddMessage()` and are removed by calling `NextMessage()`.

Each BLooper object constructs a BMessageQueue for itself; you don't need to construct one.

See also: `AddMessage()`, `NextMessage()`

~BMessageQueue()

virtual ~BMessageQueue(void)

Deletes all the objects in the queue and all the data structures used to manage the queue.

Member Functions

AddMessage()

void AddMessage(BMessage *message)

Adds *message* to the queue.

See also: `NextMessage()`

CountMessages()

int32 CountMessages(void) const

Returns the number of messages currently in the queue.

FindMessage()

BMessage *FindMessage(uint32 *what*, int32 *index* = 0) const
BMessage *FindMessage(int32 *index*) const

Returns a pointer to the BMessage that's positioned in the queue at *index*, where indices begin at 0 and count only those messages that have `what` data members matching the *what* value passed as an argument. If a *what* argument is omitted, indices count all messages in the queue. If an *index* is omitted, the first message that matches the *what* constant is found. The lower the index, the longer the message has been in the queue.

If no message matches the specified *what* and *index* criteria, this function returns NULL.

The returned message is not removed from the queue.

See also: `NextMessage()`

IsEmpty()

> bool **IsEmpty**(void) const

Returns `true` if the BMessageQueue contains no messages, and `false` if it has at least one.

See also: `CountMessages()`

Lock(), Unlock()

> bool **Lock**(void)

> void **Unlock**(void)

These functions lock and unlock the BMessageQueue, so that another thread won't alter the contents of the queue while it's being read. `Lock()` doesn't return until it has the queue locked; it always returns `true`. `Unlock()` releases the lock so that someone else can lock it. Calls to these functions can be nested.

See also: `BLooper::Lock()`

NextMessage()

> BMessage ***NextMessage**(void)

Returns the next message—the message that has been in the queue the longest—and removes it from the queue. If the queue is empty, this function returns NULL.

RemoveMessage()

> void **RemoveMessage**(BMessage *message*)

Removes a particular *message* from the queue and deletes it.

See also: FindMessage()

Unlock()   *see Lock()*

BMessenger

Derived from: *none*

Declared in: be/app/Messenger.h

Library: libbe.so

Overview

A BMessenger is an agent for sending messages to a destination. Each BMessenger object targets a particular BLooper and possibly a specific BHandler for that BLooper. The messages it sends are delivered to the BLooper and dispatched by the BLooper to the BHandler. The destination objects can belong to the same application as the message sender, but typically are in a remote application. Within the same application, it takes fewer steps to post a message directly to a BLooper than to construct a BMessenger and ask it to send the message—however, the result is the same and both methods are equally efficient.

BMessenger objects can be transported across application boundaries. You can create one for a particular BHandler/BLooper combination in your application and pass it by value to a remote application. That application can then use the BMessenger to target the objects in your application. This is, in fact, the only way for an application to get a BMessenger that can target a remote object (other than a remote BApplication object).

Constructor and Destructor

BMessenger()

```
BMessenger(const char *signature,
           team_id team = –1,
           status_t *error = NULL)
BMessenger(const BHandler *handler,
           const BLooper *looper = NULL,
           status_t *error = NULL)
BMessenger(const BMessenger &messenger)
BMessenger(void)
```

Initializes the BMessenger so that it can send messages to an application identified by its *signature* or by its *team*. The application must be running when the BMessenger is constructed.

If the *signature* passed is NULL, the application is identified by its team only. If the *team* specified is −1, as it is by default, the application is identified by its signature only. If both a real *signature* and a valid *team* identifier are passed, they must match—the *signature* must identify the *team* application. If more than one instance of the *signature* application happens to be running, the *team* picks out a particular instance as the BMessenger's target. Without a valid *team* argument, the constructor arbitrarily picks one of the instances.

BMessengers constructed in this way send messages to the main thread of the remote application, where they're received and handled by that application's BApplication object. This type of messenger is needed to initiate communication with another application.

A BMessenger can also be aimed at a particular BHandler object—or at the preferred handler for a particular BLooper. For this type of BMessenger, you must pass the constructor a pointer to a BHandler or BLooper living in your application:

- If a target *handler* is specified, the BMessenger will send messages to the BLooper associated with that BHandler object, and the BLooper will dispatch them to the BHandler. The target BHandler must be able to tell the BMessenger (through its Looper() function) which BLooper object it's associated with. The BMessenger asks for this information at the time of construction. Therefore, the *handler* must either be a BLooper itself or have been added to a BLooper's list of eligible handlers.

  Because the *handler* identifies its BLooper, there's no need to separately specify the BLooper to the constructor. The *looper* argument can be left NULL, as it is by default. If a specific *looper* is named, it must match the object that Looper() returns for the *handler*.

- A target *looper* must be specified only if the *handler* is NULL. In this case, the BMessenger will send messages to the BLooper and the BLooper will dispatch them to whatever object happens to be its preferred handler at the time. This permits the targeting decision to be made dynamically.

- The target *handler* and *looper* cannot both be NULL, for obvious reasons.

A primary purpose for constructing BMessengers for local BHandlers and BLoopers is to give remote applications access to those objects. You can add a BMessenger to a message and send the message to the remote application. That application can then use the BMessenger to target a BHandler and BLooper in your application.

The constructor reports its success or failure by placing an error code in the status_t variable that the *error* argument points to, provided that the argument isn't omitted or NULL. If it can't make a connection to the *signature* application—possibly because no such application is running—it reports a B_BAD_VALUE error. If passed an invalid *team* identifier, it registers a B_BAD_TEAM_ID error. If the *team* and the *signature* don't match, it conveys a B_MISMATCHED_VALUES error.

If it can't discover a BLooper from the target BHandler, the constructor reports a B_BAD_HANDLER error. If a *looper* is specified but the BHandler is associated with another BLooper object, it registers a B_MISMATCHED_VALUES error. If neither a *handler* nor a *looper* is specified, it reports a B_BAD_VALUE error.

If all goes well, the constructor puts B_OK in the *error* variable. It's a good idea to check for an error before asking the new BMessenger to send a message.

A BMessenger can also be constructed as a copy of another BMessenger,

```
BMessenger newOne(anotherMessenger);
```

or be assigned from another object:

```
BMessenger newOne = anotherMessenger;
```

If the construction of a BMessenger fails for any reason, the IsValid() function will report that the resulting object is not to be trusted:

```
BMessenger messenger(localHandler);
if ( messenger.IsValid() ) {
    . . .
}
```

A BMessenger constructed without arguments is invalid until it's initialized with another BMessenger.

A BMessenger object can send messages to only one destination. Once constructed, you can cache it and reuse it repeatedly to communicate with that destination. It should be freed after it's no longer needed (or it becomes invalid). The BRoster object can provide signature and team information about possible destinations.

See also: the BInvoker, BRoster, and BMessage classes, Target(), IsValid()

~BMessenger()

~BMessenger(void)

Frees all memory allocated by the BMessenger, if any was allocated at all.

Member Functions

IsTargetLocal()   *see Target()*

IsValid()

   bool **IsValid**(void) const

Returns `true` if the BMessenger is connected to a destination BLooper, and `false` if not. A BMessenger might become disconnected from its target if, for example, the user quit the destination application or that application destroyed the target BLooper.

This function doesn't check whether the target BHandler is valid; it reports only on the status of the target BLooper.

LockTarget(), LockTargetWithTimeout()

   bool **LockTarget**(void) const

   status_t **LockTargetWithTimeout**(bigtime_t *timeout*) const

These functions lock the BLooper that the BMessenger targets, but only if the target is local (only if the BLooper is in the same team as the BMessenger). They work exactly like the counterpart BLooper `Lock()` and `LockWithTimeout()` functions, and they return what those functions return, with this additional stipulation: If the target BLooper isn't local, `LockTarget()` returns `false` and `LockTargetWithTimeout()` returns B_BAD_VALUE.

Each successful lock must be balanced by a call to unlock the BLooper using the BLooper's `Unlock()` function. For example:

```
if ( myMessenger.LockTarget() ) {
    BLooper *myLooper;
    BHandler *myHandler = myMessenger.Target(&myLooper);
    . . .
    myLooper->Unlock();
}
```

The BMessenger functions have only one advantage over their BLooper counterparts. If you keep a pointer to a BLooper object and call `Lock()` through the pointer,

```
if ( myLooper->Lock() ) {
    . . .
    myLooper->Unlock();
}
```

it may return `true` even though it's not locking the object you think it is. This strange result can happen if the BLooper is deleted and another object, perhaps another BLooper, is allocated in the same memory space. The pointer won't register the difference. However, the BMessenger is not fooled. If it's target goes away, `LockTarget()` will return `false` and `LockTargetWithTimeout()` will return `B_BAD_VALUE`.

See also: `BLooper::Lock()`

SendMessage()

> status_t **SendMessage**(BMessage *message,
> > BMessage *reply,
> > bigtime_t *sendTimeout* = B_INFINITE_TIMEOUT,
> > bigtime_t *replyTimeout* = B_INFINITE_TIMEOUT) const
>
> status_t **SendMessage**(BMessage *message,
> > BHandler *replyHandler = NULL,
> > bigtime_t *sendTimeout* = B_INFINITE_TIMEOUT) const
>
> status_t **SendMessage**(uint32 *command*, BMessage *reply) const
> status_t **SendMessage**(uint32 *command*, BHandler *replyHandler = NULL) const

Sends a *message* to the destination that was designated when the BMessenger was constructed. The caller retains responsibility for the *message* passed to this function; the destination thread will receive a copy.

You can ask for a synchronous reply to the message you send or designate a BHandler for an asynchronous reply:

• Supplying a *reply* argument requests a message back from the destination. Before returning, `SendMessage()` waits for an answer and fills in the *reply* BMessage with the information it receives. The caller is responsible for allocating and deleting the *reply* message. Typically, the *reply* BMessage is an empty container for the reply allocated on the stack:

```
BMessage message(STAY_THE_COURSE);
BMessage reply;
myMessenger.SendMessage(&message, &reply);
```

If the destination doesn't send a reply before the message is deleted, the system sends one with `B_NO_REPLY` as the what data member. Check the reply message before proceeding. If there's an error in receiving the reply message, `SendMessage()` will return an error, such as `B_BAD_PORT_ID`, indicating that something went wrong.

• If a *reply* isn't requested, `SendMessage()` returns immediately; any reply to the *message* will be received asynchronously. If a *replyHandler* is specified, the reply will be directed to that BHandler object. If a handler isn't specified, it will be directed to the BApplication object.

The *replyHandler* is subject to the same restriction as a target BHandler passed to the BMessenger construtcor: It must be associated with a BLooper object (or be a BLooper itself).

By default, `SendMessage()` doesn't return until it delivers the message. If it can't do so immediately (for example, if the destination BLooper's port queue is full), it blocks until it can accomplish its mission.

However, you can limit how long it will block by setting a timeout in microseconds. The *sendTimeout* argument is the number of microseconds you give the function to place the message in the destination BLooper's port. If `SendMessage()` is unable to deliver the message in the specified amount of time, it fails and returns an error (`B_TIMED_OUT`). Separate *sendTimeout* and *replyTimeout* limits can be set for sending the message and for receiving a synchronous reply. There is no time limit if a timeout value is set `B_INFINITE_TIMEOUT`—as it is by default.

If a *command* is passed instead of a full *message*, `SendMessage()` constructs a BMessage object with *command* as its what data member and sends it just like any other message. This is simply a convenience for sending messages that contain no data. The following line of code

```
myMessenger->SendMessage(NEVERMORE);
```

is roughly equivalent to:

```
BMessage message(NEVERMORE);
myMessenger->SendMessage(&message);
```

You cannot set timeouts for the *command* versions of this function. They block without a time limit (`B_INFINITE_TIMEOUT`).

If all goes well, `SendMessage()` returns `B_OK`. If not, it returns an error code, typically `B_BAD_PORT_ID` or `B_TIMED_OUT`.

(It's an error for a thread to send a message to itself and expect a synchronous reply. The thread can't respond to the message and wait for a reply at the same time.)

See also: `BMessage::SendReply()`

Target(), IsTargetLocal()

BHandler *__Target__(BLooper **__looper__) const

bool __IsTargetLocal__(void) const

`Target()` returns a pointer to the BHandler object that's targeted to respond to the messages that the BMessenger sends. It also places a pointer to the BLooper that receives its messages in the variable that *looper* refers to. If the BMessenger is targeted to the BLooper's preferred handler, `Target()` returns `NULL` but identifies the *looper*.

`Target()` can't provide valid pointers to objects that live in other applications. Therefore, for remote targets, it returns `NULL` and sets the *looper* pointer to `NULL`. These values could also indicate that the BMessenger hadn't been initialized. `IsTargetLocal()` can distinguish between these case. It returns `true` if the BMessenger is in the same application as its target, and `false` if its target is remote or nonexistent.

Team()

> inline team_id **Team**(void) const

Returns the identifier for the team that receives the messages the BMessenger sends.

Operators

= (assignment)

> BMessenger &**operator** =(const BMessenger&)

Assigns one BMessenger to another. After the assignment the two objects are identical and independent copies of each other, with no shared data.

== (equality)

> bool **operator** ==(const BMessenger&) const

Returns `true` if the two BMessengers have the same targets for the messages they send, and `false` if not.

BRoster

Derived from: *none*

Declared in: be/app/Roster.h

Library: libbe.so

Overview

The BRoster object represents a service that keeps a roster of all applications currently running. It can provide information about any of those applications, activate one of them, add another application to the roster by launching it, or get information about an application to help you decide whether to launch it.

There's just one roster and it's shared by all applications. When an application starts up, a BRoster object is constructed and assigned to a global variable, `be_roster`.

You always access the roster through this variable; you never have to instantiate a BRoster in application code.

The BRoster identifies applications in three ways:

- By `entry_ref` references to the executable files where they reside.

- By their signatures. The signature is a unique identifier for the application assigned as a file-system attribute or resource at compile time or by the BApplication constructor at run time. You can obtain signatures for the applications you develop by contacting Be's developer support staff. They can also tell you what the signatures of other applications are.

- At run time, by their `team_ids`. A team is a group of threads sharing an address space; every application is a team.

If an application is launched more than once, the roster will include one entry for each instance of the application that's running. These instances will have the same signature, but different team identifiers.

Constructor and Destructor

BRoster()

> BRoster(void)

Sets up the object's connection to the roster service.

When an application constructs its BApplication object, the system constructs a BRoster object and assigns it to the `be_roster` global variable. A BRoster is therefore readily available from the time the application is initialized until the time it quits; you don't have to construct one. The constructor is public only to give programs that don't have BApplication objects access to the roster.

~BRoster()

> ~BRoster(void)

Does nothing.

Member Functions

ActivateApp()

> status_t ActivateApp(team_id *team*) const

Activates the *team* application (by bringing one of its windows to the front and making it the active window). This function works only if the target application has a

window on-screen. The newly activated application is notified with a
B_APP_ACTIVATED message.

See also: BApplication::AppActivated()

Broadcast()

> status_t **Broadcast**(BMessage *message*) const

Sends the *message* to every running application, except to those applications
(B_ARGV_ONLY) that don't accept messages. The message is sent asynchronously with
a timeout of 0. As is the case for other message-sending functions, the caller retains
ownership of the *message*.

This function returns immediately after setting up the broadcast operation. It doesn't
wait for the messages to be sent and doesn't report any errors encountered when
they are. It returns an error only if it can't start the broadcast operation. If successful
in getting the operation started, it returns B_OK.

See also: BMessenger::SendMessage()

FindApp()

> status_t **FindApp**(const char *type*, entry_ref *app*) const
> status_t **FindApp**(entry_ref *file*, entry_ref *app*) const

Finds the application associated with the MIME data *type* or with the specified *file*,
and modifies the *app* entry_ref structure so that it refers to the executable file for
that application. If the *type* is an application signature, this function finds the
application that has that signature. Otherwise, it finds the preferred application for the
type. If the *file* is an application executable, FindApp() merely copies the file
reference to the *app* argument. Otherwise, it finds the preferred application for the
file type.

In other words, this function goes about finding an application in the same way that
Launch() finds the application it will launch.

If it can translate the *type* or *file* into a reference to an application executable,
FindApp() returns B_OK. If not, it returns an error code, typically one describing a
file system error.

See also: Launch()

GetAppInfo(), GetRunningAppInfo(), GetActiveAppInfo()

> status_t **GetAppInfo**(cons char *signature*, app_info *appInfo*) const
> status_t **GetAppInfo**(entry_ref *executable*, app_info *appInfo*) const

status_t **GetRunningAppInfo**(team_id *team*, app_info **appInfo*) const

status_t **GetActiveAppInfo**(app_info **appInfo*) const

These functions provide information about the application identified by its *signature*, by a reference to its *executable* file, by its *team*, or simply by its status as the current active application. They place the information in the structure referred to by *appInfo*.

GetRunningAppInfo() reports on a particular instance of a running application, the one that was assigned the *team* identifier at launch. GetActiveAppInfo() similarly reports on a running application, the one that happens to be the current active application.

If it can, GetAppInfo() also tries to get information about an application that's running. If a running application has the *signature* identifier or was launched from the *executable* file, GetAppInfo() queries it for the information. If more than one instance of the *signature* application is running, or if more than one instance was launched from the same *executable* file, it arbitrarily picks one of the instances to report on.

Even if the application isn't running—if none of the applications currently in the roster are identified by *signature* or were launched from the *executable* file— GetAppInfo() can still provide some information about it, perhaps enough information for you to call Launch() to get it started.

If they're able to fill in the **app_info** structure with meaningful values, these functions return B_OK. However, GetActiveAppInfo() returns B_ERROR if there's no active application. GetRunningAppInfo() returns B_BAD_TEAM_ID if *team* isn't, on the face of it, a valid team identifier for a running application. GetAppInfo() returns B_ERROR if the application isn't running.

The **app_info** structure contains the following fields:

thread_id **thread**
> The identifier for the application's main thread of execution, or −1 if the application isn't running. (The main thread is the thread in which the application is launched and in which its main() function runs.)

team_id **team**
> The identifier for the application's team, or −1 if the application isn't running. (This will be the same as the *team* passed to GetRunningAppInfo().)

port_id **port**
> The port where the application's main thread receives messages, or −1 if the application isn't running.

uint32 **flags**
> A mask that contains information about the behavior of the application.

entry_ref **ref**

> A reference to the file that was, or could be, executed to run the application. (This will be the same as the *executable* passed to `GetAppInfo()`.)

char **signature[]**

> The signature of the application. (This will be the same as the *signature* passed to `GetAppInfo()`.)

The `flags` mask can be tested (with the bitwise `&` operator) against these two constants:

- `B_BACKGROUND_APP`. The application won't appear in the DeskBar (because it doesn't have a user interface or because it can't become the active application).

- `B_ARGV_ONLY`. The application can't receive messages. Information can be passed to it at launch only, in an array of argument strings (as on the command line).

The `flags` mask also contains a value that explains the application's launch behavior. This value must be filtered out of `flags` by combining `flags` with the `B_LAUNCH_MASK` constant. For example:

```
unit32 behavior = theInfo.flags & B_LAUNCH_MASK;
```

The result will match one of these three constants:

- `B_EXCLUSIVE_LAUNCH`. The application can be launched only if an application with the same signature isn't already running.

- `B_SINGLE_LAUNCH`. The application can be launched only once from the same executable file. However, an application with the same signature might be launched from a different executable. For example, if the user copies an executable file to another directory, a separate instance of the application can be launched from each copy.

- `B_MULTIPLE_LAUNCH`. There are no restrictions. The application can be launched any number of times from the same executable file.

These flags affect BRoster's `Launch()` function. `Launch()` can always start up a `B_MULTIPLE_LAUNCH` application. However, it can't launch a `B_SINGLE_LAUNCH` application if a running application was already launched from the same executable file. It can't launch a `B_EXCLUSIVE_LAUNCH` application if an application with the same signature is already running.

See also: `Launch()`, `BApplication::GetAppInfo()`

GetAppList()

> void **GetAppList**(BList *teams*) const
> void **GetAppList**(const char *signature*, BList *teams*) const

Fills in the *teams* BList with team identifiers for applications in the roster. Each item in the list will be of type `team_id`. It must be cast to that type when retrieving it from the list, as follows:

```
BList *teams = new BList;
be_roster->GetAppList(teams);
team_id who = (team_id)teams->ItemAt(someIndex);
```

The list will contain one item for each instance of an application that's running. For example, if the same application has been launched three times, the list will include the `team_ids` for all three running instances of that application.

If a *signature* is passed, the list identifies only applications running under that signature. If a *signature* isn't specified, the list identifies all running applications.

See also: `TeamFor()`, the BMessenger constructor

IsRunning()   *see TeamFor()*

Launch()

```
status_t Launch(const char *type,
                BMessage *message = NULL,
                team_id *team = NULL) const
status_t Launch(const char *type,
                BList *messages,
                team_id *team = NULL) const
status_t Launch(const char *type,
                int argc,
                char **argv,
                team_id *team = NULL) const

status_t Launch(entry_ref *file,
                BMessage *message = NULL,
                team_id *team = NULL) const
status_t Launch(entry_ref *file,
                BList *messages,
                team_id *team = NULL) const
status_t Launch(entry_ref *file,
                int argc,
                char **argv,
                team_id *team = NULL) const
```

Launches the application associated with a MIME *type* or with a particular *file*. If the MIME *type* is an application signature, this function launches the application with that signature. Otherwise, it launches the preferred application for the type. If the *file* is an application executable, it launches that application. Otherwise, it launches the preferred application for the file type and passes the *file* reference to the application in a B_REFS_RECEIVED message. In other words, Launch() finds the application to launch just as FindApp() finds the application for a particular *type* or *file*.

If a *message* is specified, it will be sent to the application on-launch where it will be received and responded to before the application is notified that it's ready to run. Similarly, if a list of *messages* is specified, each one will be delivered on-launch. The caller retains ownership of the BMessage objects (and the container BList); they won't be deleted for you.

Sending an on-launch message is appropriate if it helps the launched application configure itself before it starts getting other messages. To launch an application and send it an ordinary message, call Launch() to get it running, then set up a BMessenger object for the application and call BMessenger's SendMessage() function.

If the target application is already running, Launch() won't launch it again, unless it permits multiple instances to run concurrently (it doesn't wait for the messages to be sent or report errors encountered when they are). It fails for B_SINGLE_LAUNCH and B_EXCLUSIVE_LAUNCH applications that have already been launched. Nevertheless, it assumes that you want the messages to get to the application and so delivers them to the currently running instance.

Instead of messages, you can launch an application with an array of argument strings that will be passed to its main() function. *argv* contains the array and *argc* counts the number of strings. If the application accepts messages, this information will also be packaged in a B_ARGV_RECEIVED message that the application will receive on-launch.

If successful, Launch() places the identifier for the newly launched application in the variable referred to by *team* and returns B_OK. If unsuccessful, it sets the *team* variable to –1 and returns an error code, typically one of the following:

- B_BAD_VALUE. The *type* or *file* is not valid, or an attempt is being made to send an on-launch message to an application that doesn't accept messages (that is, to a B_ARGV_ONLY application).

- B_ALREADY_RUNNING. The application is already running and can't be launched again (it's a B_SINGLE_LAUNCH or B_EXCLUSIVE_LAUNCH application).

- B_LAUNCH_FAILED. The attempt to launch the application failed for some other reason, such as insufficient memory.

- A file system error. The *file* or *type* can't be matched to an application.

See also: the BMessenger class, GetAppInfo(), FindApp()

TeamFor(), IsRunning()

team_id **TeamFor**(const char *signature*) const
team_id **TeamFor**(entry_ref *executable*) const

bool **IsRunning**(const char *signature*) const
bool **IsRunning**(entry_ref *executable*) const

Both these functions query whether the application identified by its *signature* or by a reference to its *executable* file is running. `TeamFor()` returns its team identifier if it is, and `B_ERROR` if it's not. `IsRunning()` returns `true` if it is, and `false` if it's not.

If the application is running, you probably will want its team identifier (to set up a BMessenger, for example). Therefore, it's most economical to simply call `TeamFor()` and forego `IsRunning()`.

If more than one instance of the *signature* application is running, or if more than one instance was launched from the same *executable* file, `TeamFor()` arbitrarily picks one of the instances and returns its `team_id`.

See also: `GetAppList()`

Global Variables, Constants, and Defined Types

This section lists the global variables, constants, and defined types that are defined in the Application Kit. There are three global variables—be_app, be_roster, and be_clipboard—just a few defined types, and a handful of constants. Error codes are documented in Chapter 6, *The Support Kit.*

Although the Application Kit defines the constants for all system messages (such as `B_REFS_RECEIVED` and `B_KEY_DOWN`), only those that objects in this kit handle are listed here. Those that designate interface messages are documented in Chapter 4, *The Interface Kit.*

Global Variables

be_app

be/app/Application.h

BApplication *be_app

This variable provides global access to the BApplication object. It's initialized by the BApplication constructor.

See also: the BApplication class

be_clipboard

`be/app/Clipboard.h`

BClipboard **be_clipboard**

This variable gives applications access to the system clipboard—the shared repository of data for cut, copy, and paste operations. It's initialized at startup.

See also: the BClipboard class

be_roster

`be/app/Roster.h`

const BRoster **be_roster**

This variable points to the application's global BRoster object. The BRoster keeps a roster of all running applications and can add applications to the roster by launching them. It's initialized when the application starts up.

See also: the BRoster class

Constants

Application Flags

`be/app/Roster.h`

Constant
B_BACKGROUND_APP
B_ARGV_ONLY
B_LAUNCH_MASK

These constants are used to get information from the `flags` field of an `app_info` structure.

See also: `BRoster::GetAppInfo()`, "Launch Constants" below

Application Messages

`be/app/AppDefs.h`

Constant
B_QUIT_REQUESTED
B_READY_TO_RUN
B_APP_ACTIVATED

Constant
_____

B_ABOUT_REQUESTED

B_QUIT_REQUESTED

B_ARGV_RECEIVED

B_REFS_RECEIVED

B_PULSE
_____

These constants represent the system messages that are recognized and given special treatment by BApplication and BLooper dispatchers. Application messages concern the application as a whole, rather than any particular window thread. See the introduction to this chapter and the BApplication class for details.

See also: "Application Messages" on page 41 of the BApplication class

Cursor Constants

be/app/AppDefs.h

const unsigned char **B_HAND_CURSOR[]**

const unsigned char **B_I_BEAM_CURSOR[]**

These constants contain all the data needed to set the cursor to the default hand image or to the standard I-beam image for text selection.

See also: BApplication::SetCursor()

filter_result Constants

be/app/MessageFilter.h

Constant
_____

B_SKIP_MESSAGE

B_DISPATCH_MESSAGE
_____

These constants list the possible return values of a filter function.

See also: BMessageFilter::Filter()

Launch Constants

`be/app/Roster.h`

Constant
B_MULTIPLE_LAUNCH
B_SINGLE_LAUNCH
B_EXCLUSIVE_LAUNCH

These constants explain whether an application can be launched any number of times, only once from a particular executable file, or only once for a particular application signature. This information is part of the `flags` field of an `app_info` structure and can be extracted using the `B_LAUNCH_MASK` constant.

See also: `BRoster::GetAppInfo()`, "Application Flags" above

Looper Port Capacity

`be/app/Looper.h`

Constant
B_LOOPER_PORT_DEFAULT_CAPACITY

This constant records the default capacity of a BLooper's port. The default is 100 slots; a greater or smaller number can be specified when constructing the BLooper.

See also: the BLooper constructor

Message Constants

`be/app/AppDefs.h`

Constant
B_REPLY
B_NO_REPLY
B_MESSAGE_NOT_UNDERSTOOD
B_SAVE_REQUESTED
B_CANCEL
B_SIMPLE_DATA
B_MIME_DATA
B_ARCHIVED_OBJECT
B_UPDATE_STATUS_BAR
B_RESET_STATUS_BAR

Constant
B_NODE_MONITOR
B_QUERY_UPDATE
B_CUT
B_COPY
B_PASTE
B_SELECT_ALL
B_SET_PROPERTY
B_GET_PROPERTY
B_CREATE_PROPERTY
B_DELETE_PROPERTY
B_GET_SUPPORTED_SUITES

These constants mark messages that the system sometimes puts together, but that aren't dispatched like system messages. See "Standard Messages" in the *Message Protocols* appendix for details.

See also: BMessage::SendReply(), the BTextView class in the Interface Kit

message_delivery Constants

    be/app/MessageFilter.h

Constant
B_ANY_DELIVERY
B_DROPPED_DELIVERY
B_PROGRAMMED_DELIVERY

These constants distinguish the delivery criterion for filtering a BMessage.

See also: the BMessageFilter constructor

message_source Constants

    be/app/MessageFilter.h

Constant
B_ANY_SOURCE
B_REMOTE_SOURCE
B_LOCAL_SOURCE

These constants list the possible constraints that a BMessageFilter might impose on the source of the messages it filters.

See also: the BMessageFilter constructor

Message Specifiers

```
be/app/Message.h
```

Constant
B_NO_SPECIFIER
B_DIRECT_SPECIFIER
B_INDEX_SPECIFIER
B_REVERSE_INDEX_SPECIFIER
B_RANGE_SPECIFIER
B_REVERSE_RANGE_SPECIFIER
B_NAME_SPECIFIER
B_SPECIFIERS_END = 128

These constants fill the `what` slot of specifier BMessages. Each constant indicates what other information the specifier contains and how it should be interpreted. For example, a `B_REVERSE_INDEX_SPECIFIER` message has an "index" field with an index that counts backwards from the end of a list. A `B_NAME_SPECIFIER` message includes a "name" field that names the requested item.

Defined Types

app_info

```
be/app/Roster.h

typedef struct {
    thread_id thread;
    team_id team;
    port_id port;
    uint32 flags;
    entry_ref ref;
    char signature[B_MIME_TYPE_LENGTH];
    app_info(void);
    ~app_info(void);
} app_info
```

This structure is used by BRoster's `GetAppInfo()`, `GetRunningAppInfo()`, and `GetActiveAppInfo()` functions to report information about an application. Its constructor ensures that its fields are initialized to invalid values. To get meaningful values for an actual application, you must pass the structure to one of the BRoster functions. See those functions for a description of the various fields.

See also: `BRoster::GetAppInfo()`

filter_result

> `be/app/MessageFilter.h`

> typedef enum { . . . } **filter_result**

This type distinguishes between the `B_SKIP_MESSAGE` and `B_DISPATCH_MESSAGE` return values for a filter function.

See also: `BMessageFilter::Filter()`

message_delivery

> `be/app/MessageFilter.h`

> typedef enum { . . . } **message_delivery**

This type enumerates the delivery criteria for filtering a message.

See also: the BMessageFilter constructor

message_source

> `be/app/MessageFilter.h`

> typedef enum { . . . } **message_source**

This type enumerates the source criteria for filtering a message.

See also: the BMessageFilter constructor

CHAPTER THREE

The Storage Kit

Storage Kit Inheritance Hierarchy

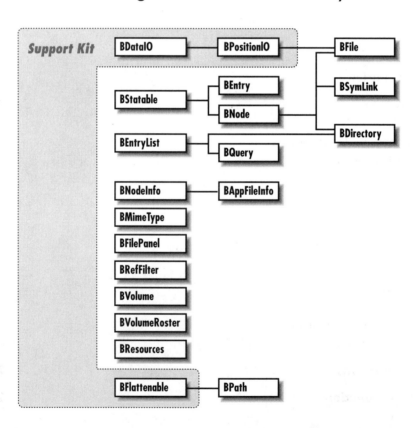

CHAPTER THREE

The Storage Kit

The Storage Kit is a set of C++ classes and C functions that let you access the file system; in particular, the kit lets you:

- Navigate the file hierarchy
- Read and write files
- Monitor changes to specific files (the Node Monitor)
- Ask for a set of files based on their characteristics (queries and attributes)

The basic functionality of the kit—such as reading and writing files—is also provided by the Be-supported POSIX functions (`open()`, `read()`, `write()`, `close()`, and so on) such that if you don't want to use the Storage Kit, you don't have to. But keep in mind that the Storage Kit's classes are *not* covers for POSIX functions. The POSIX functions and the Storage Kit classes are separate branches that dissolve into the same implementation—the one isn't implemented in terms of the other. POSIX is straight C, so it avoids the C++ overhead; but language efficiency aside, the POSIX functions aren't innately faster than the Storage Kit class functions.

The Storage Kit includes some additional C functions (beyond the standard POSIX implementation) so that almost everything that can be done from the C++ level can also be done in C, and vice versa. There are a few exceptions, notably these two:

- You can't create a file system index from the C++ classes.
- You can't create a live query with the C functions.

The next few sections provide some basic Storage Kit concepts, but most of the interesting stuff is in the class descriptions. The C functions that "imitate" the C++ layer are described at the end of the chapter.

NOTE

The standard POSIX functions are not documented in this book. Refer to an authorized POSIX pamphlet if you're interested in learning more about these functions.

File System Architecture

All file systems that the BeOS recognizes are organized hierarchically. Most file systems use hierarchical organization naturally; any other type of organization must be adapted at the "file system handler" level to simulate a hierarchy (in order to be recognized by the BeOS). The result is that all file systems can be treated similarly in terms of their organizational architecture.

Hierarchical Organization

The tenets of a Be-recognized hierarchical file system are these:

- Data is organized as a tree of directories and files.

- Directories contain files.

- Each file is a member of only one directory (at a time). The directory is said to be the file's "parent." Once hard links are supported (as explained below) the one-parent rule will no longer hold.

- Similarly, each directory has a single parent (directory).

- The hierarchy "fans out" from the file system's *root directory*. The root directory is the common ancestor for all files and directories in the hierarchy.

- Every file and directory has a "leaf" name; leaf names must be unique within the containing directory.

- The only illegal character in a leaf name (in the Be File System) is "/". Also, every directory automatically contains entries named "." and "..".

In the BeOS, more than one file system can be mounted at a time. Each distinct file system is mounted within the *root file system* (described in the next section). Because of this, all (non-root) file systems maintain distinct boundaries. However, these otherwise-tidy boundaries are smudged a bit by symbolic links.

Symbolic Links

The BeOS recognizes *symbolic links*. A symbolic link (or "symlink") is a file that "points to" some other *entry* (another file, directory, or symbolic link). The pointed-to entry can live anywhere—in some other directory, or even in another file system.

Because of symbolic links, the graph of the hierarchy isn't acyclic: As you follow a path through the hierarchy, it's possible to get into a loop. (If you leave symbolic links out of the picture, the graph *is* acyclic.)

WARNING

Currently, the BeOS does *not* recognize *hard links* (although it will in the future). A hard link associates an entry in the hierarchy with a specific chunk of data (a *node*). The attraction of hard links is that more than one entry can be associated with the same node.

File System Layout and the Root File System

Before looking at the file system layout, let's get one thing clear. The term "file system" is a heavily loaded monicker:

- At the lowest level, it means a "file system format." Currently, the BeOS recognizes BFS, HFS (Macintosh), and ISO9660 (CD-ROM) file system formats (other file systems are being ported).

- "File system" can also mean the agent that knows how to turn bytes on a disk (or even in memory, as described in "Virtual File Systems") into the sort of hierarchy that the OS wants to see. When you pop in a floppy, for example, a file system handler must wrangle the disk format to convert its contents into a recognized hierarchy. When we say that the BeOS recognizes HFS, we're really saying that we provide an HFS file system handler. See "File System Handlers" for more information.

- Yet another meaning of "file system" is that part of the OS that manages and lays out all the file systems that are mounted. It's the *über*-system for all hierarchies.

In the BeOS, this *über*-system is part of the kernel. The first thing it does is mount the *root file system*. All other file systems are mounted within the root file system.

The structure of the root file system is a simple, two-level hierarchy:

- The root directory of the root file system is "/". This is the only directory in the entire hierarchy that doesn't have a parent.

- The nodes in the root file system are directories and symlinks *only*. In other words, the root file system contains no real files.

Directories at Root

The directories in the root file system have a prescribed purpose:

- The directories are *mount points* for other file systems. A mount point becomes the root directory for the file system that's mounted there. (More accurately, the *name* of the mount point becomes the *name* of the root directory; the mount point directory itself is "obscured" when a file system is mounted on it.)

- You can create your own directories in the root file system, but they can only be used as mount points—you can't use them to store files.

Symlinks at Root

The symlinks in the root file system are less restricted. The OS creates some number of symlinks automatically (as described below), but other than that, you're free to put whatever symlinks you want in the root file system. However, root level symlinks are simply a convenience for developers—the user won't be able to see them since the Tracker doesn't display the root file system.

Default Root Nodes

When BeOS is launched, some number of directories and symlinks are automatically created in the root file system. The directories are:

- For each "persistent" file system that the OS finds (hard disks, CD-ROM, floppy, etc.), a mount point directory is created and the file system is mounted. The mount point for the file system that was used to boot the OS is */boot*; the other mount point names are taken from the storage devices themselves (if you name your floppy "fido", the floppy will be mounted at */fido*).

- The OS also creates two *virtual file systems*, mounted at */dev* and */pipe*. We'll look at virtual file systems later. Briefly, a virtual file system is one that only exists in memory—it has no persistent storage. (The root file system itself is a virtual file system.)

And the symlinks are:

- A link is made from */boot_disk_name* to */boot*.

- Links are made from */bin*, */system*, and */etc* to similarly named subdirectories of */boot/beos*.

- Links are made from */var* to */boot/var* and from */tmp* to */boot/var/tmp*.

If you cd to / in a shell and list the files, you'll see something like this (where "MyDisk" is the name of the boot disk, and "fido" is a floppy):

```
l---------  1  users     0 Jun 19 22:11 bin -> /boot/beos/bin
drwx------  1  users  2048 Jun 19 21:58 boot
drwxr-x---  1  users     0 Jun 19 22:11 dev
l---------  1  users     0 Jun 19 22:11 etc -> /boot/beos/etc
drwxr-xr-x  1  users  2048 Jun 19 22:12 fido
l---------  1  users     0 Jun 19 22:11 MyDisk -> /boot
drwxrwxrwx  1  users     0 Jun 19 22:11 pipe
```

```
l---------  1  users     0 Jun 19 22:11 system -> /boot/beos/system
l---------  1  users     0 Jun 19 22:11 tmp -> /boot/var/tmp
l---------  1  users     0 Jun 19 22:11 var -> /boot/var
```

If you invoke df, you'll see the list of mounted file systems:

```
Mount            Type     Total    Free      Flags Device
---------------  -------- -------- --------  ----- ------------------------
/                rootfs        0        0        0
/dev             devfs         0        0        0
/pipe            pipefs        0        0        0
/boot            bfs      532950   395715    70004 /dev/disk/scsi/050/0_2
/fido            bfs        1440      904    70004 /dev/disk/floppy/raw
```

All file systems, both persistent and virtual, are displayed by df. The virtual file systems are the ones that have 0 size.

Navigating the File System

If your application needs to get to a well-defined watering hole (such as the directory where a user's preference settings are stored, or where apps are kept), use the symbolic pathname constants to the find_directory() function. The constants are listed in the "Global Constants and Defined Types" section of this chapter. find_directory() is documented at the end of BDirectory description.

Virtual File Systems

A virtual file system has no backing storage. The hierarchy that it represents is maintained in memory. When you shut down the OS, all virtual file systems disappear.

Currently, the BeOS provides three virtual file system handlers:

- *rootfs* handles the root file system (described above). The root file system is mounted at "/". It's always the first file system to be mounted, and provides mount points for all other file systems.

- *devfs* is the handler for the *device file system*, mounted at */dev*. This system contains entry points for access to hardware devices, including hard disks, CD-ROMs, and so on.

- *pipefs* is the handler for the *pipe file system*, mounted at */pipe*. A "pipe" is a location through which the POSIX pipe mechanism reads and writes data.

From the developer's perspective, a virtual file system isn't much different from a persistent file system: You can create a BVolume object to represent it, you can walk through it's hierarchy, look at its contents, and so on.

But virtual file systems are hidden from the Tracker user: **The Tracker does not display virtual file systems, nor does it let the user form a query on a virtual file system.**

File System Handlers

When the kernel attempts to mount a file system, if must first find a *file system handler* that understands the file system's format. In other words, the handler is an intermediary between the kernel and the bytes on a disk (for example).

All file system handlers are add-ons. The kernel loads the handler add-on that it needs, and talks to it through a set of well-defined functions. The advantage of this approach is that the kernel doesn't need to know about specific file systems, it only needs to know how to talk to the handlers.

Currently, you can't create your own file system handler. The handler API will be released sometime in the future.

Entries and Nodes

The most important concept that you should keep in mind when you're using the Storage Kit is that a file is considered both an *entry* and a *node*:

- The entry part of a file is its location in the file hierarchy. An entry is similar to a pathname: It tells you where a file is (or should be), but it doesn't let you look at its contents.

- The node part of a file is its data. A node is an actual "thing" that's separate from the file's entry—when you rename a file, for example, all you're doing is tagging the node with a different pathname (or, in our lingo, you move the node from one entry to another). Just as entries don't know about data, nodes don't know anything about entries: A node doesn't know where its entry is located.

This concept really isn't new: If you're familiar with POSIX, then you've already dealt with entries and nodes, except you called them pathnames and file descriptors.

Entries

In the Storage Kit, entries are represented three ways:

- As pathnames
- As `entry_ref` structures
- As BEntry objects

Any entry can be given by any of these representations. Furthermore, the representations are fairly easily converted: Given an `entry_ref`, it's trivial to get a BEntry, from which you can easily get a pathname, which can be turned into an `entry_ref`. Which representation you use depends on what you're doing:

- You use pathnames or `entry_ref`s to keep track of the entries you're interested in.

- You use BEntry objects to query and manipulate the entries. For example, if you want to know if an entry is a directory or a file, you need a BEntry object.

Nodes

Nodes are represented in two ways:

- As `node_ref` structures
- As BNode objects

Here, again, the representations are easily converted. As for use:

- `node_refs` are used for purposes that we're going to ignore for now (we're just covering the basics, here).
- The BNode class is where the action is. If you want to read and write the data in a file, you need a BNode object—more specifically, you need an instance of the BFile class, which derives from BNode.

Every node has a type, or *flavor*. There are three node flavors:

- Plain files
- Directories
- Symbolic links

These flavors are represented by subclasses of BNode: BFile, BDirectory, and BSymLink. Note that a `node_ref` doesn't know its node's flavor.

More Facts

Some more facts you should be aware of:

- Every node has an entry; not every entry has a node.

  If you've got your hands on a node, then you can assume that there's an entry somewhere that "contains" that node. (This isn't entirely true, but it's true enough for now. For the real story, see "Lies.")

  The converse isn't true: An entry needn't have any data. Such entries are called "abstract." Abstract entries are useful for expressing the location of a file before it's created (for example). But don't be misled: Abstract entries do *not* exist in the file hierarchy, they're simply placeholders that your app uses to designate a location. This leads us to our next fact:

- Every file in the file hierarchy has an entry and a node.

This might seem obvious; if it does, then go to the next fact. For the skeptics, here's the gospel: The files that "normal" apps work with are real—they actually exist as bytes on a disk. Such files have a location in the hierarchy, and they contain data.

- You can convert an entry into a node, but not the other way around.

  The BNode class accepts any form of entry representation as an argument to its constructor. In other words, given a pathname, `entry_ref`, or BEntry object, you can create a BNode. But once you've got your BNode, you can't go back: There's no way to get an entry from a node.

Returning to the BNode constructor: You can *only* create a BNode by passing the constructor an entry (in one of its representations). This is an important point that we'll pick up in the next section.

Lies

Here are some more facts, slight alterations to the near truths spoken above.

A Node Can Lose Its Entry

Consider this scenario: You create a BFile object to some file. While you're reading and writing the file, the user deletes the file through the Tracker or from a Terminal. What the user has done is delete the node's entry, not the node itself. The node isn't destroyed until all references to the node, including your BFile, are deleted (or, more accurately, "closed"). The twist is that your BFile by itself has no way of knowing that the entry is gone.

So what are you supposed to do? In general, whenever you free a BFile object, you should first check to make sure the entry still exists; of course, the BFile itself can't tell you (remember: A node doesn't know about its entry), so you have to save the entry that was used to create the BFile. You ask the entry if it still exists, and then do whatever you have to do if it doesn't, such as alert the user, ask for a new entry name, and so on.

Unfortunately, this problem has another wrinkle: What if the user *moves* the entry while you're using the entry's node? In this case, the node isn't going to be destroyed, but if you ask the generative entry (the entry that was used to create the BFile object), it *looks* like the entry is gone.

There's no generic solution to the entire problem. Not because it's impossible to implement, but because the "right" solution depends on what the user meant by deleting or moving the entry. Most applications take this approach: The user knows files as entries, not as nodes. If a user opens a file through your app, moves the entry (through some other vehicle, such as the Tracker), and then asks your app to save the file, what the user really want is for you to save the node under the same name that was used to open the node.

A BDirectory Knows Its Entry

BDirectory is an exception to the "ignorant node" rule: You can ask a BDirectory object for its entry (through its `GetEntry()` function).

MIME and File Types

MIME (Multipurpose Internet Mail Extensions) is a way to describe the content or intent of a parcel of data. As the name implies, MIME was invented to make e-mail smarter: Want to send a GIF image through e-mail? If your mail program understands MIME, it can encode the image, tag it with a MIME string (in this case, "image/gif"), as well as some other header information (such as the encoding protocol) before sending the message out across the wires. Any MIME-savvy recipient program will be able to properly display the message based (primarily) on the content-type string.

MIME in the BeOS

The Be file system adds a MIME string to every file in the (native) file system, and tries to figure out an appropriate MIME type for foreign files, as well. MIME types are used by the Tracker, for example, to figure out what icon it should use to represent a particular file. Another example: When the user double-clicks a file, the MIME type (for that file) is used to identify the application that will open the file. Your application can perform similar deductions: When the user drag-drops a file, your application can look at the file's MIME type and proceed (or reject) accordingly.

There are two parts to Be's MIME support:

- **File Types.** The first part is the inclusion of a MIME string as part of every file, as mentioned above. This is called the file's *file type*. The MIME string is added as an attribute—it's not part of the file's data. Every file—whether it's a document, an application, or even a directory has its own file type attribute. For more on getting and setting a file's type, see the BNodeInfo class.

- **The File Type Database.** The second part is the system's *File Type database*. The database contains information about the file types that the system recognizes. The user can get to the database through the `FileTypes` preferences application. Programmatically, you access it through the BMimeType and BAppFileInfo classes.

BAppFileInfo

Derived from: BNodeInfo

Declared in: be/storage/AppFileInfo.h

Library: libbe.so

Overview

BAppFileInfo lets you get and set information about a specific application (executable) file. The class knows about:

- The application's signature; this is the MIME type by which the application is known to the File Type database.

- The file types that the application knows how to deal with (its "supported types").

- The application's icons, for itself as well as its supported types.

- The flags that are applied when the app is launched.

- Version information about the application.

- If you're setting information through a BAppFileInfo object, you must have a running application object.

Initialization

You initialize a BAppFileInfo object by passing it an open BFile object. The BAppFileInfo object has its own pointer to the BFile you pass in: It doesn't take ownership of the BFile, nor does it create a separate file descriptor to the file.

Like BNodeInfo, BAppFileInfo can get information even if the BFile isn't open for reading. But (unlike its parent), the BFile must be open for writing if you want to set information (as explained in the next section).

If the BFile that you use to initialize the BAppFileInfo is open for writing, the file will be locked until you re-initialize (or delete) the BAppFileInfo object. The BFile should be unlocked when you pass it in.

To initialize a BAppFileInfo to point to the executable of **be_app**, you do this:

```
/* To get app file info for be_app. */
app_info ai;
BFile file;
BAppFileInfo afi;

be_app->GetAppInfo(&ai);
file.SetTo(&ai.ref, B_READ_WRITE);
afi.SetTo(&file);
```

For any other running app, you have to consult the roster:

```
/* To get app file info for any app. */
app_info ai;
BFile file;
BAppFileInfo afi;

/* Here we look for the app by its signature; we could also
 * call GetRunningAppInfo(), or walk down the app list, etc.
 */
be_roster->GetAppInfo("application/whatever", &ai);
file.SetTo(&ai.ref, B_READ_WRITE);
afi.SetTo(&file);
```

Attributes and Resources

When you ask a BAppFileInfo object to get some information, it looks in its file's attributes. But when you ask to *set* some information, the info is written to the file's attributes *and* it's stored in the resources portion of the file, as well. This explains why the BFile must be open for writing. Also, because the resources portion must be open, BAppFileInfo isn't just a cover for attribute-accessing functions, the way BNodeInfo is.

The File Type Database and the App's Signature

In some cases, the information that you set through a BAppFileInfo object is also recorded in the File Type database (based on the app's signature) and in the app roster. This only works, however, if the application's signature is recognized by the database. The BAppFileInfo class *doesn't* tell the database about the signature; to do this, you have to go through a BMimeType object:

```
char buf[B_MIME_TYPE_LENGTH];
BMimeType mime;

if (afi.GetSignature(buf) == B_NO_ERROR) {
   mime.SetTo(buf);
   mime.Install();
}
```

Errors

Unlike most of the other Storage Kit classes, when you ask a BAppFileInfo to retrieve some information by reference, the object *doesn't* clear the reference argument if it fails. Because of this, you should always check the error code that's returned by the Get...() functions.

Constructor and Destructor

BAppFileInfo()

> **BAppFileInfo**(void)
> **BAppFileInfo**(BFile *_file_)

The default constructor creates a new, uninitialized BAppFileInfo object. To initialize you have to follow this construction with a call to `SetTo()`.

The BFile version initializes the BAppFileInfo by passing the argument to `SetTo()`. See `SetTo()` for details (and error codes).

~BAppFileInfo()

> **~BAppFileInfo**(void)

Destroys the object. The BFile object that was used to initialize the object isn't touched.

Member Functions

GetAppFlags(), SetAppFlags()

> status_t **GetAppFlags**(uint32 *_flags_) const

> status_t **SetAppFlags**(uint32 _flags_)

These functions get and set the application's "app flags." These are the constants that determine whether the app can only be launched once, whether it runs in the background, and so on. The app flag constants are defined in *be/app/Roster.h*; an application's flags must include one of the following...

B_SINGLE_LAUNCH
B_MULTIPLE_LAUNCH
B_EXCLUSIVE_LAUNC H

...plus either of these two:

B_BACKGROUND_APP
B_ARGV_ONLY

While an app is running, it records its app flags in the `flags` field of its `app_info` structure. See the BApplication and BRoster classes (in the Application Kit) for details.

Return values:

B_NO_ERROR. The flags were successfully retrieved or set.

B_NO_INIT. The BAppFileInfo is uninitialized.

B_NO_INIT. (Set) The BFile isn't open for writing.

B_ERROR. (Set) The BFile was locked when you initialized this object.

Attribute errors. See the error codes for BNode::ReadAttr() and BNode::WriteAttr().

BResources errors. See the error codes for BResources::WriteResource().

GetIcon(), SetIcon()

status_t **GetIcon**(BBitmap **icon,* icon_size *which*) const

status_t **SetIcon**(const BBitmap **icon,* icon_size *which*)

GetIcon() and SetIcon() get and set the icons that are stored in the app file. You specify which icon you want (large or small) by passing B_LARGE_ICON or B_SMALL_ICON as the *which* argument.

WARNING

The *which* value does not default the way it does for BNodeInfo.

The icon is passed in or returned through the *icon* argument:

- If you're getting the icon, the *icon* argument must be allocated; the icon data is copied into your BBitmap object.

- If you're setting the icon, the bitmap must be the proper size: 32x32 for the large icon, 16x16 for the small one. In BRect lingo, that's BRect(0, 0, 31, 31) and BRect(0, 0, 15, 15). The icons that you set through SetIcon() are also recorded in the File Type database, based on the application's signature.

- You can remove an app's icon by passing NULL as the *icon* argument to SetIcon().

Return values:

B_NO_ERROR. The icon was successfully found or set.

B_NO_INIT. The BAppFileInfo is uninitialized.

B_NO_INIT. (Set) The BFile isn't open for writing.

B_ERROR. (Set) The BFile was locked when you initialized this object.

B_BAD_VALUE. (Get) NULL BBitmap pointer.

B_BAD_VALUE. (Set) The bitmap data isn't the proper size.

Attribute errors. See the error codes for BNode::ReadAttr() and BNode::WriteAttr().

BResources errors. See the error codes for BResources::WriteResource().

GetIconForType(), SetIconForType()

status_t **GetIconForType**(const char *file_type,
              BBitmap *icon,
              icon_size which) const

status_t **SetIconForType**(const char *file_type,
              const BBitmap *icon,
              icon_size which)

These functions get and set the icons that this application uses to display the given file type.

- *file_type* must be a valid MIME string.

- The icon and which rules are the same as for GetIcon()/SetIcon().

The icons that you set are recorded in the File Type database, based on the app's signature.

Return values:
  B_NO_ERROR. The icon was found or set.
  B_NO_INIT. The BAppFileInfo is uninitialized.
  B_NO_INIT. (Set) The BFile isn't open for writing.
  B_ERROR. (Set) The BFile was locked when you initialized this object.
  B_BAD_VALUE. (Get) NULL BBitmap pointer, or *file_type* is invalid.
  B_BAD_VALUE. (Set) The bitmap data isn't the proper size, or *file_type* is invalid.
  Attribute errors. See the error codes for BNode::ReadAttr() and BNode::WriteAttr().
  BResources errors. See the error codes for BResources::WriteResource().

GetPreferredApp(), SetPreferredApp()

WARNING

Don't use these functions. An application's preferred app is itself; mucking with this setting is asking for trouble. These functions are inherited from BNodeInfo.

GetSignature(), SetSignature()

status_t **GetSignature**(char *signature) const
status_t **SetSignature**(const char *signature)

These functions get and set the signature (a MIME string) by which this application is known to the File Type database.

- The *signature* buffer that you pass to `GetSignature()` should be at least `B_MIME_TYPE_LENGTH` characters long; the signature is copied into the buffer.

- The length of the signature you pass to `SetSignature()` must be no longer than `B_MIME_TYPE_LENGTH`.

WARNING

`SetSignature()` does *not* install the signature (as a file type) in the File Type database. See "The File Type Database and the App's Signature" for details.

Return values:

`B_NO_ERROR`. The signature was found or set.

`B_NO_INIT`. The BAppFileInfo is uninitialized.

`B_NO_INIT`. (`Set`) The BFile isn't open for writing.

`B_ERROR`. (`Set`) The BFile was locked when you initialized this object.

`B_ENTRY_NOT_FOUND`. (`Get`) The app doesn't have a signature.

`B_BAD_VALUE`. (`Set`) *signature* is too long.

Attribute errors. See the error codes for `BNode::ReadAttr()` and `BNode::WriteAttr()`.

BResources errors. See the error codes for `BResources::WriteResource()`.

GetSupportedTypes(), SetSupportedTypes()

status_t **GetSupportedTypes**(BMessage *types*) const
status_t **SetSupportedTypes**(const BMessage *types*)

These functions get and set the file types that this app understands.

- If you're getting the types, you'll find them copied into your BMessage's "types" field (the BMessage must be allocated). They're given as an indexed array of strings (`B_STRING_TYPE`).

- Similarly, you pass in the supported types by adding strings to the message's "types" field.

- The BMessage's what field is unimportant.

Here we print all the supported types for a particular app:

```
/* afi is a valid BAppFileInfo object. */
BMessage msg;
uint32 i=0;
char *ptr;

if (afi.GetSupportedTypes(&msg) != B_NO_ERROR)
   /* Handle the error. */

while (true) {
   if (msg.FindString("types", i++, &ptr)
```

```
        != B_NO_ERROR)
    break;
  printf("> Supported Type:  %s\n", ptr);
}
```

The supported types that you set are recorded in the File Type database, based on the app's signature, *and* they're recorded by the app roster

When you set a new supported type, the File Type database makes sure that the type is "installed" (that the type is understood by the database). If the type wasn't previously installed, the type's preferred app is set to this app's signature.

WARNING

SetSupportedTypes() clobbers an app's existing set of supported types. If you want to augment an app's supported types, you should retrieve the existing set, add the new ones, and *then* call SetSupportedTypes().

Return values:

B_NO_ERROR. The types were found (including no types) or set.

B_NO_INIT. The BAppFileInfo is uninitialized.

B_NO_INIT. (Set) The BFile isn't open for writing.

B_NO_MEMORY. Insufficient memory to copy the types.

B_ERROR. (Set) The BFile was locked when you initialized this object.

Attribute errors. See the error codes for BNode::ReadAttr() and BNode::WriteAttr().

BResources errors. See the error codes for BResources::WriteResource().

GetType(), SetType()

virtual status_t **GetType**(char *type*) const
virtual status_t **SetType**(const char *type*)

These functions get and set the app's file type. The file type, passed in or returned through *type*, is a MIME string.

A Be-native application's default file type is "application/x-be-executable".

Return values:

B_NO_ERROR. The type was found (including no type) or set.

B_NO_INIT. The BAppFileInfo is uninitialized.

B_NO_INIT. (Set) The BFile isn't open for writing.

B_ERROR. (Set) The BFile was locked when you initialized this object.

B_BAD_VALUE. (Set) *type* is too long.

Attribute errors. See the error codes for BNode::ReadAttr() and BNode::WriteAttr().

BResources errors. See the error codes for BResources::WriteResource().

GetVersionInfo(), SetVersionInfo(), version_info, version_kind

status_t **GetVersionInfo**(version_info *_info_, version_kind *kind*) const
status_t **SetVersionInfo**(const version_info *_info_, version_kind *kind*)

struct **version_info** {}

The functions get and set the application's "version info." The information is recorded in the `version_info` structure:

```
struct version_info {
   uint32 major;

uint32 middle;
   uint32 minor;
   uint32 variety;
   uint32 internal;
   char short_info[64];
   char long_info[64];
}
```

The fields have no prescribed uses: You can stuff whatever information you want in them. Obviously, the field names (and types) provide suggestions for the type of info they want to store.

There are two kinds of version info; the kind you want to look at or set is encoded in the *kind* argument:

- `B_APP_VERSION_KIND` records information about this specific app.
- `B_SYSTEM_VERSION_KIND` records information about the "suite," or other grouping of apps, that this app belongs to.

Again, the uses of the two kinds is up to the app developer—currently, nothing in the BeOS depends on any information being stored in either `version_info` structure.

Return values:
   `B_NO_ERROR`. The `version_info` was found or set.
   `B_NO_INIT`. The BAppFileInfo is uninitialized.
   `B_NO_INIT`. (`Set`) The BFile isn't open for writing.
   `B_ERROR`. (`Set`) The BFile was locked when you initialized this object.
   `B_ENTRY_NOT_FOUND`. (`Get`) the app doesn't have the requested version info.
   Attribute errors. See the error codes for `BNode::ReadAttr()` and `BNode::WriteAttr()`.
   BResources errors. See the error codes for `BResources::WriteResource()`.

InitCheck()

status_t **InitCheck**(void) const

Returns the status of the most recent initialization.

Return values:

B_NO_ERROR. The object was successfully initialized.

B_NO_INIT. The object is uninitialized.

See `SetTo()` for more error codes.

SetAppFlags() *see GetAppFlags()*

SetIcon() *see GetIcon()*

SetIconForType() *see GetIconForType()*

SetPreferredApp() *see GetPreferredApp()*

SetSignature() *see GetSignature()*

SetSupportedTypes() *see GetSupportedTypes()*

SetTo()

status_t **SetTo**(BFile *file*)

Initializes the BAppFileInfo object by pointing it to *file*, which must be a valid (initialized) BFile object. The BFile is not copied, or re-opened by BAppFileInfo. In particular, the BAppFileInfo uses *file*'s file descriptor.

If the BFile is open for writing, it will be locked by this function. The BFile should be unlocked when you pass it in.

Return values:

B_NO_ERROR. The object was successfully initialized.

B_BAD_VALUE. *file* is uninitialized.

SetType() *see GetTypes()*

SetVersionInfo() *see GetVersionInfo()*

BDirectory

Derived from: BNode, BEntryList

Declared in: be/storage/Directory.h

Library: libbe.so

Overview

A BDirectory object gives you access to the contents of a directory. A BDirectory's primary features are:

- **It can iteratively retrieve the entries in the directory**. The entries are returned as BEntry objects, `entry_refs`, or `dirent` structures (`GetNextEntry()`, `GetNextRef()`, `GetNextDirents()`).

- **It can find a specific entry**. You can ask if the entry exists (`Contains()`), and you can retrieve the entry as a BEntry (`FindEntry()`).

- **It can create new entries**. Through the aptly named `CreateFile()`, `CreateDirectory()` and `CreateSymLink()` functions.

Unlike the other BNode classes, a BDirectory knows its own entry (`GetEntry()`), and can be initialized with a `node_ref` structure.

Retrieving Entries

The BDirectory functions that let you iterate over a directory's entries are inherited from BEntryList:

```
status_t GetNextEntry(BEntry *entry, bool traverse = true);
status_t GetNextRef(entry_ref *ref);
int32 GetNextDirents(dirent *buf, size_t length, int32 count = INT_MAX)
```

For the basic story on these functions, see the BEntryList class and the function descriptions below. In addition to the info you'll find there, you should be aware of the following:

- **Entries are returned in "directory order."** This is, roughly, the ASCII order of their names.

- **Try not to alter the directory while you're getting its entries**. Entries are delivered on demand. If you do something to change the contents of the directory while you're iterating through those contents (such as change the name of the file "aaa" to "zzz") you could end up seeing an entry more than once (technically, you'll see the same node under the guise of different entries), or you could miss an entry.

- **Counting entries uses the same iterator that retrieves entries**. You mustn't call `CountEntries()` while you're looping over a `GetNext...()` function.

Creating New Directories

To create a new directory, you can use BDirectory's `CreateDirectory()` function. The function creates a single new directory as identified by its argument. The new directory will be a subdirectory of the invoked-upon BDirectory's directory.

You can also create an entire path full of new directories through the global `create_directory()` function. This convenient function attempts to create *all* "missing" directories along the path that you pass in.

Finding a Directory

The `find_directory()` function gives you the pathnames for pre-defined directories. These directories, such as those that store Be-supplied applications and user-defined preferences settings, are represented by `directory_which` constants. These constants are not strings; you can't use them directly. You have to pass them through `find_directory()`.

Note that the BDirectory class itself doesn't let you find directories on the basis of the `directory_which` constants—you have to use the `find_directory()` function (which is documented at the end of this class description).

Node Monitoring a Directory

NOTE

The following description is a brief, directory-specific view into the Node Monitor. For the full story, see "The Node Monitor" section of this chapter.

You can monitor changes to the contents of a directory by passing a BDirectory's `node_ref` and the `B_WATCH_DIRECTORY` flag to the Node Monitor's `watch_node()` function. As with all invocations of `watch_node()`, you also have to pass a BMessenger (the "target") that will receive the Node Monitor notifications; here, we use `be_app_messenger`:

```
BDirectory dir("/boot/home");
node_ref nref;
status_t err;

if (dir.InitCheck() == B_OK) {
   dir.GetNodeRef(&nref);
   err = watch_node(&nref, B_WATCH_DIRECTORY, be_app_messenger);
   if (err != B_OK)
      /* handle the error */
}
```

The following changes to the monitored directory cause BMessages to be sent to the target. The `what` field for all Node Monitor messages is `B_NODE_MONITOR`; the "opcode" field (an integer code) describes the activity:

- An entry was created (opcode = `B_ENTRY_CREATED`).

- An entry was moved to a different name in the same directory (`B_ENTRY_RENAMED`).

- An entry was moved from this directory to a different directory, or vice versa (B_ENTRY_MOVED).

- An entry (and the node it represents) was deleted from the file system (B_ENTRY_REMOVED).

The B_WATCH_DIRECTORY flag (by itself) *doesn't* monitor changes to the directory's own entry. For example, if you change the name of the directory that you're monitoring, the target isn't sent a message. If you want a BDirectory to watch changes to itself, you have to throw in one of the other Node Monitor flags (B_WATCH_NAME, B_WATCH_STAT, or B_WATCH_ATTR).

The other fields in the Node Monitor message describe the entry that changed. The set of fields depends on the opcode (the following is a summary of the list given in "Notification Messages" in the Node Monitor documentation):

B_ENTRY_CREATED

Field	Type	Description
"device"	B_INT32_TYPE	dev_t of the directory's device.
"directory"	B_INT64_TYPE	ino_t (node number) of the directory.
"node"	B_INT64_TYPE	ino_t of the new entry's node.
"name"	B_STRING_TYPE	The name of the new entry.

B_ENTRY_MOVED

The "device", "node", and "name" fields are the same as for B_ENTRY_CREATED, plus...

Field	Type	Description
"from_directory"	B_INT64_TYPE	The ino_t number of the old directory.
"to_directory"	B_INT64_TYPE	The ino_t number of the new directory.

B_ENTRY_REMOVED

The B_ENTRY_REMOVED message takes the same form as B_ENTRY_CREATED, but without the "name" field. This, obviously, can be a problem—what good is it if you're told that a file has been removed, but you're not told the file's name? In some cases, simply being told that a file has been removed actually *is* good enough: You can simply re-read the contents of the directory.

Constructor and Destructor

BDirectory()

BDirectory(const entry_ref *ref*)
BDirectory(const node_ref *nref*)
BDirectory(const BEntry *entry*)
BDirectory(const char *path*)
BDirectory(const BDirectory *dir*, const char *path*)

BDirectory(void)
BDirectory(const BDirectory &directory*)

Creates a new BDirectory object that represents the directory as given by the arguments. See the analogous `SetTo()` functions for descriptions of the flavorful constructors.

- The default constructor does nothing; it should be followed by a call to `SetTo()`.

- The copy constructor points the BDirectory to the same directory as is represented by the argument. The two objects have their own entry iterators.

To check to see if an initialization was successful, call `InitCheck()`.

~BDirectory()

virtual ~**BDirectory**()

Deletes the object.

Member Functions

Contains()

bool **Contains**(const char *path*, int32 *nodeFlags* = B_ANY_NODE)
bool **Contains**(const BEntry *entry*, int32 *nodeFlags* = B_ANY_NODE)

Returns `true` if *path* or *entry* is contained within this directory, or in any of its subdirectories (no matter how deep). You can use the *nodeFlags* argument to limit the search to a particular flavor of node:

- `B_FILE_NODE` looks for a "plain" file.
- `B_DIRECTORY_NODE` looks for a directory.
- `B_SYMLINK_NODE` looks for a symbolic link.
- `B_ANY_NODE` (the default) doesn't discriminate between flavors.

CountEntries()   *see GetNextEntry()*

CreateDirectory()   *see CreateFile()*

CreateFile(), CreateDirectory(), CreateSymLink()

status_t **CreateFile**(const char **path*,
                BFile **file*,
                bool *failIfExists*)

status_t **CreateDirectory**(const char **path*, BDirectory **dir*)

status_t **CreateSymLink**(const char **path*,
                    const char **linkToPath*,
                    BSymLink **link*)

These functions create a new file, directory, or symbolic link. The new node is located at *path*, where *path* must be relative and is reckoned off of the directory represented by this BDirectory.

- `CreateFile()` fails if the file already exists and *failIfExists* is `true`. If the flag is `false` (and the file exists), the old file is clobbered and a new one is created. If successful, the BFile argument that you pass in is opened on the new file in `B_READ_WRITE` mode.

- `CreateDirectory()` and `CreateSymLink()` fail if *path* already exists—you can't clobber an existing directory or link.

- The *linkToPath* argument (`CreateSymLink()`) is the path that the new symbolic link will be linked to.

In all cases, the object argument (the BDirectory, BFile, or BSymLink) must be allocated before it's passed in. If the function fails, the argument is `Unset()`.

Return values:

B_OK. Success.
B_BAD_VALUE. Illegal *path*, *file*, *dir*, or *link* specified; may be NULL. *path* may be empty.
B_BUSY. A busy node could not be accessed.
B_ENTRY_NOT_FOUND. The specified *path* does not exist or is an empty string.
B_FILE_ERROR. A file system error prevented the operation.
B_FILE_EXISTS. The file specified by *path* already exists.
B_LINK_LIMIT. A cyclic loop has been detected in the file system.
B_NAME_TOO_LONG. The *path* specified is too long.
B_NO_MEMORY. Insufficient memory to perform the operation.
B_NO_MORE_FDS. All file descriptors are in use (too many open files).
B_IS_A_DIRECTORY. Can't replace a directory with a file.
B_NOT_A_DIRECTORY. A component of the *path* is not a directory.

B_NOT_ALLOWED. The volume is read-only.

B_PERMISSION_DENIED. Create access is denied in the specified *path*.

E2BIG. *linkToPath* is too long (`CreateSymLink()` only).

CreateSymLink()   *see CreateFile()*

FindEntry()

status_t **FindEntry**(const char **path*,
                    BEntry **entry*,
                    bool *traverse* = false)

Finds the entry with the given name, and sets the second argument to refer to that entry.

- *path* must be a relative pathname. It's reckoned off of the BDirectory's directory.

- You *are* allowed to look for "." and "..". The former represents this directory's entry. The latter refers to this directory's parent.

- The *entry* argument must be allocated before it's passed in (it needn't be initialized).

- The *traverse* applies to symbolic links: If the flag is `true`, the link is traversed. If it's `false`, you get the BEntry that points to the link itself.

If *path* isn't found, the second argument is automatically `Unset()`. To find out why the lookup failed, invoke `InitCheck()` on the *entry* argument:

```
BEntry entry;
status_t err;

if (dir.FindEntry("aFile", &entry) != B_OK) {
   err = entry.InitCheck();
}
```

The direct return value is also informative, but it may not be as precise as the `InitCheck()` value.

Return values:

B_OK. Success.

B_BAD_VALUE. Invalid *path* specified; it may be NULL or empty.

B_ENTRY_NOT_FOUND. The specified *path* does not exist.

B_NAME_TOO_LONG. The *path* specified is too long.

B_LINK_LIMIT. A cyclic loop has been detected in the file system.

B_NO_MEMORY. Insufficient memory to perform the operation.

B_FILE_ERROR. An invalid file prevented the operation.

GetEntry()

> status_t GetEntry(BEntry *entry)

Initializes *entry* to represent this BDirectory. If the initialization fails, *entry* is Unset().

Return values:
> B_OK. Success.
> B_NAME_TOO_LONG. The path specified by *entry* is too long.
> B_ENTRY_NOT_FOUND. The specified path does not exist.
> B_LINK_LIMIT. A cyclic loop has been detected in the file system.
> B_BAD_VALUE. *entry* is uninitialized.
> B_NO_MEMORY. Insufficient memory to perform the operation.
> B_BUSY. A busy node could not be accessed.
> B_FILE_ERROR. An invalid file prevented the operation.
> B_NO_MORE_FDS. All file descriptors are in use (too many open files).
> B_NOT_A_DIRECTORY. The path includes non-directory entries.

GetNextDirents()   *see GetNextEntry()*

GetNextEntry(), GetNextRef(), GetNextDirents(), CountEntries(), Rewind()

> status_t **GetNextEntry**(BEntry *entry*, bool *traverse* = false) const
> status_t **GetNextRef**(entry_ref *ref*) const
> int32 **GetNextDirents**(dirent *buf*, size_t *bufsize,* int32 *count* = MAX_INT) const

> int32 **CountEntries**(void) const

> status_t **Rewind**(void)

The three GetNext...() functions retrieve the "next" entry that lives in the BDirectory and returns it as a BEntry, entry_ref, or dirent structure.

- GetNextEntry() returns the entry as a BEntry object. If *traverse* is true and the entry is a symbolic link, the link is traversed. In other words, *entry* could end up being in a different directory than the one referred to by this. When all entries have been visited, the function returns B_ENTRY_NOT_FOUND. The *entry* argument must be allocated before it's passed in.

- GetNextRef() return the next entry in *ref.* Since an entry_ref doesn't supply enough information to determine if the entry is a link, there's no question of traversal: The entry_ref points to *exactly* the next entry. When all entries have been visited, the function returns B_ENTRY_NOT_FOUND. The *ref* argument must be allocated before it's passed in.

- GetNextDirents() returns some number of dirent structures, either as many as can be stuffed into *buf* (where *bufsize* gives the size of *buf*), or *count* structures, whichever is smaller. The function returns the number of structures that were stuffed into *buf*; when all entries have been visited, it returns 0.

WARNING

Currently, GetNextDirents() only reads one dirent at a time, no matter how many you ask for.

GetNextEntry() and GetNextRef() are reasonably clear; the dirent version deserves more explanation. You'll find this explanation (and an example) in the BEntryList class. Also, keep in mind that the set of candidate entries is different for the dirent version: GetNextDirents() finds *all* entries, including the entries for "." and "..". The other two versions skip these entries.

When you're done reading the BDirectory's entries, you can rewind the object's entry iterator by calling Rewind().

CountEntries() returns the number of entries (not counting "." and "..") in the directory.

WARNING

Never call CountEntries() while you're iterating through the directory. CountEntries() does a rewind, iterates through the entries, and then rewinds again.

Return values:
   B_OK. Success.
   B_FILE_ERROR. BDirectory object has not been properly initialized.
   B_NOT_A_DIRECTORY. The directory is invalid.
   B_NAME_TOO_LONG. The dirent's name is too long.
   B_ENTRY_NOT_FOUND. End of directory reached.
   B_LINK_LIMIT. A cyclic loop has been detected in the file system.
   B_BAD_VALUE. Invalid input specified, or BDirectory object has not been properly initialized.
   B_NO_MEMORY. Insufficient memory to perform the operation.

GetNextRef()   *see GetNextEntry()*

GetStatFor()

status_t **GetStatFor**(const char *path*, stat *st*) const

Gets the `stat` structure for the entry designated by *path*. *path* must be relative, and is reckoned off of the BDirectory's directory. This is, primarily, a convenience function; but it's also provided for efficiency.

Return values:

B_OK. Success.

B_FILE_ERROR. An invalid file prevented the operation.

B_NAME_TOO_LONG. The *path* specified is too long.

B_ENTRY_NOT_FOUND. The specified *path* does not exist.

B_LINK_LIMIT. A cyclic loop has been detected in the file system.

B_BAD_VALUE. Invalid input specified; the *path* may be NULL or empty.

B_NO_MEMORY. Insufficient memory to perform the operation.

InitCheck()

status_t **InitCheck**(void) const

Returns the status of the previous construction, assignment operation, or `SetTo()` call.

Return values:

B_OK. The initialization was successful.

B_NO_INIT. The object is uninitialized (this includes `Unset()`).

See `SetTo()` for other errors.

IsRootDirectory()

bool **IsRootDirectory**(void)

Returns `true` if this BDirectory represents a *root directory*. A root directory is the directory that's at the root of a volume's file hierarchy. Every volume has exactly one root directory; all other files in the volume's hierarchy descend from the root directory.

Rewind()   *see GetNextEntry()*

SetTo(), Unset()

status_t **SetTo**(const entry_ref *ref*)
status_t **SetTo**(const node_ref *nref*)
status_t **SetTo**(const BEntry *entry*)
status_t **SetTo**(const char *path*)
status_t **SetTo**(const BDirectory *dir*, const char *path*)

void **Unset**(void)

Closes the BDirectory's current directory (if any), and initializes the object to open the directory as given by the arguments.

- In the *path* version, *path* can be absolute or relative, and can contain "." and ".." elements. If *path* is relative, it's reckoned off of the current working directory.

- In the *dir/path* version, *path* must be relative. It's reckoned off of the directory given by *dir*.

If the specification results in a symbolic link that resolves to a directory, then the linked-to directory is opened. If the specification is (or resolves to) a regular file, the initialization fails.

Return values:

B_OK. Success.

B_NAME_TOO_LONG. The *path* specified is too long.

B_ENTRY_NOT_FOUND. The directory does not exist.

B_LINK_LIMIT. A cyclic loop has been detected in the file system.

B_BAD_VALUE. Invalid input specified.

B_NO_MEMORY. Insufficient memory to perform the operation.

B_BUSY. A busy node could not be accessed.

B_FILE_ERROR. An invalid file prevented the operation.

B_NO_MORE_FDS. All file descriptors are in use (too many open files).

Operators

= (assignment)

BDirectory& operator=(const BDirectory &*directory*)

In the expression

```
BDirectory a = b;
```

BDirectory *a* is initialized to refer to the same directory as *b*. To gauge the success of the assignment, you should call InitCheck() immediately afterwards. Assigning a BDirectory to itself is safe.

Assigning from an uninitialized BDirectory is "successful": The assigned-to BDirectory will also be uninitialized (B_NO_INIT).

==, != (comparison)

bool operator==(const BDirectory &*directory*) const
bool operator!=(const BDirectory &*directory*) const

Two BDirectory objects are said to be equal if they refer to the same directory, or if they're both uninitialized.

C Functions

create_directory()

status_t **create_directory**(const char *path, mode_t *mode*)

Creates all missing directories along the path specified by *path*.

- The pathname can be absolute or relative. If it's relative, the path is reckoned of the current working directory. If any symlinks are found in the existing portion of the path, they're traversed.

- *path* can contain ".", but it may not contain "..".

- *mode* is the permissions setting (typically expressed as an octal number) that's assigned to all directories that are created. To set the directories to be readable, writable, and "enterable" by all (for example), you would set the mode to 0777.

Return values:

B_OK. *path* now fully exists (or did in the first place).

B_BAD_VALUE. *path* is NULL, is empty, or contains "..".

B_NOT_ALLOWED. Read-only volume.

B_NO_MEMORY. Insufficient memory to perform the operation.

find_directory()

status_t **find_directory**(directory_which *which*,
                dev_t *volume*,
                bool *create_it*,
                char *path_string*,
                int32 *length*)

status_t **find_directory**(directory_which *which*,
                BPath *path_obj*,
                bool *create_it* = false,
                BVolume *volume* = NULL)

NOTE

The first version of this function can be used in either C or C++ code. The second version is for C++ code only.

Finds the path to the directory symbolized by *which* and copies it into *path_string*, or uses it to initializes *path_obj*.

- The *create_it* argument tells the function to create the function if it doesn't already exist.

- *volume* identifies the volume (as a `dev_t` identifier or BVolume object) on which you want to look. The C++ default (`NULL`) means to look in the boot volume.

- The *length* argument (first version only) gives the length of *path*.

The `directory_which` constants are described in the "Global Constants and Defined Types" section at the end of this chapter.

Return values:
   B_OK. The directory was found.
   Other codes. The directory wasn't found or couldn't be created.

BEntryList

Derived from: *none*

Declared in: be/storage/EntryList.h

Library: *none*

Overview

BEntryList is a pure abstract class that defines the protocol for iterating over a set of file system entries. Each derived class must figure out how to create (or "discover") the entry list in the first place: BEntryList only supplies functions for getting entries out of the list, it doesn't let you put them in. The BEntryList class has two derived classes: BDirectory and BQuery.

At the heart of the BEntryList class are the three `GetNext...()` functions, which let you retrieve the entries as:

- BEntry objects (`GetNextEntry()`),
- `entry_ref` structures (`GetNextRef()`),
- or `dirent` ("directory entry") structures (`GetNextDirents()`).

You call these functions iteratively; each call gets the "next" entry (or set of entries in the case of `GetNextDirents()`). You check the `GetNext...()` return value to detect the end of the list:

- For `GetNextEntry()` and `GetNextRef()`, `B_ENTRY_NOT_FOUND` indicates that there are no more entries to get.

- `GetNextDirents()` returns 0 when it's at the end of the list.

To get back to the top of an entry list, you call `Rewind()`, but note the following:

WARNING

`Rewind()` applies to BDirectories only. You can't rewind a BQuery's entry list.

Here's an example of an iteration over all the entries in a BDirectory, retrieved as BEntry objects:

```
BDirectory dir("/boot/home/fido");
BEntry entry;

dir.Rewind();
while (dir.GetNextEntry(&entry) == B_NO_ERROR)
   /* do something with entry here. */
```

The final BEntryList function, `CountEntries()`, also only applies to BDirectories; but even there you shouldn't depend on it. The count is stale as soon as `CountEntries()` returns. The user could create a new file or delete a file in the directory while you're iterating over the entries. Also, `CountEntries()` shares the entry list pointer with the `GetNext...()` functions. You mustn't intermingle a `CountEntries()` call within your `GetNext...()` loop.

One more BDirectory wrinkle:

- Entries are retrieved in "directory order". (This is a POSIX term that means, roughly, ASCII order.) If the user renames a file while you're iterating over the directory, it's possible that the file won't be seen, or will show up under its old name *and* its new name.

The Entry List Pointer

Each BEntryList object has a single iterator pointer that's shared by all three `GetNext...()` formats (and `CountEntries()`). Thus, each successive call to a `GetNext...()` function gets the next entry, regardless of the format. For example:

```
BEntry entry;
entry_ref ref;

dir.GetNextEntry(&entry);
dir.GetNextRef(&ref);
```

Here, `entry` represents the first entry in the directory, and `ref` represents the second entry.

Multiple Retrieval

`GetNextDirents()` is different from the other two flavors in that it can retrieve more than one entry at a time. Or it will, someday; currently `GetNextDirents()` retrieves only one entry at a time, no matter how many you ask for.

Choosing an Iterator

So, which flavor of `GetNext...()` should you use? Here's how they compare:

- `GetNextDirents()` is by far the fastest (even in the current one-struct-at-a-time version), but it's also the least wieldy—the protocol isn't nearly as nice as the other two functions. The `dirent` structure, while jam-packed with fun facts, usually has to be turned into other structures (`node_refs` or `entry_refs`) in order to be useful.

- `GetNextRef()` is slower, but the `entry_ref` structure can be immediately usable (or, at least, cachable). Nonetheless, you're still a step away from a "real" object.

- `GetNextEntry()` is the slowest, but at least it hands you an object that you can sink your teeth into.

The actual timing numbers depend on your machine, the class that you're invoking the functions through, and some other factors. But the difference is (ahem) significant: `GetNextDirents()` is about an order of magnitude faster than `GetNextEntry()`, with `GetNextRef()` right about in the middle.

If, for example, you're simply compiling a list of leaf names, you should certainly use `GetNextDirents()` (painful though it may be). But if you plan on actually *doing* something with each and every entry that you retrieve, then bite the bullet: Use `GetNextEntry()`.

The dirent Structure and GetNextDirents()

Of the three iterator functions, `GetNextDirents()` needs some explanation. The `dirent` structure, which is what the function returns, describes aspects of the retrieved entry:

```
typedef struct dirent {
   dev_t d_dev;
   ino_t d_ino;
   dev_t d_pdev;
   ino_t d_pino;
   unsigned short d_reclen;
   char d_name[1];
} dirent;
```

The fields are:

- `d_dev` is a device id that identifies the device (file system) on which this entry lies.
- `d_ino` is the node number for this entry's node.
- `d_pdev` and `d_pino` are the device and inode numbers for the parent directory.
- `d_reclen` is the length of this dirent structure. The length is variable because...
- `d_name` is a buffer that's allocated to hold the (`NULL`-terminated) name of this entry.

So—let's pretend we've retrieved a dirent and we want to do something with it. In addition to looking at individual fields, we can combine some of them to make other structures:

- d_dev + d_ino = node_ref of the entry's node
- d_pdev + d_pino = node_ref of the parent directory
- d_pdev + d_pino + d_name = entry_ref for the entry

In code:

```
dirent *dent;
entry_ref ref;
node_ref nref;
node_ref pnref;

/* Allocate and fill the dirent here... */
...

/* Make a node_ref to this entry's node. */
nref.device = dirent->d_dev;
nref.node = dirent->d_ino;

/* Make a node_ref to this entry's parent. */
pnref.device = dirent->d_pdev;
pnref.node = dirent->d_pino;

/* Make an entry_ref to this entry. */
ref.device = dirent->d_pdev;
ref.directory = dirent->d_pino;
ref.set_name(dirent->d_name);
```

Where you go from here is a simple matter of programming. Me? I'm going to lunch.

Getting a dirent

Now that we know what to do with a dirent, let's see how to get one. The GetNextDirents() protocol looks like this:

int32 GetNextDirents (dirent *buf, size_t bufsize, int32 count = INT_MAX)

By default, the function stuffs as many dirent structs as it can into the first bufsize bytes of buf. These structures represent the next N entries in the entry list. The count argument lets you set a limit to the number of structures that you want to be retrieved at a time. The function returns the number of structures that it actually got.

WARNING

Keep in mind that currently GetNextDirents() can only read one dirent at a time, regardless of the size of buf, or the value of count.

Let's try it. For the purposes of this example, we'll convert each `dirent` into an `entry_ref`, as described in the previous section.

```
/* This is the buffer that we'll stuff structures into. */
char buf[4096];
dirent *dent;
entry_ref ref;

/* We'll assume dir is a valid BDirectory object. */
while ((count = dir.GetNextDirents((dirent *)buf, 4096) > 0) {
   dent = (dirent *)buf;

   /* Now we step through the dirents. */
   while (count-- > 0) {
      ref.device = dent->d_pdev;
      ref.directory = dent->d_pino;
      ref.set_name(dent->d_name);

      /* Do something with the ref. */
      ...

      /* Bump the pointer. */
      dent = (dirent *)((char *)dent + dent->d_reclen);
   }
}
```

Remember, the structure is variable length—you have to increment the pointer by hand, as shown here.

Member Functions

CountEntries()

> virtual int32 **CountEntries**(void) = 0

Returns the number of entries that are in the entry list.

WARNING

> For BQuery this is a no-op. Also, BDirectory's implementation manipulates the entry list pointer; thus, you shouldn't call `CountEntries()` while you're iterating through the directory's entries.

GetNextEntry(), GetNextRef(), GetNextDirents()

> virtual status_t **GetNextEntry**(BEntry *entry) = 0

> virtual status_t **GetNextRef**(entry_ref *ref) = 0

> virtual int32 **GetNextDirents**(dirent *buf, size_t bufsize, int32 count = INT_MAX) = 0

These functions return the "next" entry in the entry list as a BEntry, entry_ref, or dirent structure. The end of the list is signalled by:

- GetNextEntry() and GetNextRef() return B_ENTRY_NOT_FOUND.

- GetNextDirents() returns 0.

See the Overview for more information.

Rewind()

virtual status_t **Rewind**(void)

Rewinds the entry list pointer so it points to the first element in the list.

WARNING

For BQuery this is a no-op.

BEntry

Derived from: BStatable

Declared in: be/storage/Entry.h

Library: libbe.so

Overview

The BEntry class defines objects that represent "locations" in the file system hierarchy. Each location (or *entry*) is given as a name within a directory. For example, when you create a BEntry thus,

```
BEntry entry("/boot/home/fido");
```

you're telling the BEntry object to represent the *location* of the file called *fido* within the directory "/boot/home".

A BEntry doesn't care whether the entry you tell it to represent is a plain file, a directory, or a symbolic link—it doesn't even care if the entry even *exists* (but we'll get to that later in "Abstract Entries"):

- All the BEntry cares about is a *name* in a *directory*.

The most important implication of this is the object's attitude towards data. **BEntries don't know how to operate on data.** You can't use a BEntry to read or write a file's data or attributes. For data operations, you have to turn your BEntry into a BNode.

Nonetheless, it's often convenient to speak of a BEntry as *having* data; for example, the phrase "the entry's data" really means "the data that lies in the file that's located by the entry."

Talents and Abilities

A properly initialized BEntry object (we'll get to the rules of initialization later) knows the following:

- **Location info.** A BEntry knows its own (leaf) name (`GetName()`), its full pathname (`GetPath()`), and the identity of its parent directory (`GetParent()`).

- **BStatable info.** As a descendant of BStatable, a BEntry can return statistical information about the entry's data—its size, creation date, owner, and so on.

- `entry_ref` **identifier.** A BEntry can return the `entry_ref` that globally identifies the entry (`GetRef()`).

A BEntry can do these things:

- **Perform hierarchical operations.** A BEntry can change the name of its entry (`Rename()`), move it to another directory (`Move()`), and remove it from the file hierarchy (`Remove()`).

- **Initialize BNode objects.** The constructors and `SetTo()` initializers for BNode and its children (BFile, BDirectory, and BSymLink) accept BEntry arguments.

As mentioned above, the most important thing that a BEntry *can't* do is access its own data: **A BEntry can't read or write data or attributes.** To do these things you need a BNode object.

(Actually, this isn't entirely true: A BEntry *can* set the size of its data through the `BStatable::SetSize()` function. The function only works on plain files.)

Initializing and Traversing

To initialize a BEntry, you have to tell it which entry to represent; in other words, you have to identify a directory and a name. You can initialize a BEntry object directly:

- during construction,
- through the `SetTo()` function,
- or through the assignment operator.

or you can have some other object initialize your BEntry for you, by passing the BEntry as an argument to one of the following:

- BDirectory's `FindEntry()` or `GetEntry()` function
- BEntryList's `GetNextEntry()` function (implemented by BDirectory and BQuery)
- BEntry's `GetParent()` function

In all cases (except the assignment operator) you're asked if you want to "traverse" the entry during initialization. Traversal is used to "resolve" symbolic links:

- **If you traverse**: The BEntry will point to the entry that the symbolic link is linked to.

- **If you don't traverse**: The BEntry will point to the symbolic link itself.

For example, let's say */boot/home/fidoLink* is linked to */fido*, to wit:

```
$ cd /boot/home
$ ln -s ./fido fidoLink
```

Now let's make a traversed BEntry for *fidoLink*:

```
/* The second argument is the traversal bool. */
BEntry entry("/boot/home/fidoLink", true);
```

If we ask for the entry's pathname,

```
BPath path;
entry.GetPath(&path);
printf("Pathname: %s\n", path.Path());
```

we see

```
Pathname:  /boot/home/fido
```

In other words, the BEntry refers to *fido*, not *fidoLink*.

Traversal resolves nested links—it really wants to find a "real" file (or directory). If the entry that you're initializing to isn't a link, then the traversal flag is ignored.

When to Traverse

When should you traverse, and when not? Here are a few rules of thumbs:

- If somebody hands you a file reference—if your app gets a `RefsReceived()` message—then you probably want to traverse the entry.

- If you're pawing over the contents of a directory (through BDirectory's `GetNextEntry()`), then you probably don't want to traverse.

- If you're looking at the result of a query (through BQuery's `GetNextEntry()`), then you almost *certainly* don't want to traverse. The query finds entries that satisfy certain criteria; if a symbolic link is in the list, it's because the link itself was a winner. If the linked-to file is also a winner, it will show up on its own.

Traverso Post Facto

Let's say you create a BEntry (to a symlink) without traversing, but then you decide that you *do* want to resolve the link. Unfortunately, you can't resolve in-place;

instead, you have to initialize another BEntry using info (`entry_ref` or pathname) that you get from the link entry:

```
BEntry entry1("/boot/home/fidoLink", false);
BEntry entry2;
entry_ref ref;

/* First we check to see if it's a link. */
if (entry1.IsSymLink()) {
   /* Get the link's entry_ref... */
   entry1.GetRef(&ref);

   /* ...and use it to initialize the other BEntry. */
   entry2.SetTo(&ref, true);
}
```

Abstract Entries

As we all should know by now, a BEntry identifies a name within a specific directory. The directory that a BEntry identifies must exist, but the entry that corresponds to the name doesn't have to. In other words:

• A BEntry can represent a file that doesn't exist. The entry is said to be "abstract."

For example, the following construction creates a BEntry object based on a BDirectory and a name:

```
BEntry entry(someDir, "myFile.h");
```

Let's assume that *myFile.h* doesn't exist. As long as the directory that's referred to by `someDir` *does* exist, then the construction is legal. Some of the BEntry functions (those inherited from BStatable, for instance) won't work, but the object itself is valid.

But validity doesn't equal existence:

• `SetTo()` and `InitCheck()` *do not* tell you if a BEntry's entry actually exists. Don't be confused; a return value of `B_OK` simply means the object is valid.

If you want to know if a BEntry's entry actually exists, use the `Exists()` function.

Creating a File From an Abstract Entry

To turn an abstract BEntry into a real entry (or, more accurately, a real node), you have to specify the flavor of node that you want. There are two methods for creating a node; the first is general, the second applies to plain files only.

The General Approach. BDirectory's `CreateFile()`, `CreateDirectory()`, and `CreateSymLink()` functions create nodes of the designated flavor. The functions don't take BEntry arguments directly; instead, you invoke the functions on the BEntry's directory, passing the entry's leaf name as an argument. Here we turn an abstract entry (`entry`) into a directory:

```
BPath path;
char name[B_FILE_NAME_LENGTH]; /* A buffer for the name. */
BDirectory parent;  /* The parent of our entry. */
BDirectory target_dir; /* The product of the transformation. */

if (!entry.Exists()) {
   entry.GetParent(&path);
   entry.GetName(name);
   parent.SetTo(&path);
   parent.CreateDirectory(name, &dir);
}
```

The Plain-File-Only Approach. You can create a plain file by passing the BEntry to the BFile constructor or `SetTo()` function. To do this, you also have to add `B_CREATE_FILE` to the "open mode" flags:

```
BFile file;
```

```
if (!entry.Exists())
   file.SetTo(&entry, B_CREATE_FILE|B_READ_WRITE);
```

Subtleties and Details

The following details understand you should, particularly if you want to participate in bedevtalk.

File Descriptors

Although it's not intuitively obvious, a BEntry object *does* consume a file descriptor. The file descriptor is opened on the entry's directory.

Your app has a limited number of file descriptors (currently 128, max), so you may not want to cache BEntry objects as your primary means for identifying an entry. If you're going to be dealing with a lot of entries and you want to keep track of them all, it's better to cache `entry_ref` structures or BPath objects.

Directories Are Persistent, Names Are Not

One more time: A BEntry identifies an entry as a name in a directory. As described above, the directory is maintained internally as a file descriptor; the name is simply a string. This means:

- **The directory for a given BEntry is persistent**. If you move the directory, the file descriptor, and so the BEntry, moves with it.

- **The name isn't persistent**. If the user renames the leaf that a BEntry is pointing to, the BEntry will become abstract.

For example, take the following BEntry:

```
BEntry entry("/boot/home/lbj/footFetish.jpeg");
```

If the user moves the directory:

```
$ cd /boot/home
$ mv lbj jfk
```

The BEntry (entry) "moves" with the directory. If you print the pathname and ask if the BEntry's entry exists,

```
BPath path;
entry.GetPath(&path);
printf("> Foot movie:  %s\n", path.Path());
printf("> Exists?  %s\n", entry.Exists()?"Oui":"Non");
```

you'll see this:

```
> Foot movie:  /boot/home/jfk/footFetish.jpeg
> Exists?  Oui
```

The same isn't so for the name portion of a BEntry. If the user now moves *footFetish.jpeg*:

```
$ cd /boot/home/jfk
$ mv footFetish.jpeg hammerToe.jpeg
```

your BEntry *will not* follow the file (it doesn't "follow the data"). The object will still represent the entry called *footFetish.jpeg*. The BEntry will, in this case, become abstract.

Don't be confused: The BEntry only "loses track" of a renamed entry if the name change is made behind the object's back. Manipulating the entry name through the BEntry object's `Rename()` function (for example), doesn't baffle the object. For example:

```
BPath path;
BEntry entry("/boot/home/lbj/footFetish.jpeg");

entry.Rename("hammerToe.jpeg");
entry.GetPath(&path);
printf("> Foot movie:  %s\n", path.Path());
printf("> Exists?  %s\n", entry.Exists()?"Oui":"Non");
```

and we see:

```
> Foot movie:  /boot/home/lbj/hammerToe.jpeg
> Exists?  Oui
```

BEntries and Locked Nodes

You can't lock an entry, but you can lock the entry's node (through BNode's `Lock()` function). Initializing a BEntry to point to a locked node is permitted, but **the entry's directory must *not* be locked**. If the directory is locked, the BEntry constructor and `SetTo()` function fail and set `InitCheck()` to B_BUSY.

Furthermore, the destination directories in BEntry's `Rename()` and `MoveTo()` must be unlocked for the functions to succeed. And *all* directories in the path to the entry must be unlocked for `GetPath()` to succeed.

If you get a `B_BUSY` error, you may want to try again—it's strongly advised that locks be held as briefly as possible.

Constructor and Destructor

BEntry()

BEntry(const BDirectory *dir*, const char *path*, bool *traverse* = FALSE)
BEntry(const entry_ref *ref*, bool *traverse* = FALSE)
BEntry(const char *path*, bool *traverse* = FALSE)

BEntry(void)
BEntry(const BEntry &*entry*)

Creates a new BEntry object that represents the entry described by the arguments. See the analogous `SetTo()` functions for descriptions of the flavorful constructors.

The default constructor does nothing; it should be followed by a call to `SetTo()`.

The copy constructor points the new object to the entry that's represented by the argument. The two objects themselves maintain separate representation of the entry; in other words, they each contain their own **a)** file descriptor and **b)** string to identify the entry's **a)** directory and **b)** name.

To see if the initialization was successful, call `InitCheck()`.

~BEntry

~BEntry()

Closes the BEntry's file descriptor and destroys the BEntry object.

Member Functions

GetName(), GetPath()

status_t **GetName**(char *buffer*) const

status_t **GetPath**(BPath *path*) const

These functions return the leaf name and full pathname of the BEntry's entry. The arguments must be allocated before they're passed in.

GetName() copies the leaf name into *buffer*. The buffer must be large enough to accommodate the name; B_FILE_NAME_LENGTH is a 100% safe bet:

```
char name[B_FILE_NAME_LENGTH];
entry.GetName(name);
```

If GetName() fails, **buffer* is pointed at NULL.

GetPath() takes the entry's full pathname and initializes the BPath argument with it. To retrieve the path from the BPath object, call BPath::Path():

```
BPath path;
entry.GetPath(&path);
printf(">Entry pathname:  %s\n", path.Path());
```

If GetPath() fails, the argument is Unset().

Return values:

> B_NO_ERROR. The information was successfully retrieved.
>
> B_NO_INIT. The BEntry isn't initialized.
>
> B_BUSY (GetPath() only). A directory in the entry's path is locked.

GetParent()

> status_t **GetParent**(BEntry **entry*) const
>
> status_t **GetParent**(BDirectory **dir*) const

Gets the directory, as a BEntry or BDirectory object, in which the object's entry lives. The argument must be allocated before it's passed in.

If the function is unsuccessful, the argument is Unset(). Because of this, you should be particularly careful if you're using the BEntry-argument version to destructively get a BEntry's parent:

```
if (entry.GetParent(&entry) != B_NO_ERROR) {
   /* you just lost 'entry' */
}
```

This example *is* legal; for example, you can use destructive iteration to loop your way up to the root directory. When you reach the root ("/"), GetParent() returns B_ENTRY_NOT_FOUND:

```
BEntry entry("/boot/home/fido");
status_t err;
char name[B_FILE_NAME_LENGTH];

/* Spit out the path components backwards, one at a time. */
do {
   entry.GetName(name);
   printf("> %s\n", name);
} while ((err=entry.GetParent(&entry)) == B_NO_ERROR);
```

```
/* Complain for reasons other than reaching the top. */
if (err != B_ENTRY_NOT_FOUND)
    printf(">> Error: %s\n", strerror(err));
```

This produces:

```
> fido
> home
> boot
> /
```

Return values:

B_NO_ERROR. The information was successfully retrieved.

B_NO_INIT. This BEntry isn't initialized.

B_ENTRY_NOT_FOUND. Attempt to get the parent of the root directory.

B_NO_MORE_FDS. Couldn't get another file descriptor.

GetRef()

status_t **GetRef**(entry_ref *ref*) const

Gets the `entry_ref` for the object's entry; *ref* must be allocated before it's passed in. As with BEntry objects, `entry_ref` structures can be abstract—getting a valid `entry_ref` does *not* guarantee that the entry actually exists.

If the function isn't successful, *ref* is unset.

Return values:

B_NO_ERROR. The `entry_ref` was successfully retrieved.

B_NO_INIT. This object isn't initialized.

B_NO_MEMORY. Storage for the `entry_ref`'s name couldn't be allocated.

GetPath()   *see GetName()*

InitCheck()

status_t **InitCheck**(void) const

Returns the status of the previous construction, assignment operation, or `SetTo()` call.

Return values:

B_NO_ERROR. The initialization was successful.

B_NO_INIT. The object is uninitialized (this includes `Unset()`).

See `SetTo()` for other errors.

MoveTo()   *see Rename()*

Remove()

status_t **Remove**(void)

`Remove()` "unlinks" the entry from its directory. The entry's node isn't destroyed until all file descriptors that are open on the node are closed. This means that if you create BFile based on a BEntry, and then `Remove()` the BEntry, the BFile will still be able to read and write the file's data—the BFile has no way of knowing that the entry is gone. When the BFile is deleted, the node will be destroyed as well.

NOTE

`Remove()` does *not* invalidate the BEntry. It simply makes it abstract (see "Abstract Entries").

Return values:
B_NO_ERROR. Success.
B_NO_INIT. The BEntry is not initialized.
B_BUSY. The entry's directory is locked.

Rename(), MoveTo()

status_t **Rename**(const char *path*, bool *clobber* = false)

status_t **MoveTo**(BDirectory *dir*, const char *path* = NULL, bool *clobber* = false)

These functions move the BEntry's entry and node to a new location. In both cases, the BEntry must *not* be abstract—you can't rename or move an abstract entry.

`Rename()` moves the entry to a new name, as given by *path*. *path* is usually a simple leaf name, but it can be a relative path. In the former case (simple leaf) the entry is renamed within its current directory. In the latter, the entry is moved into a subdirectory of its current directory, as given by the argument.

`MoveTo()` moves the entry to a different directory and optionally renames the leaf. Again, *path* can be a simple leaf or a relative path; in both cases, *path* is reckoned off of *dir*. If path is NULL, the entry is moved to *dir*, but retains its old leaf name.

If the entry's new location is already taken, the *clobber* argument decides whether the existing entry is removed to make way for yours. If it's `true`, the existing entry is removed; if it's `false`, the `Rename()` or `MoveTo()` function fails.

Upon success, `this` is updated to reflect the change to its entry. For example, when you invoke `Rename()` on a BEntry, the name of *that specific* BEntry object also changes. If the rename or move-to isn't successful, `this` isn't altered.

Return values:
B_NO_ERROR. Success.
B_NO_INIT. The BEntry is not initialized.

B_ENTRY_NOT_FOUND. A directory to the new location doesn't exist, or this is an abstract entry.

B_FILE_EXISTS. The new location is already taken (and you're not clobbering).

B_BUSY. The directory that you're moving the entry into is locked.

SetTo(), Unset()

status_t **SetTo**(const entry_ref *ref*, bool *traverse* = TRUE)

status_t **SetTo**(const const char *path*, bool *traverse* = TRUE)

status_t **SetTo**(const BDirectory *dir*,
             const char *path*,
             bool *traverse* = TRUE)

void **Unset**(void)

Frees the BEntry's current entry reference, and initializes it to refer to the entry identified by the argument(s):

- In the *ref* version, the BEntry is initialized to refer to the given entry_ref.
- In the *path* version, *path* can be absolute or relative, and can contain "." and ".." elements. If *path* is relative, it's reckoned off of the current working directory.
- In the *dir/path* version, *path* must be relative. It's reckoned off of the directory given by *dir*.

The *traverse* argument is used to resolve (or not) entries that are symlinks:

- If *traverse* is true, the link is resolved.
- If *traverse* is false, the BEntry refers to the link itself.

See "Initializing and Traversing" on page 184 for more information.

When you initialize a BEntry, you're describing a leaf name within a directory. The directory *must* exist, but the leaf doesn't have to. This allows you to create a BEntry to a file that doesn't exist (yet). See "Abstract Entries" on page 186 for more information.

NOTE

Remember—successfully initializing a BEntry consumes a file descriptor. When you re-initialize, the old file descriptor is closed.

Unset() removes the object's association with its current entry, and sets InitCheck() to B_NO_INIT.

Return values:

    B_NO_ERROR. The BEntry was successfully initialized.

    B_BAD_VALUE. Bad argument value; uninitialized *ref* or *dir*.

    B_ENTRY_NOT_FOUND. A directory in the path to the entry doesn't exist.

    B_BUSY. The entry's directory is locked.

Unset()   *see SetTo()*

Operators

= (assignment)

    BEntry& operator=(const BEntry &*entry*)

In the expression

```
BEntry a = b;
```

BEntry *a* is initialized to refer to the same entry as *b*. To gauge the success of the assignment, you should call InitCheck() immediately afterwards. Assigning a BEntry to itself is safe.

Assigning from an uninitialized BEntry is "successful": The assigned-to BEntry will also be uninitialized (B_NO_INIT).

==, != (comparison)

    bool operator==(const BEntry &*entry*) const
    bool operator!=(const BEntry &*entry*) const

Two BEntry objects are said to be equal if they refer to the same entry (even if the entry is abstract), or if they're both uninitialized.

BFile

Derived from:	BNode, BPositionIO
Declared in:	be/storage/File.h
Library:	libbe.so

Overview

A BFile lets you read and write the data portion of a file. It does this by implementing the Read()/Write() and ReadAt()/WriteAt() functions that are declared by the BPositionIO class.

Initializing and Opening

When you construct (or otherwise initialize) a BFile, the file is automatically opened. The file is closed when you re-initialize or destroy the object.

At each initialization, you're asked to supply an "open mode" value. this is a combination of flags that tells the object whether you want to read and/or write the file, create it if it doesn't exist, truncate it, and so on.

You can also initialize a BFile, and create a new file at the same time, through BDirectory's `CreateFile()` function. In this case, you don't have to supply an open mode—the BFile that's returned to you will automatically be open for reading and writing. (You *are* asked if you want the creation to fail if the named file already exists.)

Access to Directories and Symbolic Links

Although BFiles are meant to be used to access regular files, you aren't prevented from opening and reading a directory (you won't be able to write the directory, however). This isn't exactly a feature—there's not much reason to access a directory this way—you should simply be aware that it's not an error.

Symbolic links, however, *can't* be opened by a BFile—not because it's illegal, but because if you ask to open a symbolic link, the link is automatically traversed. The node that the BFile ends up opening will be the file or directory that the link points to.

This *is* a feature; very few applications should ever need to look at a symbolic link. (If yours is one of the few that *does* want to, you should go visit the BSymLink class.)

Constructor and Destructor

BFile()

> **BFile**(void)
> **BFile**(const BFile &*file*)
>
> **BFile**(const entry_ref **ref,* uint32 *openMode*)
> **BFile**(const BEntry **entry,* uint32 *openMode*)
> **BFile**(const char **path,* uint32 *openMode*)
> **BFile**(BDirectory **dir,* const char **path,* uint32 *openMode*)

Creates a new BFile object, initializes it according to the arguments, and sets `InitCheck()` to return the status of the initialization.

The default constructor does nothing and sets `InitCheck()` to `B_NO_INIT`. To initialize the object, call `SetTo()`.

The copy constructor creates a new BFile that's open on the same file as that of the argument. Note that the two objects maintain *separate* data pointers into the *same* file:

- **Separate pointers**: Reading and writing through one object *does not* affect the position of the data pointer in the other object.

- **Same file**: If one object writes to the file, the other object will see the written data.

For information on the other constructors, see the analogous SetTo() functions.

~BFile()

virtual ~BFile()

Closes the object's file, frees its file descriptor, and destroys the object.

Member Functions

GetSize(), SetSize()

status_t **GetSize**(off_t *size*) const
status_t **SetSize**(off_t *&size*)

These functions get and set the size, in bytes, of the object's file.

GetSize() returns the size of the file's data portion in the *size* argument; the measurement doesn't include attributes.

SetSize() sets the size of the data portion to the size given by the argument:

- Enlarging a file adds (uninitialized) bytes to its end.
- Shrinking a file removes bytes from the end.

Return values:
B_NO_ERROR. The file's size was successfully gotten or set.
B_NOT_ALLOWED. (SetSize()) The file lives on a read-only volume.
B_DEVICE_FULL. (SetSize()) No more room on the file's device.

InitCheck()

status_t **InitCheck**(void) const

Returns the status of the most recent initialization.

Return values:
B_NO_ERROR. The object is initialized.
B_NO_INIT. The object is uninitialized.
See SetTo() *for other errors.*

IsReadable(), IsWritable()

> bool **IsReadable**(void) const
> bool **IsWritable**(void) const

These functions tell you whether the BFile was initialized to read or write its file. If the object isn't (properly) initialized, they both return `false`.

Note that these functions don't query the actual file to check permissions, they only tell you what the access request was when the BFile object was initialized.

Position()   *see Seek()*

Read(), ReadAt(), Write(), WriteAt()

> ssize_t **Read**(void *buffer*, size_t *size*)
> ssize_t **ReadAt**(off_t *location*, void *buffer*, size_t *size*)
>
> ssize_t **Write**(const void *buffer*, size_t *size*)
> ssize_t **WriteAt**(off_t *location*, const void *buffer*, size_t *size*)

These functions, which are inherited from BPositionIO, read and write the file's data; note that they don't touch the file's attributes.

The `Read()` and `ReadAt()` functions read *size* bytes of data from the file and place this data in *buffer*. The buffer that *buffer* points to must already be allocated, and must be large enough to accommodate the read data. Note that the read-into buffer is *not* null-terminated by the reading functions.

The two functions differ in that:

- `Read()` reads the data starting at the current location of the file's data pointer, and increments the file pointer as it reads.

- `ReadAt()` reads the data from the location specified by the *location* argument, which is taken as a measure in bytes from the beginning of the file. `ReadAt()` does *not* bump the file's data pointer.

`Write()` and `WriteAt()` write *size* bytes of data into the file; the data is taken from the *buffer* argument. The two functions differ in their use (or non-use) of the file's data pointer in the same manner as `Read()` and `ReadAt()`.

All four functions return the number of bytes that were actually read or written; negative return values indicate an error.

Reading fewer-than-*size* bytes isn't uncommon—consider the case where the file is smaller than the size of your buffer. If you want your buffer to be NULL-terminated, you can use the return value to set the NULL:

```
char buf[1024];
ssize_t amt_read;

if ((amt_read = file.Read((void *)buf, 1024)) < 0)
   /* handle errors first */
else
   /* otherwise set null */
   buf[amt_read] = '\0';
```

A successful `Write()` or `WriteAt()`, on the other hand, will always write exactly the number of bytes you requested. In other words, `Write()` returns either the *size* value that you passed to it, or else it returns a negative (error) value.

Return values:

Positive values (and 0). The number of bytes read or written.

B_NOT_ALLOWED. (`Write`) The file lives on a read-only volume.

B_DEVICE_FULL. (`Write`) No more room on the file's device.

Seek(), Position()

off_t **Seek**(off_t *offset*, int32 *seekMode*)
off_t **Position**(void) const

`Seek()` sets the location of the file's data pointer. The new location is reckoned as *offset* bytes from the position given by the *seekMode* constant:

Constant	Meaning
SEEK_SET	Seek from the beginning of the file.
SEEK_CUR	Seek from the pointer's current position.
SEEK_END	Seek from the end of the file.

If you `Seek()` to a position that's past the end of the file and then do a `Write()`, the file will be extended (padded with garbage) from the old end of file to the `Seek()`'d position. If you don't follow the `Seek()` with a `Write()`, the file isn't extended.

`Seek()` returns the new position as measured (in bytes) from the beginning of the file.

`Position()` returns the current position as measured (in bytes) from the beginning of the file. It doesn't move the pointer.

Return values:

B_ERROR. Attempted to `Seek()` "before" the beginning of the file, or you called `Position()` after such a `Seek()`. You also get B_ERROR if you call `Seek()` on an uninitialized file.

B_BAD_FILE. `Position()` called on an uninitialized file.

WARNING

If you do a "before the beginning" seek, subsequent `Read()` and `Write()` calls *do not fail.* But they almost certainly aren't doing what you want (you shouldn't be "before the file," anyway). The moral: Always check your `Seek()` return.

SetSize()   *see GetSize()*

SetTo(), Unset()

> status_t **SetTo**(const entry_ref *ref*, uint32 *openMode*)
> status_t **SetTo**(const BEntry *entry*, uint32 *openMode*)
> status_t **SetTo**(const char *path*, uint32 *openMode*)
> status_t **SetTo**(BDirectory *dir*, const char *path*, uint32 *openMode*)

> void **Unset**(void)

Closes the BFile's current file (if any), and opens the file specified by the arguments. If the specified file is a symbolic link, the link is automatically traversed (recursively, if necessary). Note that you're not prevented from opening a directory as a BFile, but you are prevented from writing it.

- In the *path* function, *path* can be absolute or relative, and can contain "." and ".." elements. If *path* is relative, it's reckoned off of the current working directory.

- In the *dir/path* function, *path* must be relative and is reckoned off of *dir*.

openMode is a combination of flags that determines how the file is opened and what this object can do with it once it is open. There are two sets of flags; you must pass one (and only one) of the following "read/write" constants:

Constant	Meaning
B_READ_ONLY	This object can read, but not write, the file.
B_WRITE_ONLY	This object can write, but not read, the file.
B_READ_WRITE	This object can read and write the file.

You can also pass any number of the following (these are optional):

Constant	Meaning
B_CREATE_FILE	Create the file if it doesn't already exist.
B_FAIL_IF_EXISTS	If the file already exists, the initialization (of the BFile object) fails.
B_ERASE_FILE	If the file already exists, erase all its data and attributes.
B_OPEN_AT_END	Sets the data pointer to point to the end of the file.

To open a file for reading and writing, for example, you simply pass:

```
file.SetTo(entry, B_READ_WRITE);
```

Here we create a new file or erase its data if it already exists:

```
file.SetTo(entry, B_READ_WRITE | B_CREATE_FILE | B_ERASE_FILE);
```

And here we create a new file, but only if it doesn't already exist:

```
file.SetTo(entry, B_READ_WRITE | B_CREATE_FILE | B_FAIL_IF_EXISTS);
```

`Unset()` closes the object's file and sets its `InitCheck()` value to `B_NO_INIT`.

Return values:

> `B_NO_ERROR`. The file was successfully opened.
> `B_BAD_VALUE`. NULL *path* in *dir/path*, or some other argument is uninitialized.
> `B_ENTRY_NOT_FOUND`. File not found, or couldn't create the file.
> `B_FILE_EXISTS`. File exists (and you set `B_FAIL_IF_EXISTS`).
> `B_PERMISSION_DENIED`. Read or write permission request denied.
> `B_NO_MEMORY`. Couldn't allocate necessary memory to complete the operation.

Write()   *see Read()*

WriteAt()   *see Read()*

Operators

= (assignment)

> BFile& operator=(const BFile &*File*)

In the expression

```
BFile a = b;
```

BFile *a* is initialized to refer to the same file as *b*. To gauge the success of the assignment, you should call `InitCheck()` immediately afterwards. You can't assign a BFile to itself (`B_BAD_VALUE`).

Assigning to an uninitialized BFile is "successful": The assigned-to BFile will also be uninitialized (`B_NO_INIT`).

==, != (comparison)

> bool operator == (const BFile &*file*) const
> bool operator != (const BFile &*file*) const

Two BFile objects are said to be equal if they refer to the same file, or if they both refer to nothing.

BFilePanel

Derived from: none

Declared in: be/storage/FilePanel.h

Library: libtracker.so

Overview

BFilePanel knows how to create and display an "Open File" or "Save File" panel, and provides the means for filtering and responding to the user's actions on the panel. The Save Panel looks like this:

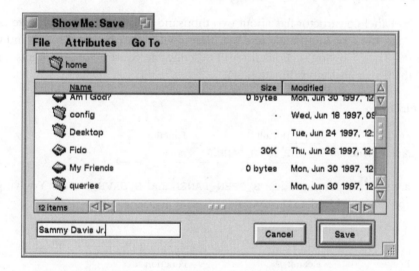

The Open Panel looks pretty much the same, but without the text view in the lower left corner.

Creating and Using a BFilePanel

To create and use a BFilePanel, follow these steps:

1. **Construct a BFilePanel object** in response to the user's request (most likely, a click on an "Open" or "Save"/"Save As" menu item). When you construct the panel, you have to specify its "mode" (Open or Save).

2. **Fine-tune the panel** by telling it which directory to display, whether it allows multiple selection, whether it can open a directory, which target it should send notifications to, and so on. (Most of these parameters can also be set in the constructor.)

3. Invoke Show() on the panel, and then wait for the user to confirm a selection (or close the panel).

4. **Receive a message**. When the user confirms a selection (or cancels the panel), the panel disappears and a notification message (Open, Save, or Cancel) is sent to the panel's target. The message identifies the confirmed file(s).

5. **Delete the BFilePanel object...or don't**. When the user closes a file panel, the object is not automatically deleted; you have to do it yourself. But you may not want to. If you don't delete the panel, you can simply call Show() the next time you want to display it; the state from the previous invocation (the panel's size and location, the directory it points to) is remembered.

Constructing and Fine-Tuning the Panel

The BFilePanel constructor has about two thousand arguments. They all have default values, and most of the parameters that they control can be set through individual functions. The following sections list and describe the constructor arguments and tell you if there's an analogous function.

Panel Mode

Argument	Default	Function
file_panel_mode *mode*	B_OPEN_PANEL	none

There are two file panel modes: B_OPEN_PANEL and B_SAVE_PANEL. You've got to make up your mind in the constructor.

Target

Argument	Default	Function
BMessenger *target*	be_app_messenger	SetTarget()

The target represents the BLooper/BHandler that will receive the Open, Save, and Cancel messages.

Panel Directory

Argument	Default	Function
entry_ref *panel_directory*	cwd	SetPanelDirectory()

When a panel is first displayed, it has to show the contents of some directory; this is called the "panel directory." The panel directory defaults to the current working directory.

Confirmable Node Flavors

Argument	Default	Function
uint32 *node_flavors*	B_FILE_NODE	none

NOTE

This parameter applies to Open panels only.

There are three node flavors: B_FILE_NODE, B_DIRECTORY_NODE, and B_SYMLINK_NODE. You combine these constants to declare the flavors that you want the user to be able to confirm. Before describing the flavor settings, keep this in mind...

- **Double-clicking a directory in the file list always enters the directory, regardless of the panel's flavor setting.**

If you understand the following, you can save yourself some reading:

- If your app wants to open files only, then stick with the default (B_FILE_NODE); the user will be able to confirm files and symlinks to files. If you want directories as well (for example, a compression app might want to work on files *and* directories) then add in B_DIRECTORY_NODE (symlinks to directories are okay, as well). If you only want directories (unusual, but possible), then leave B_FILE_NODE out of it.

If you're not convinced, read on:

- If the setting includes B_FILE_NODE and the user selects and confirms a file or a symlink to a file, the file (or symlink) is delivered to your target. If it doesn't include B_FILE_NODE and the user selects a file (or symlink to a file), the Open button is disabled.

- If the setting includes B_DIRECTORY_NODE and the user selects and Opens (i.e. clicks the Open button) a directory or a symlink to a directory, the directory (or symlink) is delivered to your target. If it doesn't include B_DIRECTORY_NODE and the user Opens a directory (or symlink to a directory), the directory is entered (the contents of the directory are displayed in the file list).

- If the setting includes B_SYMLINK_NODE and the user confirms a symlink, the symlink is delivered to your target. If it doesn't include B_SYMLINK_NODE and the user selects symlink, the panel's response depends on the inclusion of the other two flavors. Note that including B_SYMLINK_NODE is an odd thing to do—it only makes sense if it's not combined with either of the other two flavors, and even then it doesn't make much sense.

When the user confirms a symlink (regardless of the flavor setting), you always receive the *symlink itself* in the Open message—you don't get the file or directory it points to.

Multiple Selection

Argument	Default	Function
bool *allow_multiple_selection*	true	none

This parameter determines whether the user is allowed to select more than one item at a time. Save panels should set this to `false`.

Notification Message

Argument	Default	Function
BMessage *message*	a default BMessage	SetMessage()

By default, the format of the message that's sent to your target when the user confirms or cancels is defined by the file panel (the default formats are defined later). You can override the default by specifying your own BMessage. The BMessage is copied by the BFilePanel object. You can change this message using the `SetMessage()` function.

Ref Filter

Argument	Default	Function
BRefFilter *filter*	NULL	SetRefFilter()

When panel directory changes (this includes when the panel is constructed, and when the panel's `Refresh()` function is called), or when a new entry is added to the existing directory, the new entries are passed, one-by-one, to the panel's BRefFilter object through a BRefFilter hook function. In your implementation of the hook function, you can reject individual entries; rejected entries won't be displayed in the file list.

By default, a file panel has no BRefFilter. To supply one, you have to subclass BRefFilter (in order to implement the hook function) and pass it in.

- Note that the ref filter isn't asked to "re-review" the entry list when the file panel is `Show()`'d after being hidden.

Is Modal?

Argument	Default	Function
bool *modal*	false	none

A modal file panel has no window tab, so it can't be closed; to get rid of the panel, the user has to click a button. By default, file panels are not modal.

Hide When Done

Argument	Default	Function
bool *hide_when_done	true	SetHideWhenDone()

By default, a file panel is hidden when the user confirms or Cancels. If you set *hide_when_done* to `false`, the panel remains on the screen. Clicking the panel's close box always hides the panel.

The Target and the Messages It Sees

When the user confirms a selection or cancels a file panel, a BMessage is constructed and sent to the target of the BFilePanel object. By default, the target is `be_app_messenger`. You can specify a different target (as a BMessenger) through the BFilePanel constructor, or through the `SetTarget()` function.

The format of the BMessage that the target receives depends on whether the user is opening, saving, or canceling.

Open Notification

- By default, the `what` field is `B_REFS_RECEIVED`. You can override the default by supplying your own BMessage (`SetMessage()`).

- The "refs" field (type `B_REF_TYPE`) contains `entry_ref` structures, one for each entry that the user has confirmed.

- The message may contain other fields, as copied from the BMessage you (optionally) supplied. The data in these fields won't be changed.

If the target is `be_app_messenger` and the `what` field is `B_REFS_RECEIVED`, the BMessage shows up in the `RefsReceived()` function. Otherwise it's sent to the target's `MessageReceived()`.

Keep in mind that the refs that you receive through this message point to the literal entries that the user confirmed. In other words, if the confirmed selection is a symlink to a file, you'll receive a ref for the symlink, not the file (and similarly for a link to a directory). It's up to you to turn the symlink into a file (which is probably what you want).

If you want a BEntry object, all you have to do is pass `true` as the traverse argument to BEntry's constructor or `SetTo()`:

```
/* We'll assume that 'ref' was just plucked from an open notification. */
BEntry entry(ref, true);
```

You don't even have to check to see if the ref *is* a symlink.

If you want to turn a symlink ref into a ref to the pointed-to file, just add this line:

```
entry.GetRef(&ref);
```

Save Notification

- By default, the `what` field is `B_SAVE_REQUESTED`. You can override the default by supplying your own BMessage (`SetMessage()`).

- The "directory" field (type `B_REF_TYPE`) contains a single `entry_ref` structure that points to the directory in which the user has requested the entry be saved (in other words, the ref refers to the panel directory).

- The "name" field (`B_STRING_TYPE`) is the text the user typed in the Save Panel's text view.

- The message may contain other fields, as copied from the BMessage you (optionally) supplied. The data in these fields won't be changed.

Save notifications are always sent to the target's `MessageReceived()` function.

Note that if the user confirms a name that collides with an existing file, an alert is automatically displayed. The user can then back out of the confirmation and return to the Save Panel, or clobber the existing file. The save notification is sent after (and only if) the user agrees to clobber the file.

NOTE

The file *isn't* clobbered by the system; it's up to you (as the receiver of the save notification) to do the dirty work.

Cancel Notification

A cancel notification is sent *whenever* the file panel is hidden. This includes the Cancel button being clicked, the panel being closed, and the panel being hidden after an open or a save (given that the panel is in hide-when-done mode).

- The `what` field is always `B_CANCEL`, even if you supplied your own BMessage.

- The "old_what" field (`B_UINT32_TYPE`) records the "previous" `what` value. This is only useful (and dependable) if you supplied your own BMessage: The `what` from your message is moved to the "old_what" field. If you didn't supply a BMessage, you should ignore this field (it could contain garbage).

- The "source" (`B_POINTER_TYPE`) is a pointer to the BFilePanel object that was closed.

- The message may contain other fields, as copied from the BMessage you (optionally) supplied. The data in these fields won't be changed.

Cancel notifications are always sent to the target's `MessageReceived()` function.

Keep in mind that when a file panel is closed—regardless of how it's closed—the BFilePanel object is *not* destroyed. It's merely hidden.

Modifying the Look of the File Panel

There are two ways you can modify the look of your BFilePanel object.

- You can do some simple text twiddling by calling the label- and text-setting functions `SetButtonLabel()` and `SetSaveText()`.

- If you need to *really* change the look, you can get a handle on the panel's BWindow and BView objects in order to move them around, add your own, or whatever. You get the window through the `Window()` function. Finding specific views within the window is described below.

Finding Views in the Panel

Let's look at that Save Panel again:

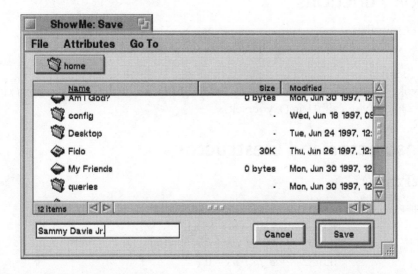

Here's how you find the views:

- The background view doesn't have a name; but it's first in the window's list of views:

  ```
  BView *background = filepanel->Window()->ChildAt(0);
  ```

- The directory popup in the top left corner is named "FileContext".
- The file list in the middle is named "PoseView".
- The Cancel button is named "cancel button".

- The Save (or Open) is named "default button".

- The text view at the bottom left (Save Panel only) is called "text view".

These last five views can be found by name:

```
BView *fileList = filepanel->Window()->FindView("PoseView");
```

What you do with the views is your business.

The C Functions

You can also display Open and Save Panels through the global C functions `run_open_panel()` and `run_save_panel()` (which are declared in *FilePanel.h*). The functions create BFilePanel objects using the default constructor settings (modulo the `file_panel_mode`, of course).

The C functions create a new file panel each time they're called, and delete the panel when the user is finished with it.

Hook Functions

`SelectionChanged()`
Invoked whenever the user changes the set of selected entries.

`WasHidden()`
Invoked just after the file panel is hidden because of the user's actions (it's not invoked if you call `Hide()` yourself).

Constructor and Destructor

BFilePanel()

BFilePanel(file_panel_mode *mode* = B_OPEN_PANEL,
                     BMessenger* *target* = NULL,
                     entry_ref *panel_directory* = NULL,
                     uint32 *node_flavors* = 0,
                     bool *allow_multiple_selection* = true,
                     BMessage *message* = NULL,
                     BRefFilter *filter* = NULL,
                     bool *modal* = false,
                     bool *hide_when_done* = true)

The constructor creates a new BFilePanel object and initializes it according to the arguments. The panel isn't displayed until you invoke `Show()`. The arguments are thoroughly described in "Constructing and Fine-Tuning the Panel."

NOTE

You may notice that some of the default arguments shown here don't jibe with the defaults listed in the section "Constructing and Fine-Tuning the Panel" on page 202. In particular, the *node_flavors* argument was described as defaulting to B_FILE_NODE, but is shown here as 0. The "Constructing..." descriptions are correct: The default values shown here are caught and converted by the BFilePanel constructor.

~BFilePanel()

virtual **~BFilePanel**(void)

Destroys the BFilePanel. The object's target and BRefFilter are not touched by this destruction. If the object is currently displaying a file panel, the panel is closed.

Member Functions
GetNextSelectedRef(), Rewind()

status_t **GetNextSelectedRef**(entry_ref *ref*)

void **Rewind**(void)

GetNextSelectedRef() initializes its arguments to point to the "next" ref in the file panel's set of currently selected items. The function returns B_ENTRY_NOT_FOUND when it reaches the end of the list. Rewind() gets you back to the top of the list.

Although you can call these functions any time you want, they're intended to be used in implementations of the SelectionChanged() hook function.

GetPanelDirectory()   *see SetPanelDirectory()*

Hide()   *see Show()*

HidesWhenDone()   *see SetHideWhenDone()*

IsShowing()   *see Show()*

Messenger()   *see SetTarget()*

PanelMode()

file_panel_mode **PanelMode**(void) const

Returns the object's mode, either B_OPEN_PANEL or B_SAVE_PANEL. The mode is set in the constructor and can't be changed thereafter.

RefFilter()   *see SetRefFilter()*

Refresh()

> void **Refresh**(void)

`Refresh()` tells the file panel to re-read the contents of the panel directory, which causes the directory's entries to be re-run through the ref filter.

You don't have to call `Refresh()` in order to keep the panel in sync with the directory's contents—the directory and file panel are kept in sync automatically.

Rewind()   *see GetNextSelectedRef()*

SelectionChanged()

> virtual void **SelectionChanged**(void)

This hook function is invoked whenever the user changes the set of selected files. Within your implementation of this function, you iterate over `GetNext-SelectedRef()` to retrieve refs to the currently selected files.

SetButtonLabel(), SetSaveText()

> void **SetButtonLabel**(file_panel_button *which_button*, const char **label*)

> void **SetSaveText**(const char **text*)

`SetButtonLabel()` lets you set the label that's displayed in the panel's buttons. The button that a specific invocation affects depends on the value of `which_button`:

- `B_DEFAULT_BUTTON` is the Open button for an Open Panel and the Save button for a Save Panel.

- `B_CANCEL_BUTTON` is the "Cancel" button.

`SetSaveText()` sets the text that's displayed in the Save Panel's text view (the area in which the user types and confirms a file name).

SetHideWhenDone(), HidesWhenDone()

> void **SetHideWhenDone**(bool *hide_when_done*)

> bool **HidesWhenDone**(void) const

By default, a file panel is hidden when the user confirms or Cancels. You can control this behavior using the `SetHideWhenDone()` function. If you set *hide_when_done* to `false`, the panel remains on the screen; if you specify `true`, the panel hides when the user confirms or Cancels. Clicking the panel's close box always hides the panel.

`HidesWhenDone()` returns the current setting of this option: `true` if the panel hides when the user is done with it or `false` if it remains on the screen.

SetMessage()

> void **SetMessage**(BMessage *_msg_)

`SetMessage()` allows you to set the format of the file panel's notification messages. The message can also be set through the constructor. See "The Target and the Messages It Sees" for more information.

A copy is made of the BMessage, so it is your responsibility to delete _msg_ when you no longer need it.

SetPanelDirectory(), GetPanelDirectory()

> void **SetPanelDirectory**(BEntry *_dirEntry_)
> void **SetPanelDirectory**(BDirectory *_dirObj_)
> void **SetPanelDirectory**(entry_ref *_dirRef_)
>
> void **GetPanelDirectory**(entry_ref *_ref_) const

The `SetPanelDirectory()` function sets the panel's "panel directory." This is the directory whose contents are displayed in the panel's file list. You can also set the panel directory through the constructor. If you don't supply a directory, the current working directory is used.

`GetPanelDirectory()` initializes _ref_ to point to the current panel directory. The argument must be allocated.

SetRefFilter(), RefFilter()

> void **SetRefFilter**(BRefFilter* filter)
> BRefFilter ***RefFilter**(void) const

Whenever the file panel's panel directory is changed or refreshed (`Refresh()`), or when a new entry is added to the current panel directory, the "new" entries are run through the panel's "ref filter." The BRefFilter class defines a single boolean hook function called `Filter()`. The function receives the entries, one-by-one, and can reject specific entries (because they're the wrong file type, for example). Rejected entries are not shown in the panel's file list.

The `SetRefFilter()` function sets the panel's ref filter. You can also set it through the constructor. Ownership of the filter is *not* handed to the panel. You mustn't delete the ref filter while the panel is still extant.

`RefFilter()` returns a pointer to the panel's ref filter.

SetSaveText()   *see SetButtonLabel()*

SetTarget(), Messenger()

> void **SetTarget**(BMessenger *bellhop*)
> BMessenger **Messenger**(void) const

`SetTarget()` sets the target of the file panel's notification messages. The target can also be set through the constructor. If you don't set a target, `be_app_messenger` is used. See the BInvoker class (in the Application Kit) for an explanation of how a BMessenger can be used as a target.

A copy is made of the BMessenger, so it is your responsibility to delete *bellhop* when you no longer need it.

`Messenger()` returns (a copy of) the messenger that's used as the file panel's target.

Show(), Hide(), IsShowing(), WasHidden()

> void **Show**(void)
> void **Hide**(void)
> bool **IsShowing**(void)
>
> virtual void **WasHidden**(void)

These functions show and hide the file panel, and tell if you the panel is currently showing.

`WasHidden()` is a hook function that's invoked whenever the user's actions causes the file panel to be hidden. If you call `Hide()` yourself, `WasHidden()` is *not* invoked.

WasHidden()   *see Show()*

Window()

> BWindow *****Window**(void) const

Returns a pointer to the file panel's window. If you want to mess around with the window's views, see "Modifying the Look of the File Panel."

BMimeType

Derived from: none

Declared in: be/storage/Mime.h

Library: libbe.so

Overview

The BMimeType class provides three services:

- **It can parse a MIME string**. It can tell you whether the string is valid, what its *supertype* component is, and whether it has a *subtype* component. (The MIME string format is described in "Valid MIME Strings.")

- **It gives you access to the File Type database**. Given a MIME type, it can look in the database and retrieve that type's icon(s), "preferred handler" application, the filename extensions that correspond to it, and so on.

- **It can regard a MIME string as an application signature**, and so get and set the executable file, the file types, and the document icons that correspond to that signature.

All three services operate on MIME *strings*. In other words, they answer questions such as "Does this *string* have a supertype?", "Is this *string* installed in the database?", and so on. You can get the MIME strings from anywhere: from a file's file type attribute, from an application's signature, from the header of an e-mail message, you can even make them up.

Valid MIME Strings

A valid MIME string takes the form:

supertype/[subtype]

where *supertype* is one of the seven "media" strings:

- Text
- Application
- Image
- Audio
- Video
- Multipart
- Message

and (the optional) *subtype* can be just about anything...Except it can't include spaces or any of these forbidden characters:

```
/ \ < > @ , ; : " ( ) [ ] ? =
```

When you initialize a BMimeType object (through the constructor or `SetTo()` function), you have to tell it what MIME string you want it to represent:

- The string can be supertype-only, or it can be supertype/subtype.

- Currently, the supertype is *not* restricted to the seven types listed above, but you're probably making a mistake if you make up a new, unrecognized supertype.

- Neither the supertype nor the subtype can include any of the forbidden characters.

- The entire string must be no longer than `B_MIME_TYPE_LENGTH` characters long. (That's about 240 characters. More than enough.)

You can check the validity of a MIME string without constructing a BMimeType object by calling the static `IsValid()` function:

```
BMimeType::IsValid("text/qwerty");
```

Constructor and Destructor

BMimeType()

> BMimeType(void)
> BMimeType(const char *MIME_string)

Constructs a new BMimeType object and initializes its MIME type to a copy of *MIME_string* (if the argument is given). The rules of validity apply (see "Valid MIME Strings," above). To see if the initialization was successful, call `InitCheck()` after you construct a new BMimeType object.

You can also set the MIME type through the `SetTo()` function.

~MimeType()

> virtual ~MimeType(void)

Frees the object's MIME string and destroys the object.

Member Functions

Delete()   *see Install()*

GetAppHint(), SetAppHint()

> status_t **GetAppHint**(entry_ref *app_ref*) const
>
> status_t **SetAppHint**(const entry_ref *app_ref*)

These functions get and set the "app hint" for the object's application signature. The app hint is an `entry_ref` that identifies the executable that should be used when launching an application that has this signature. For example, when the Tracker needs to launch an app of type "application/YourAppHere", it asks the database for the `entry_ref` hint. Of course, the `entry_ref` may not point to an application, or it might point to an application with the wrong signature (and so on)—that's why this is merely a hint.

`GetAppHint()` function initializes the `entry_ref` to the hint recorded in the database; the argument must be allocated before it's passed in.

`SetAppHint()` copies the `entry_ref` into the database. *app_ref* should point to an executable file that has the same signature as this object's MIME type. Keep in mind that `entry_ref`s aren't guaranteed to be persistent.

Return values:

B_NO_ERROR. The ref was successfully retrieved or set.

B_NO_INIT. The BMimeType is uninitialized.

B_BAD_VALUE. (Set) The ref is uninitialized.

GetIconForType(), SetIconForType()

status_t **GetIconForType**(const char *file_type,
                BBitmap *icon,
                icon_size *which*) const

status_t **SetIconForType**(const char *file_type,
                const BBitmap *icon,
                icon_size *which*)

These functions get and set the icons that an application that has this object's MIME type as a signature uses to display the given file type. *file_type* must be a valid MIME string.

The icon is passed in or returned through the *icon* argument:

• If you're getting the icon, the BBitmap must be allocated; the icon data is copied into your BBitmap object.

• If you're setting the icon, the bitmap must be the proper size: 32x32 for the large icon, 16x16 for the small one. In BRect lingo, that's BRect(0, 0, 31, 31) and BRect(0, 0, 15, 15).

• You can remove an icon by passing NULL as the *icon* argument to `SetIconForType()`.

Return values:

B_NO_ERROR. The icon was found or set.

B_NO_INIT. The BMimeType is uninitialized.

B_BAD_VALUE. (Get) NULL BBitmap pointer, or *file_type* is invalid.

B_BAD_VALUE. (Set) The bitmap data isn't the proper size, or *file_type* is invalid.

GetFileExtensions(), SetFileExtensions()

status_t **GetFileExtensions**(BMessage *msg*) const

status_t **SetFileExtensions**(const BMessage *msg*)

The database associates a list of file extensions ("*.xxx...*" filename appendages) with each file type. If a file is otherwise untyped, clients of the database can figure out its type by matching the file's extension to the lists in the database.

These functions get and set the file extensions that are associated with the object's MIME type.

- If you're getting the extensions, you'll find them copied into your BMessage's "extensions" field (the BMessage must be allocated). They're given as an indexed array of strings (B_STRING_TYPE).

- Similarly, you pass in the extensions by adding strings to the message's "extensions" field.

- The BMessage's what field is unimportant.

For example, to retrieve all the extensions that correspond to this object's MIME type, you would do the following:

```
BMessage msg();
uint32 i=0;
char *ptr;

if (mime.GetFileExtensions(&msg) != B_NO_ERROR)
   /* Handle the error. */

while (true) {
   if (msg.FindString("extensions", i++, &ptr) != B_NO_ERROR)
      break;
   printf("> Extension:  %s\n", ptr);
}
```

A given extension can be associated with more than one MIME type.

A NULL msg to SetFileExtensions() clears the type's extension list.

WARNING

SetFileExtensions() clobbers the existing set of extensions. If you want to augment a type's extensions, you should retrieve the existing set, add the new ones, and *then* call **SetFileExtensions**().

Also, there's no way to ask the database to give you a set of file types that map to a given extension. To find a type for an extension, you have to get all the installed types (GetInstalledTypes()) and ask each one for its set of extensions.

Return values:

B_NO_ERROR. The extensions were found or set.

B_NO_INIT. The BMimeType is uninitialized.

B_NO_MEMORY. Insufficient memory to copy the extensions.

GetIcon(), SetIcon()

virtual status_t **GetIcon**(BBitmap **icon*, icon_size *which*) const

virtual status_t **SetIcon**(const BBitmap **icon*, icon_size *which*)

GetIcon() and SetIcon() get and set the icons that are associated (in the database) with this object's MIME type. You specify which icon you want (large or small) by passing B_LARGE_ICON or B_SMALL_ICON as the *which* argument. The icon is passed in or returned through the *icon* argument. The icon data is copied out of or into the BBitmap object.

If you're setting the icon, the bitmap must be the proper size: 32x32 for the large icon, 16x16 for the small one. If you want to erase the node's icon, pass NULL as the *icon* argument to SetIcon().

Return values:

B_NO_ERROR. The icon was found or set.

B_NO_INIT. The BMimeType is uninitialized.

B_BAD_VALUE (Set... only). The bitmap wasn't the proper size.

GetInstalledTypes(), GetInstalledSupertypes()

static status_t **GetInstalledTypes**(BMessage **types*)

static status_t **GetInstalledTypes**(const char **supertype*, BMessage **subtypes*)

static status_t **GetInstalledSupertypes**(BMessage **supertypes*)

These static functions retrieve all the file types that are currently installed in the database, all the installed subtypes for a given supertype, and all the installed supertypes. The types are copied into the "types" field of the passed-in BMessage (which must be allocated).

Return values:

B_NO_ERROR. The types were found.

B_BAD_VALUE. The *supertype* string isn't valid.

B_NO_MEMORY. Insufficient memory to copy the types.

GetLongDescription(), SetLongDescription(), GetShortDescription(), SetShortDescription()

status_t **GetLongDescription**(char **description*) const

status_t **SetLongDescription**(const char **description*)

> status_t **GetShortDescription**(char *description) const
> status_t **SetShortDescription**(const char *description)

Each file type has a couple of human-readable description strings associated with it. Neither description string may be longer than B_MIME_TYPE_LENGTH characters.

These functions get and set the long and short description strings. The Get functions copy the string into the argument (which must be allocated). The Set functions copy the string that the argument points to.

Return values:
> B_NO_ERROR. The description was found or set.
> B_NO_INIT. The BMimeType is uninitialized.
> B_BAD_VALUE. (Set) *description* is too long.
> B_NO_MEMORY. Insufficient memory to copy the description.

GetPreferredApp(), SetPreferredApp()

> status_t **GetPreferredApp**(char *signature, app_verb *verb* = B_OPEN) const
> status_t **SetPreferredApp**(const char *signature, app_verb *verb* = B_OPEN)

These functions get and set the "preferred app" for this object's MIME type. The preferred app is the application that's used to access a file when, for example, the user double-clicks the file in a Tracker window: Unless the file identifies (in its attributes) a "custom" preferred app, the Tracker will ask the File Type database for the preferred app that's associated with the file's type.

• The preferred app is identified by *signature*, a MIME string.

• The app_verb argument specifies the type of access; currently, the only app_verb is B_OPEN.

Return values:
> B_NO_ERROR. The preferred app was found or set.
> B_NO_INIT. The BMimeType is uninitialized.
> B_BAD_VALUE (Set... only). The signature argument is too long (greater than B_MIME_TYPE_LENGTH).

GetShortDescription()   *see GetLongDescription()*

GetSupertype()   *see Type()*

GetSupportingApps(), SetSupportingApps()

> status_t **GetSupportingApps**(BMessage *msg) const
>
> status_t **SetSupportingApps**(const BMessage *msg)

These functions get and set the list of the MIME type's "supporting apps." These are the applications that know how to deal with the type. The apps are identified by their signatures.

- If you're getting the apps, you'll find their signatures copied into your BMessage's "applications" field (the BMessage must be allocated). They're given as an indexed array of strings (`B_STRING_TYPE`).
- Similarly, you pass in the signatures by adding strings to the message's "applications" field.
- The BMessage's `what` field is unimportant.

For example, to retrieve all the application (signatures) that support this object's MIME type, you would do the following:

```
BMessage msg();
uint32 i=0;
char *ptr;

if (mime.GetSupportingApps(&msg) != B_NO_ERROR)
   /* Handle the error. */

while (true) {
   if (msg.FindString("applications", i++, &ptr) != B_NO_ERROR)
      break;
   printf("> Supporting App:  %s\n", ptr);
}
```

A given application can be associated with more than one MIME type.

A `NULL` msg to `SetSupportingApps()` clears the type's application signature list.

WARNING

`SetSupportingApps()` clobbers the existing set of signatures. If you want to augment a type's signatures, you should retrieve the existing set, add the new ones, and *then* call **SetSupportingApps()**.

Return values:
> `B_NO_ERROR`. The signatures were found or set.
> `B_NO_INIT`. The BMimeType is uninitialized.
> `B_NO_MEMORY`. Insufficient memory to copy the signatures.

InitCheck()

   status_t **InitCheck**(void) const

Returns the status of the most recent construction or `SetTo()` call.

Return values:
> *See* `SetTo()`.

Install(), Delete(), IsInstalled()

> status_t **Install**(void)
> status_t **Delete**(void)
> bool **IsInstalled**(void) const

Install() adds the object's MIME type to the File Type database. `Delete()` removes the type from the database. `IsInstalled()` tells you if the type is currently installed.

None of these functions affect the object's copy of the MIME type; for instance, deleting a MIME type from the database *doesn't* uninitialize the object.

Return values:
> B_NO_ERROR. The type was successfully added or deleted.
> B_BAD_VALUE. The object is uninitialized.

WARNING

Currently, `Install()` may return a random value if the object is already installed. To avoid confusion, you should call `IsInstalled()` first:

```
if (!mime.IsInstalled())
    mime.Install();
```

IsInstalled()   *see Install()*

IsValid(), IsSupertypeOnly()

> static bool **IsValid**(const char *MIME_string*) const
> bool **IsValid**(void) const
> bool **IsSupertypeOnly**(void) const

The static `IsValid()` tests its argument for MIME validity. See "Valid MIME Strings" for the rules. The non-static version checks the validity of the object's MIME string.

`IsSupertypeOnly()` returns `true` if the object's MIME string doesn't include a subtype.

SetAppHint()   *see GetAppHint()*

SetFileExtensions()   *see GetFileExtensions()*

SetIcon()   *see GetIcon()*

SetIconForType()   *see GetIconForType()*

SetLongDescription()   *see GetLongDescription()*

SetPreferredApp()   *see GetPreferredApp()*

SetShortDescription()   *see GetLongDescription()*

SetSupportingApps()   *see GetSupportingApps()*

SetTo()

> status_t **SetTo**(const char *MIME_string*)

Initializes this BMimeType object to represent *MIME_string*. The object's previous MIME string is freed; the argument is then copied.

The argument can be a full supertype/subtype string, or simply a supertype. In any case, it must pass the validity test described in "Valid MIME Strings" on page 213.

Return values:
> These return codes are also returned by the InitCheck() function.
> B_NO_ERROR. The initialization was successful.
> B_NO_INIT. *MIME_string* is NULL or invalid.
> B_NO_MEMORY. Not enough memory to allocate a copy of the argument.

Type(), GetSupertype()

> const char ***Type**(void) const
> status_t **GetSupertype**(BMime *super*) const

Type() returns a pointer to the object's MIME string. If the object isn't initialized, this returns a pointer to NULL.

GetSupertype() initializes the argument with this object's supertype. (You can then call GetType() on the argument to see the supertype.) *super* must be allocated before it's passed in. If this object isn't initialized, *super* is uninitialized.

Return values:
> The errors apply to GetSupertype() only.
> B_NO_ERROR. Everything's fine.
> B_BAD_VALUE. This object isn't initialized.

Unset()

> void **Unset**(void)

Frees the object's current MIME string, and sets the object's status to B_NO_INIT.

BNode

Derived from: BStatable

Declared in: be/storage/Node.h

Library: libbe.so

Overview

The BNode class gives you access to the data that a file system entry (a file, directory, or symbolic link) contains. There are two parts to this data:

- The "data portion" itself
- The node's attributes

The content of the data portion depends on the node's flavor:

- If it's a regular file, the data is whatever it is that the file is meant to contain: ASCII text, binary image or sound data, executable code, and so on. Note that resources (as created by the BResources class) are kept in the data portion.

- If it's a directory, the data is the list of entries that the directory contains.

- If it's a symbolic link, the data is the path of the "linked-to" file. The path can be absolute or relative.

The content of the attributes, on the other hand, isn't qualified by the node's flavor: Any node can contain any set of attributes.

Nodes Are Dumb

Keep in mind that the concept of a "node" designates the *data parts* (data and attributes) of a file (a file, directory, or link). Contrast this with an "entry," which designates the entity's *location* within the file system: For example, you can write to a "node" (but not an entry), and you can rename an "entry" (but not a node).

This isn't just a conceptual crutch, it's the law: Nodes really don't know where they're located. For example, you can't ask a node for its name, or for the identity of its parent. This has some serious implications, the most important of which is:

- If you need to store a reference to a file (or directory, or symbolic link), don't store the node—in other words, don't cache the BNode object. Instead, store the information that you used to create the BNode (typically, a pathname or `entry_ref` structure).

Now that we've got that straight, we'll relax the rules a bit:

- BDirectory objects are node/entry hybrids. A BDirectory *does* know its own name (and parent, and so on).

This doesn't really change the "store the info" rule. Even if you're dealing exclusively with BDirectory objects, you should keep the generative information around. The primary reason for this is described in the following section.

The "Node Pool" Is Limited (File Descriptors)

Every BNode object consumes a "file descriptor." Your application can only maintain 256 file descriptors at a time. Because of this limit, you shouldn't keep BNodes around that you don't need. Keep in mind that BEntry objects also consume file descriptors (one per object).

NOTE

The file descriptor limit will probably be lifted, or at least setable, in a subsequent release. But even then you should be frugal.

Derived Classes and Their Uses

BNode has three derived classes: BFile, BDirectory, and BSymLink. The derived classes define functions that let you access the node's data portion in the appropriate style; for example:

- BFile implements `Read()` and `Write()` functions that let you retrieve arbitrary amounts of data from arbitrary positions in the file.
- BDirectory implements functions, such as `GetNextEntry()` and `FindEntry()`, that read entries from the directory.
- BSymLink's `ReadLink()` returns the pathname that it contains.

If you want to (sensibly) look at a node's data portion, you must create an instance of the appropriate derived class. In other words, if you want to browse a directory, you have to create a BDirectory instance; if you want to write to a file, you create a BFile.

Be aware that it's not (always) an error to create an instance of the "wrong" derived class; setting a BFile to a symbolic link, for example, will traverse the link such that the BFile opens the file that the symbolic link is linked to. See the individual derived class specifications for more information.

BNode Instances

In practice, you almost always want to create an instance of one of the BNode-derived classes; but if, for whatever reason, you find yourself holding a BNode instance, here's what you'll be able to do with it:

- **Read and write attributes**. The attribute-accessing functions (`ReadAttr()`, `WriteAttr()`, and so on) are general—they work without regard for the node's flavor. Thus, you don't need an instance of a specific derived class to read and write attributes.

- **Get stat information**. The BStatable functions can be invoked on any flavor of node.

- **Lock the node**. This prevents other "agents" (other objects, other apps, the user) from accessing reading or writing the node's data and attributes. See the section "Node Locking" later in this chapter.

Converting a BNode to an Instance of a Derived Class

NOTE

This section describes situations and presents solutions to problems that are a bit esoteric. If you never create direct instances of BNode (and you never *have* to), then you should skip this and go to the "Node Locking" section.

There may be times when you find yourself holding on to a BNode (instance) that you want to convert into a BFile, BDirectory, or BSymLink. However, you can't go *directly* from a BNode instance to an instance of BFile, BDirectory, or BSymLink—you can't tell your BNode to "cast itself" as one of its children.

There are solutions, however...

Converting to BDirectory

Converting from a BNode to a BDirectory, while not transparent, is pretty simple: Grab the `node_ref` out of the BNode and pass it to the BDirectory constructor or `SetTo()` function. Regard this example function:

```
void Node2Directory(BNode *node, BDirectory *dir)
{
   node_ref nref;

   if (!node || !dir) {
       dir.Unset();
       return;
   }

   node.GetNodeRef(&nref);

   /* Set the BDirectory.  If nref isn't a directory node,
    * the SetTo() will fail.
    */
   dir.SetTo(&nref);
}
```

Converting to BFile or BSymLink

Converting a BNode instance to a BFile or BSymLink isn't as neat as the foregoing. Instead, you have to cache the information that you used to initialize the BNode in the first place, and then reuse it to create the BFile or BSymLink.

For example, let's say you receive an `entry_ref`. You turn it into a BNode, but then decide you need the data-writing power of a BFile. If, in the meantime, you lost the original `entry_ref`, you're sunk—there's nothing you can do.

Node Locking

Another feature provided by the BNode class is "node locking": Through BNode's `Lock()` function you can restrict access to the node. The lock is removed when `Unlock()` is called, or when the BNode object is deleted.

- When you lock a node, you prevent other objects (or agents) from reading or writing the node's data and attributes. No other agent can even *open* the node—other BNode constructions and POSIX `open()` calls (on that node) will fail while you hold the lock.

- You can only acquire a node lock if there are no file descriptors open on the node (with one exception). This means that no other BNode may be open on the node (locked or not), nor may the node be held open because of a POSIX `open()` (or `opendir()`) call.

The one exception to the no-file descriptors rule has to do with BEntries: Let's say you lock a directory, and then you initialize a BEntry to point to an entry within that directory. Even though the BEntry creates a file descriptor to the directory (as explained in the BEntry class), the initialization *will* succeed.

Implications

For files (and, less importantly, symlinks), the implications of locking are pretty clear: No one else can read or write the file. For directories, it's worth a closer look:

- Locking a directory means that the contents of the directory can't change: You can't create new nodes in the directory, or rename or remove existing ones. (You can, however, create abstract entries within the directory; see BEntry for more on abstract entries.)

Locking a node does *not* lock the node's entry: **You can't "lock out" entry operations, such as rename, move, and remove.** Even if you have a node locked, the entry that acts as the "container" for that node could disappear. If you want to prevent such operations on a node's entry, lock the entry's parent directory.

In general, you should try to avoid locking your nodes. If you must lock, try to make it brief. The primary reason (and, pretty much, the only reason) to lock is if separate elements in the data and/or attributes must be kept in a consistent state. In such a case, you should hold the lock just long enough to ensure consistency.

WARNING

You shouldn't use locks to "privatize" data. Locking isn't meant to be used as a heightened permissions bit.

Constructor and Destructor

BNode()

BNode(const entry_ref *ref)
BNode(const BEntry *entry)
BNode(const char *path)
BNode(const BDirectory *dir, const char *path)

BNode()
BNode(const BNode &node)

Creates a new BNode object that's initialized to represent a specific file system node. To retrieve the status of the initialization, call `InitCheck()` immediately after constructing the object:

```
BNode node("/boot/lbj/FidoOnFire.gif");
if (node.InitCheck() != B_NO_ERROR)
    /* The object wasn't initialized. */
```

A successfully initialized BNode object creates a "file descriptor" through which the object reads and writes the node's data and attributes. You can only have 256 file descriptors at a time (per application). The object's file descriptor is closed when the object is deleted, reset (through `SetTo()`), or unset (`Unset()`).

- **Default constructor.** The object's status will be `B_NO_INIT,` and the file descriptor isn't allocated until you actually initialize the object with a call to `SetTo()`.

- **Copy constructor.** The new BNode is set to the same node as the argument. Each of the two BNode objects has its own file descriptor.

- **Other constructors.** See the `SetTo()` functions.

~BNode()

virtual ~**BNode**()

Frees the object's file descriptor, unlocks the node (if it was locked), and destroys the object.

Member Functions

GetAttrInfo(), attr_info

status_t **GetAttrInfo**(const char *attr*, attr_info *info*) const

typedef struct **attr_info** {}

Gets information about the attribute named by *attr*. The information is copied into *info*, which must be allocated before it's passed in.

The `attr_info` structure, defined in *be/kernel/fs_attr.h*, is:

```
typedef struct attr_info
{
    uint32 type;
    off_t size;
} attr_info;
```

- `type` is a constant (`B_STRING_TYPE`, `B_INT32_TYPE`, etc) that describes the type of data that the attribute holds.
- `size` is the size of the attribute's data, in bytes.

Return values:

`B_NO_ERROR`. Success.

`B_ENTRY_NOT_FOUND`. The node doesn't have an attribute named *attr*.

`B_FILE_ERROR`. The object is uninitialized.

GetNextAttrName(), RewindAttrs()

status_t **GetNextAttrName**(char *buffer*)

status_t **RewindAttrs**(void)

Every BNode maintains a pointer into its list of attributes. `GetNextAttrName()` retrieves the name of the attribute that the pointer is currently pointing to, and then bumps the pointer to the next attribute. The name is copied into the *buffer*, which should be at least `B_ATTR_NAME_LENGTH` characters long. The copied name is `NULL`-terminated. When you've asked for every name in the list, `GetNextAttrName()` returns an error.

WARNING

`GetNextAttrName()` does *not* clear its argument if it returns an error. This will be corrected in a subsequent release.

`RewindAttrs()` resets the BNode's attribute pointer to the first element in the list.

To visit every attribute name, you would do something like this:

```
/* Print every attribute name. */
char buf[B_ATTR_NAME_LENGTH];

while (node.GetNextAttrName(buf) == B_NO_ERROR) {
   printf("> Attr name:  %s\n", buf);
}
```

The attribute list is not static; when you ask for the next attribute name, you're asking for the next name in the list *as it exists right now.*

Furthermore, the ordinal position of an attribute within the list is indeterminate. "Newer" attributes are not necessarily added to the end of the list: If you alter the list while you're walking through it, you may get curious results—you may not see the attribute that you just now added (for example).

In general, it's best to avoid altering the list while you're iterating over it.

Return values:

> B_NO_ERROR. Success.
> B_ENTRY_NOT_FOUND. You've hit the end of the list.
> B_FILE_ERROR. The object is uninitialized.

InitCheck()

> status_t InitCheck(void) const

Returns the status of the most recent initialization.

Return values:

> B_NO_ERROR. The object was successfully initialized.
> B_NO_INIT. The object is uninitialized.
> See the SetTo() function for a list other return values.

Lock(), Unlock()

> status_t Lock(void)
> status_t Unlock(void)

Locks and unlocks the BNode's node. While the node is locked, no other object can access the node's data or attributes. More precisely, no other agent can create a file descriptor to the node. If a file descriptor already exists to this node, the Lock() function fails.

See "Node Locking" for details.

Return values:

> B_NO_ERROR. The node was successfully locked or unlocked.
>
> B_BUSY. (Lock()) The node can't be locked.
>
> B_BAD_VALUE. (Unlock()) The node isn't locked.
>
> B_FILE_ERROR. The object is uninitialized.

ReadAttr(), WriteAttr(), RemoveAttr()

> ssize_t **ReadAttr**(const char *name,
>   type_code *type*,
>   off_t *offset*,
>   void *buffer,
>   size_t *length*)

> ssize_t **WriteAttr**(const char *name,
>   type_code *type*,
>   off_t *offset*,
>   const void *buffer,
>   size_t *length*)

> status_t **RemoveAttr**(const char *attr*)

These functions read, write, and remove the node's attributes. Attributes are name/data pairs, where names must be unique (within a given node) and the data can be of arbitrary length.

ReadAttr() reads the data in the attribute named *name*, and copies it in *buffer*. The length of the buffer (the maximum number of bytes to copy) is given by *length*. Currently, the *type* and *offset* arguments are unused (or unreliable). The function returns the number of bytes that were actually read.

WriteAttr() erases the data currently held by *name* (if such an attribute exists) and replaces it with a copy of the first *length* bytes of data in *buffer*. The *type* argument *is* remembered—you can retrieve an attribute's type through GetAttrInfo(), for example—and you need to specify the correct type when you're forming a query (see BQuery and the note below). But, as mentioned above, you don't need to match types when you're reading the attribute. The *offset* argument is currently unreliable and shouldn't be used. The functions returns the number of bytes that were written.

NOTE

If you want to use the attribute in a query, its type must be either string, int32, uint32, int64, uint64, double, or float. (In other words, *type* must be B_STRING_TYPE, or B_INT32_TYPE, or B_UINT32_TYPE, and so on.)

RemoveAttr() deletes the attribute given by *name*.

Return values:

ReadAttr() and WriteAttr(), if successful, return the number of bytes read or written.

B_NO_ERROR. (Remove) The attribute was successfully removed.

B_ENTRY_NOT_FOUND. (ReadAttr() and Remove()) The attribute doesn't exist.

B_FILE_ERROR. The object is uninitialized.

B_FILE_ERROR. (WriteAttr() and Remove()) This object is a read-only BFile.

B_NOT_ALLOWED. (WriteAttr() and Remove()) The node is on a read-only volume.

B_DEVICE_FULL. (WriteAttr()) Out of disk space.

B_NO_MEMORY. (WriteAttr()) Not enough memory to complete the operation.

RemoveAttr()   *see ReadAttr()*

RenameAttr()

status_t **RenameAttr**(const char *name*, const char *new_name*)

Moves the attribute given by *name* to *new_name*. If *new_name* exists, it's clobbered.

Return values:

B_NO_ERROR. The attribute was successfully renamed.

B_ENTRY_NOT_FOUND. The *name* attribute doesn't exist.

B_FILE_ERROR. The object is uninitialized.

B_FILE_ERROR. This object is a read-only BFile.

B_NOT_ALLOWED. The node is on a read-only volume.

RewindAttrs   *see GetNextAttrName()*

SetTo(), Unset()

status_t **SetTo**(const entry_ref *ref*)
status_t **SetTo**(const BEntry *entry*)
status_t **SetTo**(const char *path*)
status_t **SetTo**(BDirectory *dir*, const char *path*)

void **Unset**(void)

Closes the BNode's current file descriptor and opens it on the node (of the entry) that's designated by the arguments.

- In the *path* version, *path* can be absolute or relative, and can contain "." and ".." elements. If *path* is relative, it's reckoned off of the current working directory.

- In the *dir/path* version, *path* must be relative. It's reckoned off of the directory given by *dir*.

BNode instances never traverse symbolic links. If the designated entry is a symbolic link, the BNode will open the link's node. (Conversely, BFile instances *always* traverse symbolic links.)

`Unset()` closes the BNode's file descriptor and sets `InitCheck()` to `B_NO_INIT`.

Return values:
 B_NO_ERROR. All is well.
 B_ENTRY_NOT_FOUND. The designated entry doesn't exist.
 B_BAD_VALUE. Uninitialized or malformed argument.
 B_BUSY. The node is locked.

Unlock()   *see Lock()*

Unset()   *see SetTo()*

WriteAttr()   *see ReadAttr()*

Operators

= (assignment)

    BNode& operator=(const BNode &*node*)

In the expression

```
BNode a = b;
```

BNode *a* is initialized to refer to the same node as *b*. To gauge the success of the assignment, you should call `InitCheck()` immediately afterwards. It's safe to assign a BNode to itself.

==, != (comparison)

    bool operator==(const BNode &*node*) const
    bool operator!=(const BNode &*node*) const

Two BNode objects are said to be equal if they're set to the same node, or if they're both `B_NO_INIT`.

BNodeInfo

Derived from:	*none*
Declared in:	be/storage/NodeInfo.h
Library:	libbe.so

Overview

BNodeInfo provides file type information about a particular node; specifically:

- The (MIME) file type.
- The node's icons, including the node-specific icon that the Tracker displays.
- The "preferred app"; this is the application that's used to access the node's contents.

Except for the Tracker icon, all this information can also be set through the BNodeInfo class. None of the information is passed on to the File Type database; if you want to record a node's file type information with the database, you have to create a BMimeType object (based on the node's file type) and go from there.

Initialization

You initialize a BNodeInfo object by passing it a BNode object. Although you can pass any flavor of node, you typically only care about files; passing a BFile object (or any subclass of BNode) is, of course, acceptable. The BNodeInfo object maintains its own pointer to the BNode you pass in. You don't have to avoid touching the BNode while a BNodeInfo is looking at it (or changing it); the only thing you shouldn't do is delete the BNode.

BNodeInfo doesn't care if the BNode is locked—there's no particular reason to lock the BNode before passing it in, but the BNodeInfo won't balk if you do. If you pass in a BFile object, BNodeInfo *does not* obey the BFile's read/write flags. For example, you can set the node info for a BFile even if you've opened it in read-only mode.

Node Info Equals Attributes

The BNodeInfo class does nothing more than look in a node's attributes for the information it sets or gets. The attribute names for the various information particles are given in the function descriptions, below. If you want, you can bypass BNodeInfo and get the node information directly by passing the attribute names to BNode's `ReadAttr()` and `WriteAttr()` functions.

The one exception to this is `GetTrackerIcon()`: This function starts by looking in the node's attributes, but then it goes out hunting if it has to (if the icon isn't found in the attributes).

BAppFileInfo

BNodeInfo has a single subclass: BAppFileInfo. You use a BAppFileInfo object to get more information about a specific executable image (file).

Errors

Unlike most of the other Storage Kit classes, when you ask a BNodeInfo to retrieve some information by reference, the object *doesn't* clear the reference argument if it fails. Because of this, you should always check the error code that's returned by the Get... functions.

Constructor and Destructor

BNodeInfo()

> **BNodeInfo**(void)
> **BNodeInfo**(BNode *node*)

The default constructor creates a new, uninitialized BNodeInfo object. To initialize you have to follow this construction with a call to SetTo().

The BNode version initializes the BNodeInfo by passing the argument to SetTo(); see SetTo() for details (and error codes).

~BNodeInfo()

> **~BNodeInfo**(void)

Destroys the object. The BNode object that was used to initialize the object isn't touched.

Member Functions

GetIcon(), SetIcon(), GetTrackerIcon()

> virtual status_t **GetIcon**(BBitmap *icon*, icon_size *which* = B_LARGE_ICON) const
> virtual status_t **SetIcon**(const BBitmap *icon*, icon_size *which* = B_LARGE_ICON)
>
> status_t **GetTrackerIcon**(BBitmap *icon*, icon_size *which* = B_LARGE_ICON)
> static status_t **GetTrackerIcon**(entry_ref *ref,
>   BBitmap *icon*,
>   icon_size *which* = B_LARGE_ICON)

GetIcon() and SetIcon() get and set the icon data that's stored in the node's attributes. You specify which icon you want (large or small) by passing B_LARGE_ICON or B_SMALL_ICON as the *which* argument. The icon is passed in or returned through the *icon* argument. The icon data is copied out of or into the BBitmap object.

If you're setting the icon, the bitmap must be the proper size: 32x32 for the large icon, 16x16 for the small one. If you want to erase the node's icon, pass NULL as the *icon* argument to SetIcon().

NOTE

The icon attributes are stored as "BEOS: L:STD_ICON" (large icon) and "BEOS: M:STD_ICON" (small, or "mini" icon).

GetTrackerIcon() finds the icon that the Tracker uses to display the node. The static version lets you identify the node as an entry_ref. Both versions follow the same ordered path in trying to find the icon:

First (1) it looks in the node's attributes. If the attribute doesn't exist, it (2) gets the node's preferred app (as a signature), and asks the File Type database if that signature declares an icon for this node's file type. If the node doesn't have a preferred app, or if the app doesn't designate an icon for the node's type, the function (3) asks the File Type database for the icon based on the node's file type. If still empty-handed, the function (4) asks the File Type database for the preferred app based on the node's file type, and then asks that app for the icon it uses to display this node's file type. If still nothing, we (5) quit.

The function doesn't tell you which branch of the path it found the icon in.

Return values:
   B_NO_ERROR. The icon was found or set.
   B_NO_INIT. The BNodeInfo is uninitialized.
   B_BAD_VALUE (Set... only). The bitmap wasn't the proper size.
   Attribute errors. See the error codes for BNode::ReadAttr() and BNode::WriteAttr().

GetPreferredApp(), SetPreferredApp()

   status_t **GetPreferredApp**(char *signature*, app_verb *verb* = B_OPEN) const
   status_t **SetPreferredApp**(const char *signature*, app_verb *verb* = B_OPEN)

These functions get and set the node's "preferred app." This is the application that's used to access the node when, for example, the user double-clicks the node in a Tracker window.

• The preferred app is identified by *signature*, a MIME string.

• The app_verb argument specifies the type of access; currently, the only app_verb is B_OPEN.

If a node doesn't have a preferred app, the Tracker looks in the File Type database for an app that can open the node's file type.

NOTE

The attribute that stores the preferred app is named "BEOS:PREF_APP".

Return values:

B_NO_ERROR. The preferred app was found or set.

B_NO_INIT. The BNodeInfo is uninitialized.

B_BAD_VALUE (Set... only). The signature argument is too long (greater than B_MIME_TYPE_LENGTH).

Attribute errors. See the error codes for BNode::ReadAttr() and BNode::WriteAttr().

GetTrackerIcon()   *see GetIcon()*

GetType(), SetType()

virtual status_t **GetType**(char *type*) const
virtual status_t **SetType**(const char *type*)

These functions get and set the node's file type. The file type, passed in or returned through *type*, is a MIME string.

NOTE

The attribute that stores the file type is named "BEOS:TYPE".

Return values:

B_NO_ERROR. The type was found or set.

B_NO_INIT. The BNodeInfo is uninitialized.

Attribute errors. See the error codes for BNode::ReadAttr() and BNode::WriteAttr().

InitCheck()

status_t **InitCheck**(void) const

Returns the status of the most recent initialization.

Return values:

B_NO_ERROR. The object was successfully initialized.

B_NO_INIT. The object is uninitialized.

See SetTo() for more error codes.

SetIcon()   *see GetIcon()*

SetPreferredApp()   *see GetPreferredApp()*

SetTo()

status_t **SetTo**(BNode *node*)

Initializes the BNodeInfo object by pointing it to *node*, which must be a valid (initialized) BNode object. The BNodeInfo maintains its own BNode pointer: You shouldn't delete *node* while the BNodeInfo is accessing it; other changes to the BNode are permitted, but you may want to avoid such antics. Re-initializing a BNodeInfo doesn't affect the previous BNode object.

Return values:
B_NO_ERROR. The object was successfully initialized.
B_BAD_VALUE. *node* is uninitialized.

SetType() *see GetType()*

The Node Monitor

Derived from: *none—these are C functions*

Declared in: be/storage/NodeMonitor.h

Library: libbe.so

Overview

The Node Monitor is a service that lets you ask to be notified of certain file system changes. You can ask to be told when a change is made to:

* The contents of a specific directory.
* The name of a specific entry.
* Any stat field of a specific entry.
* Any attribute of a specific entry.

You can also ask to be notified when:

* Volumes are mounted and unmounted.

NOTE

Volume monitoring is also provided by the BVolumeRoster class: BVolume-Roster can talk to the Node Monitor for you. The BVolumeRoster volume-watching API is more humane than that which you'll find here.

When something interesting happens, the Node Monitor lets you know by sending a BMessage to the target of your choice.

Node Monitor Functions

There are two Node Monitor functions, `watch_node()` and `stop_watching()`. The names are a wee bit misleading, so before we go on to the full technical descriptions, let's nip some buds:

- `watch_node()` tells the Node Monitor to start *or stop* watching a *specific* node, or to watch for volumes being mounted and unmounted. Memorize the emphasized words.

- `stop_watching()` tells the Node Monitor to stop sending notifications to a particular target.

watch_node()

> status_t **watch_node**(const node_ref *nref,
>   uint32 *flags*,
>   BMessenger *messenger*)

> status_t **watch_node**(const node_ref *nref,
>   uint32 *flags*,
>   const BHandler *handler,
>   const BLooper *looper = NULL)

`watch_node()` tells the Node Monitor to:

- Start paying attention to the node specified by the `node_ref` argument. If you're watching for volumes (only), *nref* can be NULL. The easiest way to get a `node_ref` is to invoke `BStatable::GetNodeRef()` on any BEntry or BNode object.

- The *flags* argument lists the changes that you want the Monitor to pay attention to. See below for details.

- The target of the change notification messages is specified either as a BMessenger, or as a BHandler*/BLooper* pair. (The target specification follows the `BInvoker::SetTarget()` protocol; see the BInvoker class for details.) The notification shows up as a BMessage in the target's `MessageReceived()` function.

NOTE

You can't tell the Node Monitor to send its notifications to another application. Currently, the BMessenger that you specify must identify a target in the caller's team.

Jumping ahead a bit, here's a sample function that tells the Node Monitor to watch for name and attribute changes to a given entry. The Monitor's notifications will be sent to the application's main loop:

```
status_t WatchThis(BEntry *entry)
{
```

```
    node_ref nref;
    entry->GetNodeRef(&nref);
    return (watch_node(&nref,
            B_WATCH_NAME | B_WATCH_ATTR,
            be_app_messenger));
}
```

Monitor Flags

`watch_node()`'s *flags* argument is a combination of the following:

- **B_WATCH_NAME** watches for name changes. This includes moving the node to a different directory, or removing the node altogether.

- **B_WATCH_STAT** watches for *any* change to the node's `stat` structure. This includes changes to the size, modification date, owner, and so on. See "The stat Structure" on page 285 in the BStatable class for a description of what's in the `stat` structure.

- **B_WATCH_ATTR** watches for changes to *any* of the node's attributes. This includes adding and removing attributes.

- **B_WATCH_DIRECTORY** only applies to nodes that are directories. The flag tells the Monitor to watch for changes (new entries, entry deletions, entries being renamed) to the directory. (You can apply the other flags to a directory, as well). It's not an error to set **B_WATCH_DIRECTORY** on a node that isn't a directory—but it doesn't *do* anything for you.

- **B_WATCH_ALL**. This is a convenience that combines all the above.

- **B_WATCH_MOUNT** watches for volumes being mounted and unmounted. As mentioned above, the *nref* argument isn't needed (it can be **NULL**) if all you're doing is watching volumes. **B_WATCH_MOUNT** *isn't* included in **B_WATCH_ALL**.

There's one other constant, which lives in a class by itself:

- **B_STOP_WATCHING** tells the Node Monitor to stop watching the *nref* argument.

You can't combine **B_STOP_WATCHING** with any of the others in an attempt to stop watching a specific category of changes. For example, if you call:

```
watch_node(&nref, B_WATCH_STAT, be_app_messenger);
watch_node(&nref, B_WATCH_ATTR, be_app_messenger);
```

and then call:

```
watch_node(&nref, B_STOP_WATCHING, be_app_messenger);
```

both of the previous Monitor calls are stopped.

WARNING

B_STOP_WATCHING does *not* apply to volume watching. The only way to stop monitoring volume un/mounts is to call `stop_watching()`.

Combining Flags and the 4096 Limit

If you can, you should combine as many flags as you're going to need in single calls to `watch_node()`. Recall the example used above:

```
watch_node(&nref,
      B_WATCH_NAME | B_WATCH_ATTR,
      be_app_messenger);
```

This is better than making separate `watch_node()` calls (one to pass **B_WATCH_NAME** and another to pass **B_WATCH_ATTR**)—not only because the single call is naturally more efficient than two, but also because **the Node Monitor can only monitor 4096 nodes at a time**. Every call to `watch_node()` consumes a Node Monitor slot, even if you're *already* monitoring the requested node.

If you want to watch all aspects of a node, just pass **B_WATCH_ALL** to every `watch_node()` call. This will consume only a single Node Monitor slot.

Notification Messages

A BMessage notification sent by the Node Monitor looks like this:

- The `what` value is `B_NODE_MONITOR`.
- The field named "opcode" is an `int32` constant that tells you what happened.
- Additional fields give you information (device, node, name, and so on) about the node (or volume) that it happened to.

The "opcode" constants and additional fields are described in "Opcode Constants." In general, the opcodes correspond to the flags that you passed to `watch_node()`; however, this correspondence isn't always one-to-one.

There are seven opcode constants:

```
B_ENTRY_CREATED

B_ENTRY_REMOVED

B_ENTRY_MOVED

B_STAT_CHANGED

B_ATTR_CHANGED

B_DEVICE_MOUNTED

B_DEVICE_UNMOUNTED
```

Return values:

  B_NO_ERROR. The Node Monitor is off and running.

  B_BAD_VALUE. Bad *nref* argument (not applicable to mount-only watches), or poorly formed target.

B_NO_MEMORY. Couldn't allocate resources, or out of Node Monitor slots.

B_ERROR. Some cases of bad *nref* arguments erroneously return B_ERROR. This will be fixed.

stop_watching()

status_t **stop_watching**(BMessenger *messenger*)

status_t **stop_watching**(const BHandler *handler,* const BLooper *looper*)

Tells the Node Monitor to stop sending notifications to the target described by the arguments. All the Node Monitor "slots" that were allocated to the target are freed. Keep in mind that are only 4096 slots for the entire system.

Return values:

B_NO_ERROR. The target is now out of the Node Monitor loop.

B_BAD_VALUE. Badly formed target description.

Opcode Constants

The following sections describe the "opcode" constants; these are the values that appear in the "opcode" field of the BMessages that are generated by the Node Monitor. Note that in these descriptions, the use of the terms "entry" and "node" is sometimes blurred.

B_ENTRY_CREATED

- A completely new entry was created in a monitored directory. (This doesn't include entries that are moved into this directory from some other directory—see B_ENTRY_MOVED.)

You get this notification if you applied B_WATCH_DIRECTORY to the directory in which the entry was created. The message's fields are:

Field	Type code	Description
"opcode"	B_INT32_TYPE	B_ENTRY_CREATED
"name"	B_STRING_TYPE	The name of the new entry.
"directory"	B_INT64_TYPE	The ino_t (node) number for the directory in which the entry was created.
"device"	B_INT32_TYPE	The dev_t number of the device on which the new entry resides.

Parsing and Tricks

In your code, you would parse a B_ENTRY_CREATED message like this:

```
void MyTarget::MessageReceived(BMessage *msg)
{
    int32 opcode;
    dev_t device;
    ino_t directory;
    ino_t node;
    const char *name;

    if (msg->what == B_NODE_MONITOR) {
        if (msg->FindInt32("opcode", &opcode) == B_OK) {
            switch (opcode) {
                case B_ENTRY_CREATED:
                    msg->FindInt32("device", &device);
                    msg->FindInt64("directory", &directory);
                    msg->FindInt64("node", &node);
                    msg->FindString("name", &name);
                    break;
                ...
```

So, what do you do with these fields?

Create an `entry_ref` to the entry. The "device", "directory", and "name" fields can be used to create an `entry_ref` to the new entry:

```
entry_ref ref;
const char *name;
...
msg->FindInt32("device", &ref.device);
msg->FindInt64("directory", &ref.directory);
msg->FindString("name", &name);
ref.set_name(name);
```

Create a `node_ref` to the entry. If you want to start Node Monitoring the new entry (or, more accurately, the node of the new entry), you stuff "device" and "directory" into a `node_ref`:

```
node_ref nref;
status_t err;

...
msg->FindInt32("device", &nref.device);
msg->FindInt64("node", &nref.node);

err = watch_node(&nref, B_WATCH_ALL, be_app_messenger);
```

Create a `node_ref` to the entry's parent. Note that the "directory" field is a node number. By combining this number with the "device" field, you can create a `node_ref` that points to the entry's parent. From there, you're a `SetTo()` away from a BDirectory object:

```
node_ref nref;
BDirectory dir;
status_t err;
```

```
...
msg->FindInt32("device", &nref.device);
msg->FindInt64("directory", &nref.node);
err = dir.SetTo(&nref);
```

B_ENTRY_REMOVED

•   A node was removed (deleted) from a directory.

You get this if you applied **B_WATCH_NAME** on the node itself, or **B_WATCH_DIRECTORY** on the directory that the node lived in. The message's fields are:

Field	Type code	Description
"opcode"	B_INT32_TYPE	B_ENTRY_REMOVED
"directory"	B_INT64_TYPE	The ino_t (node) number of the directory from which the entry was removed.
"device"	B_INT32_TYPE	The dev_t number of the device that the removed node used to live on.
"node"	B_INT64_TYPE	The ino_t number of the node that was removed.

WARNING

Since this message is telling you that the node was removed, the "node" value will be invalid. The node number *can* be useful (and sometimes necessary) for comparison with cached node numbers (as demonstrated below).

Parsing the message is the same as for **B_ENTRY_CREATED**, but without the "name" field. See "Parsing and Tricks," above.

Note that the **B_ENTRY_REMOVED** message is sent as soon as the node's entry is "unlinked" from its directory. The node itself may linger for while after that. Follow this logic:

•   When a file (regardless of flavor) is removed, the entry for that file is *immediately* removed ("unlinked") from the file hierarchy, and the Node Monitor message is *immediately* sent—even if you have an object that has opened the file's node.

•   The node isn't actually destroyed until the last open object (to that node) is destroyed. (In POSIX speak, the node is destroyed when the last file descriptor to the node is closed.)

•   Until the node is destroyed, the open objects (file descriptors) can still access the node's data.

You can take advantage of this to warn a user that a file is going to go away, or to make a backup, or whatever. For example, let's say you have an application that lets the user open files; each time a file is opened, your `OpenFile()` function creates a BFile object and starts the Node Monitor running:

```
status_t YourApp::OpenFile(const char *pathname)
{
   BFile *file;
   node_ref nref;
   status_t err;

   file = new BFile(pathname, B_READ_WRITE);
   if ((err=file->InitCheck()) != B_OK)
      return err;

   file->GetNodeRef(&nref);
   err = watch_node(&nref, B_WATCH_NAME, be_app_messenger);

   if (err != B_OK) {
      delete file;
      return err;
   }

   /* We've got the file and we're monitoring it; now we cache
    * the BFile by adding it to a BList (data member).
    * function.  There's a race condition between the
    * watch_node() call above and the following AddItem().
    */
   return ((FileList->AddItem((void *)file)) ? B_OK : B_ERROR);

}
```

Now we receive a Node Monitor message telling us the node has been removed. We stuff the "device" and "node" fields into a **node_ref** and pass them to a (fictitious) `AlertUser()` function:

```
void YourApp::MessageReceived(BMessage *msg)
{
   int32 opcode;
   node_ref nref;

   if (msg->what == B_NODE_MONITOR) {
      if (msg->FindInt32("opcode", &opcode) == B_OK) {
         switch (opcode) {
            case B_ENTRY_REMOVED:
               msg->FindInt32("device", &nref.device);
               msg->FindInt64("node", &nref.node);
               GoodbyeFile(nref);
   ...
}
```

The implementation of `GoodbyeFile()` (which we won't show here) would walk down the BFile list looking for a **node_ref** that matches the argument:

```
void YourApp::GoodbyeFile(node_ref nref)
{
   BFile *filePtr;
```

```
    int32 ktr = 0;
    node_ref cref;

    while ((*filePtr = (BFile *)FileList->ItemAt(ktr++))) {
        filePtr->GetNodeRef(&cref);
        if (nref == cref) {
            /* We found it.  Now we do whatever
             * we need to do.
             */
        }
    }
}
```

If a match is found, your app could then do whatever it needs to do. Remember—the node's data is still valid until your BFile is destroyed or re-initialized.

B_ENTRY_MOVED

• A node was moved from one directory to a different directory.

You get this if you applied **B_WATCH_NAME** on the node itself, or **B_WATCH_DIRECTORY** on *either* of the directories. The message's fields are:

Field	Type code	Description
"opcode"	B_INT32_TYPE	B_ENTRY_MOVED
"name"	B_STRING_TYPE	The name of the entry that moved.
"from directory"	B_INT64_TYPE	The `ino_t` (node) number of the directory the node was removed from.
"to directory"	B_INT64_TYPE	The `ino_t` (node) number of the directory that the node was added to.
"device"	B_INT32_TYPE	The `dev_t` number of the device that the moved node entry lives on. (You can't move a file between devices, so this value will be applied to the file's old and new locations.)
"node"	B_INT64_TYPE	The `ino_t` number of the node that moved.

NOTE

Moving a node *does not* change its `ino_t` number.

Parsing the message is much the same as for **B_ENTRY_CREATED**, modulo the directory field changes. See "Parsing and Tricks."

Moving a node doesn't affect the objects that hold the node open. They (the objects) can continue to read and write data from the node.

B_STAT_CHANGED

- A field in the node's `stat` structure changed (this doesn't include the `stat` structure disappearing because the node was deleted).

You get this if you applied `B_WATCH_STAT` on the node itself. The message's fields are:

Field	Type code	Description
"opcode"	B_INT32_TYPE	B_STAT_CHANGED
"node"	B_INT64_TYPE	The `ino_t` number of the node.
"device"	B_INT32_TYPE	The `dev_t` number of the node's device.

The `stat` structure is described in "The stat Structure" on page 285 in the BStatable class. The fields that you can change are:

- Owner (`st_uid`), group (`st_gid`), and permissions (low four bytes of `st_mode`).
- Creation (`st_ctime`), modification (`st_mtime`), and access times (`st_atime`; currently unused).
- The size of the node's data (`st_size`). The measurement doesn't include attributes.

A couple of important points:

- The `B_STAT_CHANGED` message doesn't give you enough information to construct an object from which you can get a `stat` structure. In other words, you can't play the same games that were described in "Parsing and Tricks."
- The message also doesn't tell you which `stat` field changed.

In most uses of the `B_STAT_CHANGED` message, you have to cache the objects that you're monitoring so you can compare their `node_ref`s to the message fields (an example of this is given in `B_ENTRY_REMOVED`). Furthermore, you may want to cache the objects' `stat` structures so you can figure out which field changed.

B_ATTR_CHANGED

- An attribute of the node changed.

You get this if you applied `B_WATCH_ATTR` on the node itself. The message's fields are:

Field	Type code	Description
"opcode"	B_INT32_TYPE	B_ATTR_CHANGED
"node"	B_INT64_TYPE	The `ino_t` number of the node.
"device"	B_INT32_TYPE	The `dev_t` number of the node's device.

Attributes are key/value pairs that can be "attached" to any file (regardless of flavor). They're described in the BNode class.

As with `B_STAT_CHANGED` messages, you may not be able to use the `B_ATTR_CHANGED` information directly. Instead, you have to cache references to the (BNode) objects that you're monitoring so you can compare their `node_ref`s to the message fields (an example of this is given in `B_ENTRY_REMOVED`).

B_DEVICE_MOUNTED

- A file system device (in other words, a *volume*) was mounted.

You get this if you passed `B_WATCH_MOUNT` to `watch_node()`. The message's fields are:

Field	Type code	Description
"opcode"	B_INT32_TYPE	B_DEVICE_MOUNTED
"new device"	B_INT32_TYPE	The `dev_t` number of the newly-mounted device.
"device"	B_INT32_TYPE	The `dev_t` number of the device that holds the directory of the new device's mount point.
"directory"	B_INT64_TYPE	The `ino_t` (node) number of the directory that acts as the new device's mount point.

Obviously, there's no node involved here, so the first argument to the `watch_node()` call can be `NULL`:

```
watch_node(NULL, B_WATCH_MOUNT, be_app_messenger);
```

Unlike with the other "watch flags," the only way to stop the mount-watching is to call `stop_watching()`.

B_DEVICE_UNMOUNTED

- A file system device (in other words, a *volume*) was unmounted.

You get this if you passed `B_WATCH_MOUNT` to `watch_node()`. The message's fields are:

Field	Type code	Description
"opcode"	B_INT32_TYPE	B_DEVICE_UNMOUNTED
"new device"	B_INT32_TYPE	The `dev_t` number of the unmounted device.

Be careful with the device number: `dev_t`s are quickly recycled. You should only need this number if you're keeping a list of the `dev_t`s of all mounted disks and you want to remove the `dev_t` for this recently-unmounted volume (keeping in mind that a device-mounted message bearing this `dev_t` may arrive in the meantime).

BPath

Derived from: BFlattenable

Declared in: be/storage/Path.h

Library: libbe.so

Overview

A BPath object represents an absolute pathname, and provides some simple path manipulation and querying functions. The primary features of the class are:

- **It allocates storage for you.** When you tell your BPath object which pathname you want it to represent, the object allocates storage for the pathname automatically. When you delete the object, the storage is freed.

- **It always represents an absolute path.** The pathname strings that you use to initialize a BPath can be relative, and they can include references to "." and "..". The BPath "normalizes" the passed-in strings to create an absolute pathname, as described in "Initializing and Normalizing".

BPaths are handy, but don't expect them to actually *do* very much: **A BPath is just a pathname**. It identifies the location of a file, but it can't manipulate the file, nor can it change the structure of the file system.

So what do you use BPaths for?

- **You can use your BPaths to initialize other, more powerful objects** (BEntry, BNode and its kids). See "Converting a BPath" on page 251.

- **BPaths can be passed through BMessages.** To add a BPath to a BMessage, you have to flatten it first: BPath implements BFlattenable for exactly this reason. The receiver of the BMessage can resurrect the flattened object as a BPath object or as an `entry_ref` structure. See "Passing a BPath in a BMessage".

- **BPath objects are ideal for caching references to files.** BPaths don't consume much in the way of system resources—they don't contain file descriptors, for example. So they're great for keeping track of the files that your application is interested in.

In the way that they're used, BPaths and `entry_refs` are nearly identical. In particular, `entry_refs` can do all three of the things listed here. Whether you use BPaths (pathnames in general) or `entry_refs` is largely a matter of taste.

Initializing and Normalizing

You initialize a BPath—in other words, you establish the path that the object represents—by passing a string (or two, or a BDirectory and a string) to the constructor or to the `SetTo()` function. Upon initialization, the BPath object concatenates the strings and then "normalizes" the passed-in strings *if it has to* (this emphasis is important, as we'll see in a moment). The following elements trigger normalization:

- A relative pathname (after concatenation; e.g., "boot/lbj")
- The presence of "." or ".." ("/boot/lbj/../lbj/./fido")
- Redundant slashes ("/boot//lbj")
- A trailing slash ("/boot/lbj/")

During normalization, BPath conjures up an absolute pathname in the form

$$/dir1/dir2/.../dirN/leaf$$

It does this by applying the following rules:

- Relative pathnames are reckoned off of the current working directory.
- "." is ignored (at the head of a path, it's taken as the cwd).
- ".." bumps up one directory level.
- Redundant slashes are coalesced.
- A trailing slash is removed.

(The one exception to this final rule is "/" as a full pathname.)

There's a subtle side effect that you get with normalization: **When you normalize a pathname, all the elements in the path up to but not including the leaf must exist.** In other words, a normalized BPath object gives you the *same* guarantee of existence as does an `entry_ref` structure. The subtlety, here, is that an unnormalized BPath *needn't exist at all.*

For example, here we create a BPath for a pathname that contains a nonexistent directory:

```
/* We'll assume that "/abc/def/" doesn't exist. */
BPath path("/abc/def/ghi.jkl");

/* Nonetheless, the BPath is successfully initialized.
 * The Path() function returns a pointer to the object's
 * pathname string.
 */
printf("Path:  %s\n". path.Path());
```

On the command line we see:

```
$ Path:  /abc/def/ghi.jkl
```

But if we tickle the normalization machine...

```
/* The redundant slash causes a normalization. */
BPath path("/abc/def//ghi.jkl");
```

....the object is invalid:

```
$ Path:  (null)
```

Forcing Initialization

Both the constructor and the `SetTo()` function carry an optional argument that lets you force the passed-in path to be normalized:

```
/* The trailing bool forces normalization. */
BPath path("/abc/def/ghi.jkl", true);
printf("Path:  %s\n", path.Path());
```

In this case, the forced normalization nullifies the object:

```
$Path:  (null)
```

Normalization by Default?

Since forcing normalization makes BPath's behavior more consistent and reliable, why not always normalize? Because **normalization can be expensive**.

During normalization, the pathname is `stat`'d and prodded rather heavily. If you're planning on using your BPath's pathname to initialize a BEntry or BNode, this prodding will happen again. Rather than incur the expense twice, you may want to live with unnormalized BPath objects, and take the normalization hit during the subsequent initialization.

Other Normalization Details

* You can't force the BPath constructor or SetTo() function to skip the normalization. If the path *needs* to be normalized, it *will* be normalized.

* BPath doesn't let you ask if its pathname was normalized.

The BPath Calling Convention

BPath objects are passed back to you (by reference) by a number of Storage Kit functions. However, you shouldn't find any functions that ask for a BPath object. This is a convention of usage:

* If an API element returns a pathname to you, it does so in the form of a BPath. If it asks for a pathname from you (as an argument), it asks for a `const char *`.

As an example of a function that returns a BPath to you, recall BEntry's `GetPath()` function:

```
status_t BEntry::GetPath(BPath *path)
```

(As an aside, this is where the auto-allocation comes in handy—because BPath allocates the pathname storage for you, you don't have to mess around with ugly buffer and length arguments.)

On the other hand, BEntry's `SetTo()` takes a pathname as a `const char *`:

```
status_t BEntry::SetTo(const char *path)
```

If you've got a BPath loaded up with a pathname, you would call this function thus:

```
entry.SetTo(path.Path());
```

The constructors and `SetTo()` functions in (most of) the Storage Kit classes have `const char *` versions that can be called as shown here.

Passing a BPath in a BMessage

Let's say you've got a BPath object that you want to send to some other application. To do this, you have to add it to a BMessage object through the latter's `AddFlat()` function. As an inheritor from BFlattenable, the BPath knows how to flatten itself for just this purpose.

```
BMessage msg;
BPath path("/boot/lbj/fido");

/* The check here is important, as we'll describe
 * in a moment.
 */
if (msg.AddFlat("pathname", &path) != B_NO_ERROR)
   /* handle the error */
```

The receiver of the message can retrieve the pathname as a BPath object by calling `FindFlat()`:

```
void MyApp::MessageReceived(BMessage *msg)
{
   BPath path;

   if (msg->FindFlat("pathname", &path) != B_NO_ERROR)
      /* handle the error */
   ...
}
```

Alternatively, the pathname can be retrieved as an `entry_ref` through `FindRef()`:

```
void MyApp::MessageReceived(BMessage *msg)
{
   entry_ref ref;

   if (msg->FindRef("pathname", &ref) != B_NO_ERROR)
      /* handle the error */
   ...
}
```

If you want to skip all the conversion business and simply pass the pathname as a string, use `AddString()`. The receiver, of course, would have to call `FindString()` to retrieve your pathname string.

What's Really Going On

When you add a flattened BPath to a BMessage, the object's pathname is turned into an `entry_ref`. If the message receiver asks for a BPath (through `FindFlat()`), the `entry_ref` is turned back into a BPath object. Therefore, it's more efficient to retrieve a flattened BPath as an entry_ref than it is to unflatten it as a BPath object.

The BPath to `entry_ref` conversion has another, more subtle implication: Adding a BPath through AddFlat() performs an implicit normalization on the data that's added to the BMessage.

If the normalization fails, the `AddFlat()` function returns an error and the data isn't added to the BMessage. The original BPath is untouched, regardless of the result of the normalization.

Converting a BPath

As mentioned earlier, most of the Storage Kit classes have constructors and `SetTo()` functions that accept `const char *` arguments. If you want to turn your BPath into a BFile (for example), you would do this (including error checks):

```
status_t err;

BFile file(path.Path());
err = InitCheck();
```

or:

```
err = file.SetTo(path.Path());
```

To convert a BPath to an `entry_ref`, pass the pathname to the `get_ref_for_path()` function:

```
entry_ref ref;
status_t err;

err = get_ref_for_path(path.Path(), &ref);
```

For you Node Monitor users: You can't convert directly to a **node_ref** structure. The quickest way from here to there is:

```
node_ref nref;
status_t err;

/* We'll skip InitCheck() and catch errors in GetNodeRef(). */
BEntry entry(path.Path());
err = entry.GetNodeRef(&nref);
```

Immutability

Remember, a BPath represents a pathname, not a node. It isn't "updated" when the file system changes:

- A BPath's pathname string never changes behind your back, even if the entry that it originally pointed to is renamed, moved, or deleted.

For example:

```
BEntry entry;
BPath path;

/* Set a BPath, construct a BEntry from it, rename
 * the entry, and then print the BPath's pathname.
 */
if (path.SetTo("/boot/lbj/fido") == B_NO_ERROR)
   if (entry.SetTo(&path) == B_NO_ERROR)
      if (entry.Rename("rover") == B_NO_ERROR)
         printf("Pathname: %s\n", path.Path());
```

We see:

```
$ Pathname:  /boot/lbj/fido
```

even though the entry that the BPath was constructed to represent has been renamed.

Constructor and Destructor

BPath()

BPath(const char *path*,
            const char *leaf* = NULL,
            bool *normalize* = false)

BPath(const BDirectory *dir*,
            const char *leaf* = NULL,
            bool *normalize* = false)

BPath(void)
BPath(const BPath &*path*)

Creates a new BPath object that represents the path that's created from the arguments. See the analogous `SetTo()` functions for descriptions of the flavorful constructors.

- The default constructor does nothing; it should be followed by a call to `SetTo()`.
- The copy constructor makes a copy of the argument's pathname.

The constructor automatically allocates memory for the object's stored pathname. The memory is freed when the object is deleted.

To check to see if an initialization was successful, call InitCheck().

~BPath

> virtual ~**BPath**()

Frees the object's pathname storage and extinguishes the object.

Member Functions

Append()

> status_t **Append**(const char *_path_, bool _normalize_ = false)

Appends the pathname given by _path_ to the object's current pathname. _path_ must be relative. If normalize is true, the new pathname is normalized; otherwise, it's normalized only if necessary.

Note that this:

```
Append("subdir/file")
```

is the same as (and is implemented as):

```
path.SetTo(path.Path(), "subdir/file");
```

The Append() return value is picked up from the SetTo() call.

Return values:
> B_NO_ERROR. Success.
> B_BAD_VALUE. _path_ contained a leading "/", or this is uninitialized.
> See SetTo() for other return values.

GetParent()

> status_t **GetParent**(BPath *_path_) const

Initializes the argument with the pathname to the parent directory of this. Destructive parenting is acceptable (sociologically, it's a given):

```
BPath path("/boot/lbj/fido");

path.GetParent(&path);
```

Other details...

- GetParent() makes a call to SetTo(), but it's guaranteed not to tickle the normalization machine.
- You can't get the parent of "/".

Return values:

> B_NO_ERROR. Hello, mother.
>
> B_ENTRY_NOT_FOUND. You tried to get the parent of "/".
>
> B_BAD_VALUE. *path* is NULL.
>
> B_NO_MEMORY. Couldn't allocate storage for the pathname.

If the initialization isn't successful, the argument's InitCheck() is set to B_NO_INIT.

InitCheck()

> status_t **InitCheck**(void) const

Returns the status of the most recent construction or SetTo() call.

Return values:

> B_NO_ERROR. The initialization was successful.
>
> B_NO_INIT. The object is uninitialized (this includes Unset()).
>
> See SetTo() for other errors.

Path(), Leaf()

> const char ***Path**(void) const
>
> const char ***Leaf**(void) const

These functions return the object's full path and leaf name, respectively. For example:

```
BPath path("/boot/lbj/fido");
printf("Path:  %s\n", path.Path());
printf("Leaf:  %s\n", path.Leaf());
```

produces:

```
$ Path:  /boot/lbj/fido
$ Leaf:  fido
```

In both cases, the returned pointers belong to the BPath object. When the BPath is deleted, the pointers go with it.

If the BPath isn't initialized, the functions return pointers to NULL.

SetTo(), Unset()

> status_t **SetTo**(const char *path*,
>   const char **leaf* = NULL,
>   bool *normalize* = false)

> status_t **SetTo**(const BDirectory *dir*,
>   const char **leaf* = NULL,
>   bool *normalize* = false)

> void **Unset**(void)

The `SetTo()` function frees the pathname that the object currently holds, and re-initializes the object according to the arguments:

- The first version concatenates the *path* and *leaf* strings (interposing a "/" if necessary). If *path* is relative, the concatenated pathname is appended to the current working directory. Note that you don't have to split your pathname into two parts to call this constructor; the optional *leaf* argument is provided simply as a convenience.

- The second version performs a similar operation using the path of the BDirectory as the initial part of the pathname.

Regarding the *leaf* argument:

- The *leaf* string can contain directories—it needn't be *just* a leaf name.
- However, *leaf* must be a relative pathname (it can't start with "/").

If set to `true`, the *normalize* argument tells the object to normalize the new pathname. By default (`false`), the pathname is normalized only if necessary. Note that the default *doesn't* mean that the object absolutely won't normalize, it just won't do it if it doesn't think it's necessary. See "Initializing and Normalizing" on page 247 for the full story on normalizing a pathname, including the conditions that trigger default normalization.

Storage for the pathname is allocated by the BPath object and is freed when the object is deleted (or when you re-initialize through `SetTo()`). The *path* and *leaf* arguments are copied into the allocated storage.

Other details...

- Destructive setting is safe:

```
/* This works... */
path.SetTo(path.Path(), ...);
```

- Currently, `SetTo()` only checks pathname and filename length if it has to normalize.

`Unset()` frees the object's pathname storage and sets the `InitCheck()` value to `B_NO_INIT`.

Return values:

 `B_NO_ERROR`. Successful initialization.

 `B_BAD_VALUE`. *path* is `NULL`, *leaf* isn't relative (it starts with a "/"), or *dir* is uninitialized.

 `B_BAD_VALUE`. A directory in the path doesn't exist (normalization only).

 `B_NAME_TOO_LONG`. A pathname element is too long (normalization only).

 `B_NO_MEMORY`. Couldn't allocate storage for the pathname.

The return value is also recorded in `InitCheck()`.

BFlattenable Functions

The following functions are implemented in accordance with the rules set down by the BFlattenable class. You never need to invoke these functions directly; they're implemented so a BPath can added to a BMessage (see "Passing a BPath in a BMessage" on page 250). But in case you're interested...

AllowsTypeCode()

> virtual bool **AllowsTypeCode**(type_code *code*) const

Returns `true` if *code* is `B_REF_TYPE`, and `false` otherwise.

Flatten()

> virtual status_t **Flatten**(void **buffer*, ssize_t *size*) const

Converts the object's pathname to an `entry_ref` and writes it into *buffer*. Currently, *size* is ignored.

Return values:
>   `B_NO_ERROR`. Peachy.
>   `B_NAME_TOO_LONG`. The pathname is too long (> 1024 characters).
>   `B_ENTRY_NOT_FOUND`. A directory in the path doesn't exist.

FlattenedSize()

> virtual ssize_t **FlattenedSize**() const

Returns the size of the `entry_ref` that represents the flattened pathname.

IsFixedSize()

> virtual bool **IsFixedSize**() const

Returns `false`.

TypeCode()

> virtual type_code **TypeCode**() const

Returns `B_REF_TYPE`.

Unflatten()

> virtual status_t **Unflatten**(type_code *code*,
>   const void **buffer*,
>   ssize_t *size*)

Initializes the BPath with the flattened `entry_ref` data that's found in *buffer*. The type code must be `B_REF_TYPE`.

Return values:

> `B_NO_ERROR`. Success.
>
> `B_BAD_VALUE`. Wrong type code (not `B_REF_TYPE`).
>
> `B_ENTRY_NOT_FOUND`. A directory in the `entry_ref` data doesn't exist.

The `Unflatten()` return value is recorded in `InitCheck()`.

Operators

= (assignment)

> BPath& operator=(const BPath &*path*)
> BPath& operator=(const char **string*)

Initializes `this` with a copy of the pathname that's gotten from the argument. Also sets `InitCheck()`.

==, != (comparison)

> bool operator==(const BPath &*path*) const
> bool operator==(const char **string*) const

> bool operator!=(const BPath &*path*) const
> bool operator!=(const char **string*) const

Compares `this`'s pathname with the pathname taken from the argument. The comparison is a simple `strcmp()`; neither path is normalized or otherwise altered before the comparison is made. For example:

```
BPath path("/boot/lbj/fido");

chdir("/boot");
printf("Are they equal?  %d\n", path == "lbj/fido");
```

Displays:

```
$ Are they equal? 0
```

BQuery

Derived from:	BEntryList
Declared in:	be/storage/Query.h
Library:	libbe.so

Overview

A *query* is a means of asking the file system for a set of entries that satisfy certain criteria. As examples, you can ask for all the entries with names that start with a certain letter, or that have nodes that are bigger than a certain size, or that were modified within the last *N* days, and so on.

The BQuery class lets you create objects that represent specific queries. To use a BQuery you have to follow these steps:

1. **Initialize**. The first thing you have to do is initialize the object; there are two parts to the initialization: You have to set the volume that you want to query over (`SetVolume()`), and set the query's "criteria formula" (`SetPredicate()`).

2. **Fetch**. After the BQuery has been properly initialized, you invoke `Fetch()`. The function returns immediately while the query executes in the background.

3. **Read**. As soon as `Fetch()` returns, you can start reading the list of winning entries by making iterative calls to the entry-list functions `GetNextRef()`, `GetNextEntry()`, and `GetNextDirents()`. If you ask for entries faster than the query can deliver them, your `GetNext...()` call will block until the next entry arrives. The function returns an error when there are no more entries to retrieve.

The set of entries that the `GetNext...()` calls retrieve (for a given fetch) are called the query's "static" entries. This distinction will become useful when we speak of "live" queries, below.

Reusing your BQuery

Want to go around again? You can, but first you have to clear the object:

• Between each "fetching session," you have to invoke `Clear()` on your BQuery object.

Clearing erases the object's predicate, volume, target (which we'll get to later), and list of static entries—in other words, clearing gets you back to a fresh BQuery object.

And speaking of going around again, be aware that the `Rewind()` function, which BQuery inherits from BEntryList, is implemented to be a no-op: **You can't rewind a BQuery's list of static entries**. After you've performed a fetch, you should read the entry list as quickly as possible and get on with things; you can't turn back or start over.

`CountEntries()` **is also a no-op**. This function is also defined by BEntryList. It doesn't apply to BQueries.

Live Queries

A live query is the gift that keeps on giving. After you tell a live query to fetch, you walk through the entry list (as described above), and then you wait for "query update" messages to be sent to your "target." A query update message describes a single entry that has changed so that...

- it now satisfies the predicate (where it didn't use to), or
- it no longer satisfies the predicate (where it did before).

Not every BQuery is live; you have to tell it you want it to be live. To do this, all you have to do is set the object's target, through the `SetTarget()` function. The target is a BMessenger that identifies a BHandler/BLooper pair (as described in the `SetTarget()` function). Also:

- **Live query notifications stop when you `Clear()` or destroy the BQuery object.**

Another important point regarding live queries is that you can start receiving updates *before* you're done looking at all the static entries (in other words, before you've reached the end of the `GetNext...()` loop). It's possible that your target could receive an "entry dropped out" update before you retrieve the entry through a `GetNext...()` call. If you're using live queries, you should take care in synchronizing the `GetNext...()` iteration with the target's message processing.

We'll look at the format of the update message in a moment; first, let's fill in some gaps.

The Predicate, Attributes, and Indices

A BQuery's predicate is a logical expression that evaluates to true or false. The "atoms" of the expression are comparisons in the form:

attribute op value

where *attribute* is the name of an existing indexed attribute, *op* is a constant that represents a comparison operation (==, <, >, etc), and *value* is the value that you want to compare the attribute to.

Attributes

As mentioned above, the attribute part of a query is a name. When you tell the query to fetch, the file system looks for all nodes that have an attribute with that name and then compares the attribute's value to the appropriate value in the predicate. However:

- **You can only use attributes that are indexed.**
- **The query mechanism only knows about attributes that were written *after* the index (for that attribute) was created.**

To index an attribute, you call the `fs_create_index()` function. Unfortunately, there's currently no way to retroactively include existing attributes in a newly created index. (Such a utility would be simple enough to write, but it would take a long time to execute since it would have to look at every file in the file system.)

Only string and numeric attributes can be queried. Although an attribute can hold any type of data (it's stored as raw bytes), the query mechanism can only perform string and numeric comparisons.

On the bright side, every file gets three attributes for free:

- "name" is the name of the entry.

- "size" is the size of the data portion of the entry's node. The size is a 64-bit integer, and doesn't include the node's attributes.

- "last_modified" is the time the entry's node was last modified (data and attributes), measured in seconds since January 1, 1970. The modification time is recorded as a 32-bit integer.

Technically, "name", "size", and "last_modified" aren't actually attributes—you can't get them through `BNode::ReadAttr()`, for example. But they're always eligible as the attribute component in a query.

Values

The *value* part of the "*attribute op value*" equation is any expression that can be evaluated at the time the predicate is set. Once evaluated, the value doesn't change. For example, you can't specify another attribute as the value component in hopes of comparing, file by file, the value of one attribute to the value of another. The value is just data. And data is data.

The type of the value should match the type of the attribute: You compare string attributes to strings; numeric attributes to numbers. You aren't prevented from comparing a string to a number (for example), but it may not give you the result you expect.

Constructing a Predicate

There are two ways to construct a predicate:

- You can set the predicate formula as a string through `SetPredicate()`, or

- You can construct the predicate by "pushing" the components in Reverse Polish Notation (or "postfix") order through the `PushAttr()`, `PushValue()`, and `PushOp()` functions. There are seven value-pushing functions that push specific types: string, int32, uint32, int64, uint64, float, and double.

You can't combine the methods: Pushing the predicate *always* takes precedence over `SetPredicate()`, regardless of the order in which the methods are deployed.

SetPredicate() features:

- Comparison operators: = < > <= >= !=
- Logical operators: | | &&
- Negation operator: !
- Grouping: ()
- String (value) wildcard: * (prefix and/or postfix only)
- String (value) quoting: ' '

The following are all legitimate strings that you can pass to `SetPredicate()`:

    size < 500

    (name = fido) | | (size >= 500)

    (! ((name = *id*) | | ('final utterance' = 'pass the salt'))) && (last_modified > 1024563)

Push features:

- The `PushOp()` function takes operator symbols, such as `B_EQ` (equals), `B_GT` (greater than), `B_LT` (less than), and so on. The complete list is given in the `PushOp()` function description.

- Value strings passed as arguments to `PushString()` are naturally quoted, so you don't have to single-quote to embed spaces or other odd characters.

- The "*" wildcard is allowed, or you can use special "contains", "begins with", and "ends with" operators.

In Reverse Polish Notation, the operator is postfixed. You then push the components from left to right. For example, this:

    size < 500

becomes:

    size 500 <

The push sequence is:

```
query.PushAttr("size");
query.PushInt32(500);
query.PushOp(B_LT);
```

Another example; this:

    (name = fido) | | (size >= 500)

becomes:

    (name fido =) (size 500 >=) | |

In code:

```
query.PushAttr("name");
query.PushString("fido");
query.PushOp(B_EQ);
query.PushAttr("size");
query.PushInt32(500);
query.PushOp(B_GE);
query.PushOp(B_OR);
```

There are no grouping operators in this notation; they're not needed—grouping is implied by the order in which the components are pushed.

When you're performing a numeric comparison, the `Push...()` function that you choose doesn't have to exactly match the natural type of the attribute, but you can't mix integers and floating point. For example, even though "size" is a 64 bit value, you can compare it to an int32:

```
query.PushAttr("size");
query.PushInt32(2000);
query.PushOp(B_GE);
```

But you can't (or shouldn't) compare it to a float:

```
query.PushAttr("size");
query.PushInt32(2000);
query.PushOp(B_GE);
```

Query Update Messages

The BMessages that are delivered by a live query have a **what** field of `B_QUERY_UPDATE`. The rest of the message depends on what happened:

- If the update is telling you that an entry has passed the predicate, the message's "opcode" field will be `B_ENTRY_CREATED`.

- If the update is telling you that an entry has been eliminated from the query, the "opcode" field will be `B_ENTRY_REMOVED`.

Note that the format of the messages that a live query generates are the same as the similarly-opcoded Node Monitor messages. The only difference is the **what** field (the what for Node Monitor messages is `B_NODE_MONITOR`).

Entry Created

The `B_ENTRY_CREATED` opcode means an entry has changed so that it now passes the query's predicate. The message's fields are:

Field	Type code	Description
"opcode"	B_INT32_TYPE	B_ENTRY_CREATED
"name"	B_STRING_TYPE	The name of the new entry.

Field	Type code	Description
"directory"	B_INT64_TYPE	The ino_t (node) number for the directory in which the entry was created.
"device"	B_INT32_TYPE	The dev_t number of the device on which the new entry resides.
"node"	B_INT64_TYPE	The ino_t number of the new entry itself. (More accurately, it identifies the node that corresponds to the entry.)

If you want to cache a reference to the entry, notice that you can create an entry_ref and a node_ref with the data in the message's fields:

```
/* Create an entry_ref */
entry_ref ref;
const char *name;
...
msg->FindInt32("device", &ref.device);
msg->FindInt64("directory", &ref.directory);
msg->FindString("name", &name);
ref.set_name(name);

/* Create a node_ref */
node_ref nref;
status_t err;

...
msg->FindInt32("device", &nref.device);
msg->FindInt64("node", &nref.node);
```

The node_ref is handy because you may want to start monitoring the node (through a call to the Node Monitor). We'll get back to this point when discussing B_ENTRY_REMOVED messages.

Entry Removed

The B_ENTRY_REMOVED opcode means an entry used to pass the predicate, but something has changed (in the entry or the entry's node) so that now it doesn't.

Field	Type code	Description
"opcode"	B_INT32_TYPE	B_ENTRY_REMOVED
"directory"	B_INT64_TYPE	The ino_t (node) number of the directory from which the entry was removed.
"device"	B_INT32_TYPE	The dev_t number of the device that the removed node used to live on.
"node"	B_INT64_TYPE	The ino_t number of the node that was removed.

Notice that the B_ENTRY_REMOVED message doesn't tell you the name of the entry. This is an unfortunate oversight that will be corrected. In the meantime, if you need to match the node in this message to an entry from a previous B_ENTRY_CREATED (or that you got from a `GetNext...()` invocation), you have to keep track of the entry/node yourself. However, the location of the entry that "contains" the node may have changed since the time that the entry passed the predicate. Follow this outline:

1. You set up a live query that asks for entries that have nodes larger than 500 bytes.

2. The query mechanism tells you (either in the static set or through a `B_ENTRY_CREATED` message) that "/boot/home/fido/data" satisfies the predicate.

3. You create an `entry_ref` and a `node_ref` to the entry, and cache them away somewhere.

4. *The user then renames or moves the entry.* The query mechanism doesn't tell you about this change—it only cares about the size of the node, not its name

5. You get a `B_ENTRY_REMOVED` message. You create a `node_ref` from the message and match it to your cache—and get an out-of-date `entry_ref`.

To get around the lack of a "name" field, you should monitor the nodes that you receive in your initial `GetNext...()` calls and `B_ENTRY_CREATED` messages.

Constructor and Destructor

BQuery()

BQuery(void)

Creates a new BQuery object. To use the object, you have to set its predicate and volume, and then tell it to `Fetch()`. If you want to fetch again, you have to call `Clear()` first (and reset the predicate and volume.)

~BQuery()

virtual ~BQuery(void)

Destroys the BQuery. If the query is live, the query is shot dead. You stop receiving live query updates when you delete the BQuery object.

Member Functions

Clear()

status_t **Clear**(void)

Erases the BQuery's predicate, sets the volume and target to `NULL`, and turns off live query updates (if the query is live). You call `Clear()` if you want to `Fetch()` more than once: You have to `Clear()` before each `Fetch()` (except the first).

Return values:

Clear() always return B_NO_ERROR.

CountEntries(), Rewind()

WARNING

Don't use these functions. They're no-ops for the BQuery class.

Fetch()

status_t **Fetch**(void)

Tells the BQuery to go fetch the entries that satisfy the predicate. After you've fetched, you can retrieve the set of "static" entries through calls to GetNextEntry(), GetNextRef(), or GetNextDirents().

If you've set the BQuery's target, then this query is live. The live query update messages start rolling in when you tell the object to Fetch(). They stop when you Clear() or destroy the object.

The fetch fails if the object's predicate or volume isn't set, or if you've already fetched but haven't Clear()'d since then.

Return values:

B_NO_ERROR. The fetch is running.

B_NO_INIT. The volume or predicate isn't set.

B_BAD_VALUE. The predicate is improper.

B_NOT_ALLOWED. You've already fetched; Clear() the object and start again.

GetNextEntry(), GetNextRef(), GetNextDirents()

virtual status_t **GetNextEntry**(BEntry *entry*, bool *traverse* = false)

virtual status_t **GetNextRef**(entry_ref *ref*)

virtual int32 **GetNextDirents**(dirent *buf*,
    size_t *bufsize*,
    int32 *count* = INT_MAX)

These functions return the next entry in the "static" entry list. You can retrieve the entry as a BEntry, entry_ref, or dirent structure. The static entry list is the set of entries that initially satisfy the predicate; entries found by the live query mechanism are not included in this list.

When you reach the end of the entry list, the `Get...()` function returns an indicative value:

- `GetNextRef()` and `GetNextEntry()` return `B_ENTRY_NOT_FOUND`.
- `GetNextDirents()` returns 0.

You can only cycle over the list once; the `Rewind()` function is not defined for BQuery. See the BEntryList class for more information on these functions.

Return values:

> `GetNextDirents()` returns the number of `dirents` it retrieved (currently, it can only retrieve one at a time). The other two functions return these codes:
> `B_NO_ERROR`. The entry was retrieved.
> `B_ENTRY_NOT_FOUND`. You're at the end of the list.

GetPredicate()   *see SetPredicate()*

IsLive()   *see SetTarget()*

PredicateLength()   *see SetPredicate()*

PushAttr(), PushOp(), PushUInt32(), PushInt32(), PushUInt64(), PushInt64(), PushFloat(), PushDouble(), PushString(), query_op

> void **PushAttr**(const char *attr_name*)
>
> void **PushOp**(query_op *operator*)
>
> void **PushUInt32**(uint32 *value*)
> void **PushInt32**(int32 *value*)
> void **PushUInt64**(uint64 *value*)
> void **PushInt64**(int64 *value*)
> void **PushFloat**(float *value*)
> void **PushDouble**(double *value*)
> void **PushString**(const char *string*, bool *case_insensitive* = false)

You use these functions to construct the BQuery's predicate. They create a predicate expression by pushing attribute names, operators, and values in Reverse Polish Notation (post-fix) order.

- `PushAttr()` pushes an attribute name.
- `PushOp()` pushes one of the `query_op` operators listed below.
- The rest of the functions push values of the designated types.

For details on how the push method works, see "Constructing a Predicate."

The predicate that you construct through these functions can be returned as a string through the `GetPredicate()` function.

The `query_op` constants are:

Constant	Operation
B_EQ	=
B_NE	!=
B_GT	>
B_LT	<
B_GE	>=
B_LE	<=
B_CONTAINS	string contains value ("*value*")
B_BEGINS_WITH	string begins with value ("value*")
B_ENDS_WITH	string ends with value ("*value")
B_AND	&&
B_OR	||
B_NOT	!

Rewind(), CountEntries()

WARNING

Don't use these functions. They're no-ops for the BQuery class.

SetTarget(), IsLive()

status_t **SetTarget**(BMessenger *target*)

bool **IsLive**(void) const

Sets the BQuery's target. The target identifies the BLooper/BHandler pair (*a la* the BInvoker target protocol) that will receive subsequent live query update messages. Calling this function declares the query to be live.

If *target* is NULL, the BQuery is told to be "not live". However, you can only turn off liveness (in this way) before you `Fetch()`. In other words, if you set the target, and then call `Fetch()` and *then* call `SetTarget(NULL)`, the BQuery will think that it (itself) is not live, but it really is.

`IsLive()` tells you if the BQuery is live. The "liveness" needn't be actuated yet—live queries don't start operating until you tell the BQuery to `Fetch()`. The live query is killed when you delete or `Clear()` the BQuery object.

Return values:
   B_NO_ERROR. The target was set (including set to NULL).
   B_BAD_VALUE. *target* doesn't identify a proper looper/handler pair.
   B_NOT_ALLOWED. You've already `Fetch()`'d; you need to `Clear()`.

SetVolume()

status_t **SetVolume**(const BVolume *volume*)

A query can only look in one volume at a time. This is where you set the volume that you want to look at.

Return values:
B_NO_ERROR. The volume was set.
B_NOT_ALLOWED. You've already fetched, you need to Clear() before you can reset the volume.

WARNING

Currently, SetVolume() doesn't complain if *volume* is invalid. However, the subsequent Fetch() will fail (B_NO_INIT).

SetPredicate(), GetPredicate(), PredicateLength()

status_t **SetPredicate**(const char *expr*)

status_t **GetPredicate**(char *buf*, size_t *length*)

size_t **PredicateLength**(void)

SetPredicate() sets the BQuery's predicate as a string. Predicate strings can be simple, single comparison expressions:

```
"name = fido"
```

Or they can be more complex:

```
"((name = fid*) || (size > 500)) && (last_modified < 243567)"
```

For the complete rules on setting the predicate as a string, see "Constructing a Predicate."

You can also set the predicate through the Push...() functions. You can't combine the methods: Pushing the predicate *always* takes precedence over SetPredicate(), regardless of the order in which the methods are deployed.

GetPredicate() copies the predicate into *buf*; *length* gives the length of *buf*, in bytes. If you want to find out how much storage you need to allocate to accommodate the predicate, call PredicateLength() first.

If you set the predicate through the Push...() functions, GetPredicate() converts the pushed construction into a string, and returns a copy of the string to you.

PredicateLength() returns the length of the predicate string, regardless of how it's created.

WARNING

GetPredicate() and PredicateLength() **both clear the push stack**. This is important, because it means that you can't build up a portion of your predicate, then call `GetPredicate()`, build a little more, look again, build some more, etc. When you call `GetPredicate()`, you're done. Your next step should be a `Fetch()`.

Return values:

B_NO_ERROR. The predicate was successfully set or gotten.

B_NO_INIT. (Get) The predicate isn't set.

B_BAD_VALUE. (Get) *length* is shorter than the predicate's length.

B_NOT_ALLOWED. (Set) You've already `Fetch()`'d; you have to `Clear()`.

B_NO_MEMORY. (Set) Not enough memory to store the predicate string.

BRefFilter

Derived from: (none)

Declared in: be/storage/FilePanel.h

Library: (none)

Overview

The BRefFilter class lets you filter the items that a file panel is about to display. This filtering is performed by the class' only function, `Filter()`. `Filter()` is a hook function; to use a BRefFilter, you have to create a derived class and implement the `Filter()` function.

To assign your BRefFilter object to a file panel, you invoke BFilePanel's `SetRefFilter()` function. (The BFilePanel constructor also lets you set the filter.) If you don't specifically assign a filter, the file panel will not have one—there is no "default" ref filter object. You maintain ownership of the BRefFilter that you assign to a file panel; the file panel doesn't delete or otherwise change your object.

You can assign the same filter to more than one file panel. However, the `Filter()` function isn't told which panel it's being invoked for.

Hook Functions

Filter()
    Look down there.

Member Functions

Filter()

> virtual bool **Filter**(const entry_ref *ref,
>   BNode *node,
>   struct stat *st,
>   const char *filetype)

`Filter()` is a hook function that's invoked whenever the file panel to which it's been assigned reads the entries in its "panel directory." The function is invoked once for each entry in the directory. All the arguments to the function refer to the entry currently under consideration. (Note that the function is never sent an abstract entry, so the *node, st,* and *filetype* arguments will always be valid.)

Your implementation of `Filter()` can use any or all of the arguments to figure out if the entry is a valid candidate for display in the file panel's file list. Simply return `true` or `false` to indicate if the entry is a winner or a loser.

Technically, `Filter()` is invoked when:

- the file panel's panel directory is set, either through the BFilePanel constructor or the `SetPanelDirectory()`, and when

- the file panel's `Refresh()` function is called.

A BRefFilter can be assigned to more than one BFilePanel object (assignation is performed through BFilePanel's constructor or `SetRefFilter()` function). But it's probably not a great idea to do so: At any particular invocation of `Filter()`, the BRefFilter doesn't know which BFilePanel object it's working for.

You maintain ownership of the BRefFilter objects that you create. Assigning a ref filter to a file panel does *not* hand ownership of the BRefFilter to the BFilePanel. You shouldn't delete a BRefFilter while a BFilePanel is still using it; but it's your responsibility to delete it when it's done.

BResources

Derived from: *none*

Declared in: be/storage/Resources.h

Library: libbe.so

Overview

NOTE

You may not want to be here...The BResources class was designed for a specific purpose: To provide a means to bundle application "resources" (icons, in particular) within the application executable itself. If you want to add new resources to your own application (resources that you want to have "stick" to the executable), then you've come to the right place. But you shouldn't use BResources to add data to a regular data file—use attributes instead.

The data that a file contains is either "flat," or it's "structured." To read a flat file, you simply open it (through a BFile object) and start `Read()`'ing. Structured data requires that you understand the structure. Typically, an application understands the structure either because it's a well-known format, or because the application itself wrote the file in the first place.

The BResources class defines a simple design for storing structured data. The structure is a series of "resources," where each resource is key/value pair. A single "resource file" can hold an unlimited number of resources; a single resource within a resource file can contain an unlimited amount of data.

Resources are sort of like attributes in that they store chunks of data that are looked up through the use of a key. But note these differences:

- Resources are stored in the file itself, such that if you copy the file, you copy the resources, as well.

- Resources can't be queried.

- Only plain files can have resources. (In other words, directories and symbolic links can't have resources.)

Initializing a BResources Object

The BResources class provides the means for reading and writing a file's resources, but it doesn't let you access the file directly. Instead, you must initialize the BResources object by passing it a valid BFile object, either in the constructor or the `SetTo()` function. Note the following:

- The BFile that you pass in is copied by the BResources object. Thus, initializing a BResources object opens a new file descriptor into the file. You can delete the "original" BFile immediately after you use it to initialize the BResources object.

- If the BFile that you pass in is open with write permission, the file is automatically locked by the BResources object (the object `Lock()`'s its copy of the BFile that you passed in). It's unlocked when you re-initialize or delete the BResources.

- If you want to write resources, the BFile must *not* be locked when you pass it in. The BResources needs to be able to lock its copy of your object.

- The BFile *must* be open for reading (at least).

- Unfortunately, BResources lacks an `InitCheck()` function. If you want to check initialization errors, you should always initialize through `SetTo()`, rather than through the constructor.

Identifying and Creating Resource Files

You can't use just any old file as a BResources initializer: The file must be an actual resource file. Simply initializing a BResources object with an existing non-resource file will *not* transform the file into a resource file—unless you tell the initializer to clobber the existing file.

For example, this initialization fails:

```
/* "fido" exists, but isn't a resource file. */
BFile file("/boot/home/fido", B_READ_WRITE);
BResources res;
status_t err;

if ((err = res.SetTo(&file)) != B_NO_ERROR)
...
```

And this one succeeds...

```
/* The second arg to SetTo() is the "clobber?" flag. */
if ((err = res.SetTo(&file, true)) != B_NO_ERROR)
...
```

...but at a price: *fido*'s existing data is destroyed (truncated to 0 bytes), and a new "resource header" is written to the file. Having gained a resource header, *fido* can thereafter be used to initialize a BResources object.

Clobber-setting a resource file is possible, but, as mentioned at the top of this class description, you'll probably never create resource files directly yourself.

So where do resource files come from if you don't create them yourself? Step right up...

Executables as Resource Files

The only files that are naturally resource-ful are application executables. For example, here we initialize a BResources object with the *IconWorld* executable:

```
BPath path;
BFile file;
BResources res;

find_directory(B_APPS_DIRECTORY, &path);
path.Append("IconWorld");
```

```
file.SetTo(&path, B_READ_ONLY);

if (res.SetTo(&file) != B_NO_ERROR)
   ...
```

The BResources object is now primed to look at *IconWorld*'s resources. But be aware that an application's "app-like" resources (its icons, signature, app flags) should be accessed through the BAppFileInfo class.

Resource Data

After you've initialized your BResources object, you use the *Fiddle*Resource() functions to examine and manipulate the file's resources:

Generative Functions

- `AddResource()` adds a new resource to the file.
- `RemoveResource()` removes an existing resource from the file.

Data Functions

- `WriteResource()` writes some amount of new data into an existing resource.
- `ReadResource()` reads a range of data from a resource and gives you a copy.
- `FindResource()` returns a pointer to a resource's data.

Info Functions

- `HasResource()` tells you if the file contains a specified resource.
- `GetResourceInfo()` returns information about a resource.

As mentioned earlier, the BFile that you use to initialize a BResources object must be open for reading. If you also want to modify the resources (by adding, removing, or writing) the BFile must also be open for writing.

Identifying a Resource Within a Resource File

A single resource within a resource file is tagged with a data type, an ID, and a name:

- The data type is one of the `type_code` types (`B_INT32_TYPE`, `B_STRING_TYPE`, and so on) that characterize different types of data. The data type that you assign to a resource doesn't restrict the type of data that the resource can contain, it simply serves as a way to label the type of data that you're putting into the resource so you'll know how to cast it when you retrieve it.

- The ID is an arbitrary integer that you invent yourself. It need only be meaningful to the application that uses the resource file.

- The name is optional, but can be useful: You can look up a resource by its name, if it has one.

Taken singly, none of these tags needs to be unique: Any number of resources (within the same file) can have the same data type, ID, or name. It's the *combination* of the data type constant and the ID that uniquely identifies a resource within a file. The name, on the other hand, is more of a convenience; it never needs to be unique when combined with the data type or with the ID.

Data Format

All resource data is assumed to be "raw": If you want to store a NULL-terminated string in a resource, for example, you have to write the NULL as part of the string data, or the application that reads the resource from the resource must apply the NULL itself. Put more generally, the data in a resource doesn't assume any particular structure or format, it's simply a vector of bytes.

Data Ownership

The resource-manipulating functions cause data to be read from or written to the resource file directly and immediately. In other words, the BResources object doesn't create its own "resource cache" that acts as an intermediary between your application and the resource file. This has a couple of implications:

- Resource data that you retrieve from or write to a BResources object belongs to your application. For example, the data that's pointed to by the FindResource() function is allocated by the object for you—it's your responsibility to free the data when you're finished with it. Similarly, the data that you pass to AddResource() (to be added as a resource in the file) must be freed by your application after the function returns.

- The individual changes that you make to the resources are visible to other BResources (that are open on the same file) as soon as they are made. You can't, for example, bundle up a bunch of changes and then "commit" them all at the same time.

Reading and Writing a Resource File as a Plain File

Just because a file is a resource file, that doesn't mean that you're prevented from reading and writing it as a plain file (through the BFile object). For example, it's possible to create a resource file, add some resources to it, and then use a BFile object to seek to the end of the file and write some flat data. But you have to keep track of the "data map" yourself—if you go back and add more resources to the file (or extend the size of the existing ones), your flat data will be overwritten: The BResources object doesn't preserve non-resource data that lives in the file that it's operating on.

Constructor and Destructor

BResources()

> **BResources**(void)
> **BResources**(BFile *file*, bool *clobber* = false)

Creates a new BResources object. You can initialize the object by passing a pointer to a valid BFile; without the argument, the object won't refer to a file until `SetTo()` is called.

If *clobber* is true, the file that's referred to by BFile is truncated (its data is erased), and a new resource file header is written to the file. If *clobber* is false and the file doesn't otherwise have a resource header, the initialization fails.

BResources copies the BFile argument; after the constructor returns, you can, for example, delete the BFile that you passed in.

~BResources()

> virtual **~BResources**(void)

Destroys the BResources object.

Member Functions

AddResource()

> status_t **AddResource**(type_code *type*,
>   int32 *id,*
>   const void *data,*
>   size_t *length,*
>   const char *name* = NULL)

Adds a new resource to the file. For this function to have an effect, the file must be open for writing. The arguments are:

- *type* is one of the `type_code` constants defined in *be/support/TypeConstants.h*.

- *id* is the ID number that you want to assign to the resource. The value of the ID has no meaning other than that which your application gives it; the only restriction on the ID is that the combination of it and the data type constant must be unique across all resources in this resource file.

- *data* is a pointer to the data that you want the resource to hold.

- *length* is the length of the *data* buffer, in bytes.

- *name* is optional, and needn't be unique. Or even interesting.

Ownership of the *data* pointer isn't assigned to the BResources object by this function; after `AddResource()` returns, your application can free or otherwise manipulate the buffer that *data* points to without affecting the data that was written to the file.

Return values:

B_NO_ERROR. The resource was successfully added.

B_ERROR. The file isn't open for writing, the resource already exists, or the resource couldn't otherwise be written.

WARNING

Currently, `AddResource()` *will* write over an existing resource. In this case, the function returns a positive integer (specifically, it returns the number of bytes that it just wrote), but it *doesn't* change the name of the resource. To work around this bug, you should call `RemoveResource()` just before calling `AddResource()`.

FindResource()

void *FindResource(type_code *type,*
                   int32 *id,*
                   size_t **length*)

void *FindResource(type_code *type,*
                   const char **name,*
                   size_t **length*)

Finds the resource identified by the first two arguments, and returns a pointer to a copy of the resource's data. The size of the data, in bytes, is returned by reference in **length*.

It's the caller's responsibility to free the pointer that's returned by this function.

If the first two arguments don't identify an existing resource, NULL is returned.

GetResourceInfo()

bool **GetResourceInfo**(int32 *byIndex,*
                        type_code **typeFound,*
                        int32 **idFound,*
                        char ***nameFound,*
                        size_t **lengthFound*)

bool **GetResourceInfo**(type_code *byType,*
                        long *andIndex,*
                        int32 **idFound,*

```
                char **nameFound,
                size_t *lengthFound)
```

bool **GetResourceInfo**(type_code *byType*,
                long *andId*,
                char **nameFound*,
                size_t *lengthFound*)

bool **GetResourceInfo**(type_code *byType*,
                char *andName*,
                int32 *idFound*,
                size_t *lengthFound*)

These functions return information about a specific resource, as identified by the first one or two arguments:

- The first version (*byIndex*) searches for the *byIndex*'th resource in the file.
- The second (*byType*/*andIndex*) searches for the *byIndex*'th resource that has the given type.
- The third (*byType*/*andId*) looks for the resource with the unique combination of type and ID.
- The third (*byType*/*andName*) looks for the first resource that has the given type and name.

The other arguments return the other statistics about the resource (if found).

The pointer that's returned in *foundName* belongs to the BResources. Don't free it.

The functions return **true** if a resource was found, and **false** otherwise.

HasResource()

bool **HasResource**(type_code *type*, int32 *id*)

bool **HasResource**(const char *name*, type_code *type*)

Returns **true** if the resource file contains a resource as identified by the arguments, otherwise it returns **false**.

Keep in mind that there may be more than one resource in the file with the same *name* and *type* combination. The *type* and *id* combo, on the other hand, is unique. See "Identifying a Resource Within a Resource File."

ReadResource()

status_t **ReadResource**(type_code *type*,
                  int32 *id,*
                  void **data,*
                  off_t *offset,*
                  size_t *length*)

Reads data from an existing resource (identified by *type* and *id*) and copies it into the *data* buffer. *offset* gives the location (measured in bytes from the start of the resource data) from which the read commences, and *length* is the number of bytes you want to read. The *data* buffer must already be allocated and should be at least *length* bytes long.

You can ask for more data than the resource contains; in this case, the buffer is filled with as much resource data as exists (or from *offset* to the end of the resource). However, note that the function *doesn't* tell you how much data it actually read.

Return values:
B_NO_ERROR. The resource was found and read.
B_ERROR. The resource wasn't found.

RemoveResource()

status_t **RemoveResource**(type_code *type*, int32 *id*)

Removes the resource identified by the arguments. See "Identifying a Resource Within a Resource File."

Return values:
B_NO_ERROR. The resource was removed.
B_ERROR. The resource wasn't found, or the file isn't open for writing.

SetTo()

status_t **SetTo**(BFile **file*)

Unlocks and closes the object's previous BFile, and re-initializes it to refer to a copy of the argument. If the new BFile is open for writing, the BResources' copy of the BFile is locked.

Return values:
B_NO_ERROR. The resource was removed.
B_BAD_VALUE. The argument BFile is invalid (uninitialized).
B_ERROR. The BResources couldn't be initialized (for whatever reason).

WriteResource()

status_t **WriteResource**(type_code *type*,
                    int32 *id*,
                    void **data*,
                    off_t *offset*,
                    size_t *length*)

Writes data into an existing resource, possibly overwriting the data that the resource currently contains.

- The *type* and *id* arguments identify the target resource; this resource must already be present in the file—`WriteResource()` doesn't create a new resource if the *type/id* combination fails to identify a winner. See "Identifying a Resource Within a Resource File."

- *data* is a pointer to the new data that you want to place in the resource.

- *length* is the length of the data buffer.

- *offset* gives the location at which you want the new data to be written; the offset is taken as the number of bytes from the beginning of the existing resource data.

If the new data is placed such that it exceeds the size of the current resource data, the resource grows to accommodate the new data.

You can't use this function to "shrink" a resource. To remove a portion of data from a resource, you have to remove the resource and then re-add it.

Return values:
    B_NO_ERROR. The resource was written.
    B_ERROR. The resource wasn't found, or the file isn't open for writing.

BStatable

Derived from: *none*

Declared in: be/storage/Statable.h

Library: libbe.so

Overview

BStatable is a pure abstract class that provides functionality for its two derived classes, BEntry and BNode. The BStatable functions let you get and set "statistical" information about a node in the file system. You can:

- Determine whether the node is a file, directory, or symbolic link.
- Get and set a node's owner, group, and permissions.

- Get and set the node's creation, modification, and access times.
- Get the size of the node's data (*not* counting attributes).
- Get a BVolume object for the node's volume.
- Get the node_ref of the node (and pass it to watch_node(), most likely).

Nodes and Entries

Technically, BStatable information pertains to *nodes*, not *entries*. The fact that BEntry implements the BStatable functions is a (slightly confusing) convenience: When you invoke a BStatable function on a BEntry object, what you're really doing is asking for information about the node that corresponds to the object.

Abstract Entries

As explained in BEntry, it's possible to create "abstract" BEntry objects; in other words, objects that don't correspond to actual files (nodes) on the disk. You can't get (or set) BStatable information for abstract entries. The BStatable functions return B_BAD_VALUE if the invoked-upon entry is abstract.

Relationship to stat()

The BStatable functions are covers for the POSIX stat() call. stat() retrieves a file-specific stat structure, which records the statistics listed above (and then some). Although BStatable was designed to hide stat details, you *can* get the stat structure through the GetStat() function. The stat structure is described in "The stat Structure" at the end of this specification.

stat() is notorious for being expensive. Furthermore, the stat structure is stale as soon as it gets back from the stat() call. If you're concerned with efficiency, be aware that *every* BStatable function (the "setters" as well as the "getters") performs a stat(). For example, calling GetOwner() and then GetGroup() results in two stat() calls. If you want to look at lot of fields (within the same stat structure) all at once, you might consider using BStatable's GetStat() function.

As for integrity, BStatable info-getting functions are obviously in the same boat as the stat() call itself: The retrieved data isn't guaranteed to be in sync with the actual state of the stat()'d item.

The BDirectory class also defines a stat-retrieving function that, in some cases, can be more efficient than the GetStat() function defined here:

- The BDirectory::GetStatFor() function retrieves the stat structure for the node of a named entry within a directory. If you're interested in getting stat information for a series of nodes within the same directory, you should use this function. You have to call it iteratively (once for each named entry), but the accumulation of the iterated calls will be faster than the `GetStat()` calls made on the analogous BEntry objects.

Accessing Unreadable and Unwritable Entries

BStatable isn't thwarted by file permissions: If you can construct a valid BEntry or BNode to an item, then you can invoke any of the info-getting BStatable functions on that object:

- The BStatable functions aren't denied even if the node that you're looking at is read-protected. However, you can only invoke the info-setting functions if the node allows writing.

- Similarly, you can get `stat` info for a locked node, but you won't be able to write the info (through functions such as `SetOwner()`) unless your object holds the lock. See BNode for more on locking.

Other Details

You rarely set `stat` information. In practice, you rarely use BStatable's info-setting functions. Setting information such as when a file was created, who owns it, or how big it is, is the responsibility of the system and the privilege of the user. For example, when you `Write()` to a BFile object, the system automatically updates the size and modification date for the file.

Member Functions

GetAccessTime()   *see GetCreationTime()*

GetCreationTime(), SetCreationTime(), GetModificationTime(), SetModificationTime(), GetAccessTime(), SetAccessTime()

```
status_t GetCreationTime(time_t *ctime) const
status_t SetCreationTime(time_t ctime)

status_t GetModificationTime(time_t *mtime) const
status_t SetModificationTime(time_t mtime)

status_t GetAccessTime(time_t *atime) const
status_t SetAccessTime(time_t atime)
```

WARNING

Access time is currently unused.

These functions let you get and set the time at which the item was created, last modified, and last accessed (opened). The measure of time is given as seconds since (the beginning of) January 1, 1970.

NOTE

The time quanta that `stat` uses is *seconds*; the rest of the BeOS measures time in *microseconds* (`bigtime_t`).

Return values:
- B_NO_ERROR. Success.
- B_NOT_ALLOWED. You tried to set a time field for a file on a read-only volume.
- B_NO_MEMORY. Couldn't get the necessary resources to complete the transaction.
- B_BAD_VALUE. The node doesn't exist (abstract entry).

GetGroup()   *see GetOwner()*

GetNodeRef()

status_t **GetNodeRef**(node_ref *nref*) const

Copies the item's `node_ref` structure into the *nref* argument, which must be allocated.

Typically, you use an node's `node_ref` as a key to the Node Monitor by passing the `node_ref` structure to the `watch_node()` function. The Node Monitor watches the node for specific changes; see "The Node Monitor" section of this chapter for details.

As a convenience, you can use a `node_ref` structure to initialize a BDirectory object (through the constructor or `BDirectory::SetTo()` function).

Return values:
- B_NO_ERROR. Success.
- B_NO_MEMORY. Couldn't get the necessary resources to complete the transaction.
- B_BAD_VALUE. The node doesn't exist (abstract entry).

GetModificationTime()   *see GetCreationTime()*

GetOwner(), SetOwner(), GetGroup(), SetGroup(), GetPermissions(), SetPermissions()

status_t **GetOwner**(uid_t *owner*) const
status_t **SetOwner**(uid_t *owner*)

status_t **GetGroup**(gid_t *group*) const
status_t **SetGroup**(gid_t *group*)

status_t **GetPermissions**(mode_t *perms*) const
status_t **SetPermissions**(mode_t *perms*)

These functions set and get the owner, group, and read/write/execute permissions for the node:

- The *owner* identifier encodes the identity of the user that "owns" the file.
- The *group* identifier encodes the "group" that is permitted group access to the file (as declared by the permissions).
- The *permissions* value records nine "permission facts": Whether the file can be read, written, and executed by the node's owner, by users in the node's group, and by everybody else (read/write/execute * owner/group/others = 9 items).

The uid_t, gid_t, and mode_t types used here are standard POSIX types. All three are 32-bit unsigned integers and are defined in *posix/sys/types.h*.

The *owner* and *group* encodings must match values found in the system's user and group files (which are as currently unimplemented).

The *permissions* value is a combination of the following bitfield constants (defined in *posix/sys/stat.h*):

- S_IRUSR owner's read bit.
- S_IWUSR owner's write bit.
- S_IXUSR owner's execute bit.
- S_IRGRP group's read bit.
- S_IWGRP group's write bit.
- S_IXGRP group's execute bit.
- S_IROTH others' read bit.
- S_IWOTH others' write bit.
- S_IXOTH others' execute bit.

For example:

```
/* Is a file readable by everybody? */
mode_t perms;
if (node.GetPermissions(&perms) < B_NO_ERROR)
   /* handle the error... */

if (perms & S_ISROTH)
   // Yes it is
else
   // No it isn't
```

Return values:

B_NO_ERROR. Success.

B_NOT_ALLOWED. You tried to set permissions on a read-only volume.

B_BAD_VALUE. The node doesn't exist (abstract entry).

GetPermissions()   *see GetOwner()*

GetSize()

status_t **GetSize**(off_t *size*) const

Sets the size of the node's data portion (in bytes). Only the "used" portions of the node's file blocks are counted; the amount of storage the node actually requires (i.e., the number of blocks the node consumes) may be larger than the size given here.

The size measurement *doesn't* include the node's attributes.

Return values:
   B_NO_ERROR. Success.
   B_NO_MEMORY. Couldn't get the necessary resources to complete the transaction.
   B_BAD_VALUE. The node doesn't exist (abstract entry).

GetStat()

virtual status_t **GetStat**(struct stat *st*) const

GetStat() returns the stat structure for the node. The structure is copied into the *st* argument, which must be allocated. The stat structure is described in "The stat Structure", below. The BStatable object does *not* cache the stat structure; every time you call GetStat(), fresh stat information is retrieved.

Return values:
   B_NO_ERROR. Success.
   B_NO_MEMORY. Couldn't get the necessary resources to complete the transaction.
   B_BAD_VALUE. The node doesn't exist (abstract entry).

SetAccessTime()   *see GetCreationTime()*

SetCreationTime()   *see GetCreationTime()*

SetGroup()   *see GetOwner()*

SetModificationTime()   *see GetCreationTime()*

SetOwner()   *see GetOwner()*

SetPermissions()   *see GetOwner()*

The stat Structure

Declared in: posix/sys/stat.h

The stat structure looks like this:

```
struct stat {
    dev_t st_dev;
    ino_t st_ino;
    mode_tst_mode;
    nlink_tst_nlink;
    uid_t st_uid;
    gid_t st_gid;
    off_t st_size;
    dev_t st_rdev;
    size_tst_blksize;
    time_tst_atime;
    time_tst_mtime;
    time_tst_ctime;
} stat;
```

And the fields are:

- `st_dev` identifies the node's device.
- `st_ino` is the node's "inode" number.

By combining `st_dev` and `st_ino` you can roll your own `node_ref`:

```
node_ref nref;
stat st;

if (file.GetStat(&st) == B_NO_ERROR) {
   nref.dev = st.st_dev;
   nref.node = st.st_ino;
}
```

Meanwhile...

- `st_mode` describes the node's flavor: plain file, directory or symbolic link. To test the field, pass it to the `S_ISREG()`, `S_ISDIR()`, and `S_ISLINK()` boolean macros:

```
if (S_ISREG(st.st_mode))
   /* it's a "regular" file */
   else if (S_ISDIR(st.st_mode))
      /* it's a directory */
      else if (S_ISLINK(st.st_mode))
         /* it's a symbolic link */
```

- `st_nlink` is the number of "hard links" that point to this node.
- `st_uid` and `st_gid` are the user (owner) and group ids that were described in the `GetOwner()` function.
- `st_rdev` is, well, no one really knows. It's provided for System V compatibility (hold your applause), but it's unused.

- **st_blksize** is the "preferred block size" that's used during copying. The **cp** command line program and **BFile::CopyTo()** functions allocate buffers of this size when they're copying the file's data.

- **st_atime**, **st_mtime**, and **st_ctime** are the access, modification, and creation times in seconds since January 1, 1970. Access time (**st_atime**) is currently unused.

BSymLink

Derived from:	BNode
Declared in:	be/storage/SymLink.h
Library:	libbe.so

Overview

A "symbolic link" or *symlink* is a file that "points to" some other entry. The pointed-to (or, better, "linked-to") entry can be a plain file, directory, or another symlink (which links to yet another entry, and so on). Furthermore, the entry can be abstract—you can create a symlink to an entry that doesn't exist.

The data in a symlink is the pathname to the linked-to entry. The pathname can be absolute or relative. If it's relative, the linked-to entry is found by reckoning the pathname of off the directory in which the symlink lives. Relative pathnames can contain "." and ".." components.

The thing to keep in mind, when dealing with symlinks, is that they link to *entries*, not *nodes*. If you link a symlink to an (existing) entry named "/boot/home/fido" and then the user moves *fido* to *rover* (or deletes *fido*), the symlink is not updated. It will still link to "/boot/home/fido".

Furthermore, symlinks that contain relative pathnames have a further "problem": Let's say you create a symlink in */boot/home* that links to "fido". If you move the symlink to some other directory, it will link to the entry named "fido" in the new directory.

The BSymLink class creates objects that know how to read a symlink's data. The class does not create new symlinks; to create a symlink, you use BDirectory's **CreateSymLink()** function.

NOTE

BSymLink objects are no smarter than the symlinks files themselves. For example, BSymLinks can't resolve the fido/rover "problem."

The only really useful BSymLink function is `ReadLink()`. This function returns the data that the symlink contains. The other functions are convenient, but they're not essential.

Initialization and File Descriptors

When you initialize a BSymLink object, you pass in a pathname or `entry_ref` (or whatever) that refers to an existing symlink. The BSymLink object then represents that symlink—it doesn't represent the (node of the) linked-to entry. Furthermore, you can't ask a BSymLink to "resolve itself"—it can't pass you back a BEntry object that represents the linked-to entry.

If you want the BEntry of the linked-to entry, simply initialize a BEntry object with the ref (or whatever) to the symlink and tell it to traverse (set the trailing argument to `true`).

For example, in the following code, `link` is a BSymLink to the symlink "/boot/home/fidoLink" and `entry` is a BEntry to the entry that the symlink links-to:

```
BSymLink link("/boot/home/fidoLink");
BEntry entry("/boot/home/fidoLink", true);
```

Like all nodes, BSymLink allocates a file descriptor. Remember, this is a file descriptor that's open on the symlink node itself, not the (node of the) linked-to entry.

Constructor and Destructor

BSymLink()

>BSymLink(void)
>BSymLink(const BSymLink &*link*)
>
>BSymLink(const entry_ref **ref*)
>BSymLink(const BEntry **entry*)
>BSymLink(const char **path*)
>BSymLink(BDirectory **dir*, const char **path*)

Creates a new BSymLink object, initializes it according to the arguments, and sets `InitCheck()` to return the status of the initialization.

- The default constructor does nothing and sets `InitCheck()` to `B_NO_INIT`. To initialize the object, call `SetTo()`.

- The copy constructor creates a new BSymLink that's open on the same node as that of the argument.

- For information on the other constructors, see the analogous `SetTo()` functions in the BNode class; BSymLink inherits them without change.

~BSymLink()

virtual ~BSymLink()

Closes the object's file descriptor and destroys the object.

Member Functions

IsAbsolute()

bool **IsAbsolute**(void)

Returns true if the symlink contains an absolute pathname.

MakeLinkedPath()

ssize_t **MakeLinkedPath**(BDirectory *dir*, BPath *path*) const

ssize_t **MakeLinkedPath**(const char *dirPath*, BPath *path*) const

This function creates an absolute pathname to the linked-to entry and returns it as a BPath object. For this to work you have to tell the object which directory you want to reckon off of (in case the symlink specifies a relative path). This should be the directory in which the symlink itself lives.

* Remember—a BSymLink is a node, and nodes don't know what directory they live in. That's why you have to tell it here.

If the symlink contains an absolute path, then the *dir* or *dirPath* arguments are ignored. Nonetheless, they must be supplied.

The function returns the length of the pathname that's set in BPath (or an error).

Return values:
B_FILE_ERROR. The object is uninitialized.
B_BAD_VALUE. The object doesn't refer to a symlink, or *dir/dirPath* is NULL.
B_NAME_TOO_LONG. They concatenated pathname is too long.

ReadLink()

ssize_t **ReadLink**(char *buf*, size_t *length*)

Copies the contents of the symlink into *buf*. *length* is the size of the buffer; to be perfectly safe, the buffer should be B_PATH_NAME_LENGTH characters long. The function returns the number of bytes that were copied (or it returns an error).

The symlink's contents is the pathname (relative or absolute) to the linked-to entry. Note that since the pathname might be relative, ReadLink() can't give you a BPath object. If you want a BPath to the linked-to entry, see MakeLinkedPath().

Return values:
    B_FILE_ERROR. The object is uninitialized.
    B_BAD_VALUE. The object doesn't refer to a symlink.

BVolume

Derived from: *none*

Declared in: be/storage/Volume.h

Library: libbe.so

Overview

The BVolume class lets you ask questions about specific "volumes," where a volume is any independent file system. Most applications are usually only interested in "persistent" volumes, such as hard disks, floppies, or CD-ROMs, but you can also create BVolumes to virtual file systems, such as */pipe*. Here's what a BVolume knows:

• The volume's name, device ID, and "root directory."

• Its storage capacity, and the currently available storage.

• If the volume is on a media that's removable.

• If the volume's storage is persistent (as opposed to the ephemeral storage you get with virtual file systems).

• If the volume is accessed through the network.

• If the file system uses MIME as file types, if it responds to queries, and if it knows about attributes.

Initializing a BVolume

There are two ways to initialize a BVolume:

• You can initialize it directly using a device ID (dev_id) that you pass to the BVolume constructor or SetTo() function. You can get a device ID from the device field of an entry_ref or node_ref structure. This method is useful if you have a file and you want to know which volume it lives on.

• If you want to iterate over all the mounted volumes, you can ask a BVolumeRoster object to get you the "next" volume (BVolumeRoster::GetNextVolume()). You can also ask the BVolumeRoster for the "boot" volume. This is the volume that was used to boot the computer.

Mount and Unmount

A BVolume object can't tell you directly whether the device that it represents is still mounted. If you want to ask, you can call a `status_t`-returning BVolume function; if the function returns `B_BAD_VALUE`, the device is no longer mounted.

Furthermore, you can't ask a BVolume to unmount itself. If you want to be told when devices are mounted and unmounted, you have to ask the Node Monitor to help you. Call `watch_node()` thus:

```
watch_node(NULL, B_WATCH_MOUNT, messenger);
```

messenger is a BMessenger object that acts as the target of subsequent mount and unmount notifications. See "The Node Monitor" section of this chapter for details.

Constructor and Destructor

BVolume()

BVolume(void)

BVolume(dev_id *device*)

BVolume(BVolume &*volume*)

Creates a new BVolume object and initializes it according to the argument. The status of the initialization is recorded by the `InitCheck()` function.

- The default constructor does nothing and sets `InitCheck()` to `B_NO_INIT`.
- The *device* constructor sets the BVolume to point to the volume represented by the argument. See the `SetTo()` function for status codes.
- The copy constructor sets the object to point to the same device as does the argument.

~BVolume

~BVolume(void)

Destroys the BVolume object.

Member Functions

Capacity(), FreeBytes()

off_t **Capacity**(void) const

off_t **FreeBytes**(void) const

Returns the volume's total storage capacity and the amount of storage that's currently unused. Both measurements are in bytes.

Device()

dev_t **Device**(void) const

Returns the object's `dev_t` number.

GetName()

status_t **GetName**(char *buffer) const

Copies the name of the volume into *buffer*.

GetRootDirectory()

status_t **GetRootDirectory**(BDirectory *dir*) const

Initializes dir (which must be allocated) to refer to the volume's "root directory." The root directory stands at the "root" of the volume's file hierarchy. Note that this isn't necessarily the root of the entire file hierarchy.

IsRemovable(), IsReadOnly(), IsPersistent(), IsShared()

bool **IsRemovable**(void) const
bool **IsReadOnly**(void) const
bool **IsPersistent**(void) const
bool **IsShared**(void) const

These functions answer media-related questions about the volume:

- `IsRemovable()`. Can the media be removed?
- `IsReadOnly()`. Can it be read but not written to?
- `IsPersistent()`. Is the storage persistent (such as on a floppy or hard disk)?
- `IsShared()`. Is it accessed through the network (as opposed to being directly connected to this computer)?

KnowsMime(), KnowsQuery(), KnowsAttr()

> bool **KnowsMime**(void) const
> bool **KnowsQuery**(void) const
> bool **KnowsAttr**(void) const

These functions answer questions about the file system on the volume:

- `KnowsMime()`. Does it use MIME to type files?
- `KnowsQuery()`. Can it respond to queries?
- `KnowsAttr()`. Do its files accept attributes?

SetTo(), Unset()

> status_t **SetTo**(dev_t *dev*)

> void **Unset**(void)

`SetTo()` initializes the BVolume object to represent the volume (device) identified by the argument.

`Unset()` uninitializes the BVolume.

Operators

= (assignment)

> BVolume& operator=(const BEntry &*volume*)

In the expression

```
BVolume a = b;
```

BVolume *a* is initialized to refer to the same volume as *b*. To gauge the success of the assignment, you should call `InitCheck()` immediately afterwards. Assigning a BVolume to itself is safe.

Assigning from an uninitialized BVolume is "successful": The assigned-to BVolume will also be uninitialized (`B_NO_INIT`).

==, != (comparison)

> bool operator==(const BVolume &*volume*) const
> bool operator!=(const BVolume &*volume*) const

Two BVolume objects are said to be equal if they refer to the same volume, or if they're both uninitialized.

BVolumeRoster

Derived from: none

Declared in: be/storage/VolumeRoster.h

Library: libbe.so

Overview

The BVolumeRoster class keeps track of the volumes that are mounted in the file system hierarchy. It lets you know about volumes in two ways:

- It lists the volumes that are currently mounted. You can step through the list through iterative calls to the `GetNextVolume()` function.

- It lets you know when new volumes are mounted, and when existing volumes are unmounted. (See `StartWatching()`.)

How you create your BVolumeRoster object depends on what you're going to do with it:

- If you simply want to step through the volume list, then creating a BVolumeRoster on the stack is sufficient.

- However, if you want to watch for volumes being mounted and unmounted, then you *must* keep your BVolumeRoster object around. The watching stops when the object is deleted.

A single BVolumeRoster object can perform both functions: You can use it to step through the volume list at the same time that it's watching volumes.

Constructor and Destructor

BVolumeRoster()

BVolumeRoster(void)

Creates a new BVolumeRoster object. You don't have to "initialize" the object before using it (as you do with most other Storage Kit classes). You can call `GetNextVolume()` (or whatever) immediately after constructing.

~BVolumeRoster()

~BVolumeRoster(void)

Destroys the object. If this BVolumeRoster object was watching volumes, the watch is called off.

Member Functions

GetBootVolume()

> status_t **GetBootVolume**(BVolume *boot_vol)

Initializes *boot_vol* to refer to the "boot volume." This is the volume that was used to boot the computer. *boot_vol* must be allocated before you pass it in. If the boot volume can't be found, the argument is uninitialized.

(Currently, this function looks for the volume that's mounted at */boot*. The only way to fool the system into thinking that there isn't a boot volume is to rename */boot*—not a smart thing to do.)

Return values:
> B_NO_ERROR. The boot volume was successfully retrieved.
> B_ENTRY_NOT_FOUND. The boot volume wasn't found.

GetNextVolume(), Rewind()

> status_t **GetNextVolume**(BVolume *volume)
> void **Rewind**(void)

GetNextVolume() retrieves the "next" volume from the volume list and uses it to initialize the argument (which must be allocated). When the function returns B_BAD_VALUE, you've reached the end of the list.

Rewind() rewinds the volume list such that the next GetNextVolume() will return the first element in the list.

Return values:
> B_NO_ERROR. The next volume was successfully retrieved.
> B_BAD_VALUE. You've reached the end of the volume list.

StartWatching(), StopWatching(), Messenger()

> status_t **StartWatching**(BMessenger *messenger* = be_app_messenger)
> status_t **StopWatching**(void)
> BMessenger **Messenger**(void) const

These functions start and stop the BVolumeRoster's volume-watching facility. (This is actually just a convenient cover for the Node Monitor.)

- StartWatching() registers a request for notifications of volume mounts and unmounts. The notifications are sent (as BMessages) to the BHandler/BLooper pair specified by the argument. There are separate messages for mounting and unmounting; their formats are described below. The caller retains possession of the BHandler/BLooper that the BMessenger represents. The volume watching continues until this BVolumeRoster object is destroyed, or until you call...

- `StopWatching()`. This function tells the volume-watcher to stop watching. In other words, notifications of volume mounts and unmounts are no longer sent to the BVolumeRoster's target.

- `Messenger()` returns a copy of the BMessenger object that was set in the previous `StartWatching()` call.

There are separate notifications (BMessages) for volume-mounted and volume-unmounted events. See the B_DEVICE_MOUNTED and B_DEVICE_UNMOUNTED descriptions in "The Node Monitor" section of this chapter.

Return values:

B_NO_ERROR. The volume-watcher was successfully started or stopped.

B_BAD_VALUE. Poorly formed BMessenger.

B_NO_MEMORY. Couldn't allocate resources.

Global C Functions

The next four sections document the straight C interface to attributes, indices, queries, and file system information. Technically, these functions are part of the Kernel Kit—their definitions live in header files in be/kernel, and their code is in *libroot.so*.

These functions use a global error variable (an integer), called `errno`, to register errors. You can look at the `errno` value directly in your code after a file system function fails. Alternatively, you can use the `errno()` function which prints, to standard error, its argument followed by a system-generated string that describes the current state of `errno`.

- Each thread maintains its own `errno` variable.

- `errno` is only set if there's an error—it never indicates success.

- `errno` is never cleared. If call A fails, then you call B, C, and D, `errno` will still record the error from A.

Attribute C Functions

Declared in: be/kernel/fs_attr.h

Library: libroot.so

Overview

The BeOS supports a powerful system of attributes that can be attached to files. Once these attributes are attached, you can query the file system for attributes whose values match certain specifications; this is discussed in the section on the `fs_query` functions, and in the section on the BQuery class.

Before you can perform these queries, however, you need to attach attributes to the file. There are two ways to do this. The typical mechanism for attaching attributes to files is through the BNode class, which provides a convenient interface for doing this. This section discusses the lower-level way to do this, by calling the C `fs_attr` functions directly.

This collection of functions also lets you look at the attributes attached to a file, get their names and sizes, and read their contents.

The `fs_attr` functions make use of directory pointers (DIR *). While these are true directory pointers, the data they hold aren't useful outside the `fs_attr` API; they're basically magic cookies that represent the file's attribute directory. Likewise, the dirent structures returned by some of these functions are also not useful outside this API.

An Example

Before dropping straight into the reference on the `fs_attr` API, let's have a look at a simple sample of how to use some of its features. The sample code fragment below opens the attribute directory for a file named */boot/home/dirtylaundry* and scans through all the attributes in the file, fetching their names and values.

```
DIR *d;
dirent_t *ent;
attr_info info;
int fd;
char *buffer;

d = fs_open_attr_dir("/boot/home/dirtylaundry");
if (d) {
   while (ent = fs_read_attr_dir(d)) {
   fd = open("/boot/home/dirtylaundry", O_RDONLY);
   fs_stat_attr(fd, ent->d_name, &info);
   buffer = (char *) malloc((size_t) info.size);
   if (buffer)
       fs_read_attr(fd, ent->d_name, info.type, 0, buffer,
               info.size);
   ...
   close(fd);
   fs_close_attr_dir(d);
}
```

This snippet begins by opening the attribute directory for the file, using the `fs_open_attr_dir()` function. If this is successful, it returns a pointer to a directory that contains the list of attributes. A `while` loop is used to read into *ent* each attribute from the attribute directory by calling `fs_read_attr_dir()`. The information this call provides includes the size and type of the attribute, as well as its name.

Once we know the name of the attribute, we can obtain the type and size of the attribute by calling `fs_stat_attr()`; now we have all the information needed to get the value of the attribute. After allocating a buffer to contain the value of the attribute, we pass the attribute's name (ent->d_name), and the type and size (info.type and info.size) into the `fs_read_attr()` function. The value of the attribute is stored in the *buffer* we specify.

This sample skimps a bit on error handling; you'll do better, of course.

Attribute Functions

fs_close_attr_dir

> int **fs_close_attr_dir**(DIR *dirp*)

Closes the specified attribute directory. You should pass into this function the pointer returned when you called `fs_open_attr_dir()` or `fs_fopen_attr_dir()`.

If successful, this function returns 0; otherwise it returns -1 and sets **errno** to a descriptive code.

Errno values:
> B_FILE_ERROR. Invalid directory reference specified.

fs_fopen_attr_dir()   *see fs_open_attr_dir()*

fs_open_attr_dir(), fs_fopen_attr_dir()

> DIR *fs_open_attr_dir**(const char *path*)

> DIR *fs_fopen_attr_dir**(int *fd*)

Opens the attribute directory for the file specified by pathname or file descriptor.

The attribute directory for a file contains a list of the attributes that are attached to the file. Once the attribute directory is open, you can use the `fs_read_attr_dir()` function to find out which attributes are present.

If the directory is opened successfully, a pointer to the directory structure is returned. This pointer should be passed to the other `fs_attr` functions to read entries from the attribute directory, as well as to close the directory when you're finished with it.

If an error occurs while opening the attribute directory, this function returns `NULL` and sets `errno` to one of the values listed below.

Errno values:

B_FILE_ERROR. Invalid file descriptor, or a file error prevented the operation.

B_ENTRY_NOT_FOUND. No matching attribute was found for the specified file.

B_NAME_TOO_LONG. *path* is longer than B_PATH_NAME_LENGTH characters.

B_LINK_LIMIT. A loop was detected in the directory structure.

B_NO_MEMORY. Insufficient memory to complete the operation.

B_BUSY. The specified file is currently in use.

B_NO_MORE_FDS. Too many open files; all file descriptors are in use.

fs_read_attr

ssize_t **fs_read_attr**(int *fd*,
             const char **attribute*,
             uint32 *type*,
             off_t *pos*,
             void **buffer*,
             size_t *count*)

Reads the attribute of the type and name specified by *type* and *attribute* from the file descriptor *fd*. The attribute's data is read starting at the offset *pos* and stored in the *buffer*. *count* specifies the maximum number of bytes to be read.

The *type* can be any of the standard BeOS type definitions, such as B_STRING_TYPE. See the header file *be/support/TypeConstants.h* for a complete list of these types. Note that the type of the attribute is a hint only; there's no reason you can't read a B_STRING_TYPE attribute as an integer (except that the data would probably not make any sense if you did).

If the attribute is read successfully, `fs_read_attr()` returns the actual number of bytes of data read from the attribute into the buffer. If an error occurs, this function returns -1 and sets `errno` to an appropriate value.

Errno values:

B_FILE_ERROR. Invalid file descriptor *fd* specified.

B_ENTRY_NOT_FOUND. No matching attribute was found for the specified file descriptor.

fs_read_attr_dir

> struct dirent *fs_read_attr_dir(DIR *dirp)

Reads the current attribute from the specified attribute directory, and bumps the *dirp* so it points to the next attribute. The *dirp* pointer that you pass to this function should have been retrieved through a previous call to `fs_open_attr_dir()` or `fs_fopen_attr_dir()`.

A pointer to a `dirent` structure is returned. This structure contains information about the attribute. Do not dispose of or alter the data contained by this pointer; it belongs to the operating system.

Once a file's attribute directory has been opened, you can loop over this function to iteratively retrieve the names of all the attributes in the file. An attribute's name is recorded in the `d_name` field of the `dirent` structure; see the example in "An Example" on page 296.

This function *doesn't* let you get the type or value of an attribute. For that, use `fs_stat_attr()`.

If you're looking for files that have a particular value for one or more attributes, however, you should try using the `fs_query` functions, which allow you to more easily establish complex search operations on the values of one or more attributes.

If an error occurs (including reaching the end of the directory), this function returns NULL.

Errno values:

> B_FILE_ERROR. Invalid directory reference specified.
> B_NOT_A_DIRECTORY. The attribute directory is invalid.
> B_ENTRY_NOT_FOUND. You've reached the end of the attribute directory.

fs_remove_attr()

> int fs_remove_attr(int *fd*, const char *attribute)

Deletes the named *attribute* from the file given by the file descriptor *fd*.

If the function is successful, `fs_remove_attr()` returns 0. Otherwise, it returns -1 and sets `errno` to an appropriate value.

Errno values:

> B_FILE_ERROR. *fd* is invalid, or file opened with read-only access.
> B_BAD_VALUE. Invalid attribute name specified.
> B_NOT_ALLOWED. Disk containing the file is read-only.
> B_ENTRY_NOT_FOUND. No matching attribute was found.

fs_rewind_attr_dir()

> int **fs_rewind_attr_dir**(DIR *dirp*)

Rewinds the attribute directory to the beginning. This lets you start over again at the top of a file's attribute directory and read your way down toward the bottom.

Returns a result code specifying whether or not the operation was successful.

NOTE

Unlike most of the other file system C functions, `fs_rewind_attr_dir()` doesn't set `errno`.

Return values:
> B_OK. Success.
> B_FILE_ERROR. Invalid directory reference specified.

fs_stat_attr

> int **fs_stat_attr**(int *fd*,
>   const char *name*,
>   struct attr_info *info*)

Returns, in the `attr_info` structure pointed to by *info*, the type and size of the specified attribute on the file whose descriptor is specified by *fd*.

The `attr_info` structure is defined as follows:

```
typedef struct attr_info
{
   uint32 type;
   off_t  size;
}
```

type contains a code defining the format of the data contained by the attribute; standard values for this field are defined in the *be/support/TypeConstants.h* header file.

size specifies the size of the data the attribute contains.

Upon success, the function returns 0. Otherwise, it returns -1 and sets `errno` to an appropriate value.

Errno values:
> B_ENTRY_NOT_FOUND. The requested attribute was not found for the file.
> B_FILE_ERROR. Invalid file descriptor specified.

fs_write_attr()

ssize_t **fs_write_attr**(int *fd*,
>   const char **attribute*,
>   uint32 *type*,
>   off_t *pos*,
>   const void **buffer*,
>   size_t *count*)

Sets the value of the named *attribute* to the data in the specified *buffer*. The data's type is specified by *type* and should be one of the codes defined in *be/support/TypeConstants.h*. The length of the data to be written is specified by *count*.

NOTE

At this time, writing at an offset within an attribute is not fully supported, so you should always specify a *pos* of 0 to write at the beginning of the attribute.

If the attribute already has a value, this function wholly replaces that value with the new data—even if the new data is smaller than the existing data.

WARNING

Under the Be File System, files have a special attribute storage area which contains the smaller attributes. When this space is filled up, or an attribute too large to fit into the space is added to the file, additional disk blocks are allocated for the new attributes. However, only one attribute is written per block in these additional blocks. The moral of the story is: use attributes wisely. They can be your friends, but if you overuse them, you'll bloat your files.

Upon success, the function returns the number of bytes that were actually written. Otherwise, it returns -1 and sets `errno` to an appropriate value.

Errno values:
>   `B_BAD_VALUE`. The attribute name is too long or is an empty string.
>   `B_NO_MEMORY`. Insufficient memory to complete the operation.
>   `B_FILE_ERROR`. Invalid file descriptor *fd* specified, or the file is read-only.

Index C Functions

Declared in: be/kernel/fs_index.h

Library: libroot.so

Overview

Before a query can be performed on a file system, indices need to be established in which to search. Much like the card catalog in a library, these indices contain a list of files that can be searched given a particular attribute and the desired value.

An index directory is, essentially, a list of the indices on a particular disk; it keeps track of the attributes that can be searched upon. Each disk has its own index directory. For instance, a disk might have the following indices in its index directory:

- MAIL:subject
- MAIL:from
- MAIL:to
- MAIL:priority

Each of these is the name of an index that can be queried using either the `fs_query` API or the BQuery class.

For example, if an e-mail program wishes to allow searching on the name of the sender of a message, it needs to create an index for the "sender" attribute. Once this index is established, any file that has the "sender" attribute added to it will be added to the "sender" index.

Files which had the "sender" attribute attached *before* the "sender" index was created, however, will *not* be in the index until their "sender" attribute is updated, at which time they will be added to the index. For this reason, you should consider installing your indices when your application is installed, or when it is initially launched.

Since each disk has its own index directory, if you want all disks to have your indices available, you need to create them on each device. You can do this by using the functions described here in conjunction with the `fs_info` functions.

There are three indices that are present on every disk:

Index	Meaning
name	The name of the file.
size	The size, in bytes, of the file.
last_modified	The date the file was last changed.

You can always perform queries in these indices. Their names are reserved; you can't create or remove indices by these names.

The Index Directory

The following sample function opens the index directory for a specified device and, in a loop, reads every entry, printing their names to standard output. This presents a list of each index available on the disk.

```
void ListIndex(int32 device)
{
    DIR *d;
    index_info info;
    struct dirent *ent;

    d = fs_open_index_dir(device);
    if (!d) {
        fprintf(stderr, "Unable to open index.\n");
        return;
    }

    while (ent = fs_read_index_dir(d)) {
        printf("%s\n", ent->d_name);
    }
    fs_close_index_dir(d);
}
```

After calling `fs_open_index_dir()` to open the index directory for the device passed into the function (and handling the error that might occur if that function fails), a `while` loop iterates through all the entries in the directory, calling `fs_read_index_dir()` to obtain the desired information, then printing that information to standard output.

When there are no indices left, `fs_read_index_dir()` returns NULL and the `while` loop exits. At this point, `fs_close_index_dir()` is called to close the index directory.

Installing and Removing Indices

If you want query operations to be available for an attribute you attach to your files, it is first necessary to create an index for that attribute; you can't search for an attribute that hasn't been indexed.

To install a new index, use the `fs_create_index()` function. For example, to create an index for the attribute "GOLF:Handicap" on device 4 you would do this:

```
fs_create_index(4, "GOLF:Handicap", B_INT16_TYPE, 0);
```

This creates an empty index for the golf handicap attribute, which is stored as a 16-bit integer. Once the index has been created, any file that gets a "GOLF:Handicap" attribute added or changed will be indexed.

(You usually shouldn't hard-code a device number, of course; you can obtain a device number for a specific disk by using the `fs_info` functions or `stat()`.)

If you later need to remove the index, call `fs_remove_index()`, like this:

```
fs_remove_index(4, "GOLF:Handicap");
```

You should be careful when deciding to delete an index. If the user still has files around that contain indexed attributes that they want to be able to search for—using the Find panel in the Tracker, for example—they will not be able to do so after the index has been removed. So you need to decide when it is appropriate to remove indices; the choice is yours, but choose wisely, or you might annoy users.

Index Functions

fs_close_index_dir()

> int **fs_close_index_dir**(DIR *dirp*)

Closes the specified index directory and frees *dirp*. You should pass into this function the pointer returned from a previous `fs_open_index_dir()`.

You should always use this function to close index directories after you finish using them.

If successful, this function returns 0; otherwise it returns -1 and sets `errno` to one of the following codes.

Errno values:
  `B_FILE_ERROR`. Invalid directory reference specified.
  `B_BAD_FILE`. Invalid directory reference specified.

fs_create_index()

> int **fs_create_index**(dev_t *device*,
>   const char **name*,
>   int *type*,
>   uint *flags*)

Creates a new index called *name* on the specified *device*. Once this has been done, adding an attribute named *name* to a file causes the file to be added to the *name* index, such that subsequent queries will be able to search for files that contain the *name* attribute.

type indicates the kind of data the attribute will contain. Standard types are defined in the *be/support/TypeConstants.h* header file.

flags is currently unused and should always be 0.

If successful, this function returns 0; otherwise it returns -1 and sets `errno` to one of the following codes.

Errno values:

B_BAD_VALUE. The device does not exist, or *name* is reserved.

B_NOT_ALLOWED. The device is read-only.

B_NO_MEMORY. Insufficient memory to complete the operation.

B_FILE_EXISTS. The index *name* already exists.

B_DEVICE_FULL. There's not enough room on the device to create the index.

B_FILE_ERROR. Invalid directory reference.

fs_open_index_dir()

DIR *fs_open_index_dir(dev_t *device*)

Opens the index directory for the volume identified by *device*. Once open, you can retrieve the names of the indices on the volume by calling `fs_read_index_dir()`.

When you have finished using the index directory, call `fs_close_index_dir()` to close it.

If the index directory is opened successfully, a pointer to a directory structure is returned. This pointer should be passed to the other `fs_index` functions to read entries from the index directory, as well as to close the directory when you're finished with it.

If an error occurs while opening the index directory, this function returns `NULL` and sets `errno` to an appropriate value.

Errno values:

B_FILE_ERROR. A file error prevented the operation.

B_BAD_VALUE. Invalid device number specified.

B_LINK_LIMIT. A cyclic loop was detected in the directory structure.

B_NO_MEMORY. Insufficient memory to complete the operation.

B_BUSY. The specified file is currently in use.

B_NO_MORE_FDS. Too many open files; all file descriptors are in use.

fs_read_index_dir()

struct dirent *fs_read_index_dir(DIR *dirp*)

Reads the current entry from the open index directory referenced by *dirp*, and bumps the pointer to point to the next entry. dirp should have been obtained through a previous call to `fs_open_index_dir()`. The returned `dirent` pointer contains information about the index entry, including the name of the attribute represented by the index. This pointer belongs to the system; you must not delete it.

Through repeated calls to `fs_read_index_dir()`, you can obtain a list of all the indices available on the device. When you reach the end of the list, `errno` is set to `B_ENTRY_NOT_FOUND`.

If an error occurs, this function returns `NULL` and sets `errno` to an appropriate value.

Errno values:

    `B_FILE_ERROR`. Invalid file descriptor *fd* specified.

    `B_NOT_A_DIRECTORY`. *dirp* does not represent a valid index directory.

    `B_ENTRY_NOT_FOUND`. You've reached the end of the list.

fs_remove_index()

    int **fs_remove_index(**dev_t *device*, const char **index_name*)

Deletes the index named *index_name* from the specified *device*. Once the index is deleted, it will no longer be possible to use the query system to search for files with the corresponding attribute.

Use this function to remove an index that you no longer wish or need to be able to search upon. For example, if your application is being uninstalled by your user-friendly uninstaller program, and it's no longer meaningful to be able to search on a given attribute, you should use this function to delete the index for that attribute.

You should be careful when deciding whether or not to delete an index, however. If the user still has files around that they want to be able to search, using the Tracker's Find panel, for instance, and you've deleted the index for that attribute, they'll be most displeased. There's a grey area you need to wade through in determining whether or not to delete your indices; your decision needs to be based on the specifics of what your application does and how it will be used.

If the index is removed successfully, `fs_remove_index()` returns 0. Otherwise, it returns -1 and sets `errno` to an appropriate value.

Errno values:

    `B_FILE_ERROR`. A file system error prevented the operation.

    `B_BAD_VALUE`. Invalid device number specified.

    `B_NOT_ALLOWED`. Can't remove a system-reserved index ("name," "size," "last_modified"), or the device is read-only.

    `B_NO_MEMORY`. Insufficient memory to complete the operation.

    `B_ENTRY_NOT_FOUND`. The specified index does not exist.

fs_rewind_index_dir()

>   int **fs_rewind_index_dir**(DIR *_dirp_)

Rewinds the specified index directory to the beginning of its list of indices. This allows you to start over again at the top of a device's index directory and make your way down toward the bottom.

Returns a result code specifying whether or not the operation was successful.

NOTE

Unlike the most of the other file system functions, `fs_rewind_index_dir()` _doesn't_ set `errno`.

Return values:
>   B_OK. Success.
>   B_FILE_ERROR. Invalid directory reference specified.

fs_stat_index()

>   int **fs_stat_index**(dev_t _device_,
>   const char *_index_name_,
>   struct index_info *_info_)

Returns, in the `index_info` structure pointed to by _info_, information about the index named _index_name_ on the specified _device_.

The `index_info` structure is defined as follows:

```
typedef struct index_info
{
   uint32 type;
   off_t  size;
   time_t modification_time;
   time_t creation_time;
   uid_t  uid;
   gid_t  gid;
}
```

type contains a code defining the format of the data contained by the attribute represented by the index; standard values for this field are defined in the _be/support/TypeConstants.h_ header file.

- `size` specifies the size of the data the attribute contains.

- `modification_time` contains the time the index was last changed, in seconds since January 1, 1970.

- `creation_time` contains the date and time the index was originally created, in seconds since January 1, 1970.

- `uid` contains the user ID of the owner of the index.

- `gid` contains the group ID of the owner of the index.

If the function is successful, it returns 0; otherwise, it returns -1 and sets `errno` to an appropriate value

Errno values:
> `B_ENTRY_NOT_FOUND`. The requested index was not found.
> `B_BAD_VALUE`. Invalid device number specified.

Query C Functions

Declared in: be/kernel/fs_query.h

Library: libroot.so

Overview

Normally, when you want to perform a file system query, you would use the BQuery class, which is a nice, clean, object-oriented way to do it. If you have an aversion to object-oriented programming, however, or you're writing a simple C program and would rather use C functions instead, then you've come to the right place.

Be aware that, currently, you can't perform "live" queries at the C level. If you want a live query, you have to use a BQuery object.

Opening, Reading, and Closing a Query

To begin a query, you call `fs_open_query()`. `fs_open_query()` performs a "one-shot" query: It lets you ask for all the files that fulfill certain criteria right now. This criteria is expressed as a "predicate" string. This is a formula that lists the attribute values that you're interested in. A simple predicate takes the form:

> *attribute op value*

For example, you can look for files that are larger than 5K by supplying a string that looks like this:

`"size > 5000"`

Simple predicates can be grouped and combined to create more complex predicates. Here we look for files named "fido" that are greater than 5K:

`"(name = fido) && (size > 5000)"`

For a full description of the predicate format, see "The Predicate, Attributes, and Indices" in the BQuery class description, but be aware of this difference:

- The `fs_query` functions don't let you "push" elements onto the predicate; all predicates must be expressed as strings.

Once the query has been opened, you can step through the files that fulfill the predicate through iterated calls to `fs_read_query()`. When all the winning files have been visited, `fs_read_query()` returns `NULL`.

When you've finished using your query, you must close it by using the `fs_close_query()` function.

An Example

The following sample demonstrates very briefly how to perform a simple, non-live query. In this example, we're searching for all C header files on the device specified by *devnum*.

```
void sample_query(dev_t devnum) {
   DIR    *q;
   dirent_t*d;

   q = fs_open_query(devnum, "name=*.h", 0);
   if (q) {
      while (d = fs_read_query(q)) {
         ...
      }
      fs_close_query(q);
   }
}
```

The code opens the query by calling `fs_open_query()` and then calls `fs_read_query()` in a loop until `NULL` is returned. Once that happens, `fs_close_query()` is used to close the query.

Query Functions

fs_close_query()

int **fs_close_query**(DIR *`dir`)

Closes a query which was previously opened using the `fs_open_query()` function. You pass in the DIR * returned by either of these functions. The pointer *dir* is freed by this function.

If the query closes successfully, `fs_close_query()` returns 0; otherwise, it returns -1 and sets `errno` to an appropriate value.

Errno values:

`B_FILE_ERROR`. A file system error prevented the operation from succeeding.

fs_open_query()

> DIR *fs_open_query(dev_t *device*,
>   const char *query*,
>   uint32 *flags*)

Opens a new query on the specified device. The *query* string is the criteria or "predicate" that describes the files that you're looking for. For information on how to construct the *query* string, see the BQuery class. Note that you can't use the "push" method: `fs_open_query()` only understands predicate strings.

flags is currently unused; pass 0 as its value.

The pointer returned by this function is used to identify your query to the other query functions; you should not dispose of it yourself—this will be done for you when you call `fs_close_query()`. If the query couldn't be opened, the function returns NULL and sets errno to an appropriate value.

Errno values:

> B_ENTRY_NOT_FOUND. *path* does not exist, or is NULL or an empty string.
> B_BAD_VALUE. *device* does not specify a valid device, *query* is NULL or an invalid expression, or a live query was requested without specifying a valid *port*.
> B_NO_MEMORY. Insufficient memory to complete the operation.
> B_FILE_ERROR. A file system error prevented the operation from succeeding.
> B_BUSY. A busy node could not be accessed.
> B_NO_MORE_FDS. All file descriptors are in use (too many open files).
> E2BIG. *query* expression is too big.

fs_read_query()

> dirent *fs_read_query(DIR *d*)

Returns the next item that matches the specified query. The *d* argument should have been gotten from a previous call to `fs_open_query()`; it identifies the particular query from which to read.

You mustn't free the pointer returned to you by this function.

If an error occurs while reading the query, this function returns NULL and sets errno to an appropriate value.

Errno values:

> B_FILE_ERROR. A file system error prevented the operation from succeeding.
> B_BAD_VALUE. An error occurred processing the query predicate.
> B_ENTRY_NOT_FOUND. No more matches.
> B_NOT_A_DIRECTORY. A non-directory node was found where a directory was expected.

B_INTERRUPTED. A signal interrupted the read.

E2BIG. Query predicate is too big.

File System Info C Functions

Declared in: be/kernel/fs_info.h

Library: libroot.so

Overview

From time to time, it can be useful to know certain information about the capabilities of the file system on a device. While the BVolume class provides you easy access to this information, it can occasionally be helpful to have more direct access to this information.

This section describes three C functions which can be used to obtain information about the file system on a device. One of these functions, `fs_stat_dev()`, returns this information given a device number. The other two functions, `dev_for_path()` and `next_dev()`, provide two ways to obtain a device number for use with `fs_stat_dev()`.

Note that these functions *don't* set `errno`.

C Functions

dev_for_path()

    dev_t **dev_for_path**(const char *path*)

Given a pathname, returns the device number of the device on which the path is located. If the result is negative, it is a return code specifying an error.

Return values:
    B_ENTRY_NOT_FOUND.   *path* does not exist, or is NULL or an empty string.
    B_BAD_VALUE. *path* is null or an empty string.
    B_NAME_TOO_LONG. *path* is too long.
    B_NO_MEMORY. Insufficient memory to complete the operation.
    B_FILE_ERROR. A file system error prevented the operation from succeeding.

next_dev()

    dev_t **next_dev**(int32 *pos*)

The `next_dev()` function allows you to iterate through all devices, receiving their device numbers as a result each time. If the result is negative, it is an error code.

When the end of the device list is reached, the return value `B_BAD_VALUE` is returned.

You should initially set *pos* to 0, then call `next_dev()` in a loop to obtain each device number until an error occurs. For example:

```
void ScanDevices(void) {
    int pos;

    pos = 0;
    while(next_dev(&pos) >=0) {
        do_something(pos);
    }
}
```

Return values:

> `B_BAD_VALUE`. No matching device found.

fs_stat_dev()

> int **fs_stat_dev**(dev_t *dev*, fs_info *info*)

> struct {} **fs_info**

`fs_stat_dev()` returns information about the specified device. This can be used in conjunction with `next_dev()` to scan all devices and record information your application requires.

This function returns 0 if the request was successful or -1 if an error occurred. Use the `errno()` function to determine what error in particular occurred.

The `fs_info` structure is defined as:

```
typedef struct fs_info {
    dev_t  dev;
    ino_t  root;
    uint32 flags;
    off_t  block_size;
    off_t  io_size;
    off_t  total_blocks;
    off_t  free_blocks;
    off_t  total_nodes;
    off_t  free_nodes;
    char   device_name[128];
    char   volume_name[B_FILE_NAME_LENGTH];
    char   fsh_name[B_OS_NAME_LENGTH];
};
```

The structure's fields are:

- `dev`. The device number of the device.
- `root`. The inode of the root of the device.
- `flags`. Flags describing the device's capabilities.
- `block_size`. The fundamental block size of the device.
- `io_size`. Optimal I/O size of the device.
- `total_blocks`. The total number of blocks on the device.
- `free_blocks`. The number of free (unused) blocks on the device.
- `total_nodes`. The total number of nodes on the device.
- `free_nodes`. The number of free (unused) nodes on the device.
- `device_name`. Name of the device holding the file system.
- `volume_name`. Name of the volume contained by the device.
- `fsh_name`. Name of the file system handler for the device.

The `flags` can be any combination of the following values, which specify the attributes of the file system on the device:

- `B_FS_IS_READONLY`. The file system on the device is read-only.
- `B_FS_IS_REMOVABLE`. The device contains removable media.
- `B_FS_IS_PERSISTENT`. Data written to the device remains even while the device is off.
- `B_FS_IS_SHARED`. The file system is being shared on a network.
- `B_FS_HAS_MIME`. The file system supports the MIME typing system used by the BeOS.
- `B_FS_HAS_ATTR`. The file system supports node attributes.
- `B_FS_HAS_QUERY`. The file system supports the BeOS query mechanism.

The information in the `fs_info` structure is guaranteed to be internally consistent, but the structure as a whole should be considered to be out-of-date as soon as you receive it. It provides a picture of a device as it exists just before the info-retrieving function returns. In particular, the number of free blocks and of free nodes can easily change immediately after you receive this information.

Return values:
    `B_OK`. The device was found; *info* contains valid information.
    `B_BAD_VALUE`. *dev* doesn't identify an existing device.

Global Constants and Defined Types

This section lists parts of the Storage Kit that aren't contained in classes.

Constants

Limits Constants

`be/storage/StorageDefs.h`

Constant	Meaning
B_FILE_NAME_LENGTH	Number of characters allowed in a file name.
B_PATH_NAME_LENGTH	Number of characters allowed in a path name.
B_ATTR_NAME_LENGTH	Number of characters allowed in an attribute name.
B_MIME_TYPE_LENGTH	Number of characters allowed in a MIME type name.
B_MAX_SYMLINKS	Number of nested symlinks allowed.

These constants define the maximum values for several Storage Kit related items, including file and path name strings, attribute name strings, and MIME type strings. B_MAX_SYMLINKS specifies how many symbolic links may be linked through each other.

File Open Mode Constants

`be/storage/StorageDefs.h`

Constant	Meaning
B_READ_ONLY	Open the file with read-only access.
B_WRITE_ONLY	Open the file with write-only access.
B_READ_WRITE	Open the file for both reading and writing.
B_FAIL_IF_EXISTS	Don't open the file if it already exists.
B_CREATE_FILE	Create the file before opening it.
B_ERASE_FILE	Erase the previous contents before opening the file.
B_OPEN_AT_END	Open with the pointer at the end of the file.

These constants are used when opening files using either the POSIX `open()` function or using the BFile class. They specify the mode in which the file is to be opened. For instance, if write-only access is desired, and you want the operation to fail if the file exists, you would do the following:

```
fd = open("foobar.data", B_WRITE_ONLY | B_FAIL_IF_EXISTS);
```

Node Flavors

be/storage/StorageDefs.h

Constant	Meaning
B_FILE_NODE	Files only
B_SYMLINK_NODE	Symbolic links only
B_DIRECTORY_NODE	Directories only
B_ANY_NODE	Matches any node

These constants are used when making a request that can be qualified based on the "flavor" of a node—in other words, whenever you wish to perform an operation on only files, directories, or symbolic links. This is used when opening a file panel, for instance, so that you can specify what types of items you want the user to be able to select.

Version Kinds

be/storage/AppFileInfo.h

Constant	Meaning
B_APP_VERSION_KIND	Records information about a specific application.
B_SYSTEM_VERSION_KIND	Records information about a "suite," or other grouping of applications, that the application belongs to.

These constants are used when setting or retrieving the version information attached to an application. There are two version information records for each application, and these two constants select which one you wish to reference. Although there is no prescribed use for these structures or their constants, it is suggested that B_APP_VERSION_KIND be used for application-specific version information, and B_SYSTEM_VERSION_KIND be used for information about the suite of applications to which the application belongs.

Directories

be/storage/FindDirectory.h

Constant	Meaning
B_DESKTOP_DIRECTORY	Desktop directory.
B_TRASH_DIRECTORY	Trash directory.
B_APPS_DIRECTORY	Applications directory.
B_PREFERENCES_DIRECTORY	Preferences directory.
B_BEOS_DIRECTORY	BeOS directory.

Constant	Meaning
B_BEOS_SYSTEM_DIRECTORY	System directory.
B_BEOS_ADDONS_DIRECTORY	BeOS add-ons directory.
B_BEOS_BOOT_DIRECTORY	Boot volume's root directory.
B_BEOS_FONTS_DIRECTORY	BeOS fonts directory.
B_BEOS_LIB_DIRECTORY	BeOS libraries directory.
B_BEOS_SERVERS_DIRECTORY	BeOS servers directory.
B_BEOS_APPS_DIRECTORY	BeOS applications directory.
B_BEOS_BIN_DIRECTORY	*/bin* directory.
B_BEOS_ETC_DIRECTORY	*/etc* directory.
B_BEOS_DOCUMENTATION_DIRECTORY	BeOS documentation directory.
B_BEOS_PREFERENCES_DIRECTORY	BeOS preferences directory.
B_COMMON_DIRECTORY	The common directory, shared by all users.
B_COMMON_SYSTEM_DIRECTORY	The shared system directory.
B_COMMON_ADDONS_DIRECTORY	The shared addons directory.
B_COMMON_BOOT_DIRECTORY	The shared boot directory.
B_COMMON_FONTS_DIRECTORY	The shared fonts directory.
B_COMMON_LIB_DIRECTORY	The shared libraries directory.
B_COMMON_SERVERS_DIRECTORY	The shared servers directory.
B_COMMON_BIN_DIRECTORY	The shared */bin* directory.
B_COMMON_ETC_DIRECTORY	The shared */etc* directory.
B_COMMON_DOCUMENTATION_DIRECTORY	The shared documentation directory.
B_COMMON_SETTINGS_DIRECTORY	The shared settings directory.
B_COMMON_DEVELOP_DIRECTORY	The shared develop directory.
B_COMMON_LOG_DIRECTORY	The shared log directory.
B_COMMON_SPOOL_DIRECTORY	The shared spool directory.
B_COMMON_TEMP_DIRECTORY	The shared temporary items directory.
B_COMMON_VAR_DIRECTORY	The shared */var* directory.
B_USER_DIRECTORY	The user's home directory.
B_USER_CONFIG_DIRECTORY	The user's config directory.
B_USER_ADDONS_DIRECTORY	The user's add-ons directory.
B_USER_BOOT_DIRECTORY	The user's */boot* directory.
B_USER_FONTS_DIRECTORY	The user's fonts directory.
B_USER_LIB_DIRECTORY	The user's libraries directory.
B_USER_SETTINGS_DIRECTORY	The user's settings directory.
B_USER_DESKBAR_DIRECTORY	The user's Deskbar directory.

These constants are used when calling the `find_directory()` function to determine the pathname of a particular directory of interest.

`B_DESKTOP_DIRECTORY` and `B_TRASH_DIRECTORY` are per-volume directories; if you don't specify the volume you wish to locate these directories on, `find_directory()` will assume you mean the boot disk.

`B_APPS_DIRECTORY` and `B_PREFERENCES_DIRECTORY` are global directories, and always refer to the standard *apps* and *preferences* directories.

The `B_BEOS_*` constants refer to BeOS-owned directories, the `B_COMMON_*` constants refer to directories that are common to all users of the system, and the `B_USER_*` constants refer to the current user's directories (currently these are all in a subtree rooted at */boot/home*). By using these constants properly, your code will be compatible with future generations of the BeOS.

Icon Sizes

    be/storage/Mime.h

Constant	Meaning
B_LARGE_ICON	Large (32x32) icon.
B_MINI_ICON	Small (16x16) icon.

These constants are used when selecting icons from a meta MIME file; they let you fetch the large and small variations of a file's icon.

watch_node() Flags

    be/storage/NodeMonitor.h

Constant	Meaning
B_STOP_WATCHING	Stop watching the node.
B_WATCH_NAME	Watch for changes to the name of the node.
B_WATCH_STAT	Watch for stat changes.
B_WATCH_ATTR	Watch for attribute changes.
B_WATCH_DIRECTORY	Watch for changes to the directory's contents.
B_WATCH_ALL	Watch everything (except mounting).
B_WATCH_MOUNT	Watch for disk mounts and unmounts.

These constants are used to control what type of monitoring to perform on a node. `B_WATCH_ALL` is a convenience constant that allows you to monitor changes to the name, stat information, attributes, and directory of a node. B_WATCH_MOUNT, which is not included in B_WATCH_ALL, monitors volumes being mounted and unmounted.

B_WATCH_DIRECTORY applies only to directory nodes.

Node Monitor Opcodes

be/storage/NodeMonitor.h

Constant	Meaning
B_ENTRY_CREATED	A new entry has been created.
B_ENTRY_REMOVED	An entry has been removed.
B_ENTRY_MOVED	An entry has been moved.
B_STAT_CHANGED	Stat information has changed.
B_ATTR_CHANGED	An attribute has been changed.
B_DEVICE_MOUNTED	A volume has been mounted.
B_DEVICE_UNMOUNTED	A volume has been unmounted.

These constants are returned by the Node Monitor to let you know what sort of change has occurred to a node being monitored.

Query Operation Constants

be/storage/Query.h

Constant	Operation
B_EQ	=
B_NE	!=
B_GT	>
B_LT	<
B_GE	>=
B_LE	<=
B_CONTAINS	string contains value ("*value*")
B_BEGINS_WITH	string begins with value ("value*")
B_ENDS_WITH	string ends with value ("*value")
B_AND	&&
B_OR	||
B_NOT	!

These constants define the operations that can be used to specify a query. They are used in conjunction with the push functions for constructing a query.

Defined Types

entry_ref

```
be/storage/Entry.h
```

```
struct entry_ref {
        entry_ref();
        entry_ref(dev_t device, ino_t dir, const char *name);
        entry_ref(const entry_ref &ref);
        ~entry_ref();

    status_t set_name(const char *name);
    bool    operator==(const entry_ref &ref) const;
    bool    operator!=(const entry_ref &ref) const;
    entry_ref &operator=(const entry_ref &ref);

    dev_t  device;
    ino_t  directory;
    char   *name;
}
```

The `entry_ref` structure describes a single entry in a directory.

`entry_ref()`
`entry_ref(dev_t device, ino_t dir, const char *name)`
`entry_ref(const entry_ref &ref)`

> The constructor for the `entry_ref` structure. The first of these creates an empty `entry_ref`, the second accepts a device number, directory inode number, and a file name and constructs an `entry_ref` referring to that entry, and the last version of the constructor duplicates an existing `entry_ref`.

`~entry_ref()`

> The destructor for `entry_ref`.

`status_t set_name(const char *name)`

> Lets you change the name of the file referred to by the `entry_ref` structure.

`operator ==`

> Lets you perform comparisons of `entry_ref` structures to see if they refer to the same entry.

`operator !=`

> Lets you test to see if two `entry_ref` structures refer to different entries.

device contains the device number on which the entry's target is located.

directory contains the inode of the directory that contains the entry's target.

name contains the name of the entry.

node_ref

```
be/storage/Node.h
```

```
struct node_ref {
        node_ref();
        node_ref(const node_ref &ref);
        ~node_ref();

    bool   operator==(const node_ref &ref) const;
    bool   operator!=(const node_ref &ref) const;
    node_ref &operator=(const node_ref &ref);

    dev_t  device;
    ino_t  node;
}
```

The `node_ref` structure describes a node in a file system.

`node_ref()`
`node_ref(const node_ref &ref)`

  The constructor for the `node_ref` structure. The first of these creates an empty `node_ref`, and the second duplicates an existing `node_ref`.

`~node_ref()`

  The destructor for `node_ref`.

operator ==

  Lets you perform comparisons of `node_ref` structures to see if they refer to the same node.

operator !=

  Lets you test to see if two `node_ref` structures refer to different nodes.

device contains the device number on which the node is located.

node contains the inode of the node.

version_info

be/storage/AppFileInfo.h

```
struct version_info {
    uint32 major;
    uint32 middle;
    uint32 minor;
    uint32 variety;
    uint32 internal;
    char    short_info[64];
    char    long_info[256];
}
```

The `version_info` structure is used to contain version information about an application. Although none of these fields has prescribed uses, and you can use them for anything you want, their names do hint at their suggested uses.

CHAPTER FOUR

The Interface Kit

Interface Kit Inheritance Hierarchy

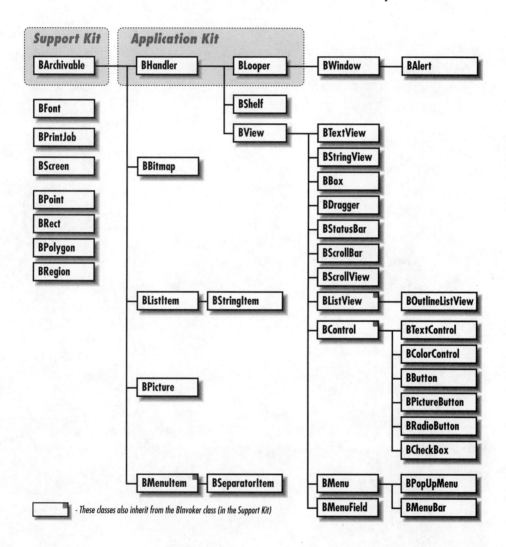

CHAPTER FOUR

The Interface Kit

Most applications have an interactive graphic user interface. When an app starts, it displays a set of windows in which the user can click and type. The application responds to the user's actions, and updates its window to show the user that it's listening.

To run this kind of user interface, an application has to:

- Manage a set of windows
- Draw within the windows
- Respond to the users's actions (reported as *interface messages*)

The Interface Kit defines a set of C++ classes that provide a structure for these operations. This chapter first introduces the conceptual framework for the user interface, then describes all the classes, functions, types, and constants the kit defines.

Framework for the User Interface

A graphical user interface is organized around windows. In a multitasking environment, any number of applications might be running at the same time, each with its own set of windows on-screen. The windows of all running applications must cooperate in a common interface. The Application Server manages this mess. It's the conduit for an application's message input and drawing output:

- It monitors the keyboard and mouse and sends messages reporting each user keystroke and mouse action to the application.

- It receives drawing instructions from the application and interprets them to render images within windows.

BWindow Objects

Every window in an application is represented by a separate BWindow object. Constructing the BWindow establishes a connection to the Application Server. When you call BWindow's window-manipulating functions (`Show()`, `MoveTo()`, `SetTitle()` and so on), the object sends a message to the server, which performs the actual manipulation.

The BWindow class inherits from BLooper. Every BWindow object spawns a thread (in the application's address space) where it receives and responds to interface messages from the server.

All other Interface Kit objects play roles that depend on a BWindow. They draw in a window, respond to interface messages received by a window, or act in support of other objects that draw and respond to messages.

BView Objects

A window is divided into smaller rectangular areas called *views*. Each view corresponds to one part of what the window displays—a scroll bar, a document, a list, and so on.

An application sets up a view by constructing a BView object and associating it with a particular BWindow. The BView object is responsible for drawing within the view rectangle and for handling interface messages directed at that area.

Drawing in a View

A window can retain and display rendered images, but it can't draw them; for that it needs a set of BViews. A BView is an agent for drawing, but it can't render the images it creates; for that it needs a BWindow. The two objects work hand in hand.

Each BView object is an autonomous graphics environment for drawing: It has its own coordinate system, current colors, drawing mode, clipping region, font, pen position, and so on. The BView class also defines functions that represent elemental drawing operations such as line stroking, character drawing, and image blitting.

Handling Messages in a View

When the user acts, system messages that report the resulting events are sent to the BWindow object, which determines which BView elicited the user action and should respond to it. For example, a BView that draws typed text can expect to respond to messages reporting the user's keystrokes. A BView that draws a button gets to handle the messages that are generated when the button is clicked. The BView class derives from BHandler, so BView objects are eligible to handle messages dispatched by the BWindow.

The View Hierarchy

A window typically contains a number of different views—all arranged in a hierarchy beneath the *top view*, a view that's exactly the same size as the content area of the window. The top view is a companion of the window; it's created by the BWindow object when the BWindow is constructed. When the window is resized, the top view is resized to match. Unlike other views, the top view doesn't draw or respond to messages; it serves merely to connect the window to the views that the application creates and places in the hierarchy.

As illustrated in the following diagram, the view hierarchy can be represented as a branching tree structure with the top view at its root. All views in the hierarchy (except the top view) have one, and only one, parent view. Each view (including the top view) can have any number of child views.

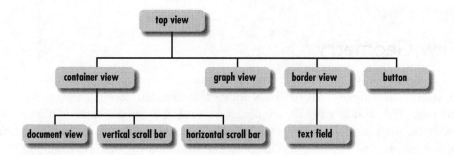

In this diagram, the top view has four children, the container view has three, and the border view one.

When a new BView object is created, it isn't attached to a window and it has no parent. It's added to a window by making it a child of a view already in the view hierarchy. This is done with the `AddChild()` function. A view can be made a child of the window's top view by calling BWindow's version of `AddChild()`.

Until it's assigned to a window, a BView can't draw and won't receive reports of events. BViews know how to produce images, but it takes a window to display and retain the images they create.

Drawing and Message Handling in the View Hierarchy

The view hierarchy determines what's displayed where on-screen, and also how user actions are associated with the responsible BView object:

- When the views in a window are called on to draw, parents draw before their children; children draw in front of their ancestors.

- Mouse events are associated with the view where the cursor is located.

Overlapping Siblings

Siblings don't draw in any predefined order. If they overlap, it's indeterminate which view will draw last—that is, which one will draw in front of the other. Similarly, it's indeterminate which view will be associated with mouse events in the area the siblings share.

Therefore, it's strongly recommended that sibling views should be arranged so that they don't overlap.

Drawing

This section discusses the framework in which BViews draw, beginning with the placement of view rectangles in the coordinate system. Detailed descriptions of the functions mentioned here can be found in the BView and BWindow class descriptions.

View Geometry

As a convenience, each view is assigned a coordinate system of its own. By default, the coordinate origin—(0.0, 0.0)—is located at the left top corner of the view rectangle. The *x*-axis extends to the right and the *y*-axis extends downward; coordinate units count screen pixels. (For a detailed discussion of the coordinate systems assumed by the Interface Kit, see "The Coordinate Space" on page 368.)

When a view is added as a child of another view, it's located within the coordinate system of its parent. A child is considered part of the contents of the parent view. If the parent moves, the child moves with it; if the parent view scrolls its contents, the child view is shifted along with everything else in the view.

Since each view retains its own internal coordinate system no matter who its parent is, where it's located within the parent, or where the parent is located, a BView's drawing and message-handling code doesn't need to be concerned about anything exterior to itself. To do its work, a BView need look no farther than the boundaries of its own view rectangle.

Frame and Bounds Rectangles

Although a BView doesn't have to look outside its own boundaries, it does have to know where those boundaries are. It can get this information in two forms:

- Since a view is located within the coordinate system of its parent, the view rectangle is initially defined in terms of the parent's coordinates. This defining rectangle for a view is known as its *frame rectangle*. (See the BView constructor and the `Frame()` function.)

- When translated from the parent's coordinates to the internal coordinates of the view itself, the same rectangle is known as the *bounds rectangle*. (See the Bounds() function.)

The following illustration shows a child view 180.0 units wide and 135.0 units high. When viewed from the outside, from the perspective of its parent's coordinate system, it has a frame rectangle with left, top, right, and bottom coordinates at 90.0, 60.0, 270.0, and 195.0, respectively. But when viewed from the inside, in the view's own coordinate system, it has a bounds rectangle with coordinates at 0.0, 0.0, 180.0, and 135.0:

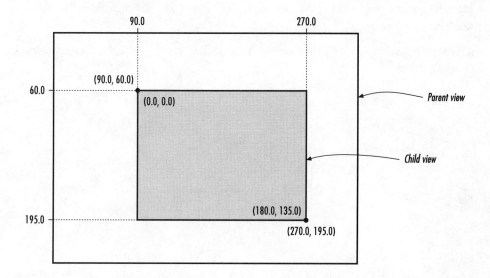

When a view moves to a new location in its parent, its frame rectangle changes but not its bounds rectangle. When a view scrolls its contents, its bounds rectangle changes, but not its frame. The frame rectangle positions the view in the world outside; the bounds rectangle positions the contents inside the view.

Since a BView does its work in its own coordinate system, it refers to the bounds rectangle more often than to the frame rectangle.

Nonfractional Coordinates

Because views are areas within windows and windows are displayed on-screen, the edges of a view must line up on rows and columns of screen pixels. It's easy to achieve this result, since coordinate units correspond to screen pixels; one unit is the distance from the center of a pixel to the center of an adjacent pixel. Therefore, all you must do is define the view rectangle with nonfractional coordinates, as in the illustration above.

Pixel and Coordinate Dimensions

It was mentioned that the child view in the illustration above is 180.0 coordinate units wide and 135.0 units high. However, this view actually covers 181 pixel columns and 136 pixel rows on-screen.

Two facts conspire to determine this result. First, as stated, coordinate units correspond to screen pixels. Second, in a departure from other systems, the coordinate axes don't lie between pixels but right in the middle of them. The *x*-axis splits a row of pixels and the *y*-axis runs down the center of a column of pixels; the coordinate origin where they meet is at the very center of a pixel. Therefore, a view rectangle covers one more pixel in each direction than its coordinate dimensions would indicate.

Imagine, for example, an implausibly tiny frame rectangle like the one in the following diagram:

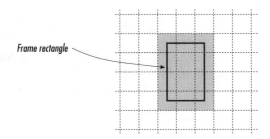

Since the pixels on the edges of this 2.0 × 3.0 rectangle are treated as being inside the rectangle, the view covers a 3 pixel × 4 pixel area.

This fact is important when laying out views and drawing in the bounds rectangle (or drawing any rectangle, for that matter). However, when discussing view coordinates and rectangles in general, it's easier and more accurate to speak in terms of coordinate values, not pixels—and that's the practice in this chapter. However, see "Mapping Coordinates to Pixels" on page 371 for more on how coordinate values relate to pixels.

Scrolling

A BView scrolls its contents by shifting coordinate values within the view rectangle—that is, by altering the bounds rectangle. If, for example, the top of a view's bounds rectangle is at 100.0 and its bottom is at 200.0, scrolling downward 50.0 units would put the top at 150.0 and the bottom at 250.0. Contents of the view with *y*-coordinate values of 150.0 to 200.0, originally displayed in the bottom half of the view, would be shifted to the top half. Contents with *y*-coordinate values from 200.0 to 250.0, previously unseen, would become visible at the bottom of the view, as shown in the following illustration:

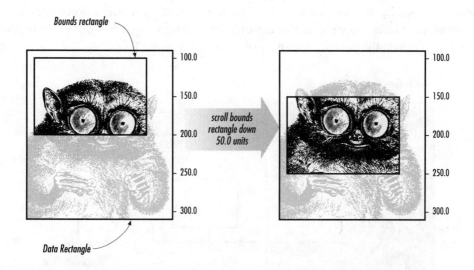

Scrolling doesn't move the view—it doesn't alter the frame rectangle—it moves only what's displayed inside the view. In the illustration above, a "data rectangle" encloses everything the BView is capable of drawing. For example, if the view is able to display an entire book, the data rectangle would be large enough to enclose all the lines and pages of the book laid end to end. However, since a BView can draw only within its bounds rectangle, everything in the data rectangle with coordinates that fall outside the bounds rectangle would be invisible. To make unseen data visible, the bounds rectangle must change the coordinates that it encompasses. Scrolling can be thought of as sliding the view's bounds rectangle to a new position on its data rectangle, as is shown in the illustration above. However, as it appears to the user, it's moving the data rectangle under the bounds rectangle. The view doesn't move; the data does.

The Clipping Region

The Application Server clips the images that a BView produces to the region where it's permitted to draw.

This region is never any larger than the view's bounds rectangle; a view cannot draw outside its bounds. Furthermore, since a child is considered part of its parent, a view can't draw outside the bounds rectangle of its parent either—or, for that matter, outside the bounds rectangle of any ancestor view. In addition, since child views draw after, and therefore logically in front of, their parents, a view concedes some of its territory to its children.

Thus, the *visible region* of a view is the part of its bounds rectangle that's inside the bounds rectangles of all its ancestors, minus the frame rectangles of its children. This is illustrated in the following figure. It shows a hierarchy of three views—X, Y, and Z. The area filled with a crosshatch pattern is the visible region of view X; it omits the area occupied by its child, view Y. The visible region of view Y is colored dark gray; it omits the part of the view that lies outside its parent. View Z has no visible region, for it lies outside the bounds rectangle of its ancestor, view X:

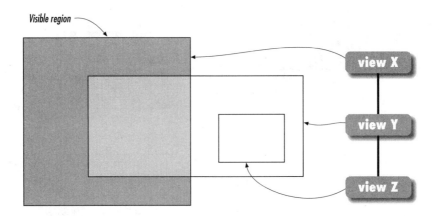

The visible region of a view might be further restricted if its window is obscured by another window or if the window it's in lies partially off-screen. The visible region includes only those areas that are actually visible to the user. For example, if the three views in the previous illustration were in a window that was partially blocked by another, their visible regions might be much smaller, as shown in the next figure:

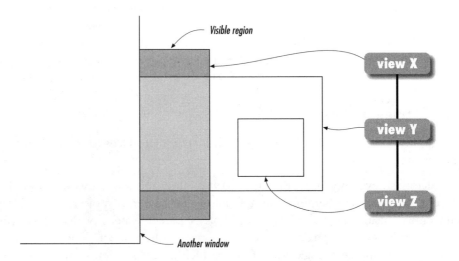

Note that in this case, view X has a discontinuous visible region.

The Application Server clips the drawing that a view does to a region that's never any larger than the visible region. On occasion, it may be smaller. For the sake of efficiency, while a view is being automatically updated, the *clipping region* excludes portions of the visible region that don't need to be redrawn:

- When a view is scrolled, the Application Server may be able to shift some of its contents from one portion of the visible region to another. The clipping region excludes any part of the visible region that the server was able to update on its own; it includes only the part where the BView must produce images that were not previously visible.

- If a view is resized larger, the clipping region may include only the new areas that were added to the visible region. (But see the *flags* argument for the BView constructor.)

- If only part of a view is invalidated (by the `Invalidate()` function), the clipping region is the intersection of the visible region and the invalid rectangle.

An application can also limit the clipping region for a view by passing a BRegion object to `ConstrainClippingRegion()`. The clipping region won't include any areas that aren't in the region passed. The Application Server calculates the clipping region as it normally would but intersects it with the specified region.

You can obtain the current clipping region for a view by calling `GetClippingRegion()`. (See also the BRegion class description.)

The View Color

Every view has a basic, underlying color. It's the color that fills the view rectangle before the BView does any drawing. The Application Server paints the view with this color before any view-specific drawing functions are called. The user may catch a glimpse of the color when the view is first shown on-screen, when it's resized larger, and when it's erased in preparation for an update. It will also be seen wherever the BView fails to draw in the visible region.

In a sense, the view color is the canvas on which the BView draws. It doesn't enter into any of the object's drawing operations except to provide a background. Although it's one of the BView's graphics parameters, it's not one that any drawing functions refer to.

The default view color is white. You can assign a different color to a view by calling BView's `SetViewColor()` function. If you set the view color to `B_TRANSPARENT_32_BIT`, the Application Server won't erase the view's clipping region before an update. This is appropriate only if the view erases itself by touching every pixel in the clipping region when it draws.

The Mechanics of Drawing

Views draw through the following set of primitive functions:

- `DrawString()` draws a string of characters. `DrawChar()` is a variant of this function; it draws just a single character.

- `DrawPicture()` executes a set of recorded drawing instructions.

- `DrawBitmap()` produces an image from a bitmap.

- `CopyBits()` copies an image from one location to another.

- `FillEllipse()`, `FillRegion()`, and other `Fill...()` functions fill closed shapes.

- `StrokeLine()`, `StrokeArc()`, and other `Stroke...()` functions stroke lines along defined paths.

- `BeginLineArray()`, `AddLine()`, and `EndLineArray()` draw a set of straight lines, all of the same width, but possibly in different colors.

The way these functions work depends not only on the values that they're passed—the particular string, bitmap, arc, or ellipse that's to be drawn—but on previously set values in the BView's graphics environment.

Graphics Environment

Each BView object maintains its own graphics environment for drawing. The view color, coordinate system, and clipping region are fundamental parts of that environment, but not the only parts. It also includes a number of parameters that can be set and reset at will to affect the next image drawn. These parameters are:

- Font attributes that determine the appearance of text the BView draws. (See `SetFont()` and the BFont class.)

- Two pen parameters—a location and a size. The pen location determines where the next drawing will occur, and the pen size determines the thickness of stroked lines. (See `MovePenBy()` and `SetPenSize()`.)

- Two current colors—a *high color* and a *low color*—that can be used either alone or in combination to form a pattern or halftone. The high color is used for most drawing. The low color is sometimes set to the underlying view color so that it can be used to erase other drawing or, because it matches the view background, make it appear that drawing has not touched certain pixels.

   (The high and low colors roughly match what other systems call the fore and back, or foreground and background, colors. However, neither color truly represents the color of the foreground or background. The terminology *high* and *low* is meant to keep the sense of two opposing colors and to match how they're defined in a pattern. A pattern bit is turned on for the high color and turned off for the low color. See the `SetHighColor()` and `SetLowColor()` functions in the BView class description and the "Patterns" section on page 343.)

- A drawing mode that determines how the next image is to be rendered. (See "Drawing Modes" on page 345 and the `SetDrawingMode()` function.)

By default, a BView's graphics parameters are set to the following values:

Font	The system plain font (`be_plain_font`)
Pen position	(0.0, 0.0)
Pen size	1.0 coordinate units
High color	Black (red, green, and blue components all equal to 0)
Low color	White (red, green, and blue components all equal to 255)
Drawing mode	Copy mode (`B_OP_COPY`)
View color	White (red, green, and blue components all equal to 255)
Clipping region	The visible region of the view
Coordinate system	Origin at the left top corner of the bounds rectangle

However, as "Views and the Server" on page 349 explains, these values have meaning only when the BView is assigned to a window.

The Pen

The pen is a fiction that encompasses two properties of a view's graphics environment: the current drawing location and the thickness of stroked lines.

The pen location determines where the next image will be drawn—but only if another location isn't explicitly passed to the drawing function. Some drawing functions alter the pen location—as if the pen actually moves as it does the drawing—but usually it's set by calling `MovePenBy()` or `MovePenTo()`.

The pen that draws lines (through the various `Stroke...()` functions) has a malleable tip that can be made broader or narrower by calling the `SetPenSize()` function. The larger the pen size, the thicker the line that it draws.

The pen size is expressed in coordinate units, which must be translated to a particular number of pixels for the display device. This is done by scaling the pen size to a device-specific value and rounding to the closest integer. For example, pen sizes of 2.6 and 3.3 would both translate to 3 pixels on-screen, but to 7 and 10 pixels respectively on a 300-dpi printer.

The size is never rounded to 0; no matter how small the pen may be, the line never disappears. If the pen size is set to 0.0, the line will be as thin as possible—it will be drawn using the fewest possible pixels on the display device. (In other words, it will be rounded to 1 for all devices.)

If the pen size translates to a tip that's broader than 1 pixel, the line is drawn with the tip centered on the path of the line. Roughly the same number of pixels are colored on both sides of the path.

A later section, "Picking Pixels to Stroke and Fill" on page 372, illustrates how pens of different sizes choose the pixels to be colored.

Colors

The high and low colors are specified as `rgb_color` values—full 32-bit values with separate red, green, and blue color components, plus an alpha component for transparency. Although there may sometimes be limitations on the colors that can be rendered on-screen, there are no restrictions on the colors that can be specified.

Color Spaces

The way colors are specified for a bitmap depends on the color space in which they're interpreted. The color space determines the *depth* of the bitmap data (how many bits of information are stored for each pixel), the *interpretation* of the data (whether it represents shades of gray or true colors, whether it's segmented into color components, what the components are, and so on), and the *arrangement* of components within the data (whether big-endian or little-endian). These five basic color spaces are recognized:

B_MONOCHROME_1_BIT	One bit of data per pixel, where 1 is black and 0 is white.
B_GRAYSCALE_8_BIT	Eight bits of data per pixel, where a value of 255 is black and 0 is white.
B_COLOR_8_BIT	Eight bits of data per pixel, interpreted as an index into a list of 256 colors. The list is part of the system color map and is the same for all applications.
B_RGB_16_BIT	Four components of data per pixel—alpha, red, green, and blue, in that order—with 5 bits each for red, green, and blue, and 1 bit for alpha. (This color space is not currently implemented.)
B_RGB_32_BIT	Four components of data per pixel—alpha, red, green, and blue, in that order—with 8 bits per component. A component value of 255 yields the maximum amount of red, green, or blue, and a value of 0 indicates the absence of that color. (The alpha component is currently ignored. It will specify the coverage of the color—how transparent or opaque it is.)

The components in the `B_RGB_32_BIT` and `B_RGB_16_BIT` color spaces are meshed rather than separated into distinct planes; all four components are specified for the first pixel before the four components for the second pixel, and so on. The order of bytes for these two types is little-endian, which means that for `B_RGB_32_BIT` data, the component bytes appear in the order alpha, blue, green, and red.

Two counterpart color spaces are defined for big-endian data. `B_BIG_RGB_32_BIT` is equivalent to `B_RGB_32_BIT` and `B_BIG_RGB_16_BIT` is the same as `B_RGB_16_BIT`—except for the order of bytes. The Be operating system retains data in the little-endian formats; the big-endian color spaces are defined only to label noncompatible data that the system must convert and to allow drivers to communicate precise formats to the operating system.

The Screen

The screen can be configured to display colors in either the `B_COLOR_8_BIT` color space or the `B_RGB_32_BIT` color space. When it's in the `B_COLOR_8_BIT` color space, specified `rgb_colors` are displayed as the closest 8-bit color in the color list. (See the BBitmap and BScreen classes.)

Patterns

Most functions that stroke a line or fill a closed shape don't draw directly in either the high or the low color. Rather they take a *pattern*, an arrangement of one or both colors that's repeated over the entire surface being drawn. A pattern might consist of just the high color, just the low color, or some combination of the two.

By combining the low color with the high color, patterns can produce dithered colors that lie somewhere between two hues in the `B_COLOR_8_BIT` color space. Patterns also permit drawing with less than the solid high color (for intermittent or broken lines, for example) and can take advantage of drawing modes that treat the low color as if it were transparent, as discussed in the next section.

A pattern is defined as an 8-pixel by 8-pixel square. The `pattern` type is 8 bytes long, with 1 byte per row and 1 bit per pixel. Rows are specified from top to bottom and pixels from left to right. Bits marked 1 designate the high color; those marked 0 designate the low color. For example, a pattern of wide diagonal stripes could be defined as follows:

```
pattern stripes = { 0xc7, 0x8f, 0x1f, 0x3e,
                    0x7c, 0xf8, 0xf1, 0xe3 };
```

Patterns repeat themselves across the screen, like tiles laid side by side. The pattern defined above looks like the following figure.

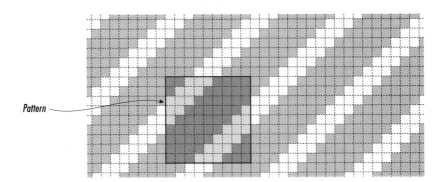

Pattern

The dotted lines in this illustration show the separation of the screen into pixels. The thicker black line outlines one 8 × 8 square that the pattern defines.

The outline of the shape being filled or the width of the line being stroked determines where the pattern is revealed. It's as if the screen was covered with the pattern just below the surface, and stroking or filling allowed some of it to show through. For example, stroking a 1-pixel wide horizontal path in the pattern illustrated above would result in a dotted line, with the dashes (in the high color) slightly longer than the spaces between (in the low color):

When stroking a line or filling a shape, the pattern serves as the source image for the current drawing mode, as explained in "Drawing Modes" next. The nature of the mode determines how the pattern interacts with the destination image, the image already in place.

The Interface Kit defines three patterns:

B_SOLID_HIGH	Consists only of the high color.
B_SOLID_LOW	Has only the low color.
B_MIXED_COLORS	Mixes the two colors evenly, like the pattern on a checkerboard.

B_SOLID_HIGH is the default pattern for all drawing functions. Applications can define as many other patterns as they need.

Drawing Modes

When a BView draws, it in effect transfers an image to a target location somewhere in the view rectangle. The drawing mode determines how the image being transferred interacts with the image already in place at that location. The image being transferred is known as the *source image*; it might be a bitmap or a pattern of some kind. The image already in place is known as the *destination image*.

In the simplest and most straightforward kind of drawing, the source image is simply painted over the destination; the source replaces the destination. However, there are other possibilities. There are ten different drawing modes—ten distinct ways of combining the source and destination images. The modes are designated by `drawing_mode` constants that can be passed to `SetDrawingMode()`:

B_OP_COPY	B_OP_ADD
B_OP_OVER	B_OP_SUBTRACT
B_OP_ERASE	B_OP_BLEND
B_OP_INVERT	B_OP_MIN
B_OP_SELECT	B_OP_MAX

`B_OP_COPY` is the default mode and the simplest. It transfers the source image to the destination, replacing whatever was there before. The destination is ignored.

In the other modes, however, some of the destination might be preserved, or the source and destination might be combined to form a result that's different from either of them. For these modes, it's convenient to think of the source image as an image that exists somewhere independent of the destination location, even though it's not actually visible. It's the image that would be rendered at the destination in `B_OP_COPY` mode.

Bitmaps and Patterns

The modes work for all BView drawing functions—including those that stroke lines and fill shapes, those that draw characters, and those that image bitmaps. The way they work depends foremost on the nature of the source image—whether it's a *pattern* or a *bitmap*. For the `Fill...()` and `Stroke...()` functions, the source image is a pattern that has the same shape as the area being filled or the area the pen touches as it strokes a line. For `DrawBitmap()`, the source image is a rectangular bitmap.

In a sense, a pattern is simply a bitmap that's one bit deep. It's a bitmap consisting of two colors, one which maps to the current high color and another that maps to the current low color. As we shall see later, a B_MONOCHROME_1_BIT bitmap acts just like a pattern. However, patterns and bitmaps generally behave differently:

- Only a source pattern has designated high and low colors. Even if a source bitmap has colors that match the current high and low colors, they're not handled like the colors in a pattern; they're treated just like any other color in the bitmap.

- On the other hand, only a source bitmap can have transparent pixels. In the B_COLOR_8_BIT color space, a pixel is made transparent by assigning it the B_TRANSPARENT_8_BIT value. In the B_RGB_32_BIT color space, a pixel assigned the B_TRANSPARENT_32_BIT value is considered transparent. These values have meaning only for source bitmaps, not for source patterns. If the current high or low color in a pattern happens to have a transparent value, it's still treated as the high or low color, not like transparency in a bitmap.

Drawing Modes and Color Spaces

The way the drawing modes work also depends on the color space of the source image and the color space of the destination. The following discussion concentrates on drawing where the source and destination both contain colors. This is the most common case, and also the one that's most general.

The source and destination images can have different color spaces. For example, a source bitmap might be defined in the B_COLOR_8_BIT space while the destination is displayed in the full color B_RGB_32_BIT color space. The drawing operation merely combines the colors in the two images in some way. It doesn't transfer the color space of the source image to the destination. The image that results from the drawing operation will always be in the color space of the destination image.

Mode Definitions

When applied to colors, the ten drawing modes fall naturally into four groups:

- The B_OP_COPY mode, which copies the source image to the destination.

- The B_OP_OVER, B_OP_ERASE, B_OP_INVERT, and B_OP_SELECT modes, which—despite their differences—all treat the low color in a pattern as if it were transparent.

- The B_OP_ADD, B_OP_SUBTRACT, and B_OP_BLEND modes, which combine colors in the source and destination images.

- The B_OP_MIN and B_OP_MAX modes, which choose between the source and destination colors.

The following paragraphs describe each of these groups in turn.

Copy mode. In B_OP_COPY mode, the source image replaces the destination. This is the default drawing mode and the one most commonly used. Because this mode doesn't have to test for particular color values in the source image, look at the colors in the destination, or compute colors in the result, it's also the fastest of the modes.

If the source image contains transparent pixels, their transparency will be retained in the result; the transparent value is copied just like any other color. However, the appearance of a transparent pixel when shown on-screen is indeterminate. If a source image has transparent portions, it's best to transfer it to the screen in B_OP_OVER or another mode. In all modes other than B_OP_COPY, a transparent pixel in a source bitmap preserves the color of the corresponding destination pixel.

Transparency modes. Four drawing modes—specifically, B_OP_OVER, B_OP_ERASE, B_OP_INVERT, and B_OP_SELECT—are designed to make use of transparency in the source image; they're able to preserve some of the destination image. In these modes (and only these modes) the low color in a source pattern acts just like transparency in a source bitmap.

Each of these modes has a different effect on the destination image—but only in those places where the source image is not transparent. One of the modes, B_OP_OVER, transfers some of the source image to the destination. The other three modes play with the destination in some way—erase it, invert it, or select colors in it—without regard to the source image. For these modes, the only thing that matters about the source image is where it's transparent and where it's not. Each of the four modes is described below:

- The B_OP_OVER mode places the source image "over" the destination; the source provides the foreground and the destination the background. In this mode, the source image replaces the destination image (just as in the B_OP_COPY mode)— except where a source bitmap has transparent pixels and a source pattern has the low color. Transparency in a bitmap and the low color in a pattern retain the destination image in the result.

  By masking out the unwanted parts of a rectangular bitmap with transparent pixels, this mode can place an irregularly shaped source image in front of a background image. Transparency in the source foreground lets the destination background show through. The versatility of B_OP_OVER makes it the second most commonly used mode, after B_OP_COPY.

- The B_OP_ERASE mode doesn't draw the source image at all. Instead, it erases the destination image. Like B_OP_OVER, it preserves the destination image wherever a source bitmap is transparent or a source pattern has the low color. But everywhere else—where the source bitmap isn't transparent and the source pattern has the high color—it removes the destination image, replacing it with the low color.

  Although this mode can be used for selective erasing, it's simpler to erase by filling an area with the B_SOLID_LOW pattern in B_OP_COPY mode.

- The B_OP_INVERT mode, like B_OP_ERASE, doesn't draw the source image. Instead, it inverts the colors in the destination image. As in the case of the B_OP_OVER and B_OP_ERASE modes, where a source bitmap is transparent or a source pattern has the low color, the destination image remains unchanged in the result. Everywhere else, the color of the destination image is inverted.

  The inversion of an rgb_color is the complement of its color components. For example, the inversion of a red value of 58 would be 197 (255–58).

- The B_OP_SELECT mode also doesn't draw the source image. It replaces the high color in the destination image with the low color and the low color with the high color. As for the other modes in this group, where a source bitmap is transparent or a source pattern has the low color, the destination image remains unchanged in the result. Everywhere else, the high and low colors are switched.

  This is similar to the B_OP_INVERT mode, except that B_OP_SELECT affects at most only two colors in the destination image. The destination is preserved not only where the source is transparent, but also where its colors don't match the current high and low colors.

These four modes also work for monochrome images. If the source image is monochrome, the distinction between source bitmaps and source patterns breaks down. Two rules apply:

- If the source image is a monochrome bitmap, it acts just like a pattern. A value of 1 in the bitmap designates the current high color, and a value of 0 designates the current low color. Thus, 0, rather than B_TRANSPARENT_32_BIT or B_TRANSPARENT_8_BIT, becomes the transparent value.

- If the source and destination are both monochrome, the high color is necessarily black (1), and the low color is necessarily white (0)—but otherwise the drawing modes work as described. With the possible colors this severely restricted, the three modes are reduced to boolean operations: B_OP_OVER is the same as a logical *OR*, B_OP_INVERT and B_OP_SELECT are the same as logical *exclusive OR*, and B_OP_ERASE is the same as an inversion of logical *AND*.

Blending modes. Three drawing modes—B_OP_ADD, B_OP_SUBTRACT, and B_OP_BLEND—combine the source and destination images, pixel by pixel, and color component by color component. As in most of the other modes, transparency in a source bitmap preserves the destination image in the result. Elsewhere, the result is a combination of the source and destination. The high and low colors of a source pattern aren't treated in any special way; they're handled just like other colors.

- B_OP_ADD adds each component of the source color to the corresponding component of the destination color, with a component value of 255 as the limit. Colors become brighter, closer to white.

By adding a uniform gray to each pixel in the destination, for example, the whole destination image can be brightened by a constant amount.

- `B_OP_SUBTRACT` subtracts each component of the source color from the corresponding component of the destination color, with a component value of 0 as the limit. Colors become darker, closer to black.

  For example, by subtracting a uniform amount from the red component of each pixel in the destination, the whole image can be made less red.

- `B_OP_BLEND` averages each component of the source and destination colors (adds the source and destination components and divides by 2). The two images are merged into one.

These modes work only for color images, not for monochrome ones. If the source or destination is specified in the `B_COLOR_8_BIT` color space, the color will be expanded to a full `B_RGB_32_BIT` value to compute the result; the result is then contracted to the closest color in the `B_COLOR_8_BIT` color space.

Selection modes. Two drawing modes—`B_OP_MAX` and `B_OP_MIN`—compare each pixel in the source image to the corresponding pixel in the destination image and select one to keep in the result. If the source pixel is transparent, both modes select the destination pixel. Otherwise, `B_OP_MIN` selects the darker of the two colors and `B_OP_MAX` selects the brighter of the two. If the source image is a uniform shade of gray, for example, `B_OP_MAX` would substitute that shade for every pixel in the destination image that was darker than the gray.

Like the blending modes, `B_OP_MIN` and `B_OP_MAX` work only for color images.

Views and the Server

Windows lead a dual life—as on-screen entities provided by the Application Server and as BWindow objects in the application. BViews have a similar dual existence— each BView object has a shadow counterpart in the server. The server knows the view's location, its place in the window's hierarchy, its visible area, and the current state of its graphics parameters. Because it has this information, the server can more efficiently associate a user action with a particular view and interpret the BView's drawing instructions.

BWindows become known to the Application Server when they're constructed; creating a BWindow object causes the server to produce the window that the user will eventually see on-screen. A BView, on the other hand, has no effect on the server when it's constructed. It becomes known to the server only when it's attached to a BWindow. The server must look through the application's windows to see what views it has.

A BView that's not attached to a window therefore lacks a counterpart in the server. This restricts what some functions can do. Three groups of functions are affected:

- Drawing functions—`DrawBitmap()`, `FillRect()`, `StrokeLine()`, and so on—don't work for unattached views. A BView can't draw unless it's in a window.

- The scrolling functions—`ScrollTo()` and `ScrollBy()`—require the BView to be in a window. Manipulations of a view's coordinate system are carried out in its server counterpart.

- Functions that indirectly depend on a BView's graphics parameters—such as `GetMouse()`, which reports the cursor location in the BView's coordinates—also require the BView to belong to a window. These functions need information that an unattached BView can't provide.

However, the functions that set and return graphics parameters—such as `SetFont()`, `SetDrawingMode()`, `PenLocation()`, and `SetHighColor()`—are not restricted. A view's graphic state is kept within the server (where it's needed to carry out drawing instructions), but also cached by the BView. Therefore, it's possible to assign a value to a graphics parameter before the server knows about the view. The value is simply cached until the view becomes part of a window's view hierarchy; the BView then hands it to the server. The server and the client-side cache are always kept in synch.

Attaching to a Window

Although you can set a BView's graphics parameters before it belongs to a window and has a counterpart in the Application Server, some of its initialization may need to wait until the BView receives an `AttachedToWindow()` notification informing it that it has been added to a window's view hierarchy. For example, if a view acts like a chameleon and adapts itself to the background color of its parent, something that's quiet common for objects defined in the Interface Kit, it can only set the view color in `AttachedToWindow()`:

```
void MyView::AttachedToWindow(void)
{
    if ( Parent() )
        SetViewColor(Parent()->ViewColor());
    . . .
}
```

`AttachedToWindow()` is called for each view that's added to a window, beginning with the root view being attached, followed by each of its children, and so on down the hierarchy. After all views have been notified with an `AttachedToWindow()` function call, they each get an `AllAttached()` notification, but in the reverse order. A parent view that must adjust itself to calculations made by a child view when it's attached to a window can wait until `AllAttached()` to do the work.

These two function calls are matched by another pair—DetachedFromWindow()
and AllDetached()—which notify BViews that they're about to be removed from
the window.

Preparing to Draw

A BView doesn't have to draw anything within its frame rectangle; it can just be a
container for other BViews that do draw there. However, most views that you
implement will draw, which means that they must do two things:

- Implement a Draw() function. This function is called upon to present the view
  on-screen (or, when printing, on a page). It's implemented using the primitive
  drawing functions listed above.
- Set the B_WILL_DRAW flag. This flag informs the Application Server that it cannot
  overlook the view when updating the window. The update mechanism is
  discussed next.

The B_WILL_DRAW flag is set on construction. For example:

```
MyView *view = new MyView(frameRect, "my view", B_FOLLOW_ALL_SIDES,
                          B_WILL_DRAW | B_NAVIGIBLE);
```

This flag must also be set if the BView's background color is anything but white (or
transparent), even if it's just a container and has no drawing functions of its own.
Drawing a background other than white is a view-specific drawing operation.

The Update Mechanism

The Application Server sends a message to a BWindow whenever any of the views
within the window need to be updated. The BWindow then calls the Draw()
function of each out-of-date BView so that it can redraw the contents of its on-screen
display.

Update messages can arrive at any time. A BWindow receives one whenever:

- The window is first placed on-screen, or is shown again after having been hidden.
- Any part of the window becomes visible after being obscured.
- The views in the window are rearranged—for example, if a view is resized or a
  child is removed from the hierarchy.
- Something happens to alter what a particular view displays. For example, if the
  contents of a view are scrolled, the BView must draw any new images that
  scrolling makes visible. If one of its children moves, it must fill in the area the
  child view vacated.
- The application forces an update by "invalidating" a view, or a portion of a view.

Update messages take precedence over other kinds of messages. To keep the on-screen display as closely synchronized with event handling as possible, the window acts on update messages as soon as they arrive. They don't need to wait their turn in the message queue.

Update messages do their work quietly and behind the scenes. You won't find them in the BWindow's message queue, they aren't handled by BWindow's `DispatchMessage()` function, and they aren't returned by BLooper's `CurrentMessage()`.

Forcing an Update

When a user action or a BView function alters a view in a window—for example, when a view is resized or its contents are scrolled—the Application Server knows about it. It makes sure that an update message is sent to the window so the view can be redrawn.

However, if code that's specific to your application alters a view, you'll need to inform the server that the view needs updating. This is done by calling the `Invalidate()` function. For example, if you write a function that changes the number of elements a view displays, you might invalidate the view after making the change, as follows:

```
void MyView::SetNumElements(long count)
{
    if ( numElements == count )
        return;
    numElements = count;
    Invalidate();
}
```

`Invalidate()` ensures that the view's `Draw()` function—which presumably looks at the new value of the *numElements* data member—will be called automatically.

At times, the update mechanism may be too slow for your application. Update messages arrive just like other messages sent to a window thread, including the interface messages that report events. Although they take precedence over other messages, update messages must wait their turn. The window thread can respond to only one message at a time; it will get the update message only after it finishes with the current one.

Therefore, if your application alters a view and calls `Invalidate()` while responding to an interface message, the view won't be updated until the response is finished and the window thread is free to turn to the next message. Usually, this is soon enough. But if it's not, if the response to the interface message includes some time-consuming operations, the application can request an immediate update by calling BWindow's `UpdateIfNeeded()` function.

Erasing the Clipping Region

Just before sending an update message, the Application Server prepares the clipping region of each BView that is about to draw by erasing it to the view background color. Note that only the clipping region is erased, not the entire view, and perhaps not the entire area where the BView will, in fact, draw.

The server forgoes this step only if the BView's background color is set to the magical B_TRANSPARENT_32_BIT color. See "The View Color" above.

Drawing During an Update

While drawing, a BView may set and reset its graphics parameters any number of times—for example, the pen position and high color might be repeatedly reset so that whatever is drawn next is in the right place and has the right color. These settings are temporary. When the update is over, all graphics parameters are reset to their initial values.

If, for example, Draw() sets the high color to a shade of light blue:

```
SetHighColor(152, 203, 255);
```

it doesn't mean that the high color will be blue when Draw() is called next. If this line of code is executed during an update, light blue would remain the high color only until the update ends or SetHighColor() is called again, whichever comes first. When the update ends, the previous graphics state, including the previous high color, is restored.

Although you can change most graphics parameters during an update—move the pen around, reset the font, change the high color, and so on—the coordinate system can't be touched; a view can't be scrolled while it's being updated. If the view's coordinate system were to change, it would alter the current clipping region and confuse the update mechanism.

Drawing Outside of an Update

Graphics parameters that are set outside the context of an update are not limited; they remain in effect until they're explicitly changed. For example, if application code calls Draw(), perhaps in response to an interface message, the parameter values that Draw() last sets would persist even after the function returns. They would become the default values for the view and would be assumed the next time Draw() is called.

Default graphics parameters are typically set as part of initializing the BView once it's attached to a window—in an AttachedToWindow() function. If you want a Draw() function to assume the values set by AttachedToWindow(), it's important to restore those values after any drawing the BView does that's not the result of an update. For example, if a BView invokes SetHighColor() while drawing in response to an interface message, it will need to restore the default high color when done.

If `Draw()` is called outside of an update, it can't assume that the clipping region will have been erased to the view color, nor can it assume that default graphics parameters will be restored when it's finished.

Responding to the User

The BWindow and BView classes together define a structure for responding to user actions on the keyboard and mouse. These actions generate *interface messages* that are delivered to BWindow objects. The BWindow distributes responsibility for the messages it receives to other objects, typically BViews.

Interface Messages

Eighteen interface messages are currently defined. Two of them command the window to do something in particular:

- A `B_ZOOM` instruction tells the window to zoom to a larger size—or to return to its normal size having previously been zoomed larger. The message is typically caused by the user operating the zoom button in the window's title tab.

- A `B_MINIMIZE` instruction tells the window to remove itself from the screen so that only a token is left to represent it—or to restore itself to the screen, having previously been minimized. This message is typically caused by the user double-clicking the window tab (or invoking the token).

  In the current incarnation of the Be user interface, the window token is a menu item under the application name in the track bar. Applications don't have access to the item, which is partially dimmed when the window is minimized.

All other interface messages report *events*—something that happened, rather than something that the application must do. In most cases, the message merely reports what the user did on the keyboard or mouse. However, in some cases, the event may reflect the way the Application Server interpreted or handled a user action. The server might respond directly to the user and pass along a message that indicates what it did—moved a window or changed a value, for example. In a few cases, the message may even reflect what the application thinks the user intended—that is, an application might interpret one or more generic user actions as a more specific event.

The following five messages report atomic user actions on the keyboard and mouse:

- A `B_KEY_DOWN` message reports character input from the keyboard. It's typically sent when the user presses a character key. After the initial key-down event (and a brief threshold), most keys generate repeated `B_KEY_DOWN` messages—as long as the user continues to hold the key down and doesn't press another key. Only character keys produce the event; the modifier keys—Shift, Control, Caps Lock, and so on—may affect the character that's reported for another key, but don't generate keyboard input on their own.

If a key is mapped to a string of characters, one B_KEY_DOWN message is generated for each character. In effect, one event is mapped to a series of messages.

Similarly, B_KEY_DOWN messages may also report a string of characters consolidated by an input method. Input methods are used where the keyboard can't be directly mapped to a full set of characters, even with the Option modifier and dead keys, either because the full set is too large or because the choice of character depends on context (or typically both). For example, input methods permit users to type languages like Japanese and Chinese from a standard keyboard. As the user types phonetically, the input method translates the typing to a set of candidate strings. The user picks a string from the list, which is then reported in a series of B_KEY_DOWN message, one for each character.

- A B_KEY_UP message reports that the user released the character key; a normal keystroke produces B_KEY_DOWN and B_KEY_UP messages in quick succession. If the user holds a repeating key down, it produces a series of B_KEY_DOWN messages, but only one B_KEY_UP. If a key is mapped to a string of characters, it produces a B_KEY_DOWN message for each character, followed by a matching series of B_KEY_UP messages, one for each character.

- A B_MOUSE_DOWN message reports that the user pressed one of the mouse buttons while the cursor was over the content area of a window. The message is generated only for the first button the user presses—that is, only if no other mouse buttons are down at the time.

- A B_MOUSE_UP message reports that the user released the mouse button. The message is produced only for the last button the user releases—that is, only if no other mouse button remains down.

- A B_MOUSE_MOVED message captures some small portion of the cursor's movement into, within, or out of a window. If the cursor isn't over a window, it's movement isn't reported. (All interface messages are associated with windows.) Repeated messages are generated as the user moves the mouse.

The five messages above are all directed at particular views—the view where the cursor is located or where typed input appears. Three others also concern views:

- A B_VIEW_MOVED message is sent when a view is moved within its parent's coordinate system. This can be a consequence of a programmatic action or of the parent view being automatically resized. If the parent view is being continuously resized because the user is resizing the window, repeated view-moved events may be reported.

- A B_VIEW_RESIZED message is delivered when a view is resized, perhaps because the program resized it or possibly as an automatic consequence of the window being resized. If the resizing is continuous, because the user is resizing the window, repeated view-resized events are reported.

- A B_VALUE_CHANGED message reports that the Application Server changed a value associated with an object. Currently, a value-changed event occurs only for BScrollBar objects. Repeated messages are sent as the user manipulates a scroll bar.

A few messages concern events that affect the window itself:

- A B_WINDOW_ACTIVATED message reports an activation event. This event occurs when a window becomes the active window and again when it gives up that status. The single action of clicking a window to make it active might result in four messages—one for the window that gains active-window status and another for the window that relinquishes it, plus B_MOUSE_DOWN and B_MOUSE_UP messages.

- A B_QUIT_REQUESTED message is interpreted by a BWindow object as a request to close the window. Quit-requested events occur when the user clicks a window's close button, or when the system perceives some other reason to request the window to quit.

- A B_WINDOW_MOVED message records the new location of a window that has been moved, either programmatically or by the user. When the user drags a window, repeated messages are generated, each one capturing a small portion of the window's continuous movement. Only one window-moved event is reported when the program moves a window.

- A B_WINDOW_RESIZED message reports that a window has been resized, again either programmatically or by the user. The message is generated repeatedly as the user resizes the window, but only once each time the application resizes it.

A few messages report changes to the on-screen environment for a window:

- A B_SCREEN_CHANGED message reports that the configuration of the screen—the size of the pixel grid it displays or the color space of the frame buffer—has changed. Such changes may require the window to take compensatory measures.

- A B_WORKSPACE_ACTIVATED message reports that the active workspace (the one displayed on-screen) has changed. All windows that live in the previously active workspace and in the one that has been newly activated are notified of the change.

- A B_WORKSPACES_CHANGED message notifies the window that the set of workspaces in which it can be displayed has changed.

Finally, there's one message that doesn't derive from a user action:

- Periodic **B_PULSE** messages are posted at regularly spaced intervals, like a steady heartbeat. Pulses don't involve any communication between the application and the Server. They're generated as long as no other events are pending, but only if the application asks for them.

An application doesn't have to wait for a message to discover what the user is doing on the keyboard and mouse. A global function, `get_key_info()`, takes a snapshot of the current state of the keyboard. BView's `GetMouse()` checks on the state of the mouse buttons and the location of the cursor.

Hook Functions for Interface Messages

Interface messages are generated and delivered to the application as the user acts. Keyboard messages are delivered to the current active window; mouse messages are sent to the window where the cursor is located. The BWindow object handles some of these messages itself, and passes others to the appropriate BView object.

An interface message is dispatched by calling a virtual function that's matched to the message. The chart below lists the virtual functions, and the base class where each is declared.

Message type	Hook function	Class
B_ZOOM	Zoom()	BWindow
B_MINIMIZE	Minimize()	BWindow
B_KEY_DOWN	KeyDown()	BView
B_KEY_UP	KeyUp()	BView
B_MOUSE_DOWN	MouseDown()	BView
B_MOUSE_UP	MouseUp()	BView
B_MOUSE_MOVED	MouseMoved()	BView
B_VIEW_MOVED	FrameMoved()	BView
B_VIEW_RESIZED	FrameResized()	BView
B_VALUE_CHANGED	ValueChanged()	BScrollBar
B_WINDOW_ACTIVATED	WindowActivated()	BWindow and BView
B_QUIT_REQUESTED	QuitRequested()	BLooper
B_WINDOW_MOVED	FrameMoved()	BWindow
B_WINDOW_RESIZED	FrameResized()	BWindow
B_SCREEN_CHANGED	ScreenChanged()	BWindow
B_WORKSPACE_ACTIVATED	WorkspaceActivated()	BWindow
B_WORKSPACES_CHANGED	WorkspacesChanged()	BWindow
B_PULSE	Pulse()	BView

B_MOUSE_UP messages aren't dispatched by calling a virtual function. A BView can determine when a mouse button goes up by calling GetMouse() from within its MouseDown() function. As it reports information about the location of the cursor and the state of the mouse buttons, GetMouse() removes mouse messages from the BWindow's message queue, so the same information won't be reported twice.

A BWindow reinterprets a B_QUIT_REQUESTED message, originally defined for the BLooper class in the Application Kit, to mean a user request to close the window. However, it doesn't redeclare the QuitRequested() hook function that it inherits from BLooper.

Dispatching

Notice, from the chart above, that the BWindow class declares the functions that handle instructions and events directed at the window itself. FrameMoved() is called when the user moves the window, FrameResized() when the user resizes it, WindowActivated() when it becomes, or ceases to be, the active window, Zoom() when it should zoom larger, and so on.

Although the BWindow handles some interface messages, the most common ones—those reporting direct user actions on the keyboard and mouse—are handled by BViews. When the BWindow receives a keyboard or mouse message, it must decide which view is responsible.

This decision is relatively easy for messages reporting mouse events. The cursor points to the affected view:

- When the user presses a mouse button, the BWindow calls the MouseDown() virtual function of the view under the cursor.

- When the user moves the mouse, it calls the MouseMoved() function of each view the cursor travels through.

- When the user releases the mouse, it will, in a future release, call the MouseUp() function both of the view that was under the cursor when the mouse button went down and of the view that is currently under the cursor (if it's a different view in the same window). (MouseUp() is not currently called.)

However, there's no cursor attached to the keyboard, so the BWindow object must keep track of the view that's responsible for messages reporting key-down and key-up events. That view is known as the *focus view*.

The Focus View

The focus view is whatever view happens to be displaying the current selection (possibly an insertion point) within the window, or whatever check box, button, or other gadget is currently marked to show that it can be operated from the keyboard.

The focus view is expected to respond to the user's keyboard actions when the window is the active window. When the user presses a key on the keyboard, the BWindow calls the focus view's `KeyDown()` function. If the focus view displays editable data, it's also expected to handle user actions that target the current selection, such as commands to cut, copy, or paste data.

The focus typically doesn't stay on one view all the time; it shifts from view to view. It may change as the user changes the current selection in the window—from text field to text field, for example. Or it changes when the user navigates from one view to another by pressing the Tab key. Only one view in the window can be in focus at a time.

Views put themselves in focus when they're selected by a user action of some kind. For example, when a BView's `MouseDown()` function is called, notifying it that the user has selected the view, it can grab the focus by calling `MakeFocus()`. When a BView makes itself the focus view, the previous focus view is notified that it has lost that status.

A view should become the focus view if it fits one of the following criteria:

- It has a `KeyDown()` function to display typed characters.
- It has a `KeyDown()` function so that the user can operate it from the keyboard.
- It can show the current selection, whether or not it has a `KeyDown()` function.

A view should highlight the current selection only while it's in focus.

BViews make themselves the focus view (with the `MakeFocus()` function), but BWindows report which view is currently in focus (with the `CurrentFocus()` function).

Kinds of Keyboard Messages

The focus view gets most keyboard messages, but not all. Three kinds of `B_KEY_DOWN` messages are conscripted for special tasks:

- If the user holds a Command key down while pressing a character key, the Command-character combination is interpreted as a keyboard shortcut (typically for a menu item, but possibly for some other control device). Instead of assigning the message to a view, the BWindow tries to issue the command associated with the shortcut.

- If the user holds an Option key down while pressing the Tab key, the Option-Tab combination is interpreted as an instruction to change the focus view. Instead of assigning the message to a view, the BWindow forces the change. This is done to enable keyboard navigation in all circumstances.

- If the window has a default button and the user presses the Enter key, the window assigns the message to the button, so that it can respond to the key-down event as it would to a click. A "default button" is simply a button that can be operated from the Enter key on the keyboard.

In all other cases, the BWindow assigns the message to the current focus view and its KeyDown() function is called.

B_KEY_UP messages have a simpler distribution: They all are assigned to the view that's in focus when the user releases the key—even if the previous B_KEY_DOWN message performed a shortcut, forced keyboard navigation, or was assigned to the default button.

Moreover, a focus view that gets a B_KEY_DOWN message may not also get the following B_KEY_UP. If the user changes the focus view after pressing the key but before releasing it, the two messages will go to different views. The B_KEY_UP message will go to an entirely different window if the user changes the active window.

Message Protocols

The BMessage objects that convey interface messages typically contain various kinds of data describing the events they report or clarifying the instructions they give. In most cases, the message contains more information than is passed to the function that starts the application's response. For example, a MouseDown() function is passed the point where the cursor was located when the user pressed the mouse button. But a B_MOUSE_DOWN BMessage also includes information about when the event occurred, what modifier keys the user was holding down at the time, which mouse button was pressed, whether the event counts as a solitary mouse-down, the second event of a double-click, or the third of a triple-click, and so on.

A MouseDown() function can get this information by taking it directly from the BMessage. The BMessage that the window thread is currently responding to can be obtained by calling the CurrentMessage() function, which the BWindow inherits from BLooper. For example, a MouseDown() function might check whether the event is a single-click or the second of a double-click as follows:

```
void MyView::MouseDown(BPoint point)
{
    int32 num;
    Window()->CurrentMessage()->FindInt32("clicks", &num);
    if ( num == 1 ) {
        . . .
    }
    else if ( num == 2 ) {
        . . .
    }
    . . .
}
```

Appendix A, *Message Protocols*, lists the contents of all interface messages.

The User Interface

Since they provide the content that's displayed within windows, BViews carry most of the burden of implementing an application's user interface. Often this is simply a matter of how a BView implements a hook function—how `Draw()` presents the view or how `MouseDown()` handles a double-click.

However, in some cases the Interface Kit provides a mechanism that derived classes can participate in, if they coordinate with kit-defined code. Two such mechanisms are described below—keyboard navigation and the drag-and-drop delivery of messages.

Keyboard Navigation

Keyboard navigation is a mechanism for allowing users to manipulate views—especially buttons, check boxes, and other control devices—from the keyboard. It gives users the ability to:

- Move the focus of keyboard actions from view to view within a window by pressing the Tab key.

- Operate the view that's currently in focus by pressing the space bar and Enter key (to invoke it) or the arrow keys (to move around inside it).

The first ability—navigation between views—is implemented by the Interface Kit. The second—navigation within a view—is up to individual applications (although the BControl class helps a little), as are most view-specific aspects of the user interface. The only trick, and it's not a difficult one, is to make the two kinds of navigation work together.

To participate in the navigation mechanism, a class derived from BView needs to coordinate three aspects of its code—setting navigation flags, drawing an indication that the BView is in focus, and responding to keyboard events. The following sections discuss each of these elements.

Setting Navigation Flags

The `B_NAVIGABLE` flag marks a BView as an eligible target for keyboard navigation. It's one flag in a mask that the BView constructor sets, along with other view attributes. For example:

```
MyView::MyView(BRect frame, const char *name,
                        uint32 resizingMode, uint32 flags)
    : BView(frame, name, resizingMode, flags|B_NAVIGIBLE|B_WILL_DRAW)
{
    . . .
}
```

When the user presses the Tab key, the focus moves from one B_NAVIGIBLE target to the next, working first down and then across the view hierarchy. That is, if a BView has both B_NAVIGIBLE children and B_NAVIGIBLE siblings, the children will be targeted before the siblings.

The flag should be removed from the mask when the view is disabled or cannot become the focus view for any reason, and included again when it's re-enabled. The mask can be altered with the SetFlags() function:

```
if ( /* cannot become the focus view */ )
    SetFlags(Flags() & ~B_NAVIGIBLE);
else
    SetFlags(Flags() | B_NAVIGIBLE);
```

Most navigable BViews are control devices and derive from the BControl class. All BControls are navigable by default and BControl has a SetEnabled() function that turns the B_NAVIGIBLE flag on and off, so this work is already done for objects that inherit from BControl.

You may also want to set the B_NAVIGIBLE_JUMP flag to permit larger jumps between navigable views. Pressing the Control-Tab combination moves the focus from one group of views to another, where the groups are (hopefully) obvious to the user from their arrangement in the window.

B_NAVIGIBLE_JUMP marks positions in the view hierarchy for these larger jumps. When the user presses Control-Tab, the focus lands on the first B_NAVIGIBLE view at or after the B_NAVIGIBLE_JUMP marker. If a B_NAVIGABLE_JUMP view is not also flagged B_NAVIGABLE, the system searches for the next available B_NAVIGABLE view and jumps to it. The search descends the view hierarchy and moves from one sibling view to another as each branch of the view hierarchy is exhausted. For example, if a B_NAVIGABLE_JUMP parent view is not navigable itself but has navigable children, Control-Tab will land on its first B_NAVIGABLE child.

Unlike B_NAVIGABLE, B_NAVIGABLE_JUMP should not be turned on and off.

Drawing the Focus Indicator

When the user navigates to a view, the BView needs to draw some sort of visual indication that it's the current focus for keyboard actions. Guidelines are forthcoming on what the indication should be. Currently, Be-defined views underline text (for example, a button label) when the view is in focus, or draw a rectangular outline of the view. The underline and outline are drawn in the color returned by keyboard_navigation_color(). Using this color lends consistency to the user interface.

A BView learns that the focus has changed when its MakeFocus() hook function is called. It's up to MakeFocus() to ensure that the focus indicator is drawn or erased, depending on the BView's new status. It's usually simplest for `MakeFocus()` to call `Draw()` and have it do the work. For example:

```
void MyView::MakeFocus(bool focused)
{
    if ( focused != IsFocus() ) {
        BView::MakeFocus(focused);
        Draw(Bounds());
        Flush();
        . . .
    }
}
```

The BControl class has a `MakeFocus()` function that calls `Draw()` (though it doesn't look exactly like the one above), so if your class derives from BControl, all you need to do is implement `Draw()`. `Draw()` can call `IsFocus()` to test the BView's current status. Here's a rough example:

```
void MyView::Draw(BRect updateRect)
{
    rbg_color navigationColor = keyboard_navigation_color();
    BRect r = Bounds()
    r.InsetBy(2.0, 2.0)
    . . .
    rgb_color c = HighColor();
    if ( IsFocus() ) {
        /* draw the indicator */
        SetHighColor(navigationColor);
        StrokeRect(r);
        SetHighColor(c);
    }
    else {
        /* erase the indicator */
        SetHighColor(ViewColor());
        StrokeRect(r);
        SetHighColor(c);
    }
    . . .
}
```

This example is diagrammatic; it may not show an appropriate way for the BViews in your application to draw. (Note that when `MakeFocus()` called `IsFocus()`, it returned the BView's previous status, but when `Draw()` called it, it returned the updated status.)

Handling Keyboard Actions

Finally, your BView may need to override `KeyDown()` to handle the keystrokes that are used to operate the view (for view-internal navigation). Always incorporate the inherited version of `KeyDown()` so that it can take care of navigation between views. For example:

```
void MyView::KeyDown(const char *bytes, int32 numBytes)
{
    switch ( bytes[0] ) {
        case B_ENTER:
        case B_SPACE:
            /* take action */
            break;
        case B_UP_ARROW:
        case B_DOWN_ARROW:
        case B_RIGHT_ARROW:
        case B_LEFT_ARROW:
            /* move within the view */
            break;
        default:
            BView::KeyDown(bytes, numBytes);
            break;
    }
}
```

Again, the BControl class implements a `KeyDown()` function that invokes the control device when the user presses the space bar or Enter key. If your class derives from BControl and it doesn't have to do any other view-internal navigation, the BControl function may be adequate for your needs.

Drag and Drop

The BView class supports a drag-and-drop user interface. The user can transfer a parcel of information from one place to another by dragging an image from a source view and dropping it on a destination view—perhaps a view in a different window in a different application.

A source BView initiates dragging by calling `DragMessage()` from within its `MouseDown()` function. The BView bundles all information relevant to the dragging session into a BMessage object and passes it to `DragMessage()`. It also passes an image or a rectangle to represent the data package on-screen. For example:

```
void MyView::MouseDown(BPoint point)
{
    . . .
    if ( aRect.Contains(point) ) {
        BMessage message(SOME_WORDS_OF_ENCOURAGEMENT);
        message.AddString("words", theEncouragingWords);
        DragMessage(&message, aRect);
    }
    . . .
}
```

The Application Server then takes charge of the BMessage object and animates the image as the user drags it on-screen. As the image moves across the screen, the views it passes over are informed with `MouseMoved()` function calls. These notifications give views a chance to show the user whether or not they're willing to accept the message being dragged. When the user releases the mouse button, dropping the dragged message, the message is delivered to the BWindow and targeted to the destination BView.

A BView is notified that a message has arrived by a `MessageReceived()` function call. This is the same function that announces the arrival of other messages. By calling `WasDropped()`, you can ask the message whether it was dropped on the view or delivered in some other way. If it was dropped, you can find out where by calling `DropPoint()`. For example:

```
void AnotherView::MessageReceived(BMessage *message)
{
    switch ( Message->what ) {
        . . .
        case SOME_WORDS_OF_ENCOURAGEMENT:
        {
            char *words;
            if ( message->FindString("words", &words) != B_OK )
                return;
            if ( message->WasDropped() ) {
                BPoint where = DropPoint();
                ConvertFromScreen(&where);
                PleaseInsertTheseWords(words, where);
            }
            break;
        }
        . . .
        default:
            BView::MessageReceived(message);
    }
}
```

Aside from creating a BMessage object and passing it to `DragMessage()`, or implementing `MouseMoved()` and `MessageReceived()` functions to handle any messages that come its way, there's nothing an application needs to do to support a drag-and-drop user interface. The bulk of the work is done by the Application Server and Interface Kit.

Character Encoding

The BeOS encodes characters using the UTF-8 transformation of Unicode character values. Unicode is a standard encoding scheme for all the major scripts of the world—including, among others, extended Latin, Cyrillic, Greek, Devanagiri, Telugu, Hebrew, Arabic, Tibetan, and the various character sets used by Chinese, Japanese, and Korean. It assigns a unique and unambiguous 16-bit value to each character, making it possible for characters from various languages to co-exist in the same document. Unicode makes it simpler to write language-aware software (though it doesn't solve all the problems). It also makes a wide variety of symbols available to an application, even if it's not concerned with covering more than one language.

Unicode's one disadvantage is that all characters have a width of 16 bits. Although 16 bits are necessary for a universal encoding system and a fixed width for all characters is important for the standard, there are many contexts in which byte-sized characters would be easier to work with and take up less memory (besides being more familiar and backwards compatible with existing code). UTF-8 is designed to address this problem.

UTF-8

UTF-8 stands for "UCS Transformation Format, 8-bit form" (and UCS stands for "Universal Multiple-Octet Character Set," another name for Unicode). UTF-8 transforms 16-bit Unicode values into a variable number of 8-bit units. It takes advantage of the fact that for values equal to or less than 0x007f, the Unicode character set matches the 7-bit ASCII character set—in other words, Unicode adopts the ASCII standard, but encodes each character in 16 bits. UTF-8 strips ASCII values back to 8 bits and uses two or three bytes to encode Unicode values over 0x007f.

The high bit of each UTF-8 byte indicates the role it plays in the encoding:

* If the high bit is 0, the byte stands alone and encodes an ASCII value.
* If the high bit is 1, the byte is part of a multiple-byte character representation.

In addition, the first byte of a multibyte character indicates how many bytes are in the encoding: The number of high bits that are set to 1 (before a bit is 0) is the number of bytes it takes to represent the character. Therefore, the first byte of a multibyte character will always have at least two high bits set. The other bytes in a multibyte encoding have just one high bit set.

To illustrate, a character encoded in one UTF-8 byte will look like this (where a "1" or a "0" indicates a control bit specified by the standard and an "x" is a bit that contributes to the character value):

$$0xxxxxxx$$

A character encoded in two bytes has the following arrangement of bits:

$$110xxxxx\ 10xxxxxx$$

And a character encoded in three bytes is laid out as follows:

$$1110xxxx\ 10xxxxxx\ 10xxxxxx$$

Note that any 16-bit value can be encoded in three UTF-8 bytes. However, UTF-8 discards leading zeroes and always uses the fewest possible number of bytes—so it can encode Unicode values less than 0x0080 in a single byte and values less than 0x0800 in two bytes.

In addition to the codings illustrated above, UTF-8 takes four bytes to translate a Unicode *surrogate pair*—two conjoined 16-bit values that together encode a character that's not part of the standard. Surrogates are extremely rare.

ASCII Compatibility

The UTF-8 encoding scheme has several advantages:

- The single byte that encodes an ASCII value can't be confused with a byte that's part of a multiple-byte encoding. You can test a UTF-8 byte for an ASCII value without considering surrounding bytes; if there's a match, you can be sure the byte is the ASCII character. UTF-8 is fully compatible with ASCII.

- The first (or only) byte of a character can't be confused with a byte inside a multibyte sequence. It's simple to find where a character begins. For example, this macro will do it:

```
#define BEGINS_CHAR(byte) ((byte & 0xc0) != 0x80)
```

- The string functions in the standard C library—for example, `strcat()` and `strlen()`—can operate on a UTF-8 string.

  However, it's important to remember that `strlen()` measures the string in bytes, not characters. Some Interface Kit functions, like `GetEscapements()` in the BFont class, ask for a character count; `strlen()` can't provide the answer. Instead, you need to do something like this to count the characters in a string:

```
int32 count = 0;
while ( *p != '\0' ) {
    if ( BEGINS_CHAR(*p) )
        count++;
    p++;
}
```

- UTF-8 preserves the numerical ordering of Unicode character values. String comparison functions—such as `strcasecmp()`—will put UTF-8 strings in the correct order.

  However, you should be careful when using the string comparison functions to order a set of UTF-8 strings. Unicode tries for a universal encoding and orders characters in a way that's generically correct, but it may not be correct for specific characters in specific languages. (Because it follows ASCII, UTF-8 is correct for English.)

- For European languages, UTF-8 generally yields more compact data representations than would Unicode. Most of the characters in a string can be encoded in a single byte. In many other cases, UTF-8 is no less compact than Unicode.

UTF-8 and the BeOS

The BeOS assumes UTF-8 encoding in most cases. For example, a B_KEY_DOWN message reports the character that's mapped to the key the user pressed as a UTF-8 value. That value is then passed as a string to KeyDown() along with the byte count:

virtual void KeyDown (const char *bytes, int32 numBytes);

You can expect the bytes string to always contain at least one byte. And, of course, you can test it for an ASCII value without caring whether it's UTF-8:

```
if ( bytes[0] == B_TAB )
     . . .
```

Similarly, objects that display text in the user interface—such as window titles and button labels—expect to be passed UTF-8 encoded strings, and hand you a UTF-8 string if you ask for the title or label. These objects display text using a system font—either the system plain font (be_plain_font) or the bold font (be_bold_font). The BFont class allows other character encodings, which you may need to use in limited circumstances from time to time, but the system fonts are constrained to UTF-8 (B_UNICODE_UTF8 encoding). The FontPanel preferences application doesn't permit users to change the encoding of a system font.

Unicode and UTF-8 are documented in *The Unicode Standard, Version 2.0*, published by Addison-Wesley. See that book for complete information on Unicode and for a description of how UTF-8 encodes surrogate pairs.

The Coordinate Space

To locate screens, windows, and views, draw in them, and report where the cursor is positioned, it's necessary to have some conventional way of talking about the display surface. The same conventions are used whether the display device is a monitor that shows images on a screen or a printer that puts them on a page.

Two-Dimensional Coordinates

In Be software, the display surface is described by a standard two-dimensional coordinate system where the *y*-axis extends downward and the *x*-axis extends to the right, as shown in the next illustration.

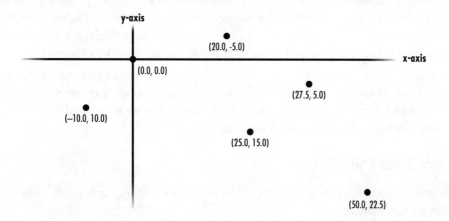

y-coordinate values are greater towards the bottom of the display and smaller towards the top, *x*-coordinate values are greater to the right and smaller to the left.

The axes define a continuous coordinate space where distances are measured by floating-point values of the type `float`. All quantities in this space—including widths and heights, *x*- and *y*-coordinates, font sizes, angles, and the size of the pen—are floating-point numbers.

Floating-point coordinates permit precisely stated measurements that can take advantage of display devices with higher resolutions than the screen. For example, a vertical line 0.4 units wide would be displayed using a single column of pixels on-screen, the same as a line 1.4 units wide. However, a 300 dpi printer would use two columns of pixels to print the 0.4-unit line and six to print the 1.4-unit line.

A coordinate unit is 1/72 of an inch, roughly equal to a typographical point. However, all screens are considered to have a resolution of 72 pixels per inch (regardless of the actual dimension), so coordinate units count screen pixels. One unit is the distance between the centers of adjacent pixels on-screen.

Coordinate Systems

Specific coordinate systems are associated with the screen, with windows, and with the views inside windows. They differ only in where the two axes are located:

* The global or *screen coordinate system* has its origin, (0.0, 0.0), at the left top corner of the main screen. It's used for positioning windows on-screen, for arranging multiple screens connected to the same machine, and for comparing coordinate values that weren't originally stated in a common coordinate system. (Multiple screens are not currently supported.)

- A *window coordinate system* has its origin at the left top corner of the content area of a window. It's used principally for positioning views within the window. Each window has its own coordinate system so that locations within the window can be specified without regard to where the window happens to be on-screen.

- A *view coordinate system* has its default origin at the left top corner of the view rectangle. However, scrolling can shift view coordinates and move the origin. View-specific coordinates are used for all drawing operations and to report the cursor location in most system messages.

Coordinate Data Types

The Interface Kit defines a handful of basic classes for locating points and areas within a coordinate system:

- A BPoint object is the simplest way to specify a coordinate location. Each object stores two values—an *x*-coordinate and a *y*-coordinate—that together locate a specific point, (*x*, *y*), within a given coordinate system.

- A BRect object represents a rectangle; it's the simplest way to designate an area within a coordinate system. The BRect class defines a rectangle as a set of four coordinate values—corresponding to the rectangle's left, top, right, and bottom edges, as shown in this illustration:

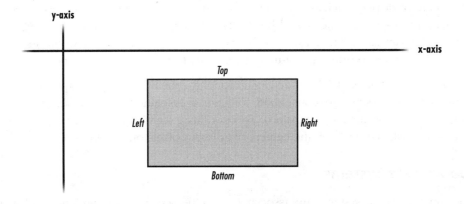

The sides of the rectangle are therefore parallel to the coordinate axes. The left and right sides delimit the range of *x*-coordinate values within the rectangle, and the top and bottom sides delimit the range of *y*-coordinate values. For example, if a rectangle's left top corner is at (0.8, 2.7) and its right bottom corner is at (11.3, 49.5), all points having *x*-coordinates ranging from 0.8 through 11.3 and *y*-coordinates from 2.7 through 49.5 lie inside the rectangle.

If the top of a rectangle is the same as its bottom, or its left the same as its right, the rectangle defines a straight line. If the top and bottom are the same and also the left and right, it collapses to a single point. Such rectangles are still valid—they specify real locations within a coordinate system. However, if the top is greater than the bottom or the left greater than the right, the rectangle is invalid; it has no meaning.

- A BPolygon object represents a polygon, a closed figure with an arbitrary number of sides. The polygon is defined as an ordered set of points. It encloses the area that would be outlined by connecting the points in order, then connecting the first and last points to close the figure. Each point is therefore a potential vertex of the polygon.

- A BRegion object defines a set of points. A region can be any shape and even include discontinuous areas. It's equivalent to a set of rectangles.

Mapping Coordinates to Pixels

The device-independent coordinate space described above must be mapped to the pixel grid of a particular display device—the screen, a printer, or some other piece of hardware that's capable of rendering an image. For example, to display a rectangle, it's necessary to find the pixel columns that correspond to its right and left sides and the pixel rows that correspond to its top and bottom.

This depends entirely on the resolution of the device. In essence, each device-independent coordinate value must be translated internally to a device-dependent value—an integer index to a particular column or row of pixels. In the coordinate space of the device, one unit equals one pixel.

This translation is easy for the screen, since, as mentioned above, there's a one-to-one correspondence between coordinate units and pixels. It reduces to rounding floating-point coordinates to integers. For other devices, however, the translation means first scaling the coordinate value to a device-specific value, then rounding. For example, the point (12.3, 40.8) would translate to (12, 41) on the screen, but to (51, 170) on a 300 dpi printer.

Screen Pixels

To map coordinate locations to device-specific pixels, you need to know only two things:

- The resolution of the device
- The location of the coordinate axes relative to pixel boundaries

The axes are located in the same place for all devices: The *x*-axis runs left to right along the middle of a row of pixels, and the *y*-axis runs down the middle of a pixel column. They meet at the very center of a pixel.

Because coordinate units match pixels on the screen, this means that all integral coordinate values (those without a fractional part) fall midway across a screen pixel. The following illustration shows where various *x*-coordinate values fall on the *x*-axis. The broken lines represent the division of the screen into a pixel grid:

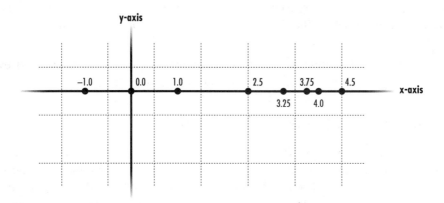

As this illustration shows, it's possible to have coordinate values that lie on the boundary between two pixels. The next section describes how these values are mapped to one pixel or the other.

Picking Pixels to Stroke and Fill

This section discusses how the various BView `Stroke...()` and `Fill...()` functions pick specific pixels to color. (Since pixels are small, this is not a topic that you necessarily need to be concerned about, especially as you begin programming for the BeOS.)

Pixels are chosen after the pen size and all coordinate values have been translated to device-specific units. Device-specific values measure distances by counting pixels; 1 unit equals 1 pixel on the device.

A device-specific value can be derived from a coordinate value using a formula that takes the size of a coordinate unit and the resolution of the device into account. For example:

```
device_value = coordinate_value × ( dpi / 72 )
```

dpi is the resolution of the device in dots (pixels) per inch, 72 is the number of coordinate units in an inch, and *device_value* is rounded to the closest integer.

To describe where lines and shapes fall on the pixel grid, this section mostly talks about pixel units rather than coordinate units. The accompanying illustrations magnify the grid so that pixel boundaries are clear. As a consequence, they can show only very short lines and small shapes. By blowing up the image, they exaggerate the phenomena they illustrate.

Stroking Thin Lines

The thinnest possible line is drawn when the pen size translates to 1 pixel on the device. Setting the size to 0.0 coordinate units guarantees a 1-pixel pen on all devices.

A 1-pixel pen follows the path of the line it strokes and makes the line exactly 1 pixel thick at all points. If the line is perfectly horizontal or vertical, it touches just one row or one column of pixels, as illustrated below. (The grid of broken lines shows the separation of the display surface into pixels.)

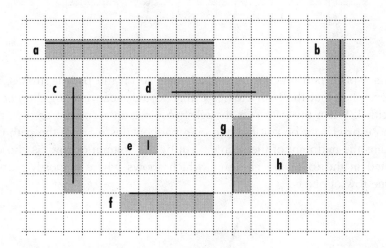

Only pixels that the line path actually passes through are colored to display the line. If a path begins or ends on a pixel boundary, as it does for examples (a) and (b) in the illustration, the pixels at the boundary aren't colored unless the path crosses into the pixel. The pen touches the fewest possible number of pixels.

A line path that doesn't enter any pixels, but lies entirely on the boundaries between pixels, colors the pixel row beneath it or the pixel column to its right, as illustrated by lines (f) and (g). A path that reduces to a single point lying on the corner of four pixels, as does (h), colors the pixel at its lower right. (However, currently, it's indeterminate which column or row of adjacent pixels would be used to display vertical and horizontal lines like (f) and (g). Point (h) would not be visible.)

1-pixel lines that aren't exactly vertical or horizontal touch just one pixel per row or one per column. If the line is more vertical than horizontal, only one pixel in each row is used to color the line. If the line is more horizontal than vertical, only one pixel in each column is used. Some illustrations of slanted 1-pixel thick lines are given below:

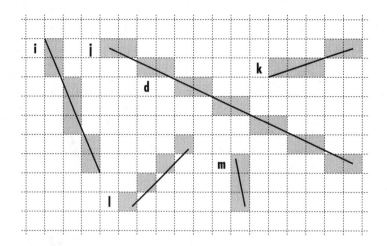

Although a 1-pixel pen touches only pixels that lie on the path it strokes, it won't touch every pixel that the path crosses if that would mean making the line thicker than specified. When the path cuts though two pixels in a column or row, but only one of those pixels can be colored, the one that contains more of the path (the one that contains the midpoint of the segment cut by the column or row) is chosen. This is illustrated in the following close-up, which shows where a mostly vertical line crosses one row of pixels:

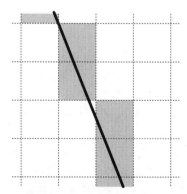

However, before a choice is made as to which pixel in a row or column to color, the line path is normalized for the device. For example, if a line is defined by two endpoints, it's first determined which pixels correspond to those endpoints. The line path is then treated as if it connected the centers of those pixels. This may alter which pixels get colored, as is illustrated below. In this illustration, the solid black line is the line path as originally specified and the broken line is its normalized version:

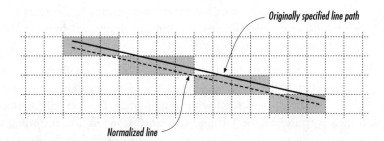

This normalization is nothing more than the natural consequence of the rounding that occurs when coordinate values are translated to device-specific pixel values.

Stroking Curved Lines

Although all the diagrams above show straight lines, the principles they illustrate apply equally to curved line paths. A curved path can be treated as if it were made up of a large number of short straight segments.

Filling and Stroking Rectangles

The following illustration shows how some rectangles, represented by the solid black line, would be filled with a solid color.

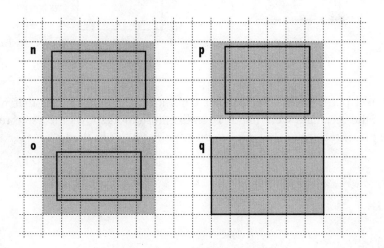

A rectangle includes every pixel that it encloses and every pixel that its sides pass through. However, as rectangle (q) illustrates, it doesn't include pixels that its sides merely touch at the boundary.

If the pixel grid in this illustration represents the screen, rectangle (q) would have left, top, right, and bottom coordinates with fractional values of .5. Rectangle (n), on the other hand, would have coordinates without any fractional parts. Nonfractional coordinates lie at the center of screen pixels.

Rectangle (n), in fact, is the normalized version of all four of the illustrated rectangles. It shows how the sides of the four rectangles would be translated to pixel values. Note that for a rectangle like (q), with edges that fall on pixel boundaries, normalization means rounding the left and top sides upward and rounding the right and bottom sides downward. This follows from the principal that the fewest possible number of pixels should be colored.

Although the four rectangles above differ in size and shape, when filled they all cover a 6×4 pixel area. You can't predict this area from the dimensions of the rectangle. Because the coordinate space is continuous and x and y values can be located anywhere, rectangles with different dimensions might have the same rendered size, as shown above, and rectangles with the same dimensions might have different rendered sizes, as shown below:

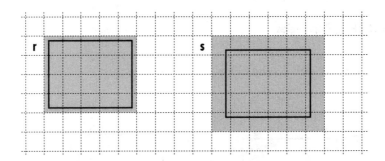

If a one-pixel pen strokes a rectangular path, it touches only pixels that would be included if the rectangle were filled. The next illustration shows the same rectangles that were presented above, but strokes them rather than fills them.

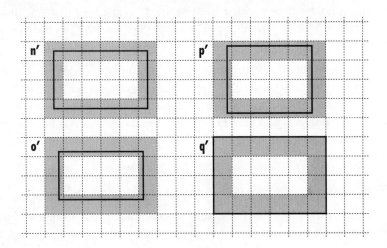

Each of the rectangles still covers a 6 × 4 pixel area. Note that even though the path of rectangle (q′) lies entirely on pixel boundaries, pixels below it and to its right are not touched by the pen. The pen touches only pixels that lie within the rectangle.

If a rectangle collapses to a straight line or to a single point, it no longer contains any area. Stroking or filling such a rectangle is equivalent to stroking the line path with a one-pixel pen, as was discussed in the previous section.

Filling and Stroking Polygons

The figure below shows a polygon as it would be stroked by a one-pixel pen and as it would be filled:

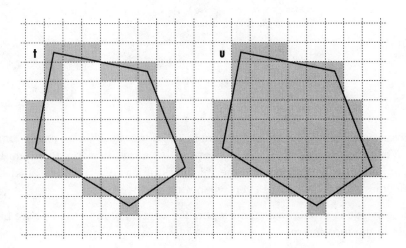

The same rules apply when stroking each segment of a polygon as would apply if that segment were an independent line. Therefore, the pen may not touch every pixel the segment passes through.

When the polygon is filled, no additional pixels around its border are colored. As is the case for a rectangle, the displayed shape of filled polygon is identical to the shape of the polygon when stroked with a one-pixel pen. The pen doesn't touch any pixels when stroking the polygon that aren't colored when the polygon is filled. Conversely, filling doesn't color any pixels at the border of the polygon that aren't touched by a one-pixel pen.

Stroking Thick Lines

A pen that's thicker than one pixel touches the same pixels that a one-pixel pen does, but it adds extra columns and rows adjacent to the line path. A thick pen tip is, in effect, a linear brush that's held perpendicular to the line path and kept centered on the line. The illustration below shows two short lines, each five pixels thick:

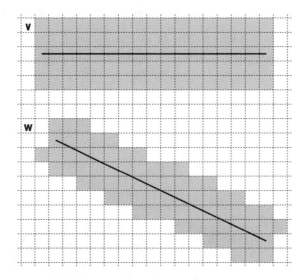

The thickness or a vertical or horizontal line can be measured in an exact number of pixels. When the line is slanted, as it is for (t) above, the stroking algorithm tries to make the line visually approximate the thickness of a vertical or horizontal line. In this way, lines retain their shape even when rotated.

When a rectangle is stroked with a thick pen, the corners of the rectangle are filled in, as shown in the next figure.

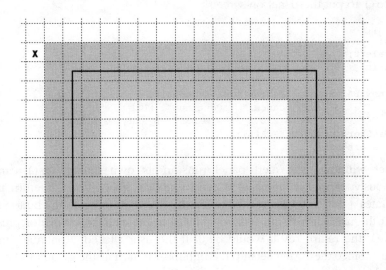

BAlert

Derived from: public BWindow

Declared in: be/interface/Alert.h

Library: libbe.so

Overview

A BAlert places a modal window on-screen in front of other windows. The window is an *alert panel* that has a message for the user to read and one or more buttons the user can operate. The message might warn the user of something or convey some information that the application doesn't want the user to overlook. Typically, it asks a question that the user must answer. Operating a button chooses a course of action and dismisses the panel (closes the window).

The alert panel stays on-screen until the user operates one of the buttons. As long as it's on-screen, other parts of the application's user interface are disabled. However, the user can continue to move windows around and work in other applications.

To use a BAlert object, all you do is:

- Construct the object.
- Call SetShortcut() if you want the user to be able to operate window buttons from the keyboard. (The button on the right is automatically made the default button and can be operated by the Enter key.)

- Call `Go()` to put the panel on-screen.

For example:

```
BAlert *alert;
long result;

alert = new BAlert("", "Do you want to continue?",
                        "Cancel", "Continue", NULL,
                        B_WIDTH_FROM_WIDEST, B_WARNING_ALERT);
alert->SetShortcut(0, B_ESCAPE);
result = alert->Go();
```

Like other windows, the alert panel runs in its own thread. `Go()` can run it synchronously or asynchronously. If synchronously, `Go()` doesn't return until the user operates a button to dismiss the panel. It returns an index to the button the user picked. If the user clicked the "Cancel" button in the example above or pressed the Escape key, the return result would be 0. If the user clicked "Continue", the result would be 1. Since the BAlert sets up the rightmost button as the default button for the window, the user could also operate the "Continue" button by pressing the Enter key.

If it runs the panel asynchronously, `Go()` returns immediately with, of course, no indication of which button the user will choose. If it's important to take some action when the user acts, a BInvoker object must be passed to the function:

```
alert->Go(someInvoker);
```

The BInvoker will send its message when the user acts. The index of the button the user chose is stuffed into the message as an `int32` under the name "which".

In either case, when the user dismisses the panel, the window thread is killed, and the BAlert object is deleted.

Constructor

BAlert()

> **BAlert**(const char *title*, const char *text*,
>   const char *firstButton*,
>   const char *secondButton* = NULL,
>   const char *thirdButton* = NULL,
>   button_width *width* = B_WIDTH_AS_USUAL,
>   alert_type *type* = B_INFO_ALERT)
> **BAlert**(BMessage *archive*)

Creates an alert panel as a modal window. The window displays some *text* for the user to read, and can have up to three buttons. There must be at least a *firstButton*; the others are optional. The BAlert must also have a *title*, even though the panel doesn't have a title tab to display it. The title can be NULL or an empty string.

The buttons are arranged in a row at the bottom of the panel so that one is always in the right bottom corner. They're placed from left to right in the order specified to the constructor. If labels for three buttons are provided, *firstButton* will be on the left, *secondButton* in the middle, and *thirdButton* on the right. If only two labels are provided, *firstButton* will come first and *secondButton* will be in the right bottom corner. If there's just one label (*firstButton*), it will be at the right bottom location.

By default, the user can operate the rightmost button by pressing the Enter key. If a "Cancel" button is included, it should be assigned the `B_ESCAPE` character as a keyboard shortcut. Other buttons can be assigned other shortcut characters. Use BAlert's `SetShortcut()` function to set up the shortcuts, rather than BWindow's `AddShortcut()`. Shortcuts added by a BWindow require the user to hold down a Command key, while those set by a BAlert don't.

By default, all the buttons have a standard, minimal width (`B_WIDTH_AS_USUAL`). This is adequate for most buttons, but may not be wide enough to accommodate an especially long label. To adjust the width of each button to the width of its label, set the *width* parameter to `B_WIDTH_FROM_LABEL`. To ensure that the buttons are all the same width, yet wide enough to display the widest label, set the *width* parameter to `B_WIDTH_FROM_WIDEST`.

For more hands-on manipulation of the buttons, you can get the BButton objects that the BAlert creates by calling the `ButtonAt()` function. To get the BTextView object that displays the *text* string, you can call `TextView()`.

There are various kinds of alert panels, depending on the content of the textual message and the nature of the options presented to the user. The *type* parameter should classify the BAlert object as one of the following:

`B_EMPTY_ALERT`

`B_INFO_ALERT`

`B_IDEA_ALERT`

`B_WARNING_ALERT`

`B_STOP_ALERT`

Currently, the alert *type* is used only to select a representative icon that's displayed at the left top corner of the window. A `B_EMPTY_ALERT` doesn't have an icon.

After the BAlert is constructed, `Go()` must be called to place it on-screen. The object is deleted when the user closes the window; you don't need to write code to delete it.

Static Functions

Instantiate()

> static BAlert ***Instantiate**(BMessage *archive)

Returns a new BAlert object, allocated by new and created with the version of the constructor that takes a BMessage *archive*. However, if the *archive* message doesn't contain data for a BAlert object, the return value will be NULL.

See also: BArchivable::Instantiate(), instantiate_object(), Archive()

Member Functions

Archive()

> virtual status_t **Archive**(BMessage *archive, bool *deep* = true) const

Calls the inherited version of Archive(), then adds the BAlert's type, buttons, keyboard shortcuts, preferred button width, and the text it displays to the BMessage *archive*.

See also: BArchivable::Archive(), Instantiate() static function

ButtonAt()

> BButton ***ButtonAt**(int32 *index*) const

Returns a pointer to the BButton object for the button at *index*. Indices begin at 0 and count buttons from left to right. The BButton belongs to the BAlert object and should not be freed.

See also: TextView()

FrameResized()

> virtual void **FrameResized**(float *width*, float *height*)

Overrides the BView function to adjust the layout within the panel when its dimensions change. This function is called as the panel is being resized; there's no need to call it or override it in application code.

Go()

> int32 **Go**(void)
> status_t **Go**(BInvoker *invoker)

Sets the modal loop for the BAlert in motion and calls the `Show()` virtual function to place the panel on-screen. `Go()` can operate synchronously or asynchronously:

- If called without an argument, `Go()` returns only when the modal loop has quit and the window has been closed. The value it returns is the index of the button that the user operated to close the window. Buttons are indexed from left to right, beginning with 0.

- If called with an argument, `Go()` returns immediately (the return value is invariably `B_OK`). The panel remains on-screen until the user closes it. This option frees the calling thread (usually a main window) to keep working while the panel is on-screen.

  This version of `Go()` is passed a BInvoker object, which the BAlert will use to send a message when the user operates a button to close the panel. The index of the button the user chooses is added to the message as a 32-bit value under the name "which". This is in addition to the "when" field added by the BInvoker.

  If you don't need to know what action the user takes, *invoker* can be `NULL`.

To put an alert panel on-screen, simply construct a BAlert object, set its keyboard shortcuts, if any, and call this function. See the example code in the "Overview" section above.

Before returning, this function deletes the BAlert object, and all the objects it created.

MessageReceived()

> virtual void **MessageReceived**(BMessage **message*)

Closes the window in response to messages posted from the window's buttons. There's no need for your application to call or override this function.

SetShortcut(), Shortcut()

> void **SetShortcut**(int32 *index*, char *shortcut*)

> char **Shortcut**(int32 *index*) const

These functions set and return a *shortcut* character that the user can type to operate the button at *index*. Buttons are indexed from left to right beginning with 0. By default, `B_ENTER` is the shortcut for the rightmost button.

A "Cancel" button should be assigned the `B_ESCAPE` character as a shortcut.

The shortcut doesn't require the user to hold down a Command key or other modifier (except for any modifiers normally required to produce the *shortcut* character).

The shortcut is valid only while the window is on-screen.

TextView()

BTextView ***TextView**(void) const

Returns a pointer to the BTextView object that contains the textual information that's displayed in the panel. The object is created and the text is set when the BAlert is constructed. The BTextView object belongs to the BAlert and should not be freed.

BBitmap

Derived from: . public BArchivable

Declared in: be/interface/Bitmap.h

Library: libbe.so

Overview

A BBitmap object is a container for an image bitmap; it stores pixel data—data that describes an image pixel by pixel. The class provides a way of specifying a bitmap from raw data, and also a way of creating the data from scratch using the Interface Kit graphics mechanism.

BBitmap functions manage the bitmap data and provide information about it. However, they don't do anything with the data. Placing the image somewhere so that it can be seen is the province of BView functions—such as `DrawBitmap()` and `DragMessage()`—not this class.

Bitmap Data

An image bitmap records the color values of pixels within a rectangular area. The pixels in the rectangle, as on the screen, are arranged in rows and columns. The data is specified in rows, beginning with the top row of pixels in the image and working downward to the bottom row. Each row of data is aligned on a long word boundary and is read from left to right.

New BBitmap objects are constructed with two pieces of information that prepare them to store bitmap data—a bounds rectangle and a color space. For example, this code:

```
BRect rect(0.0, 0.0, 79.0, 39.0);
BBitmap *image = new BBitmap(rect, B_COLOR_8_BIT);
```

constructs a bitmap of 40 rows and 80 pixels per row. Each pixel is specified by an 8-bit color value.

The Bounds Rectangle

A BBitmap's bounds rectangle serves two purposes:

- It sets the size of the image. A bitmap covers as many pixels as its bounds rectangle encloses—under the assumption that one coordinate unit equals one pixel, as it does when the display device is the screen.

  Since a bitmap can't contain a fraction of a pixel, the bounds rectangle shouldn't contain any fractional coordinates. Without fractional coordinates, each side of the bounds rectangle will be aligned with a column or a row of pixels. The pixels around the edge of the rectangle are included in the image, so the bitmap will contain one more column of pixels than the width of the rectangle and one more row than the rectangle's height. (See the BRect class for an illustration.)

- It establishes a coordinate system that can be used later by drawing functions, such as `DrawBitmap()` and `DragMessage()`, to designate particular points or portions of the image.

  For example, if one BBitmap was constructed with this bounds rectangle:

  ```
  BRect firstRect(0.0, 0.0, 60.0, 100.0);
  ```

  and another with this rectangle:

  ```
  BRect secondRect(60.0, 100.0, 120.0, 200.0);
  ```

  they would both have the same size and shape. However, the coordinates (60.0, 100.0) would designate the right bottom corner of the first bitmap, but the left top corner of the second.

If a BBitmap object enlists BViews to create the bitmap data, it must have a bounds rectangle with (0.0, 0.0) at the left top corner.

The Color Space

The color space of a bitmap determines its depth (how many bits of information are stored for each pixel) and its interpretation (what the data values mean). These five color spaces are currently defined:

```
B_MONOCHROME_1_BIT
```

```
B_GRAYSCALE_8_BIT
```

```
B_COLOR_8_BIT
```

```
B_RGB_16_BIT
```

```
B_RGB_32_BIT
```

Currently, bitmap data is stored only in the `B_RGB_32_BIT`, `B_COLOR_8_BIT`, and `B_MONOCHROME_1_BIT` color spaces. The `B_GRAYSCALE_8_BIT` and `B_RGB_16_BIT` color spaces are not used at the present time.

In the `B_RGB_32_BIT` color space, the color of each pixel is specified by its red, green, and blue components. In the `B_COLOR_8_BIT` color space, colors are specified as byte indices into the color map. In the `B_MONOCHROME_1_BIT` color space, a value of 1 means black and 0 means white. (A more complete description of the five color spaces can be found under "Colors" in the "Drawing" section of this chapter.)

Specifying the Image

BBitmap objects begin life empty. When constructed, they allocate sufficient memory to store an image of the size and color space specified. However, the memory isn't initialized. The actual image must be set after construction. This can be done by explicitly assigning pixel values with the `SetBits()` function:

```
image->SetBits(rawData, numBytes, 0, COLOR_8_BIT);
```

You can also get the `Bits()` pointer to the memory buffer and copy image data directly to it:

```
uchar *bits (uchar *)image->Bits();
memcpy(bits, sourceData, numBytes);
```

In this case, you must make sure the data is written in the internal format of the BBitmap object.

In addition to these functions, BView objects can be enlisted to produce the bitmap. Views are assigned to a BBitmap object just as they are to a BWindow (by calling the `AddChild()` function). In reality, the BBitmap sets up a private, off-screen window for the views. When the views draw, the window renders their output into the bitmap buffer. The rendered image has the same format as the data captured by the `SetBits()` function. `SetBits()` and BViews can be used in combination to create a bitmap.

The BViews that construct a bitmap behave a bit differently than the BViews that draw in regular windows:

• In contrast to BViews attached to an ordinary window, the BViews assigned to a BBitmap can create an image off-screen. When an ordinary window is hidden, it doesn't render images; its BViews may draw, but they don't produce image data. However, the BViews assigned to a BBitmap produce an off-screen bitmap.

• Because they never appear on-screen, the BViews that produce a bitmap image never handle events and never get update messages telling them to draw. You must call their drawing functions directly in your own code.

- Because there are no update messages, the output buffer to the Application Server isn't automatically flushed. You must flush it explicitly in application code. This is best done by calling Sync(), rather than Flush(), so that you can be sure the entire image has been rendered before the bitmap is used.

- A BBitmap has no background color against which images are drawn. Your code must color every pixel within the bounds rectangle.

- Views that are attached to a BWindow normally draw in the window's thread. However, views attached to a BBitmap don't draw in a separate thread; the BBitmap doesn't set up an independent thread for its private window.

If BViews are used to produce a static image, one that will not change, you need to have them draw just once. After creating the image, they can be discarded; they'll never be called upon to update the image. However, if the bitmap will change—perhaps to reflect decisions the user makes as the program runs—the BViews can be retained to make the changes. The BBitmap will serve as an offscreen buffer for a dynamic display.

So that you can manage the BViews that are assigned to a BBitmap, the BBitmap class duplicates a number of BWindow functions—such as AddChild(), FindView(), and ChildAt().

A BBitmap that enlists views to produce the bitmap consumes more system resources than one that relies solely on SetBits(). Therefore, by default, BBitmaps refuse to accept BViews. If BViews will be used to create bitmap data, the BBitmap constructor must be informed so that it can set up the off-screen window and prepare the rendering mechanism.

Transparency

Color bitmaps can have transparent pixels. When the bitmap is imaged in a drawing mode other than B_OP_COPY, its transparent pixels won't be transferred to the destination view. The destination image will show through wherever the bitmap is transparent.

To introduce transparency into a B_COLOR_8_BIT bitmap, a pixel can be assigned a value of B_TRANSPARENT_8_BIT. In a B_RGB_32_BIT bitmap, a pixel can be assigned the special value of B_TRANSPARENT_32_BIT. (Or B_TRANS-PARENT_32_BIT can be made the high or low color of the BView drawing the bitmap.)

Transparency is covered in more detail under "Drawing Modes" on page 345.

See also: system_colors()

Constructor and Destructor

BBitmap()

> BBitmap(BRect *bounds*, color_space *space*,
>   bool *acceptsViews* = false, bool *needsContiguousMemory* = false)
> BBitmap(BMessage **archive*)

Initializes the BBitmap to the size and internal coordinate system implied by the *bounds* rectangle and to the depth and color interpretation specified by the *space* color space.

This function allocates enough memory to store data for an image the size of *bounds* at the depth required by *space*, but does not initialize any of it. All pixel data should be explicitly set using the SetBits() function, by copying it to the address returned by Bits(), or by enlisting BViews to produce the bitmap. If BViews are to be used, the constructor must be informed by setting the *acceptsViews* flag to true. This permits it to set up the mechanisms for rendering the image, including an off-screen window to contain the views.

If the *needsContiguousMemory* flag is true, the BBitmap will make sure that the memory it allocates is one contiguous chunk. This should matter only to drivers doing direct DMA into physical memory. If the flag is false, as it is by default, allocated memory may or may not be contiguous.

Currently, only B_RGB_32_BIT, B_COLOR_8_BIT, and B_MONOCHROME_1_BIT are acceptable as the color space *mode*. B_RGB_16_BIT is not supported for the present release and B_GRAYSCALE_8_BIT is reinterpreted as B_COLOR_8_BIT.

If the BBitmap accepts BViews, the left and top sides of its *bounds* rectangle must be located at 0.0.

~BBitmap()

> virtual ~BBitmap(void)

Frees all memory allocated to hold image data, deletes any BViews used to create the image, gets rid of the off-screen window that held the views, and severs the BBitmap's connection to the Application Server.

Static Functions

Instantiate()

> static BBitmap *Instantiate(BMessage **archive*)

Returns a new BBitmap object, allocated by new and created with the version of the constructor that takes a BMessage *archive*. However, if the *archive* doesn't contain data for a BBitmap object, Instantiate() returns NULL.

See also: BArchivable::Instantiate(), instantiate_object(), Archive()

Member Functions

AddChild()

> virtual void **AddChild**(BView *aView*)

Adds *aView* to the hierarchy of views associated with the BBitmap, attaching it to an off-screen window (one created by the BBitmap for just this purpose) by making it a child of the window's top view. If *aView* already has a parent, it's removed from that view hierarchy and adopted into this one. A view can serve only one window at a time.

Like AddChild() in the BWindow class, this function calls the BView's AttachedToWindow() function to inform it that it now belongs to a view hierarchy. Every view that descends from *aView* also becomes attached to the BBitmap's off-screen window and receives its own AttachedToWindow() notification.

AddChild() fails if the BBitmap was not constructed to accept views.

See also: BWindow::AddChild(), BView::AttachedToWindow(), RemoveChild(), the BBitmap constructor

Archive()

> virtual status_t **Archive**(BMessage *archive*, bool *deep* = true) const

Archives the BBitmap by recording its bounds rectangle and color space in the BMessage *archive* along with the bitmap data. If the *deep* flag is true and the BBitmap employs BViews to produce the image, it also archives all the BView objects.

See also: BArchivable::Archive(), Instantiate() static function

Bits()

> void *Bits(void) const

Returns a pointer to the bitmap data. The data lies in memory shared by the application and the Application Server. The length of the data can be obtained by calling BitsLength()—or it can be calculated from the height of the bitmap (the number of rows) and the number of bytes per row.

A B_RGB_32_BIT bitmap holds the data in an internal format that's most natural for screen display devices. In this format, the color components are ordered BGRA (blue, green, red, alpha).

See also: Bounds(), BytesPerRow(), BitsLength()

BitsLength()

int32 **BitsLength**(void) const

Returns the number of bytes that were allocated to store the bitmap data.

See also: Bits(), BytesPerRow()

Bounds()

BRect **Bounds**(void) const

Returns the bounds rectangle that defines the size and coordinate system of the bitmap. This should be identical to the rectangle used in constructing the object.

BytesPerRow()

int32 **BytesPerRow**(void) const

Returns how many bytes of data are required to specify a row of pixels. For example, a monochrome bitmap (one bit per pixel) 80 pixels wide would require twelve bytes per row (96 bits). The extra sixteen bits at the end of the twelve bytes are ignored. Every row of bitmap data is aligned on a long word boundary.

ChildAt(), CountChildren()

BView ***ChildAt**(int32 *index*) const

int32 **CountChildren**(void) const

ChildAt() returns the child BView at *index*, or NULL if there's no child at *index*. Indices begin at 0 and count only BViews that were added to the BBitmap (added as children of the top view of the BBitmap's off-screen window) and not subsequently removed.

CountChildren() returns the number of BViews the BBitmap currently has. (It counts only BViews that were added directly to the BBitmap, not BViews farther down the view hierarchy.)

These functions fail if the BBitmap wasn't constructed to accept views.

ColorSpace()

color_space **ColorSpace**(void) const

Returns the color space of the data being stored (not necessarily the color space of the data passed to the `SetBits()` function). Once set by the BBitmap constructor, the color space doesn't change.

CountChildren() *see ChildAt()*

FindView()

BView ***FindView**(BPoint *point*) const
BView ***FindView**(const char *_name_) const

Returns the BView located at *point* within the bitmap or the BView tagged with *name*. The point must be somewhere within the BBitmap's bounds rectangle, which must have the coordinate origin, (0.0, 0.0), at its left top corner.

If the BBitmap doesn't accept views, this function fails. If no view draws at the *point* given, or no view associated with the BBitmap has the *name* given, it returns `NULL`.

IsValid()

bool **IsValid**(void) const

Returns `true` if there's memory for the bitmap (if the address returned by `Bits()` is valid), and `false` if not.

Lock(), Unlock()

bool **Lock**(void)

void **Unlock**(void)

These functions lock and unlock the off-screen window where BViews associated with the BBitmap draw. Locking works for this window and its views just as it does for ordinary on-screen windows.

`Lock()` returns `false` if the BBitmap doesn't accept views or if its off-screen window is unlockable (and therefore unusable) for some reason. Otherwise, it doesn't return until it has the window locked and can return `true`.

RemoveChild()

virtual bool **RemoveChild**(BView *_aView_)

Removes *aView* from the hierarchy of views associated with the BBitmap, but only if *aView* was added to the hierarchy by calling BBitmap's version of the `AddChild()` function.

If *aView* is successfully removed, `RemoveChild()` returns `true`. If not, it returns `false`.

SetBits()

void **SetBits**(const void **data*, int32 *length*, int32 *offset*, color_space *mode*)

Assigns *length* bytes of *data* to the BBitmap object. The new data is copied into the bitmap beginning *offset* bytes (*not* pixels) from the start of allocated memory. To set data beginning with the first (left top) pixel in the image, the *offset* should be 0; to set data beginning with, for example, the sixth pixel in the first row of a `B_RGB_32_BIT` image, the offset should be 20. The offset counts any padding required to align rows of data.

The source data is specified in the *mode* color space, which may or may not be the same as the color space that the BBitmap uses to store the data. If not, the following conversions are automatically made:

- `B_MONOCHROME_1_BIT` and `B_RGB_32_BIT` to `B_COLOR_8_BIT`.
- `B_COLOR_8_BIT` and `B_GRAYSCALE_8_BIT` to `B_RGB_32_BIT`.

Colors may be dithered in a conversion to `B_COLOR_8_BIT` so that the resulting image will match the original as closely as possible, despite the lost information.

If the color space *mode* is `B_RGB_32_BIT`, the *data* should be triplets of three 8-bit components—red, green, and blue, in that order—without an alpha component. Although stored as 32-bit quantities with the components in BGRA order, the input data is only 24 bits in RGB order. Rows of source data do not need to be aligned.

However, if the source data is in any *mode* other than `B_RGB_32_BIT`, padding must be added so that each row is aligned on a `int32` word boundary.

This function works for all BBitmaps, whether or not BViews are also enlisted to produce the image.

BBox

Derived from:	public BView
Declared in:	be/interface/Box.h
Library:	libbe.so

Overview

A BBox draws a labeled border around other views. It serves only to label those views and organize them visually. It doesn't respond to messages.

The border is drawn inside the edge of the view's frame rectangle. If the BBox has a label, the border at the top of box is broken where the label appears (and the border is inset from the top somewhat to make room for the label).

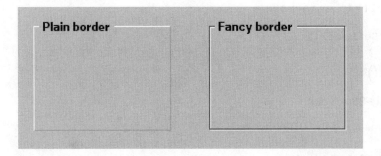

The current pen size of the view determines the width of the border; by default it's 1.0 coordinate unit. This size produces the best results, especially for fancy borders. If you make the border thicker, it will be inset somewhat so that none of it is clipped by the BBox's frame rectangle. The label is drawn in the current font, which by default is the system bold font, and the current high color; the default high color is black.

The views that the box encloses should be made children of the BBox object.

Constructor and Destructor

BBox()

> **BBox**(BRect *frame*, const char **name* = NULL,
>   uint32 *resizingMode* = B_FOLLOW_LEFT | B_FOLLOW_TOP,
>   uint32 *flags* = B_WILL_DRAW | B_FRAME_EVENTS |
>   B_NAVIGABLE_JUMP,
>   border_style *border* = B_FANCY_BORDER)
>
> **BBox**(BMessage **archive*)

Initializes the BBox by passing the *frame, name, resizingMode,* and *flags* to the BView constructor, and sets the style of its border to *border.* The three possible border styles are shown in the following table.

B_PLAIN_BORDER	The border is a simple line, lighter on the left and top than on the right and bottom so that the box looks raised from the surrounding surface.
B_FANCY_BORDER	The border is a fancier line that looks like a 3D groove inset into the surrounding surface of the view.
B_NO_BORDER	There is no border. This option is not that useful for a BBox object; it turns the box into something other than a box.

The constructor also sets the font for displaying the BBox's label to the system bold font (be_bold_font). However, the new object doesn't have a label; call SetLabel() to assign it one.

See also: SetLabel()

~BBox()

virtual **~BBox**(void)

Frees the label, if the BBox has one.

Static Functions

Instantiate()

static BBox ***Instantiate**(BMessage *archive)

Returns a new BBox object, allocated by **new** and created with the version of the constructor that takes a BMessage *archive*. However, if the *archive* message doesn't contain data for a Box object, Instantiate() returns NULL.

See also: BArchivable::Instantiate(), instantiate_object(), Archive()

Member Functions

Archive()

virtual status_t **Archive**(BMessage *archive, bool *deep* = true) const

Archives the BBox by recording its label and border style in the BMessage *archive*, after calling the inherited version of the function.

See also: BArchivable::Archive(), Instantiate() static function

AttachedToWindow()

virtual void **AttachedToWindow**(void)

Makes the BBox's background view color and its low color match the background color of its new parent, after calling the inherited version of AttachedToWindow().

Border()   *see SetBorder()*

Draw()

virtual void **Draw**(BRect *updateRect*)

Draws the box and its label. This function is called automatically in response to update messages.

FrameResized()

virtual void **FrameResized**(float *width*, float *height*)

Makes sure that the parts of the box that change when it's resized are redrawn.

See also: BView::FrameResized()

Label()   *see SetLabel()*

SetBorder(), Border()

virtual void **SetBorder**(border_style *border*)

border_style **Border**(void) const

These functions set and return the style of border the BBox draws—B_PLAIN_BORDER, B_FANCY_BORDER, or B_NO_BORDER. The border style is initially set by the BBox constructor.

SetLabel(), Label()

void **SetLabel**(const char **string*)

const char ****Label**(void) const

These functions set and return the label that's displayed along the top edge of the box. SetLabel() copies *string* and makes it the BBox's label, freeing the previous label, if any. If *string* is NULL, it removes the current label and frees it.

Label() returns a pointer to the BBox's current label, or NULL if it doesn't have one.

BButton

Derived from: public BControl

Declared in: be/interface/Button.h

Library: libbe.so

Overview

A BButton object draws a labeled button on-screen and responds when the button is clicked or when it's operated from the keyboard. If the BButton is the *default button* for its window and the window is the active window, the user can operate it by pressing the Enter key.

BButtons have a single state. Unlike check boxes and radio buttons, the user can't toggle a button on and off. However, the button's value changes while it's being operated. During a click (while the user holds the mouse button down and the cursor points to the button on-screen), the BButton's value is set to 1 (B_CONTROL_ON). Otherwise, the value is 0 (B_CONTROL_OFF).

This class depends on the control framework defined in the BControl class. In particular, it calls these BControl functions:

- SetValue() to make each change in the BControl's value. This is a hook function that you can override to take collateral action when the value changes.

- Invoke() to post a message each time the button is clicked or operated from the keyboard. You can designate the object that should handle the message by calling BControl's SetTarget() function. A model for the message is set by the BButton constructor (or by BControl's SetMessage() function).

- IsEnabled() to determine how the button should be drawn and whether it's enabled to post a message. You can call BControl's SetEnabled() to enable and disable the button.

A BButton is an appropriate control device for initiating an action. Use a BCheckBox, a BPictureButton, or BRadioButtons to set a state.

Hook Functions

MakeDefault()

Makes the BButton the default button for its window or removes that status; can be augmented by derived classes to take note when the status of the button changes.

Constructor and Destructor

BButton()

BButton(BRect *frame*, const char **name*,
const char **label*,
BMessage **message*,
uint32 *resizingMode* = B_FOLLOW_LEFT | B_FOLLOW_TOP,
uint32 *flags* = B_WILL_DRAW | B_NAVIGABLE)
BButton(BMessage **archive*)

Initializes the BButton by passing all arguments to the BControl constructor. BControl initializes the button's *label* and assigns it a model *message* that identifies the action that should be carried out when the button is invoked.

The *frame*, *name*, *resizingMode*, and *flags* arguments are the same as those declared for the BView class and are passed up the inheritance hierarchy to the BView constructor without change.

When the button is attached to a window, it will be resized to its preferred height; the height of BButton's *frame* rectangle will exactly accommodate the button border and label, given the BButton's current font.

See also: the BControl and BView constructors, `BControl::Invoke()`

~BButton()

virtual **~BButton**(void)

Does nothing; a BButton has no data to free.

Static Functions

Instantiate()

static BButton ****Instantiate**(BMessage **archive*)

Returns a new BButton object—or NULL, if the *archive* message doesn't contain data for a BButton object. The new object is allocated by new and created with the version of the constructor that takes a BMessage *archive*.

See also: `BArchivable::Instantiate()`, `instantiate_object()`, `Archive()`

Member Functions

Archive()

> virtual status_t **Archive**(BMessage *archive*, bool *deep* = true) const

Calls the inherited version of `Archive()` and records the BButton's label and whether or not it's the default button for its window in the BMessage *archive*.

See also: `BArchivable::Archive()`, `Instantiate()` static function

AttachedToWindow()

> virtual void **AttachedToWindow**(void)

Augments the BControl version of this function to set the background color of the button so that it matches the background color of its parent. This function also resizes the button vertically so that its height is just adequate to display the label and the button border. The height of the label depends on the BView's font.

Finally, if `MakeDefault()` had already been called to make the BButton the default button for its window, this function informs the BWindow of that fact.

See also: `BView::AttachedToWindow()`, `BControl::AttachedToWindow()`, `MakeDefault()`

Draw()

> virtual void **Draw**(BRect *updateRect*)

Draws the button and labels it. If the BButton's value is anything but 0, the button is highlighted. If it's disabled, it drawn in muted shades of gray. Otherwise, it's drawn in its ordinary, enabled, unhighlighted state.

See also: `BView::Draw()`

GetPreferredSize()

> virtual void **GetPreferredSize**(float *width*, float *height*)

Calculates how big the button needs to be to display its label in the current font, and writes the results into the variables that the *width* and *height* arguments refer to. `ResizeToPreferred()`, defined in the BView class, resizes a view's frame rectangle to the preferred size, keeping its left and top sides constant. A button is automatically resized to its preferred height (but not to its preferred width) by `AttachedToWindow()`.

IsDefault()   *see MakeDefault*

KeyDown()

> virtual void **KeyDown**(const char *bytes*, int32 *numBytes*)

Augments the inherited version of `KeyDown()` to respond to messages reporting that the user pressed the Enter key or the space bar. Its response is to:

- Momentarily highlight the button and change its value.
- Call `Invoke()` to deliver a copy of the model BMessage to the target receiver.

The BButton gets `KeyDown()` function calls when it's the focus view for the active window (which results when the user navigates to it) and also when it's the default button for the window and the character the user types is B_ENTER.

See also: `BControl::Invoke()`, `BView::KeyDown()`, `MakeDefault()`

MakeDefault(), IsDefault()

> virtual void **MakeDefault**(bool *flag*)
>
> bool **IsDefault**(void) const

`MakeDefault()` makes the BButton the default button for its window when *flag* is `true`, and removes that status when *flag* is `false`. The default button is the button the user can operate by striking the Enter key when the window is the active window. `IsDefault()` returns whether the BButton is currently the default button.

A window can have only one default button at a time. Setting a new default button, therefore, may deprive another button of that status. When `MakeDefault()` is called with an argument of `true`, it generates a `MakeDefault()` call with an argument of `false` for previous default button. Both buttons are redisplayed so that the user can see which one is currently the default.

The default button can also be set by calling BWindow's `SetDefaultButton()` function. That function makes sure that the button that's forced to give up default status and the button that obtains it are both notified through `MakeDefault()` function calls.

`MakeDefault()` is therefore a hook function that can be augmented to take note each time the default status of the button changes. It's called once for each change in status, no matter which function initiated the change.

See also: `BWindow::SetDefaultButton()`

MouseDown()

> virtual void **MouseDown**(BPoint *point*)

Overrides the BView version of `MouseDown()` to track the cursor while the user holds the mouse button down. As the cursor moves in and out of the button, the BButton's value is reset accordingly. The `SetValue()` virtual function is called to make the change each time.

If the cursor is inside the BButton's bounds rectangle when the user releases the mouse button, this function posts a copy of the model message so that it will be dispatched to the target object.

See also: `BView::MouseDown()`, `BControl::Invoke()`, `BControl::SetTarget()`

SetLabel()

> virtual void **SetLabel**(const char **string*)

Overrides the BControl version of this function to make sure that calculations based on the width of the label won't assume cached results for the previous label.

See also: `BControl::SetLabel()`

BCheckBox

Derived from: public BControl

Declared in: be/interface/CheckBox.h

Library: libbe.so

Overview

A BCheckBox object draws a labeled check box on-screen and responds to a keyboard action or a click by changing the state of the device. A check box has two states: An "X" is displayed in the box when the object's value is 1 (`B_CONTROL_ON`), and is absent when the value is 0 (`B_CONTROL_OFF`). The BCheckBox is invoked (it posts a message to the target receiver) whenever its value changes in either direction—when it's turned on *and* when it's turned off.

A check box is an appropriate control device for setting a state—turning a value on and off. Use menu items or buttons to initiate actions within the application.

Constructor and Destructor

BCheckBox()

> **BCheckBox**(BRect *frame*, const char **name*,
> > const char **label*,
> > BMessage **message*,
> > uint32 *resizingMode* = B_FOLLOW_LEFT | B_FOLLOW_TOP,
> > uint32 *flags* = B_WILL_DRAW | B_NAVIGABLE)
>
> **BCheckBox**(BMessage **archive*)

Initializes the BCheckBox by passing all arguments to the BControl constructor. BControl initializes the *label* of the check box and assigns it a *message* that encapsulates the action that should be taken when the state of the check box changes.

The *frame, name, resizingMode,* and *flags* arguments are the same as those declared for the BView class and are passed unchanged to the BView constructor.

When the BCheckBox is attached to a window, the height of its *frame* rectangle will be adjusted so that it has exactly the right amount of room to display the check box icon and the label, given its current font. The object draws at the vertical center of its frame rectangle beginning at the left side.

See also: the BControl and BView constructors, `AttachedToWindow()`

~CheckBox()

> virtual **~CheckBox**(void)

Does nothing; a BCheckBox doesn't require any cleanup when it's deleted.

Static Functions

Instantiate()

> static BCheckBox ****Instantiate**(BMessage **archive*)

Returns a new BCheckBox object, allocated by `new` and created with the version of the constructor that takes a BMessage *archive*. However, if the *archive* doesn't contain data for a BCheckBox object, this function returns NULL.

See also: `BArchivable::Instantiate()`, `instantiate_object()`, `Archive()`

Member Functions

Archive()

> virtual status_t **Archive**(BMessage *archive, bool *deep* = true) const

Calls the inherited version of `Archive()`, then adds the BCheckBox class name to the archive BMessage.

See also: `BArchivable::Archive()`, `Instantiate()` static function

AttachedToWindow()

> virtual void **AttachedToWindow**(void)

Augments the BControl version of `AttachedToWindow()` to set the view and low colors of the BCheckbox to the match its parent's view color, and to resize the view vertically to fit the height of the label it displays. The height of the label depends on the BCheckBox's font, which the BControl constructor sets to system plain font (`be_plain_font`).

See also: `BControl::AttachedToWindow()`

Draw()

> virtual void **Draw**(BRect *updateRect*)

Draws the check box and its label. If the current value of the BCheckBox is 1 (`B_CONTROL_ON`), it's marked with an "X". If the value is 0 (`B_CONTROL_OFF`), it's empty.

See also: `BView::Draw()`

GetPreferredSize()

> virtual void **GetPreferredSize**(float *width, float *height)

Calculates the most optimal size for the check box to display the icon and the label in the current font; and reports the results in the variables that the *width* and *height* arguments refer to. `ResizeToPreferred()`, defined in the BView class, resizes a view's frame rectangle to the preferred size, keeping its left and top sides constant. `AttachedToWindow()` automatically resizes a check box to its preferred height, but doesn't modify its width.

See also: `BView::GetPreferredSize()`, `AttachedToWindow()`

MouseDown()

virtual void **MouseDown**(BPoint *point*)

Responds to a mouse-down event within the check box by tracking the cursor while the user holds the mouse button down. If the cursor is inside the bounds rectangle when the user releases the mouse button, this function toggles the value of the BCheckBox and calls `Draw()` to redisplay it.

When the value of the BCheckBox changes, a copy of the model BMessage is delivered to the object's target handler. See BInvoker's `Invoke()` and `SetTarget()` functions for more information. The message is dispatched by calling the target's `MessageReceived()` virtual function.

The target object can get a pointer to the source BCheckBox from the message, and use it to discover the object's new value. For example:

```
void MyHandler::MessageReceived(BMessage *message)
{
    BHandler *handler;
    if ( message->FindPointer("source", &handler) ) {
        BCheckBox *box = cast_as(handler, BCheckBox);
        if ( box ) {
            . . .
        }
    }
    . . .
}
```

BColorControl

Derived from: public BControl

Declared in: be/interface/ColorControl.h

Library: libbe.so

Overview

A BColorControl object displays an on-screen device that permits users to pick a color. It reports the color as its current value—an `rgb_color` data structure stored as a 32-bit integer. If a model message is provided, it announces each change in value by sending a copy of the message to a designated target.

When the screen is 8 bits deep, the BColorControl object presents users with a matrix of the 256 available colors. The user chooses a color by pressing the primary mouse button while the cursor is over one of the cells in the matrix. Dragging from cell to cell changes the selected color. The arrow keys can similarly change the selection when the object is the focus view. The BColorControl's value changes each time the selection does.

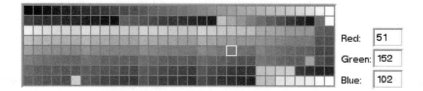

When the screen is 32 bits deep, the BColorControl object displays ramps for each color component. The user changes the current color by modifying a red, green, or blue component value.

In addition to the color matrix and ramp, a BColorControl has three text fields where the user can set a color by typing in its red, green, and blue component values. The text fields (BTextControl objects) are children of the BColorControl.

Constructor and Destructor

BColorControl()

> BColorControl(BPoint *leftTop*, color_control_layout *matrix*, float *cellSide*,
>   const char **name*, BMessage **message* = NULL,
>   bool *bufferedDrawing* = false)
> BColorControl(BMessage **archive*)

Initializes the BColorControl so that the left top corner of its frame rectangle will be located at the stated *leftTop* point in the coordinate system of its parent view. The frame rectangle will be large enough to display 256 color cells arranged in the specified *matrix*, which can be any of the following constants:

B_CELLS_4x64	B_CELLS_8x32	B_CELLS_16x16
B_CELLS_64x4	B_CELLS_32x8	

For example, B_CELLS_4x64 lays out a matrix with four cell columns and 64 rows; B_CELLS_32x8 specifies 32 columns and 8 rows. Each cell is a square *cellSide* coordinate units on a side; since the number of units translates directly to screen pixels, *cellSide* should be a whole number.

When the screen is 32 bits deep, the same frame rectangle will display four color ramps, one each for the red, green, and blue components, plus a disabled ramp for the alpha component. You might choose *matrix* and *cellSize* values with a view toward how the resulting bounds rectangle would be divided into four horizontal rows.

The *name* argument assigns a name to the object as a BHandler. It's the same as the argument declared by the BView constructor.

If a model *message* is supplied, the BColorControl will announce every change in color value by calling Invoke() (defined in the BControl class) to post a copy of the message to a designated target.

If the *bufferedDrawing* flag is true, all changes to the on-screen display will first be made in an off-screen bitmap and then copied to the screen. This makes the drawing smoother, but it requires more memory.

The initial value of the new object is 0, which when translated to an rgb_color structure, means black.

See also: BHandler::SetName(), BControl::Invoke()

~BColorControl()

> virtual ~BColorControl(void)

Gets rid of the off-screen bitmap, if one was requested when the object was constructed.

Static Functions

Instantiate()

> static BColorControl *Instantiate(BMessage *archive)

Returns a new BColorControl object, allocated by new and created with the version of the constructor that takes a BMessage *archive*. However, if the *archive* doesn't contain data for a BColorControl object, this function returns NULL.

See also: BArchivable::Instantiate(), instantiate_object(), Archive()

Member Functions

Archive()

> virtual status_t **Archive**(BMessage *archive*, bool *deep* = true) const

Calls the inherited version of `Archive()`, then adds the layout, cell size, and whether the object uses buffered drawing to the BMessage *archive*.

See also: `BArchivable::Archive()`, `Instantiate()` static function

AttachedToWindow()

> virtual void **AttachedToWindow**(void)

Augments the BControl version of this function to set the BColorControl's view color and low color to be the same as its parent's view color and to set up the BTextControl objects where the user can type red, green, and blue color values. If the object uses buffered drawing, this function makes sure the offscreen images are displayed on-screen.

See also: `BControl::AttachedToWindow()`, `BView::SetViewColor()`

CellSize()   *see SetCellSize()*

Draw()

> virtual void **Draw**(BRect *updateRect*)

Overrides the BView version of this function to draw the color control.

See also: `BView::Draw()`

GetPreferredSize()

> virtual void **GetPreferredSize**(float *width*, float *height*)

Calculates how large the color control needs to be given its layout, cell size, and current font; the results are reported in the variables that the *width* and *height* arguments refer to.

See also: `BView::GetPreferredSize()`

KeyDown()

> virtual void **KeyDown**(const char *bytes*, int32 *numBytes*)

Augments the BControl version of `KeyDown()` to allow the user to navigate within the color control using the arrow keys.

See also: `BControl::KeyDown()`

Layout() *see SetLayout()*

MessageReceived()

virtual void **MessageReceived**(BMessage *message*)

Responds to internal messages that change the color.

See also: `BHandler::MessageReceived()`

MouseDown()

virtual void **MouseDown**(BPoint *point*)

Overrides the BView version of `MouseDown()` to allow the user to operate the color control with the mouse.

See also: `BView::MouseDown()`

SetCellSize(), CellSize()

virtual void **SetCellSize**(float *cellSide*)

float **CellSize**(void) const

These functions set and return the size of a single cell in the BColorControl's matrix of 256 colors. A cell is a square *cellSide* coordinate units on a side. The size is first set by the BColorControl constructor.

See also: the BColorControl constructor

SetEnabled()

virtual void **SetEnabled**(bool *enabled*)

Augments the BControl version of `SetEnabled()` to disable and re-enable the text fields for setting the color components as the BColorControl is disabled and re-enabled. The inherited `IsEnabled()` function doesn't need augmenting and therefore isn't reimplemented.

See also: `BControl::SetEnabled()`

SetLayout(), Layout()

virtual void **SetLayout**(color_control_layout *layout*)

color_control_layout **Layout**(void) const

These functions set and return the layout of the matrix of 256 color cells. The matrix is first arranged by the constructor. See the constructor for permissible *layout* values.

See also: the BColorControl constructor

SetValue(), ValueAsColor()

virtual void **SetValue**(int32 *color*)
inline void **SetValue**(rgb_color *color*)

rgb_color **ValueAsColor**(void)

These functions set and return the BColorControl's current value—the last color that the user selected.

The virtual version of `SetValue()` takes an `int32` argument and is essentially the same as the BControl version of the function, which it modifies only to take care of class-internal housekeeping details. The inline version, on the other hand, takes an `rgb_color` argument and is unique to this class. It packs color information from the structure into a 32-bit integer and passes it to the virtual version of the function. Like all other objects that derive from BControl, a BColorControl stores its current value as an `int32`; no information is lost in the translation from an `rgb_color` structure to an integer.

`SetValue()` is called to make every change to the BControl's value. If you override this function to be notified of the changes, you should override the virtual version. (However, due to the peculiarities of C++, overriding any version of an overloaded function hides all versions of the function. For continued access to the `rgb_color` version of `SetValue()` without explicitly specifying the "BColorControl::" prefix, copy the inline code from *interface/ColorControl.h* to the derived class.)

`ValueAsColor()` is an alternative to the `Value()` function inherited from the BControl class. It returns the object's current value as an `rgb_color`; `Value()` returns it as an `int32`.

See also: `BControl::SetValue()`

BControl

Derived from: public BView, public BInvoker

Declared in: be/interface/Control.h

Library: libbe.so

Overview

BControl is an abstract class for views that draw control devices on the screen. Objects that inherit from BControl emulate, in software, real-world control devices— like the switches and levers on a machine, the check lists and blank lines on a form to fill out, or the dials and knobs on a home appliance.

Controls translate the messages that report generic mouse and keyboard events into other messages with more specific instructions for the application. A BControl object can be customized by setting the message it posts when invoked and the target object that should handle the message.

Controls also register a current value, stored as an `int32` integer that's typically set to `B_CONTROL_ON` or `B_CONTROL_OFF`. The value is changed only by calling `SetValue()`, a virtual function that derived classes can implement to be notified of the change.

Derived Classes

The Interface Kit currently includes six classes derived from BControl—BButton, BPictureButton, BRadioButton, BCheckBox, BColorControl, and BTextControl. In addition, it has two classes—BListView and BMenuItem—that implement control devices but are not derived from this class. BListView and its subclass, BOutlineListView, share an interface with the BList class (of the Support Kit) and BMenuItem is designed to work with the other classes in the menu system. Like BControl, BListView and BMenuItem inherit from the Application Kit's BInvoker class.

As BListView and BMenuItem demonstrate, it's possible to implement a control device that's not a BControl. However, it's simpler to take advantage of the code that's already provided by the BControl class. That way you can keep a simple programming interface and avoid reimplementing functions that BControl has defined for you. If your application defines its own control devices—dials, sliders, selection lists, and the like—they should be derived from BControl.

Scripting Support

The BControl class implements the suite called "suite/vnd.Be-control" consisting of the following messages:

Property name: "Label" for the label on the control device
Specifiers: B_DIRECT_SPECIFIER only
Messages: B_SET_PROPERTY and B_GET_PROPERTY
Data type: A null-terminated character string (char *)

Property name: "Value" for the current value of the object
Specifiers: B_DIRECT_SPECIFIER only
Messages: B_SET_PROPERTY and B_GET_PROPERTY
Data type: int32

See "Scripting" in Chapter 2, *The Application Kit*, for more on scripting and message suites.

Hook Functions

SetEnabled()
  Enables and disables the control device; can be augmented by derived classes to note when the state of the object has changed.

SetValue()
  Changes the value of the control device; can be augmented to take collateral action when the change is made.

Constructor and Destructor

BControl()

BControl(BRect *frame*, const char **name*,
                const char **label*, BMessage **message*,
                uint32 *resizingMode*, uint32 *flags*)
BControl(BMessage **archive*)

Initializes the BControl by setting its initial value to 0 (B_CONTROL_OFF), assigning it a *label*, and registering a model *message* that captures what the control does—the command it gives when it's invoked and the information that accompanies the command. The *label* and the *message* can each be NULL.

The *label* is copied, but the *message* is not. The BMessage object becomes the property of the BControl; it should not be deleted, posted, assigned to another object, or otherwise used in application code. The label and message can be altered after construction with the SetLabel() and SetMessage() functions.

The BControl class doesn't define a `Draw()` function to draw the label or a `MouseDown()` function to post the message. (It does define `KeyDown()`, but only to enable keyboard navigation between controls.) It's up to derived classes to determine how the *label* is drawn and how the *message* is to be used. Typically, when a BControl object needs to take action (in response to a click, for example), it calls the `Invoke()` function, which copies the model message and delivers the copy to the designated target. By default, the target is the window where the control is located, but `SetTarget()` can designate another handler.

Before delivering the message, `Invoke()` adds two data field to it, under the names "when" and "source". These names should not be used for data items in the model.

The *frame, name, resizingMode,* and *flags* arguments are identical to those declared for the BView class and are passed unchanged to the BView constructor.

The BControl begins life enabled, and the system plain font is made the default font for all control devices.

See also: the BView constructor, `BLooper::PostMessage()` in the Application Kit, `SetLabel()`, `SetMessage()`, `SetTarget()`, `Invoke()`

~BControl()

virtual **~BControl**(void)

Frees the model message and all memory allocated by the BControl.

Static Functions

Instantiate()

static BControl ***Instantiate**(BMessage *archive)

Returns a new BControl object, allocated by `new` and created with the version of the constructor that takes a BMessage *archive*. However, if the *archive* doesn't contain data for a BControl object, `Instantiate()` returns NULL.

See also: `BArchivable::Instantiate()`, `instantiate_object()`, `Archive()`

Member Functions

Archive()

virtual status_t **Archive**(BMessage *archive, bool *deep* = true) const

Archives the BControl by recording its label, current value, model message, and whether or not it's disabled in the BMessage *archive*.

See also: `BArchivable::Archive()`, `Instantiate()` static function

AttachedToWindow()

virtual void **AttachedToWindow**(void)

Overrides BView's version of this function to set the BControl's low color and view color so that it matches the view color of its new parent. It also makes the BWindow to which the BControl has become attached the default target for the `Invoke()` function, provided that another target hasn't already been set.

`AttachedToWindow()` is called for you when the BControl becomes a child of a view already associated with the window.

See also: `BView::AttachedToWindow()`, `BView::SetFontName()`, `Invoke()`, `SetTarget()`

GetSupportedSuites()

virtual status_t **GetSupportedSuites**(BMessage *message*)

Adds the name "suite/vnd.Be-control" to the *message*. See "Scripting Support" in the class overview and "Scripting" in Chapter 2 for more information.

See also: `BHandler::GetSupportedSuites()`

Invoke()

virtual status_t **Invoke**(BMessage *message* = NULL)

Copies the BControl's model BMessage and sends the copy so that it will be dispatched to the designated target (which may be a BLooper's preferred handler). The following two pieces of information are added to the copy before it's delivered:

Data name	Type code	Description
"when"	B_INT64_TYPE	When the control was invoked, as measured in the number of milliseconds since 12:00:00 AM January 1, 1970.
"source"	B_OBJECT_TYPE	A pointer to the BControl object. This permits the message handler to request more information from the source of the message.

These two names shouldn't be used for data fields in the model.

BControl's version of `Invoke()` overrides the version that the BInvoker class defines. It's designed to be called by derived classes in their `MouseDown()` and `KeyDown()` functions; it's not called for you in BControl code. It's up to each derived class to define what user actions trigger the call to `Invoke()`—what activity constitutes "invoking" the control.

This function doesn't check to make sure the BControl is currently enabled. Derived classes should make that determination before calling `Invoke()`.

See also: `BInvoker::Invoke()`, `SetEnabled()`

IsEnabled()   *see SetEnabled()*

IsFocusChanging()

protected:
  bool **IsFocusChanging**(void) const

Returns `true` if the BControl is being asked to draw because the focus changed, and `false` if not. If the return value is `true`, either the BControl has just become the focus view or it has just lost that status and the `Draw()` function has been called to update the on-screen display.

This function can be called from inside `Draw()` to learn whether it's necessary to draw or erase the visible indication that the BControl is the focus view. `IsFocus()` will return the new status of the view.

See also: `MakeFocus()`

KeyDown()

  virtual void **KeyDown**(const char *bytes*, int32 *numBytes*)

Augments the BView version of `KeyDown()` to toggle the BControl's value and call `Invoke()` when the character encoded in *bytes* is either B_SPACE or B_ENTER. This is done to facilitate keyboard navigation and make all derived control devices operable from the keyboard. Some derived classes—BCheckBox in particular—find this version of the function to be adequate. Others, like BRadioButton, reimplement it.

`KeyDown()` is called only when the BControl is the focus view in the active window. (However, if the window has a default button, B_ENTER events will be passed to that object and won't be dispatched to the focus view.)

See also: `BView::KeyDown()`, `MakeFocus()`

Label()   *see SetLabel()*

MakeFocus()

  virtual void **MakeFocus**(bool *focused* = true)

Augments the BView version of this function to call the BControl's `Draw()` function when the focus changes. This is done to aid keyboard navigation among control devices. If the Draw() function of a derived class has a section of code that checks whether the object is in focus and marks the on-screen display to show that it is (and removes any such marking when it isn't), the visual part of keyboard navigation will be taken care of. The derived class doesn't have to reimplement MakeFocus(). Most of the derived classes implemented in the Interface Kit depend on this version of the function.

When Draw() is called from this function, IsFocusChanging() returns true.

See also: BView::MakeFocus(), KeyDown(), IsFocusChanging()

MessageReceived()

virtual void **MessageReceived**(BMessage *message*)

Handles scripting messages for the BControl. See "Scripting Support" on page 410 for a description of the messages.

See also: BHandler::MessageReceived()

ResolveSpecifier()

virtual BHandler *ResolveSpecifier(BMessage *message*, int32 *index*,
            BMessage *specifier*, int32 *command*, const char *property*)

Resolves specifiers for the "Label" and "Value" properties. See "Scripting Support" in the class overview and "Scripting" in Chapter 2 for more information.

See also: BHandler::ResolveSpecifier()

SetEnabled(), IsEnabled()

virtual void **SetEnabled**(bool *enabled*)

bool **IsEnabled**(void) const

SetEnabled() enables the BControl if the *enabled* flag is true, and disables it if *enabled* is false. IsEnabled() returns whether or not the object is currently enabled. BControls are enabled by default.

While disabled, a BControl won't let the user navigate to it; the B_NAVIGABLE flag is turned off if *enabled* is false and turned on again if *enabled* is true.

Typically, a disabled BControl also won't post messages or respond visually to mouse and keyboard manipulation. To indicate this nonfunctional state, the control device is displayed on-screen in subdued colors. However, it's left to each derived class to carry out this strategy in a way that's appropriate for the kind of control it implements. The BControl class merely marks an object as being enabled or disabled; none of its functions take the enabled state of the device into account.

Derived classes can augment `SetEnabled()` (override it) to take action when the control device becomes enabled or disabled. To be sure that `SetEnabled()` has been called to actually make a change, its current state should be checked before calling the inherited version of the function. For example:

```
void MyControl::SetEnabled(bool enabled)
{
    if ( enabled == IsEnabled() )
        return;
    BControl::SetEnabled(enabled);
    /* Code that responds to the change in state goes here. */
}
```

Note, however, that you don't have to override `SetEnabled()` just to update the on-screen display when the control becomes enabled or disabled. If the BControl is attached to a window, the kit's version of `SetEnabled()` always calls the `Draw()` function. Therefore, the device on-screen will be updated automatically—as long as `Draw()` has been implemented to take the enabled state into account.

See also: the BControl constructor

SetLabel(), Label()

> virtual void **SetLabel**(const char *string)

> const char *__Label__(void) const

These functions set and return the label on a control device—the text that's displayed, for example, on top of a button or alongside a check box or radio button. The label is a null-terminated string.

`SetLabel()` frees the old label, replaces it with a copy of *string*, and updates the control on-screen so the new label will be displayed to the user—but only if the *string* that's passed differs from the current label. The label is first set by the constructor and can be modified thereafter by this function.

`Label()` returns the current label. The string it returns belongs to the BControl and may be altered or freed in due course.

See also: the BControl constructor, `BView::AttachedToWindow()`, `BView::SetFontName()`

SetValue(), Value()

virtual void **SetValue**(int32 *value*)

int32 **Value**(void) const

These functions set and return the value of the BControl object.

`SetValue()` assigns the object a new value. If the *value* passed is in fact different from the BControl's current value, this function calls the object's `Draw()` function so that the new value will be reflected in what the user sees on-screen; otherwise it does nothing.

`Value()` returns the current value.

Classes derived from BControl should call `SetValue()` to change the value of the control device in response to user actions. The derived classes defined in the Be software kits change values only by calling this function.

Since `SetValue()` is a virtual function, you can override it to take note whenever a control's value changes. However, if you want your code to act only when the value actually changes, you must check to be sure the new value doesn't match the old before calling the inherited version of the function. For example:

```
void MyControl::SetValue(int32 value)
{
    if ( value != Value() ) {
        BControl::SetValue(value);
        /* MyControl's additions to SetValue() go here */
    }
}
```

Remember that the BControl version of `SetValue()` does nothing unless the new value differs from the old.

Value()   *see SetValue()*

WindowActivated()

virtual void **WindowActivated**(bool *active*)

Makes sure that the BControl, if it's the focus view, is redrawn when the window is activated or deactivated.

See also: `BView::WindowActivated()`

BDragger

Derived from: public BView

Declared in: be/interface/Dragger.h

Library: libbe.so

Overview

A BDragger is a view that lets users drag and drop some other view. The other view is the *target* of the BDragger and its immediate relative—a sibling, a parent, or an only child. The BDragger draws a handle, usually at the corner of the target view, that the user can grab. When the user drags the handle the target view appears to move with the handle.

When dragged in this way, the target view itself doesn't actually move. Instead, the view is archived in a BMessage object and the BMessage is dragged. When the BMessage is dropped, the target BView can be reconstructed from the archive (along with the BDragger). The new object is a duplicate—a replicant—of the target view.

This class works closely with the BShelf class. A BShelf object accepts dragged BViews, reconstructs them from their archives, and installs them in another view hierarchy.

BDraggers are under the control of DeskBar's "Show Replicants" / "Hide Replicants" menu item. Showing replicants means that the BDragger handles are visible on-screen; hiding replicants means that the handles are hidden.

Constructor and Destructor

BDragger()

> **BDragger**(BRect *frame*, BView **target*, uint32 *resizingMode* = B_FOLLOW_NONE,
>   uint32 *flags* = B_WILL_DRAW)
> **BDragger**(BMessage **archive*)

Creates a new BDragger and sets its target view. The BDragger and the target BView must be directly related in the view hierarchy (as parent-child or as siblings); but, note well, the constructor doesn't establish this relationship for you. After you construct your BDragger, you have to do one of three things:

- Add the target as a child of the dragger
- Add the dragger as a child of the target
- Add the dragger as a sibling of the target

If you add the target as a child of BDragger, it should be the only child that the BDragger has.

A BDragger draws in the right bottom corner of its *frame* rectangle. If the target view is a parent or a sibling of the BDragger, that rectangle needs to be no larger than the image the BDragger draws (the handle). However, if the target is the BDragger's child, the dragger's frame rectangle must enclose the target's frame (so that the dragger doesn't clip the target).

A BDragger is fully functional once it has been constructed and attached to the view hierarchy of its target. You don't need to call any other functions. However, the whole endeavor fails if the target BView can't be archived.

~BDragger()

virtual ~**BDragger**(void)

Frees all memory the BDragger allocated (principally for the bitmap image it draws).

Static Functions

HideAllDraggers(), ShowAllDraggers(), AreDraggersDrawn()

static status_t **HideAllDraggers**(void)

static status_t **ShowAllDraggers**(void)

static bool **AreDraggersDrawn**(void)

These functions communicate with all BDragger objects in all applications (provided they're attached to a window). `HideAllDraggers()` hides the BDragger objects so that they're not visible on-screen. `ShowAllDraggers()` undoes the effect of `HideAllDraggers()` and causes all BDragger objects to draw their handles. The Show Replicants / Hide Replicants menu item does its work through these functions.

`HideAllDraggers()` may or may not hide the BDragger view in the way that BView's `Hide()` function does. The BDragger may still be visible, although it won't draw anything until `ShowAllDraggers()` is called. Therefore, if the target BView is the BDragger's child, it will not be hidden when `HideAllDraggers()` erases its parent.

`AreDraggersDrawn()` returns `true` when the BDraggers are shown and `false` when they're hidden.

Instantiate()

static BDragger ***Instantiate**(BMessage *archive)

Returns a new BDragger object, allocated by new and created with the version of the constructor that takes a BMessage *archive*. If the *archive* message doesn't contain and archived BDragger, Instantiate() returns NULL.

ShowAllDraggers()   *see HideAllDraggers()*

Member Functions

Archive()

> virtual status_t Archive(BMessage *archive*, bool *deep* = true) const

Records the BDragger's hierarchical relationship to the target view and then calls BView::Archive(). The *deep* flag has no significance for BDragger itself, but note that the flag is passed on to the BView version.

AttachedToWindow(), DetachedFromWindow()

> virtual void AttachedToWindow(void)

> virtual void DetachedFromWindow(void)

AttachedToWindow() makes sure that the BDragger is under the control of the HideAllDraggers() and ShowAllDraggers() functions, makes its low and background view colors match the view color of its parent, and determines the BDragger's precise relationship to its target view. To make this determination, the target must be in the view hierarchy; it can't be added to the window after the BDragger is. For example, if the target is the BDragger's child, it should be added to the BDragger and then the BDragger added to the window.

DetachedFromWindow() removes the BDragger from the control of the HideAllDraggers() and ShowAllDraggers() functions.

Draw()

> virtual void Draw(BRect *updateRect*)

Draws the handle—or fails to draw it and has the parent view draw in that area instead, if all BDraggers are hidden.

IsVisibilityChanging()

protected:
> bool IsVisibilityChanging(void) const

Returns true if two things are true:

- The BDragger is the parent of its target.

- The BDragger handle was visible but now should not be, or it wasn't visible and now should be.

Otherwise, this function returns false.

What's this function for? It's in the API so derived classes can implement their own versions of Draw(). If the BDragger isn't the parent of its target, the visibility of the BDragger view can be controlled by the Hide() and Show() functions rather than Draw().

MessageReceived()

virtual void **MessageReceived**(BMessage *message*)

Responds to messages that regulate the visibility of the BDragger handle.

MouseDown()

virtual void **MouseDown**(BPoint *where*)

Responds to a B_MOUSE_DOWN message by archiving the target view (and the BDragger) and initiating a drag-and-drop operation, or by taking other appropriate action.

BFont

Derived from:	*none*
Declared in:	be/interface/Font.h
Library:	libbe.so

Overview

A BFont object records a set of font attributes, such as the font's family, style, size, and so on. You can set most of these attributes to modify the font and then use the object to set the font of a BView. A BView's font determines how the characters that it draws (with the DrawString() and DrawChar() functions) will be rendered.

A BFont object can perform calculations based on the metrics of the particular font it represents. For example, it can tell you how much screen real estate it needs to display a given line of text.

To find which fonts are currently installed on the system, call `get_font_family()` and `get_font_style()`.

Using a BFont Object

A BFont object by itself doesn't do anything. To be able to draw characters in the font, the object must be passed to BView's `SetFont()` function (or BTextView's `SetFontAndColor()`).

A BFont object is always a full representation of a font; all attributes are always set. However, you can choose which of these attributes will modify a BView's current font by passing a mask to `SetFont()` (or `SetFontAndColor()`). For example, this code sets only the font shear and spacing:

```
BFont font;
font.SetShear(60.0);
font.SetSpacing(B_CHAR_SPACING);
myView->SetFont(&font, B_FONT_SHEAR | B_FONT_SPACING);
```

Alternatively, the BView's font could have been modified and reset as follows:

```
BFont font;
myView->GetFont(&font);
font.SetShear(60.0);
font.SetSpacing(B_CHAR_SPACING);
myView->SetFont(&font);
```

Notice that we had to explicitly reset the view's font (through `SetFont()`) after changing the font's attributes.

System Fonts

The Interface Kit constructs three BFont objects (plain, bold, and fixed)for each application when the application starts up. The values of these fonts are set by the user through the FontPanel preferences application. You can get to these objects through global pointers:

const BFont *`be_plain_font`
> The font that's used to display most gadgets in the user interface, such as check box labels and menu items. All BControl objects use this font.

const BFont *`be_bold_font`
> The font that's used to display window titles and BBox labels.

const BFont *`be_fixed_font`
> The font that's used to display fixed-width characters.

The global fonts are `const` objects that can't be modified by your application, and aren't updated by the system, even if the user changes their definitions while your app is running. The new values take effect the next time your application is launched.

To use a system font in a view, simply call `SetFont()`:

```
myView->SetFont(be_bold_font);
```

If you want to modify some attributes of a system font, you have to make a copy of it first (and modify the copy):

```
BFont font(be_bold_font);
font.SetSize(13.0);
myView->SetFont(&font);
```

Applications should respect the user's choices and base all font choices on these three system fonts, rather than hard-code font names into the application. You should not try to predict the fonts that will be installed on the user's machine.

Constructor

BFont()

> **BFont**(const BFont &*font*)
> **BFont**(const BFont *font*)
> **BFont**(void)

Initializes the new BFont object as a copy of another *font*. If no font is specified, `be_plain_font` is used.

The system BFont objects, including `be_plain_font`, are initialized only when you create a BApplication object for your application. Therefore, the default settings of BFont objects constructed before the BApplication object will be invalid.

See also: `BView::SetFont()`, `BTextView::SetFontAndColor()`

Member Functions

CountTuned()   *see GetTunedInfo()*

Direction()

> font_direction **Direction**(void) const

Returns `B_FONT_LEFT_TO_RIGHT` if the font displays text that's read from left to right, and `B_FONT_RIGHT_TO_LEFT` if it displays text that's read from right to left. This is an inherent property of the font and cannot be set.

The direction of the font affects the direction in which DrawString() draws the characters in a string, but not the direction in which it moves the pen.

See also: BView::DrawString()

Encoding()   *see SetEncoding()*

Face()   *see SetFace()*

FamilyAndStyle()   *see SetFamilyAndStyle()*

Flags()   *see SetFlags()*

GetEscapements(), GetEdges()

> void **GetEscapements**(const char *charArray*[], int32 *numChars*,
> > float *escapementArray*[]) const

> void **GetEscapements**(const char *charArray*[], int32 *numChars*,
> > escapement_delta **delta*, float *escapementArray*[]) const

> void **GetEdges**(const char *charArray*[], int32 *numChars*,
> > edge_info *edgeArray*[]) const

These two functions provide the information required to precisely position characters on the screen or printed page. For each character passed in the *charArray*, they write information about the horizontal dimension of the character into the *escapementArray* or the *edgeArray*. Both functions provide this information in "escapement units" that yield standard coordinate units (72.0 per inch) when multiplied by the font size.

GetEscapements() and GetEdges() expect the character array they're passed to contain at least *numChar* characters; neither function checks the *charArray* for a null terminator. Because the array may hold multibyte characters (in B_UNICODE_UTF8 encoding), the number of bytes in the array may be greater than the number of characters specified. The *escapementArray* and *edgeArray* should be long enough to hold an output value for every input character.

Escapements

A character's escapement measures the amount of horizontal space it requires. It includes the space needed to display the character itself, plus some extra room on the left and right edges to separate the character from its neighbors. The illustration below shows the approximate escapements for the letters "l" and "p"; the escapement for each character is the distance between the vertical lines.

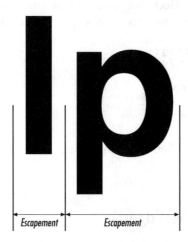

GetEscapements() measures the same space that functions such as StringWidth() and BTextView's LineWidth() do, but it measures each character individually and records its width in per-point-size escapement units. To translate the escapement value to the width of the character, you must multiply by the point size of the font:

```
float width = escapementArray[i] * font.Size();
```

Because of rounding errors, there may be some difference between the value returned by StringWidth() and the width calculated from the individual escapements of the characters in the string.

The escapement value is scalable if the spacing mode of the font is B_CHAR_SPACING. In other words, given B_CHAR_SPACING and the same set of font characteristics, GetEscapements() will report the same measurement for a character regardless of the font size. You can cache one value per character and use it for all font sizes. For the other spacing modes, the reported escapement depends on the font size and therefore can't be scaled.

For most spacing modes, a character has a constant escapement in all contexts; it depends only on the font. However, for B_STRING_SPACING, each character's escapement is also contextually dependent on the string it's in. To find the escapement of a character within a particular string, you must pass the entire string in the input *charArray*.

In the B_BITMAP_SPACING and B_FIXED_SPACING modes, all characters have integral widths (without a fractional part). For these modes, multiplying an escapement by the font size should yield an integral value. In B_FIXED_SPACING mode, all characters have the same escapement.

If a *delta* argument is provided, `GetEscapements()` will adjust the escapements it reports so that, after multiplying by the font size, the character widths will include the specified increments. An `escapement_delta` structure contains two values:

float `nonspace`
> The amount to add to the width of each character with a visible glyph.

float `space`
> The amount to add to each whitespace character (characters like `B_TAB` and `B_SPACE` with an escapement but no visible glyph).

A similar argument can be passed to BView's `DrawString()` to adjust the spacing of the characters as they're drawn.

Edges

Edge values measure how far a character outline is inset from its left and right escapement boundaries. `GetEdges()` putss the edge values in an array of `edge_info` structures. Each structure has a `left` and a `right` data member, as follows:

```
typedef struct {
    float left;
    float right;
} edge_info
```

Edge values, like escapements, are stated in per-point-size units that need to be multiplied by the font size.

The illustration below shows typical character edges. As in the illustration above, the solid vertical lines mark escapement boundaries. The dotted lines mark off the part of each escapement that's an edge, the distance between the character outline and the escapement boundary:

Escapement boundary

This is the normal case. The left edge is a positive value measured rightward from the left escapement boundary. The right edge is a negative value measured leftward from the right escapement boundary.

However, if the characters of a font overlap, the left edge can be a negative value and the right edge can be positive. This is illustrated below:

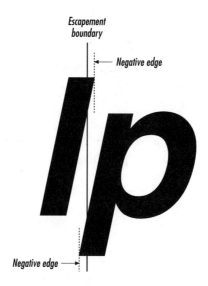

Note that the italic "*l*" extends beyond its escapement to the right, and that the "*p*" begins before its escapement to the left. In this case, instead of separating the adjacent characters, the edges determine how much they overlap.

Edge values are specific to each character and depend on nothing but the character and the font. They don't take into account any contextual information; for example, the right edge for italic "*l*" would be the same no matter what letter followed. Edge values therefore aren't sufficient to decide how character pairs can be kerned. Kerning is contextually dependent on the combination of two particular characters.

See also: `StringWidth()`, `SetSpacing()`

GetFamilyAndStyle()   *see SetFamilyAndStyle()*

GetHeight()

> void **GetHeight**(font_height **height*) const

Writes the three components that determine the height of the font into the structure that the *height* argument refers to. A `font_height` structure has the following fields:

float **ascent**

How far characters can ascend above the baseline.

float **descent**

How far characters can descend below the baseline.

float **leading**

How much space separates lines (the distance between the descent of the line above and the ascent of the line below).

If you need to round the font height, or any of its components, to an integral value (to figure the spacing between lines of text on-screen, for example), you should always round them up to reduce the amount of vertical character overlap.

See also: `BView::GetFontHeight()`

GetStringWidths()   *see StringWidth()*

GetTruncatedStrings()

> void **GetTruncatedStrings**(const char *inputStringArray*[], int32 *numStrings*,
>   uint32 *mode*, float *maxWidth*,
>   char *truncatedStringArray*[]) const

Truncates a set of strings so that each one (and an ellipsis to show where the string was cut) will fit into the *maxWidth* horizontal space. This function is useful for shortening long strings that are displayed to the user—for showing path names in a list, for example.

The *numStrings* argument states how many strings in the *inputStringArray* should be shortened. The *mode* argument states where the string should be cut. It can be:

B_TRUNCATE_BEGINNING	Cut from the beginning of the string until it fits within the specified width.
B_TRUNCATE_MIDDLE	Cut from the middle of the string.
B_TRUNCATE_END	Cut from the end of the string.
B_TRUNCATE_SMART	Cut anywhere, but do so intelligently, so that all the strings remain different after being cut. For example, if a set of similar path names are passed in the *inputStringArray*, this mode would attempt to cut from the identical parts of the path names and preserve the parts that are different. This mode also pays attention to word boundaries, separators, punctuation, and the like. However, it's not implemented for the current release.

Each output string is written to the *truncatedStringArray*—into memory that the caller must provide—at an index that matches the index of the full string in the *inputStringArray*. The *truncatedStringArray* is a list of pointers to string buffers. Each buffer should be allocated separately and should be at least 3 bytes longer than the matching input string. The 3 bytes allow for the worst-case scenario: `GetTruncatedStrings()` cuts a one-byte character from the input string and replaces it with an ellipsis character, which takes three bytes in UTF-8 encoding, for a net gain of 2 bytes. It then adds a null terminator for the third byte.

The output strings are null-terminated. The input strings should likewise be null-terminated.

See also: `StringWidth()`

GetTunedInfo(), CountTuned()

> void **GetTunedInfo**(int32 *index*, tuned_font_info *info*) const

> int32 **CountTuned**(void) const

These functions are used to get information about fonts that have been "tuned" to look good when displayed on-screen. A tuned font is a set of character bitmaps, originally produced from the standard outline font and then modified so that the characters are well proportioned and spaced when displayed at the low resolution of the screen (1 pixel per point).

Because it's a bitmap font, a tuned font captures a specific configuration of font attributes, including size, style, shear, and rotation. A tuned font is a counterpart to an outline font with the same settings. If a BView's current font has a tuned counterpart, `DrawString()` automatically chooses it when drawing on-screen. Tuned fonts are not used for printing.

`CountTuned()` returns how many tuned fonts there are for the family and style represented by the BFont object. `GetTunedInfo()` writes information about the tuned font at *index* into the structure the *info* argument refers to. Indices begin at 0 and count only tuned fonts for the BFont's family and style. A `tuned_font_info` structure has fields for five properties of the font:

```
typedef struct {
    float size;
    float shear;
    float rotation;
    uint32 flags;
    uint16 face;
} tuned_font_info
```

With this information, you can set the BFont to values that match those of a tuned font. When a BView draws to the screen, it picks a tuned font if there's one that corresponds to its current font in all respects.

See also: `get_font_family()`

PrintToStream()

void **PrintToStream**(void) const

Writes the following information about the font to the standard output:

family
style
size (in points)
shear (in degrees)
rotation (in degrees)
ascent
descent
leading

However, the information in printed on a single line rather than arranged vertically.

Rotation()   *see SetRotation()*

SetEncoding(), Encoding()

void **SetEncoding**(uint8 *encoding*)

uint8 **Encoding**(void) const

These functions set and return the encoding that maps character values to characters. The following encodings are supported:

B_UNICODE_UTF8 (UTF-8)	B_ISO_8859_6 (Latin/Arabic)
B_ISO_8859_1 (Latin 1)	B_ISO_8859_7 (Latin/Greek)
B_ISO_8859_2 (Latin 2)	B_ISO_8859_8 (Latin/Hebrew)
B_ISO_8859_3 (Latin 3)	B_ISO_8859_9 (Latin 5)
B_ISO_8859_4 (Latin 4)	B_ISO_8859_10 (Latin 6)
B_ISO_8859_5 (Latin/Cyrillic)	B_MACINTOSH_ROMAN

UTF-8 is an 8-bit encoding for Unicode and is part of the Unicode standard. It matches ASCII values for all 7-bit character codes, but uses multibyte characters for values over 127. The other encodings take only a single byte to represent a character; they therefore necessarily encompass a far smaller set of characters. Most of them represent standards in the ISO/IEC 8859 family of character codes that extend the ASCII set. B_MACINTOSH_ROMAN stands for the standard encoding used by the Mac OS.

The encoding affects both input and output functions of the BView. It determines how DrawString() interprets the character values it's passed and also how KeyDown() encodes character values for the keys the user pressed.

UTF-8 is the preferred encoding and the one that's most compatible with objects defined in the software kits. For example, a BTextView expects all text it takes from the clipboard or from a dragged and dropped message to be UTF-8 encoded. If it isn't, the results are not defined. The more that applications stick with UTF-8 encoding, the more freely they'll be able to exchange data.

See also: "Character Encoding" on page 365 of this chapter, `convert_to_utf8()`, `BView::DrawString()`, `BView::KeyDown()`

SetFace(), Face()

>   void **SetFace**(uint16 *face*)
>
>   uint16 **Face**(void) const

These functions set and return a mask that record secondary characteristics of the font, such as whether characters are underlined or drawn in outline. The values that form the *face* mask have not been defined for this release.

SetFamilyAndStyle(), GetFamilyAndStyle(), FamilyAndStyle()

>   void **SetFamilyAndStyle**(const font_family *family*, const font_style *style*)
>   void **SetFamilyAndStyle**(uint32 *code*)
>
>   void **GetFamilyAndStyle**(font_family **family*, font_style **style*) const
>
>   uint32 **FamilyAndStyle**(void) const

`SetFamilyAndStyle()` sets the family and style of the font. The *family* passed to this function must be one of the families enumerated by the `get_font_family()` global function and *style* must be one of the styles associated with that family, as reported by `get_font_style()`. If the *family* is `NULL`, `SetFamilyAndStyle()` sets only the style; if *style* is `NULL`, it sets only the family.

`GetFamilyAndStyle()` writes the names of the current family and style into the `font_value` and `font_style` variables provided.

Internally, the BFont class encodes each family and style combination as a unique integer. `FamilyAndStyle()` returns that code, which can then be passed to `SetFamilyAndStyle()` to set another BFont object. The integer code is not persistent; its meaning may change when the list of installed fonts changes and when the machine is rebooted.

See also: `get_font_family()`

SetFlags(), Flags()

void **SetFlags**(uint32 *flags*)

uint32 **Flags**(void) const

These functions set and return a mask that records various behaviors of the font. Currently, there's just one flag, B_DISABLE_ANTIALIASING, which turns off all antialiasing for characters displayed in the font. The default mask has antialiasing turned on.

SetRotation(), Rotation()

void **SetRotation**(float *rotation*)

float **Rotation**(void) const

These functions set and return the rotation of the baseline for characters displayed in the font. The baseline rotates counterclockwise from an axis on the left side of the character. The default (horizontal) baseline is at 0°. For example, this code:

```
BFont font;
font.SetRotation(45.0);
myView->SetFont(&font, B_FONT_ROTATION);
myView->DrawString("to the northeast");
```

would draw a string that extended upwards and to the right.

Rotation is not supported by some Interface Kit classes, including BTextView.

SetShear(), Shear()

void **SetShear**(float *shear*)

float **Shear**(void) const

These functions set and return the angle at which characters are drawn relative to the baseline. The default (perpendicular) shear for all font styles, including oblique and italic ones, is 90.0°. The shear is measured counterclockwise and can be adjusted within the range 45.0° (slanted to the right) through 135.0° (slanted to the left). If the *shear* passed falls outside this range, it will be adjusted to the closest value within range.

SetSize(), Size()

void **SetSize**(float *size*)

float **Size**(void) const

These functions set and return the size of the font in points. Valid sizes range from less than 1.0 point through 10,000 points.

See also: BView::SetSize()

SetSpacing(), Spacing()

void **SetSpacing**(uint8 *spacing*)

uint8 **Spacing**(void) const

These functions set and return the mode that determines how characters are horizontally spaced relative to each other when they're drawn. The mode also affects the width or "escapement" of each character as reported by GetEscapements().

There are four *spacing* modes:

B_CHAR_SPACING
Positions each character according to its own inherent width, without adjustment. This produces good results on high-resolution devices like printers, and is the best mode to use for printing. However, when character widths are rounded for the screen, the results are generally poor. Characters are not well-separated and can collide or overlap at small font sizes.

B_STRING_SPACING
Keeps the string at the same width as it would have for B_CHAR_SPACING, but optimizes the position of each character within that space. The position of a character depends on the surrounding characters and the overall width of the string. Collisions are unlikely in this mode, but because the width of the string constrains what can be done, characters may touch each other.

This mode is preferred when it's important to have the screen match the printed page—for example, to have lines break on-screen where they will break when the display is printed. As the user types new characters into a line of text, the application must redraw the entire line to add each character. The characters in the line may therefore appear to "jiggle" or jump around as new ones are added. New optimal positions are calculated for each character as the width and composition of the string changes.

B_BITMAP_SPACING
Calculates the width of each character according to its bitmap appearance on-screen. The widths are chosen for optimal spacing, so that characters never collide and rarely touch. This mode increases the B_CHAR_SPACING width of a string if necessary to keep characters separated. (For a small-sized bold font, it may increase the string width substantially.)

In this mode, the spacing between characters is regular and not contextually dependent. Character widths are integral values. This is the best mode for drawing small amounts of text in the user interface; it's the mode that BTextView objects use and it works for both proportional and fixed-width fonts. However, the spacing of text shown on-screen won't correspond to the spacing when the text is printed in B_CHAR_SPACING mode.

B_FIXED_SPACING

Positions characters according to a constant, integral width. This mode can be used for both proportional and fixed-width fonts, though it treats proportional fonts as if they were fixed-width. All characters have the same escapement.

The B_CHAR_SPACING mode is the preferred mode for printing. It's also somewhat faster than B_STRING_SPACING or B_BITMAP_SPACING. In all modes other than B_STRING_SPACING, it's possible to change the character displayed at the end of a string by erasing it and drawing a new character. However, in B_STRING_SPACING mode, it's necessary to erase the entire string and redraw it. The longer the string, the better the results.

The B_STRING_SPACING and B_BITMAP_SPACING modes are relevant only for font sizes in a range of about 7.0 points to 18.0 points. Above that range, B_CHAR_SPACING achieves reasonable results on-screen and may be used even where one of the other two modes is specified. Below that range, the screen resolution isn't great enough for the different modes to produce significantly different results, so again B_CHAR_SPACING is used.

In addition, B_CHAR_SPACING is always used for rotated or sheared text and when antialiasing is disabled.

See also: BView::DrawString(), GetEscapements()

Shear()   *see SetShear()*

Size()   *see SetSize()*

Spacing()   *see SetSpacing()*

StringWidth(), GetStringWidths()

float **StringWidth**(const char *string*) const
float **StringWidth**(const char *string*, int32 *length*) const

void **GetStringWidths**(const char *stringArray*[], const int32 *lengthArray*[],
              uint32 *numStrings*, float *widthArray*[]) const

`StringWidth()` returns how much room is required to draw a *string* in the font. It measures the characters encoded in *length* bytes of the string—or, if no *length* is specified, the entire string up to the null character, "\0", which terminates it. The return value totals the width of all the characters in coordinate units; it's the length of the baseline required to draw the string.

`GetStringWidth()` provides the same information for a group of strings. It works its way through the *stringArray* looking at a total of *numStrings*. For each string, it gets the length at the corresponding index from the *lengthArray* and places the width of the string in the *widthArray* at the same index.

These functions take all the attributes of the font—including family, style, size, and spacing—into account.

See also: `BView::StringWidth()`

Operators

= (assignment)

> BFont& **operator** =(const BFont&)

Assigns one BFont object to another. After the assignment, the two objects are identical to each other and do not share any data.

== (equality), != (inequality)

> bool **operator** ==(const BFont&) const
>
> bool **operator** !=(const BFont&) const

These operators test whether two BFont objects are identical in all respects. If all settable font attributes are the same in both objects, they're equal. If not, they're unequal.

BListItem

Derived from:	public BArchivable
Declared in:	be/interface/ListItem.h
Library:	libbe.so

Overview

A BListItem is an object that can cooperate with a BListView, including a BOutlineListView, to display one item in a list. The BListItem draws the item and keeps track of its current state. The BListView manages the list, responds to messages, provides its items with the graphics environment they need to draw, and calls upon them to draw when needed.

BListItem is an abstract class; derived classes must implement a `DrawItem()` function to draw the item. The BStringItem class is the only implementation of a BListItem available in the Interface Kit. It draws the item as a line of text.

A BListItem records some properties that are relevant only if it's part of a BOutlineListView—in particular, the level of the item in the outline and whether it's expanded (its subitems are displayable) or collapsed (its subitems are not displayable). Other properties apply to all lists—for example, whether or not the item is selected and whether it's enabled or disabled.

The class provides functions to set and return these properties. However, setting a BListItem property doesn't by itself alter the display or inform the container BView. The view communicates with the BListItem, but the item doesn't reciprocate and communicate with the BListView. Therefore, once a BListItem has been added to a list, it's generally best to manipulate it through BListView (and BOutlineListView) functions, rather than directly through its own functions.

Hook Functions

`DrawItem()`
Must be implemented to draw the item.

`UpdateInfo()`
Can be implemented to update cached information.

Constructor and Destructor

BListItem()

BListItem(uint32 *level* = 0, bool *expanded* = true)
BListItem(BMessage **archive*)

Marks the BListItem as being at the specified outline *level* and as controlling an expanded section of the outline if the expanded flag is `true` or a collapsed section if expanded is `false`. Outline levels are indicated by an index, with 0 as the outer level, 1 for one level of indentation, 2 for two levels of indentation, and so on.

Initially, the item has a width and height of 0.0 coordinate units, is enabled, and is not selected.

~BListItem()

virtual ~BListItem(void)

Does nothing.

Member Functions

Archive()

virtual status_t **Archive**(BMessage *archive*, bool *deep* = true) const

Calls the inherited version of `Archive()`, then adds four pieces of information to the *archive* BMessage:

- The outline level of the item
- Whether the item controls a collapsed or an expanded part of the list
- Whether the item is currently selected or not
- Whether or not the item is currently enabled

See also: BArchivable::Archive(), Instantiate() static function

Deselect()   *see Select()*

DrawItem()

virtual void **DrawItem**(BView *owner*, BRect *itemRect*, bool *complete* = false) = 0

Implemented by derived classes to draw the item in the *itemRect* portion of the *owner* BView. If the *complete* flag is `true`, this function should touch every pixel in the *itemRect* rectangle. If the flag is `false`, it can assume that background pixels are already the correct color.

To draw the item, this function should call the graphic functions of the owner BView. For example:

```
void MyItem:DrawItem(BView * owner, BRect itemRect, bool complete)
{
    if ( complete ) {
        rgb_color color;
        if ( IsSelected() ) {
            color = my_highlight_color;
        else
            color = owner->ViewColor();
        owner->SetHighColor(color);
        owner->FillRect(itemRect);
    }
    . . .
}
```

`DrawItem()` should be implemented to visually reflect the state of the item, highlighting it if it's selected, dimming it if it's disabled, and so on. However, it should not consider the outline level. If the level is important, the *owner* BView will have already taken it into account in calculating the *itemRect* rectangle.

See also: `BListView::Draw()`

Height()   *see SetHeight()*

IsEnabled()   *see SetEnabled()*

IsExpanded()   *see SetExpanded()*

IsSelected()   *see Select()*

OutlineLevel()

uint32 **OutlineLevel**(void) const

Returns the outline level of the item. The greater the return value, the deeper the level. The outermost level is 0.

See also: the BOutlineListView class

Select(), Deselect(), IsSelected()

void **Select**(void)

void **Deselect**(void)

bool **IsSelected**(void) const

`Select()` and `Deselect()` mark the item as being selected or unselected. However, these functions don't inform the BListView of the change. To select and deselect items that have been added to a view, call the container BListView's `Select()` and `Deselect()` functions instead. Those functions update the display on-screen and mark the BListItem accordingly.

`IsSelected()` returns `true` if the item is selected and `false` if not.

See also: `BListView::Select()`, `BListView::Deselect()`

SetEnabled(), IsEnabled()

void **SetEnabled**(bool *enabled*)

bool **IsEnabled**(void) const

SetEnabled() marks the BListItem as being enabled if the *enabled* flag is true, or disabled if it is false. IsEnabled() returns the current enabled state of the item.

SetEnabled() doesn't alter how the item is displayed; you must take steps to invalidate the region of the BView where the item is displayed so that DrawItem() will be called.

See also: BListView::InvalidateItem()

SetExpanded(), IsExpanded()

> void **SetExpanded**(bool *expanded*)
>
> bool **IsExpanded**(void) const

SetExpanded() marks the item as controlling an expanded section of the list if the *expanded* flag is true, or as controlling a collapsed section if *expanded* is false. IsExpanded() returns the current state of the BListItem.

SetExpanded() doesn't affect the on-screen display. If the item is in a BOutlineListView in a window, it's better to call that view's Collapse() and Expand() functions so that the changes can take effect immediately.

See also: BOutlineListView::Collapse()

SetHeight(), SetWidth(), Height(), Width()

> void **SetHeight**(float *height*)
>
> void **SetWidth**(float *width*)
>
> float **Height**(void) const
>
> float **Width**(void) const

These functions set and return the width and height of the item. The item's dimensions are adjusted when Update() is called.

See also: Update()

Update()

> virtual void **Update**(BView **owner*, const BFont **font*)

Modifies the width of the BListItem to match the width of the *owner* BView where it will draw and modifies the item's height to fit the height of the BView's current *font*. This function is called whenever an item is assigned to a BListView (including a BOutlineListVIew) and when the owning object undergoes a change that might affect the item.

Derived classes can augment this function to record the *owner* BView, cache the *font*, query the owner about other aspects of the graphics environment, or take any other action that's required to keep the item up to date.

Width()   *see* SetHeight()

BListView

Derived from: public BView, public BInvoker

Declared in: be/interface/ListView.h

Library: libbe.so

Overview

A BListView displays a list of items the user can select and invoke. Each item is a kind of BListItem object—typically a BStringItem, which simply draws a line of text. The BListView manages the layout of the list and the interaction with the user; it leaves the display of each item to the BListItem object. A BListItem is not a view and draws only when called upon by the BListView.

A derived class, BOutlineListView, can arrange items in a hierarchical outline, indent items to show the level of the hierarchy they occupy, and collapse and expand sections of the hierarchy. A BListView, on the other hand, displays all items unindented at a single level.

Lists and List Views

This class is based on the BList class of the Support Kit. It implements counterparts for *all* BList member functions, so you can treat a BListView object just like a BList. BListView simply makes the list visible.

BListView functions work identically to their BList counterparts, except for two things:

- A BListView assumes that the list contains pointers to BListItem objects, not void* pointers.

- A BListView makes sure that the on-screen display is properly updated whenever the items in the list change.

In both classes, the list keeps track of data pointers—void* pointers in the case of BList and pointers to BListItems in the case of BListView. Adding an item to the list adds only the pointer; the pointed-to object isn't copied.

Updating the List

When the contents of the list change, the BListView makes sure the visible list on-screen is updated. However, since it records only pointers to data, it can know that something changed only when a BListItem is added or removed. If an item pointer remains the same but the data the item displays is altered, the BListView won't know about it. In this case, you must force the list to be redrawn (by calling the `InvalidateItem()` function or BView's `Invalidate()`).

Selecting and Invoking Items

The user can click an item in the list to select it and double-click an item to both select and invoke it. The user can also select and invoke items from the keyboard. The navigation keys (such as Down Arrow, Home, and Page Up) select items; Enter and the space bar invoke them.

By default, a BListView permits only one item to be selected at a time. However, at construction and with the `SetListType()` function, you can set it up to allow multiple selections. The user can make contiguous extensions to the current selection by holding down a Shift key, and discontiguous extensions by holding down an Option key.

The BListView highlights items as they're selected, but otherwise it doesn't define what, if anything, should take place when the selection changes. You can determine that yourself either by implementing a `SelectionChanged()` function in a derived class or by registering a *selection message* (a BMessage object) with the BListView. The function is called and the message is delivered to a target destination whenever the user modifies the selection.

Similarly, the BListView doesn't define what it means to "invoke" an item. You can register a separate *invocation message* that's sent whenever the user double-clicks an item or presses Enter or the space bar while items are selected. For example, if the user double-clicks an item in a list of file names, the message might tell the BApplication object to open that file.

A BListView doesn't have default selection and invocation messages. Messages are sent only if registered with the `SetSelectionMessage()` and `SetInvocationMessage()` functions. Before sending either type of message, the BListView adds information to it identifying itself and the items that are currently selected. See the `Invoke()` function for details.

See also: the BList class in the Support Kit, the BOutlineListView and BListItem classes

Hook Functions

`InitiateDrag()`

Can be implemented to permit users to drag items—for example, to reorder items in the list.

`SelectionChanged()`

Can be implemented to take collateral action each time the selection changes.

Constructor and Destructor

BListView()

BListView(BRect *frame*, const char **name*,
            list_view_type *type* = B_SINGLE_SELECTION_LIST,
            uint32 *resizingMode* = B_FOLLOW_LEFT | B_FOLLOW_TOP,
            uint32 *flags* = B_WILL_DRAW | B_NAVIGABLE |
            B_FRAME_EVENTS)

BListView(BMessage **archive*)

Initializes the new BListView. The *frame*, *name*, *resizingMode*, and *flags* arguments are identical to those declared for the BView class and are passed unchanged to the BView constructor.

The list *type* can be either:

B_SINGLE_SELECTION_LIST	The user can select only one item in the list at a time. This is the default setting.
B_MULTIPLE_SELECTION_LIST	The user can select any number of items by holding down an Option key (for discontiguous selections) or a Shift key (for contiguous selections).

The list begins life empty. Call `AddItem()` or `AddList()` to put items in the list. Call `Select()` to select one of the items so that it's highlighted when the list is initially displayed to the user.

See also: the BView constructor, `AddItem()`

~BListView()

virtual **~BListView**(void)

Frees the selection and invocation messages, if any, and any memory allocated to hold the list of items, but not the items themselves.

Static Functions

Instantiate()

> static BListView ***Instantiate**(BMessage *archive)

Returns a new BListView object, allocated by **new** and created with the version of the constructor that takes a BMessage *archive*. However, if the *archive* message doesn't contain data for a BListView object, this function returns NULL.

See also: BArchivable::Instantiate(), instantiate_object(), Archive()

Member Functions

AddItem()

> virtual bool **AddItem**(BListItem *item, int32 *index*)
> virtual bool **AddItem**(BListItem *item)

Adds an *item* to the BListView at *index*—or, if no index is supplied, at the end of the list. If necessary, additional memory is allocated to accommodate the new item.

Adding an item never removes an item already in the list. If the item is added at an index that's already occupied, items currently in the list are bumped down one slot to make room.

If *index* is out of range (greater than the current item count, or less than zero), this function fails and returns false. Otherwise, it returns true.

See also: BList::AddItem()

AddList()

> virtual bool **AddList**(BList *list, int32 *index*)
> virtual bool **AddList**(BList *list)

Adds the contents of another *list* to this BListView. The items from the BList are inserted at *index*—or, if no index is given, they're appended to the end of the list. If the index is out of range, the function fails and returns false. If successful, it returns true.

The BListView doesn't check to be sure that all the items it adds from the *list* are pointers to BListItem objects. It assumes that they are; if the assumption is false, subsequent BListView operations will fail.

See also: AddItem(), BList::AddList()

Archive()

> virtual status_t **Archive**(BMessage *archive*, bool *deep* = true) const

Calls the inherited version of `Archive()`, then adds the BListView's type (`B_SINGLE_SELECTION_LIST` or `B_MULTIPLE_SELECTION_LIST`) and model invocation and selection messages, if any, to the BMessage *archive*. If the *deep* flag is true, all the items are also archived.

See also: `BArchivable::Archive()`, `Instantiate()` static function

AttachedToWindow()

> virtual void **AttachedToWindow**(void)

Sets up the BListView and makes the BWindow to which it has become attached the target for the messages it sends when items are selected or invoked—provided another target hasn't already been set. In addition, this function calls `Update()` for each item in the list to give it a chance to adjust its layout. The BListView's vertical scroll bar is also adjusted.

This function is called for you when the BListView becomes part of a window's view hierarchy.

See also: `BView::AttachedToWindow()`, `BInvoker::SetTarget()`,
`BListItem::Update()`

CountItems()

> int32 **CountItems**(void) const

Returns the number of BListItems currently in the list.

See also: `BList::CountItems()`

CurrentSelection()

> int32 **CurrentSelection**(int32 *index* = 0) const

Returns the index of a currently selected item in the list, or a negative number if no item is selected. The domain of the *index* passed as an argument is the current set of selected items; the first selected item is at *index* 0, the second at *index* 1, and so on, even if the selection is not contiguous. The domain of the returned index is the set of all items in the list.

To get all currently selected items, increment the passed index until the function returns a negative number:

```
BListItem *item;
int32 selected;
while ( (selected = myListView->CurrentSelection(i)) >= 0 ) {
    item = ItemAt(selected);
    . . .
}
```

See also: `Select()`

Deselect(), DeselectAll(), DeselectExcept()

void **Deselect**(int32 *index*)

void **DeselectAll**(void)

void **DeselectExcept**(int32 *start*, int32 *finish*)

These functions deselect the item at *index*, all the items, or all the items except those from index *start* through index *finish*.

See also: `Select()`

DoForEach()

void **DoForEach**(bool (**func*)(BListItem *))
void **DoForEach**(bool (**func*)(BListItem *, void *), void **arg2*)

Calls the *func* function once for each item in the BListView. BListItems are visited in order, beginning with the first one in the list (index 0) and ending with the last. If a call to *func* returns `true`, the iteration is stopped, even if some items have not yet been visited.

func must be a function that takes one or two arguments. The first argument is a pointer to the BListItem; the second argument, if *func* requires one, is passed to `DoForEach()` as *arg2*.

See also: `BList::DoForEach()`

Draw()

virtual void **Draw**(BRect *updateRect*)

Calls upon every item in the *updateRect* area of the view to draw itself.

`Draw()` is called for you whenever the list view is to be updated or redisplayed; you don't need to call it yourself. You also don't need to reimplement it; to change the way items are drawn, define a new version of `DrawItem()` in a class derived from BListItem.

See also: `BView::Draw()`, `BListItem::DrawItem()`

FirstItem()   *see ItemAt()*

FrameResized()

virtual void **FrameResized**(float *width*, float *height*)

Updates the on-screen display in response to a notification that the BListView's frame rectangle has been resized. In particular, this function looks for a vertical scroll bar that's a sibling of the BListView. It adjusts this scroll bar to reflect the way the list view was resized, under the assumption that it must have the BListView as its target.

`FrameResized()` is called automatically at the appropriate times; you shouldn't call it yourself.

See also: `BView::FrameResized()`

HasItem()

bool **HasItem**(BListItem **item*) const

Returns `true` if *item* is in the list, and `false` if not.

See also: `BList::HasItem()`

IndexOf()

int32 **IndexOf**(BListItem **item*) const
int32 **IndexOf**(BPoint **point*) const

Returns the index where a particular *item*—or the item whose display rectangle includes a particular *point*—is located in the list. If the *item* is in the list more than once, the index returned will be the position of its first occurrence. To determine whether an item lies at the specified *point*, only the *y*-coordinate value of the point is considered.

If the *item* isn't in the list or the *y*-coordinate of the *point* doesn't intersect with the data rectangle of the BListView, the return value will be a negative number.

See also: `BList::IndexOf()`

InitiateDrag()

> virtual bool **InitiateDrag**(BPoint *point*, int32 *index*, bool *wasSelected*)

Implemented by derived classes to permit users to drag items. This function is called from the BListView's `MouseDown()` function; it should initiate the drag-and-drop operation and return `true`, or refuse to do so and return `false`. By default, it always returns `false`.

The *point* that's passed to `InitiateDrag()` is the same as the point passed to `MouseDown()`; it's where the cursor was located when the user pressed the mouse button. The *index* of the item under the cursor (the item that would be dragged) is passed as the second argument, and the *wasSelected* flag indicates whether or not the item was selected before the mouse button went down.

A BListView allows users to autoscroll the list by holding the mouse button down and dragging outside its frame rectangle. If a derived class implements `InitiateDrag()` to drag an item each time the user moves the mouse with a button down, it will hide this autoscrolling behavior. Therefore, derived classes typically permit users to drag items only if they're already selected (if *wasSelected* is `true`). In other words, it takes two mouse-down events to drag an item—one to select it and one to begin dragging it.

See also: `BView::DragMessage()`

InvalidateItem()

> void **InvalidateItem**(int32 *index*)

Invalidates the item at *index* so that an update message will be sent forcing the BListView to redraw it.

See also: `BView::Invalidate()`

Invoke()

> virtual status_t **Invoke**(BMessage **message* = NULL) const

Augments the BInvoker version of `Invoke()` to add three pieces of information to each message the BListView sends:

Data name	Type code	Description
"when"	B_INT64_TYPE	When the message is sent, as measured by the number of microseconds since 12:00:00 AM 1970.
"source"	B_POINTER_TYPE	A pointer to the BListView object.
"index"	B_INT32_TYPE	An array containing the index of every selected item.

This function is called to send both the selection message and the invocation message. It can also be called from application code. The default target of the message (established by `AttachedToWindow()`) is the BWindow where the BListView is located.

What it means to "invoke" selected items depends entirely on the invocation BMessage and the receiver's response to it. This function does nothing but send the message.

See also: `Select()`, `SetInvocationMessage()`, `BInvoker::SetTarget()`

IsEmpty()

bool **IsEmpty**(void) const

Returns `true` if the list is empty (if it contains no items), and `false` otherwise.

See also: `MakeEmpty()`, `BList::IsEmpty()`

IsItemSelected()

bool **IsItemSelected**(int32 *index*) const

Returns `true` if the item at *index* is currently selected, and `false` if it's not.

See also: `CurrentSelection()`

ItemAt(), FirstItem(), LastItem()

BListItem *`*ItemAt`(int32 *index*) const

BListItem *`*FirstItem`(void) const

BListItem *`*LastItem`(void) const

The first of these functions returns the BListItem at *index*, or NULL if the index is out of range. The other two functions return the very first and very last items in the list, or NULL if the list is empty. None of the functions alters the contents of the list—they don't remove the returned item.

See also: `Items()`, `BList::FirstItem()`, `BList::LastItem()`, `BList::ItemAt()`

ItemFrame()

BRect **ItemFrame**(int32 *index*)

Returns the frame rectangle of the BListItem at *index*. The rectangle is stated in the coordinate system of the BListView and defines the area where the item is drawn. Items can differ in height, but all have the same width.

See also: `DrawItem()`

Items()

const BListItem **Items**(void) const

Returns a pointer to the BListView's list of BListItems. You can index directly into the list of items if you're certain that the index is in range:

```
BListItem *item = Items()[index];
```

Although the practice is discouraged, you can also step through the list of items by incrementing the list pointer that `Items()` returns. Be aware that the list isn't null-terminated—you have to detect the end of the list by some other means. The simplest method is to count items:

```
BListItem **ptr = myListView->Items();

for ( long i = myListView->CountItems(); i > 0; i-- )
{
    . . .
    *ptr++;
}
```

You should never use the item's pointer to alter the contents of the list.

See also: `DoForEach()`, `SortItems()`, `BList::Items()`

KeyDown()

virtual void **KeyDown**(const char *bytes*, int32 *numBytes*)

Permits the user to operate the list using the following keys:

Keys	Perform Action
Up Arrow and Down Arrow	Select the items that are immediately before and immediately after the currently selected item.
Page Up and Page Down	Select the items that are one viewful above and below the currently selected item—or the first and last items if there's no item a viewful away.
Home and End	Select the first and last items in the list.
Enter and the space bar	Invoke the current selection.

This function also incorporates the inherited BView version so that the Tab key can navigate to another view.

KeyDown() is called to report B_KEY_DOWN messages when the BListView is the focus view of the active window; you shouldn't call it yourself.

See also: BView::KeyDown(), Select(), Invoke()

LastItem() *see ItemAt()*

MakeEmpty()

 virtual void **MakeEmpty**(void)

Empties the BListView of all its items, without freeing the BListItem objects.

See also: IsEmpty(), RemoveItem(), BList::MakeEmpty()

MakeFocus()

 virtual void **MakeFocus**(bool *focused* = true)

Overrides the BView version of MakeFocus() to draw an indication that the BListView has become the focus for keyboard events when the *focused* flag is true, and to remove that indication when the flag is false.

See also: BView::MakeFocus()

MouseDown()

 virtual void **MouseDown**(BPoint *point*)

Responds to B_MOUSE_DOWN messages by selecting items, invoking them (if the mouse-down event is the second of a double-click), and autoscrolling the list (when the user drags with a mouse button down). This function also calls InitiateDrag() to give derived classes the opportunity to drag items. You can implement that function; you shouldn't override (or call) this one.

See also: BView::MouseDown(), Select(), Invoke(), InitiateDrag()

RemoveItem(), RemoveItems()

 virtual BListItem ***RemoveItem**(int32 *index*)
 virtual bool **RemoveItem**(BListItem **item*)

 virtual bool **RemoveItems**(int32 *index*, int32 *count*)

RemoveItem() removes a single item from the BListView. If passed an *index*, it removes the item at that index and returns it. If there's no item at the index, it returns NULL. If passed an *item*, this function looks for that particular item in the list, removes it, and returns `true`. If it can't find the item, it returns `false`. If the item is in the list more than once, this function removes only its first occurrence.

`RemoveItems()` removes *count* number of items from the BListView, beginning with the item at *index*. If the list doesn't contain *count* items between *index* and the end of the list, this function removes as many items as there are.

The list is compacted after an item is removed. Therefore, you shouldn't try to empty a list (or a range within a list) by removing items incrementing indices. You should either start with the highest index and move towards the head of the list, or remove at the same index (the lowest in the range) some number of times. As an example of the latter, the following code removes the first five items in the list:

```
for ( int32 i = 0; i <= 4; i++ )
    myListView->RemoveItem(0);
```

See also: `MakeEmpty()`, `BList::RemoveItem()`

ScrollTo()

> virtual void **ScrollTo**(BPoint *point*)
> inline void **ScrollTo**(float *x*, float *y*)

Augments the BView version of `ScrollTo()` to do some class-internal housekeeping when the list is scrolled. For all practical purposes, these functions are identical to their BView counterparts.

See also: `BView::ScrollTo()`

ScrollToSelection()

> void **ScrollToSelection**(void)

Scrolls the list so that the first item in the current selection is visible.

Select()

> void **Select**(int32 *index*, bool *extend* = false)

> void **Select**(int32 *start*, int32 *finish*, bool *extend* = false)

Selects the item located at *index*—or all the items from the *start* index through the *finish* index—provided that none of the indices are out of range. If the *extend* flag is `false`, as it is by default, this function removes the highlighting from the previously selected item(s) and highlights the new selection, scrolling the list, if necessary, so that at least one selected item is visible. However, if the *extend* flag is `true`, the newly selected items are added to the current selection.

Select() can be called to set an initial selection in the list or change the current selection. It permits the program to select a number of items, even for a B_SINGLE_SELECTION_LIST list.

If this function succeeds in changing the selection, it calls SelectionChanged() to notify the BListView. If a model selection message has been registered with the BListView, it also calls Invoke() to send the message. If a message hasn't been registered and SelectionChanged() hasn't been implemented, "selecting" items simply means to highlight them and mark them as being selected for other functions, such as CurrentSelection().

Typically, BListViews are set up to send a message when items are invoked, but not when they're selected.

See also: SetSelectionMessage(), Invoke(), SelectionChanged()

SelectionChanged()

> virtual void **SelectionChanged**(void)

Implemented by derived classes to do whatever they please when the selection changes.

See also: Select()

SetInvocationMessage(), InvocationMessage(), InvocationCommand()

> virtual void **SetInvocationMessage**(BMessage *message*)
>
> BMessage *****InvocationMessage**(void) const
>
> uint32 **InvocationCommand**(void) const

These functions set and return information about the BMessage that the BListView sends when currently selected items are invoked.

SetInvocationMessage() assigns *message* to the BListView, freeing any message previously assigned. The message becomes the responsibility of the BListView object and will be freed only when it's replaced by another message or the BListView is freed; you shouldn't free it yourself. Passing a NULL pointer to this function deletes the current message without replacing it.

When sending the message, the Invoke() function makes a copy of it and adds two pieces of relevant information—"when" the message is sent and the "source" BListView. These names should not be used for any data that you add to the invocation *message*.

`InvocationMessage()` returns a pointer to the BMessage and `InvocationCommand()` returns its what data member. The message belongs to the BListView; it can be altered by adding or removing data, but it shouldn't be deleted. To get rid of the current message, pass a `NULL` pointer to `SetInvocationMessage()`.

See also: `Invoke()`, the BMessage class

SetListType(), ListType()

virtual void **SetListType**(list_view_type *type*)

list_view_type **ListType**(void) const

These functions set and return the list type—whether or not it permits multiple selections. The `list_view_type` must be either `B_SINGLE_SELECTION_LIST` or `B_MULTIPLE_SELECTION_LIST`. The type is first set when the BListView is constructed.

See also: the BListView constructor

SetSelectionMessage(), SelectionMessage(), SelectionCommand()

virtual void **SetSelectionMessage**(BMessage **message*)

BMessage *****SelectionMessage**(void) const

uint32 **SelectionCommand**(void) const

These functions set, and return information about, the message that a BListView sends whenever a new item is selected. They're exact counterparts to the functions described above under `SetInvocationMessage()`, except that the selection message is sent whenever an item in the list is selected, rather than when invoked. It's more common to take action (to initiate a message) when invoking an item than when selecting one.

See also: `Select()`, `SetInvocationMessage()`, `Invoke()`, the BMessage class

SortItems()

void *****SortItems**(int (**compareFunc*)(const void *, const void *))

Rearranges the items in the list. The items are sorted using the *compareFunc* comparison function passed as an argument. This function should return a negative number if the first item is ordered before the second, a positive number if the second comes before the first, and 0 if the two items are ordered equivalently.

Although the comparison function is, in the usual manner for such functions, declared to take two `void*` arguments, each argument should be a pointer to an item in the list—in other words, a pointer to a BListItem pointer:

```
int compare_func(BListItem **firstArg, BListItem **secondArg);
```

See also: `Items()`, `BList::SortItems()`

TargetedByScrollView()

virtual void **TargetedByScrollView**(BScrollView *view*)

Notes the fact that the BListView is the target of a BScrollView and arranges for the border of the BScrollView to be highlighted when the BListView is the current focus view of the active window.

See also: `BScrollView::SetBorderHighlighted()`

WindowActivated()

virtual void **WindowActivated**(bool *active*)

Makes sure that the BScrollView that targets the BListView is redrawn when the window is activated and deactivated, if the BListView is the current focus view. This gives the BScrollView a chance to highlight or unhighlight its border, as appropriate.

See also: `BView::WindowActivated()`

BMenu

Derived from:	public BView
Declared in:	be/interface/Menu.h
Library:	libbe.so

Overview

A BMenu object displays a pull-down or pop-up list of menu items. Menus organize the features of an application—the common ones as well as the more obscure—and provide users with points of entry for most everything the application can do. The arrangement of menus presents an outline of how the various parts of the application fit together.

Menu Hierarchy

Menus are hierarchically arranged; an item in one menu can control another menu. The controlled menu is a *submenu*; the menu that contains the item that controls it is its *supermenu*. A submenu remains hidden until the user operates the item that controls it; it becomes hidden again when the user is finished with it. A submenu can have its own submenus, and those submenus can have submenus of their own, and so on—although it becomes hard for users to find their way in a menu hierarchy that becomes too deep.

The menu at the root of the hierarchy is displayed in a window as a list—perhaps a list of just one item. Since it, unlike other menus, doesn't have a controlling item, it must remain visible. A root menu is therefore a special kind of menu in that it behaves more like an ordinary view than do other menus, which stay hidden. Root menus should belong to the BMenuBar class, which is derived from BMenu. The typical root menu is a menu bar displayed across the top of a window (hence the name of the class).

Menu Items

Each item in a menu is a kind of BMenuItem object. An item can be marked (displayed with a check mark to its left), assigned a keyboard shortcut, enabled and disabled, and given a "trigger" character that the user can type to invoke the item when its menu is open on-screen.

Every item has a particular job to do. If an item controls a submenu, its job is to show the submenu on-screen and hide it again. All other items give instructions to the application. When invoked by the user, they deliver a BMessage to a target BHandler. What the item does depends on the content of the BMessage and the BHandler's response to it.

Hook Functions

ScreenLocation() Can be implemented to have the menu appear on-screen at some location other than the default.

Constructor and Destructor

BMenu()

BMenu(const char *name, menu_layout *layout* = B_ITEMS_IN_COLUMN)
BMenu(const char *name, float *width*, float *height*)
BMenu(BMessage *archive*)

protected:
    BMenu(BRect *frame*, const char **name*, uint32 *resizingMode*, uint32 *flags*,
            menu_layout *layout*, bool *resizeToFit*)

Initializes the BMenu object. The *name* of the object becomes the initial label of the supermenu item that controls the menu and brings it to the screen. (It's also the name that can be passed to BView's `FindView()` function.)

A new BMenu object doesn't contain any items; you need to call `AddItem()` to set up its contents.

A menu can arrange its items in any of three ways:

`B_ITEMS_IN_COLUMN`
    The items are stacked vertically in a column, one on top of the other, as in a typical menu.

`B_ITEMS_IN_ROW`
    The items are laid out horizontally in a row, from end to end, as in a typical menu bar.

`B_ITEMS_IN_MATRIX`
    The items are arranged in a custom fashion, such as a matrix.

Either `B_ITEMS_IN_ROW` or the default `B_ITEMS_IN_COLUMN` can be passed as the *layout* argument to the public constructor. (A column is the default for ordinary menus; a row is the default for BMenuBars.) This version of the constructor isn't designed for `B_ITEMS_IN_MATRIX` layouts.

A BMenu object can arrange items that are laid out in a column or a row entirely on its own. The menu will be resized to exactly fit the items that are added to it.

However, when items are laid out in a custom matrix, the menu needs more help. First, the constructor must be informed of the exact *width* and *height* of the menu rectangle. The version of the constructor that takes these two parameters is designed just for matrix menus—it sets the layout to `B_ITEMS_IN_MATRIX`. Then, when items are added to the menu, the BMenu object expects to be informed of their precise positions within the specified area. The menu is *not* resized to fit the items that are added. Finally, when items in the matrix change, you must take care of any required adjustments in the layout yourself.

The protected version of the constructor is supplied for derived classes that don't simply devise different sorts of menu items or arrange them in a different way, but invent a different kind of menu. If the *resizeToFit* flag is `true`, it's expected that the *layout* will be `B_ITEMS_IN_COLUMN` or `B_ITEMS_IN_ROW`. The menu will resize itself to fit the items that are added to it. If the layout is `B_ITEMS_IN_MATRIX`, the *resizeToFit* flag should be `false`.

~BMenu()

virtual ~**BMenu**(void)

Deletes all the items that were added to the menu and frees all memory allocated by the BMenu object. Deleting the items serves also to delete any submenus those items control and, thus, the whole branch of the menu hierarchy.

Static Functions

Instantiate()

static BMenu ***Instantiate**(BMessage *_archive_)

Returns a new BMenu object, allocated by **new** and created with the version of the constructor that takes a BMessage _archive_. However, if the _archive_ message doesn't contain data for a BMenu object, `Instantiate()` returns `NULL`.

See also: `BArchivable::Instantiate()`, `instantiate_object()`, `Archive()`

Member Functions

AddItem()

bool **AddItem**(BMenuItem *_item_)
bool **AddItem**(BMenuItem *_item_, int32 _index_)
bool **AddItem**(BMenuItem *_item_, BRect _frame_)
bool **AddItem**(BMenu *_submenu_)
bool **AddItem**(BMenu *_submenu_, int32 _index_)
bool **AddItem**(BMenu *_submenu_, BRect _frame_)

Adds an item to the menu list at _index_—or, if no _index_ is mentioned, to the end of the list. If items are arranged in a matrix rather than a list, it's necessary to specify the item's _frame_ rectangle—the exact position where it should be located in the menu view. Assume a coordinate system for the menu that has the origin, (0.0, 0.0), at the left top corner of the view rectangle. The rectangle will have the width and height that were specified when the menu was constructed.

The versions of this function that take an _index_ (even an implicit one) can be used only if the menu arranges items in a column or row (`B_ITEMS_IN_COLUMN` or `B_ITEMS_IN_ROW`); it's an error to use them for items arranged in a matrix. Conversely, the versions of this function that take a _frame_ rectangle can be used only if the menu arranges items in a matrix (`B_ITEMS_IN_MATRIX`); it's an error to use them for items arranged in a list.

If a *submenu* is specified rather than an *item,* `AddItem()` constructs a controlling BMenuItem for the submenu and adds the item to the menu.

If it's unable to add the item to the menu—for example, if the *index* is out-of-range or the wrong version of the function has been called—`AddItem()` returns `false`. If successful, it returns `true`.

See also: the BMenu constructor, the BMenuItem class, `RemoveItem()`

AddSeparatorItem()

> bool **AddSeparatorItem**(void)

Creates an instance of the BSeparatorItem class and adds it to the end of the menu list, returning `true` if successful and `false` if not (a very unlikely possibility). This function is a shorthand for:

```
BSeparatorItem *separator = new BSeparatorItem;
AddItem(separator);
```

A separator serves only to separate other items in the list. It counts as an item and has an indexed position in the list, but it doesn't do anything. It's drawn as a horizontal line across the menu. Therefore, it's appropriately added only to menus where the items are laid out in a column.

See also: `AddItem()`, the BSeparatorItem class

Archive()

> virtual status_t **Archive**(BMessage **archive,* bool *deep* = true) const

Calls the inherited version of `Archive()`, then archives the BMenu by recording its layout and all current settings in the BMessage *archive.* If the *deep* flag is `true`, all of the menu items are also archived.

See also: `BArchivable::Archive()`, `Instantiate()` static function

AreTriggersEnabled() *see SetTriggersEnabled()*

AttachedToWindow()

> virtual void **AttachedToWindow**(void)

Finishes initializing the BMenu object by laying out its items and resizing the BMenu view to fit. This function is called for you each time the BMenu is assigned to a window. For a submenu, that means each time the menu is shown on-screen.

See also: `BView::AttachedToWindow()`

CountItems()

> int32 **CountItems**(void) const

Returns the total number of items in the menu, including separator items.

Draw()

> virtual void **Draw**(BRect *updateRect*)

Draws the menu. This function is called for you whenever the menu is placed on-screen or is updated while on-screen. It's not a function you need to call yourself.

See also: BView::Draw()

FindItem()

> BMenuItem *****FindItem**(const char *****label*) const
> BMenuItem *****FindItem**(uint32 *command*) const

Returns the item with the specified *label*—or the one that sends a message with the specified *command*. If there's more than one item in the menu hierarchy with that particular *label* or associated with that particular *command*, this function returns the first one it finds. It recursively searches the menu by working down the list of items in order. If an item controls a submenu, it searches the submenu before returning to check any remaining items in the menu.

If none of the items in the menu hierarchy meet the stated criterion, FindItem() returns NULL.

FindMarked()

> BMenuItem *****FindMarked**(void)

Returns the first marked item in the menu list (the one with the lowest index), or NULL if no item is marked.

See also: SetRadioMode(), BMenuItem::SetMarked()

GetMaxContentWidth()   *see SetMaxContentWidth()*

Hide(), Show()

protected:
> void **Hide**(void)

> void **Show**(bool *selectFirst*)
> virtual void **Show**(void)

These functions hide the menu (remove the BMenu view from the window it's in and remove the window from the screen) and show it (attach the BMenu to a window and place the window on-screen). If the *selectFirst* flag passed to Show() is true, the first item in the menu will be selected when it's shown. If *selectFirst* is false, the menu is shown without a selected item.

The version of Show() that doesn't take an argument simply calls the version that does and passes it a *selectFirst* value of false.

These functions are not ones that you'd ordinarily call, even when implementing a derived class. You'd need them only if you're implementing a nonstandard menu of some kind and want to control when the menu appears on-screen.

See also: BView::Show(), Track()

IndexOf()

int32 **IndexOf**(BMenuItem *item*) const
int32 **IndexOf**(BMenu *submenu*) const

Returns the index of the specified menu *item*—or the item that controls the specified *submenu*. Indices record the position of the item in the menu list. They begin at 0 for the item at the top of a column or at the left of a row and include separator items.

If the menu doesn't contain the specified *item*, or the item that controls *submenu*, the return value will be B_ERROR.

See also: AddItem()

InvalidateLayout()

void **InvalidateLayout**(void)

Forces the BMenu to recalculate the layout of all menu items and, consequently, its own size. It can do this only if the items are arranged in a row or a column. If the items are arranged in a matrix, it's up to you to keep their layout up-to-date.

All BMenu and BMenuItem functions that change an item in a way that might affect the overall menu automatically invalidate the menu's layout so it will be recalculated. For example, changing the label of an item might cause the menu to become wider (if it needs more room to accommodate the longer label) or narrower (if it no longer needs as much room as before).

Therefore, you don't need to call InvalidateLayout() after using a kit function to change a menu or menu item; it's called for you. You'd call it only when making some other change to a menu.

See also: the BMenu constructor

IsEnabled()   *see SetEnabled()*

IsLabelFromMarked()   *see SetLabelFromMarked()*

IsRadioMode()   *see SetRadioMode()*

ItemAt(), SubmenuAt()

BMenuItem ***ItemAt**(int32 *index*) const

BMenu ***SubmenuAt**(int32 *index*) const

These functions return the item at *index*—or the submenu controlled by the item at *index*. If there's no item at the index, they return NULL. SubmenuAt() is a shorthand for:

```
ItemAt(index)->Submenu()
```

It returns NULL if the item at *index* doesn't control a submenu.

See also: AddItem()

KeyDown()

virtual void **KeyDown**(const char **bytes*, int32 *numBytes*)

Handles keyboard navigation through the menu. This function is called to respond to messages reporting key-down events. It should not be called from application code.

See also: BView::KeyDown()

Layout()

protected:
    menu_layout **Layout**(void) const

Returns B_ITEMS_IN_COLUMN if the items in the menu are stacked in a column from top to bottom, B_ITEMS_IN_ROW if they're stretched out in a row from left to right, or B_ITEMS_IN_MATRIX if they're arranged in some custom fashion. By default BMenu items are arranged in a column and BMenuBar items in a row.

The layout is established by the constructor.

See also: the BMenu and BMenuBar constructors

MaxContentWidth()   *see SetMaxContentWidth()*

RemoveItem()

BMenuItem *RemoveItem(int32 *index*)
bool **RemoveItem**(BMenuItem *item*)
bool **RemoveItem**(BMenu *submenu*)

Removes the item at *index*, or the specified *item*, or the item that controls the specified *submenu*. Removing the item doesn't free it.

- If passed an *index*, this function returns a pointer to the item so you can free it. It returns a NULL pointer if the item couldn't be removed (for example, if the *index* is out-of-range).

- If passed an *item*, it returns true if the item was in the list and could be removed, and false if not.

- If passed a *submenu*, it returns true if the submenu is controlled by an item in the menu and that item could be removed, and false otherwise.

When an item is removed from a menu, it loses its target; the cached value is set to NULL. If the item controls a submenu, it remains attached to the submenu even after being removed.

See also: AddItem()

ResizeToPreferred()   *see GetPreferredSize()*

ScreenLocation()

protected:
virtual BPoint **ScreenLocation**(void)

Returns the point where the left top corner of the menu should appear when the menu is shown on-screen. The point is specified in the screen coordinate system.

This function is called each time a hidden menu (a submenu of another menu) is brought to the screen. It can be overridden in a derived class to change where the menu appears. For example, the BPopUpMenu class overrides it so that a pop-up menu pops up over the controlling item.

See also: the BPopUpMenu class

SetEnabled(), IsEnabled()

virtual void **SetEnabled**(bool *enabled*)

bool **IsEnabled**(void) const

SetEnabled() enables the BMenu if the *enabled* flag is true, and disables it if *enabled* is false. If the menu is a submenu, this enables or disables its controlling item, just as if SetEnabled() were called for that item. The controlling item is updated so that it displays its new state, if it happens to be visible on-screen.

Disabling a menu disables its entire branch of the menu hierarchy. All items in the menu, including those that control other menus, are disabled.

IsEnabled() returns true if the BMenu, and every BMenu above it in the menu hierarchy, is enabled. It returns false if the BMenu, or any BMenu above it in the menu hierarchy, is disabled.

See also: BMenuItem::SetEnabled()

SetItemMargins(), GetItemMargins()

protected:

void **SetItemMargins**(float *left*, float *top*, float *right*, float *bottom*)

void **GetItemMargins**(float **left*, float **top*, float **right*, float **bottom*)

These functions set and get the margins around each item in the BMenu. For the purposes of this function, you should assume that all items are enclosed in a rectangle of the same size, one big enough for the largest item. Keyboard shortcuts are displayed in the right margin and check marks in the left.

See also: SetMaxContentWidth()

SetLabelFromMarked(), IsLabelFromMarked()

protected:

void **SetLabelFromMarked**(bool *flag*)

bool **IsLabelFromMarked**(void)

SetLabelFromMarked() determines whether the label of the item that controls the menu (the label of the superitem) should be taken from the currently marked item within the menu. If *flag* is true, the menu is placed in radio mode and the superitem's label is reset each time the user selects a different item. If *flag* is false, the setting for radio mode doesn't change and the label of the superitem isn't automatically reset.

IsLabelFromMarked() returns whether the superitem's label is taken from the marked item (but not necessarily whether the BMenu is in radio mode).

See also: SetRadioMode()

SetMaxContentWidth(), MaxContentWidth()

virtual void **SetMaxContentWidth**(float *width*)

float **MaxContentWidth**(void) const

These functions set and return the maximum width of an item's content area. The content area is where the item label is drawn; it excludes the margin on the left where a check mark might be placed and the margin on the right where a shortcut character or a submenu symbol might appear. The content area is the same size for all items in the menu.

Normally, a menu will be wide enough to accommodate its longest item. However, items wider than the maximum set by `SetMaxContentWidth()` are truncated to fit.

See also: `SetItemMargins()`, `BMenuItem::TruncateLabel()`

SetRadioMode(), IsRadioMode()

virtual void **SetRadioMode**(bool *flag*)

bool **IsRadioMode**(void)

`SetRadioMode()` puts the BMenu in radio mode if *flag* is `true` and takes it out of radio mode if *flag* is `false`. In radio mode, only one item in the menu can be marked at a time. If the user selects an item, a check mark is placed in front of it automatically (you don't need to call BMenuItem's `SetMarked()` function; it's called for you). If another item was marked at the time, its mark is removed. Selecting a currently marked item retains the mark.

`IsRadioMode()` returns whether the BMenu is currently in radio mode. The default radio mode is `false` for ordinary BMenus, but `true` for BPopUpMenus.

`SetRadioMode()` doesn't change any of the items in the menu. If you want an initial item to be marked when the menu is put into radio mode, you must mark it yourself.

When `SetRadioMode()` turns radio mode off, it calls `SetLabelFromMarked()` and passes it an argument of `false`—turning off the feature that changes the label of the menu's superitem each time the marked item changes. Similarly, when `SetLabelFromMarked()` turns on this feature, it calls `SetRadioMode()` and passes it an argument of `true`—turning radio mode on.

See also: `BMenuItem::SetMarked()`, `SetLabelFromMarked()`

SetTargetForItems()

virtual status_t **SetTargetForItems**(BHandler *handler*)
virtual status_t **SetTargetForItems**(BMessenger *messenger*)

Assigns the same target *handler* or *messenger* to all the items in the menu. This function is simply a convenient way to call `SetTarget()` for all of a menu's items when they share the same target. It works through the list of BMenuItems in order, calling `SetTarget()` for each one and passing it the specified BHandler or BMessenger object. The proposed target is therefore subject to the restrictions imposed by the `SetTarget()` function that BMenuItem inherits from BInvoker in the Application Kit. See that function for further information.

If it's unable to set the target of any item, `SetTargetForItems()` aborts and returns the error it encountered. If successful in setting the target of all items, it returns `B_OK`.

This function doesn't work recursively; it acts only on items currently in the BMenu, not on items in submenus nor on items that might be added later.

See also: `BInvoker::SetTarget()`

SetTriggersEnabled(), AreTriggersEnabled()

> virtual void **SetTriggersEnabled**(bool *flag*)

> bool **AreTriggersEnabled**(void) const

`SetTriggersEnabled()` enables the triggers for all items in the menu if *flag* is `true` and disables them if *flag* is `false`. `AreTriggersEnabled()` returns whether the triggers are currently enabled or disabled. They're enabled by default.

Triggers are displayed to the user only if they're enabled, and only when keyboard actions can operate the menu.

Triggers are appropriate for some menus, but not for others. `SetTriggers-Enabled()` is typically called to initialize the BMenu when it's constructed, not to enable and disable triggers as the application is running. If triggers are ever enabled for a menu, they should always be enabled; if they're ever disabled, they should always be disabled.

See also: `BMenuItem::SetTrigger()`

Show() *see Hide()*

SubmenuAt() *see ItemAt()*

Superitem(), Supermenu()

> BMenuItem *****Superitem**(void) const

> BMenu *****Supermenu**(void) const

These functions return the supermenu item that controls the BMenu and the supermenu where that item is located. The supermenu could be a BMenuBar object. If the BMenu hasn't been made the submenu of another menu, both functions return NULL.

See also: `AddItem()`

Track()

protected:

BMenuItem *__Track__(bool *openAnyway* = false, BRect **clickToOpenRect* = NULL)

Initiates tracking of the cursor within the menu. This function passes tracking control to submenus (and submenus of submenus) depending on where the user moves the mouse. If the user ends tracking by invoking an item, `Track()` returns the item. If the user didn't invoke any item, it returns NULL. The item doesn't have to be located in the BMenu; it could, for example, belong to a submenu of the BMenu.

If the *openAnyway* flag is `true`, `Track()` opens the menu and leaves it open even though a mouse button isn't held down. This enables menu navigation from the keyboard. If a *clickToOpenRect* is specified and the user has set the click-to-open preference, `Track()` will leave the menu open if the user releases the mouse button while the cursor is inside the rectangle. The rectangle should be stated in the screen coordinate system.

`Track()` is called by the BMenu to initiate tracking in the menu hierarchy. You would need to call it yourself only if you're implementing a different kind of menu that starts to track the cursor under nonstandard circumstances.

BMenuBar

Derived from:	public BMenu
Declared in:	be/interface/MenuBar.h
Library:	libbe.so

Overview

A BMenuBar is a menu that can stand at the root of a menu hierarchy. Rather than appear on-screen when commanded to do so by a user action, a BMenuBar object has a settled location in a window's view hierarchy, just like other views. Typically, the root menu is the menu bar that's drawn across the top of the window. It's from this use that the class gets its name.

However, instances of this class can also be used in other ways. A BMenuBar might simply display a list of items arranged in a column somewhere in a window. Or it might contain just one item, where that item controls a pop-up menu (a BPopUpMenu object). Rather than look like a "menu bar," the BMenuBar object would look something like a button.

The Key Menu Bar

The "real" menu bar at the top of the window usually represents an extensive menu hierarchy; each of its items typically controls a submenu.

The user should be able to operate this menu bar from the keyboard (using the arrow keys and Enter). There are two ways that the user can put the BMenuBar and its hierarchy in focus for keyboard events:

- Clicking an item in the menu bar. If the "click to open" preference is not turned off, this opens the submenu the item controls so that it stays visible on-screen and puts the submenu in focus.

- Pressing the Menu key or Command-Escape. This puts the BMenuBar in focus and selects its first item.

Either method opens the entire menu hierarchy to keyboard navigation.

If a window's view hierarchy includes more than one BMenuBar object, the Menu key (or Command-Escape) must choose one of them to put in focus. By default, it picks the last one that was attached to the window. However, the `SetKeyMenuBar()` function defined in the BWindow class can be called to designate a different BMenuBar object as the "key" menu bar for the window.

A Kind of BMenu

BMenuBar inherits most of its functions from the BMenu class. It reimplements the `AttachedToWindow()`, `Draw()`, and `MouseDown()` functions that set up the object and respond to messages, but these aren't functions that you'd call from application code; they're called for you.

The only real function (other than the constructor) that the BMenuBar class adds to those it inherits is `SetBorder()`, which determines how the list of items is bordered.

Therefore, for most BMenuBar operations—adding submenus, finding items, temporarily disabling the menu bar, and so on—you must call inherited functions and treat the object like the BMenu that it is.

See also: the BMenu class

Constructor and Destructor

BMenuBar()

BMenuBar(BRect *frame*, const char **name*,
　　　　　uint32 *resizingMode* = B_FOLLOW_LEFT_RIGHT |
　　　　　B_FOLLOW_TOP,
　　　　　menu_layout *layout* = B_ITEMS_IN_ROW,
　　　　　bool *resizeToFit* = true)
BMenuBar(BMessage **archive*)

Initializes the BMenuBar by assigning it a *frame* rectangle, a *name*, and a *resizing-Mode*, just like other BViews. These values are passed up the inheritance hierarchy to the BView constructor. The default resizing mode (B_FOLLOW_LEFT_RIGHT plus B_FOLLOW_TOP) is designed for a true menu bar (one that's displayed along the top edge of a window). It permits the menu bar to adjust itself to changes in the window's width, while keeping it glued to the top of the window frame.

The *layout* argument determines how items are arranged in the menu bar. By default, they're arranged in a row as befits a true menu bar. If an instance of this class is being used to implement something other than a horizontal menu, items can be laid out in a column (B_ITEMS_IN_COLUMN) or in a matrix (B_ITEMS_IN_MATRIX).

If the *resizeToFit* flag is turned on, as it is by default, the frame rectangle of the BMenuBar will be automatically resized to fit the items it displays. This is generally a good idea, since it relieves you of the responsibility of testing user preferences to determine what size the menu bar should be. Because the font and font size for menu items are user preferences, items can vary in size from user to user.

When *resizeToFit* is true, the *frame* rectangle determines only where the menu bar is located, not how large it will be. The rectangle's left and top data members are respected, but the right and bottom sides are adjusted to accommodate the items that are added to the menu bar.

Two kinds of adjustments are made if the *layout* is B_ITEMS_IN_ROW, as it typically is for a menu bar:

- The height of the menu bar is adjusted to the height of a single item.
- If the *resizingMode* includes B_FOLLOW_LEFT_RIGHT, the width of the menu bar is adjusted to match the width of its parent view. This means that a true menu bar (one that's a child of the window's top view) will always be as wide as the window.

Two similar adjustments are made if the menu bar *layout* is B_ITEMS_IN_COLUMN:

- The width of the menu bar is adjusted to the width of the widest item.
- If the *resizingMode* includes B_FOLLOW_TOP_BOTTOM, the height of the menu bar is adjusted to match the height of its parent view.

After setting up the key menu bar and adding items to it, you may want to set the minimum width of the window so that certain items won't be hidden when the window is resized smaller.

Change the *resizingMode*, the *layout*, and the *resizeToFit* flag as needed for BMenuBars that are used for a purpose other than to implement a true menu bar.

See also: the BMenu constructor, `BWindow::SetSizeLimits()`

~BMenuBar()

virtual **~BMenuBar**(void)

Frees all the items and submenus in the entire menu hierarchy, and all memory allocated by the BMenuBar.

Static Functions

Instantiate()

static BMenuBar ***Instantiate**(BMessage *archive*)

Returns a new BMenuBar object, allocated by **new** and created with the version of the constructor that takes a BMessage *archive*. However, if the *archive* message doesn't contain data for a BMenuBar object, this function returns **NULL**.

See also: `BArchivable::Instantiate()`, `instantiate_object()`, `Archive()`

Member Functions

Archive()

virtual status_t **Archive**(BMessage *archive*, bool *deep* = true) const

Calls the inherited version of `Archive()`, which serves to archive the BMenuBar's current state and, if the *deep* flag is **true**, all its menu items. This function then adds the BMenuBar's border style to the BMessage *archive*.

See also: `BArchivable::Archive()`, `BMenu::Archive()`, `Instantiate()` static function

AttachedToWindow()

virtual void **AttachedToWindow**(void)

Finishes the initialization of the BMenuBar by setting up the whole hierarchy of menus that it controls, and by making the BWindow to which it has become attached the target handler for all items in the menu hierarchy, except for those items for which a target has already been set.

This function also makes the BMenuBar the key menu bar, the BMenuBar object whose menu hierarchy the user can navigate from the keyboard. If a window contains more than one BMenuBar in its view hierarchy, the last one that's added to the window gets to keep this designation. However, the key menu bar should always be the real menu bar at the top of the window. It can be explicitly set with BWindow's SetKeyMenuBar() function.

See also: BWindow::SetKeyMenuBar()

Border()   *see SetBorder()*

Draw()

virtual void **Draw**(BRect *updateRect*)

Draws the menu—whether as a true menu bar, as some other kind of menu list, or as a single item that controls a pop-up menu. This function is called as the result of update messages; you don't need to call it yourself.

See also: BView::Draw()

Hide(), Show()

virtual void **Hide**(void)

virtual void **Show**(void)

These functions override their BMenu counterparts to restore the normal behavior for views when they're hidden and unhidden. When an ordinary BMenu is hidden, the window that displays it is also removed from the screen. But it would be a mistake to remove the window that displays a BMenuBar. Hiding a BMenuBar is like hiding a typical view; only the view is hidden, not the window.

See also: BView::Hide()

MouseDown()

virtual void **MouseDown**(BPoint *point*)

Initiates mouse tracking and keyboard navigation of the menu hierarchy. This function is called to notify the BMenuBar of a mouse-down event.

See also: BView::MouseDown()

SetBorder(), Border()

void **SetBorder**(menu_bar_border *border*)

menu_bar_border **Border**(void) const

`SetBorder()` determines how the menu list is bordered. The *border* argument can be any of three values:

B_BORDER_FRAME	The border is drawn around the entire frame rectangle.
B_BORDER_CONTENTS	The border is drawn around just the list of items.
B_BORDER_EACH_ITEM	A border is drawn around each item.

`Border()` returns the current setting. The default is B_BORDER_FRAME.

BMenuField

Derived from:	public BView
Declared in:	be/interface/MenuField.h
Library:	libbe.so

Overview

A BMenuField object displays a labeled pop-up menu. It's a simple object that employs a BMenuBar object to control a BMenu. All it adds to what a BMenuBar can do on its own is a label and a more control-like user interface that includes keyboard navigation.

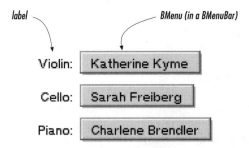

The functions defined in this class resemble those of a BControl (`SetLabel()`, `IsEnabled()`), especially a BTextControl (`SetDivider()`, `Alignment()`). However, unlike a real BControl object, a BMenuField doesn't maintain a current value and it can't be invoked to send a message. All the control work is done by items in the BMenu.

Constructor and Destructor

BMenuField()

> BMenuField(BRect *frame*, const char **name*,
>   const char **label*,
>   BMenu **menu*,
>   uint32 *resizingMode* = B_FOLLOW_LEFT | B_FOLLOW_TOP,
>   uint32 *flags* = B_WILL_DRAW | B_NAVIGABLE)
> BMenuField(BMessage **archive*)

Initializes the BMenuField object with the specified *frame* rectangle, *name*, *resizingMode*, and *flags*. These arguments are the same as for any BView object and are passed unchanged to the BView constructor. When the object is attached to a window, the height of its frame rectangle will be adjusted to fit the height of the text it displays, which depends on the user's preferred font for menus.

By default, the frame rectangle is divided horizontally in half, with the *label* displayed on the left and the *menu* on the right. This division can be changed with the SetDivider() function. The *menu* is assigned to a BMenuBar object and will pop up under the user's control. For most uses, the *menu* should be a BPopUpMenu object.

~BMenuField()

> virtual ~BMenuField(void)

Frees the label, the BMenuBar object, and other memory allocated by the BMenuField.

Static Functions

Instantiate()

> static BMenuField *Instantiate(BMessage **archive*)

Returns a new BMenuField object, allocated by new and created with the version of the constructor that takes a BMessage *archive*. However, if the *archive* message doesn't contain data for a BMenuField object, this function returns NULL.

See also: BArchivable::Instantiate(), instantiate_object(), Archive()

Member Functions

Alignment()   *see SetAlignment()*

Archive()

> virtual status_t **Archive**(BMessage *archive*, bool *deep* = **true**) const

Calls the inherited version of `Archive()`, which will, in the normal course of things, archive the child BMenuBar and the BMenu it displays, provided the *deep* flag is `true`. This function then adds the label, divider, and current state of the BMenuField to the BMessage *archive*.

See also: `BArchivable::Archive()`, `Instantiate()` static function

AttachedToWindow(), AllAttached()

> virtual void **AttachedToWindow**(void)

> virtual void **AllAttached**(void)

These functions override their BView counterparts to make the BMenuField's background color match the color of its parent view and to adjust the height of the view to the height of the BMenuBar child it contains. The height of the child depends on the size of the user's preferred font for menus.

See also: `BView::AttachedToWindow()`

Divider()   *see SetDivider()*

Draw()

> virtual void **Draw**(BRect *updateRect*)

Overrides the BView version of this function to draw the view's border and label. The way the menu field is drawn depends on whether it's enabled or disabled and whether or not it's the current focus for keyboard actions.

See also: `BView::Draw()`

IsEnabled()   *see SetEnabled()*

KeyDown()

> virtual void **KeyDown**(const char *bytes*, int32 *numBytes*)

Augments the BView version of `KeyDown()` to permit keyboard navigation to and from the view and to allow users to open the menu by pressing the space bar.

See also: `BView::KeyDown()`

Label() *see SetLabel()*

MakeFocus()

> virtual void **MakeFocus**(bool *focused*)

Augments the BView version of `MakeFocus()` to enable keyboard navigation. This function calls `Draw()` when the BMenuField becomes the focus view and when it loses that status.

See also: `BView::MakeFocus()`

Menu(), MenuBar()

> BMenu ***Menu**(void) const

> BMenuBar ***MenuBar**(void) const

`Menu()` returns the BMenu object that pops up when the user operates the BMenuField; `MenuBar()` returns the BMenuBar object that contains the menu. The BMenuBar is created by the BMenuField; the menu is assigned to it during construction.

See also: the BMenuField constructor

MouseDown()

> virtual void **MouseDown**(BPoint *point*)

Overrides the BView version of `MouseDown()` to enable users to pop up the menu using the mouse, even if the cursor isn't directly over the menu portion of the bounds rectangle.

See also: `BView::MouseDown()`

SetAlignment(), Alignment()

> virtual void **SetAlignment**(alignment *label*)

> alignment **Alignment**(void) const

These functions set and return the alignment of the label in its portion of the frame rectangle.

B_ALIGN_LEFT	The label is aligned at the left side of the bounds rectangle.
B_ALIGN_RIGHT	The label is aligned at the right boundary of its portion of the bounds rectangle.
B_ALIGN_CENTER	The label is centered in its portion of the bounds rectangle.

The default is B_ALIGN_LEFT.

SetDivider(), Divider()

virtual void **SetDivider**(float *xCoordinate*)

float **Divider**(void) const

These functions set and return the *x* coordinate value that divides the bounds rectangle between the label's portion on the left and the portion that holds the menu on the right. The coordinate is expressed in the BMenuField's coordinate system.

The default divider splits the bounds rectangle in two equal sections. By resetting it, you can provide more or less room for the label or the menu.

SetEnabled(), IsEnabled()

virtual void **SetEnabled**(bool *enabled*)

bool **IsEnabled**(void) const

SetEnabled() enables the BMenuField if the *enabled* flag is true, and disables it if the flag is false. IsEnabled() returns whether or not the object is currently enabled. When disabled, the BMenuField doesn't respond to mouse and keyboard manipulations.

If the *enabled* flag changes the current state of the object, SetEnabled() causes the view to be redrawn, so that its new state can be displayed to the user.

SetLabel(), Label()

virtual void **SetLabel**(const char **string*)

const char ****Label**(void) const

SetLabel() frees the current label and, if the argument it's passed is not NULL, replaces it with a copy of *string*. Label() returns the current label. The string it returns belongs to the BMenuField object.

See also: the BMenuField constructor

WindowActivated()

virtual void **WindowActivated**(bool *active*)

Makes sure that the BMenuField is redrawn when the window is activated and deactivated, provided that it's the current focus view.

See also: `BView::WindowActivated()`

BMenuItem

Derived from: public BInvoker, public BArchivable

Declared in: be/interface/MenuItem.h

Library: libbe.so

Overview

A BMenuItem object displays one item within a menu and contains the state associated with the item. By default, menu items are displayed simply as textual labels, like "Format" or "Save As...". Derived classes can be defined to draw something other than a label—or something in addition to the label.

Kinds of Items

Some menu items set up the menu hierarchy by giving users access to submenus. A submenu remains hidden until the user operates the item that controls it.

Other items accomplish specific actions. When the user invokes the item, it sends a message to a target BLooper and BHandler, usually the window where the menu at the root of the hierarchy (a BMenuBar object) is displayed. The action that the item initiates, or the state that it sets, depends entirely on the message and the target's response to it.

The message and the target can be customized for every item. BMenuItem derives in part from the BInvoker class, so each item retains a model for the BMessage it sends and can have a target that's different from other items in the same menu.

Items can also have a visual presence, but do nothing. Instances of the BSeparatorItem class, which is derived from BMenuItem, serve only to visually separate groups of items in the menu.

Shortcuts and Triggers

Any menu item (except for those that control submenus) can be associated with a keyboard shortcut, a character the user can type in combination with a Command key (and possibly other modifiers) to invoke the item. The shortcut character is displayed in the item to the right of the label. All shortcuts for menu items require the user to hold down the Command key.

A shortcut works even when the item it invokes isn't visible on-screen. It, therefore, has to be unique within the window (within the entire menu hierarchy).

Every menu item is also associated with a *trigger*, a character that the user can type (without the Command key) to invoke the item. The trigger works only while the menu is both open on-screen and can be operated using the keyboard. It therefore must be unique only within a particular branch of the menu hierarchy (within the menu).

The trigger is one of the characters that's displayed within the item—either the keyboard shortcut or a character in the label. When it's possible for the trigger to invoke the item, the character is underlined. Like shortcuts, triggers are case-insensitive.

For an item to have a keyboard shortcut, the application must explicitly assign one. However, by default, the Interface Kit chooses and assigns triggers for all items. The default choice can be altered by the `SetTrigger()` function.

Marked Items

An item can also be marked (with a check mark drawn to the left of the label) in order to indicate that the state it sets is currently in effect. Items are marked by the `SetMarked()` function. A menu can be set up so that items are automatically marked when they're selected and exactly one item is marked at all times. (See `SetRadioMode()` in the BMenu class.)

Disabled Items

Items can also be enabled or disabled (by the `SetEnabled()` function). A disabled item is drawn in muted tones to indicate that it doesn't work. It can't be selected or invoked. If the item controls a specific action, it won't post the message that initiates the action. If it controls a submenu, it will still bring the submenu to the screen, but all the items in submenu will be disabled. If an item in the submenu brings its own submenu to the screen, items in that submenu will also be disabled. Disabling the superitem for a submenu in effect disables a whole branch of the menu hierarchy.

See also: the BMenu class, the BSeparatorItem class

Hook Functions

All BMenuItem hook functions are protected. They should be implemented only if you design a special type of menu item that displays something other than a textual label.

`Draw()`
    Draws the entire item; can be reimplemented to draw the item in a different way.

`DrawContents()`
    Draws the item label; can be reimplemented to draw something other than a label.

`GetContentSize()`
    Provides the width and height of the item's content area, which is based on the length of the label and the current font; can be reimplemented to provide the size required to draw something other than a label.

`Highlight()`
    Highlights the item when it's selected; can be reimplemented to do highlighting in some way other than the default.

`TruncateLabel()`
    Cuts characters from the item's label so the item will fit in the space provided; can be reimplemented to cut intelligently taking the content of the label into account.

Constructor and Destructor

BMenuItem()

> BMenuItem(const char *label*, BMessage *message*,
>   char *shortcut* = NULL, uint32 *modifiers* = NULL)
> BMenuItem(BMenu *submenu*, BMessage *message* = NULL)
> BMenuItem(BMessage *archive*)

Initializes the BMenuItem to display *label* (which can be NULL if the item belongs to a derived class that's designed to display something other than text) and assigns it a model *message* (which also can be NULL).

Whenever the user invokes the item, the model message is copied and the copy is posted and marked for delivery to the target handler. Three pieces of information are added to the copy before it's posted:

Data name	Type code	Description
"when"	B_INT64_TYPE	The time the item was invoked, as measured by the number of microseconds since 12:00:00 AM January 1, 1970.
"source"	B_POINTER_TYPE	A pointer to the BMenuItem object.
"index"	B_INT32_TYPE	The index of the item, its ordinal position in the menu. Indices begin at 0.

These names should not be used for any data that you place in the *message*.

By default, the target of the message is the window associated with the item's menu hierarchy—the window where the BMenuBar at the root of the hierarchy is located. Another target can be designated by calling the `SetTarget()` function.

The constructor can also optionally set a keyboard shortcut for the item. The character that's passed as the *shortcut* parameter will be displayed to the right of the item's label. It's the accepted practice to display uppercase shortcut characters only, even though the actual character the user types may not be uppercase.

The *modifiers* mask, not the *shortcut* character, determines which modifier keys the user must hold down for the shortcut to work—including whether the Shift key must be down. The mask can be formed by combining any of the modifiers constants, especially these:

```
B_SHIFT_KEY
B_CONTROL_KEY
B_OPTION_KEY
B_COMMAND_KEY
```

However, `B_COMMAND_KEY` is required for all keyboard shortcuts; it doesn't have to be explicitly included in the mask. For example, setting the *shortcut* to 'U' with no *modifiers* would mean that the letter 'U' would be displayed alongside the item label and Command-*u* would invoke the item. The same *shortcut* with a `B_SHIFT_KEY` *modifiers* mask would mean that the uppercase character (Command-Shift-*U*) would invoke the item.

If the BMenuItem is constructed to control a *submenu*, it can't take a shortcut and it typically doesn't post messages—its role is to bring up the submenu. However, it can be assigned a model *message* if the application must take some collateral action when the submenu is opened. The item's initial label will be taken from the name of the submenu. It can be changed after construction by calling `SetLabel()`.

See also: `BInvoker::SetTarget()`, `BInvoker::SetMessage()`, `SetLabel()`

~BMenuItem()

virtual ~BMenuItem(void)

Frees the item's label and its model BMessage object. If the item controls a submenu, that menu and all its items are also freed. Deleting a BMenuItem destroys the entire menu hierarchy under that item.

Static Functions

Instantiate()

> static BMenuItem ***Instantiate**(BMessage *_archive_)

Returns a new BMenuItem object, allocated by `new` and created with the version of the constructor that takes a BMessage _archive_. However, if the _archive_ message doesn't contain data for a BMenuItem object, `Instantiate()` returns `NULL`.

See also: `BArchivable::Instantiate()`, `instantiate_object()`, `Archive()`

Member Functions

Archive()

> virtual status_t **Archive**(BMessage *_archive_, bool _deep_ = true) const

Calls the inherited version of `Archive()`, then adds a complete description of the item to the BMessage _archive_, including its label, shortcut, trigger, and whether it's marked or not. If the _deep_ flag is `true` and the BMenuItem controls a submenu, this function also adds the submenu to the archive.

See also: `BArchivable::Archive()`, `Instantiate()` static function

ContentLocation()

protected:
> BPoint **ContentLocation**(void) const

Returns the left top corner of the content area of the item, in the coordinate system of the BMenu to which it belongs. The content area of an item is the area where it displays its label (or whatever graphic substitutes for the label). It doesn't include the part of the item where a check mark or a keyboard shortcut could be displayed, nor the border and background around the content area.

You would need to call this function only if you're implementing a `DrawContent()` function to draw the contents of the menu item (likely something other than a label). The content rectangle can be calculated from the point returned by this function and the size specified by `GetContentSize()`.

If the item isn't part of a menu, the return value is indeterminate.

See also: `GetContentSize()`, `DrawContent()`

Draw(), DrawContent()

protected:

> virtual void **Draw**(void)

> virtual void **DrawContent**(void)

These functions draw the menu item and highlight it if it's currently selected. They're called by the `Draw()` function of the BMenu where the item is located whenever the menu is required to display itself; they don't need to be called from within application code.

However, they can both be overridden by derived classes that display something other than a textual label. The `Draw()` function is called first. It draws the background for the entire item, then calls `DrawContent()` to draw the label within the item's content area. After `DrawContent()` returns, it draws the check mark (if the item is currently marked) and the keyboard shortcut (if any). It finishes by calling `Highlight()` if the item is currently selected.

Both functions draw by calling functions of the BMenu in which the item is located. For example:

```
void MyItem::DrawContent()
{
    .  .  .
    Menu()->DrawBitmap(image);
    .  .  .
}
```

A derived class can override either `Draw()`, if it needs to draw the entire item, or `DrawContent()`, if it needs to draw only within the content area. A `Draw()` function can find the frame rectangle it should draw within by calling the BMenuItem's `Frame()` function; a `DrawContent()` function can calculate the content area from the point returned by `ContentLocation()` and the dimensions provided by `GetContentSize()`.

When `DrawContent()` is called, the pen is positioned to draw the item's label and the high color is appropriately set. The high color may be a shade of gray, if the item is disabled, or black if it's enabled. If some other distinction is used to distinguish disabled from enabled items, `DrawContent()` should check the item's current state by calling `IsEnabled()`.

NOTE

> If a derived class implements its own `DrawContent()` function, but still wants to draw a textual string, it should do so by assigning the string as the BMenu-Item's label and calling the inherited version of `DrawContent()`, not by calling

`DrawString()`. This preserves the BMenuItem's ability to display a trigger character in the string.

See also: `Highlight()`, `Frame()`, `ContentLocation()`, `GetContentSize()`

Frame()

BRect **Frame**(void) const

Returns the rectangle that frames the entire menu item, in the coordinate system of the BMenu to which the item belongs. If the item hasn't been added to a menu, the return value is indeterminate.

See also: `BMenu::AddItem()`

GetContentSize()

protected:
virtual void **GetContentSize**(float **width*, float **height*)

Writes the size of the item's content area into the variables referred to by *width* and *height*. The content area of an item is the area where its label (or whatever substitutes for the label) is drawn.

A BMenu calls `GetContentSize()` for each of its items as it arranges them in a column or a row; the function is not called for items in a matrix. The information it provides helps determine where each item is located and the overall size of the menu.

`GetContentSize()` must report a size that's large enough to display the content of the item (and separate one item from another). By default, it reports an area just large enough to display the item's label. This area is calculated from the label and the BMenu's current font.

If you design a class derived from BMenuItem and implement your own `Draw()` or `DrawContent()` function, you should also implement a `GetContentSize()` function to report how much room will be needed to draw the item's contents.

See also: `DrawContent()`, `ContentLocation()`

Highlight()

protected:
virtual void **Highlight**(bool *flag*)

Highlights the menu item when *flag* is `true`, and removes the highlighting when *flag* is `false`. Highlighting simply inverts all the colors in the item's frame rectangle (except for the check mark).

This function is called by the `Draw()` function whenever the item is selected and needs to be drawn in its highlighted state. There's no reason to call it yourself, unless you define your own version of `Draw()`. However, it can be reimplemented in a derived class, if items belonging to that class need to be highlighted in some way other than simple inversion.

See also: `Draw()`

Invoke()

private:
    virtual status_t **Invoke**(BMessage **message* = NULL)

Augments the BInvoker version of `Invoke()` to ensure that only enabled menu items that are attached to a menu hierarchy can be invoked. This function appropriately marks items when the user invokes them. Before sending a message, it adds "when", "source", and "index" field to it, as explained under the BMenuItem constructor.

See also: `BInvoker::Invoke()`

IsEnabled()   *see SetEnabled()*

isMarked()   *see SetMarked()*

IsSelected()

protected:
    bool **IsSelected**(void) const

Returns `true` if the menu item is currently selected, and `false` if not. Selected items are highlighted.

Label()   *see SetLabel()*

Menu()

    BMenu ****Menu**(void) const

Returns the menu where the item is located, or `NULL` if the item hasn't yet been added to a menu.

See also: `BMenu::AddItem()`

SetEnabled(), IsEnabled()

virtual void **SetEnabled**(bool *enabled*)

bool **IsEnabled**(void) const

`SetEnabled()` enables the BMenuItem if the *enabled* flag is `true`, disables it if *enabled* is `false`, and updates the item if it's visible on-screen. If the item controls a submenu, this function calls the submenu's `SetEnabled()` virtual function, passing it the same flag. This ensures that the submenu is enabled or disabled as well.

`IsEnabled()` returns `true` if the BMenuItem is enabled, its menu is enabled, and all menus above it in the hierarchy are enabled. It returns `false` if the item is disabled or any objects above it in the menu hierarchy are disabled.

Items and menus are enabled by default.

When using these functions, keep in mind that:

- Disabling a BMenuItem that controls a submenu serves to disable the entire menu hierarchy under the item.

- Passing an argument of `true` to `SetEnabled()` is not sufficient to enable the item if it's located in a disabled branch of the menu hierarchy. It can only undo a previous `SetEnabled()` call (with an argument of `false`) on the same item.

See also: `BMenu::SetEnabled()`

SetLabel(), Label()

virtual void **SetLabel**(const char **string*)

const char ****Label**(void) const

`SetLabel()` frees the item's current label and copies *string* to replace it. If the menu is visible on-screen, it will be redisplayed with the item's new label. If necessary, the menu will become wider (or narrower) so that it fits the new label.

The Interface Kit calls this virtual function to:

- Set the initial label of an item that controls a submenu to the name of the submenu, and

- Subsequently set the item's label to match the marked item in the submenu, if the submenu was set up to have this feature.

`Label()` returns a pointer to the current label.

See also: `BMenu::SetLabelFromMarked()`, the BMenuItem constructor

SetMarked(), IsMarked()

virtual void **SetMarked**(bool *flag*)

bool **IsMarked**(void) const

`SetMarked()` adds a check mark to the left of the item label if *flag* is `true`, or removes an existing mark if *flag* is `false`. If the menu is visible on-screen. it's redisplayed with or without the mark.

`IsMarked()` returns whether the item is currently marked.

See also: `BMenu::SetLabelFromMarked()`, `BMenu::FindMarked()`

SetShortcut(), Shortcut()

virtual void **SetShortcut**(char *shortcut*, uint32 *modifiers*)

char **Shortcut**(uint32 **modifiers* = NULL) const

`SetShortcut()` sets the *shortcut* character that's displayed at the right edge of the menu item and the set of *modifiers* that are associated with the character. These two arguments work just like the arguments passed to the BMenuItem constructor. See the constructor for a more complete description.

`Shortcut()` returns the character that's used as the keyboard shortcut for invoking the item, and writes a mask of all the modifier keys the shortcut requires to the variable referred to by *modifiers*. Since the Command key is required to operate the keyboard shortcut for any menu item, `B_COMMAND_KEY` will always be part of the *modifiers* mask. The mask can also be tested against the `B_CONTROL_KEY`, `B_OPTION_KEY`, and `B_SHIFT_KEY` constants.

The shortcut is initially set by the BMenuItem constructor.

See also: the BMenuItem constructor

SetTrigger(), Trigger()

virtual void **SetTrigger**(char *trigger*)

char **Trigger**(void) const

`SetTrigger()` sets the *trigger* character that the user can type to invoke the item while the item's menu is open on-screen. If a *trigger* is not set, the Interface Kit will select one for the item, so it's not necessary to call `SetTrigger()`.

The character passed to this function has to match a character displayed in the item— either the keyboard shortcut or a character in the label. The case of the character doesn't matter; lowercase arguments will match uppercase characters in the item and uppercase arguments will match lowercase characters. When the item can be invoked by its trigger, the trigger character is underlined.

If more than one character in the item matches the character passed, `SetTrigger()` tries first to mark the keyboard shortcut. Failing that, it tries to mark an uppercase letter at the beginning of a word. Failing that, it marks the first instance of the character in the label.

If the *trigger* doesn't match any characters in the item, the item won't have a trigger, not even one selected by the system.

`Trigger()` returns the character set by `SetTrigger()`, or `NULL` if `SetTrigger()` didn't succeed or if `SetTrigger()` was never called and the trigger is selected automatically.

See also: `BMenu::SetTriggersEnabled()`

Shortcut()   *see SetShortcut()*

Submenu()

> BMenu ***Submenu**(void) const

Returns the BMenu object that the item controls, or `NULL` if the item doesn't control a submenu.

See also: the BMenuItem constructor, the BMenu class

Trigger()   *see SetTrigger()*

TruncateLabel()

protected:
> virtual void **TruncateLabel**(float *maxWidth*, char **newLabel*)

Removes characters from the middle of the item label and replaces them with an ellipsis. This is done so that the label will fit within *maxWidth* coordinate units. The shortened string is copied into the *newLabel* buffer.

This function is called by the BMenuItem when it draws the item's label, but only if it's necessary to fit a long item into a smaller space. It can be reimplemented by derived classes to do a better job of shortening the string based on the actual content of the label.

Your version of `TruncateLabel()` should be careful to not cut the trigger character from the string.

See also: `BFont::GetTrunctatedStrings()`

BOutlineListView

Derived from: public BListView

Declared in: be/interface/OutlineListView.h

Library: libbe.so

Overview

A BOutlineListView displays a list of items that can be structured like an outline, with items grouped under other items. The levels of the outline are indicated by successive levels of indentation.

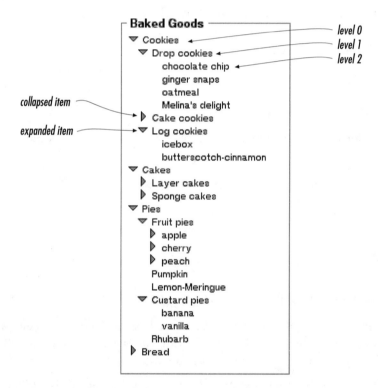

Outline Structure

If an item has other items under it—that is, if the immediately following item in the list is at a deeper level of the outline—it is a *superitem*; the items grouped under it are its *subitems*. Superitems are marked by a triangular icon or *latch*, in the usual interface for hypertext lists.

The user can collapse or expand sections of the outline by manipulating the latch. When a section is collapsed, only the superitem for that section is visible (and the latch points to the superitem). All items that follow the superitem are hidden, up to the next item that's not at a deeper outline level. When a section is expanded, subitems are visible (and the latch points downward).

Inherited Functions

The BOutlineListView class inherits most of its functionality from the BListView class. However, inherited functions are concerned only with the expanded sections of the list, not with sections that are hidden because they're collapsed. If an inherited function returns an index or takes an index as an argument, the index counts just the items that are shown on-screen (or could be shown on-screen if they were scrolled into the visible region of the view). `DoForEach()` skips items that can't be displayed. `CountItems()` counts items only in the expanded sections of the list.

However, the functions that the BOutlineListView class itself defines are concerned with all sections of the list, expanded or collapsed. For its functions, an index counts all items in the list, whether visible or not.

The class defines some functions that match those it inherits, but its versions prefix `FullList...` to the function name and don't ignore any items. For example, `FullListCountItems()` counts every item in the list and `FullListDoForEach()` doesn't skip items in collapsed sections.

In some cases, BOutlineListView simply overrides an inherited function without adding the `FullList...` prefix. You should always use the BOutlineListView versions of these functions, not the BListView versions. For example, BOutlineListView's version of `MakeEmpty()` truly empties the list; BListView's version would remove items from the screen, but not from the real list.

Constructor and Destructor

BOutlineListView()

> BOutlineListView(BRect *frame*, const char **name*,
>   list_view_type *type* = B_SINGLE_SELECTION_LIST,
>   uint32 *resizingMode* = B_FOLLOW_LEFT | B_FOLLOW_TOP,
>   uint32 *flags* =   B_WILL_DRAW | B_FRAME_EVENTS |
>   B_NAVIGABLE)
> BOutlineListView(BMessage **archive*)

Initializes the BOutlineListView. This constructor matches the BListView constructor in every detail, including default arguments. All argument values are passed to the

BListView constructor without change. The BOutlineListView class doesn't do any initialization of its own.

See also: the BListView constructor

~BOutlineListView()

> virtual **~BOutlineListView**(void)

Does nothing; this class relies on the BListView destructor.

Static Functions

Instantiate()

> static BOutlineListView ***Instantiate**(BMessage **archive*)

Returns a new BOutlineListView object, allocated by **new** and created with the version of the constructor that takes a BMessage *archive*. However, this function returns **NULL** if the specified *archive* doesn't contain data for a BOutlineListView object.

See also: `BArchivable::Instantiate()`, `instantiate_object()`, `Archive()`

Member Functions

AddItem(), AddUnder()

> virtual bool **AddItem**(BListItem **item*)
> virtual bool **AddItem**(BListItem **item*, int32 *index*)
>
> virtual bool **AddUnder**(BListItem **item*, BListItem **superitem*)

These functions add an *item* to the list. `AddItem()` adds the item at *index*—where the index counts all items assigned to the BOutlineListView—or, if an *index* isn't specified, at the end of the list. The two versions of this function override their BListView counterparts to ensure that the item is correctly entered into the outline. If the item is added to a portion of the list that is collapsed, it won't be visible.

`AddUnder()` adds an *item* immediately after another item in the list and at one outline level deeper. The level of the *item* is modified accordingly. Thus, the item already in the list becomes the superitem for the newly added *item*. If its new superitem is collapsed or is in a collapsed part of the list, the item will not be visible.

Unlike `AddUnder()`, `AddItem()` respects the outline level of the item. By setting the item's level before calling `AddItem()`, you can add it as a subitem to an item at a higher outline level or insert it as a superitem to items at a lower level.

See also: the BListItem class

AddList()

> virtual bool **AddList**(BList *newItems)
>
> virtual bool **AddList**(BList *newItems, int32 index)

Adds a group of items to the list just as `AddItem()` adds a single item. The index counts all items assigned to the BOutlineListView. The *newItems* BList must contain pointers to BListItem objects.

See also: `BListView::AddList()`

AddUnder()   *see AddItem()*

Archive()

> virtual status_t **Archive**(BMessage *archive, bool *deep* = true) const

Archives the BOutlineListView object much as the `Archive()` function in the BListView class does, but makes sure that all items are archived, including items in collapsed sections of the list, when the *deep* flag is true.

See also: `BListView::Archive()`, `Instantiate()` static function

Collapse(), Expand()

> void **Collapse**(BListItem *item)
>
> void **Expand**(BListItem *item)

These functions collapse and expand the section of the list controlled by the *item* superitem. If *item* isn't a superitem, it is nevertheless flagged as expanded or collapsed so that it will behave appropriately in case it does become a superitem.

See also: `BListItem::SetExpanded()`

FullListCountItems(), FullListCurrentSelection(), FullListFirstItem(), FullListLastItem(), FullListIndexOf(), FullListItemAt(), FullListHasItem(), FullListIsEmpty(), FullListDoForEach()

> int32 **FullListCountItems**(void) const
>
> int32 **FullListCurrentSelection**(int32 *index* = 0) const
>
> BListItem ***FullListFirstItem**(void) const
>
> BListItem ***FullListLastItem**(void) const

int32 **FullListIndexOf**(BPoint *point*) const
int32 **FullListIndexOf**(BListItem **item*) const

BListItem ****FullListItemAt**(int32 *index*) const

bool **FullListHasItem**(BListItem **item*) const

bool **FullListIsEmpty**(void) const

void **FullListDoForEach**(bool (**func*)(BListItem *))
void **FullListDoForEach**(bool (**func*)(BListItem *, void *), void *)

These functions parallel a similar set of functions defined in the BListView class. The BListView functions have identical names, but without the `FullList...` prefix. When applied to a BOutlineListView object, the inherited functions consider only items in sections of the outline that can be displayed on-screen—that is, they skip over items in collapsed portions of the list.

These BOutlineListView functions, on the other hand, consider all items in the list. For example, `IndexOf()` and `FullListIndexOf()` both return an index to a given *item*. However, for `IndexOf()` the index is to the position of the item in the list that can be currently displayed, but for `FullListIndexOf()` it's to the item's position in the full list, including collapsed sections.

IsExpanded()

bool **IsExpanded**(int32 *index*)

Returns `true` if the item at *index* is marked as controlling an expanded section of the list, and `false` if it's marked as controlling a collapsed section or if there's no item at that index. If a superitem is expanded, the BOutlineListView can display its subitems; if not, the subitems are hidden.

The *index* passed to this function is to the full list of items assigned to the BOutlineListView.

See also: `BListItem::IsExpanded()`

KeyDown()

virtual void **KeyDown**(const char **bytes*, int32 *numBytes*)

Augments the inherited version of `KeyDown()` to allow users to navigate the outline hierarchy using the arrow keys and to expand or collapse sections of the outline using Control–arrow key combinations.

See also: `BListView::KeyDown()`

MakeEmpty()

virtual void **MakeEmpty**(void)

Overrides the BListView version of `MakeEmpty()` to remove all items from the list. The BListView version of this function won't work as advertised on a BOutlineListView.

See also: `BListView::MakeEmpty()`

MouseDown()

virtual void **MouseDown**(BPoint *point*)

Augments the inherited version of `MouseDown()` to permit users to expand and collapse sections of the outline by clicking on an item's latch.

See also: `BView::MouseDown()`

RemoveItem(), RemoveItems()

virtual bool **RemoveItem**(BListItem **item*)
virtual BListItem ****RemoveItem**(int32 *index*)

virtual bool **RemoveItems**(int32 *index*, int32 *count*)

These functions work like their BListView counterparts, except that:

- They can remove items from any part of the list, including collapsed sections. The *index* counts all items assigned to the BOutlineListView; the specified *item* can be hidden.

- If the item being removed is a superitem, they also remove all of its subitems.

NOTE

The BListView versions of these functions will not produce reliable results when applied to a BOutlineListView, even if the item being removed is in an expanded section of the list and is not a superitem.

See also: `BListView::RemoveItem()`

Superitem()

BListItem ****Superitem**(const BListItem **item*)

Returns the superitem for the *item* passed as an argument—that is, the item under which the argument *item* is grouped—or NULL if the *item* is at the outermost level of the outline (level 0) or isn't in the list.

BPicture

Derived from: public BArchivable

Declared in: be/interface/Picture.h

Library: libbe.so

Overview

A BPicture object holds a set of drawing instructions in the Application Server, where they can be reused over and over again simply by passing the object to BView's `DrawPicture()` function. Because it contains instructions for producing an image, not the rendered result of those instructions, a picture (unlike a bitmap) is independent of the resolution of the display device.

Recording a Picture

Drawing instructions are captured by bracketing them with calls to a BView's `BeginPicture()` and `EndPicture()` functions. An empty BPicture object is passed to `BeginPicture()`; `EndPicture()` returns the same object, fully initialized. For example:

```
BPicture *myPict;
someView->BeginPicture(new BPicture);
/* drawing code goes here */
myPict = someView->EndPicture();
```

The BPicture object records all of the drawing instructions given to the BView following the `BeginPicture()` call and preceding the `EndPicture()` call. Only drawing that the BView does is recorded; drawing done by children and other views attached to the window is ignored, as is everything except drawing code.

Drawing instructions that are captured between `BeginPicture()` and `EndPicture()` do not also produce a rendered image; ignored instructions may be rendered if they draw into the visible region of an on-screen window.

If the BPicture object passed to `BeginPicture()` isn't empty, the new drawing is appended to the code that's already in place.

The Picture Definition

The picture captures everything that affects the image that's drawn. It takes a snapshot of the BView's graphics parameters—the pen size, high and low colors, font size, and so on—at the time `BeginPicture()` is called. It then captures all subsequent modifications to those parameters, such as calls to `MovePenTo()`,

SetLowColor(), and SetFontSize(). However, changes to the coordinate system (ScrollBy() and ScrollTo()) are ignored.

The picture records all primitive drawing instructions—such as, DrawBitmap(), StrokeEllipse(), FillRect(), and DrawString(). It can even include a call to DrawPicture(); one picture can incorporate another.

The BPicture traces exactly what the BView would draw if the drawing code were not bracketed by BeginPicture() and EndPicture() calls, and reproduces it precisely. For example, whatever pen size happens to be in effect when a line is stroked will be the pen size that the picture records, whether it was explicitly set while the BPicture was being recorded or assumed from the BView's graphics environment.

The picture makes its own copy of any data that's passed during the recording session. For example, it copies the bitmap passed to DrawBitmap() and the picture passed to DrawPicture(). If that bitmap or picture later changes, it won't affect what was recorded.

See also: BView::BeginPicture(), BView::DrawPicture(), the BPictureButton class

Constructor and Destructor

BPicture()

> **BPicture**(void)
> **BPicture**(const BPicture &*picture*)
> **BPicture**(void **data*, int32 *size*)
> **BPicture**(BMessage **archive*)

Initializes the BPicture object by ensuring that it's empty, by copying data from another *picture*, or by copying *size* bytes of picture *data*. The data should be taken, directly or indirectly, from another BPicture object.

~BPicture()

> virtual **~BPicture**(void)

Destroys the Application Server's record of the BPicture object and deletes all its picture data.

Static Functions

Instantiate()

   static BPicture *Instantiate(BMessage *archive)

Returns a new BPicture object, allocated by new and created with the version of the constructor that takes a BMessage archive. However, if the archive message doesn't contain BPicture data, this function returns NULL.

See also: BArchivable::Instantiate(), instantiate_object(), Archive()

Member Functions

Archive()

   virtual status_t Archive(BMessage *archive, bool deep = true) const

Calls the inherited version of Archive(), then adds the picture data to the BMessage archive.

See also: BArchivable::Archive(), Instantiate() static function

Data()

   const void *Data(void) const

Returns a pointer to the data contained in the BPicture. The data can be copied from the object, stored on disk (perhaps as a resource), and later used to initialize another BPicture object.

See also: the BPicture constructor

DataSize()

   int32 DataSize(void) const

Returns how many bytes of data the BPicture object contains.

See also: Data()

BPictureButton

Derived from: public BControl

Declared in: be/interface/PictureButton.h

Library: libbe.so

Overview

A BPictureButton object draws a button with a graphic image on its face, rather than a textual label. The image is set by a BPicture object.

Like other BControl objects, BPictureButtons can have two values, B_CONTROL_OFF and B_CONTROL_ON. A separate BPicture object is associated with each value. How the BPictureButton displays these pictures depends on its behavior—whether it's set to remain in one state or to toggle between two states:

- A one-state BPictureButton usually has a value of 0 (B_CONTROL_OFF), and it displays the BPicture associated with that value. However, while it's being operated (while the cursor is over the button on-screen and the user keeps the mouse button down), its value is set to 1 (B_CONTROL_ON) and it displays the alternate picture. That picture should be a highlighted version of the picture that's normally shown.

  This behavior is exactly like an ordinary, labeled BButton object. Just as a BButton displays the same label, a one-state BPictureButton shows the same picture. Both kinds of objects are appropriate devices for initiating an action of some kind.

- A two-state BPictureButton toggles between the B_CONTROL_OFF and B_CONTROL_ON values. Each time the user operates the button, it's value changes. The picture that's displayed changes with the value. The two BPictures are alternatives to each other. The B_CONTROL_ON picture might be a highlighted version of the B_CONTROL_OFF picture, but it doesn't need to be. The value of the object changes only after it has been toggled to the other state, not while it's being operated.

  This behavior is exactly like a BCheckBox or an individual BRadioButton. Like those objects, a two-state BPictureButton is an appropriate device for setting a state.

Every BPictureButton must be assigned at least two BPictures. If it's a one-state button, one picture will be the one that's normally shown and another will be shown while the button is being operated. If it's a two-state button, one picture is shown when the button is turned on and one when it's off.

If a one-state button can be disabled, it also needs to be assigned an image that can be shown while it's disabled. If a two-state button can be disabled, it needs two additional images—one in case it's disabled while in the B_CONTROL_OFF state and another if it's disabled in the B_CONTROL_ON state.

Often the BPictures that are assigned to a BPictureButton simply wrap around a bitmap image. For example:

```
BPicture *myPict;
someView->BeginPicture(new BPicture);
someView->DrawBitmap(&buttonBitmap);
myPict = someView->EndPicture();
```

See also: the BPicture class

Constructor and Destructor

BPictureButton()

> BPictureButton(BRect *frame*, const char* *name*,
>   BPicture *off*,
>   BPicture *on*,
>   BMessage *message*,
>   uint32 *behavior* = B_ONE_STATE_BUTTON,
>   uint32 *resizingMode* = B_FOLLOW_LEFT | B_FOLLOW_TOP,
>   uint32 *flags* = B_WILL_DRAW | B_NAVIGABLE)
> BPictureButton(BMessage *archive*)

Initializes the BPictureButton by assigning it two images—an *off* picture that will be displayed when the object's value is B_CONTROL_OFF and an *on* picture that's displayed when the value is B_CONTROL_ON—and by setting its *behavior* to either B_ONE_STATE_BUTTON or B_TWO_STATE_BUTTON. A one-state button displays the *off* image normally and the *on* image to highlight the button as it's being operated by the user. A two-state button toggles between the *off* image and the *on* image (between the B_CONTROL_OFF and B_CONTROL_ON values). The initial value is set to B_CONTROL_OFF.

If the BPictureButton can be disabled, it will need additional BPicture images that indicate its disabled state. They can be set by calling SetDisabledOff() and SetDisabledOn().

All the BPictures assigned to the BPictureButton object become its property. It takes responsibility for deleting them when they're no longer needed.

The *message* parameter is the same as the one declared for the BControl constructor. It establishes a model for the messages the BPictureButton sends to a target object each time it's invoked.

The *frame*, *name*, *resizingMode*, and *flags* parameters are the same as those declared for the BView constructor. They're passed up the inheritance hierarchy to the BView class unchanged. See the BView constructor for details.

See also: the BControl and BView constructors, `SetEnabledOff()`, `BControl::Invoke()`, `BInvoker::SetMessage()`, `BInvoker::SetTarget()`

~BPictureButton()

> virtual ~**BPictureButton**(void)

Deletes the model message and the BPicture objects that have been assigned to the BPictureButton.

Static Functions

Instantiate()

> static BPictureButton ***Instantiate**(BMessage *archive*)

Returns a new BPictureButton object, allocated by **new** and created with the version of the constructor that takes a BMessage *archive*. However, if the *archive* message doesn't contain data for a BPictureButton object, the return value will be NULL.

See also: `BArchivable::Instantiate()`, `instantiate_object()`, `Archive()`

Member Functions

Archive()

> virtual status_t **Archive**(BMessage *archive*, bool *deep* = true) const

Calls the inherited version of `Archive()`, then adds the behavior flag (B_ONE_STATE_BUTTON or B_TWO_STATE_BUTTON) to the BMessage *archive*. If the *deep* flag is true, all the BPictures the object displays are also archived.

See also: `BArchivable::Archive()`, `Instantiate()` static function

Behavior()   *see SetBehavior()*

Draw()

> virtual void **Draw**(BRect *updateRect*)

Draws the BPictureButton. This function is called as the result of an update message to draw the button in its current appearance; it's also called from the `MouseDown()` function to draw the button in its highlighted state.

See also: `BView::Draw()`

KeyDown()

> virtual void **KeyDown**(const char *bytes*, int32 *numBytes*)

Augments the inherited version of `KeyDown()` so that users can correctly operate both one-state and two-state buttons by pressing the Enter key or the space bar (`B_ENTER` or `B_SPACE`).

See also: `BView::KeyDown()`, `BControl::Invoke()`

MouseDown()

> virtual void **MouseDown**(BPoint *point*)

Responds to a mouse-down event in the button by tracking the cursor while the user holds the mouse button down. If the BPictureButton is a one-state object, this function resets its value as the cursor moves in and out of the button on-screen. The `SetValue()` virtual function is called to make the change each time. If it's a two-state object, the value is not reset. (However, the picture corresponding to the `B_CONTROL_ON` value is shown while the cursor is in the button on-screen and the mouse button remains down.)

If the cursor is inside the BPictureButton's bounds rectangle when the user releases the mouse button, this function posts a copy of the model message so that it will be dispatched to the target handler. If it's a one-state object, it's value is reset to `B_CONTROL_OFF`. If it's a two-state object, its value is toggled on or off and the corresponding picture is displayed.

See also: `BView::MouseDown()`, `BControl::Invoke()`, `SetBehavior()`

SetBehavior(), Behavior()

> virtual void **SetBehavior**(uint32 *behavior*)

> uint32 **Behavior**(void) const

These functions set and return whether the BPictureButton is a `B_ONE_STATE_BUTTON` or a `B_TWO_STATE_BUTTON`. If it's a one-state button, its value is normally set to `B_CONTROL_OFF` and it displays a fixed image (the *off* picture passed to the constructor or the one passed to `SetEnabledOff()`). Its value is reset as its being operated and it displays the alternate image (the *on* picture passed to the constructor or the one passed to `SetEnabledOn()`).

If it's a two-state button, its value toggles between `B_CONTROL_OFF` and `B_CONTROL_ON` each time the user operates it. The image the button displays similarly toggles between two pictures (the *off* and *on* images passed to the constructor or the ones passed to `SetEnabledOff()` and `SetEnabledOn()`).

See also: the BPictureButton constructor

SetEnabledOff(), SetEnabledOn(), SetDisabledOff(), SetDisabledOn(), EnabledOff(), EnabledOn(), DisabledOff(), DisabledOn

> virtual void **SetEnabledOff**(BPicture *picture)
>
> virtual void **SetEnabledOn**(BPicture *picture)
>
> virtual void **SetDisabledOff**(BPicture *picture)
>
> virtual void **SetDisabledOn**(BPicture *picture)
>
> BPicture ***EnabledOff**(void) const
>
> BPicture ***EnabledOn**(void) const
>
> BPicture ***DisabledOff**(void) const
>
> BPicture ***DisabledOn**(void) const

These functions set and return the images the BPictureButton displays. Each BPictureButton object needs to be assigned at least two BPicture objects—one corresponding to the `B_CONTROL_OFF` value and another corresponding to the `B_CONTROL_ON` value. These are the images that are displayed when the BPictureButton is enabled, as it is by default. They're initially set when the object is constructed and can be replaced by calling the `SetEnabledOff()` and `SetEnabledOn()` functions.

If a BPictureButton can be disabled, it needs to display an image that indicates its disabled condition. A two-state button might be disabled when its value is either `B_CONTROL_OFF` or `B_CONTROL_ON`, so it needs two BPictures to indicate disabling, one corresponding to each value. They can be set by calling `SetDisabledOff()` and `SetDisabledOn()`.

The value of a one-state button is always `B_CONTROL_OFF` (except when it's being operated), so it needs only a single BPicture to indicate disabling; you can set it by calling `SetDisabledOff()`.

All four of the Set...() functions free the image previously set, if any, and replace it with *picture*. The *picture* belongs to the BPictureButton; it should not be freed or assigned to any other object.

The last four functions listed above return the BPictureButton's four images, or NULL if it hasn't been assigned a BPicture object in the requested category.

BPoint

Derived from: *none*

Declared in: be/interface/Point.h

Library: libbe.so

Overview

BPoint objects represent points on a two-dimensional coordinate grid. Each object holds an *x* coordinate value and a *y* coordinate value declared as public data members. These values locate a specific point, (*x*, *y*), relative to a given coordinate system.

Because the BPoint class defines a basic data type for graphic operations, its data members are publicly accessible and it declares no virtual functions. It's a simple class that doesn't inherit from BArchivable or any other class and doesn't have any virtual functions, not even a destructor. In the Interface Kit, BPoint objects are typically passed and returned by value, not through pointers.

For an overview of coordinate geometry for the BeOS, see "The Coordinate Space" on page 368.

Data Members

float x
    The coordinate value measured horizontally along the *x*-axis.

float y
    The coordinate value measured vertically along the *y*-axis.

Constructor

BPoint()

    inline **BPoint**(float *x*, float *y*)
    inline **BPoint**(const BPoint& *point*)
    inline **BPoint**(void)

Initializes a new BPoint object to (*x, y*), or to the same values as *point*. For example:

```
BPoint somePoint(155.7, 336.0);
BPoint anotherPoint(somePoint);
```

Here, both *somePoint* and *anotherPoint* are initialized to (155.7, 336.0).

If no coordinate values are assigned to the BPoint when it's declared:

```
BPoint emptyPoint;
```

its initial values are indeterminate.

BPoint objects can also be initialized or modified using the `Set()` function:

```
emptyPoint.Set(155.7, 336.0);
anotherPoint.Set(221.5, 67.8);
```

or the assignment operator:

```
somePoint = anotherPoint;
```

See also: `Set()`, the assignment operator

Member Functions

ConstrainTo()

> void **ConstrainTo**(BRect *rect*)

Constrains the point so that it lies inside the *rect* rectangle. If the point is already contained in the rectangle, it remains unchanged. However, if it falls outside the rectangle, it's moved to the nearest edge. For example, this code:

```
BPoint point(54.9, 76.3);
BRect rect(10.0, 20.0, 40.0, 80.0);
point.Constrain(rect);
```

modifies the point to (40.0, 76.3).

See also: `BRect::Contains()`

PrintToStream()

> void **PrintToStream**(void) const

Prints the contents of the BPoint object to the standard output stream (`stdout`) in the form:

```
"BPoint(x, y)"
```

where *x* and *y* stand for the current values of the BPoint's data members.

Set()

inline void **Set**(float *x*, float *y*)

Assigns the coordinate values *x* and *y* to the BPoint object. For example, this code

```
BPoint point;
point.Set(27.0, 53.4);
```

is equivalent to:

```
BPoint point;
point.x = 27.0;
point.y = 53.4;
```

See also: the BPoint constructor

Operators

= (assignment)

inline BPoint& **operator** =(const BPoint&)

Assigns the *x* and *y* values of one BPoint object to another BPoint:

```
BPoint a, b;
a.Set(21.5, 17.0);
b = a;
```

Point *b*, like point *a*, is set to (21.5, 17.0).

== (equality)

bool **operator** ==(const BPoint&) const

Compares the data members of two BPoint objects and returns `true` if each one exactly matches its counterpart in the other object, and `false` if not. In the following example, the equality operator would return `false`:

```
BPoint a(21.5, 17.0);
BPoint b(17.5, 21.0);
if ( a == b )
    . . .
```

!= (inequality)

bool **operator** !=(const BPoint&) const

Compares two BPoint objects and returns `true` unless their data members match exactly (the two points are the same), in which case it returns `false`. This operator is the inverse of the == (equality) operator.

+ (addition)

BPoint **operator** +(const BPoint&) const

Combines two BPoint objects by adding the x coordinate of the second to the x coordinate of the first and the y coordinate of the second to the y coordinate of the first, and returns a BPoint object that holds the result. For example:

```
BPoint a(77.0, 11.0);
BPoint b(55.0, 33.0);
BPoint c = a + b;
```

Point c is initialized to (132.0, 44.0).

+= (addition and assignment)

BPoint& **operator** +=(const BPoint&)

Modifies a BPoint object by adding another point to it. As in the case of the + (addition) operator, the members of the second point are added to their counterparts in the first point:

```
BPoint a(77.0, 11.0);
BPoint b(55.0, 33.0);
a += b;
```

Point a is modified to (132.0, 44.0).

− (subtraction)

BPoint **operator** −(const BPoint&) const

Subtracts one BPoint object from another by subtracting the x coordinate of the second from the x coordinate of the first and the y coordinate of the second from the y coordinate of the first, and returns a BPoint object that holds the result. For example:

```
BPoint a(99.0, 66.0);
BPoint b(44.0, 88.0);
BPoint c = a - b;
```

Point c is initialized to (55.0, −22.0).

−= (subtraction and assignment)

BPoint& **operator** −=(const BPoint&)

Modifies a BPoint object by subtracting another point from it. As in the case of the − (subtraction) operator, the members of the second point are subtracted from their counterparts in the first point. For example:

```
BPoint a(99.0, 66.0);
BPoint b(44.0, 88.0);
a -= b;
```

Point *a* is modified to (55.0, –22.0).

BPolygon

Derived from:	*none*
Declared in:	be/interface/Polygon.h
Library:	libbe.so

Overview

A BPolygon object represents a *polygon*—a closed, many-sided figure that describes an area within a two-dimensional coordinate system. It differs from a BRect object in that it can have any number of sides and the sides don't have to be aligned with the coordinate axes.

A BPolygon is defined as a series of connected points. Each point is a potential vertex in the polygon. An outline of the polygon could be constructed by tracing a straight line from the first point to the second, from the second point to the third, and so on through the whole series, then by connecting the first and last points if they're not identical.

The BView functions that draw a polygon—StrokePolygon() and FillPolygon()—take BPolygon objects as arguments. StrokePolygon() offers the option of leaving the polygon open—of not stroking the line that connects the first and last points in the list. The polygon therefore won't look like a polygon, but like an chain of lines fastened at their endpoints.

Constructor and Destructor

BPolygon()

BPolygon(const BPoint *pointList*, int32 *numPoints*)
BPolygon(const BPolygon *polygon*)
BPolygon(void)

Initializes the BPolygon by copying *numPoints* from *pointList*, or by copying the list of points from another *polygon*. If one polygon is constructed from another, the original and the copy won't share any data; independent memory is allocated for the copy to hold a duplicate list of points.

If a BPolygon is constructed without a point list, points must be set with the `AddPoints()` function.

See also: `AddPoints()`

~BPolygon()

> virtual **~BPolygon**(void)

Frees all the memory allocated to hold the list of points.

Member Functions

AddPoints()

> void **AddPoints**(const BPoint *pointList*, int32 *numPoints*)

Appends *numPoints* from *pointList* to the list of points that already define the polygon.

See also: the BPolygon constructor

CountPoints()

> int32 **CountPoints**(void) const

Returns the number of points that define the polygon.

Frame()

> BRect **Frame**(void) const

Returns the polygon's frame rectangle—the smallest rectangle that encloses the entire polygon.

MapTo()

> void **MapTo**(BRect *source*, BRect *destination*)

Modifies the polygon so that it fits the *destination* rectangle exactly as it originally fit the *source* rectangle. Each vertex of the polygon is modified so that it has the same proportional position relative to the sides of the destination rectangle as it originally had to the sides of the source rectangle.

The polygon doesn't have to be contained in either rectangle. However, to modify a polygon so that it's exactly inscribed in the destination rectangle, you should pass its frame rectangle as the source:

```
BRect frame = myPolygon->Frame();
myPolygon->MapTo(frame, anotherRect);
```

PrintToStream()

    void **PrintToStream**(void) const

Prints the BPolygon's point list to the standard output stream (`stdout`). The BPoint version of this function is called to report each point as a string in the form

    "BPoint(*x*, *y*)"

where x and y stand for the coordinate values of the point in question.

See also: `BPoint::PrintToStream()`

Operators

= (assignment)

    BPolygon& **operator =**(const BPolygon&)

Copies the point list of one BPolygon object and assigns it to another BPolygon. After the assignment, the two objects describe the same polygon, but are independent of each other. Destroying one of the objects won't affect the other.

BPopUpMenu

Derived from: public BMenu

Declared in: be/interface/PopUpMenu.h

Library: libbe.so

Overview

A BPopUpMenu is a specialized menu that's typically used in isolation, rather than as part of an extensive menu hierarchy. By default, it operates in radio mode—the last item selected by the user, and only that item, is marked in the menu.

A menu of this kind can be used to choose one from among a limited set of mutually exclusive states—to pick a paper size or paragraph style, for example, or to select a category of information. It should not be used to group different kinds of choices (as other menus may), nor should it include items that initiate actions rather than set states, except in certain well-defined cases.

A pop-up menu can be used in any of three ways:

• It can be controlled by a BMenuBar object, often one that contains just a single item. The BMenuBar, in effect, functions as a button that pops up a list. The label of the marked item in the list can be displayed as the label of the controlling item in the BMenuBar. In this way, the BMenuBar is able to show the current state of the hidden menu. When this is the case, the menu pops up so its marked item is directly over the controlling item.

- A BPopUpMenu can also be controlled by a view other than a BMenuBar. It might be associated with a particular image the view displays, for example, and appear over the image when the user moves the cursor there and presses the mouse button. Or it might be associated with the view as a whole and come up under the cursor wherever the cursor happens to be. When the view is notified of a mouse-down event, it calls BPopUpMenu's Go() function to show the menu on-screen.

- The BPopUpMenu might also be controlled by a particular mouse button, typically the secondary mouse button. When the user presses the button, the menu appears at the location of the cursor. Instead of passing responsibility for the mouse-down event to a BView, the BWindow would intercept it and place the menu on-screen.

Other than Go() (and the constructor), this class implements no functions that you ever need to call from application code. In all other respects, a BPopUpMenu can be treated like any other BMenu.

Constructor and Destructor

BPopUpMenu()

> **BPopUpMenu**(const char *name*, bool *radioMode* = true,
>   bool *labelFromMarked* = true,
>   menu_layout *layout* = B_ITEMS_IN_COLUMN)
> **BPopUpMenu**(BMessage *archive*)

Initializes the BPopUpMenu object. If the object is added to a BMenuBar, its *name* also becomes the initial label of its controlling item (just as for other BMenus).

If the *labelFromMarked* flag is `true` (as it is by default), the label of the controlling item will change to reflect the label of the item that the user last selected. In addition, the menu will operate in radio mode (regardless of the value passed as the *radioMode* flag). When the menu pops up, it will position itself so that the marked item appears directly over the controlling item in the BMenuBar.

If *labelFromMarked* is `false`, the menu pops up so that its first item is over the controlling item.

If the *radioMode* flag is `true` (as it is by default), the last item selected by the user will always be marked. In this mode, one and only one item within the menu can be marked at a time. If *radioMode* is `false`, items aren't automatically marked or unmarked.

However, the *radioMode* flag has no effect unless the *labelFromMarked* flag is false. As long as *labelFromMarked* is true, radio mode will also be true.

The *layout* of the items in a BPopUpMenu can be either B_ITEMS_IN_ROW or the default B_ITEMS_IN_COLUMN. It should never be B_ITEMS_IN_MATRIX. The menu is resized so that it exactly fits the items that are added to it.

The new BPopUpMenu is empty; you add items to it by calling BMenu's AddItem() function.

See also: BMenu::SetRadioMode(), BMenu::SetLabelFromMarked()

~BPopUpMenu()

virtual **~BPopUpMenu**(void)

Does nothing. The BMenu destructor is sufficient to clean up after a BPopUpMenu.

Static Functions

Instantiate()

static BPopUpMenu ***Instantiate**(BMessage *archive*)

Returns a new BPopUpMenu object, allocated by new and created with the version of the constructor that takes a BMessage *archive*. However, if the *archive* message doesn't contain data for a BPopUpMenu, this function returns NULL.

See also: BArchivable::Instantiate(), instantiate_object(), BMenu::Archive()

Member Functions

Go()

BMenuItem ***Go**(BPoint *screenPoint*,
            bool *deliversMessage* = false,
            bool *openAnyway* = false,
            bool *asynchronous* = false)
BMenuItem ***Go**(BPoint *screenPoint*,
            bool *deliversMessage*,
            bool *openAnyway*,
            BRect *clickToOpenRect*,
            bool *asynchronous* = false)

Places the pop-up menu on-screen so that its left top corner is located at *screenPoint* in the screen coordinate system. If the *asynchronous* flag is `true`, `Go()` returns right away; the return value is `NULL`. Otherwise, it doesn't return until the user dismisses the menu from the screen. If the user invoked an item in the menu, it returns a pointer to the item. If no item was invoked, it returns `NULL`.

`Go()` is typically called from within the `MouseDown()` function of a BView. For example:

```
void MyView::MouseDown(BPoint point)
{
    BMenuItem *selected;
    BMessage *copy;
    . . .
    ConvertToScreen(&point);
    selected = myPopUp->Go(point);
    . . .
    if ( selected ) {
        BLooper *looper;
        BHandler *target = selected->Target(&looper);
        looper->PostMessage(selected->Message(), target);
    }
    . . .
}
```

`Go()` operates in two modes:

- If the *deliversMessage* flag is `true`, the BPopUpMenu works just like a menu that's controlled by a BMenuBar. When the user invokes an item in the menu, the item posts a message to its target.

- If the *deliversMessage* flag is `false`, a message is not posted. Invoking an item doesn't automatically accomplish anything. It's up to the application to look at the returned BMenuItem and decide what to do. It can mimic the behavior of other menus and post the message—as shown in the example above—or it can take some other course of action.

`Go()` always puts the pop-up menu on-screen, but ordinarily keeps it there only as long as the user holds a mouse button down. When the user releases the button, the menu is hidden and `Go()` returns. However, the *openAnyway* flag and the *clickToOpenRect* arguments can alter this behavior so that the menu will stay open even when the user releases the mouse button (or even if a mouse button was never down). It will take another user action—such as invoking an item in the menu or clicking elsewhere—to dismiss the menu.

If the *openAnyway* flag is `true`, `Go()` keeps the menu on-screen even if no mouse buttons are held down. This permits a user to open and operate a pop-up menu from the keyboard. If *openAnyway* is `false`, mouse actions determine whether the menu stays on-screen.

If the user has the click-to-open menu preference turned on and releases the mouse button while the cursor lies inside the *clickToOpenRect* rectangle, Go() interprets the action as clicking to open the menu and keeps it on-screen. If the cursor is outside the rectangle when the mouse button goes up, the menu is removed from the screen and Go() returns. The rectangle should be stated in the screen coordinate system.

See also: BMenuItem::SetMessage()

ScreenLocation()

protected:
  virtual BPoint **ScreenLocation**(void)

Determines where the pop-up menu should appear on-screen (when it's being run automatically, not by Go()). As explained in the description of the class constructor, this largely depends on whether the label of the superitem changes to reflect the item that's currently marked in the menu. The point returned is stated in the screen coordinate system.

This function is called only for BPopUpMenus that have been added to a menu hierarchy (a BMenuBar). You should not call it to determine the point to pass to Go(). However, you can override it to change where a customized pop-up menu defined in a derived class appears on-screen when it's controlled by a BMenuBar.

See also: BMenu::SetLabelFromMarked(), BMenu::ScreenLocation(), the BPopUpMenu constructor

BPrintJob

Derived from: *none*

Declared in: be/interface/PrintJob.h

Library: libbe.so

Overview

A BPrintJob object runs a printing session. It negotiates everything after the user's initial request to print—from engaging the Print Server to calling upon BViews to draw and spooling the results to the printer. It also handles a secondary and somewhat separate matter related to printing—configuring the page layout.

Setting Up the Page Layout

Users typically don't decide how a document fits on a page—the size of the paper, the width of the margins, the orientation of the image, and so on—each time they print. These decisions are usually made when setting up the document, perhaps from a Page Layout menu item, rather than Print.

To set up the page parameters for a document, an application should create a BPrintJob object, assign it a name, and call `ConfigPage()`:

```
status_t MyDocumentManager::SetUpPage()
{
    BPrintJob job("document");
    return job.ConfigPage();
}
```

`ConfigPage()` has the Print Server interact with the user to set up the page configuration. Configuration settings are stored in a BMessage object that will be handed to the server when the document is printed. The BMessage is important to the server, but it contains nothing that an application needs to look at. However, you may want to get the object and store it with the document so that the configuration can be reused whenever the document is printed—and so that the user's previous choices can be the default settings when `ConfigPage()` is called again. `Settings()` returns the page configuration the user set up; `SetSettings()` initializes the configuration that's presented to the user. For example:

```
BMessage *setup;
  . . .
status_t MyDocumentManager::SetUpPage()
{
    BPrintJob job("document");
    status_t err;

    if ( setup )
        job.SetSettings(new BMessage(setup));
    if ( (err = job.ConfigPage()) == B_OK ) {
        delete setup;
        setup = job.Settings();
    }
    return err;
}
```

In this example, the `setup` BMessage presumably is flattened and saved with the document whenever the document is saved, and unflattened whenever the document is open and the page settings are needed.

Printing

To print a document, an application must go through several ordered steps:

- Engaging the Print Server and setting parameters for the job
- Setting up a spool file to hold image data
- Asking BViews to draw each page

- After each page is drawn, putting the data for the page in the spool file
- Committing the spool file to the Print Server

A BPrintJob object has member functions that assist with each step.

Setting Up a Print Job

A print job begins when the user requests the application to print something. In response, the application should create a BPrintJob object, assign the job a name, and call `ConfigJob()` to initialize the printing environment. For example:

```
BMessage *setup;
. . .
status_t MyDocumentManager::Print()
{
    BPrintJob job("document");
    status_t err;

    if ( setup )
        job.SetSettings(new BMessage(setup));
    if ( (err = job.ConfigJob()) == B_OK ) {
        delete setup;
        setup = job.Settings();
    }
    . . .
}
```

So far, this looks much like the code for configuring the page presented in the previous "Setting Up the Page Layout" section. The idea is the same. `ConfigJob()` gets the Print Server ready for a new printing session and has it interact with the user to set up the parameters for the job—which pages, how many copies, and so on. It uses the same settings BMessage to record the user's choices as `ConfigPage()` did, though it records information that's more immediate to the particular printing session.

Again, you may want to store the user's choices with the document so that they can be used to set the initial configuration for the job when the document is next printed. By calling `Settings()`, you can get the job configuration the user set up; `SetSettings()` initializes the configuration that's presented to the user.

Information about the page layout will be required while printing. If that information isn't available in the `Settings()` BMessage, `ConfigJob()` will begin, in essence, by calling `ConfigPage()` so that the server can ask the user to supply it.

To discover which pages the user wants to print, you can call the `FirstPage()` and `LastPage()` functions after `ConfigJob()` returns:

```
int32 pageCount = job.LastPage() - job.FirstPage() + 1;
```

The Spool File

The next step after configuring the job is to call `BeginJob()` to set up a spool file and begin the production of pages. After all the pages are produced, `CommitJob()` is called to commit them to the printer.

```
job.BeginJob();
/* draw pages here */
job.CommitJob();
```

`BeginJob()` and `CommitJob()` bracket all the drawing that's done during the job.

Cancellation

A number of things can happen to derail a print job after it has started—most significantly, the user can cancel it at any time. To be sure that the job hasn't been canceled or something else hasn't happened to defeat it, you can call `CanContinue()` at critical junctures in your code. This function will tell you whether it's sensible to continue with the job. In the following example, `CanContinue()` checks before each page is drawn:

```
job.BeginJob();
for ( int32 i = 0; i < pageCount; i++ ) {
    if ( !job.CanContinue() )
        break;
    /* draw each page here */
job.CommitJob();
```

Drawing on the Page

A page is produced by asking one or more BViews to draw within a rectangle that can be mapped to a sheet of paper (excluding the margins at the edge of the paper). `DrawView()` requests one BView to draw some portion of its data and specifies where the data should appear on the page. You can call `DrawView()` any number of times for a single page to ask any number of BViews to contribute to the page. After all views have drawn, `SpoolPage()` spools the data to the file that will eventually be committed to the printer. `SpoolPage()` is called just once for each page. For example:

```
for ( int i = job.FirstPage(); i <= job.LastPage(); i++ ) {
    if ( job.CanContinue() ) {
        . . .
        job.DrawView(someView, viewRect, pointOnPage);
        job.DrawView(anotherView, anotherRect, differentPoint);
        . . .
        job.SpoolPage();
    }
    else
        break;
}
```

DrawView() calls the BView's Draw() function. That function must be prepared to draw either for the screen or on the printed page. It can test the destination of its output by calling the BView IsPrinting() function.

Drawing Coordinates

When a BView draws for the printer, it draws within the *printable rectangle* of a page—a rectangle that matches the size of a sheet of paper minus the unprinted margin around the paper's edge. The PaperRect() function returns a rectangle that measures a sheet of paper and PrintableRect() returns the printable rectangle, as illustrated in this diagram:

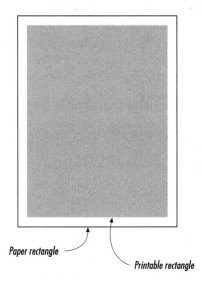

Paper rectangle

Printable rectangle

Both rectangles are stated in a coordinate system that has its origin at the left top corner of the page. Thus, the left and top sides of the rectangle returned by PaperRect() are always 0.0. PrintableRect() locates the printable rectangle on the paper rectangle. However, DrawView() assumes coordinates that are local to the printable rectangle—that is, an origin at the left top corner of the printable rectangle rather than the paper rectangle.

The diagram below shows the left top coordinates of the printable rectangle as PrintableRect() would report them and as DrawView() would assume them, given a half-inch margin.

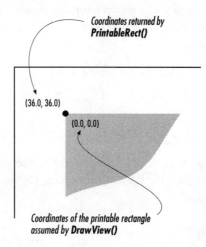

Draw() always draws in the BView's own coordinate system. Those coordinates are mapped to locations in the printable rectangle as specified by the arguments passed to DrawView().

See also: BView::IsPrinting()

Constructor and Destructor

BPrintJob()

> BPrintJob(const char *name*)

Initializes the BPrintJob object and assigns the job a *name*. The Print Server isn't contacted until ConfigPage() or ConfigJob() is called. The spool file isn't created until BeginJob() prepares for the production of pages.

See also: ConfigJob(), BeginJob()

~BPrintJob()

> virtual ~BPrintJob(void)

Frees all memory allocated by the object.

Member Functions

BeginJob()

> void BeginJob(void)

Opens a spool file for the job and prepares for the production of a series of pages. Call this function only once per printing session—just after initializing the job and just before drawing the first page.

See also: `CommitJob()`, "The Spool File" in the class overview

CancelJob()

void **CancelJob**(void)

Cancels the print job programmatically and gets rid of the spool file. The job cannot be restarted; you must destroy the BPrintJob object. Create a new object to renew printing.

CanContinue()

bool **CanContinue**(void)

Returns `true` if there's no impediment to continuing with the print job, and `false` if the user has canceled the job, the spool file has grown too big, or something else has happened to terminate printing. It's a good idea to liberally sprinkle `CanContinue()` queries throughout your printing code to make sure that the work you're about to do won't be wasted.

See also: "Cancellation" in the class overview

CommitJob()

void **CommitJob**(void)

Commits all spooled pages to the printer. This ends the print job; when `CommitJob()` returns, the BPrintJob object can be deleted. `CommitJob()` can be called only once per job.

See also: `BeginJob()`, "The Spool File" in the class overview

ConfigPage(), ConfigJob()

int32 **ConfigPage**(void)

int32 **ConfigJob**(void)

These functions contact the Print Server and have the server interact with the user to lay out the document on a page (in the case of `ConfigPage()`) or to define a print job (in the case of `ConfigJob()`). The page layout includes such things as the orientation of the image (portrait or landscape), the dimensions of the paper on which the document will be printed, and the size of the margins. The job definition includes such things as which pages are to be printed and the number of copies.

Both functions record the user's choices in a BMessage object that `Settings()` returns.

If `SetSettings()` has been called to establish a default configuration for the page layout or the job, these functions will pass it to the Print Server so the server can present it to the user. Otherwise, the server will choose a default configuration to show the user.

These two functions return `status_t` error codes, despite having return values that are declared `int32`. They return `B_ERROR` if they have trouble communicating with the server or if the job can't be established for any reason. They return `B_OK` if all goes well.

See also: `SetSettings()`, "Setting Up the Page Layout" and "Setting Up a Print Job" in the class overview

DrawView(), SpoolPage()

   virtual void **DrawView**(BView **view*, BRect *rect*, BPoint *point*)

   void **SpoolPage**(void)

`DrawView()` calls upon a *view* to draw the *rect* portion of its display at *point* on the page. As a result, the *view*'s `Draw()` function will be called with *rect* passed as the update rectangle. The rectangle should be stated in the BView's coordinate system. The *point* should be stated in a coordinate system that has the origin at the top left corner of the printable rectangle. Together the *rect* and *point* should be fashioned so that the entire rectangle lies within the boundaries of the page's printable area.

The *view* must be attached to a window; that is, it must be known to the Application Server. However, when printing, a BView can be asked to draw portions of its display that are not visible on-screen. Its drawing is not limited by the clipping region, its bounds rectangle, or the frame rectangles of ancestor views.

`DrawView()` doesn't look down the view hierarchy; it asks only the named *view* to draw, not any of its children. However, any number of BViews can draw on a page if they are subjects of separate `DrawView()` calls.

After all views have drawn and the page is complete, `SpoolPage()` adds it to the spool file. `SpoolPage()` must be called once to terminate each page.

See also: `PrintableRect()`, `BView::Draw()`, "Drawing on the Page" in the class overview

FirstPage(), LastPage()

int32 **FirstPage**(void)

int32 **LastPage**(void)

These functions return the first and last pages that should be printed as part of the current job. If the pages are not set (for example, if the current job has been canceled), `FirstPage()` returns 0 and `LastPage()` returns a very large number (`LONG_MAX`).

LastPage()   *see FirstPage()*

PaperRect(), PrintableRect()

BRect **PaperRect**(void)

BRect **PrintableRect**(void)

`PaperRect()` returns a rectangle that records the presumed size of the paper that the printer will use. Its left and top sides are at 0.0, so its right and bottom coordinates reflect the size of a sheet of paper. The size depends on choices made by the user when setting up the page layout.

`PrintableRect()` returns a rectangle that encloses the portion of a page where printing can appear. It's stated in the same coordinate system as the rectangle returned by `PaperRect()`, but excludes the margins around the edge of the paper. When drawing on the printed page, the left top corner of this rectangle is taken to be the coordinate origin, (0.0, 0.0).

The "Drawing Coordinates" section in the class overview illustrates these rectangles and their coordinate systems.

See also: `DrawView()`

SetSettings(), Settings()

void **SetSettings**(BMessage *configuration*)

BMessage *__Settings__(void)

These functions set and return the group of parameters that define how a document should be printed. The parameters include some that capture the page layout of the document and some that define the current job. They're recorded in a BMessage object that can be regarded as a black box; the data in the message are interpreted by the Print Server and will be documented where the print driver API is documented.

Instead of looking in the `Settings()` BMessage, rely on BPrintJob functions to provide specific information about the layout and the print job. Currently, there are only two functions—`FirstPage()` and `LastPage()`, which return the first and last pages that need to be printed.

`Settings()` can be called to get the current configuration message, which can then be flattened and stored with the document. You can retrieve it later and pass it to `SetSettings()` to set initial configuration values the next time the document is printed, as discussed in the "Setting Up the Page Layout" and "Setting Up a Print Job" sections of the class overview.

`SetSettings()` assumes ownership of the object it's passed. If your application needs to retain the object, pass a copy to `SetSettings()`:

```
print_job_object.SetSettings(new BMessage(settings_message));
```

On the other hand, `Settings()` transfers ownership of the object it returns to the caller; you don't need to make a copy.

See also: `ConfigPage()`

SpoolPage()   *see DrawView()*

BRadioButton

Derived from:	public BControl
Declared in:	be/interface/RadioButton.h
Library:	libbe.so

Overview

A BRadioButton object draws a labeled, two-state button that's displayed in a group along with other similar buttons. The button itself is a round icon that has a filled center when the BRadioButton is turned on, and is empty when it's off. The label appears next to the icon.

Only one radio button in the group can be on at a time; when the user clicks a button to turn it on, the button that's currently on is turned off. One button in the group must be on at all times; the user can turn a button off only by turning another one on. The button that's on has a value of 1 (`B_CONTROL_ON`); the others have a value of 0 (`B_CONTROL_OFF`).

The BRadioButton class handles the interaction between radio buttons in the following way: A direct user action can only turn on a radio button, not turn it off.

However, when the user turns a button on, the BRadioButton object turns off all siblings BRadioButtons—that is, all BRadioButtons that have the same parent as the one that was turned on.

This means that a parent view should have no more than one group of radio buttons among its children. Each set of radio buttons should be assigned a separate parent—perhaps an empty BView that simply contains the radio buttons and does no drawing of its own.

Constructor and Destructor

BRadioButton()

> **BRadioButton**(BRect *frame*, const char **name*,
>   const char **label*,
>   BMessage **message*,
>   uint32 *resizingMode* = B_FOLLOW_LEFT | B_FOLLOW_TOP,
>   uint32 *flags* = B_WILL_DRAW | B_NAVIGABLE)
> **BRadioButton**(BMessage **archive*)

Initializes the BRadioButton by passing all arguments to the BControl constructor without change. BControl initializes the radio button's *label* and assigns it a model *message* that identifies the action that should be taken when the radio button is turned on. When the user turns the button on, the BRadioButton posts a copy of the *message* so that it can be delivered to the target handler.

The *frame*, *name*, *resizingMode*, and *flags* arguments are the same as those declared for the BView class and are passed without change from BControl to the BView constructor.

The BRadioButton draws at the bottom of its frame rectangle beginning at the left side. It ignores any extra space at the top or on the right. (However, the user can click anywhere within the *frame* rectangle to turn on the radio button.) When the object is attached to a window, the height of the rectangle will be adjusted so that there is exactly the right amount of room to accommodate the label.

See also: the BControl and BView constructors, `AttachedToWindow()`

~BRadioButton()

> virtual **~BRadioButton**(void)

Does nothing; a BRadioButton doesn't need to clean up after itself when it's deleted.

Static Functions

Instantiate()

static BRadioButton ***Instantiate**(BMessage *archive)

Returns a new BRadioButton object, allocated by new and created with the version of the constructor that takes a BMessage archive. However, if the message doesn't contain data for an archived BRadioButton object, this function returns NULL.

See also: BArchivable::Instantiate(), instantiate_object(), Archive()

Member Functions

Archive()

virtual status_t **Archive**(BMessage *archive, bool deep = true) const

Calls the inherited version of Archive() and doesn't add anything specific to the BRadioButton class to the BMessage archive.

See also: BArchivable::Archive(), Instantiate() static function

AttachedToWindow()

virtual void **AttachedToWindow**(void)

Augments the BControl version of AttachedToWindow() to set the view and low colors of the BRadioButton to the match its parent's view color, and to resize the radio button vertically to fit the height of the label it displays. The height of the label depends on the BRadioButton's font.

See also: BControl::AttachedToWindow()

Draw()

virtual void **Draw**(BRect updateRect)

Draws the radio button—the circular icon—and its label. The center of the icon is filled when the BRadioButton's value is 1 (B_CONTROL_ON); it's left empty when the value is 0 (B_CONTROL_OFF).

See also: BView::Draw()

GetPreferredSize()

> virtual void **GetPreferredSize**(float *width*, float *height*)

Calculates the optimal size for the radio button to display the icon and the label in the current font, and places the result in the variables that the *width* and *height* arguments refer to. `ResizeToPreferred()`, defined in the BView class, resizes a view's frame rectangle to the preferred size, keeping its left and top sides constant. `AttachedToWindow()` automatically resizes a radio button to its preferred height, but doesn't modify its width.

See also: BView::GetPreferredSize(), AttachedToWindow()

KeyDown()

> virtual void **KeyDown**(const char *bytes*, int32 *numBytes*)

Augments the inherited versions of `KeyDown()` to turn the radio button on and deliver a message to the target BHandler when the character passed in *bytes* is B_SPACE or B_ENTER.

See also: BView::KeyDown(), SetValue()

MouseDown()

> virtual void **MouseDown**(BPoint *point*)

Responds to a mouse-down event in the radio button by tracking the cursor while the user holds the mouse button down. If the cursor is pointing to the radio button when the user releases the mouse button, this function turns the button on (and consequently turns all sibling BRadioButtons off), calls the BRadioButton's `Draw()` function, and posts a message that will be delivered to the target BHandler. Unlike a BCheckBox, a BRadioButton posts the message—it's "invoked"—only when it's turned on, not when it's turned off.

See also: BControl::Invoke(), BControl::SetTarget(), SetValue()

SetValue()

> virtual void **SetValue**(int32 *value*)

Augments the BControl version of `SetValue()` to turn all sibling BRadioButtons off (set their values to 0) when this BRadioButton is turned on (when the *value* passed is anything but 0).

See also: BControl::SetValue()

BRect

Derived from: *none*

Declared in: be/interface/Rect.h

Library: libbe.so

Overview

A BRect object represents a *rectangle*, one with sides that parallel the x and y coordinate axes. The rectangle is defined by its left, top, right, and bottom coordinates, as illustrated below:

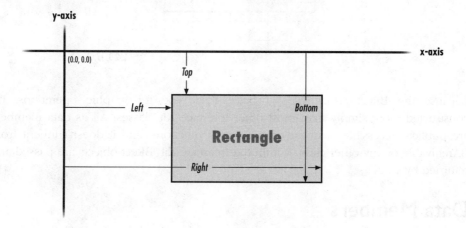

In a valid rectangle, the top y coordinate value is never greater than the bottom y coordinate, and the left x coordinate value is never greater than the right.

A BRect is the simplest, most basic way of specifying an area in a two-dimensional coordinate system. Windows, scroll bars, buttons, text fields, and the screen itself are all specified as rectangles.

When used to define the frame of a window or a view, or the bounds of a bitmap, the sides of the rectangle must line up on screen pixels. For this reason, the rectangle can't have any fractional coordinates. Coordinate units have a one-to-one correspondence with screen pixels.

Integral coordinates fall at the center of screen pixels, so frame rectangles cover a larger area than their coordinate values would indicate. Just as the number of elements in an array is one greater than the largest index, a frame rectangle covers one more column of pixels than its width and one more row than its height.

The figure below illustrates why this is the case. It shows a rectangle with a right side 8.0 units from its left (62.0–54.0) and a bottom 4.0 units below its top (17.0–13.0). Because the pixels that lie on all four sides of the rectangle are considered to be inside it, there's an extra pixel in each direction. When the rectangle is filled on-screen, it covers a 9-pixel-by-5-pixel area.

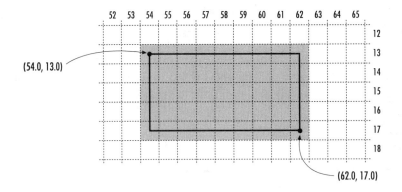

Because the BRect structure is a basic data type for graphic operations, it's constructed more simply than most other Interface Kit classes: All its data members are publicly accessible, it doesn't have virtual functions, and it doesn't inherit from BArchivable or any other class. Within the Interface Kit, BRect objects are passed and returned by value.

Data Members

float **left**
> The coordinate value of the rectangle's leftmost side (the smallest x coordinate in a valid rectangle).

float **top**
> The coordinate value of the rectangle's top (the smallest y coordinate in a valid rectangle).

float **right**
> The coordinate value of the rectangle's rightmost side (the largest x coordinate in a valid rectangle).

float **bottom**
> The coordinate value of the rectangle's bottom (the largest y coordinate in a valid rectangle).

Constructor

BRect()

> inline **BRect**(float *left*, float *top*, float *right*, float *bottom*)
> inline **BRect**(BPoint *leftTop*, BPoint *rightBottom*)
> inline **BRect**(const BRect& *rect*)
> inline **BRect**(void)

Initializes a BRect with its four coordinate values—*left*, *top*, *right*, and *bottom*. The four values can be directly stated:

```
BRect rect(11.0, 24.7, 301.5, 99.0);
```

or they can be taken from two points designating the rectangle's left top and right bottom corners:

```
BPoint leftTop(11.0, 24.7);
BPoint rightBottom(301.5, 99.0);
BRect rect(leftTop, rightBottom);
```

or they can be copied from another rectangle:

```
BRect anotherRect(11.0, 24.7, 301.5, 99.0);
BRect rect(anotherRect);
```

A rectangle that's not assigned any initial values:

```
BRect rect;
```

is constructed to be invalid (its top and left are greater than its right and bottom), until a specific assignment is made, typically with the `Set()` function:

```
rect.Set(77.0, 2.25, 510.8, 393.0);
```

See also: `Set()`

Member Functions

Contains()

> bool **Contains**(BPoint *point*) const
> bool **Contains**(BRect *rect*) const

Returns `true` if *point*—or *rect*—lies inside the area the BRect defines, and `false` if not. A rectangle contains a point even if the point coincides with one of the rectangle's corners or lies on one of its edges.

One rectangle contains another if their union is the same as the first rectangle and their intersection is the same as the second—that is, if the second rectangle lies entirely within the first. A rectangle is considered to be inside another rectangle even if they have one or more sides in common. Two identical rectangles contain each other.

See also: `Intersects()`, the & (intersection) and | (union) operators, `BPoint::ConstrainTo()`

Height() *see Width()*

InsetBy()

> void **InsetBy**(float *horizontal*, float *vertical*)
> void **InsetBy**(BPoint *point*)

Modifies the BRect by insetting its left and right sides by *horizontal* units and its top and bottom sides by *vertical* units. (If a *point* is passed, its *x* coordinate value substitutes for *horizontal* and its *y* coordinate value substitutes for *vertical.*)

For example, this code:

```
BRect rect(10.0, 40.0, 100.0, 140.0);
rect.InsetBy(20.0, 30.0);
```

produces a rectangle identical to one that could be constructed as follows:

```
BRect rect(30.0, 70.0, 80.0, 110.0);
```

If *horizontal* or *vertical* is negative, the rectangle becomes larger in that dimension, rather than smaller.

See also: `OffsetBy()`

IntegerWidth(), IntegerHeight()

> inline int32 **IntegerWidth**(void) const

> inline int32 **IntegerHeight**(void) const

These functions return the width and height of the rectangle expressed as integers. Fractional widths and heights are rounded up to the next whole number.

See also: `Width()`

Intersects()

> bool **Intersects**(BRect *rect*) const

Returns `true` if the BRect has any area—even a corner or part of a side—in common with *rect*, and `false` if it doesn't.

See also: the & (intersection) operator

IsValid()

inline bool **IsValid**(void) const

Returns `true` if the BRect's right side is greater than or equal to its left and its bottom is greater than or equal to its top, and `false` otherwise. An invalid rectangle doesn't designate any area, not even a line or a point.

LeftBottom()   *see SetLeftBottom()*

LeftTop()   *see SetLeftTop()*

OffsetBy(), OffsetTo()

void **OffsetBy**(float *horizontal*, float *vertical*)
void **OffsetBy**(BPoint *point*)

void **OffsetTo**(BPoint *point*)
void **OffsetTo**(float *x*, float *y*)

These functions reposition the rectangle in its coordinate system, without altering its size or shape.

`OffsetBy()` adds *horizontal* to the left and right coordinate values of the rectangle and *vertical* to its top and bottom coordinates. (If a *point* is passed, *point.x* substitutes for *horizontal* and *point.y* for *vertical*.)

`OffsetTo()` moves the rectangle so that its left top corner is at *point*—or at (x, y). The coordinate values of all its sides are adjusted accordingly.

See also: `InsetBy()`

PrintToStream()

void **PrintToStream**(void) const

Prints the contents of the BRect object to the standard output stream (`stdout`) in the form:

`"BRect(left, top, right, bottom)"`

where *left*, *top*, *right*, and *bottom* stand for the current values of the BRect's data members.

RightBottom()   *see SetRightBottom()*

RightTop()   *see SetRightTop()*

Set()

> inline void **Set**(float *left*, float *top*, float *right*, float *bottom*)

Assigns the values *left*, *top*, *right*, and *bottom* to the BRect's corresponding data members. The following code:

```
BRect rect;
rect.Set(0.0, 25.0, 50.0, 75.0);
```

is equivalent to:

```
BRect rect;
rect.left = 0.0;
rect.top = 25.0;
rect.right = 50.0;
rect.bottom = 75.0;
```

See also: the BRect constructor

SetLeftBottom(), LeftBottom()

> void **SetLeftBottom**(const BPoint *point*)

> inline BPoint **LeftBottom**(void) const

These functions set and return the left bottom corner of the rectangle. SetLeftBottom() alters the BRect so that its left bottom corner is at *point*, and LeftBottom() returns its current left and bottom coordinates as a BPoint object.

See also: SetLeftTop(), SetRightBottom(), SetRightTop()

SetLeftTop(), LeftTop()

> void **SetLeftTop**(const BPoint *point*)

> inline BPoint **LeftTop**(void) const

These functions set and return the left top corner of the rectangle. SetLeftTop() alters the BRect so that its left top corner is at *point*, and LeftTop() returns its current left and top coordinates as a BPoint object.

See also: SetLeftBottom(), SetRightTop(), SetRightBottom()

SetRightBottom(), RightBottom()

> void **SetRightBottom**(const BPoint *point*)

> inline BPoint **RightBottom**(void) const

These functions set and return the right bottom corner of the rectangle. `SetRightBottom()` alters the BRect so that its right bottom corner is at *point*, and `RightBottom()` returns its current right and bottom coordinates as a BPoint object.

See also: `SetRightTop()`, `SetLeftBottom()`, `SetLeftTop()`

SetRightTop(), RightTop()

void **SetRightTop**(const BPoint *point*)

inline BPoint **RightTop**(void) const

These functions set and return the right top corner of the rectangle. `SetRightTop()` alters the BRect so that its right top corner is at *point*, and `RightTop()` returns its current right and top coordinates as a BPoint object.

See also: `SetRightBottom()`, `SetLeftTop()`, `SetLeftBottom()`

Width(), Height()

inline float **Width**(void) const

inline float **Height**(void) const

These functions return the width of the rectangle (the difference between the coordinates of its left and right sides) and its height (the difference between its top and bottom coordinates). If either value is negative, the rectangle is invalid.

The width and height of a rectangle are not accurate guides to the number of pixels it covers on-screen. As illustrated in the "Overview" to this class, a rectangle without fractional coordinates covers an area that's one pixel broader than its coordinate width and one pixel taller than its coordinate height.

See also: `IntegerWidth()`

Operators

= (assignment)

inline BRect& **operator** =(const BRect&)

Assigns the data members of one BRect object to another BRect:

```
BRect a(27.2, 36.8, 230.0, 359.1);
BRect b;
b = a;
```

Rectangle *b* is made identical to rectangle *a*.

== (equality)

bool **operator** ==(BRect) const

Compares the data members of two BRect objects and returns `true` if each one exactly matches its counterpart in the other object, and `false` if any of the members don't match. In the following example, the equality operator would return `false`, since the two objects have different right boundaries:

```
BRect a(11.5, 22.5, 66.5, 88.5);
BRect b(11.5, 22.5, 46.5, 88.5);
if ( a == b )
    . . .
```

!= (inequality)

char **operator** !=(BRect) const

Compares two BRect objects and returns `true` unless their data members match exactly (the two rectangles are identical), in which case it returns `false`. This operator is the inverse of the == (equality) operator.

& (intersection)

BRect **operator** &(BRect) const

Returns the intersection of two rectangles—a rectangle enclosing the area they have in common. The shaded area below shows where the two outlined rectangles intersect.

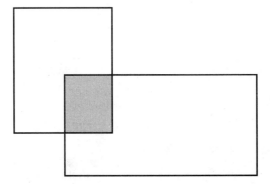

The intersection is computed by taking the greatest left and top coordinate values of the two rectangles, and the smallest right and bottom values. In the following example,

```
BRect a(10.0, 40.0, 80.0, 100.0);
BRect b(35.0, 15.0, 95.0, 65.0);
BRect c = a & b;
```

rectangle *c* will be identical to one constructed as follows:

```
BRect c(35.0, 40.0, 80.0, 65.0);
```

If the two rectangles don't actually intersect, the result will be invalid. You can test for this by calling the `Intersects()` function on the original rectangles, or by calling `IsValid()` on the result.

See also: `Intersects()`, `IsValid()`, the | (union) operator

| (union)

   BRect **operator** |(BRect) const

Returns the union of two rectangles—the smallest rectangle that encloses them both. The shaded area below illustrates the union of the two outlined rectangles. Note that it includes areas not in either of them.

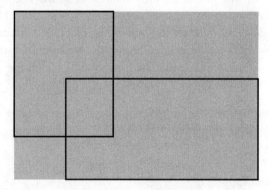

The union is computed by selecting the smallest left and top coordinate values from the two rectangles, and the greatest right and bottom coordinate values. In the following example,

```
BRect a(10.0, 40.0, 80.0, 100.0);
BRect b(35.0, 15.0, 95.0, 65.0);
BRect c = a | b;
```

rectangle *c* will be identical to one constructed as follows:

```
BRect c(10.0, 15.0, 95.0, 100.0);
```

Note that two rectangles will have a valid union even if they don't intersect.

See also: the & (intersection) operator

BRegion

Derived from: *none*

Declared in: be/interface/Region.h

Library: libbe.so

Overview

A BRegion object describes an arbitrary area within a two-dimensional coordinate system. The area can have irregular boundaries, contain holes, or be discontinuous. It's often convenient to think of a region as a set of locations or points, rather than as a closed shape like a rectangle or a polygon.

The points that a region includes can be described by a set of rectangles. Any point that lies within at least one of the rectangles belongs to the region. You can define a region incrementally by passing rectangles to functions like Set(), Include(), and Exclude(). By calling CountRects() and RectAt(), you can also look at the rectangles the BRegion object keeps to define the region. Since the object optimizes its description of the region, these rectangles may differ from the ones you passed to it.

BView's GetClippingRegion() function modifies a BRegion object so that it represents the current clipping region of the view. A BView can pass GetClippingRegion() a pointer to an empty BRegion,

```
BRegion temp;
GetClippingRegion(&temp);
```

then call BRegion's Intersects() and Contains() functions to test whether the potential drawing it might do falls within the region:

```
if ( temp.Intersects(someRect) )
    . . .
```

BView's FillRegion() fills a region with a specified pattern. This is equivalent to filling all the rectangles that define the region.

Constructor and Destructor

BRegion()

> **BRegion**(const BRegion& *region*)
> **BRegion**(void)

Initializes the BRegion object to have the same area as another *region*—or, if no other region is specified, to an empty region.

The original BRegion object and the newly constructed one each have their own copies of the data describing the region. Altering or freeing one of the objects will not affect the other.

BRegion objects can be allocated on the stack and assigned to other objects:

```
BRegion regionOne(anotherRegion);
BRegion regionTwo = regionOne;
```

However, due to their size, it's more efficient to pass them by pointer than by value.

~BRegion

> virtual **~BRegion**(void)

Frees any memory that was allocated to hold data describing the region.

Member Functions

Contains()

> bool **Contains**(BPoint *point*) const

Returns `true` if *point* lies within the region, and `false` if not.

CountRects()   *see RectAt()*

Exclude()

> void **Exclude**(BRect *rect*)
> void **Exclude**(const BRegion **region*)

Modifies the region so that it excludes all points contained within *rect* or *region* that it might have included before.

See also: `Include()`, `IntersectWith()`

Frame()

BRect **Frame**(void) const

Returns the frame rectangle of the BRegion—the smallest rectangle that encloses all the points within the region.

If the region is empty, the rectangle returned won't be valid.

See also: `BRect::IsValid()`

Include()

void **Include**(BRect *rect*)

void **Include**(const BRegion **region*)

Modifies the region so that it includes all points contained within the *rect* or *region* passed as an argument.

See also: `Exclude()`

IntersectWith()

void **IntersectWith**(const BRegion **region*)

Modifies the region so that it includes only those points that it has in common with another *region*.

See also: `Include()`

Intersects()

bool **Intersects**(BRect *rect*) const

Returns `true` if the BRegion has any area in common with *rect*, and `false` if not.

MakeEmpty()

void **MakeEmpty**(void)

Empties the BRegion of all its points. It will no longer designate any area and its frame rectangle won't be valid.

See also: the BRegion constructor

OffsetBy()

void **OffsetBy**(int32 *horizontal*, int32 *vertical*)

Offsets all points contained within the region by adding *hoSrizontal* to each *x* coordinate value and *vertical* to each *y* coordinate value.

PrintToStream()

> void **PrintToStream**(void) const

Prints the contents of the BRegion to the standard output stream (`stdout`) as an array of strings. Each string describes a rectangle in the form:

`"BRect(left, top, right, bottom)"`

where *left*, *top*, *right*, and *bottom* are the coordinate values that define the rectangle.

The first string in the array describes the BRegion's frame rectangle. Each subsequent string describes one portion of the area included in the BRegion.

See also: `BRect::PrintToStream()`, `Frame()`

RectAt(), CountRects()

> BRect **RectAt**(int32 *index*)

> int32 **CountRects**(void)

These functions provide access to the array of rectangles that define the region. Each coordinate point or pixel that's included within a rectangle is part of the region; points or pixels not inside a rectangle are not in the region.

`CountRects()` returns the total number of rectangles in the array; `RectAt()` returns the rectangle at a particular *index* in the array.

Set()

> void **Set**(BRect *rect*)

Modifies the BRegion so that it describes an area identical to *rect*. A subsequent call to `Frame()` should return the same rectangle (unless some other change was made to the region in the interim).

See also: `Include()`, `Exclude()`

Operators

= (assignment)

> BRegion& **operator** =(const BRegion&)

Assigns the region described by one BRegion object to another BRegion:

`BRegion region = anotherRegion;`

After the assignment, the two regions will be identical, but independent, copies of one another. Each object allocates its own memory to store the description of the region.

BScreen

Derived from: *none*

Declared in: be/interface/Screen.h

Library: libbe.so

Overview

A BScreen object represents a screen, a monitor that's connected to the computer and the graphics card that serves the monitor. The object's main purpose is to provide information about the screen—its pixel dimensions, depth, color map, color space, and so on. However, it can also set one screen parameter, the background "desktop" color. Nevertheless, the configuration of the screen (including the desktop color) should be left to users and a preferences application; most applications should be content just to get information from the BScreen object.

Multiple Screens

Currently, the BeOS supports only one screen. However, in the future, it will allow you to hook up more than one monitor to your computer. One of the screens, the *main screen*, will have the origin of the screen coordinate system at its left top corner. Other screens will be located elsewhere in the same coordinate system. If there's just one screen, it's the main screen.

A BScreen object represents just one screen. An application can have more than one object referring to the same screen, but you'll need a different BScreen object for each screen you want to query.

When multiple screens are supported, a `screen_id` identifier will be assigned to each one. Currently, `B_MAIN_SCREEN_ID` is the only identifier.

Locking and Allocation

When a BScreen object is constructed, it locks the screen in its current configuration, preventing all changes (except to the desktop color). The screen is unlocked when the object is destroyed, unless another BScreen object still has it locked. Therefore, you should keep a BScreen object for as short a period as possible, only until it has finished revealing the information you need. BScreen objects should not be cached or dynamically allocated. Allocate one on the stack each time you need information about the screen and make sure it's in a block of code that won't linger for long.

If a BScreen object is being used to get just one piece of information about the screen, it can be constructed anonymously (without assigning it to a variable). For example:

```
BRect screenRect = BScreen(myWindow).Frame();
```

However, anonymous construction doesn't mean that the object goes away after its single use. The normal rules of engagement for static construction apply—the object will be destroyed when the flow of execution leaves the braces that enclose the block of code it's in.

Constructor and Destructor

BScreen()

> BScreen(BWindow *window)
> BScreen(screen_id id = B_MAIN_SCREEN_ID)

Initializes the BScreen object so that it represents the screen where window is displayed or the screen identified by id. If window is NULL, the window is hidden, or the id is invalid, the BScreen will represent the main screen (which is currently the only possibility anyway).

Since multiple monitors are not currently supported, there's no API for getting screen identifiers other than for the main screen.

Constructing a BScreen object locks the screen configuration; the user won't be able to change its depth or resolution until the object is destroyed. Therefore, you should keep the object for only as brief a time as possible. It's best to construct it statically in a block of code that will be executed quickly.

To be sure the new object was correctly constructed, call IsValid().

See also: IsValid()

~BScreen()

> ~BScreen(void)

Unlocks the screen and invalidates the BScreen object.

Member Functions

BaseAddress(), BytesPerRow()

> void *BaseAddress(void)

> uint32 BytesPerRow(void)

`BaseAddress()` returns the base address for the frame buffer for the screen and `BytesPerRow()` returns the number of bytes in the frame buffer for each row of pixel data. The count includes bytes that hold pixel values and possibly bytes at the end of each row to make sure the next row is aligned on an appropriate boundary.

These are dangerous functions. Although the BScreen object locks the current configuration of the screen, the screen itself is not locked. You cannot safely read from the frame buffer or write to it. Use the BWindowScreen class in the Game Kit to get direct access to the frame buffer.

ColorForIndex()   *see IndexForColor()*

ColorMap()

   const color_map *`ColorMap`(void)

Returns a pointer to the color map for the screen. The color map defines the set of 256 colors that can be displayed in the `B_COLOR_8_BIT` color space. A single set of colors is shared by all applications that display on the screen.

The `color_map` structure is defined in *interface/GraphicsDefs.h* and contains the following fields:

int32 **id**

   An identifier that the Application Server uses to distinguish one color map from another.

rgb_color **color_list**[256]

   A list of the 256 colors, expressed as `rgb_color` structures. Indices into the list can be used to specify colors in the `B_COLOR_8_BIT` color space. See `IndexForColor()`.

uint8 **inversion_map**[256]

   A mapping of each color in the `color_list` to its opposite color. Indices are mapped to indices. An example of how this map might be used is given below.

uint8 **index_map**[32768]

   An array that maps RGB colors—specified using 5 bits per component—to their nearest counterparts in the color list. An example of how to use this map is also given below.

The `inversion_map` is a list of indices into the `color_list` where each index locates the "inversion" of the original color. The inversion of the *n*th color in `color_list` would be found as follows:

```
BScreen screen;
const color_map *map = screen.ColorMap();
```

```
uint8 inversionIndex = map->inversion_map[n];
rgb_color inversionColor = map->color_list[inversionIndex];
```

Inverting an inverted index returns the original index, so this code:

```
uint8 color = map->inversion_map[inversionIndex];
```

would return *n*. The InvertIndex() function is an alternative to indexing into the inversion_map in this way, though it carries the overhead of a function call for each operation.

Inverted colors are used, primarily, for highlighting. Given a color, its highlight complement is its inversion.

The index_map maps every RGB combination that can be expressed in 15 bits (5 bits per component) to a single color_list index that best approximates the original RGB data. The following example demonstrates how to squeeze 24-bit RGB data into a 15-bit number that can be used as an index into the index_map:

```
long rgb15 = ( ((red & 0xf8) << 7) |
               ((green & 0xf8) << 2) |
               ((blue & 0xf8) >> 3) );
```

Most applications won't need to use the index map directly; the IndexForColor() function performs the same conversion with less fuss (no masking and shifting required). However, applications that implement repetitive graphic operations, such as dithering, may want to access the index map themselves, and thus avoid the overhead of an additional function call.

You should never modify or free the color_map structure returned by this function; it belongs to the BScreen object.

See also: IndexForColor(), system_colors()

ColorSpace()

color_space **ColorSpace**(void)

Returns the color space of the screen display—typically B_COLOR_8_BIT or B_RGB_32_BIT—or B_NO_COLOR_SPACE if the BScreen object is invalid. The color space is under the control of the user and the Screen preferences application.

See also: "Colors" near the beginning of this chapter for an explanation of the various color spaces

DesktopColor()   *see SetDesktopColor()*

Frame()

BRect **Frame**(void)

Returns the rectangle that locates the screen in the screen's coordinate system and defines its dimensions. For example, a screen with a resolution of 1,024 pixels × 768 pixels would have a frame rectangle with both its left and top sides at 0.0 (assuming it's the main screen), its right side at 1,023.0, and its bottom at 767.0.

If the BScreen object is invalid, all sides of the rectangle are set to 0.0.

See also: the BRect class

ID()

screen_id **ID**(void)

Returns the identifier for the screen, which for the main screen (currently the only screen) should be `B_MAIN_SCREEN_ID`.

The `screen_id` is not persistent. A new one may be assigned each time the machine is rebooted or a monitor is disconnected then reconnected.

This function currently returns `B_MAIN_SCREEN_ID` even if the BScreen object is invalid.

IndexForColor(), ColorForIndex()

inline uint8 **IndexForColor**(rgb_color *color*)
uint8 **IndexForColor**(uint8 *red*, uint8 *green*, uint8 *blue*, uint8 *alpha* = 0)

rgb_color **ColorForIndex**(const uint8 *index*)

`IndexForColor()` returns an index into the list of 256 colors that comprise the 8-bit color space for the screen. The value returned picks out the listed color that most closely matches a full 32-bit *color*—specified either as an `rgb_color` value or by its *red*, *green*, and *blue* components. (The *alpha* component is currently ignored.)

The returned index identifies a color in the `B_COLOR_8_BIT` color space. It can, for example, be passed to BBitmap's `SetBits()` function to set the color of a bitmap pixel. If the *color* is `B_TRANSPARENT_32_BIT`, the return value will be `B_TRANSPARENT_8_BIT`.

To find the fully specified color that an index picks out, you can call `ColorForIndex()` or you can get the color list for the screen and find the color directly. For example, if you first obtain the index for the "best fit" color that most closely matches an arbitrary color,

```
BScreen screen;
uint8 index = screen.IndexForColor(134, 210, 6);
```

you can then pass the index to `ColorForIndex()`,

```
rgb_color bestFit = screen.ColorForIndex(index);
```

or you can use the index to locate that color in the color list:

```
rgb_color bestFit = screen.ColorMap()->color_list[index];
```

Neither method will correctly translate B_TRANSPARENT_8_BIT to B_TRANSPARENT_32_BIT.

See also: `ColorMap()`, the BBitmap class

InvertIndex()

> uint8 **InvertIndex**(uint8 *index*)

Returns the index to the color that's the inversion (or exact opposite) of the *index* color passed as an argument. Both the return value and the argument specify colors in the B_COLOR_8_BIT color space. Inverting an inverted color returns the original color. For example:

```
uint8 inversion = InvertIndex(colorIndex);
uint8 inversionOfInversion = InvertIndex(inversion);
ASSERT(inversionOfInversion == colorIndex);
```

This function is an alternative to getting the color map and looking at the `inversion_map` yourself.

See also: `ColorMap()`

IsValid()

> bool **IsValid**(void)

Returns `true` if the BScreen object is valid (if it represents a real screen connected to the computer), and `false` if not (for example, if the screen has been disconnected).

SetDesktopColor(), DesktopColor()

> void **SetDesktopColor**(rgb_color *color*, bool *makeDefault* = true)

> rgb_color **DesktopColor**(void)

These functions set and return the color of the "desktop"—the backdrop against which windows are displayed on the screen. `SetDesktopColor()` makes an immediate change in the desktop color displayed on-screen; `DesktopColor()` returns the color currently displayed. If the *makeDefault* flag is `true`, the color that's set becomes the default color for the screen; it's the color that will be shown the next time the machine is booted. If the flag is `false`, the color is set only for the current session.

Typically, users choose the desktop color with the Screen preferences application. Other applications can look at the desktop color, but should not set it.

WaitForRetrace()

status_t **WaitForRetrace**(void)

Blocks until the monitor has finished the current vertical retrace, then returns B_OK. There are a few milliseconds available before it begins another retrace. Drawing done (changes made to the frame buffer) in this period won't cause any "flicker" on-screen.

For some graphics card drivers, this function will wait for vertical sync; for others it will wait until vertical blank, providing a few extra milliseconds. (However, it's currently not implemented and always returns B_ERROR without blocking.)

BScrollBar

Derived from:	public BView
Declared in:	be/interface/ScrollBar.h
Library:	libbe.so

Overview

A BScrollBar object displays a vertical or horizontal scroll bar that users can operate to scroll the contents of another view, a *target view*. Scroll bars usually are grouped as siblings of the target view under a common parent. Then, when the parent is resized, the target and scroll bars can be automatically resized to match. (A companion class, BScrollView, defines just such a container view; a BScrollView object sets up the scroll bars for a target view and makes itself the parent of the target and the scroll bars.)

The Update Mechanism

BScrollBars are different from other views in one important respect: All their drawing and event handling is carried out within the Application Server, not in the application. A BScrollBar object doesn't receive Draw() or MouseDown() notifications; the server intercepts updates and interface messages that would otherwise be reported to the BScrollBar and handles them itself. As the user moves the knob on a scroll bar or presses a scroll arrow, the Application Server continuously refreshes the scroll bar's image on-screen and informs the application with a steady stream of B_VALUE_CHANGED messages.

The window dispatches these messages by calling the BScrollBar's ValueChanged() function. Each function call notifies the BScrollBar of a change in its value and, consequently, of a need to scroll the target view.

Confining the update mechanism for scroll bars to the Application Server limits the volume of communication between the application and server and enhances the efficiency of scrolling. The application's messages to the server can concentrate on updating the target view as its contents are being scrolled, rather than on updating the scroll bars themselves.

Value and Range

A scroll bar's value determines what the target view displays. The assumption is that the left coordinate value of the target view's bounds rectangle should match the value of the horizontal scroll bar, and the top of the target view's bounds rectangle should match the value of the vertical scroll bar. When a BScrollBar is notified of a change of value (through `ValueChanged()`), it calls the target view's `ScrollTo()` function to put the new value at the left or top of the bounds rectangle.

The value reported in a `ValueChanged()` notification and passed to `ScrollTo()` depends on where the user moves the scroll bar's knob and on the range of values the scroll bar represents. The range is first set in the BScrollBar constructor and can be modified by the `SetRange()` function.

The range must be large enough to bring all the coordinate values where the target view can draw into its bounds rectangle. If everything the target view can draw is conceived as being enclosed in a "data rectangle," the range of a horizontal scroll bar must extend from a minimum that makes the left side of the target's bounds rectangle coincide with the left side of its data rectangle, to a maximum that puts the right side of the bounds rectangle at the right side of the data rectangle. This is illustrated in part below:

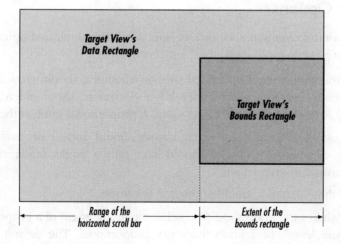

As this illustration helps demonstrate, the maximum value of a horizontal scroll bar can be no less than the right coordinate value of the data rectangle minus the width of the bounds rectangle. Similarly, for a vertical scroll bar, the maximum value can be no less than the bottom coordinate of the data rectangle minus the height of the bounds rectangle. The range of a scroll bar subtracts the dimensions of the target's bounds rectangle from its data rectangle. (The minimum values of horizontal and vertical scroll bars can be no greater than the left and top sides of the data rectangle.)

What the target view can draw may change from time to time as the user adds or deletes data. As this happens, the range of the scroll bar should be updated with the `SetRange()` function. The range may also need to be recalculated when the target view is resized.

Coordination

Scroll bars control the target view, but a target can also be scrolled without the intervention of its scroll bars (by calling `ScrollTo()` or `ScrollBy()` directly). Therefore, not only must a scroll bar know about its target, but a target view must know about its scroll bars. When a BScrollBar sets its target, the target BView is notified and records the identity of the BScrollBar.

The two objects communicate whenever the display changes: When the scroll bar is the instrument that initiates scrolling, `ValueChanged()` calls the target view's `ScrollTo()` function. To cover cases of target-initiated scrolling, `ScrollTo()` calls the BScrollBar's `SetValue()` function so that the scroll bars can be updated on-screen. `SetValue()` in turn calls `ValueChanged()`, which makes sure the exchange of function calls doesn't get too circular.

Scroll Bar Options

Users have control over some aspects of how scroll bars look and behave. With the ScrollBar preferences application, they can choose:

- Whether the knob should be a fixed size, or whether it should grow and shrink to proportionally represent how much of a document (how much of the data rectangle) is visible within the target view. A proportional knob is the default.

- Whether double, bidirectional scroll arrows should appear on each end of the scroll bar, or whether each end should have only a single, unidirectional arrow. Double arrows are the default.

- Which of three patterns should appear on the knob.

- What the size of the knob should be—the minimum length of a proportional knob or the fixed length of a knob that's not proportional. The default length is 15 pixels.

When this class constructs a new BScrollBar, it conforms the object to the choices the user has made.

See also: set_scroll_bar_info(), BView::ScrollBar(), the BScrollView class

Hook Functions

ValueChanged()
> Scrolls the target view when the BScrollBar is informed that its value has changed; can be augmented to coordinate other activities with the change in value.

Constructor and Destructor

BScrollBar()

> **BScrollBar**(BRect *frame*, const char **name*, BView **target*,
> float *min*, float *max*, orientation *posture*)
> **BScrollBar**(BMessage **archive*)

Initializes the BScrollBar and connects it to the *target* view that it will scroll. It will be a horizontal scroll bar if *posture* is B_HORIZONTAL and a vertical scroll bar if *posture* is B_VERTICAL.

The range of values that the scroll bar can represent at the outset is set by *min* and *max*. These values should be calculated from the boundaries of a rectangle that encloses the entire contents of the target view—everything that it can draw. If *min* and *max* are both 0, the scroll bar is disabled and the knob is not drawn.

The object's initial value is 0 even if that falls outside the range set for the scroll bar.

The other arguments, *frame* and *name*, are the same as for other BViews:

- The *frame* rectangle locates the scroll bar within its parent view. For consistency in the user interface, a horizontal scroll bar should be B_H_SCROLL_BAR_HEIGHT coordinate units high, and a vertical scroll bar should be B_V_SCROLL_BAR_WIDTH units wide.

- The BScrollBar's *name* identifies it and permits it to be located by the FindView() function. It can be NULL.

Unlike other BViews, the BScrollBar constructor doesn't set an automatic resizing mode. By default, scroll bars have the resizing behavior that befits their posture—horizontal scroll bars resize themselves horizontally (as if they had a resizing mode that combined B_FOLLOW_LEFT_RIGHT with B_FOLLOW_BOTTOM) and vertical scroll bars resize themselves vertically (as if their resizing mode combined B_FOLLOW_TOP_BOTTOM with B_FOLLOW_RIGHT).

~BScrollBar()

virtual **~BScrollBar**(void)

Disconnects the scroll bar from its target.

Static Functions

Instantiate()

static BScrollBar ***Instantiate**(BMessage *archive*)

Returns a new BScrollBar object, allocated by **new** and created with the version of the constructor that takes a BMessage *archive*. However, if the *archive* message doesn't contain data for a BScrollBar object, the return value will be NULL.

See also: BArchivable::Instantiate(), instantiate_object(), Archive()

Member Functions

Archive()

virtual status_t **Archive**(BMessage *archive*, bool *deep* = true) const

Calls the inherited version of Archive(), then adds the BScrollBar's range, orientation, current value and proportion, and the size of its big and little steps to the BMessage *archive*.

See also: BArchivable::Archive(), Instantiate() static function

AttachedToWindow()

virtual void **AttachedToWindow**(void)

Makes sure that the Application Server is cognizant of the BScrollBar's value, if a value was set before the object was attached to a window.

See also: BHandler::AttachedToWindow()

GetRange()   *see SetRange()*

GetSteps()   *see SetSteps()*

Orientation()

orientation **Orientation**(void) const

Returns B_HORIZONTAL if the object represents a horizontal scroll bar and B_VERTICAL if it represents a vertical scroll bar.

See also: the BScrollBar constructor

SetProportion(), Proportion()

> void **SetProportion**(float *ratio*)

> float **Proportion**(void) const

These functions set and return a value between 0.0 and 1.0 that represents the proportion of the entire document that can be displayed within the target view—the ratio of the width (or height) of the target's bounds rectangle to the width (or height) of its data rectangle. This ratio determines the size of a proportional scroll knob relative to the whole scroll bar. It's not adjusted to take into account the minimum size of the knob.

The proportion should be reset as the size of the data rectangle changes (as data is entered and removed from the document) and when the target view is resized.

SetRange(), GetRange()

> void **SetRange**(float *min*, float *max*)

> void **GetRange**(float **min*, float **max*) const

These functions modify and return the range of the scroll bar. SetRange() sets the minimum and maximum values of the scroll bar to *min* and *max*. GetRange() places the current minimum and maximum in the variables that *min* and *max* refer to.

If the scroll bar's current value falls outside the new range, it will be reset to the closest value—either *min* or *max*—within range. ValueChanged() is called to inform the BScrollBar of the change whether or not it's attached to a window.

If the BScrollBar is attached to a window, any change in its range will be immediately reflected on-screen. The knob will move to the appropriate position to reflect the current value.

Setting both the minimum and maximum to 0 disables the scroll bar. It will be drawn without a knob.

See also: the BScrollBar constructor

SetSteps(), GetSteps()

void **SetSteps**(float *smallStep*, float *bigStep*)

void **GetSteps**(float **smallStep*, float **bigStep*) const

`SetSteps()` sets how much a single user action should change the value of the scroll bar—and therefore how far the target view should scroll. `GetSteps()` provides the current settings.

When the user presses one of the scroll arrows at either end of the scroll bar, its value changes by a *smallStep* coordinate units. When the user clicks in the bar itself (other than on the knob), it changes by a *bigStep* units. For an application that displays text, the small step of a vertical scroll bar should be large enough to bring another line of text into view.

The default small step is 1.0, which should be too small for most purposes; the default large step is 10.0, which is also probably too small.

Currently, a BScrollBar's steps can be successfully set only after it's attached to a window.

See also: `ValueChanged()`

SetTarget(), Target()

void **SetTarget**(BView **view*)
void **SetTarget**(const char **name*)

BView **Target**(void) const

These functions set and return the target of the BScrollBar, the view that the scroll bar scrolls. `SetTarget()` sets the target to *view*, or to the BView identified by *name*. `Target()` returns the current target view. The target can also be set when the BScrollBar is constructed.

`SetTarget()` can be called either before or after the BScrollBar is attached to a window. If the target is set by *name*, the named view must eventually be found within the same window as the scroll bar. Typically, the target and its scroll bars are children of a container view that serves to bind them together as a unit.

When the target is successfully set, a pointer to the BScrollBar object is passed to the target view. This lets the target update its scroll bars when its contents are scrolled.

See also: the BScrollBar constructor, `ValueChanged()`, `BView::ScrollBar()`

SetValue(), Value()

void **SetValue**(float *value*)

float **Value**(void) const

These functions modify and return the value of the scroll bar. The value is usually set as the result of user actions; `SetValue()` provides a way to do it programmatically. `Value()` returns the current value, whether set by `SetValue()` or by the user.

`SetValue()` assigns a new *value* to the scroll bar and calls the `ValueChanged()` hook function, whether or not the new value is really a change from the old. If the *value* passed lies outside the range of the scroll bar, the BScrollBar is reset to the closest value within range—that is, to either the minimum or the maximum value previously specified.

If the scroll bar is attached to a window, changing its value updates its on-screen display. The call to `ValueChanged()` enables the object to scroll the target view so that it too is updated to conform to the new value.

The initial value of a scroll bar is 0.

See also: `ValueChanged()`, `SetRange()`

Target()   *see SetTarget()*

Value()   *see SetValue()*

ValueChanged()

virtual void **ValueChanged**(float *newValue*)

Responds to a notification that the value of the scroll bar has changed to *newValue*. For a horizontal scroll bar, this function interprets *newValue* as the coordinate value that should be at the left side of the target view's bounds rectangle. For a vertical scroll bar, it interprets *newValue* as the coordinate value that should be at the top of the rectangle. It calls `ScrollTo()` to scroll the target's contents into position, unless they have already been scrolled.

`ValueChanged()` is called as the result both of user actions (`B_VALUE_CHANGED` messages received from the Application Server) and of programmatic ones. Programmatically, scrolling can be initiated by the target view (calling `ScrollTo()`) or by the BScrollBar (calling `SetValue()` or `SetRange()`).

In all these cases, the target view and the scroll bars need to be kept in synch. This is done by a chain of function calls: `ValueChanged()` calls `ScrollTo()`, which in turn calls `SetValue()`, which then calls `ValueChanged()` again. It's up to

`ValueChanged()` to get off this merry-go-round, which it does by checking the target view's bounds rectangle. If *newValue* already matches the left or top side of the bounds rectangle, if forgoes calling `ScrollTo()`.

`ValueChanged()` does nothing if a target BView hasn't been set—or if the target has been set by name, but the name doesn't correspond to an actual BView within the scroll bar's window.

Derived classes can override this function to interpret *newValue* differently, or to do something in addition to scrolling the target view.

See also: `SetTarget()`, `SetValue()`, `BView::ScrollTo()`

BScrollView

Derived from:	public BView
Declared in:	be/interface/ScrollView.h
Library:	libbe.so

Overview

A BScrollView object is a container for another view, a *target view*, typically a view that can be scrolled. The BScrollView creates and positions the scroll bars the target view needs and makes itself the parent of the scroll bars and the target view. It's a convenient way to set up scroll bars for another view.

If requested, the BScrollView draws a border around its children. Otherwise, it does no drawing and simply contains the family of views it set up.

The `ScrollBar()` function provides access to the scroll bars the BScrollView creates, so you can set their ranges and values as needed.

Constructor and Destructor

BScrollView()

BScrollView(const char **name*, BView **target*,
                uint32 *resizingMode* = B_FOLLOW_LEFT | B_FOLLOW_TOP,
                uint32 *flags* = 0,
                bool *horizontal* = false,
                bool *vertical* = false,
                border_style *border* = B_FANCY_BORDER)
BScrollView(BMessage **archive*)

Initializes the BScrollView. It will have a frame rectangle large enough to contain the *target* view and any scroll bars that are requested. If *horizontal* is true, there will be a horizontal scroll bar. If *vertical* is true, there will be a vertical scroll bar. Scroll bars are not provided unless you ask for them.

The *border* argument can be set to one of three values:

B_PLAIN_BORDER	Draw a border consisting of just a simple line around the target view and scroll bars.
B_FANCY_BORDER	Draw a fancier border that looks like a 3D groove inset into the surface of the view.
B_NO_BORDER	Don't draw a border.

A BScrollView can be used without scroll bars to simply contain and border the target view.

The BScrollView adapts its frame rectangle from the frame rectangle of the target view. It makes its frame just big enough to hold the target, scroll bars, and border. It positions itself so that the target view doesn't move within the window: If there's no border, its left and top sides are exactly where the left and top sides of the target view originally were. If there is a border, its sides are adjusted to make room for it while keeping the target view constant.

The target view is notified that it has become the target of a BScrollView with a TargetedByScrollView() function call. The BScrollView then adds the target view as its child along with any requested scroll bars. In the process, it modifies the target view's frame rectangle (but not its bounds rectangle) so that it will fit within its new parent.

If the resize mode of the target view is B_FOLLOW_ALL_SIDES, it and the scroll bars will be automatically resized to fill the container view whenever the container view is resized.

The scroll bars created by the BScrollView have an initial range extending from a minimum of 0 to a maximum of 1000. You'll generally need to ask for the scroll bars (using the ScrollBar() function) and set their ranges to more appropriate values.

The *name*, *resizingMode*, and *flags* arguments are identical to those declared in the BView class and are passed to the BView constructor. If a border is requested, B_WILL_DRAW is automatically added to the *flags* mask. The other two arguments are passed to the BView class unchanged.

See also: the BView constructor, BView:TargetedByScrollView()

~BScrollView()

virtual ~**BScrollView**(void)

Does nothing.

Static Functions

Instantiate()

static BScrollView ***Instantiate**(BMessage *_archive_)

Returns a new BScrollView object, allocated by **new** and created with the version of the constructor that takes a BMessage _archive_. However, if the message doesn't contain data for an archived BScrollView object, `Instantiate()` returns **NULL**.

See also: `BArchivable::Instantiate()`, `instantiate_object()`, `Archive()`

Member Functions

Archive()

virtual status_t **Archive**(BMessage *_archive_, bool _deep_ = true) const

Calls the inherited version of `Archive()`, which will archive the target view and scroll bars if the _deep_ flag is **true**. This function then adds the BScrollView's border style to the _archive_ message.

See also: `BArchivable::Archive()`, `Instantiate()` static function

AttachedToWindow()

virtual void **AttachedToWindow**(void)

Resizes scroll bars belonging to BScrollViews that occupy the right bottom corner of a document window (B_DOCUMENT_WINDOW) so that room is left for the resize knob. This function assumes that vertical scroll bars are B_V_SCOLL_BAR_WIDTH units wide and horizontal scroll bars are B_H_SCROLL_BAR_HEIGHT units high. It doesn't check to make sure the window is actually resizable.

This function also sets the default high color to a medium shade of gray.

See also: `BView::AttachedToWindow()`

Border()   _see SetBorder()_

Draw()

> virtual void **Draw**(BRect *updateRect*)

Draws the border around the target view and scroll views, provided a border was requested when the BScrollView was constructed.

See also: the BScrollView constructor, `BView::Draw()`

IsBorderHighlighted()   *see SetBorderHighlighted()*

ScrollBar()

> BScrollBar ****ScrollBar**(orientation *posture*) const

Returns the horizontal scroll bar if *posture* is `B_HORIZONTAL` and the vertical scroll bar if *posture* is `B_VERTICAL`. If the BScrollView doesn't contain a scroll bar with the requested orientation, this function returns `NULL`.

See also: the BScrollBar class

SetBorder(), Border()

> virtual void **SetBorder**(border_style *border*)
>
> border_style **Border**(void) const

These functions set and return the style of the BScrollView's border, which may be `B_PLAIN_BORDER`, `B_FANCY_BORDER`, or `B_NO_BORDER`. The border is originally set by the constructor. The three constants and the border's effect on the BScrollView are discussed there.

See also: the BScrollView constructor

SetBorderHighlighted(), IsBorderHighlighted()

> virtual status_t **SetBorderHighlighted**(bool *highlighted*)
>
> bool **IsBorderHighlighted**(void) const

`SetBorderHighlighted()` highlights the border of the BScrollView when the *highlighted* flag is `true`, and removes the highlighting when the flag is `false`. This function works by calling `Draw()`. However, it works only for a border in the `B_FANCY_BORDER` style. If successful, it returns `B_OK`. Otherwise, it returns `B_ERROR`.

`IsBorderHighlighted()` returns whether the border is currently highlighted. The return value is always `false` for a BScrollView that doesn't have a border or has only a "plain" one.

Highlighting a BScrollView's border shows that the target view is the current focus view for the window. Typically, the target view calls `SetBorderHighlighted()` from its `MakeFocus()` function when the focus changes. (The target knows that it's inside a BScrollView because of the `TargetedByScrollView()` notification it received.) In the Interface Kit, only BListViews take the opportunity these functions afford to highlight a parent BScrollView's border.

BSeparatorItem

Derived from: public BMenuItem

Declared in: be/interface/MenuItem.h

Library: libbe.so

Overview

A BSeparatorItem is a menu item that serves only to separate the items that precede it in the menu list from the items that follow it. It's drawn as a horizontal line across the menu from the left border to the right. Although it has an indexed position in the menu list just like other items, it doesn't have a label, can't be selected, sends no messages, and is permanently disabled.

Since the separator is drawn horizontally, it's assumed that items in the menu are arranged in a column, as they are by default. It's inappropriate to use a separator in a menu bar or another menu where the items are arranged in a row.

A separator can be added to a BMenu by constructing an object of this class and calling BMenu's `AddItem()` function. As a shorthand, you can simply call BMenu's `AddSeparatorItem()` function, which constructs the object for you and adds it to the list.

A BSeparatorItem that's returned to you (by BMenu's `ItemAt()` function, for example) will always respond `NULL` to `Message()`, `Command()`, and `Submenu()` queries and `false` to `IsEnabled()`.

See also: BMenu::AddSeparatorItem()

Constructor and Destructor

BSeparatorItem()

BSeparatorItem(void)
BSeparatorItem(BMessage *archive)

Initializes the BSeparatorItem and disables it.

~BSeparatorItem()

> virtual ~**BSeparatorItem**(void)

Does nothing.

Static Functions

Instantiate()

> static BSeparatorItem ***Instantiate**(BMessage *archive)

Returns a new BSeparatorItem object, allocated by **new** and created with the version of the constructor that takes a BMessage *archive*. However, if the *archive* message doesn't contain data for a BSeparatorItem object, the return value is NULL.

See also: `BArchivable::Instantiate()`, `instantiate_object()`, `BMenuItem::Archive()`

Member Functions

Draw()

> protected:
> virtual void **Draw**(void)

Draws the item as a horizontal line across the width of the menu.

GetContentSize()

> protected:
> virtual void **GetContentSize**(float *width*, float *height*)

Provides a minimal size for the item so that it won't constrain the size of the menu.

Instantiate()   *see Archive()*

SetEnabled()

> virtual void **SetEnabled**(bool *flag*)

Does nothing. A BSeparatorItem is disabled when it's constructed and must stay that way.

BShelf

Derived from: public BHandler

Declared in: be/interface/Shelf.h

Library: libbe.so

Overview

A BShelf is an object that you "attach" to a view in order to make the view accept dropped BDragger objects (and the views that they serve). In user-talk, a shelf receives and displays replicants. Attaching a BShelf to a view (called the "container" view) is remarkably simple:

```
BShelf *shelf = new BShelf(some_view);
```

That's all there is to it: With this single line of code, `some_view` is primed to accept and (automatically) display dropped replicants. A dropped replicant becomes a child of the container view. The container view itself can be *any* BView object; you don't have to prime the view or otherwise alter it in any way.

A rule you should remember:

- **Attaching a shelf to a view is performed by the BShelf constructor only**. You can't create a BShelf and *then* decide which view you want it to serve.

Other BShelf features:

- A BShelf can configure itself from a "settings" file, and can write its contents to that file. Your only chance to associate a BShelf with a settings file is during construction. You can save the contents at any time through the `Save()` function.

- A BShelf can reject dropped replicants, and can adjust the position of the replicants that it accepts. These features are provided through hook functions (`CanAccept...` and `AdjustReplicantBy()`).

- A BShelf has a name. When a replicant message is dropped on the shelf, the shelf's name is compared to the dropped message's "shelf_name" field (if it has one). If the two don't match, the replicant is rejected. In this way, individual views can be picky about the shelves that they want to be displayed on.

Dropping into the View Hierarchy

When the user drops a replicant on a container view, the thing that the view actually receives is a `B_ARCHIVED_OBJECT` message that contains a BDragger and the dragger's target (a BView). These two objects (the BDragger and its target) are directly related as parent-child, child-parent, or as siblings (as explained in the

BDragger class). The "more elderly" of the two objects is added as a child of the container view; if they're siblings, the two objects are both added as children.

You can also send or post B_ARCHIVED_OBJECT messages to a BShelf to simulate a drag and drop.

Hook Functions

CanAcceptReplicantMessage()

Invoked when a replicant BMessage is received by the BShelf. A return value of false rejects the replicant.

CanAcceptReplicantView()

Invoked after the message has been accepted (by the above); this is the shelf's chance to reject on the basis of the view that the message contains. A return value of false rejects the replicant.

AdjustReplicantBy()

Invoked after the replicant has been accepted, but before it's displayed. The function can return a BPoint that offsets the replicant's frame.

Constructor and Destructor

BShelf()

BShelf(BView *_view_,
                bool *allowsDragging* = true,
                const char *_name_ = NULL)

BShelf(const entry_ref *_ref_,
                BView *_view_,
                bool *allowsDragging* = true,
                const char *_name_ = NULL)

BShelf(BDataIO *_stream_,
                BView *_view_,
                bool *allowsDragging* = true,
                const char *_name_ = NULL)

Initializes the BShelf object so that it serves a container _view_. The versions that accept an entry_ref or BDataIO argument prime the shelf so that it (initially) contains the replicants that are archived in the referred to file or stream. The _ref/stream_ argument is also used as the archival repository when you tell your BShelf to Save() itself.

If the _allowsDragging_ flag is true, the user will be able to drag replicant view within the container's bounds. If the flag is false, dropped views stay where they're first put.

name is the BShelf's handler name. The name can be important: It's compared to the replicant's "shelf_name" field, as explained in `AddReplicant()`.

WARNING

There's an archive-accepting version of the BShelf constructor declared in *Shelf.h*. Don't use it.

~BShelf()

virtual **~BShelf**(void)

The destructor calls `Save()`, and then frees the object.

Static Functions

Instantiate()

static BShelf ***Instantiate**(BMessage **archive*)

Returns a new BShelf object, allocated by `new` and created with the version of the constructor that takes a BMessage *archive*. If the *archive* message doesn't contain data for a BShelf object, a new object isn't created and the function returns `NULL`.

See also: `BArchivable::Instantiate()`, `instantiate_object()`, `Archive()`

Member Functions

AddReplicant()

filter_result **AddReplicant**(BMessage **archive*, BPoint *point*)

This function is invoked automatically when a replicant is dropped on the BShelf. The *archive* message contains the BDragger archive that's being dropped; *point* is where, within the container view's bounds, the message was dropped. The function goes through these steps to reject and adjust the replicant:

- First, it invokes the `CanAcceptReplicantMessage()` hook function. If the hook returns `false`, then `AddReplicant()` doesn't add the replicant.

- Next, it looks for a "shelf_name" string field in the BMessage. If it finds one and the value of the field doesn't match the BShelf's name, the replicant is rejected.

  There's no specific API for adding the "shelf_name" field to a view. If you want to configure your views to accept only certain BShelf objects, you have to add the field directly as part of the view's `Archive()` implementation.

- The archive message is then unarchived (the replicant is instantiated). If the archive doesn't contain a BView, the message is passed on to another handler (B_DISPATCH_MESSAGE is returned).

- CanAcceptReplicantView() hook function is called next (with a return of false meaning rejection).

- Finally, AdjustReplicantBy() is called, and the replicant is drawn in the container view.

Except in the case of a no-view archive, AddReplicant() returns B_SKIP_MESSAGE.

It's possible to archive a BDragger and call this function yourself, although that's not its expected use.

AdjustReplicantBy()

protected:
   virtual BPoint **AdjustReplicantBy**(BRect *destRect*, BMessage **archive*) const

This hook function is invoked automatically when a replicant is dropped on the BShelf. It gives the shelf a chance to fine-tune the placement of the BDragger and its target view.

destRect is the rectangle (in the container view's coordinates) in which the dropped replicant is about to be drawn. Exactly what the rectangle means depends on the relationship between the dragger and its target:

- If the dragger is the target's parent, then *destRect* encloses the BDragger's frame.

- Otherwise (if the target is the parent, or if the two views are siblings), *destRect* encloses the target's frame. Note that in the case of siblings, the BDragger's frame isn't included in the rectangle.

archive is the archive message that was dropped on the shelf.

The BPoint that this function returns offsets (is added into) the location of the replicant. If you don't want to move the replicant, return BPoint(0, 0). Note that the BDragger and the view are *both* moved by this offset, even in the case where *destRect* doesn't include the dragger's frame.

This function ignores the "allows dragging" flag given in the BShelf constructor. In other words, you can adjust a replicant's placement through this function even if the BShelf doesn't otherwise allow dragging.

AllowsDragging()

bool **AllowsDragging**(void)

Does this BShelf let the user drag existing replicants within the container view's frame (as specified through an argument to the constructor)?

Archive()

WARNING

`Archive()` is currently a no-op that returns `B_ERROR`. You can't archive a BShelf. If you want to archive something, archive the shelf's contents by calling `Save()`.

CanAcceptReplicantMessage(), CanAcceptReplicantView()

protected:
virtual bool **CanAcceptReplicantMessage**(BMessage *archive*) const
virtual bool **CanAcceptReplicantView**(BRect *destRect*,
      BView *view*,
      BMessage *archive*) const

These hook function are invoked from within `AddReplicant()` whenever a replicant is dropped on the BShelf. You can implement these functions to reject unwanted replicants.

`CanAcceptReplicantMessage()` is called first; the argument is the archive that (should) contain the replicated view. If you don't like the look of the archive, return `false` and the message will be thrown away. Note that you shouldn't return `false` if the archive doesn't seem to be in the correct form (specifically, if it doesn't contain any views). Rejection of such messages is handled more elegantly (and after this function is invoked) by the `AddReplicant()` function.

CanAcceptReplicantView() is invoked after the message has been unarchived. *destRect* is the rectangle that the replicant will occupy in the BShelf's container view's coordinates. *view* is the replicated view itself. *archive* is the original message.

If either function returns `false`, the replicant is rejected and the message is thrown away (it isn't passed on to another handler). A return of `true` does the obvious thing.

IsDirty() *see Save()*

Save(), SetDirty(), IsDirty()

status_t **Save**(void)

virtual void **SetDirty**(bool *flag*)

bool **IsDirty**(void)

Writes the shelf's contents (the replicants that it contains) as an archive to the `entry_ref` or BDataIO object that was specified in the constructor.

By default, the save is only performed if the object's "dirty" flag is set—in other words, if it has changed since it was last written. You can force set the dirty flag by calling `SetDirty()`.

`IsDirty()` returns the current state of the "dirty" flag.

BStatusBar

Derived from: public BView

Declared in: be/interface/StatusBar.h

Library: libbe.so

Overview

A BStatusBar object draws a status bar, also called a progress bar, that indicates the progression and pace of a time-consuming operation. It gives the user something to look at while the operation is taking place and provides some indication of how long it will take. The bar is filled with color from left to right as more and more of the operation is completed.

A BStatusBar can display a label on the far left above the bar itself and some text immediately to the right of the label. It can also display a trailing label on the far right and trailing text immediately to its left. The label and text are aligned at the left of the bar; the trailing text and trailing label are aligned at the right of the bar. In neither case is there any space between the label and text; to separate words you must add space characters to one string or the other.

The text and trailing text can change each time the bar is updated—that is, each time a bit more of the bar is filled. The label and trailing label, on the other hand, are set when the BStatusBar is constructed and remain constant throughout the display, or until the object is reset for another operation.

For example, a status bar that's displayed while a large file is being downloaded might have the file name as the label and no text. It could have the percentage completed as the trailing text and something like "% done" as the trailing label. A BStatusBar that tracks the processing of, say, 40 employee records could have "Employee: " as the label, the employee's name as the text, the number of the record being processed as the trailing text, and " of 40" as the trailing label.

The value of a BStatusBar determines how much of the bar is filled with color. The minimum value (none of the bar is filled) is 0.0; the maximum value (all of the bar is filled) is 100.0 by default, but can be set to another positive number. For example, if the maximum value is 400.0 and current value is 86.0, 21.5% (86/400) of the bar will be filled.

A BStatusBar is controlled synchronously by calling its `Update()` and `Reset()` functions. `Update()` fills a bit more of the bar each time it's called and can change the text and trailing text. `Reset()` resets the current value to 0.0 so the bar can show the progress of another operation; it can change the label and trailing label.

You can also control a BStatusBar asynchronously by making it the target of `B_UPDATE_STATUS_BAR` and `B_RESET_STATUS_BAR` messages, which indirectly call `Update()` and `Reset()`. These messages are described under the corresponding functions.

See also: `Update()`, `Reset()`

Constructor and Destructor

BStatusBar()

> **BStatusBar**(BRect *frame*, const char **name*,
>   const char **label* = NULL, const char **trailingLabel* = NULL)
> **BStatusBar**(BMessage **archive*)

Initializes the BStatusBar with a label and a trailing label, which can both be NULL. The *frame* and *name* arguments are the same as those declared for the BView constructor and are passed to the BView class unchanged along with the `B_WILL_DRAW` flag and a resizing mode that will keep the BStatusBar glued to the left and top sides of its parent.

Regardless of the *frame* rectangle, however, when the BStatusBar is attached to a window, it will be resized to a height that precisely accommodates the bar, the labels, and the text given the current font.

The default font of the BStatusBar is the system plain font, and the default color of the bar is blue (50, 150, 255). Its initial value is 0.0, the minimum, and its default maximum value is 100.0.

See also: `SetMaxValue()`, `SetBarColor()`

~BStatusBar()

virtual **~BStatusBar**(void)

Frees the labels and the text.

Static Functions

Instantiate()

static BStatusBar **Instantiate**(BMessage *archive*)

Returns a new BStatusBar object, allocated by new and created with the version of the constructor that takes a BMessage *archive*. However, if the *archive* doesn't contain data for an BStatusBar object, this function returns NULL.

See also: `BArchivable::Instantiate()`, `instantiate_object()`, `Archive()`

Member Functions

Archive()

virtual status_t **Archive**(BMessage *archive*, bool *deep* = true) const

Calls the inherited version of `Archive()`, then adds the bar color, bar height, current value, and maximum value to the BMessage *archive*, along with the current text, trailing text, label, and trailing label.

See also: `BArchivable::Archive()`, `Instantiate()` static function

AttachedToWindow()

virtual void **AttachedToWindow**(void)

Resizes the frame rectangle to the optimal height for displaying the bar, labels, and text. If the height of the bar has not been set yet, a default height is chosen for it.

This function also sets the view and low colors of the BStatusBar to match the background view color of its new parent. The low color fills the status bar when it's empty.

See also: BView::AttachedToWindow()

BarColor() *see SetBarColor()*

BarHeight() *see SetBarHeight()*

CurrentValue() *see SetMaxValue()*

Draw()

virtual void **Draw**(BRect *updateRect*)

Draws the bar, labels, and text.

See also: BView::Draw()

Label(), TrailingLabel()

const char *Label(void) const

const char *TrailingLabel(void) const

These functions return the current label and trailing label of the BStatusBar. The returned strings belong to the BStatusBar object and should not be altered. They can be set only on construction or when all values are reset.

See also: Reset()

MaxValue() *see SetMaxValue()*

MessageReceived()

virtual void **MessageReceived**(BMessage *message*)

Responds to B_UPDATE_STATUS_BAR and B_RESET_STATUS_BAR messages by calling the Update() and Reset() functions. Each message contains data that can be passed as arguments to the functions.

See also: BView::MessageReceived(), Update(), Reset(), "BStatusBar Messages" Appendix A, *Message Protocols*

Reset()

virtual void Reset(const char *label* = NULL, const char *trailingLabel* = NULL)

Empties the status bar, sets its current value to 0.0 and its maximum value to 100.0, deletes and erases the text and trailing text, and replaces the label and trailing label with copies of the strings passed as arguments. If either argument is NULL, the label or trailing label will also be deleted and erased.

This gets the BStatusBar ready to be reused for another operation. For example, if several large files are being downloaded, the BStatusBar could be reset for each one.

You can call this function indirectly (and asynchronously) through a B_RESET_STATUS_BAR message. If the message has an entry named "label" containing a string (B_STRING_TYPE), the string will be passed to the function as the first argument. If there's a string in an entry named "trailing_label", it will be passed as the second argument. If either entry is absent, the value for the corresponding argument will be NULL.

See also: SetText(), Update()

SetBarColor(), BarColor()

virtual void SetBarColor(rgb_color *color*)

rgb_color **BarColor**(void) const

These functions set and return the color that fills the bar to show how much of an operation has been completed. The default bar color is blue (50, 150, 255).

SetBarHeight(), BarHeight()

virtual void SetBarHeight(float *height*)

float **BarHeight**(void) const

These functions set and return the height of the bar itself, minus the text and labels. The default height is 16.0 coordinate units. When the BStatusBar is attached to a window, its frame rectangle is resized to a height that fits the bar height and the height of the current font for displaying the text and labels. Therefore, if you want a bar that's taller or shorter than the default height, you should call SetBarHeight() before adding the BStatusBar to a view hierarchy.

See also: AttachedToWindow()

SetMaxValue(), MaxValue(), CurrentValue()

virtual void **SetMaxValue**(float *max*)

float **MaxValue**(void) const

float **CurrentValue**(void) const

SetMaxValue() sets the maximum value of the BStatusBar, which by default is 100.0. MaxValue() returns the current maximum. The minimum value is 0.0 and cannot be changed.

CurrentValue() returns the current value of the BStatusBar, which determines how much of the bar is filled with the bar color. For example, if the maximum is 300.0 and the current value is 120.0, the bar color will fill 40% of the bar. The current value is set by Update() and reset to 0.0 by Reset().

See also: Update(), Reset()

SetText(), SetTrailingText(), Text(), TrailingText()

virtual void **SetText**(const char **string*)

virtual void **SetTrailingText**(const char **string*)

const char ****Text**(void) const

const char ****TrailingText**(void) const

These functions set and return the text and the trailing text of the BStatusBar. The Set...() functions free the previous text and replace it with a copy of the *string* that's passed. The *string* can be NULL. Both functions erase the previous text and redraw the view to display the new text. The text and trailing text can also be replaced by calling Update().

Text() and TrailingText() return pointers to the current text strings.

See also: Update()

Text()   *see SetText()*

TrailingLabel()   *see Label()*

TrailingText()   *see SetText()*

Update()

> virtual void **Update**(float *delta*, const char **text* = NULL,
>   const char **trailingText* = NULL)

Updates the BStatusBar by adding a *delta* increment to its current value and resetting its text and trailing text. For example, if the current value is 50.0 and *delta* is 8.0, the new value will be 58.0. The change in value is immediately reflected on-screen in a corresponding increment in how much of the bar is filled with color. Passing NULL for the *text* or *trailingText* argument retains the previous text or trailing text string.

You can call this function indirectly through a B_UPDATE_STATUS_BAR message. The message must have a B_FLOAT_TYPE entry named "delta" containing the value that should be passed to the function as the *delta* argument. If it also has a string in an entry named "text", the string will be passed as the *text* argument. And if it has a string entry named "trailing_text", that string will be passed as the *trailingText* argument. If either string entry is omitted, the corresponding argument will be NULL.

See also: Reset(), CurrentValue(), SetText()

BStringItem

Derived from:	public BListItem
Declared in:	be/interface/ListItem.h
Library:	libbe.so

Overview

A BStringItem is an item of text that can appear in a BListView, including a BOutlineListView. It's the only concrete representative of the abstract BListItem class that the Interface Kit defines. It simply draws the item as a string of text.

Constructor and Destructor

BStringItem()

> **BStringItem**(const char **text*, uint32 *level* = 0, bool *expanded* = true)
> **BStringItem**(BMessage **archive*)

Initializes the BStringItem by making a copy of the *text* string passed as an argument. This is the string the item will display. The *level* and *expanded* arguments are passed unchanged to the BListItem constructor; see that function for an explanation.

~BStringItem()

virtual **~BStringItem**(void)

Frees the text the item displays.

Static Functions

Instantiate()

static BStringItem ***Instantiate**(BMessage *_archive_)

Returns a new BStringItem object, allocated by **new** and created with the version of the constructor that takes a BMessage _archive_. However, if the _archive_ message doesn't contain archived data for a BStringItem, Instantiate() returns NULL.

See also: BArchivable::Instantiate(), instantiate_object(), Archive()

Member Functions

Archive()

virtual status_t **Archive**(BMessage *_archive_, bool _deep_ = true) const

Calls the inherited version of Archive(), then adds the text string to the BMessage _archive_.

See also: BArchivable::Archive(), Instantiate() static function

DrawItem()

virtual void **DrawItem**(BView *_owner_, BRect _frame_, bool _complete_ = false)

Draws the text string, dimming it if the item is disabled and highlighting it if the item is selected.

See also: BListItem::DrawItem()

SetText(), Text()

virtual void **SetText**(const char *_text_)

const char ***Text**(void) const

These functions set and return the text that the BStringItem draws. SetText() copies the string it's passed. Text() returns a pointer to the string owned by the BStringItem.

Update()

virtual void **Update**(BView *owner*, const BFont *font*)

Overrides the BListItem version of `Update()` to recalculate the width and height of the BStringItem and the placement of the text. The width of the item is based on the width of the *owner* BView. The height and text placement are based on the owner's *font*. The item must be tall enough to display the string in the current font.

See also: `BListItem::Update()`

BStringView

Derived from: public BView

Declared in: be/interface/StringView.h

Library: libbe.so

Overview

A BStringView object draws a static character string. The user can't select the string or edit it; a BStringView doesn't respond to user actions. An instance of this class can be used to draw a label or other text that simply delivers a message of some kind to the user. Use a BTextView object for selectable and editable text.

You can also draw strings by calling BView's `DrawString()` function. However, assigning a string to a BStringView object locates it in the view hierarchy. The string will be updated automatically, just like other views. And, by setting the resizing mode of the object, you can make sure that it will be positioned properly when the window or the view it's in (the parent of the BStringView) is resized.

Constructor and Destructor

BStringView()

BStringView(BRect *frame*, const char *name*, const char *text*,
                uint32 *resizingMode* = B_FOLLOW_LEFT | B_FOLLOW_TOP,
                uint32 *flags* = B_WILL_DRAW)
BStringView(BMessage *archive*)

Initializes the BStringView by assigning it a *text* string and the system plain font (`be_plain_font`). The *frame*, *name*, *resizingMode*, and *flags* arguments are the same as those declared for the BView class. They're passed unchanged to the BView constructor.

The *frame* rectangle needs to be large enough to display the entire string in the current font. The string is drawn at the bottom of the frame rectangle and, by default, is aligned to the left side. A different horizontal alignment can be set by calling `SetAlignment()`.

See also: `SetAlignment()`

~BStringView()

>   virtual ~**BStringView**(void)

Frees the text string.

Static Functions

Instantiate()

>   static BStringView ***Instantiate**(BMessage *archive*)

Returns a new BStringView object, allocated by **new** and created with the version of the constructor that takes a BMessage *archive*. However, if the *archive* message doesn't contain data for a BStringView, `Instantiate()` returns NULL.

See also: `BArchivable::Instantiate()`, `instantiate_object()`, `Archive()`

Member Functions

Alignment()   *see SetAlignment()*

Archive()

>   virtual status_t **Archive**(BMessage *archive*, bool *deep* = true) const

Calls the inherited version of `Archive()`, then adds the string and its alignment to the BMessage *archive*.

See also: `BArchivable::Archive()`, `Instantiate()` static function

AttachedToWindow()

>   virtual void **AttachedToWindow**(void)

Sets the BStringView's low color and its background view color to match the background color of its new parent view.

See also: `BView::AttachedToWindow()`

Draw()

virtual void **Draw**(BRect *updateRect*)

Draws the string along the bottom of the BStringView's frame rectangle in the current high color.

SetAlignment(), Alignment()

void **SetAlignment**(alignment *flag*)

alignment **Alignment**(void) const

These functions align the string within the BStringView's frame rectangle and return the current alignment. The alignment *flag* can be:

B_ALIGN_LEFT	The string is aligned at the left side of the frame rectangle.
B_ALIGN_RIGHT	The string is aligned at the right side of the frame rectangle.
B_ALIGN_CENTER	The string is aligned so that the center of the string falls midway between the left and right sides of the frame rectangle.

The default is B_ALIGN_LEFT.

SetText(), Text()

void **SetText**(const char **string*)

const char ****Text**(void) const

These functions set and return the text string that the BStringView draws. `SetText()` frees the previous string and copies *string* to replace it. `Text()` returns the null-terminated string.

BTextControl

Derived from: public BControl

Declared in: be/interface/TextControl.h

Library: libbe.so

Overview

A BTextControl object displays a labeled text field that behaves like other control devices. When the user presses certain keys after modifying the text in the field, it delivers a message to a designated target.

There are two parts to the view: A static label on the left, which the user cannot modify, and an editable field on the right, which behaves just like a one-line BTextView. In fact, the BTextControl installs a BTextView object as its child to handle editing chores within this part of the view. It's this child view that responds to keyboard events for the BTextControl rather than the control object itself.

Architect: Belmont Freeman

The child BTextView must become the focus view for the window before the user can enter or edit text in the field. If the user modifies the contents of the field and then causes the child to cease being the focus view, the BTextControl delivers a message to its target, just like any other BControl object when it's invoked. The message notifies the target that the user has finished making changes to the text. (It doesn't matter what causes the change in focus—a click in another text field, for example, or a B_TAB character that navigates to another view.)

The BTextControl is also invoked when the user types a B_ENTER character, though this doesn't change the focus view. It selects all the text in the field.

You can arrange for another message—a "modification message"—to be sent when the user makes the first change to the text after the child BTextView has become the focus view (or after B_ENTER caused all the text to be selected). This message notifies the target that editing has begun.

Because the label is drawn by the BTextControl itself and the editable text is drawn by its child BTextView, you can assign different properties (color or font, for example) to each string. The BTextControl has only one child; ChildAt() returns it when passed an index of 0.

Scripting Support

A BTextControl object supports the following scripting requests, but doesn't assign them a suite name:

Property name:	"Text" or "Value" for all the text assigned to the object
Specifiers:	B_DIRECT_SPECIFIER only
Messages:	B_SET_PROPERTY and B_GET_PROPERTY
Data type:	a null-terminated character string (char *)

In other words, it interprets the "Value" property declared by the BControl class to mean the text string (not the label) that the object displays. Its type is therefore

B_STRING_TYPE, rather than B_INT32_TYPE as it is for other control devices. The same data can be specified using "Text" as the property name.

See "Scripting" in Chapter 2 for more on scripting and message suites.

Constructor and Destructor

BTextControl()

> **BTextControl**(BRect *frame*, const char *name*,
>   const char **label*, const char **text*,
>   BMessage **message*,
>   uint32 *resizingMode* = B_FOLLOW_LEFT | B_FOLLOW_TOP,
>   uint32 *flags* = B_WILL_DRAW | B_NAVIGABLE)
> **BTextControl**(BMessage **archive*)

Initializes the BTextControl by assigning it a *label* and some *text*, both of which can be NULL. If the *label* is NULL, the entire bounds rectangle is assigned to the text. Otherwise, half the view is assigned to the label and half to the text, though the exact proportion can be changed by the SetDivider() function. The label always is on the left and the text always on the right. By default, both label and text are aligned at the left margins of their respective sections; call SetAlignment() to alter the alignment.

The *message* parameter is the same as the one declared for the BControl constructor. It establishes a model for the messages the BTextControl will send when it's invoked. It can be NULL. See SetMessage() and SetTarget() in the BInvoker class and Invoke() in the BControl class for more information.

The *frame, name, resizingMode*, and *flags* arguments are the same as those declared for the BView class and are passed up the inheritance hierarchy to the BView constructor without change. When the BTextControl is attached to a window, it will be resized to the optimal height for displaying the label and text.

See also: SetDivider(), SetAlignment(), BInvoker::SetMessage(),
BInvoker::SetTarget(), BControl::Invoke()

~BTextControl()

> virtual **~BTextControl**(void)

Frees memory allocated by the BTextControl and its BTextView child.

Static Functions

Instantiate()

> static BTextControl *__Instantiate__(BMessage *_archive_)

Returns a new BTextControl object, allocated by new and created with the version of the constructor that takes a BMessage _archive_. However, if the _archive_ message doesn't contain data for a BTextControl object, Instantiate() returns NULL.

See also: BArchivable::Instantiate(), instantiate_object(), Archive()

Member Functions

Archive()

> virtual status_t __Archive__(BMessage *_archive_, bool _deep_ = true) const

Calls the inherited version of Archive(), which will archive the child BTextView if the _deep_ flag is true, then adds the alignment of the label and the text, the modification message, and the divider to the BMessage _archive_.

See also: BArchivable::Archive(), Instantiate() static function

AttachedToWindow()

> virtual void __AttachedToWindow__(void)

Augments the BControl version of AttachedToWindow() to set up its child BTextView and to make the view and low colors of the BTextControl the same as the background view color of its new parent. This function also adjusts the height of the BTextControl to fit the height of the label and text, given the fonts used to display them.

See also: BView::AttachedToWindow(), BControl::AttachedToWindow()

Divider()   _see SetDivider()_

Draw()

> virtual void __Draw__(BRect _updateRect_)

Draws the label. (The BTextControl defers to its child BTextView to draw the editable text string.)

See also: BView::Draw()

GetAlignment()   *see SetAlignment()*

GetPreferredSize(), ResizeToPreferred()

virtual void **GetPreferredSize**(float **width*, float **height*)

virtual void **ResizeToPreferred**(void)

`GetPreferredSize()` calculates the optimal size for the BTextControl to display the label and the text, given its current font and the current font of its BTextView child; it places the result in the variables that the *width* and *height* arguments refer to. `ResizeToPreferred()` resizes the BTextControl to its preferred size, keeping its left and top sides constant, and adjusts the size of the BTextView to fit.

See also: `BView::GetPreferredSize()`

MakeFocus()

virtual void **MakeFocus**(bool *flag* = true)

Passes the `MakeFocus()` instruction on to the child BTextView. If the *flag* is `true`, this function selects all the text in the child BTextView, which becomes the new focus view for the window. If the *flag* is `false`, the child will no longer be the focus view. If the text has changed when the child ceases to be the focus view, the BTextControl is considered to have been invoked; a copy of its model message is posted so that it will be delivered to the target handler.

Note that the BTextControl itself never becomes the focus view, so will return `false` to all `IsFocus()` queries.

See also: `BView::MakeFocus()`

MessageReceived()

virtual void **MessageReceived**(BMessage **message*)

Handles scripting requests for the BTextControl.

See also: `BHandler::MessageReceived()`

ModificationMessage()   *see SetModificationMessage()*

MouseDown()

virtual void **MouseDown**(BPoint *point*)

Makes the child BTextView the focus view when the user clicks in the BTextControl but outside the text.

See also: `BTextView::MouseDown()`

ResizeToPreferred()   *see GetPreferredSize()*

ResolveSpecifier()

> virtual BHandler ***ResolveSpecifier**(BMessage *_message_, int32 _index_,
>   BMessage *_specifier_, int32 _command_, const char *_property_)

Resolves specifiers for the "Text" and "Value" properties. See "Scripting Support" in the class overview and "Scripting" in Chapter 2 for more information.

See also: `BHandler::ResolveSpecifier()`

SetAlignment(), GetAlignment()

> virtual void **SetAlignment**(alignment _forLabel_, alignment _forText_)

> void **GetAlignment**(alignment *_forLabel_, alignment *_forText_) const

These functions set and report the alignment of the label and the text within their respective portions of the view. Three settings are possible:

B_ALIGN_LEFT	The label or text is aligned at the left boundary of its part of the view rectangle.
B_ALIGN_RIGHT	The label or text is aligned at the right boundary of its part of the view rectangle.
B_ALIGN_CENTER	The label or text is centered within its part of the view rectangle.

The default alignment is **B_ALIGN_LEFT** for both label and text.

See also: `SetDivider()`

SetDivider(), Divider()

> virtual void **SetDivider**(float _xCoordinate_)

> float **Divider**(void) const

These functions set and return the _x_ coordinate value that marks the division between the label portion of the view rectangle on the left and the text portion on the right. It's stated in the coordinate system of the BTextControl.

See also: the BTextControl constructor

SetEnabled()

virtual void **SetEnabled**(bool *enabled*)

Disables the BTextControl if the *enabled* flag is `false`, and reenables it if *enabled* is `true`. BTextControls are enabled by default.

This function augments the BControl version of `SetEnabled()`. When the control is disabled, it makes the text unselectable (and therefore uneditable) and draws it in a way that displays its disabled state. When the control is re-enabled, it makes the text editable (and therefore selectable) and draws it as normal text.

See also: `BControl::SetEnabled()`

SetModificationMessage(), ModificationMessage()

virtual void **SetModificationMessage**(BMessage **message*)

BMessage ****ModificationMessage**(void) const

These functions set and return the message that the BTextControl sends to its target when the user begins to enter or edit text.

`SetModificationMessage()` assigns *message* to the BTextControl, freeing the message previously assigned, if any. The message becomes the responsibility of the BTextControl object and will be freed only when it's replaced by another message or the BTextControl is freed; you shouldn't free it yourself. Passing a `NULL` pointer to this function deletes the current modification message without replacing it.

The assigned BMessage becomes the model for the message that the BTextControl sends when the user first modifies the text after the child BTextView has become the focus view (or after the user pressed the Enter key). The message is sent only for the first character the user types, pastes, or deletes. Subsequent changes don't invoke the message, until after the user presses the Enter key to select all the text or after the child BTextView loses focus view status and regains it again.

Before sending the message, the BTextControl adds these two pieces of information to it:

Data name	Type code	Description
"when"	B_INT64_TYPE	When the user modified the text, as measured by the number of microseconds since 12:00:00 AM January 1, 1970.
"source"	B_POINTER_TYPE	A pointer to the BTextControl object.

These names should not be used for any data that you place in the model *message*.

`ModificationMessage()` returns the model message.

SetText(), Text()

virtual void **SetText**(const char *text*)

const char ***Text**(void) const

These functions set and return the text displayed by the BTextControl—or rather by its child BTextView. The text is first set by the constructor.

TextView()

BTextView ***TextView**(void) const

Returns the child BTextView object that handles the BTextControl's editing chores.

See also: the BTextView class

WindowActivated()

virtual void **WindowActivated**(bool *active*)

Makes sure that the BTextControl is redrawn when the window is activated and deactivated, if its child BTextView is the current focus view. This gives the BTextControl a chance to draw or erase the indication that it's the current focus for keyboard navigation.

BTextView

Derived from:	public BView
Declared in:	be/interface/TextView.h
Library:	libbe.so

Overview

A BTextView object displays formatted text on-screen. It implements a standard user interface for entering, selecting, and editing text from the keyboard and mouse; it also supports the principal editing commands—Cut, Copy, Paste, Delete, and Select All. BTextView objects are suitable for displaying small amounts of text in the user interface and for moderate text-editing tasks. Full-scale text editors and word processors will need to define their own objects to handle richer data formats.

By default, a BTextView displays all its text in a single font and color. However, if you call `SetStylable()` to turn on support for multiple character formats, you can apply different fonts and colors to different groups of characters. For example, some words might be bold or italic, some displayed in a different color or font size, and others using an entirely different font family.

On the other hand, paragraph formats—such as alignment and tab widths—are uniform for all text the BTextView displays. These properties can be set, but the setting always applies to the entire text.

Offsets

The BTextView locates particular characters in its text buffer by offsets from the beginning of the data. The offsets count bytes, not characters, and begin at 0. A single character is identified by the offset of the first byte of the character. A group of characters—the current selection, for example—is delimited by the offsets that bound its first and last characters; all characters beginning with the first offset up to, but not including, the last offset are part of the group.

For example, suppose the BTextView contains the following text in Unicode UTF-8 encoding,

The BeOS™ is . . .

and "BeOS™" is selected. `GetSelection()` would return 4 and 11 as the offsets that enclose the selection. The character "B" occupies the fourth byte of text and the space following the trademark symbol is the eleventh byte of text. The characters in "BeOS" are each encoded in one byte, but "™" takes up three bytes in UTF-8. Thus the five-character selection occupies 7 bytes (and offsets) of text.

Although offsets count bytes, they can also be thought of as designating positions between characters. The position at the beginning of the text is offset 0, the position between the space and the "B" in the example above is at offset 4, the position between the "™" and the space is at offset 11, and so on. Thus, even if no characters are selected, the insertion point (and location of the caret) can still be designated by an offset.

Most BTextView functions expect the offsets they're passed to mark positions between characters; the results are not defined if a character-internal offset is specified instead.

Graphics Primitives

The BTextView's mechanism for formatting and drawing text uses the graphics primitives it inherits from the BView class. However, it largely presents its own API for determining the appearance of the text it draws. You should not attempt to affect the BTextView by calling primitive BView functions like `MovePen()`, `SetFont()`, or `SetHighColor()`. Instead, use BTextView functions like `SetFontAndColor()` and let the object take care of formatting and drawing the text.

The one inherited function that can influence the BTextView is `SetViewColor()`. This function determines the background against which the text is drawn and the color that is used in antialiasing calculations.

Resizing

A BTextView can be made to resize itself to exactly fit the text that the user enters. This is sometimes appropriate for small one-line text fields. See the `MakeResizable()` function.

Shortcuts and Menu Items

When a BTextView is the focus view for its window, it responds to these standard keyboard shortcuts for cutting, copying, pasting, and selecting text:

- Command-x to cut text and copy it to the clipboard,
- Command-c to copy text to the clipboard without cutting it,
- Command-v to paste text taken from the clipboard, and
- Command-a to select all of the text in the BTextView.

These shortcuts work even in the absence of Cut, Copy, Paste, and Select All menu items; they're implemented by the BWindow for any view that might be the focus view. All the focus view has to do is cooperate, as a BTextView does, by handling the messages the shortcuts generate.

The only trick is to make sure that the menu items you set up are compatible with the shortcuts. Follow these guidelines if you put a menu with editing commands in a window that has a BTextView:

- Create Cut, Copy, Paste, and Select All menu items and assign them the Command-x, Command-c, Command-v, and Command-a shortcuts.

- Assign the items model `B_CUT`, `B_COPY`, `B_PASTE`, and `B_SELECT_ALL` messages. These messages don't need to contain any information (other than a `what` data member initialized to the proper constant).

- Target the messages to the BWindow's focus view (or directly to the BTextView). No changes to the BTextView are necessary. When it gets these messages, the BTextView calls its `Cut()`, `Copy()`, `Paste()`, and `SelectAll()` functions.

You can also set up menu items that trigger calls to other BTextView editing and layout functions. Simply create menu items like Align at Left that are targeted to the focus view of the window where the BTextView is located, or to the BTextView itself. The messages assigned to these items can be structured with whatever command constants and data entries you wish; the BTextView class imposes no constraints.

Then, in a class derived from BTextView, implement a `MessageReceived()` function that responds to messages posted from the menu items by calling BTextView functions like `SetAlignment()`. For example:

```
void myText::MessageReceived(BMessage *message)
{
    switch ( message->what ) {
    case ALIGN_AT_LEFT:
        SetAlignment(B_ALIGN_LEFT);
        break;
    case ALIGN_AT_RIGHT:
        SetAlignment(B_ALIGN_RIGHT);
        break;
    . . .
    default:
        BTextView::MessageReceived(message);
        break;
    }
}
```

The `MessageReceived()` function you implement should be sure to call BTextView's version of the function, which already handles B_CUT, B_COPY, B_PASTE, and B_SELECT_ALL messages.

Scripting Support

The BTextView class responds to the following scripting messages, though it doesn't give them a suite name:

Property name: "Text" for the text assigned to the BTextView
Specifiers: B_RANGE_SPECIFIER and B_REVERSE_RANGE_SPECIFIER
Messages: B_SET_PROPERTY and B_GET_PROPERTY
Data type: A null-terminated character string (B_STRING_TYPE)

Property name: "text_run_array" for character formats in a range of text
Specifiers: B_RANGE_SPECIFIER and B_REVERSE_RANGE_SPECIFIER
Messages: B_SET_PROPERTY and B_GET_PROPERTY
Data type: A text_run_array structure

Property name: "selection" for the text that's currently selected
Specifiers: B_DIRECT_SPECIFIER
Messages: B_SET_PROPERTY and B_GET_PROPERTY
Data type: int32 offsets to the beginning and end of the selection

The "index" in a specifier for the "Text" and "text_run_array" properties is a byte offset to the first byte of a character. The "range" similarly counts bytes, not characters.

The "range" for both B_RANGE_SPECIFIER and B_REVERSE_RANGE_SPECIFIER specifiers counts bytes from the "index" toward the end of the list—even if the index counts in reverse from the end of the list forward.

If a B_SET_PROPERTY message for the "Text" property lacks a "data" entry, the BTextView deletes the range of bytes specified. However, if "data" is provided, the BTextView inserts the number of bytes specified. In other words, for a deletion, the "range" entry in the specifier counts bytes in the BTextView beginning at the specified index; for an insertion the "range" entry counts bytes in the "data" entry beginning with the first byte.

See "Scripting" in Chapter 2 for more on scripting messages.

Hook Functions

AcceptsDrop()

> Determines whether a BMessage that's dragged to the BTextView has data that the object can insert; can be reimplemented to prevent the BTextView from accepting dropped text or to allow it to accept data it currently doesn't understand.

AcceptsPaste()

> Determines whether the BTextView can take data from the clipboard; can be reimplemented to prevent text from being pasted or to make the BTextView accept data it currently doesn't understand.

CanEndLine()

> Determines where a line can end; can be overridden to follow a different criterion than the default.

DeleteText()

> Deletes characters from the text; can be augmented to preview the deletions and accept or reject them before the text is removed from the display. This function is called to carry out all deletions.

FindWord()

> Finds the boundaries of a word when the user double-clicks; can be overridden to redefine what a word is or to provide a definition of a word for other languages.

InsertText()

> Inserts new characters into the text; can be augmented to preview the characters the user types, pastes, or drops and accept or reject them before they're added to the display. All insertions pass through this function.

Constructor and Destructor

BTextView()

BTextView(BRect *frame*, const char **name*, BRect *textRect*,
uint32 *resizingMode*, uint32 *flags*)
BTextView(BRect *frame*, const char **name*, BRect *textRect*,
const BFont **font*, const rgb_color **color*,
uint32 *resizingMode*, uint32 *flags*)
BTextView(BMessage **archive*)

Initializes the BTextView to the *frame* rectangle, stated in its eventual parent's coordinate system, assigns it an identifying *name*, sets its resizing behavior to *resizingMode* and its drawing behavior with *flags*. These four arguments—*frame*, *name*, *resizingMode*, and *flags*—are identical to those declared for the BView class and are passed to the BView constructor. The *frame*, *name*, and *resizingMode* arguments are passed to the BView class unchanged, but two flags are added to the *flags* argument—B_FRAME_EVENTS, so that the BTextView can reformat the text when it's resized, and B_PULSE_NEEDED, so that the caret marking the insertion point can "blink" in time with B_PULSE messages. Later, AttachedToWindow() will set the window's pulse rate to 500,000 microseconds.

The text rectangle, *textRect*, is stated in the BTextView's coordinate system. It determines where text in placed within the view's bounds rectangle:

- The first line of text is placed at the top of the text rectangle. As additional lines of text are entered into the view, the text grows downward and may actually extend beyond the bottom of the rectangle.

- The left and right sides of the text rectangle determine where lines of text are placed within the view. Lines can be aligned to either side of the rectangle, or they can be centered between the two sides. See the SetAlignment() function.

- When lines wrap on word boundaries, the width of the text rectangle determines the maximum length of a line; each line of text can be as long as the rectangle is wide. When word wrapping isn't turned on, lines can extend beyond the boundaries of the text rectangle. See the SetWordWrap() function.

The bottom of the text rectangle is ignored; it doesn't limit the amount of text the view can contain. The text can be limited by the number of characters, but not by the number of lines.

If a default *font* is provided, the BTextView will display its text in that font, unless another font is later set. Similarly, if a default *color* is specified, the text will be displayed in that color, unless the color is subsequently changed. If the *font* is NULL or not specified, the BTextView uses the system plain font, be_plain_font. If the *color* pointer is NULL or not specified, the text is drawn in black.

The constructor establishes the following default properties for a new BTextView:

- The text is selectable and editable. (See `MakeSelectable()` and `Make-Editable()`.)
- Multiple character formats are not permitted. (See `SetStylable()`.)
- The text is left-aligned. (See `SetAlignment()`.)
- The tab width is 28.0 coordinate units. (See `SetTabWidth()`.)
- Word wrapping is turned on. (See `SetWordWrap()`.)
- Automatic indenting is turned off. (See `SetAutoindent()`.)
- The maximum amount of data is permitted. (See `SetMaxBytes()`.)
- The view doesn't grow to accommodate more characters. (See `Make-Resizable()`.)
- All characters the user may type are acceptable. (See `DisallowChar()`.)

See also: `AttachedToWindow()`, `SetFontAndColor()`, the BView constructor

~BTextView()

virtual ~BTextView(void)

Frees the memory the BTextView allocated to hold the text and to store information about it.

Static Functions

FlattenRunArray(), UnflattenRunArray()

static void *FlattenRunArray(const text_run_array *runs, int32 *numBytes = NULL)

static text_run_array *UnflattenRunArray(const void *data, int32 *numBytes = NULL)

These functions flatten and unflatten a `text_run_array` structure so that it can be treated as an untyped stream of bytes. A `text_run_array` that's saved on-disk will be valid when the user reboots the machine only if it's saved as flat data. Both functions return pointers to memory they allocate (with `malloc()`). The caller is responsible for freeing the memory when it's no longer needed.

`FlattenRunArray()` flattens the *runs* text_run_array and returns the flat data. `UnflattenRunArray()` reconstructs a text_run_array from previously flattened *data* and returns a pointer to the structure.

If a *numBytes* argument is provided, both functions place the number of bytes they allocated for the data in the variable that *numBytes* refers to.

See also: `SetRunArray()`

Instantiate()

static BTextView ***Instantiate**(BMessage *archive)

Returns a new BTextView object, allocated by new and created by the version of the constructor that takes a BMessage archive. However, if the archive doesn't contain data for a BTextView object, the return value will be NULL.

See also: BArchivable::Instantiate(), Archive()

UnflattenRunArray()   see FlattenRunArray()

Member Functions

AcceptsDrop(), AcceptsPaste()

virtual bool **AcceptsDrop**(const BMessage *message)

virtual bool **AcceptsPaste**(BClipboard *clipboard)

These functions test a dragged message and a clipboard for data that can be inserted into the text. As implemented, they return true if the BTextView is editable and the message or clipboard contains data they recognize as text—B_MIME_TYPE data stored under the name "text/plain". They return false if the BTextView either is not editable or they can't find "text/plain" data in the message or clipboard. A return of false aborts the drag-and-drop and paste operations; nothing will be inserted into the text unless the return value is true.

AcceptsDrop() is called when the user drags a message into the text view and again when the message is dropped. AcceptsPaste() is called when a B_PASTE message is received. They can be augmented by derived classes to expand or restrict the range of data formats the object recognizes. Note, however, that simply modifying these functions is not enough to teach the BTextView about data it doesn't currently understand. You'll also need to augment the MessageReceived() and Paste() functions to take the data from the message and clipboard and insert it.

See also: Paste(), MessageReceived(), the BClipboard and BMessage classes in the Application Kit

Alignment()   see SetAlignment()

AllowChar()   see DisallowChar()

Archive()

> virtual status_t **Archive**(BMessage *archive*, bool *deep* = true) const

Calls the inherited version of `Archive()`, then adds the BTextView's text to the BMessage *archive* along with all current settings.

See also: `BArchivable::Archive()`, `Instantiate()` static function

AttachedToWindow()

> virtual void **AttachedToWindow**(void)

Completes the initialization of the BTextView object after it becomes attached to a window. This function sets up the object so that it can correctly format text and display it. Among other things, it sets the drawing mode to `B_OP_COPY`. If the BTextView is targeted by scroll bars, it adjusts them so that they're accurately set up for scrolling the text.

Because the BTextView uses pulses to animate (or "blink") the caret, the vertical line that marks the current insertion point, this function also enables pulsing in the window and fixes the pulse rate at 2 per second (once every 500,000 microseconds).

`AttachedToWindow()` is called for you when the BTextView becomes part a window's view hierarchy; you shouldn't call it yourself, though you can override it. A function that's implemented by a derived class should begin by incorporating the BTextView version:

```
void MyText::AttachedToWindow()
{
    BTextView::AttachedToWindow()
    . . .
}
```

If it doesn't, the BTextView won't be able to properly display the text.

See also: `BView::AttachedToWindow()`, `SetFontName()`

ByteAt()   *see Text()*

CanEndLine()

> virtual bool **CanEndLine**(int32 *offset*)

Returns `true` if the character at *offset* can be the last character in a line of text, and `false` if not. Sometimes this depends on whether the next character (if there is one) can begin a line. This function is called as the BTextView figures out where to break lines, but only if word wrapping is turned on.

As implemented, `CanEndLine()` allows the following ASCII characters to end a line regardless of the context:

B_SPACE	=	<	/	&
B_TAB	+	>	\	*
B_ENTER	−	^	|	'\0'

The default implementation also understands the line-ending conventions for Chinese and Japanese. Because these languages are written without the spaces that typically end lines in other languages, lines can potentially break anywhere. However, certain characters are prohibited from ending a line and others are prohibited from beginning a new line. `CanEndLine()` prevents lines from ending either on a prohibited ending character or on the character before a prohibited beginning character.

Derived classes can override this function to apply different criteria for where lines end, possibly looking at the context of the *offset* character. You can also augment the current implementation so that it understands the conventions for other languages.

If you override this function to look to the left or right of the character at *offset*, be sure to check that you haven't stepped beyond the range of the text. For example, this version of the function makes sure that the first hyphen of a pair doesn't break a line:

```
bool MyTextView::CanEndLine(int32 offset)
{
    if ( ByteAt[offset] == '-' ) {
        if ( TextLength() - offset > 1 ) {
            if ( ByteAt[offset + 1] == '-' )
                return false;
        }
    }
    return BTextView::CanEndLine(offset);
}
```

See also: `SetWordWrap()`

ColorSpace()   *see SetColorSpace()*

Copy()   *see Cut()*

CountLines()   *see GoToLine()*

CurrentLine()   *see GoToLine()*

Cut(), Copy(), Paste()

virtual void **Cut**(BClipboard *clipboard*)

virtual void **Copy**(BClipboard *clipboard*)

virtual void **Paste**(BClipboard *clipboard*)

These functions implement the standard cut, copy, and paste editing commands. `Cut()` and `Copy()` both copy the current selection to the specified *clipboard*; `Cut()` also deletes the text from the BTextView and removes it from the display. The text is entered in the clipboard as `B_MIME_TYPE` data under the name "text/plain". `Paste()` looks in the *clipboard* for just this type of data and pastes it into the text—but only if `AcceptsPaste()` returns `true`. The new text replaces the current selection, or is placed at the site of the current insertion point.

If the BTextView supports multiple character formats, `Cut()` and `Copy()` also place a `text_run_array` structure describing the formats of the copied text in the clipboard—as `B_MIME_TYPE` data under the name "application/x-vnd.Be-text_run_array". If the BTextView that takes text from the clipboard supports multiple formats, `Paste()` looks for the `text_run_array` in the clipboard and sets the formats of the pasted text accordingly.

In most cases, the *clipboard* argument will be identical to the global `be_clipboard` object.

See also: `AcceptsPaste()`, "Shortcuts and Menu Items" in the overview

Delete()   *see Insert()*

DeleteText()   *see InsertText()*

DetachedFromWindow()

virtual void **DetachedFromWindow**(void)

Resets the cursor to the standard hand image (`B_HAND_CURSOR`) if it's above the BTextView when the BTextView is removed from the window.

See also: `BView::DetachedFromWindow()`

DisallowChar(), AllowChar()

void **DisallowChar**(uint32 *aChar*)

void **AllowChar**(uint32 *aChar*)

These functions inform the BTextView whether the user should be allowed to enter *aChar* into the text. By default, all characters are allowed. Call `DisallowChar()` for each character you want to prevent the BTextView from accepting, preferably when first setting up the object. Although declared as `uint32`, *aChar* must be a character encoded in a single byte; it can't be a 16-bit Unicode value or a multibyte UTF-8 string.

`AllowChar()` reverses the effect of `DisallowChar()`.

Alternatively, and for more control over the context in which characters are accepted or rejected, you can implement an `InsertText()` function for the BTextView. `InsertText()` is called for all insertions, including each character the user types, all text the user drags to the BTextView, and all attempts to paste from the clipboard.

See also: `AcceptsChar()`

DoesAutoindent()   *see SetAutoindent()*

DoesWordWrap()   *see SetWordWrap()*

Draw()

   virtual void **Draw**(BRect *updateRect*)

Draws the text on-screen. The Interface Kit calls this function for you whenever the text display needs to be updated—for example, whenever the user edits the text, enters new characters, or scrolls the contents of the BTextView.

See also: `BView::Draw()`

FindWord()

   virtual void **FindWord**(int32 *offset*, int32 **start*, int32 **finish*)

Looks for a sequence of characters that qualifies as a word—that is, a sequence that the user can double-click to select—that includes the character at *offset*. This function places the offset of the word's first character in the variable that *start* refers to and the offset following the last character in the word in the variable that *finish* refers to. If the *offset* character can't be part of a word, the *start* and *finish* offsets will be identical.

As implemented, this function allows the user to select a group of similar characters with a double-click. For example, in the following line of malformed text,

`"You what!!?"`

it would allow the user to select the words "You" and "what," the group of spaces between the words, and the group of punctuation marks at the end.

The function also defines similar groups of Japanese characters that can be selected together.

FrameResized()

virtual void **FrameResized**(float *width*, float *height*)

Overrides the BView version of this function to reset the ranges of the BTextView's scroll bars and to update the sizes of their proportional knobs whenever the size of the BTextView changes.

See also: `BView::FrameResized()`

GetSelection()

void **GetSelection**(int32 **start*, int32 **finish*)

Provides the current selection by writing the offset before the first selected character into the variable referred to by *start* and the offset after the last selected character into the variable referred to by *finish*. If no characters are selected, both offsets will record the position of the current insertion point.

If the text isn't selectable, both offsets will be 0.

See also: `Select()`

GetText()   *see Text()*

GetTextRegion()

void **GetTextRegion**(int32 *start*, int32 *finish*, BRegion **region*) const

Calculates the region where the run of characters beginning at the *start* offset and ending at the *finish* offset would be displayed within the BTextView's coordinate system, and modifies the BRegion object passed as the third argument, *region*, so that it represents that region.

See also: `TextHeight()`

GoToLine(), CountLines(), CurrentLine()

void **GoToLine**(int32 *index*)

int32 **CurrentLine**(void) const

int32 **CountLines**(void) const

`GoToLine()` moves the insertion point to the beginning of the line at *index*. The first line has an index of 0, the second line an index of 1, and so on. If the *index* is out-of-range, the insertion point is moved to the beginning of the line with the nearest in-range index—that is, to either the first or the last line.

CurrentLine() returns the index of the line where the first character of the selection—or the character following the insertion point—is currently located.

CountLines() returns how many lines of text the BTextView currently contains.

Like other functions that change the selection, GoToLine() doesn't automatically scroll the display to make the new selection visible. Call ScrollToSelection() to be sure that the user can see the start of the selection.

See also: ScrollToSelection()

Highlight()

> inline void **Highlight**(int32 *start*, int32 *finish*)

Highlights (or unhighlights) the characters between the *start* and *finish* offsets. This is the function that the BTextView calls to highlight and unhighlight the current selection. You don't need to call it yourself for this purpose. It's in the public API just in case you may need to highlight a range of text in some other circumstance.

If the text is not currently highlighted, this function highlights it. But if the text is already highlighted, it unhighlights it. If you highlight some text, be sure to unhighlight it before the next editorial change; the BTextView will not do it for you.

See also: Select(), TextRegion()

Insert(), Delete()

> void **Insert**(const char **text*, const text_run_array **runs* = NULL)
> void **Insert**(const char **text*, int32 *length*, const text_run_array **runs* = NULL)
> void **Insert**(int32 *offset*, const char **text*, int32 *length*,
>   const text_run_array **runs* = NULL)
>
> void **Delete**(void)
> void **Delete**(int32 *start*, int32 *finish*)

Insert() adds *length* bytes of *text* to the BTextView—or if a *length* isn't specified, all the characters of the *text* string up to the null character that terminates it. The text is inserted at *offset*—or at the beginning of the current selection if an *offset* isn't specified. The current selection is not deleted and the insertion is not selected.

The inserted characters are displayed in the fonts and colors specified in the accompanying *runs* array, provided the BTextView allows multiple character formats. If multiple formats aren't allowed, the *runs* array is ignored. If multiple formats are allowed but a *runs* array isn't provided, the insertion is displayed in the font and color in force at the point of insertion. This generally means the font and color of the first character of the selection, or of the character immediately preceding the *offset* character.

Offsets in the *runs* array should describe the text being inserted; in other words, the first offset should be 0. See `SetRunArray()` for a description of the `text_run_array` structure.

`Insert()` doesn't assume responsibility for the *text* data or the *runs* array. It copies the information it needs.

`Delete()` removes the characters bounded by the *start* and *finish* offsets from the display and deletes them from the BTextView's text, without copying them to the clipboard. If the *start* and *finish* offsets are the same, nothing is deleted. If offsets are not provided, `Delete()` deletes the current selection.

See also: `SetText()`, `Cut()`, `SetRunArray()`

InsertText(), DeleteText()

protected:

> virtual void **InsertText**(const char *text, int32 *length*, int32 *offset*,
> > text_run_array *runs)

> virtual void **DeleteText**(int32 *start*, int32 *finish*)

These protected functions are the vehicles through which the BTextView performs every insertion and deletion of text (with one exception). They can be augmented in derived classes to take note of pending editorial changes to the text and perhaps modify them or prevent them from taking place. For example, a derived class might implement `InsertText()` to screen incoming characters for `B_ENTER` to prevent the user from typing more than one line of text.

You can implement these two functions to be notified of pending insertions and deletions, but do *not* call them to insert and delete text; call `Insert()` and `Delete()` instead.

`InsertText()` adds *length* bytes of *text* to the BTextView, inserting it at *offset* within the text buffer. The font and color of the inserted characters may be described by an accompanying *runs* array. If the BTextView doesn't support multiple character formats, the *runs* array is ignored. If multiple formats are supported but the *runs* array is NULL, the text is displayed in the font and color of the character preceding *offset* (or of the first character, if *offset* is 0).

The offsets in the *runs* data structure are relative to the inserted text; that is, the first offset in the array is 0, not *offset*.

`InsertText()` is called for every insertion, except one. The exception occurs when `SetText()` takes text from a file; in this case the text goes directly from the file to the BTextView; it's not stored in a temporary buffer while `InsertText()` is called.

`DeleteText()` removes the text bounded by the *start* and *finish* offsets. It fails if the offsets don't differ, or if the *finish* offset isn't greater than the *start* offset. This function is called for every deletion, without exception.

See also: `Insert()`, `Delete()`

IsEditable()   *see MakeEditable()*

IsSelectable()   *see MakeSelectable()*

KeyDown()

> virtual void **KeyDown**(const char **bytes*, int32 *numBytes*)

Enters text at the current selection in response to the user's typing. This function is called from the window's message loop for every report of a key-down event—typically once for every character the user types. However, it does nothing unless the BTextView is the focus view and the text it contains is editable.

If the character encoded in the *bytes* string is an editing instruction, `KeyDown()` takes the appropriate action:

- If the character is from one of the arrow keys (B_UP_ARROW, B_LEFT_ARROW, B_DOWN_ARROW, or B_RIGHT_ARROW), it extends the selection or moves the insertion point in the appropriate direction, depending on the modifiers

- If the character is B_BACKSPACE or B_DELETE, it deletes the current selection—or the character preceding or following the current insertion point.

- If the character comes from one of the paging keys (B_HOME, B_END, B_PAGE_UP, or B_PAGE_DOWN), it scrolls the display.

Otherwise, it checks whether the character was registered as unacceptable (by `DisallowChar()`). If not disallowed, it calls the `InsertText()` hook function to enter the character into the text and display it. Derived classes can preview about-to-be-inserted characters by overriding `InsertText()`.

See also: `BView::KeyDown()`, `InsertText()`, `DisallowChar()`

LineAt(), PointAt(), OffsetAt()

> int32 **LineAt**(int32 *offset*) const
> int32 **LIneAt**(BPoint *point*) const

BPoint **PointAt**(int32 *offset*, float **height* = NULL) const

int32 **OffsetAt**(BPoint *point*) const
int32 **OffsetAt**(int32 *index*) const

These functions translate between coordinate values, text offsets, and line indices. `LineAt()` returns the index of the line containing the character at *offset* in the text, or the line located at the specified *point* in the BTextView's coordinate system. Line indices begin at 0.

`PointAt()` returns the coordinate location of the character at *offset*. The point is the left top corner of a rectangle enclosing the character and is stated in the BTextView's coordinate system. The *x*-coordinate of the point is the position on the baseline where the character is (or would be) drawn; its *y*-coordinate is the top of the line where the *offset* character is located. If a *height* argument is provided, `PointAt()` returns the height of the line by reference.

`OffsetAt()` returns the offset to the character that begins the *index* line, or to the character displayed at *point*.

LineHeight(), TextHeight()

float **LineHeight**(int32 *index* = 0) const

float **TextHeight**(int32 *firstIndex*, int32 *lastIndex*) const

`LineHeight()` returns the height of the line of text at *index*, or the first line if an index isn't specified. Line indices begin at 0. The height is stated in coordinate units and depends on the font. It's the sum of how far characters can ascend above and descend below the baseline, plus the amount of leading that separates lines. If more than one font is used on the line, the ascent is taken from the tallest font and the descent and leading from the deepest.

`TextHeight()` returns the height of the set of lines from *firstIndex* through *lastIndex*.

Both functions reset out-of-range indices to be in-range—that is, to the index of the first or last line.

See also: `BFont::GetHeight()`

LineWidth()

float **LineWidth**(int32 *index* = 0) const

Returns the width of the line at *index*—or, if no index is given, the width of the first line. The value returned is the sum of the widths (in coordinate units) of all the characters in the line, from the first through the last, including tabs and spaces. Line indices begin at 0.

If the *index* passed is out-of-range, it's reinterpreted to be the nearest in-range index—that is, as the index to the first or the last line.

See also: `BFont::StringWidth()`

MakeEditable(), IsEditable()

> void **MakeEditable**(bool *flag* = true)
>
> bool **IsEditable**(void) const

The first of these functions sets whether the user can edit the text displayed by the BTextView; the second returns whether or not the text is currently editable. Text is editable by default.

When text is editable but not selectable, the user can enter and delete text at the insertion point, but can't select text to make changes to more than one character at a time.

See also: `MakeSelectable()`

MakeFocus()

> virtual void **MakeFocus**(bool *flag* = true)

Overrides the BView version of `MakeFocus()` to highlight the current selection when the BTextView becomes the focus view (when *flag* is `true`) and to unhighlight it when the BTextView no longer is the focus view (when *flag* is `false`). However, the current selection is highlighted only if the BTextView's window is the current active window.

This function is called for you whenever the user's actions make the BTextView become the focus view, or force it to give up that status.

See also: `BView::MakeFocus()`, `MouseDown()`

MakeResizable(), IsResizable()

> void **MakeResizable**(bool *resizable*, BView **containerView* = NULL)
>
> bool **IsResizable**(void) const

`MakeResizable()` gives the BTextView the ability to automatically resize itself to fit its contents if the *resizable* flag is `true`, and takes away that ability if the flag is `false`. `IsResizable()` returns whether the BTextView is currently resizable.

The frame rectangle and text rectangle of a resizable BTextView automatically grow and shrink to exactly enclose all the characters entered by the user. The object should display just a single line of text (the resizing is horizontal); if the *resizable* flag is `true`, `MakeResizable()` turns off line wrapping. The text can be aligned to the left, right, or center of the text rectangle.

The *containerView* is a view that draws a border around the text (like a BScrollView object) and is the parent of the BTextView; it's the view that's resized to fit the text. The BTextView's resizing mode should be such that it will be resized in tandem with the container (for example, `B_FOLLOW_LEFT_RIGHT` or `B_FOLLOW_ALL_SIDES`). However, if the *containerView* is `NULL`, as it is by default, the BTextView itself is resized to fit the text.

If the *resizable* flag is `false`, the *containerView* argument is ignored.

This resizing mechanism is an alternative to the automatic resizing behavior provided in the BView class. It triggers resizing on the user's entry of text, not on a change in the parent view's size. The two schemes are incompatible; the container view (or the BTextView, if there is no container) should not automatically resize itself when its parent is resized.

See also: `SetAlignment()`

MakeSelectable(), IsSelectable()

> void **MakeSelectable**(bool *flag* = true)
>
> bool **IsSelectable**(void) const

The first of these functions sets whether it's possible for the user to select text displayed by the BTextView; the second returns whether or not the text is currently selectable. Text is selectable by default.

When text is selectable but not editable, the user can select one or more characters to copy to the clipboard, but can't position the insertion point (an empty selection), enter characters from the keyboard, or paste new text into the view.

See also: `MakeEditable()`

MaxBytes()   *see SetMaxBytes()*

MessageReceived()

> virtual void **MessageReceived**(BMessage **message*)

Augments the BView version of `MessageReceived()` to handle scripting requests, dropped data, and four editing messages—`B_CUT`, `B_COPY`, `B_PASTE`, and `B_SELECT_ALL`.

If the *message* was dragged and dropped on the BTextView and it contains `B_MIME_TYPE` data under the name "text/plain", this function inserts the new text at the point where it was dropped—but only if `AcceptsDrop()` returns `true` for the *message*.

This function handles `B_CUT`, `B_COPY`, `B_PASTE`, and `B_SELECT_ALL` messages by calling the `Cut()`, `Copy()`, `Paste()`, and `SelectAll()` functions. A BTextView will get these messages, even if the application doesn't send them, when it's the focus view and the user uses the Command-*x*, Command-*c*, Command-*v*, and Command-*a* shortcuts. See "Shortcuts and Menu Items" in the class overview for information on how to set up compatible Cut, Copy, Paste, and Select All menu items.

To inherit this functionality, `MessageReceived()` functions implemented by derived classes should be sure to call the BTextView version.

See also: `BView::MessageReceived()`, `AcceptsPaste()`, `BInvoker::SetMessage()`, `BInvoker::SetTarget()`, `InsertText()`

MouseDown()

virtual void **MouseDown**(BPoint *point*)

Selects text, drags text, and positions the insertion point in response to the user's mouse actions. If the BTextView isn't already the focus view for its window, this function calls `MakeFocus()` to make it the focus view.

`MouseDown()` is called for each mouse-down event that occurs inside the BTextView's frame rectangle.

See also: `BView::MouseDown()`, `MakeFocus()`

MouseMoved()

virtual void **MouseMoved**(BPoint *point*, uint32 *transit*, BMessage **message*)

Responds to `B_MOUSE_MOVED` messages by changing the cursor to the standard I-beam image for editing text whenever the cursor enters the view and by resetting it to the standard hand image when the cursor exits the view. The cursor is changed to an I-beam for text that is selectable or editable, but only if the BTextView is the current focus view in the active window. However, when the cursor moves over the current selection, this function changes it from the I-beam back to the standard hand image. This is done to indicate that it's possible to drag and drop the current selection.

If a *message* is being dragged to the BTextView, this function tests it see whether it contains textual data and tracks it to its destination.

See also: `BView::MouseMoved()`, `AcceptsDrop()`

OffsetAt()   *see LineAt()*

PointAt()   *see LineAt()*

Paste()   *see Cut()*

Pulse()

   virtual void **Pulse**(void)

Turns the caret marking the current insertion point on and off when the BTextView is the focus view in the active window. `Pulse()` is called by the system at regular intervals.

This function is first declared in the BView class.

See also: `BView::Pulse()`

ResolveSpecifier()

   virtual BHandler ***ResolveSpecifier**(BMessage **message*, int32 *index*,
                 BMessage **specifier*, int32 *command*, const char **property*)

Resolves specifiers for the "Text", "text_run_array", and "selection" properties. See "Scripting Support" in the class overview and "Scripting" in Chapter 2 for more information.

See also: `BHandler::ResolveSpecifier()`

ScrollToOffset(), ScrollToSelection()

   virtual void **ScrollToOffset**(int32 *offset*)

   void **ScrollToSelection**(void)

These functions scroll the text so that the character at *offset*—or the character that begins the current selection—is within the visible region of the view. If the BTextView is equipped with scroll bars, the BScrollBar objects are informed so they can update themselves.

See also: `BView::ScrollTo()`

Select()

virtual void **Select**(int32 *start*, int32 *finish*)

Selects the characters from *start* up to *finish*, where *start* and *finish* are offsets into the BTextView's text. If *start* and *finish* are the same, the selection will be empty (an insertion point). See "Offsets" in the class overview for a discussion of the constraints on the offset arguments.

Normally, the selection is changed by the user. This function provides a way to change it programmatically.

If the BTextView is the current focus view in the active window, `Select()` highlights the new selection (or displays a blinking caret at the insertion point). However, it doesn't automatically scroll the contents of the BTextView to make the new selection visible. Call `ScrollToSelection()` to be sure that the user can see the start of the selection.

See also: `Text()`, `GetSelection()`, `ScrollToSelection()`, `GoToLine()`, `MouseDown()`

SelectAll()

void **SelectAll**(void)

Selects the entire text of the BTextView, and highlights it if the BTextView is the current focus view in the active window.

See also: `Select()`

SetAlignment(), Alignment()

void **SetAlignment**(alignment *where*)

alignment **Alignment**(void) const

These functions set the way text is aligned within the text rectangle and return the current alignment. Three settings are possible:

`B_ALIGN_LEFT`	Each line is aligned at the left boundary of the text rectangle.
`B_ALIGN_RIGHT`	Each line is aligned at the right boundary of the text rectangle.
`B_ALIGN_CENTER`	Each line is centered between the left and right boundaries of the text rectangle.

The default is `B_ALIGN_LEFT`.

SetAutoindent(), DoesAutoindent()

> void **SetAutoindent**(bool *flag*)

> bool **DoesAutoindent**(void) const

These functions set and return whether a new line of text is automatically indented the same as the preceding line. When set to `true` and the user types Return at the end of a line that begins with tabs or spaces, the new line will automatically indent past those tabs and spaces to the position of the first visible character.

The default value is `false`.

SetColorSpace(), ColorSpace()

> void **SetColorSpace**(color_space *space*)

> color_space **ColorSpace**(void) const

These functions set and return the color space of the offscreen bitmap that buffers the drawing the BTextView does. The default color space is `B_COLOR_8_BIT`.

See also: the BBitmap class

SetFontAndColor(), GetFontAndColor()

> void **SetFontAndColor**(int32 *start*, int32 *finish*,
>   const BFont **font*, uint32 *properties* = B_FONT_ALL,
>   rgb_color **color* = NULL)
> void **SetFontAndColor**(const BFont **font*, uint32 *properties* = B_FONT_ALL,
>   rgb_color **color* = NULL)

> void **GetFontAndColor**(int32 *offset*, BFont **font*, rgb_color **color* = NULL) const
> void **GetFontAndColor**(BFont **font*, uint32 **sameProperties*,
>   rgb_color **color* = NULL, bool **sameColor* = NULL) const

These functions set and get the font and color used to display the text. If the BTextView supports multiple character formats, `SetFontAndColor()` sets the font and color of the characters bounded by the *start* and *finish* offsets. If no offsets are given, it sets the font and color of the current selection. However, if multiple character formats are not supported, `SetFontAndColor()` ignores the offsets and formats the entire text.

`SetFontAndColor()` works like BView's `SetFont()` function. It sets the font to the attributes of the *font* BFont object that are enumerated by the *properties* mask. The mask is formed by combining the following constants:

```
B_FONT_FAMILY_AND_STYLE

B_FONT_SIZE

B_FONT_SHEAR

B_FONT_ROTATION

B_FONT_SPACING

B_FONT_ENCODING

B_FONT_FACE

B_FONT_FLAGS
```

In addition, **B_FONT_ALL** is a shorthand for all properties of the specified *font*. However, the BTextView modifies the font to ensure that:

- Characters are not rotated.
- Antialiasing is not disabled.
- The spacing mode is **B_BITMAP_SPACING**.
- The character encoding is UTF-8 (**B_UNICODE_UTF8**).

If the *font* argument is **NULL**, the font is not set and the *properties* mask is ignored.

The color of the characters is set by a pointer to an **rgb_color** structure. If the pointer is **NULL**, as it is by default, the color is not set.

GetFontAndColor() gets the font and color used to display the character at *offset*. It modifies the *font* BFont object and the *color* **rgb_color** structure so that they describe the font and color of the character.

If an *offset* isn't specified, GetFontAndColor() looks at the current selection. It provides a font and color description of the first character of the selection—or the character at the insertion point if the selection is empty. It also modifies that variable that the *sameProperties* argument refers to so that it lists all the font properties that are uniform for all characters in the selection. Similarly, it indicates, in the variable that *sameColor* refers to, whether all the characters in the selection are displayed in the same color.

See also: BView::SetFont()

SetMaxBytes(), MaxBytes()

> void **SetMaxBytes**(int32 *max*)

> int32 **MaxBytes**(void) const

These functions set and return the maximum number of bytes that the BTextView can accept. The default is the maximum number of bytes that can be designated by a signed 32-bit integer, a number sufficiently large to accommodate all uses of a

BTextView. Use this function only if you need to restrict the number of characters that the user can enter in a text field.

Note that these functions count bytes, not characters.

SetRunArray(), RunArray()

> void **SetRunArray**(int32 *start*, int32 *finish*, const text_run_array **runs*)

> text_run_array ****RunArray**(int32 *start*, int32 *finish*, int32 **length* = NULL)

These functions set and return the font and color formats of all the characters bounded by the *start* and *finish* offsets. The formats are described by a `text_run_array` structure, which has the following fields:

int32 `count`
> The number of `text_run` structures in the array.

text_run `runs[1]`
> A structure describing the font and color formats in effect at a particular offset in the BTextView's text.

The `text_run` structure describes a run of characters that share the same font and color formats. It has three fields:

int32 `offset`
> An offset to the first byte of a character in the text buffer. The text run begins with this character; it continues until another run begins.

BFont `font`
> The font that's used to display the run of characters beginning at the specified offset.

rgb_color `color`
> The color that's used to display the run of characters beginning at the specified offset.

The first offset of the first `text_run` in the array passed to `SetRunArray()` should be 0; the array returned by `RunArray()` also begins at offset 0.

If the BTextView doesn't support multiple character formats, `SetRunArray()` ignores the *start* and *finish* offsets and sets the entire text to the font and color of the first `text_run` in the array. Similarly, `RunArray()` returns a `text_run_array` with one `text_run` describing the entire text.

`RunArray()` returns a pointer to memory that it allocated (using `malloc()`). It puts the number of bytes that it allocated in the variable that the *length* argument points to. Although `RunArray()` allocated the memory, the caller is responsible for freeing it when the returned `text_run_array` is no longer needed.

SetRunArray() doesn't assume responsibility for the *runs* data it's passed; it's up to the caller to free it.

See also: SetFontAndColor()

SetStylable(), IsStylable()

> void **SetStylable**(bool *stylable*)
>
> bool **IsStylable**(void) const

SetStylable() sets whether the BTextView permits multiple character formats. If the *stylable* flag is true, the functions that set the font and color of the text can apply to particular characters in the text buffer. If the flag is false, those functions apply only to the entire text. When SetStylable() is called to turn off support for multiple formats, all the text is reformatted in the font and color of the first character.

IsStylable() returns whether multiple formats are permitted. By default, they're not.

See also: SetFontAndColor(), SetRunArray()

SetTabWidth(), TabWidth()

> void **SetTabWidth**(float *width*)
>
> float **TabWidth**(void) const

These functions set the distance between tab stops to *width* coordinate units and return the current tab width. Tabs cannot be removed nor can they be individually set; all tabs have a uniform width. The default tab width is 28.0 coordinate units.

SetText()

> void **SetText**(const char **text*, int32 *length*, const text_run_array **runs* = NULL)
> void **SetText**(const char **text*, const text_run_array **runs* = NULL)
> void **SetText**(BFile **file*, int32 *offset*, int32 *length*,
>   const text_run_array **runs* = NULL)

Removes any text currently in the BTextView and copies new text from a *text* buffer or from a *file* to replace it. This function copies *length* bytes of text from the buffer—or all the bytes in the buffer, up to the null character, if a *length* isn't specified. Or it copies *length* bytes from the *file* beginning at the *offset* byte. If the *text* or *file* is NULL or *length* is 0, it empties the BTextView without replacing the text.

If a *runs* `text_run_array` is provided, it will be used to set the font and color formats of the new text—provided that the BTextView permits multiple character formats. If not, the *runs* array is ignored.

The BTextView doesn't assume ownership of the *text* buffer, the *file*, or the *runs* array; you can delete them when `SetText()` returns.

Text taken from a file is inserted directly into the text, bypassing the `InsertText()` function. In other words, you won't receive an `InsertText()` notification for text taken from a file.

This function is typically used to set the text initially displayed in the view. If the BTextView is already attached to a window, it's updated to show its new contents.

See also: `Text()`, `TextLength()`

SetTextRect(), TextRect()

void **SetTextRect**(BRect *rect*)

BRect **TextRect**(void) const

`SetTextRect()` makes *rect* the BTextView's text rectangle—the rectangle that locates where text is placed within the view. This replaces the text rectangle originally set in the BTextView constructor. The layout of the text is recalculated to fit the new rectangle, and the text is redisplayed.

`TextRect()` returns the current text rectangle.

See also: the BTextView constructor

SetWordWrap(), DoesWordWrap()

void **SetWordWrap**(bool *flag*)

bool **DoesWordWrap**(void) const

These functions set and return whether the BTextView wraps lines on word boundaries, dropping entire words that don't fit at the end of a line to the next line. When word wrapping is turned on, the BTextView calls `CanEndLine()` to determine exactly where a line can break. If word wrapping is off, lines break only on a newline character (where the user types Return).

By default, word wrapping is turned on (`DoesWordWrap()` returns `true`).

See also: `SetTextRect()`, `CanEndLine()`

TabWidth()   *see SetTabWidth()*

Text(), GetText(), ByteAt()

const char *__Text__(void) const

void __GetText__(int32 *offset,* int32 *length,* char *__*buffer__*) const

uchar __ByteAt__(int32 *offset*) const

These functions reveal the text contained in the BTextView.

`Text()` returns a pointer to the text, which may be a pointer to an empty string if the BTextView is empty. The returned pointer can be used to read the text, but not to alter it (use `SetText()`, `Insert()`, `Delete()`, and other BTextView functions to do that).

`GetText()` copies up to *length* bytes of the text into *buffer,* beginning with the byte at *offset,* and adds a null terminator ("\0"). Fewer than *length* bytes are copied if there aren't that many between the specified *offset* and the end of the text. This function doesn't make any attempt to ensure that only full character specifications are copied; it's up to the caller to make sure that a character begins at *offset* and that the last byte copied isn't in the middle of a multibyte character. The results won't be reliable if the *offset* is out-of-range.

`ByteAt()` returns the byte located at *offset.* The offset doesn't have to be to the first byte of a character.

The pointer that `Text()` returns is to the BTextView's internal representation of the text. When it returns, the text string is guaranteed to be null-terminated and without gaps. However, the BTextView may have had to manipulate the text to get it in that condition. Therefore, there may be a performance price to pay if `Text()` is called frequently. If you're going to copy the text, it's more efficient to have `GetText()` do it for you. If you're going to index into the text, it may be more efficient to call `ByteAt()`.

The pointer that `Text()` returns may no longer be valid after the user or the program next changes the text. Even if valid, the string may no longer be null-terminated and gaps may appear.

See also: `TextLength()`

TextHeight() *see LineHeight()*

TextLength()

int32 __TextLength__(void) const

Returns the number of bytes of text data the BTextView currently contains—the number of bytes in the string that `Text()` returns (not counting the null terminator).

See also: `Text()`, `SetMaxBytes()`

TextRect()   *see SetTextRect()*

WindowActivated()

> virtual void **WindowActivated**(bool *flag*)

Highlights the current selection when the BTextView's window becomes the active window (when *flag* is `true`)—provided that the BTextView is the current focus view—and removes the highlighting when the window ceases to be the active window (when *flag* is `false`).

If the current selection is empty (if it's an insertion point), it's highlighted by turning the caret on and off (blinking it).

The Interface Kit calls this function for you whenever the BTextView's window becomes the active window or it loses that status.

See also: `BView::WindowActivated()`, `MakeFocus()`

BView

> ***Derived from:***   public BHandler
>
> ***Declared in:***   be/interface/View.h
>
> ***Library:***   libbe.so

Overview

BView objects are the agents for drawing and message handling within windows. Each object sets up and takes responsibility for a particular *view*, a rectangular area that's associated with at most one window at a time. The object draws within the view rectangle and responds to reports of events elicited by the images drawn.

Classes derived from BView implement the actual functions that draw and handle messages; BView merely provides the framework. For example, a BTextView object draws and edits text in response to the user's activity on the keyboard and mouse. A BButton draws the image of a button on-screen and responds when the button is clicked. BTextView and BButton inherit from the BView class—as do most classes in the Interface Kit.

Views and Windows

For a BView to do its work, you must attach it to a window. The views in a window are arranged in a hierarchy—there can be views within views—with those that are most directly responsible for drawing and message handling located at the terminal branches of the hierarchy and those that contain and organize other views situated closer to its trunk and root. A BView begins life unattached. You can add it to a hierarchy by calling the AddChild() function of the BWindow or of another BView.

Within the hierarchy, a BView object plays two roles:

• It's a BHandler for messages delivered to the window thread. BViews implement the functions that respond to the most common system messages—including those that report keyboard and mouse events. They can also be targeted to handle application-defined messages that affect what the view displays.

• It's an agent for drawing. Adding a BView to a window gives it an independent graphics environment. A BView draws on the initiative of the BWindow and the Application Server, whenever they determine that the appearance of any part of the view rectangle needs to be "updated." It also draws on its own initiative in response to events.

The relationship of BViews to BWindows and the framework for drawing and responding to the user were discussed in the opening sections of this chapter. The concepts and terminology presented there are assumed in this class description.

BViews can also be called upon to create bitmap images. See the BBitmap class for details.

Locking the Window

If a BView is attached to a window, any operation that affects the view might also affect the window and the BView's shadow counterpart in the Application Server. For this reason, any code that calls a BView function should first lock the window—so that one thread can't modify essential data structures while another thread is using them. A window can be locked by only one thread at a time.

Locking is accomplished through the BLooper Lock() and Unlock() functions inherited by BWindow:

```
if ( Window()->Lock() ) {
    . . .
    Window()->Unlock();
}
```

Before they do anything else, almost all BView functions check to be sure the caller has the window locked. If the window isn't properly locked, they print warning messages and fail.

Of course, a BView function can require the window to be locked only if the view has a window to lock; the requirement can't be enforced if the BView isn't attached to a window. However, as discussed in "Views and the Server" in the "Drawing" section of this chapter, some BView functions don't work at all unless the view is attached—in which case the window must be locked.

Whenever the system calls a BView function to notify it of something—whenever it calls `WindowActivated()`, `Draw()`, `MessageReceived()` or another hook function—it first locks the window thread. The application doesn't have to explicitly lock the window when responding to an update, an interface message, or some other notification; the window is already locked.

Scripting Support

The BView class implements a suite named "suite/vnd.Be-view" that opens three of its properties to scripting requests. The suite includes the following messages:

Property name: "Frame" for the frame rectangle of the BView
Specifiers: `B_DIRECT_SPECIFIER` only
Messages: `B_SET_PROPERTY` and `B_GET_PROPERTY`
Data type: BRect

Property name: "Hidden" for whether or not the BView is hidden
Specifiers: `B_DIRECT_SPECIFIER` only
Messages: `B_SET_PROPERTY` and `B_GET_PROPERTY`
Data type: `bool`

The suite also includes the ability to resolve the following specifiers by designating the specified BView as the new target of the message, regardless of what the message is:

Property name: "View" for a descendant BView object
Specifiers: `B_NAME_SPECIFIER, B_INDEX_SPECIFIER,`
               or `B_REVERSE_INDEX_SPECIFIER`

For `B_NAME_SPECIFIER`, the BView may descend the view hierarchy to find the named view. However, an index specifier picks only an immediate child of the BView.

See "Scripting" in Chapter 2 for more on scripting and suites.

Derived Classes

When it comes time for a BView to draw, its `Draw()` virtual function is called automatically. When it needs to respond to an event, a virtual function named after the kind of event is called—`MouseMoved()`, `KeyDown()`, and so on. Classes derived from BView implement these hook functions to do the particular kind of drawing and message handling characteristic of the derived class.

- Some classes derived from BView implement control devices—buttons, dials, selection lists, check boxes, and so on—that translate user actions on the keyboard and mouse into more explicit instructions for the application. In the Interface Kit, BMenu, BListView, BButton, BCheckBox, and BRadioButton are examples of control devices.

- Other BViews visually organize the display—for example, a view that draws a border around and arranges other views, or one that splits a window into two or more resizable panels. The BBox, BScrollBar, and BScrollView classes fall into this category.

- Some BViews implement highly organized displays the user can manipulate, such as a game board or a scientific simulation.

- Perhaps the most important BViews are those that permit the user to create, organize, and edit data. These views display the current selection and are the focus of most user actions. They carry out the main work of an application. BTextView is the only Interface Kit example of such a view.

Almost all the BView classes defined in the Interface Kit fall into the first two of these groups. Control devices and organizational views can serve a variety of different kinds of applications, and therefore can be implemented in a kit that's common to all applications.

However, the BViews that will be central to most applications fall into the last two groups. Of particular importance are the BViews that manage editable data. Unfortunately, these are not views that can be easily implemented in a common kit. Just as most applications devise their own data formats, most applications will need to define their own data-handling views.

Nevertheless, the BView class structures and simplifies the task of developing application-specific objects that draw in windows and interact with the user. It takes care of the lower-level details and manages the view's relationship to the window and other views in the hierarchy. You should make yourself familiar with this class before implementing your own application-specific BViews.

Hook Functions

`AllAttached()`
Can be implemented to finish initializing the BView after it's attached to a window, where the initialization depends on a descendant view's `AttachedToWindow()` function having been called.

`AllDetached()`

Can be implemented to prepare the BView for being detached from a window, where the preparations depend on a descendant view's `DetachedFromWindow()` function having been called.

`AttachedToWindow()`

Can be implemented to finish initializing the BView after it becomes part of a window's view hierarchy.

`DetachedFromWindow()`

Can be implemented to prepare the BView for its impending removal from a window's view hierarchy.

`Draw()`

Can be implemented to draw the view.

`FrameMoved()`

Can be implemented to respond to a message notifying the BView that it has moved in its parent's coordinate system.

`FrameResized()`

Can be implemented to respond to a message informing the BView that its frame rectangle has been resized.

`GetPreferredSize()`

Can be implemented to calculate the optimal size of the view.

`KeyDown()`

Can be implemented to respond to a message reporting character input from the keyboard (a key-down event).

`KeyUp()`

Can be implemented to respond to a message reporting a key-up event.

`MakeFocus()`

Makes the BView the focus view, or causes it to give up being the focus view; can be augmented to take any action the change in status may require.

`MouseDown()`

Can be implemented to respond to a message reporting a mouse-down event.

`MouseMoved()`

Can be implemented to respond to a notification that the cursor has entered the view's visible region, moved within the visible region, or exited from the view.

`Pulse()`

Can be implemented to do something at regular intervals. This function is called repeatedly when no other messages are pending.

`TargetedByScrollView()`

Can be implemented to react when the BView becomes the target of a BScrollView.

`WindowActivated()`

Can be implemented to respond to a notification that the BView's window has become the active window, or has lost that status.

Constructor and Destructor

BView()

BView(BRect *frame*, const char **name*, uint32 *resizingMode*, uint32 *flags*)
BView(BMessage **archive*)

Sets up a view with the *frame* rectangle, which is specified in the coordinate system of its eventual parent, and assigns the BView an identifying *name*, which can be NULL.

When it's created, a BView doesn't belong to a window and has no parent. It's assigned a parent by having another BView adopt it with the `AddChild()` function. If the other view is in a window, the BView becomes part of that window's view hierarchy. A BView can be made a child of the window's top view by calling BWindow's version of the `AddChild()` function.

When the BView gains a parent, the values in *frame* are interpreted in the parent's coordinate system. The sides of the view must be aligned on screen pixels. Therefore, the *frame* rectangle should not contain coordinates with fractional values. Fractional coordinates will be rounded to the nearest whole number.

The *resizingMode* mask determines the behavior of the view when its parent is resized. It should combine one constant for horizontal resizing:

```
B_FOLLOW_LEFT
B_FOLLOW_RIGHT
B_FOLLOW_LEFT_RIGHT
B_FOLLOW_H_CENTER
```

with one for vertical resizing:

```
B_FOLLOW_TOP
B_FOLLOW_BOTTOM
B_FOLLOW_TOP_BOTTOM
B_FOLLOW_V_CENTER
```

For example, if B_FOLLOW_LEFT is chosen, the margin between the left side of the view and the left side of its parent will remain constant—the view will "follow" the parent's left side. Similarly, if B_FOLLOW_RIGHT is chosen, the view will follow the parent's right side. If B_FOLLOW_H_CENTER is chosen, the view will maintain a constant relationship to the horizontal center of the parent.

If the constants name opposite sides of the view rectangle—left and right, or top and bottom—the view will necessarily be resized in that dimension when the parent is. For example, B_FOLLOW_LEFT_RIGHT means that the margin between the left side of the view and left side of the parent will remain constant, as will the margin between the right side of the view and the right side of the parent. As the parent is resized horizontally, the child will be resized with it. Note that B_FOLLOW_LEFT_RIGHT is not the same as combining B_FOLLOW_LEFT and B_FOLLOW_RIGHT, an illegal move. The *resizingMode* mask can contain only one horizontal constant and one vertical constant.

If a side is not mentioned in the mask, the distance between that side of the view and the corresponding side of the parent is free to fluctuate. This may mean that the view will move within its parent's coordinate system when the parent is resized. B_FOLLOW_RIGHT plus B_FOLLOW_BOTTOM, for example, would keep a view from being resized, but the view will move to follow the right bottom corner of its parent whenever the parent is resized. B_FOLLOW_LEFT plus B_FOLLOW_TOP prevents a view from being resized *and* from being moved.

In addition to the constants listed above, there are two other possibilities:

B_FOLLOW_ALL_SIDES

B_FOLLOW_NONE

B_FOLLOW_ALL_SIDES is a shorthand for B_FOLLOW_LEFT_RIGHT and B_FOLLOW_TOP_BOTTOM. It means that the view will be resized in tandem with its parent, both horizontally and vertically.

B_FOLLOW_NONE keeps the view at its absolute position on-screen; the parent view is resized around it. (Nevertheless, because the parent is resized, the view may wind up being moved in its parent's coordinate system.)

Typically, a parent view is resized because the user resizes the window it's in. When the window is resized, the top view is too. Depending on how the *resizingMode* flag is set for the top view's children and for the descendants of its children, automatic resizing can cascade down the view hierarchy. A view can also be resized programmatically by the ResizeTo() and ResizeBy() functions.

The resizing mode can be changed after construction with the SetResizingMode() function.

The *flags* mask determines what kinds of notifications the BView will receive. It can be any combination of the following constants:

B_WILL_DRAW

Indicates that the BView does some drawing of its own and therefore can't be ignored when the window is updated. If this flag isn't set, the BView won't receive update notifications—its Draw() function won't be called—and it won't be erased to its background view color if the color is other than white.

B_PULSE_NEEDED

Indicates that the BView should receive Pulse() notifications.

B_FRAME_EVENTS

Indicates that the BView should receive FrameResized() and FrameMoved() notifications when its frame rectangle changes—typically as a result of the automatic resizing behavior described above. FrameResized() is called when the dimensions of the view change; FrameMoved() is called when the position of its left top corner in its parent's coordinate system changes.

B_FULL_UPDATE_ON_RESIZE

Indicates that the entire view should be updated when it's resized. If this flag isn't set, only the portions that resizing adds to the view will be included in the clipping region.

B_NAVIGABLE

Indicates that the BView can become the focus view for keyboard actions. This flag makes it possible for the user to navigate to the view and put it in focus by pressing the Tab key. See "Keyboard Navigation" at the beginning of this chapter.

B_NAVIGABLE_JUMP

Marks the position of a group of views for keyboard navigation. By pressing Control-Tab, the user can jump from group to group. The focus lands on the first BView in the group that has the B_NAVIGABLE flag set. This may be the same BView that has the B_NAVIGABLE_JUMP marker, or the B_NAVIGABLE_JUMP BView may be the parent of a group of B_NAVIGABLE views.

If none of these constants applies, *flags* can be NULL. The flags can be reset after construction with the SetFlags() function.

See also: SetResizingMode(), SetFlags(), BHandler::SetName()

~BView()

virtual ~BView(void)

Frees all memory the BView allocated, and ensures that each of the BView's descendants in the view hierarchy is also destroyed.

It's an error to delete a BView while it remains attached to a window. Call RemoveChild() or RemoveSelf() before using the delete operator.

See also: RemoveChild()

Static Functions

Instantiate()

> static BView *Instantiate(BMessage *archive)

Returns a new BView object, allocated by new and created with the version of the constructor that takes a BMessage *archive*. However, if the message doesn't contain archived data for a BView, Instantiate() returns NULL.

See also: BArchivable::Instantiate(), instantiate_object(), Archive()

Member Functions

AddChild(), RemoveChild()

> void AddChild(BView *aView, BView *sibling = NULL)

> bool RemoveChild(BView *aView)

AddChild() makes *aView* a child of the BView, provided that *aView* doesn't already have a parent. The new child is added to the BView's list of children immediately before the named *sibling* BView. If the sibling is NULL (as it is by default), *aView* isn't added in front of any other view—in other words, it's added to the end of the list. If the BView is attached to a window, *aView* and all its descendants become attached to the same window. Each of them is notified of this change through AttachedToWindow() and AllAttached() function calls.

AddChild() fails if *aView* already belongs to a view hierarchy. A view can live with only one parent at a time. It also fails if *sibling* is not already a child of the BView.

RemoveChild() severs the link between the BView and *aView*, so that *aView* is no longer a child of the BView; *aView* retains all its own children and descendants, but they become an isolated fragment of a view hierarchy, unattached to a window. Each removed view is notified of this change through DetachedFromWindow() and AllDetached() function calls.

A BView must be removed from a window before it can be destroyed.

If it succeeds in removing *aView*, RemoveChild() returns true. If it fails, it returns false. It will fail if *aView* is not, in fact, a current child of the BView.

When a BView object becomes attached to a BWindow, two other connections are automatically established for it:

- The view is added to the BWindow's flat list of BHandler objects, making it an eligible target for messages the BWindow dispatches.

- The BView's parent view becomes its next handler. Messages that the BView doesn't recognize will be passed to its parent.

Removing a BView from a window's view hierarchy also removes it from the BWindow's flat list of BHandler objects; the BView will no longer be eligible to handle messages dispatched by the BWindow.

See also: `BWindow::AddChild()`, `BLooper::AddHandler()`, `BHandler::SetNextHandler()`, `RemoveSelf()`, `AttachedToWindow()`, `DetachedFromWindow()`

AddLine()   *see BeginLineArray()*

AllAttached()   *see AttachedToWindow()*

AllDetached()   *see DetachedFromWindow()*

Archive()

virtual status_t **Archive**(BMessage *archive*, bool *deep* = true) const

Calls the inherited version of `Archive()`, then records the following BView attributes in the BMessage *archive*:

- The frame rectangle
- The resizing mode
- The flags mask
- All aspects of its current graphics state (font, high and low color, and so on)

If the *deep* flag is `true`, all of the BView's descendants in the view hierarchy are also archived. If *deep* is `false`, only the BView itself is archived.

See also: `BArchivable::Archive()`, `Instantiate()` static function

AttachedToWindow(), AllAttached()

virtual void **AttachedToWindow**(void)

virtual void **AllAttached**(void)

Implemented by derived classes to complete the initialization of the BView when it's assigned to a window. A BView is assigned to a window when it, or one of its ancestors in the view hierarchy, becomes a child of a view already attached to a window.

`AttachedToWindow()` is called immediately after the BView is formally made a part of the window's view hierarchy and after it has become known to the Application Server and its graphics parameters are set. The `Window()` function can identify which BWindow the BView belongs to.

All of the BView's children, if it has any, also become attached to the window and receive their own `AttachedToWindow()` notifications. Parents receive the notification before their children, but only after all views have become attached to the window and recognized as part of the window's view hierarchy. This function can therefore depend on all ancestor and descendant views being in place.

For example, `AttachedToWindow()` can be implemented to set a view's background color to the same color as its parent, something that can't be done before the view belongs to a window and knows who its parent is.

```
void MyView::AttachedToWindow()
{
    if ( Parent() )
        SetViewColor(Parent()->ViewColor());
    BView::AttachedToWindow();
}
```

The `AllAttached()` notification follows on the heels of `AttachedToWindow()`, but works its way up the view hierarchy rather than down. When `AllAttached()` is called for a BView, all its descendants have received both `AttachedToWindow()` and `AllAttached()` notifications. Therefore, parent views can depend on any calculations that their children make in either function. For example, a parent can resize itself to fit the size of its children, where their sizes depend on calculations done in `AttachedToWindow()`.

The default (BView) version of both these functions are empty.

See also: `AddChild()`, `Window()`

BeginLineArray(), AddLine(), EndLineArray()

> void **BeginLineArray**(int32 *count*)

> void **AddLine**(BPoint *start*, BPoint *end*, rgb_color *color*)

> void **EndLineArray**(void)

These functions provide a more efficient way of drawing a large number of lines than repeated calls to `StrokeLine()`. `BeginLineArray()` signals the beginning of a series of up to *count* AddLine() calls; EndLineArray() signals the end of the series. Each AddLine() call defines a line from the *start* point to the *end* point, associates it with a particular *color*, and adds it to the array. The lines can each be a different color; they don't have to be contiguous. When EndLineArray() is called, all the lines are drawn—using the then current pen size—in the order that they were added to the array.

These functions don't change any graphics parameters. For example, they don't move the pen or change the current high and low colors. Parameter values that are in effect when EndLineArray() is called are the ones used to draw the lines. The high and low colors are ignored in favor of the *color* specified for each line.

The *count* passed to BeginLineArray() is an upper limit on the number of lines that can be drawn. Keeping the count close to accurate and within reasonable bounds helps the efficiency of the line-array mechanism. It's a good idea to keep it less than 256; above that number, memory requirements begin to impinge on performance.

See also: StrokeLine()

BeginPicture(), EndPicture()

> void **BeginPicture**(BPicture **picture*)

> BPicture ****EndPicture**(void)

BeginPicture() instructs the Application Server to begin recording a set of drawing instructions for a *picture*. EndPicture() instructs the server to end the recording session; it returns the same object that was passed to BeginPicture().

The BPicture records exactly what the BView would draw—and only what the BView would draw—were the instructions not bracketed by BeginPicture() and EndPicture() calls. The drawing of other views is ignored, as are function calls that don't draw or affect graphics parameters. The picture captures only primitive graphics operations—that is, functions defined in this class, such as DrawString(), FillArc(), and SetFont(). If a complex drawing function (such as Draw()) is called, only the primitive operations that it contains are recorded.

A BPicture can be recorded only if the BView is attached to a window. The window can be off-screen and the view itself can be hidden or reside outside the current clipping region. However, the drawing the BView does will not be seen even if the window is on-screen and the view is visible—it's captured in the *picture* rather than rendered in the window.

See also: the BPicture class, DrawPicture()

BeginRectTracking(), EndRectTracking()

void **BeginRectTracking**(BRect *rect*, uint32 *how* = B_TRACK_WHOLE_RECT)

void **EndRectTracking**(void)

These functions instruct the Application Server to display a rectangular outline that will track the movement of the cursor. `BeginRectTracking()` puts the rectangle on-screen and initiates tracking; `EndRectTracking()` terminates tracking and removes the rectangle. The initial rectangle, *rect*, is specified in the BView's coordinate system.

This function supports two kinds of tracking, depending on the constant passed as the *how* argument:

B_TRACK_WHOLE_RECT	The whole rectangle moves with the cursor. Its position changes, but its size remains fixed.
B_TRACK_RECT_CORNER	The left top corner of the rectangle remains fixed within the view while its right and bottom edges move with the cursor.

Tracking is typically initiated from within a BView's `MouseDown()` function and is allowed to continue as long as a mouse button is held down. For example:

```
void MyView::MouseDown(BPoint point)
{
    unit32 buttons;

    BRect rect(point, point);
    BeginRectTracking(rect, B_TRACK_RECT_CORNER);
    do {
        snooze(30 * 1000);
        GetMouse(&point, &buttons);
    } while ( buttons );
    EndRectTracking();

    rect.SetRightBottom(point);
    . . .
}
```

This example uses `BeginRectTracking()` to drag out a rectangle from the point recorded for a mouse-down event. It sets up a modal loop to periodically check on the state of the mouse buttons. Tracking ends when the user releases all buttons. The right and bottom sides of the rectangle are then updated from the cursor location last reported by the `GetMouse()` function.

See also: `ConvertToScreen()`, `GetMouse()`

Bounds()

BRect **Bounds**(void) const

Returns the BView's bounds rectangle. If the BView is attached to a window, this function returns the rectangle kept by the Application Server. If not, it returns a rectangle the same size as the BView's frame rectangle, but with the left and top sides at 0.0.

If Bounds() is called during an update, the BView is already aware of the current rectangle (the update message included it); it can therefore return it directly without communicating with the Application Server. However, if called at other times, Bounds() must get the latest rectangle from the server, an interaction that has a certain amount of overhead.

See also: Frame()

ChildAt()   *see Parent()*

ConstrainClippingRegion()

virtual void **ConstrainClippingRegion**(BRegion *region*)

Restricts the drawing that the BView can do to *region*.

The Application Server keeps track of a clipping region for each BView that's attached to a window. It clips all drawing the BView does to that region; the BView can't draw outside of it.

By default, the clipping region contains only the visible area of the view and, during an update, only the area that actually needs to be drawn. By passing a *region* to this function, an application can further restrict the clipping region. When calculating the clipping region, the server intersects it with the *region* provided. The BView can draw only in areas common to the *region* passed and the clipping region as the server would otherwise calculate it. The region passed can't expand the clipping region beyond what it otherwise would be.

If called during an update, ConstrainClippingRegion() restricts the clipping region only for the duration of the update.

Calls to ConstrainClippingRegion() are not additive; each *region* that's passed replaces the one that was passed in the previous call. Passing a NULL pointer removes the previous region without replacing it. The function works only for BViews that are attached to a window.

See also: GetClippingRegion(), Draw()

ConvertToParent(), ConvertFromParent()

> BPoint **ConvertToParent**(BPoint *localPoint*) const
> void **ConvertToParent**(BPoint **localPoint*) const
>
> BRect **ConvertToParent**(BRect *localRect*) const
> void **ConvertToParent**(BRect **localRect*) const
>
> BPoint **ConvertFromParent**(BPoint *parentPoint*) const
> void **ConvertFromParent**(BPoint **parentPoint*) const
>
> BRect **ConvertFromParent**(BRect *parentRect*) const
> void **ConvertFromParent**(BRect **parentRect*) const

These functions convert points and rectangles to and from the coordinate system of the BView's parent. `ConvertToParent()` converts *localPoint* or *localRect* from the BView's coordinate system to the coordinate system of its parent BView. `ConvertFromParent()` does the opposite; it converts *parentPoint* or *parentRect* from the coordinate system of the BView's parent to the BView's own coordinate system.

If the point or rectangle is passed by value, the function returns the converted value. If a pointer is passed, the conversion is done in place.

Both functions fail if the BView isn't attached to a window.

See also: `ConvertToScreen()`

ConvertToScreen(), ConvertFromScreen()

> BPoint **ConvertToScreen**(BPoint *localPoint*) const
> void **ConvertToScreen**(BPoint **localPoint*) const
>
> BRect **ConvertToScreen**(BRect *localRect*) const
> void **ConvertToScreen**(BRect **localRect*) const
>
> BPoint **ConvertFromScreen**(BPoint *screenPoint*) const
> void **ConvertFromScreen**(BPoint **screenPoint*) const
>
> BRect **ConvertFromScreen**(BRect *screenRect*) const
> void **ConvertFromScreen**(BRect **screenRect*) const

`ConvertToScreen()` converts *localPoint* or *localRect* from the BView's coordinate system to the global screen coordinate system. `ConvertFromScreen()` makes the opposite conversion; it converts *screenPoint* or *screenRect* from the screen coordinate system to the BView's local coordinate system.

If the point or rectangle is passed by value, the function returns the converted value. If a pointer is passed, the conversion is done in place.

The screen coordinate system has its origin, (0.0, 0.0), at the left top corner of the main screen.

Neither function will work if the BView isn't attached to a window.

See also: BWindow::ConvertToScreen(), ConvertToParent()

CopyBits()

void **CopyBits**(BRect *source*, BRect *destination*)

Copies the image displayed in the *source* rectangle to the *destination* rectangle, where both rectangles lie within the view and are stated in the BView's coordinate system.

If the two rectangles aren't the same size, the source image is scaled to fit.

If not all of the destination rectangle lies within the BView's visible region, the source image is clipped rather than scaled.

If not all of the source rectangle lies within the BView's visible region, only the visible portion is copied. It's mapped to the corresponding portion of the destination rectangle. The BView is then invalidated so its Draw() function will be called to update the part of the destination rectangle that can't be filled with the source image.

The BView must be attached to a window.

CountChildren()   *see Parent()*

DetachedFromWindow(), AllDetached()

virtual void **DetachedFromWindow**(void)

virtual void **AllDetached**(void)

Implemented by derived classes to make any adjustments necessary when the BView is about to be removed from a window's view hierarchy. These two functions parallel the more commonly implemented AttachedToWindow() and AllAttached() functions.

DetachedFromWindow() notifications work their way down the hierarchy of views being detached, followed by AllDetached() notifications, which work their way up the hierarchy. The second function call permits an ancestor view to take actions that depend on calculations a descendant might have to make when it's first notified of being detached.

The BView is still attached to the window when both functions are called.

See also: AttachedToWindow()

DragMessage()

> void **DragMessage**(BMessage *message,* BBitmap *image,* BPoint *point,*
>   BHandler *replyTarget* = NULL)
> void **DragMessage**(BMessage *message,* BRect *rect,*
>   BHandler *replyTarget* = NULL)

Initiates a drag-and-drop session. The first argument, *message,* is a BMessage object that bundles the information that will be dragged and dropped on the destination view. The caller retains responsibility for this object and can delete it after `DragMessage()` returns; the BView makes a copy.

The second argument, *image,* represents the message on-screen; it's the visible image that the user drags. Unlike the BMessage, this BBitmap object becomes the responsibility of the system; it will be freed when the message is dropped. If you want to keep the image yourself, make a copy to pass to `DragMessage()`. The image isn't dropped on the destination BView; if you want the destination to have the image, you must add it to the *message* as well as pass it as the *image* argument.

The third argument, *point,* locates the point within the image that's aligned with the hot spot of the cursor—that is, the point that's aligned with the location passed to `MouseDown()` or returned by `GetMouse()`. It's stated within the coordinate system of the source image and should lie somewhere within its bounds rectangle. The bounds rectangle and coordinate system of a BBitmap are set when the object is constructed.

Alternatively, you can specify that an outline of a rectangle, *rect,* should be dragged instead of an image. The rectangle is stated in the BView's coordinate system. (Therefore, a *point* argument isn't needed to align it with the cursor.)

The final argument, *replyTarget,* names the object that you want to handle a message that might be sent in reply to the dragged message. If *replyTarget* is NULL, as it is by default, any reply that's received will be directed to the BView object that initiated the drag-and-drop session.

This function works only for BViews that are attached to a window.

See also: `BMessage::WasDropped()`, the BBitmap class

Draw()

> virtual void **Draw**(BRect *updateRect*)

Implemented by derived classes to draw the *updateRect* portion of the view. The update rectangle is stated in the BView's coordinate system.

`Draw()` is called as the result of update messages whenever the view needs to present itself on-screen. This may happen when:

- The window the view is in is first shown on-screen, or shown after being hidden (see the BWindow version of the `Hide()` function).

- The view is made visible after being hidden (see BView's `Hide()` function).

- Obscured parts of the view are revealed, as when a window is moved from in front of the view or an image is dragged across it.

- The view is resized.

- The contents of the view are scrolled (see `ScrollBy()`).

- A child view is added, removed, or resized.

- A rectangle has been invalidated that includes at least some of the view (see `Invalidate()`).

- `CopyBits()` can't completely fill a destination rectangle within the view.

`Draw()` is also called from a BPrintJob object's `DrawView()` function to draw the view on a printed page. `IsPrinting()` returns `true` when the BView is drawing for the printer and `false` when it's drawing to the screen. When printing, you may want to recalculate layouts, substitute fonts, turn antialiasing off, scale the size of a coordinate unit, or make other adjustments to ensure the quality of the printed image.

When drawing to the screen, the *updateRect* is the smallest rectangle that encloses the current clipping region for the view. Since the Application Server won't render anything on-screen that's outside the clipping region, an application will be more efficient if it avoids producing drawing instructions for images that don't intersect with the rectangle. For still more efficiency and precision, you can ask for the clipping region itself (by calling `GetClippingRegion()`) and confine drawing to images that intersect with it.

When printing, the *updateRect* matches the rectangle passed to `DrawView()` and may lie outside the clipping region. The clipping region is not enforced for printing, but the Print Server clips the BView's drawing to the specified rectangle.

See also: `BWindow::UpdateIfNeeded()`, `Invalidate()`, `GetClippingRegion()`, `BPrintJob::DrawView()`, `IsPrinting()`

DrawBitmap(), DrawBitmapAsync()

    void **DrawBitmap**(const BBitmap *image)
    void **DrawBitmap**(const BBitmap *image, BPoint point)
    void **DrawBitmap**(const BBitmap *image, BRect destination)
    void **DrawBitmap**(const BBitmap *image, BRect source, BRect destination)

void **DrawBitmapAsync**(const BBitmap *_image_)
void **DrawBitmapAsync**(const BBitmap *_image_, BPoint _point_)
void **DrawBitmapAsync**(const BBitmap *_image_, BRect _destination_)
void **DrawBitmapAsync**(const BBitmap *_image_, BRect _source_, BRect _destination_)

These functions place a bitmap _image_ in the view at the current pen position, at the _point_ specified, or within the designated _destination_ rectangle. The _point_ and the _destination_ rectangle are stated in the BView's coordinate system.

If a _source_ rectangle is given, only that part of the bitmap image is drawn. Otherwise, the entire bitmap is placed in the view. The _source_ rectangle is stated in the internal coordinates of the BBitmap object.

If the source image is bigger than the destination rectangle, it's scaled to fit.

The two functions differ in only one respect: `DrawBitmap()` waits for the Application Server to finish rendering the image before it returns. `DrawBitmapAsync()` doesn't wait; it passes the image to the server and returns immediately. The latter function can be more efficient in some cases—for example, you might use an asynchronous function to draw several bitmaps and then call `Sync()` to wait for them all to finish rather than wait for each one individually:

```
DrawBitmapAsync(bitmapOne, firstPoint);
DrawBitmapAsync(bitmapTwo, secondPoint);
DrawBitmapAsync(bitmapThree, thirdPoint);
Sync();
```

Or, if you can cram some useful work between the time you send the bitmap to the Application Server and the time you need to be sure that it has appeared on-screen, `DrawBitmapAsync()` will free your thread to do that work immediately:

```
DrawBitmapAsync(someBitmap, somePoint);
/* do something else */
Sync();
```

See also: the "Drawing" section near the beginning of this chapter, the BBitmap class, `Sync()`

DrawChar()

void **DrawChar**(char _c_)
void **DrawChar**(char _c_, BPoint _point_)

Draws the character _c_ at the current pen position—or at the _point_ specified—and moves the pen to a position immediately to the right of the character. This function is equivalent to passing a string of one character to `DrawString()`. The _point_ is specified in the BView's coordinate system.

See also: `DrawString()`

DrawingMode()   *see SetDrawingMode()*

DrawPicture()

> void **DrawPicture**(const BPicture *picture*)
> void **DrawPicture**(const BPicture *picture*, BPoint *point*)

Draws the previously recorded *picture* at the current pen position—or at the specified *point* in the BView's coordinate system. The point or pen position is taken as the coordinate origin for all the drawing instructions recorded in the BPicture.

Nothing that's done in the BPicture can affect anything in the BView's graphics state—for example, the BPicture can't reset the current high color or the pen position. Conversely, nothing in the BView's current graphics state affects the drawing instructions captured in the picture. The graphics parameters that were in effect when the picture was recorded determine what the picture looks like.

See also: `BeginPicture()`, the BPicture class

DrawString()

> void **DrawString**(const char *string*,
>   escapement_delta *delta* = NULL)
> void **DrawString**(const char *string*, int32 *length*,
>   escapement_delta *delta* = NULL)
> void **DrawString**(const char *string*, BPoint *point*,
>   escapement_delta *delta* = NULL)
> void **DrawString**(const char *string*, int32 *length*, BPoint *point*,
>   escapement_delta *delta* = NULL)

Draws the characters encoded in *length* bytes of *string*—or, if the number of bytes isn't specified, all the characters in the string, up to the null terminator ("\0"). Characters are drawn in the BView's current font. The font's direction determines whether the string is drawn left-to-right or right-to-left. Its rotation determines the angle of the baseline (horizontal for an unrotated font). The spacing mode of the font determines how characters are positioned within the string and the string width.

This function places the characters on a baseline that begins at the current pen position—or at the specified *point* in the BView's coordinate system. It draws the characters to the right (assuming an unrotated font) and moves the pen to the baseline immediately past the characters drawn. For a left-to-right font, the pen will be in position to draw the next character, as shown in the following diagram.

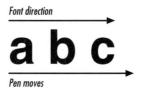

The characters are drawn in the opposite direction for a right-to-left font, but the pen still moves left-to-right:

For a font that's read from left-to-right, a series of simple `DrawString()` calls (with no *point* specified) will produce a continuous string. For example, these two lines of code:

```
DrawString("tog");
DrawString("ether");
```

will produce the same result as this one:

```
DrawString("together");
```

except if the spacing mode is `B_STRING_SPACING`. Under `B_STRING_SPACING`, character placements are adjusted keeping the string width constant. The adjustments are contextually dependent on the string and may therefore differ depending on whether there are two strings ("tog" and "ether") or just one ("together").

If a *delta* argument is provided, `DrawString()` adds the additional amounts specified in the `escapement_delta` structure to the width of each character. This structure has two fields:

float `nonspace`

   The amount to add to the width of characters that have visible glyphs (that put ink on the printed page).

float `space`

   The amount to add to the width of characters that have escapements, but don't have visible glyphs (characters that affect the position of surrounding characters but don't put ink on the page).

When drawing to the screen, DrawString() uses antialiasing—unless the BView's font disables it or the font size is large enough (over 1,000.0 points) so that its benefits aren't required. Antialiasing produces colors at the margins of character outlines that are intermediate between the color of the text (the BView's high color) and the color of the background against which the text is drawn. When drawing in B_OP_COPY mode, antialiasing requires the BView's low color to match the background color.

It's much faster to draw a string in B_OP_COPY mode than in any other mode. If you draw the same string repeatedly in the same location in B_OP_OVER mode without erasing, antialiasing will produce different, and worse, results each time as the intermediate color it previously produced is treated as the new background each time. Antialiasing doesn't produce pleasing results in B_OP_SELECT mode.

This is a graphical drawing function, so any character that doesn't have an escapement or a visible representation (including white space) is replaced by an undefined character that can be drawn (currently an empty box). This includes all control characters (those with values less than B_SPACE, 0x20).

DrawString() doesn't erase before drawing.

See also: MovePenBy(), SetFontName(), the BFont class

EndLineArray()   *see BeginLineArry()*

EndPicture()   *see BeginPicture()*

EndRectTracking()   *see BeginRectTracking()*

FillArc()   *see StrokeArc()*

FillEllipse()   *see StrokeEllipse()*

FillPolygon()   *see StrokePolygon()*

FillRect()   *see StrokeRect()*

FillRegion()

> void **FillRegion**(BRegion *region*, pattern *aPattern* = B_SOLID_HIGH) const

Fills the *region* with the pattern specified by *aPattern*—or, if no pattern is specified, with the current high color. Filling a region is equivalent to filling all the rectangles that define the region.

See also: the BRegion class

FillRoundRect()   *see StrokeRoundRect()*

FillTriangle()   *see StrokeTriangle()*

FindView()

>   BView *FindView(const char *name*) const

Returns the BView identified by *name*, or NULL if the view can't be found. Names are assigned by the BView constructor and can be modified by the SetName() function inherited from BHandler.

FindView() begins the search by checking whether the BView's name matches *name*. If not, it continues to search down the view hierarchy, among the BView's children and more distant descendants. To search the entire view hierarchy, use the BWindow version of this function.

See also: BWindow::FindView(), BHandler::SetName()

Flags()   *see SetFlags()*

Flush(), Sync()

>   void Flush(void) const

>   void Sync(void) const

These functions flush the window's connection to the Application Server. If the BView isn't attached to a window, neither function has an effect.

For reasons of efficiency, the window's connection to the Application Server is buffered. Drawing instructions destined for the server are placed in the buffer and dispatched as a group when the buffer becomes full. Flushing empties the buffer, sending whatever it contains to the server, even if it's not yet full.

The buffer is automatically flushed on every update. However, if you do any drawing outside the update mechanism—in response to interface messages, for example—you need to explicitly flush the connection so that drawing instructions won't languish in the buffer while waiting for it to fill up or for the next update. You should also flush it if you call any drawing functions from outside the window's thread.

Flush() simply flushes the buffer and returns. It does the same work as BWindow's function of the same name.

Sync() flushes the connection, then waits until the server has executed the last instruction that was in the buffer before returning. This alternative to Flush()

prevents the application from getting ahead of the server (ahead of what the user sees on-screen) and keeps both processes synchronized.

It's a good idea, for example, to call `Sync()`, rather than `Flush()`, after employing BViews to produce a bitmap image (a BBitmap object). `Sync()` is the only way you can be sure the image has been completely rendered before you attempt to draw with it.

(Note that all BViews attached to a window share the same connection to the Application Server. Calling `Flush()` or `Sync()` for any one of them flushes the buffer for all of them.)

See also: `BWindow::Flush()`, the BBitmap class

Frame()

> BRect **Frame**(void) const

Returns the BView's frame rectangle. The frame rectangle is first set by the BView constructor and is altered only when the view is moved or resized. It's stated in the coordinate system of the BView's parent.

If the BView is not attached to a window, `Frame()` reports the object's own cached conception of its frame rectangle. If it is attached, `Frame()` reports the Application Server's conception of the rectangle. When a BView is added to a window, its cached rectangle is communicated to the server. While it remains attached, the functions that move and resize the frame rectangle affect the server's conception of the view, but don't alter the rectangle kept by the object. Therefore, if the BView is removed from the window, `Frame()` will again report the frame rectangle that it had before it was attached, no matter how much it was moved and resized while it belonged to the window.

See also: `MoveBy()`, `ResizeBy()`, the BView constructor

FrameMoved()

> virtual void **FrameMoved**(BPoint *parentPoint*)

Implemented by derived classes to respond to a notification that the view has moved within its parent's coordinate system. *parentPoint* gives the new location of the left top corner of the BView's frame rectangle.

`FrameMoved()` is called only if the **B_FRAME_EVENTS** flag is set and the BView is attached to a window.

If the view is both moved and resized, `FrameMoved()` is called before `FrameResized()`. This might happen, for example, if the BView's automatic resizing mode is a combination of B_FOLLOW_TOP_BOTTOM and B_FOLLOW_RIGHT and its parent is resized both horizontally and vertically.

The default (BView) version of this function is empty.

WARNING

Currently, FrameMoved() is also called when a hidden window is shown on-screen.

See also: MoveBy(), BWindow::FrameMoved(), SetFlags()

FrameResized()

virtual void **FrameResized**(float *width*, float *height*)

Implemented by derived classes to respond to a notification that the view has been resized. The arguments state the new *width* and *height* of the view. The resizing could have been the result of a user action (resizing the window) or of a programmatic one (calling ResizeTo() or ResizeBy()).

FrameResized() is called only if the B_FRAME_EVENTS flag is set and the BView is attached to a window.

BView's version of this function is empty.

See also: ResizeBy(), BWindow::FrameResized(), SetFlags()

GetClippingRegion()

void **GetClippingRegion**(BRegion *region*) const

Modifies the BRegion object passed as an argument so that it describes the current clipping region of the BView, the region where the BView is allowed to draw. It's most efficient to allocate temporary BRegions on the stack:

```
BRegion clipper;
GetClippingRegion(&clipper);
. . .
```

Ordinarily, the clipping region is the same as the visible region of the view, the part of the view currently visible on-screen. The visible region is equal to the view's bounds rectangle minus:

• The frame rectangles of its children,

• Any areas that are clipped because the view doesn't lie wholly within the frame rectangles of all its ancestors in the view hierarchy, and

• Any areas that are obscured by other windows or that lie in a part of the window that's off-screen.

The clipping region can be smaller than the visible region if the program restricted it by calling `ConstrainClippingRegion()`. It will exclude any area that doesn't intersect with the region passed to `ConstrainClippingRegion()`.

While the BView is being updated, the clipping region contains just those parts of the view that need to be redrawn. This may be smaller than the visible region, or the region restricted by `ConstrainClippingRegion()`, if:

- The update occurs during scrolling. The clipping region will exclude any of the view's visible contents that the Application Server is able to shift to their new location and redraw automatically.

- The view rectangle has grown (because, for example, the user resized the window larger) and the update is needed only to draw the new parts of the view.

- The update was caused by `Invalidate()` and the rectangle passed to `Invalidate()` didn't cover all of the visible region.

- The update was necessary because `CopyBits()` couldn't fill all of a destination rectangle.

This function works only if the BView is attached to a window. Unattached BViews can't draw and therefore have no clipping region.

See also: `ConstrainClippingRegion()`, `Draw()`, `Invalidate()`

GetFont()   *see SetFont()*

GetFontHeight()

> void **GetFontHeight**(font_height **fontHeight*) const

Gets the height of the BView's font. This function provides the same information as BFont's `GetHeight()`. The following code:

```
font_height height;
myView->GetFontHeight(&height);
```

is equivalent to:

```
font_height height;
BFont font;
myView->GetFont(&font);
font.GetHeight(&height);
```

See the BFont class for more information.

See also: `BFont::GetHeight()`

GetMouse()

> void **GetMouse**(BPoint *cursor*, uint32 *buttons*, bool *checkQueue* = true)

Provides the location of the cursor and the state of the mouse buttons. The position of the cursor is recorded in the variable referred to by *cursor*; it's provided in the BView's own coordinates. A bit is set in the variable referred to by *buttons* for each mouse button that's down. This mask may be 0 (if no buttons are down) or it may contain one or more of the following constants:

```
B_PRIMARY_MOUSE_BUTTON

B_SECONDARY_MOUSE_BUTTON

B_TERTIARY_MOUSE_BUTTON
```

The cursor doesn't have to be located within the view for this function to work; it can be anywhere on-screen. However, the BView must be attached to a window.

If the *checkQueue* flag is set to `false`, `GetMouse()` provides information about the current state of the mouse buttons and the current location of the cursor.

If *checkQueue* is `true`, as it is by default, this function first looks in the message queue for any pending reports of mouse-moved or mouse-up events. If it finds any, it takes the one that has been in the queue the longest (the oldest message), removes it from the queue, and reports the *cursor* location and *button* states that were recorded in the message. Each `GetMouse()` call removes another message from the queue. If the queue doesn't hold any `B_MOUSE_MOVED` or `B_MOUSE_UP` messages, `GetMouse()` reports the current state of the mouse and cursor, just as if *checkQueue* were `false`.

This function is typically called from within a `MouseDown()` function to track the location of the cursor and wait for the mouse button to go up. By having it check the message queue, you can be sure that you haven't overlooked any of the cursor's movement or missed a mouse-up event (quickly followed by another mouse-down) that might have occurred before the first `GetMouse()` call.

See also: `modifiers()`

GetPreferredSize(), ResizeToPreferred()

> virtual void **GetPreferredSize**(float *width*, float *height*)

> virtual void **ResizeToPreferred**(void)

`GetPreferredSize()` is implemented by derived classes to write the preferred width and height of the view into the variables the *width* and *height* arguments refer to. Derived classes generally make this calculation based on the view's contents. For example, a BButton object reports the optimal size for displaying the button border and label given the current font.

`ResizeToPreferred()` resizes the BView's frame rectangle to the preferred size, keeping its left and top sides constant.

See also: `ResizeTo()`

GetStringWidths()   *see StringWidth()*

GetSupportedSuites()

   virtual status_t **GetSupportedSuites**(BMessage *message*)

Adds the name "suite/vnd.Be-view" to the *message*. See "Scripting Support" in the class overview for more information.

See also: `BHandler::GetSupportedSuites()`

Hide(), Show()

   virtual void **Hide**(void)

   virtual void **Show**(void)

These functions hide a view and show it again.

`Hide()` makes the view invisible without removing it from the view hierarchy. The visible region of the view will be empty and the BView won't receive update messages. If the BView has children, they also are hidden.

`Show()` unhides a view that had been hidden. This function doesn't guarantee that the view will be visible to the user; it merely undoes the effects of `Hide()`. If the view didn't have any visible area before being hidden, it won't have any after being shown again (given the same conditions).

Calls to `Hide()` and `Show()` can be nested. For a hidden view to become visible again, the number of `Hide()` calls must be matched by an equal number of `Show()` calls.

However, `Show()` can only undo a previous `Hide()` call on the same view. If the view became hidden when `Hide()` was called to hide the window it's in or to hide one of its ancestors in the view hierarchy, calling `Show()` on the view will have no effect. For a view to come out of hiding, its window and all its ancestor views must be unhidden.

Hide() and Show() can affect a view before it's attached to a window. The view will reflect its proper state (hidden or not) when it becomes attached. Views are created in an unhidden state.

See also: BWindow::Hide(), IsHidden()

HighColor()   *see SetHighColor()*

Invalidate()

> void **Invalidate**(BRect *rect*)
> void **Invalidate**(void)

Invalidates the *rect* portion of the view, causing update messages—and consequently Draw() notifications—to be generated for the BView and all descendants that lie wholly or partially within the rectangle. The rectangle is stated in the BView's coordinate system.

If no rectangle is specified, the BView's entire bounds rectangle is invalidated.

Since only BViews that are attached to a window can draw, only attached BViews can be invalidated.

See also: Draw(), GetClippingRegion(), BWindow::UpdateIfNeeded()

InvertRect()

> void **InvertRect**(BRect *rect*)

Inverts all the colors displayed within the *rect* rectangle. A subsequent InvertRect() call on the same rectangle restores the original colors.

The rectangle is stated in the BView's coordinate system.

See also: BScreen::ColorMap

IsFocus()

> bool **IsFocus**(void) const

Returns true if the BView is the current focus view for its window, and false if it's not. The focus view changes as the user chooses one view to work in and then another—for example, as the user moves from one text field to another when filling out an on-screen form. The change is made programmatically through the MakeFocus() function.

See also: BWindow::CurrentFocus(), MakeFocus()

IsHidden()

bool **IsHidden**(void) const

Returns `true` if the view has been hidden by the `Hide()` function, and `false` otherwise.

This function returns `true` whether `Hide()` was called to hide the BView itself, to hide an ancestor view, or to hide the BView's window. When a window is hidden, all its views are hidden with it. When a BView is hidden, all its descendants are hidden with it.

If the view has no visible region—perhaps because it lies outside its parent's frame rectangle or is obscured by a window in front—this function may nevertheless return `false`. It reports only whether the `Hide()` function has been called to hide the view, hide one of the view's ancestors in the view hierarchy, or hide the window where the view is located.

If the BView isn't attached to a window, `IsHidden()` returns the state that it will assume when it becomes attached. By default, views are not hidden.

See also: `Hide()`

IsPrinting()

bool **IsPrinting**(void) const

Returns `true` if the BView is being asked to draw for the printer, and `false` if the drawing it produces will be rendered on-screen (or if the BView isn't being asked to draw at all).

This function is typically called from within `Draw()` to determine whether the drawing it does is destined for the printer or the screen. When drawing to the printer, the BView may choose different parameters—such as fonts, bitmap images, or colors—than when drawing to the screen.

See also: the BPrintJob class, `Draw()`

KeyDown()

virtual void **KeyDown**(const char *bytes*, int32 *numBytes*)

Implemented by derived classes to respond to a `B_KEY_DOWN` message reporting keyboard input. Whenever a BView is the focus view of the active window, it receives a `KeyDown()` notification for each character the user types, except for those that:

- Are produced while a Command key is held down. Command key events are interpreted as keyboard shortcuts.

- Are produced by the Tab key when an Option key is held down. Option-Tab events are invariably interpreted as instructions to change the focus view (for keyboard navigation); they work even where Tab alone does not.

- Can operate the default button in a window. The BButton object's `KeyDown()` function is called, rather than the focus view's.

The first argument, *bytes*, is an array that encodes the character mapped to the key the user pressed. The second argument, *numBytes*, tells how many bytes are in the array; there will always be at least one. The *bytes* value follows the character encoding of the BView's font. Typically, the encoding is Unicode UTF-8 (`B_UNICODE_UTF8`), so there may be more than one byte per character. The *bytes* array is not null-terminated; "\0" is a valid character value.

The character value takes into account any modifier keys that were held down or keyboard locks that were on at the time of the keystroke. For example, Shift-*i* is reported as uppercase "I" (0x49) and Control-*i* is reported as a `B_TAB` (0x09).

Single-byte characters can be tested against ASCII codes and these constants:

B_BACKSPACE	B_LEFT_ARROW	B_INSERT
B_ENTER	B_RIGHT_ARROW	B_DELETE
B_RETURN	B_UP_ARROW	B_HOME
B_SPACE	B_DOWN_ARROW	B_END
B_TAB		B_PAGE_UP
B_ESCAPE	B_FUNCTION_KEY	B_PAGE_DOWN

`B_ENTER` and `B_RETURN` are the same character, a newline ("\n").

Only keys that generate characters produce key-down events; the modifier keys on their own do not.

You can determine which modifier keys were being held down at the time of the event by calling BLooper's `CurrentMessage()` function and looking up the "modifiers" entry in the BMessage it returns. If the *bytes* character is `B_FUNCTION_KEY` and you want to know which key produced the character, you can look up the "key" entry in the BMessage and test it against these constants:

B_F1_KEY	B_F6_KEY	B_F11_KEY
B_F2_KEY	B_F7_KEY	B_F12_KEY
B_F3_KEY	B_F8_KEY	B_PRINT_KEY (Print Screen)
B_F4_KEY	B_F9_KEY	B_SCROLL_KEY (Scroll Lock)
B_F5_KEY	B_F10_KEY	B_PAUSE_KEY

For example:

```
if ( bytes[0] == B_FUNCTION_KEY ) {
    BMessage *msg = Window()->CurrentMessage();
    if ( msg ) {
        int32 key;
        msg->FindInt32("key", &key);
        switch ( key ) {
        case B_F1_KEY:
            . . .
            break;
        case B_F2_KEY:
            . . .
            break;
        . . .
        }
    }
}
```

The BView version of `KeyDown()` handles keyboard navigation from view to view through B_TAB characters. If the view you define is navigable, its `KeyDown()` function should permit B_SPACE characters to operate the object and perhaps allow the arrow keys to navigate inside the view. It should also call the inherited version of `KeyDown()` to enable between-view navigation. For example:

```
void MyView::KeyDown(const char *bytes, int32 numBytes)
{
    if ( numBytes == 1 ) {
        switch ( bytes[0] ) {
        case B_SPACE:
            /* mimic a click in the view */
            break;
        case B_RIGHT_ARROW:
            /* move one position to the right in the view */
            break;
        case B_LEFT_ARROW:
            /* move one position to the left in the view */
            break;
        default:
            BView::KeyDown(bytes, numBytes);
            break;
        }
    }
}
```

If your BView is navigable but needs to respond to B_TAB characters—for example, if it permits users to insert tabs in a text string—its `KeyDown()` function should simply grab the characters and not pass them to the inherited function. Users will have to rely on the Option-Tab combination to navigate from your view.

See also: Appendix B, *Keyboard Information;* "B_KEY_DOWN" in Appendix A, *Message Protocols;* BWindow::SetDefaultButton(), modifiers()

KeyUp()

> virtual void **KeyUp**(const char *bytes*, int32 *numBytes*)

Implemented by derived classes to respond to a B_KEY_UP message reporting that the user released a key on the keyboard. The same set of keys that produce B_KEY_DOWN messages when they're pressed produce B_KEY_UP messages when they're released. The *bytes* and *numBytes* arguments encode the character mapped to the key the user released; they work exactly like the same arguments passed to KeyDown().

Some B_KEY_DOWN messages are swallowed by the system and are never dispatched by calling KeyDown(); others are dispatched, but not to the focus view. In contrast, all B_KEY_UP messages are dispatched by calling KeyUp() for the focus view of the active window. Since the focus view and active window can change between the time a key is pressed and the time it's released, this may or may not be the same BView that was notified of the B_KEY_DOWN message.

See also: KeyDown(), "B_KEY_DOWN" in Appendix A, *Message Protocols*

LeftTop()

> BPoint **LeftTop**(void) const

Returns the coordinates of the left top corner of the view—the smallest x and y coordinate values within the bounds rectangle.

See also: BRect::LeftTop(), Bounds()

LowColor()   *see SetHighColor()*

MakeFocus()

> virtual void **MakeFocus**(bool *focused* = true)

Makes the BView the current focus view for its window (if the *focused* flag is true), or causes it to give up that status (if *focused* is false). The focus view is the view that displays the current selection and is expected to handle reports of key-down events when the window is the active window. There can be no more than one focus view per window at a time.

When called to make a BView the focus view, this function invokes MakeFocus() for the previous focus view, passing it an argument of false. It's thus called twice— once for the new and once for the old focus view.

Calling MakeFocus() is the only way to make a view the focus view; the focus doesn't automatically change on mouse-down events. BViews that can display the current selection (including an insertion point) or that can accept pasted data should call `MakeFocus()` in their `MouseDown()` functions.

A derived class can override `MakeFocus()` to add code that takes note of the change in status. For example, a BView that displays selectable data may want to highlight the current selection when it becomes the focus view, and remove the highlighting when it's no longer the focus view. A BView that participates in the keyboard navigation system should visually indicate that it can be operated from the keyboard when it becomes the focus view, and remove that indication when the user navigates to another view and it's notified that it's no longer the focus view.

If the BView isn't attached to a window, this function has no effect.

See also: `BWindow::CurrentFocus()`, `IsFocus()`

MessageReceived()

> virtual void **MessageReceived**(BMessage *message*)

Augments the BHandler version of `MessageReceived()` to handle scripting messages for the BView.

See also: `BHandler::MessageReceived()`

MouseDown()

> virtual void **MouseDown**(BPoint *point*)

Implemented by derived classes to respond to a message reporting a mouse-down event within the view. The location of the cursor at the time of the event is given by *point* in the BView's coordinates.

`MouseDown()` functions are often implemented to track the cursor while the user holds the mouse button down and then respond when the button goes up. You can call the `GetMouse()` function to learn the current location of the cursor and the state of the mouse buttons. For example:

```
void MyView::MouseDown(BPoint point)
{
    uint32 buttons = 0;
    . . .
    Window()->CurrentMessage()->FindInt32("buttons", &buttons);
    while ( buttons ) {
        . . .
        snooze(20 * 1000);
        GetMouse(&point, &buttons, true);
    }
    . . .
}
```

It's important to snooze between `GetMouse()` calls so that the loop doesn't monopolize system resources; 20,000 microseconds is a minimum time to wait.

To get complete information about the mouse-down event, look inside the BMessage object returned by BLooper's `CurrentMessage()` function. The "clicks" entry in the message can tell you if this mouse-down is a solitary event or the latest in a series constituting a multiple click.

The BView version of `MouseDown()` is empty.

See also: "B_MOUSE_DOWN" in Appendix A, *Message Protocols*; `GetMouse()`

MouseMoved()

   virtual void **MouseMoved**(BPoint *point*, uint32 *transit*, const BMessage **message*)

Implemented by derived classes to respond to reports of mouse-moved events associated with the view. As the user moves the cursor over a window, the Application Server generates a continuous stream of messages reporting where the cursor is located.

The first argument, *point*, gives the cursor's new location in the BView's coordinate system. The second argument, *transit*, is one of three constants:

```
B_ENTERED_VIEW

B_INSIDE_VIEW

B_EXITED_VIEW
```

which explains whether the cursor has just entered the visible region of the view, is now inside the visible region having previously entered, or has just exited from the view. When the cursor crosses a boundary separating the visible regions of two views (perhaps moving from a parent to a child view, or from a child to a parent), `MouseMoved()` is called for each of the BViews, once with a *transit* code of `B_EXITED_VIEW` and once with a code of `B_ENTERED_VIEW`.

If the user is dragging a bundle of information from one location to another, the final argument, *message*, is a pointer to the BMessage object that holds the information. If a message isn't being dragged, *message* is `NULL`.

A `MouseMoved()` function might be implemented to ignore the `B_INSIDE_VIEW` case and respond only when the cursor enters or exits the view. For example, a BView might alter its display to indicate whether or not it can accept a message that has been dragged to it. Or it might be implemented to change the cursor image when it's over the view.

MouseMoved() notifications should not be used to track the cursor inside a view. Use the GetMouse() function instead. GetMouse() provides the current cursor location plus information on whether any of the mouse buttons are being held down.

The default version of MouseMoved() is empty.

See also: "B_MOUSE_MOVED" in Appendix A, *Message Protocols*; DragMessage()

MouseUp()

virtual void **MouseUp**(BPoint *point*)

This function is a placeholder for future releases; it isn't currently called. Although B_MOUSE_UP messages are generated, a virtual function is not now called to handle them.

See also: GetMouse()

MoveBy(), MoveTo()

void **MoveBy**(float *horizontal*, float *vertical*)

void **MoveTo**(BPoint *point*)
void **MoveTo**(float *x*, float *y*)

These functions move the view in its parent's coordinate system without altering its size.

MoveBy() adds *horizontal* coordinate units to the left and right components of the frame rectangle and *vertical* units to the top and bottom components. If *horizontal* and *vertical* are positive, the view moves downward and to the right. If they're negative, it moves upward and to the left.

MoveTo() moves the upper left corner of the view to *point*—or to (*x*, *y*)—in the parent view's coordinate system and adjusts all coordinates in the frame rectangle accordingly.

Neither function alters the BView's bounds rectangle or coordinate system.

None of the values passed to these functions should specify fractional coordinates; the sides of a view must line up on screen pixels. Fractional values will be rounded to the closest whole number.

If the BView is attached to a window, these functions cause its parent view to be updated, so the BView is immediately displayed in its new location. If it doesn't have a parent or isn't attached to a window, these functions merely alter its frame rectangle.

See also: FrameMoved(), ResizeBy(), Frame()

MovePenBy(), MovePenTo(), PenLocation()

void **MovePenBy**(float *horizontal*, float *vertical*)

void **MovePenTo**(BPoint *point*)
void **MovePenTo**(float *x*, float *y*)

BPoint **PenLocation**(void) const

These functions move the pen (without drawing a line) and report the current pen location.

`MovePenBy()` moves the pen *horizontal* coordinate units to the right and *vertical* units downward. If *horizontal* or *vertical* are negative, the pen moves in the opposite direction. `MovePenTo()` moves the pen to *point*—or to (*x*, *y*)—in the BView's coordinate system.

Some drawing functions also move the pen—to the end of whatever they draw. In particular, this is true of `StrokeLine()`, `DrawString()`, and `DrawChar()`. Functions that stroke a closed shape (such as `StrokeEllipse()`) don't move the pen.

The pen location is a parameter of the BView's graphics environment, which is maintained by both the Application Server and the BView. If the BView doesn't belong to a window, `MovePenTo()` and `MovePenBy()` cache the location, so that later, when the BView becomes attached to a window, it can be handed to the server to become the operable pen location for the BView. If the BView belongs to a window, these functions alter both the server parameter and the client-side cache.

`PenLocation()` returns the point where the pen is currently positioned in the BView's coordinate system. Because of the cache, this shouldn't entail contacting the server. The default pen position is (0.0, 0.0).

See also: `SetPenSize()`

MoveTo()   *see MoveBy()*

NextSibling()   *see Parent()*

Parent(), NextSibling(), PreviousSibling(), ChildAt(), CountChildren()

BView ****Parent**(void) const

BView ****NextSibling**(void) const

BView ****PreviousSibling**(void) const

BView *ChildAt(int32 *index*) const

int32 CountChildren(void) const

These functions provide various ways of navigating the view hierarchy. Parent() returns the BView's parent view, unless the parent is the top view of the window, in which case it returns NULL. It also returns NULL if the BView doesn't belong to a view hierarchy and has no parent.

All the children of the same parent are arranged in a linked list. NextSibling() returns the next sibling of the BView in the list, or NULL if the BView is the last child of its parent. PreviousSibling() returns the previous sibling of the BView, or NULL if the BView is the first child of its parent.

ChildAt() returns the view at *index* in the list of the BView's children, or NULL if the BView has no such child. Indices begin at 0 and there are no gaps in the list. CountChildren() returns the number of children the BView has. If the BView has no children, CountChildren() returns NULL, as will ChildAt() for all indices, including 0.

To scan the list of a BView's children, you can increment the index passed to ChildAt() until it returns NULL. However, it's more efficient to ask for the first child and then use NextSibling() to walk down the sibling list. For example:

```
BView *child;
if ( child = myView->ChildAt(0) ) {
    while ( child ) {
        . . .
        child = child->NextSibling();
    }
}
```

See also: AddChild()

PenLocation()   *see MovePenBy()*

PenSize()   *see SetPenSize()*

PreviousSibling()   *see Parent()*

Pulse()

virtual void Pulse(void)

Implemented by derived classes to do something at regular intervals. Pulses are regularly timed events, like the tick of a clock or the beat of a steady pulse. A BView receives Pulse() notifications when no other messages are pending, but only if it asks for them with the B_PULSE_NEEDED flag.

The interval between `Pulse()` calls can be set with BWindow's `SetPulseRate()` function. The default interval is around 500 milliseconds. The pulse rate is the same for all views within a window, but can vary between windows.

Derived classes can implement a `Pulse()` function to do something that must be repeated continuously. However, for time-critical actions, you should implement your own timing mechanism.

The BView version of this function is empty.

See also: `SetFlags()`, the BView constructor, `BWindow::SetPulseRate()`

RemoveChild()   *see AddChild()*

RemoveSelf()

   bool **RemoveSelf**(void)

Removes the BView from its parent and returns `true`, or returns `false` if the BView doesn't have a parent or for some reason can't be removed from the view hierarchy.

This function acts just like `RemoveChild()`, except that it removes the BView itself rather than one of its children.

See also: `AddChild()`

ResizeBy(), ResizeTo()

   void **ResizeBy**(float *horizontal*, float *vertical*)

   void **ResizeTo**(float *width*, float *height*)

These functions resize the view, without moving its left and top sides. `ResizeBy()` adds *horizontal* coordinate units to the width of the view and *vertical* units to the height. `ResizeTo()` makes the view *width* units wide and *height* units high. Both functions adjust the right and bottom components of the frame rectangle accordingly.

Since a BView's frame rectangle must be aligned on screen pixels, only integral values should be passed to these functions. Values with fractional components will be rounded to the nearest whole integer.

If the BView is attached to a window, these functions cause its parent view to be updated, so the BView is immediately displayed in its new size. If it doesn't have a parent or isn't attached to a window, these functions merely alter its frame and bounds rectangles.

See also: `FrameResized()`, `MoveBy()`, `BRect::Width()`, `Frame()`

ResizeToPreferred()   *see GetPreferredSize()*

ResizingMode()   *see SetResizingMode()*

ResolveSpecifier()

> virtual BHandler *ResolveSpecifier(BMessage *message*, int32 *index*,
> BMessage *specifier*, int32 *command*, const char *property*)

Resolves specifiers for the "Frame", "Hidden", and "View" properties. See "Scripting Support" in the class overview and "Scripting" in Chapter 2 for more information.

See also: BHandler::ResolveSpecifier()

ScrollBar()

> BScrollBar *ScrollBar(orientation *posture*) const

Returns a BScrollBar object that scrolls the BView (that has the BView as its target). The requested scroll bar has the *posture* orientation—B_VERTICAL or B_HORIZONTAL. If the BView isn't the target of a scroll bar with the specified orientation, this function returns NULL.

See also: ScrollBar::SetTarget()

ScrollBy(), ScrollTo()

> void ScrollBy(float *horizontal*, float *vertical*)

> virtual void ScrollTo(BPoint *point*)
> inline void ScrollTo(float *x*, float *y*)

These functions scroll the contents of the view, provided that the BView is attached to a window.

ScrollBy() adds *horizontal* to the left and right components of the BView's bounds rectangle, and *vertical* to the top and bottom components. This serves to shift the display *horizontal* coordinate units to the left and *vertical* units upward. If *horizontal* and *vertical* are negative, the display shifts in the opposite direction.

ScrollTo() shifts the contents of the view as much as necessary to put *point*—or (*x*, *y*)—at the upper left corner of its bounds rectangle. The point is specified in the BView's coordinate system.

Anything in the view that was visible before scrolling and also visible afterwards is automatically redisplayed at its new location. The remainder of the view is invalidated, so the BView's Draw() function will be called to fill in those parts of the display that were previously invisible. The update rectangle passed to `Draw()` will be the smallest possible rectangle that encloses just these new areas. If the view is scrolled in only one direction, the update rectangle will be exactly the area that needs to be drawn.

If the BView is the target of scroll bars, `ScrollBy()` and `ScrollTo()` notify the BScrollBar objects of the change in the display so they can update themselves to match. If the contents were scrolled horizontally, they call the horizontal BScrollBar's `SetValue()` function and pass it the new value of the left side of the bounds rectangle. If they were scrolled vertically, they call `SetValue()` for the vertical BScrollBar and pass it the new value of the top of the bounds rectangle.

The inline version of `ScrollTo()` works by creating a BPoint object and passing it to the version that's declared `virtual`. Therefore, if you want to override either function, you should override the virtual version. (However, due to the peculiarities of C++, overriding any version of an overloaded function hides all versions of the function. For continued access to the nonvirtual version without explicitly specifying the "BView::" prefix, simply copy the inline code from *interface/View.h* into the derived class.)

See also: `GetClippingRegion()`, `BScrollBar::SetValue()`

SetDrawingMode(), DrawingMode()

> virtual void **SetDrawingMode**(drawing_mode *mode*)

> drawing_mode **DrawingMode**(void) const

These functions set and return the BView's drawing mode, which can be any of the following ten constants:

B_OP_COPY	B_OP_MIN
B_OP_OVER	B_OP_MAX
B_OP_ERASE	B_OP_ADD
B_OP_INVERT	B_OP_SUBTRACT
B_OP_SELECT	B_OP_BLEND

The drawing mode is an element of the BView's graphics environment, which both the Application Server and the BView keep track of. If the BView isn't attached to a window, `SetDrawingMode()` caches the *mode*. When the BView is placed in a window and becomes known to the server, the cached value is automatically set as the current drawing mode. If the BView belongs to a window, `SetDrawingMode()` makes the change in both the server and the cache.

`DrawingMode()` returns the current mode. Because of the cache, this generally doesn't entail a trip to the server.

The default drawing mode is `B_OP_COPY`. It and the other modes are explained under "Drawing Modes" in the "Drawing" section of this chapter.

SetFlags(), Flags()

> virtual void **SetFlags**(uint32 *mask*)

> uint32 **Flags**(void) const

These functions set and return the flags that inform the Application Server about the kinds of notifications the BView should receive. The *mask* set by `SetFlags()` and the return value of `Flags()` is formed from combinations of the following constants:

B_WILL_DRAW	B_PULSE_NEEDED
B_FULL_UPDATE_ON_RESIZE	B_NAVIGABLE
B_FRAME_EVENTS	B_NAVIGABLE_JUMP

The flags are first set when the BView is constructed; they're explained in the description of the BView constructor. The mask can be 0.

To set just one of the flags, combine it with the current setting:

```
myView->SetFlags(Flags() | B_FRAME_EVENTS);
```

See also: the BView constructor, `SetResizingMode()`

SetFont(), GetFont()

> virtual void **SetFont**(const BFont **font*, uint32 *properties* = B_FONT_ALL)

> void **GetFont**(BFont **font*)

`SetFont()` sets the BView's current font so that it matches the specified *properties* of the *font* BFont object. The *properties* mask is formed by combining the following constants:

B_FONT_FAMILY_AND_STYLE	B_FONT_SPACING
B_FONT_SIZE	B_FONT_ENCODING
B_FONT_SHEAR	B_FONT_FACE
B_FONT_ROTATION	B_FONT_FLAGS

Each constant corresponds to a settable property of the BFont object. The default mask, B_FONT_ALL, is a shorthand for all the properties (including any that might be added in future releases). If the mask is 0, SetFont() won't set the BView's font.

GetFont() copies the BView's current font to the BFont object passed as an argument. Modifying this copy doesn't modify the BView's font; it takes an explicit SetFont() call to affect the BView.

For example, this code changes the size of a BView's font and turns antialiasing off:

```
BFont font;
myView->GetFont(&font);
font.SetSize(67.0);
font.SetFlags(B_DISABLE_ANTIALIASING);
myView->SetFont(&font, B_FONT_SIZE | B_FONT_FLAGS);
```

Since the BFont object that this example code alters is a copy of the BView's current font, it's not strictly necessary to name the properties that are different when calling SetFont(). However, it's more efficient and better practice to do so.

The font is part of the BView's graphic environment. Like other elements in the environment, it can be set whether or not the BView is attached to the window. Graphics parameters are kept by the Application Server and also cached by the BView object.

See also: the BFont class, get_font_family()

SetFontSize()

> void **SetFontSize**(float *points*)

Sets the size of the BView's font to *points*. This function is a shorthand for a SetFont() call that just alters the font size. For example, this line of code:

```
myView->SetFontSize(12.5);
```

does the same thing as:

```
BFont font;
font.SetSize(12.5);
myView->SetFont(&font, B_FONT_SIZE);
```

See also: the BFont class, SetFont()

SetHighColor(), HighColor(), SetLowColor(), LowColor()

> virtual void **SetHighColor**(rgb_color *color*)
> inline void **SetHighColor**(uchar *red*, uchar *green*, uchar *blue*, uchar *alpha* = 0)
>
> rgb_color **HighColor**(void) const

virtual void **SetLowColor**(rgb_color *color*)

inline void **SetLowColor**(uchar *red*, uchar *green*, uchar *blue*, uchar *alpha* = 0)

rgb_color **LowColor**(void) const

These functions set and return the current high and low colors of the BView. These colors combine to form a pattern that's passed as an argument to the `Stroke...()` and `Fill...()` drawing functions. The `B_SOLID_HIGH` pattern is the high color alone, and `B_SOLID_LOW` is the low color alone.

The default high color is black—*red, green,* and *blue* values all equal to 0. The default low color is white—*red, green,* and *blue* values all equal to 255.

NOTE

The *alpha* component of the color is currently ignored.

The inline versions of `SetHighColor()` and `SetLowColor()` take separate arguments for the *red, blue,* and *green* color components; they work by creating an `rgb_color` data structure and passing it to the corresponding function that's declared `virtual`. Therefore, if you want to override either function, you should override the virtual version. (However, due to the peculiarities of C++, overriding any version of an overloaded function hides all versions of the function. For continued access to the nonvirtual version without explicitly specifying the "BView::" prefix, simply copy the inline code from *interface/View.h* into the derived class.)

The high and low colors are parameters of the BView's graphics environment, which is kept in the BView's shadow counterpart in the Application Server and cached in the BView. If the BView isn't attached to a window, `SetHighColor()` and `SetLowColor()` cache the *color* value so that later, when the BView is placed in a window and becomes known to the server, the cached value can automatically be registered as the current high or low color for the view. If the BView belongs to a window, these functions alter both the client-side and the server-side values.

`HighColor()` and `LowColor()` return the BView's current high and low colors. Because of the cache, this shouldn't entail contacting the Application Server.

See also: "Patterns" in the "Drawing" section of this chapter, `SetViewColor()`

SetPenSize(), PenSize()

virtual void **SetPenSize**(float *size*)

float **PenSize**(void) const

`SetPenSize()` sets the size of the BView's pen—the graphics parameter that determines the thickness of stroked lines—and `PenSize()` returns the current pen size. The pen size is stated in coordinate units, but is translated to a device-specific number of pixels for each output device.

The pen tip can be thought of as a brush that's centered on the line path and held perpendicular to it. If the brush is broader than one pixel, it paints roughly the same number of pixels on both sides of the path.

The default pen size is 1.0 coordinate unit. It can be set to any nonnegative value, including 0.0. If set to 0.0, the size is translated to one pixel for all devices. This guarantees that it will always draw the thinnest possible line no matter what the resolution of the device.

Thus, lines drawn with pen sizes of 1.0 and 0.0 will look alike on the screen (one pixel thick), but the line drawn with a pen size of 1.0 will be 1/72 of an inch thick when printed, however many printer pixels that takes, while the line drawn with a 0.0 pen size will be just one pixel thick.

The pen size is a parameter of the BView's graphics environment maintained by the Application Server and cached by the BView. If the BView isn't attached to a window, `SetPenSize()` records the *size* so that later, when the BView is added to a window and becomes known to the server, the cached value can automatically be established as the operable pen size for the BView. If the BView belongs to a window, this function changes both the server and the cache.

See also: "The Pen" in the "Drawing" section of this chapter, `StrokeArc()`, `MovePenBy()`

SetResizingMode(), ResizingMode()

> virtual void **SetResizingMode**(uint32 *mode*)

> uint32 **ResizingMode**(void) const

These functions set and return the BView's automatic resizing mode. The resizing mode is first set when the BView is constructed. The various possible modes are explained where the constructor is described.

See also: the BView constructor, `SetFlags()`

SetScale()

> void **SetScale**(float *percent*)

Sets the scale of the BView's coordinate system. By default, each coordinate unit translates to one typographical point, about 1/72 of an inch. The *percent* argument scales the internal coordinate system of the view (not its frame rectangle) to a percentage of the default. For example, at a *percent* of 200.0, each coordinate unit will translate to 2 typographical points, 36 units per inch, and at a *percent* of 50.0, each unit will translate to a half point, 144 per inch.

See also: the BPrintJob class

SetViewColor(), ViewColor()

>   virtual void **SetViewColor**(rgb_color *color*)
>   inline void **SetViewColor**(uchar *red*, uchar *green*, uchar *blue*, uchar *alpha* = 0)
>
>   rgb_color **ViewColor**(void) const

These functions set and return the background color that's shown in all areas of the view rectangle that the BView doesn't cover with its own drawing. When the clipping region is erased prior to an update, it's erased to the view color. When a view is resized to expose new areas, the new areas are first displayed in the view color. The default color is white, which matches the background of the window's content area.

If you know that a BView will cover every pixel in the clipping region when it draws, you may want to avoid having the region erased to a color that will immediately be obliterated. If you set the view color to **B_TRANSPARENT_32_BIT**, the Application Server will not draw its background color before updates nor fill new areas with the background color. (Note that, despite the name, this doesn't make the view transparent—you can't see through it to what the view behind it would draw in that region.)

If you set the view color to anything but white (or **B_TRANSPARENT_32_BIT**), you must also set the **B_WILL_DRAW** flag. The flag informs the Application Server that there are specific drawing operations associated with the view. If it isn't set, the BView won't get update messages. Even if the BView does no other drawing—for example, if it doesn't implement a **Draw()** function—it must be updated to draw a background color other than white.

The version of **SetViewColor()** that takes separate arguments for the *red*, *blue*, and *green* color components works by creating an **rgb_color** data structure and passing it to the corresponding function that's declared **virtual**. Therefore, overriding only the virtual version will affect how both versions work. (However, due to the peculiarities of C++, overriding any version of an overloaded function hides all versions of the function. For continued access to the nonvirtual version without explicitly specifying the "BView::" prefix, simply copy the inline code from *interface/View.h* into the derived class.)

NOTE

The *alpha* color component is currently ignored.

It's best to set the view color before the window is shown on-screen.

The view color is a parameter of the BView's graphics environment, which both the Application Server and the BView maintain. If the BView doesn't belong to a window, SetViewColor() caches the *color* it's passed so that later, when the BView is attached to a window, it can automatically be handed to the server. If the BView belongs to a window, SetViewColor() alters both the server parameter and the client-side cache.

ViewColor() returns the current background color, which, because of the cache, doesn't normally entail contacting the Application Server.

See also: "The View Color" in the "Drawing" section of this chapter, SetHighColor()

Show()   *see Hide()*

StringWidth(), GetStringWidths()

> float **StringWidth**(const char *string) const
> float **StringWidth**(const char *string, int32 *length*) const

> void **GetStringWidths**(char *stringArray, int32 *lengthArray*[], int32 *numStrings*,
>   float *widthArray*[]) const

These functions measure how much room is required to draw a *string*, or a group of strings, in the BView's current font. They're equivalent to the identically named set of functions defined in the BFont class, except that they assume the BView's font. For example, this excerpt of code:

```
float width;
width = myView->StringWidth("Be"B_UTF8_REGISTERED);
```

produces the same result as:

```
float width;
BFont font;
myView->GetFont(&font);
width = font.StringWidth("Be"B_UTF8_REGISTERED);
```

See the BFont class for details.

See also: BFont::StringWidth(), BFont::GetEscapements()

StrokeArc(), FillArc()

> void **StrokeArc**(BRect *rect*, float *angle*, float *span*,
>   pattern *aPattern* = B_SOLID_HIGH)
> void **StrokeArc**(BPoint *center*, float *xRadius*, float *yRadius*, float *angle*, float *span*,
>   pattern *aPattern* = B_SOLID_HIGH)

void **FillArc**(BRect *rect*, float *angle*, float *span*,
                  pattern *aPattern* = B_SOLID_HIGH)
void **FillArc**(BPoint *center*, float *xRadius*, float *yRadius*, float *angle*, float *span*,
                  pattern *aPattern* = B_SOLID_HIGH)

These functions draw an arc, a portion of an ellipse. `StrokeArc()` strokes a line along the path of the arc. `FillArc()` fills the wedge defined by straight lines stretching from the center of the ellipse of which the arc is a part to the end points of the arc itself. For example:

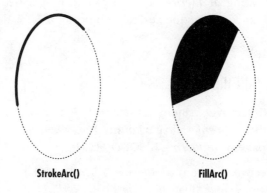

StrokeArc()   FillArc()

The arc is a section of the ellipse inscribed in *rect*—or the ellipse located at *center*, where the horizontal distance from the center to the edge of the ellipse is measured by *xRadius* and the vertical distance from the center to the edge is measured by *yRadius*.

The arc starts at *angle* and stretches along the ellipse for *span* degrees, where angular coordinates are measured counterclockwise with 0° on the right, as shown below:

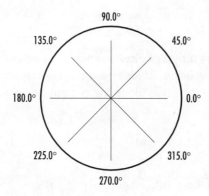

For example, if *angle* is 180.0° and *span* is 90.0°, the arc would be the lower left quarter of the ellipse. The same arc would be drawn if *angle* were 270.0° and *span* were –90.0°.

WARNING

Currently, *angle* and *span* measurements in fractions of a degree are not supported.

The width of the line drawn by `StrokeArc()` is determined by the current pen size. Both functions draw using *aPattern*—or, if no pattern is specified, using the current high color. Neither function alters the current pen position.

See also: `StrokeEllipse()`

StrokeEllipse(), FillEllipse()

> void **StrokeEllipse**(BRect *rect*, pattern *aPattern* = B_SOLID_HIGH)
> void **StrokeEllipse**(BPoint *center*, float *xRadius*, float *yRadius*,
>   pattern *aPattern* = B_SOLID_HIGH)
>
> void **FillEllipse**(BRect *rect*, pattern *aPattern* = B_SOLID_HIGH)
> void **FillEllipse**(BPoint *center*, float *xRadius*, float *yRadius*,
>   pattern *aPattern* = B_SOLID_HIGH)

These functions draw an ellipse. `StrokeEllipse()` strokes a line around the perimeter of the ellipse and `FillEllipse()` fills the area the ellipse encloses.

The ellipse has its center at *center*. The horizontal distance from the center to the edge of the ellipse is measured by *xRadius* and the vertical distance from the center to the edge is measured by *yRadius*. If *xRadius* and *yRadius* are the same, the ellipse will be a circle.

Alternatively, the ellipse can be described as one that's inscribed in *rect*. If the rectangle is a square, the ellipse will be a circle.

The width of the line drawn by `StrokeEllipse()` is determined by the current pen size. Both functions draw using *aPattern*—or, if no pattern is specified, using the current high color. Neither function alters the current pen position.

See also: `SetPenSize()`

StrokeLine()

> void **StrokeLine**(BPoint *start*, BPoint *end*, pattern *aPattern* = B_SOLID_HIGH)
> void **StrokeLine**(BPoint *end*, pattern *aPattern* = B_SOLID_HIGH)

Draws a straight line between the *start* and *end* points—or, if no starting point is given, between the current pen position and *end* point—and leaves the pen at the end point.

This function draws the line using the current pen size and the specified pattern. If no pattern is specified, the line is drawn in the current high color. The points are specified in the BView's coordinate system.

See also: `SetPenSize()`, `BeginLineArray()`

StrokePolygon(), FillPolygon()

> void **StrokePolygon**(BPolygon **polygon*,
>   bool *isClosed* = true, pattern *aPattern* = B_SOLID_HIGH)
> void **StrokePolygon**(BPoint **pointList*, int32 *numPoints*,
>   bool *isClosed* = true, pattern *aPattern* = B_SOLID_HIGH)
> void **StrokePolygon**(BPoint **pointList*, int32 *numPoints*, BRect *rect*,
>   bool *isClosed* = true, pattern *aPattern* = B_SOLID_HIGH)
>
> void **FillPolygon**(BPolygon **aPolygon*,
>   pattern *aPattern* = B_SOLID_HIGH)
> void **FillPolygon**(BPoint **pointList*, int32 *numPoints*,
>   pattern *aPattern* = B_SOLID_HIGH)
> void **FillPolygon**(BPoint **pointList*, int32 *numPoints*, BRect *rect*,
>   pattern *aPattern* = B_SOLID_HIGH)

These functions draw a polygon with an arbitrary number of sides. `StrokePolygon()` strokes a line around the edge of the polygon using the current pen size. If a *pointList* is specified rather than a BPolygon object, this function strokes a line from point to point, connecting the first and last points if they aren't identical. However, if the *isClosed* flag is `false`, `StrokePolygon()` won't stroke the line connecting the first and last points that define the BPolygon (or the first and last points in the *pointList*). This leaves the polygon open—making it not appear to be a polygon at all, but rather a series of straight lines connected at their end points. If *isClosed* is `true`, as it is by default, the polygon will appear to be a polygon, a closed figure.

`FillPolygon()` is a simpler function; it fills in the entire area enclosed by the polygon.

Both functions must calculate the frame rectangle of a polygon constructed from a point list—that is, the smallest rectangle that contains all the points in the polygon. If you know what this rectangle is, you can make the function somewhat more efficient by passing it as the *rect* parameter.

Both functions draw using the specified pattern—or, if no pattern is specified, in the current high color. Neither function alters the current pen position.

See also: SetPenSize(), the BPolygon class

StrokeRect(), FillRect()

> void **StrokeRect**(BRect *rect*, pattern *aPattern* = B_SOLID_HIGH)

> void **FillRect**(BRect *rect*, pattern *aPattern* = B_SOLID_HIGH)

These functions draw a rectangle. StrokeRect() strokes a line around the edge of the rectangle; the width of the line is determined by the current pen size. FillRect() fills in the entire rectangle.

Both functions draw using the pattern specified by *aPattern*—or, if no pattern is specified, in the current high color. Neither function alters the current pen position.

See also: SetPenSize(), StrokeRoundRect()

StrokeRoundRect(), FillRoundRect()

> void **StrokeRoundRect**(BRect *rect*, float *xRadius*, float *yRadius*,
>   pattern *aPattern* = B_SOLID_HIGH)

> void **FillRoundRect**(BRect *rect*, float *xRadius*, float *yRadius*,
>   pattern *aPattern* = B_SOLID_HIGH)

These functions draw a rectangle with rounded corners. The corner arc is one-quarter of an ellipse, where the ellipse would have a horizontal radius equal to *xRadius* and a vertical radius equal to *yRadius*.

Except for the rounded corners of the rectangle, these functions work exactly like StrokeRect() and FillRect().

Both functions draw using the pattern specified by *aPattern*—or, if no pattern is specified, in the current high color. Neither function alters the current pen position.

See also: StrokeRect(), StrokeEllipse()

StrokeTriangle(), FillTriangle()

> void **StrokeTriangle**(BPoint *firstPoint*, BPoint *secondPoint*, BPoint *thirdPoint*,
>   pattern *aPattern* = B_SOLID_HIGH)
> void **StrokeTriangle**(BPoint *firstPoint*, BPoint *secondPoint*, BPoint *thirdPoint*, BRect
>   *rect*, pattern *aPattern* = B_SOLID_HIGH)

void FillTriangle(BPoint *firstPoint*, BPoint *secondPoint*, BPoint *thirdPoint*,
        pattern *aPattern* = B_SOLID_HIGH)
void FillTriangle(BPoint *firstPoint*, BPoint *secondPoint*, BPoint *thirdPoint*,
        BRect *rect*, pattern *aPattern* = B_SOLID_HIGH)

These functions draw a triangle, a three-sided polygon. `StrokeTriangle()` strokes a line the width of the current pen size from the first point to the second, from the second point to the third, then back to the first point. `FillTriangle()` fills in the area that the three points enclose.

Each function must calculate the smallest rectangle that contains the triangle. If you know what this rectangle is, you can make the function marginally more efficient by passing it as the *rect* parameter.

Both functions do their drawing using the pattern specified by *aPattern*—or, if no pattern is specified, in the current high color. Neither function alters the current pen position.

See also: `SetPenSize()`

Sync()   *see Flush()*

TargetedByScrollView()

virtual void TargetedByScrollView(BScrollView **scroller*)

Implemented by derived classes to respond to a notification that the BView has become the target of the *scroller* BScrollView object. This function is called when the BScrollView sets its target, which it does on construction. The target is the object whose contents will be scrolled.

BView's implementation of this function is empty.

See also: the BScrollView class

Window()

BWindow **Window*(void) const

Returns the BWindow to which the BView belongs, or `NULL` if the BView isn't attached to a window. This function returns the same object that `Looper()` (inherited from the BHandler class) does—except that `Window()` returns it more specifically as a pointer to a BWindow and `Looper()` returns it more generally as a pointer to a BLooper.

See also: `BHandler::Looper()` in the Application Kit, `AddChild()`, `BWindow::AddChild()`, `AttachedToWindow()`

WindowActivated()

virtual void **WindowActivated**(bool *active*)

Implemented by derived classes to take whatever steps are necessary when the BView's window becomes the active window, or when the window gives up that status. If *active* is **true**, the window has become active. If *active* is **false**, it no longer is the active window.

All objects in the view hierarchy receive **WindowActivated()** notifications when the status of the window changes.

BView's version of this function is empty.

See also: BWindow::WindowActivated()

BWindow

Derived from:	public BLooper
Declared in:	be/interface/Window.h
Library:	libbe.so

Overview

The BWindow class defines an application interface to windows. Each BWindow object corresponds to one window in the user interface.

It's the Application Server's responsibility to provide an application with the windows it needs. The server allocates the memory each window requires, renders images in the window on instructions from the application, and manages the user interface. It equips windows with all the accouterments that let users activate, move, resize, reorder, hide, and close them. These user actions are not mediated by the application; they're handled within the Application Server alone. However, the server sends the application messages notifying it of user actions that affect the window. A class derived from BWindow can implement virtual functions such as **FrameResized()**, **QuitRequested()**, and **WindowActivated()** to respond to these messages.

A BWindow object is the application's interface to a server window. Creating the object instructs the server to produce a window that can be displayed to the user. The BWindow constructor determines what kind of window it will be and how it will behave. The window is initially hidden; the **Show()** function makes it visible on-screen.

BWindow objects communicate directly with the Application Server. However, before this communication can take place, the constructor for the BApplication object must establish an initial connection to the server. You must construct the BApplication object before the first BWindow.

View Hierarchy

A window can display images, but it can't produce them. To draw within a window, an application needs a collection of various BView objects. For example, a window might have several check boxes or radio buttons, a list of names, some scroll bars, and a scrollable display of pictures or text—all provided by objects that inherit from the BView class.

These BViews are created by the application and are associated with the BWindow by arranging them in a hierarchy under a *top view*, a view that fills the entire content area of the window. Views are added to the hierarchy by making them children of views already in the hierarchy, which at the outset means children of the top view.

A BWindow doesn't reveal the identity of its top view, but it does have functions that act on the top view's behalf. For example, AddChild() adds a view to the hierarchy as a child of the top view; FindView() searches the view hierarchy beginning with the top view.

Window Threads

Every window runs in its own thread. A BWindow object is a kind of BLooper; it spawns a *window thread* where it runs a message loop. You don't have to call Run() to get the message loop going, as you do for other BLoopers; it's called for you when you first call Show() to put the window on-screen.

The window's message loop receives messages reporting user actions associated with the window. Typically, those actions are directed at something that's drawn within the content area of the window—so the object responsible for responding is usually one of the BViews in the window's view hierarchy. Views are notified of user actions through MouseDown(), KeyDown(), MouseMoved() and other virtual function calls. However, sometimes the responsible object is the BWindow itself. It handles FrameMoved(), QuitRequested(), WindowActivated() and other notifications.

Since all these functions are called from the window thread, that thread will execute the application's responses to user activity centering on the window. This, of course, includes operations spun off from the original message. For example, if the user clicks a button in a window and this initiates a series of calculations involving a variety of objects, those calculations will be executed in the thread of the window where the button is located (unless the calculation explicitly spawns other threads or sends messages to other BLoopers).

The message loop continues running until the window is told to quit and the BWindow object is deleted. Everything the window thread does is initiated by a message of some kind.

Quitting

To "close" a window is to remove the window from the screen, quit the message loop, kill the window thread, and delete the BWindow object. As is the case for other BLoopers, this process is initiated by a request to quit—a B_QUIT_REQUESTED message.

For a BWindow, a request to quit is an event that might be reported from the Application Server (as when the user clicks a window's close button) or from within the application (as when the user operates a Close menu item).

To respond to quit-requested messages, classes derived from BWindow implement QuitRequested() functions. QuitRequested() can prevent the window from closing, or take whatever action is appropriate before the window is destroyed. It typically interacts with the user, asking, for example, whether recent changes to a document should be saved.

QuitRequested() is a hook function declared in the BLooper class; it's not documented here. See the BLooper class in the Application Kit for information on the function and on how classes derived from BWindow might implement it.

Scripting Support

BWindow objects can respond to the "suite/vnd.Be-window" suite of scripting requests. The suite includes these messages:

Property name: "Frame" for the frame rectangle of the window
Specifiers: B_DIRECT_SPECIFIER only
Messages: B_SET_PROPERTY and B_GET_PROPERTY
Data type: BRect (B_RECT_TYPE)

Property name: "Title" for the window title
Specifiers: B_DIRECT_SPECIFIER only
Messages: B_SET_PROPERTY and B_GET_PROPERTY
Data type: A null-terminated character string (B_STRING_TYPE)

The suite also includes the ability to resolve the following specifier, regardless of what the message may be:

Property name: "View" for a descendant BView object
Specifiers: B_NAME_SPECIFIER, B_INDEX_SPECIFIER,
            or B_REVERSE_INDEX_SPECIFIER

The specified BView replaces the BWindow as the designated handler for the message. For B_NAME_SPECIFIER, the BWindow searches the entire view hierarchy for the named view. For B_INDEX_SPECIFIER and B_REVERSE_INDEX_SPECIFIER, it uses the index to pick an immediate child of its top view.

See "Scripting" in Chapter 2 for more information.

Hook Functions

FrameMoved()
   Can be implemented to take note of the fact that the window has moved.

FrameResized()
   Can be implemented to take note of the fact that the window has been resized.

MenusBeginning()
   Can be implemented to make sure menu data structures are up-to-date before the menus are displayed to the user.

MenusEnded()
   Can be implemented to note that menus are no longer being displayed. The BWindow will receive a MenusBeginning() notification before they're displayed again.

Minimize()
   Removes the window from the screen and replaces it with its minimized representation, or restores the window if it was previously minimized; can be reimplemented to provide a different representation for a minimized window.

ScreenChanged()
   Makes sure the window stays visible on-screen when the size of the pixel grid changes; can be implemented to make other adjustments when the screen changes its depth or dimensions.

WindowActivated()
   Can be implemented to take whatever action is necessary when the window becomes the active window, or when it loses that status.

WorkspaceActivated()
   Can be implemented to take remedial steps when the workspace where the window lives becomes the active workspace, or when it loses that status.

WorkspacesChanged()
   Can be implemented to respond when the set of workspaces where the window can be displayed changes.

Zoom()
   Zooms the window to a larger size, or from the larger size to its previous state; can be reimplemented to modify the target window size or make other adjustments.

Constructor and Destructor

BWindow()

BWindow(BRect *frame*, const char **title*, window_type *type*, uint32 *flags*,
uint32 *workspaces* = B_CURRENT_WORKSPACE)
BWindow(BMessage **archive*)

Produces a new window with the *frame* content area, assigns it a *title* and a *type*, sets its behavioral *flags*, and determines the *workspaces* where it can be displayed. However, the constructor does not spawn a new thread of execution for the window or begin running a message loop in that thread. The thread will be created and the loop begun when Show() is called to put the window on-screen for the first time.

The first argument, *frame*, determines where the window will be located on-screen and the size of its content area; it excludes the border and the title tab at the top. The window's top view will be exactly the same size and shape as its frame rectangle—though the top view is located in the window's coordinate system and the window's frame rectangle is specified in the screen coordinate system. The width and height of *frame* must both be greater than 0.0.

For the window to become visible on-screen, the frame rectangle you assign it must lie within the frame rectangle of the screen. You can get this information by constructing a BScreen object and asking for its Frame():

```
BScreen screen(B_MAIN_SCREEN_ID);
BRect r = screen.Frame();
```

Since a window is always aligned on screen pixels, the sides of its frame rectangle must have integral coordinate values. Any fractional coordinates that are passed in *frame* will be rounded to the nearest whole number.

The second argument, *title*, does two things: It sets the title the window will display if it has a tab, and it determines the name assigned to the window thread (when Show() is called). The thread name is a string that prefixes "w>" to the title in the following format:

```
"w>title"
```

If the *title* is long, only as many characters will be used as will fit within the limited length of a thread name. (Only the thread name is limited, not the window title.) The title (and thread name) can be changed with the SetTitle() function.

The *title* can be NULL or an empty string.

The *type* of window is set by one of the following constants:

B_MODAL_WINDOW	A modal window, one that disables other activity in the application until the user dismisses it. It has a border but no tab to display a title.
B_BORDERED_WINDOW	An ordinary (nonmodal) window with a border but no title tab.
B_TITLED_WINDOW	A window with a tab that displays its title and a border that's the same on all sides.
B_DOCUMENT_WINDOW	A window with a title tab, a border, and a resize button in the bottom right corner. The border on the right and bottom sides is designed to look good next to vertical and horizontal scroll bars. The tab and border are drawn around the window's frame rectangle, but the resize button is located inside the content area of the window, in the corner where the scroll bars meet. It's drawn last and obscures whatever the application might draw in that corner.

The fourth argument, *flags*, is a mask that determines the behavior of the window. It's formed by combining constants from the following set:

B_NOT_MOVABLE	Prevents the user from being able to move the window. By default, a window with a tab at the top is movable.
B_NOT_H_RESIZABLE	Prevents the user from resizing the window horizontally. A window is horizontally resizable by default.
B_NOT_V_RESIZABLE	Prevents the user from resizing the window vertically. A window is vertically resizable by default.
B_NOT_RESIZABLE	Prevents the user from resizing the window in any direction. This constant is a shorthand that you can substitute for the combination of B_NOT_H_RESIZABLE and B_NOT_V_RESIZABLE. A window is resizable by default.
B_NOT_CLOSABLE	Prevents the user from closing the window (eliminates the close button from its tab). Windows with title tabs have a close button by default.
B_NOT_ZOOMABLE	Prevents the user from zooming the window larger or smaller (eliminates the zoom button from the window tab). Windows with tabs are zoomable by default.
B_NOT_MINIMIZABLE	Prevents the user from collapsing the window to its minimized form. Windows can be minimized by default.
B_WILL_ACCEPT_FIRST_CLICK	Enables the BWindow to receive mouse-down and mouse-up messages even when it isn't the active window. By default, a click in a window that isn't the active window brings the win-dow to the front and makes it active, but doesn't get reported to the application. If a BWindow accepts the first click, the event gets reported to the application, but it doesn't make the window active. The BView that responds to the mouse-down message must take responsibility for activating the window.
B_WILL_FLOAT	Not implemented for the current release.

If *flags* is 0, the window will be one the user can move, resize, close, and zoom. It won't float or accept the first click.

The final argument, *workspaces*, associates the window with a set of one or more workspaces. Each workspace is identified by a specific bit in a 32-bit integer; the *workspaces* mask can name up to 32 workspaces. The mask can include workspaces that don't yet exist. The window will live in those workspaces when and if the user creates them.

Two special values can be passed as the *workspaces* parameter:

B_CURRENT_WORKSPACE	Associates the window with the workspace that's currently displayed on-screen (the active workspace), whatever workspace that happens to be. This is the default choice.
B_ALL_WORKSPACES	Associates the window with all workspaces. The window will show up in all workspaces the user has created and in all future workspaces that will be created.

When created, the window is hidden and the BWindow object is locked; it must be locked when Show() is called for the first time.

See also: Hide(), SetFlags(), SetTitle()

~BWindow()

> virtual **~BWindow**(void)

Frees all memory that the BWindow allocated for itself.

Call the Quit() function to destroy the BWindow object; don't use the **delete** operator. Quit() does everything that's necessary to shut down the window—such as remove its connection to the Application Server and get rid of its views—and invokes **delete** at the appropriate time.

See also: Quit()

Static Functions

Instantiate()

> static BWindow ***Instantiate**(BMessage *archive*)

Returns a new BWindow object, allocated by **new** and created with the version of the constructor that takes a BMessage *archive*. However, if the *archive* message doesn't contain data for a BWindow object, the return value will be NULL.

See also: BArchivable::Instantiate(), instantiate_object(), Archive()

Member Functions

Activate()

> void **Activate**(bool *flag* = true)

Makes the BWindow the active window (if *flag* is true), or causes it to relinquish that status (if *flag* is false). When this function activates a window, it reorders the window to the front, highlights its tab, and makes it the window responsible for handling subsequent keyboard messages. When it deactivates a window, it undoes all these things. It reorders the window to the back and removes the highlighting from its tab. Another window (the new active window) becomes the target for keyboard messages.

When a BWindow is activated or deactivated (whether programmatically through this function or by the user), it and all the BViews in its view hierarchy receive WindowActivated() notifications.

This function will not activate a window that's hidden.

See also: WindowActivated(), BView::WindowActivated()

AddChild(), RemoveChild()

> void **AddChild**(BView **aView*, BView **sibling* = NULL)

> bool **RemoveChild**(BView **aView*)

AddChild() adds *aView* to the hierarchy of views associated with the window, making it a child of the window's top view, and assigns the BWindow object as *aView*'s next handler for unrecognized messages. The new child is inserted before the named *sibling* BView in the top view's list of children. If the sibling is NULL (as it is by default), *aView* is added to the end of the list.

However, AddChild() fails if *sibling* isn't a child of the top view. Moreover, if *aView* already has a parent, it won't be forcibly removed from that family and adopted into this one. A view can live with but one parent at a time.

If successful in adopting *aView*, AddChild() calls its AttachedToWindow() and AllAttached() functions to inform it that it now belongs to the BWindow. Every BView that descends from *aView* also becomes attached to the window and receives its own AttachedToWindow() and AllAttached() notifications. In addition, each newly attached BView is added to the BWindow's list of BHandler objects, making it eligible to receive messages the BWindow dispatches.

RemoveChild() removes *aView* from the BWindow's view hierarchy, but only if it was added to the hierarchy as a child of the window's top view (by calling the

BWindow version of AddChild()). If it succeeds in removing *aView*, RemoveChild() returns true. If not, it returns false.

When a BView is removed from a window, all its descendant views are removed with it. Every removed BView receives a DetachedFromWindow() and an AllDetached() function call to notify it of the change and it's crossed off the BWindow's list of eligible message handlers.

See also: BView::AddChild(), BLooper::AddHandler(), BView::AttachedToWindow(), BView::DetachedFromWindow(), BHandler::SetNextHandler()

AddFloater(), RemoveFloater()

void **AddFloater**(BWindow **floatingWindow*)

void **RemoveFloater**(BWindow **floatingWindow*)

These functions are not implemented for the current release.

AddShortcut(), RemoveShortcut()

void **AddShortcut**(uint32 *aChar*, uint32 *modifiers*, BMessage **message*)
void **AddShortcut**(uint32 *aChar*, uint32 *modifiers*, BMessage **message*,
        BHandler **handler*)

void **RemoveShortcut**(uint32 *aChar*, uint32 *modifiers*)

These functions set up, and tear down, keyboard shortcuts for the window. A shortcut is a character (*aChar*) that the user can type, in combination with the Command key and possibly one or more other *modifiers* to issue an instruction to the application. For example, Command-*r* might rotate what's displayed within a particular view. The instruction is issued by posting a message to the window thread.

Keyboard shortcuts are commonly associated with menu items. However, *do not* use these functions to set up shortcuts for menus; use the BMenuItem constructor instead. These BWindow functions are for shortcuts that aren't associated with a menu.

BWindows come with five built-in shortcuts:

Shortcut	Message	Target handler
Command-*x*	B_CUT	the focus view
Command-*c*	B_COPY	the focus view
Command-*v*	B_PASTE	the focus view
Command-*a*	B_SELECT_ALL	the focus view
Command-*w*	B_QUIT_REQUESTED	the BWindow

(In addition, Command-*q* sends a B_QUIT_REQUESTED message to the BApplication object.)

AddShortcut() registers a new window-specific keyboard shortcut. The first two arguments, *aChar* and *modifiers*, specify the character and the modifier states that together will issue the instruction. *modifiers* is a mask that combines any of the usual modifier constants (see the modifiers() function for the full list). Typically, it's one or more of these four (or it's 0):

B_SHIFT_KEY

B_CONTROL_KEY

B_OPTION_KEY

B_COMMAND_KEY

B_COMMAND_KEY is assumed; it doesn't have to be specified. The character value that's passed as an argument should reflect the modifier keys that are required. For example, if the shortcut is Command-Shift-*C*, *aChar* should be "C", not "c".

The instruction that the shortcut issues is embodied in a model *message* that the BWindow will copy and post to itself whenever it's notified of a key-down event matching the combination of *aChar* and *modifiers* (including B_COMMAND_KEY).

Before posting the message, it adds one data field to the copy:

Field name	Type code	Description
"when"	B_INT64_TYPE	When the key-down event occurred, as measured by the number of microseconds from 12:00:00 AM January 1, 1970.

The model *message* shouldn't contain an entry of the same name.

If a target *handler* is specified, the BWindow will dispatch the message to that BHandler object; the *handler* must be in the BWindow's list of eligible BHandlers. If the *handler* is NULL, the BWindow will dispatch the message to its preferred handler at the time, the view that's in focus when it gets the message (or to itself if no view is in focus). If a *handler* isn't specified at all, not even NULL, the BWindow will handle the message.

RemoveShortcut() unregisters a keyboard shortcut that was previously added.

See also: MessageReceived(), the BMenuItem constructor

Archive()

virtual status_t **Archive**(BMessage **archive*, bool *deep* = true) const

Archives the BWindow by recording its frame rectangle, title, type, and flags in the BMessage *archive*. If the *deep* flag is `true`, this function also archives all the views in the window's view hierarchy. If the flag is `false`, only the BWindow is archived.

See also: `BArchivable::Archive()`, `Instantiate()` static function

Bounds()

   BRect **Bounds**(void) const

Returns the current bounds rectangle of the window. The bounds rectangle encloses the content area of the window and is stated in the window's coordinate system. It's exactly the same size as the frame rectangle, but its left and top sides are always 0.0.

See also: `Frame()`

ChildAt(), CountChildren()

   BView ***ChildAt**(int32 *index*) const

   int32 **CountChildren**(void) const

The first of these functions returns the child BView at *index*, or `NULL` if there's no such child of the BWindow's top view. Indices begin at 0 and there are no gaps in the list. The second function returns how many children the top view has.

See also: `BView::Parent()`

Close()   *see Quit()*

ConvertToScreen(), ConvertFromScreen()

   BPoint **ConvertToScreen**(BPoint *windowPoint*) const
   void **ConvertToScreen**(BPoint *windowPoint*) const

   BRect **ConvertToScreen**(BRect *windowRect*) const
   void **ConvertToScreen**(BRect *windowRect*) const

   BPoint **ConvertFromScreen**(BPoint *screenPoint*) const
   void **ConvertFromScreen**(BPoint *screenPoint*) const

   BRect **ConvertFromScreen**(BRect *screenRect*) const
   void **ConvertFromScreen**(BRect *screenRect*) const

These functions convert points and rectangles to and from the global screen coordinate system. `ConvertToScreen()` converts *windowPoint* or *windowRect* from the window coordinate system to the screen coordinate system. `Convert-`

`FromScreen()` makes the opposite conversion; it converts *screenPoint* or *screenRect* from the screen coordinate system to the window coordinate system.

If the point or rectangle is passed by value, the function returns the converted value. If a pointer is passed, the conversion is done in place.

The window coordinate system has its origin, (0.0, 0.0), at the left top corner of the window's content area. The origin of the screen coordinate system is at the left top corner of the main screen.

See also: `BView::ConvertToScreen()`

CurrentFocus()

> BView *CurrentFocus(void) const

Returns the current focus view for the BWindow, or `NULL` if no view is currently in focus. The focus view is the BView that's responsible for showing the current selection and handling keyboard messages when the window is the active window.

The BWindow sets its preferred handler to be the focus view, so the inherited `PreferredHandler()` function will return the same object. `CurrentFocus()` returns the focus view as a BView object; `PreferredHandler()` returns it as a BHandler.

See also: `BView::MakeFocus()`, `BInvoker::SetTarget()`, `BLooper::SetPreferredHandler()`

DefaultButton()   *see SetDefaultButton()*

DisableUpdates(), EnableUpdates()

> void DisableUpdates(void)

> void EnableUpdates(void)

These functions disable automatic updating within the window, and re-enable it again. Updating is enabled by default, so every user action that changes a view and every program action that invalidates a view's contents causes the view to be automatically redrawn.

This may be inefficient when there are a number of changes to a view, or to a group of views within a window. In this case, you can temporarily disable the updating mechanism by calling `DisableUpdates()`, make the changes, then call `Enable-Updates()` to re-enable updating and have all the changes displayed at once.

See also: `BView::Invalidate()`, `UpdateIfNeeded()`

DispatchMessage()

virtual void **DispatchMessage**(BMessage *message*, BHandler *handler*)

Overrides the BLooper function to dispatch messages as they're received by the window thread. This function is called for you each time the BWindow takes a message from its queue. It dispatches the message by calling the virtual function that's designated to begin the application's response.

- It dispatches system messages by calling a message-specific virtual function implemented for the BWindow or the responsible BView. See "Hook Functions for Interface Messages" in the "Responding to the User" section of this chapter for a list of these functions.

- It defers to the BLooper version of this function to dispatch B_QUIT_REQUESTED messages.

- It dispatches other messages by calling the targeted *handler's* Message-Received() function.

Derived classes can override this function to make it dispatch specific kinds of messages in other ways. For example:

```
void MyWindow::DispatchMessage(BMessage *message)
{
    if ( message->what == MAKE_PREDICTIONS )
        predictor->GuessAbout(message);
    else
        BWindow::DispatchMessage(message);
}
```

However, much of the user interface depends on how the BWindow processes system messages. For example, for keyboard shortcuts and keyboard navigation to work, the BWindow object needs to get its hands on B_KEY_DOWN messages. You shouldn't implement a version of DispatchMessage() that denies these messages to the BWindow version. (Nor should you filter these messages so they never reach DispatchMessage().)

The BWindow is locked before DispatchMessage() is called. The lock remains in place until the window thread's response to the message is complete and DispatchMessage() returns. When it returns, the message loop deletes the *message*. You should not delete it in application code (unless DetachCurrentMessage() is first called to detach it from the message loop).

See also: the BMessage class, the BMessageFilter class,
BLooper::DispatchMessage(), BLooper::CurrentMessage()

EnableUpdates()   *see DisableUpdates()*

FindView()

BView *FindView(BPoint *point*) const
BView *FindView(const char *name) const

Returns the view located at *point* within the window, or the view tagged with *name*. The point is specified in the window's coordinate system (the coordinate system of its top view), which has the origin at the upper left corner of the window's content area.

If no view is located at the point given, or no view within the window has the name given, this function returns NULL.

See also: BView::FindView()

Flush()

void Flush(void) const

Flushes the window's connection to the Application Server, sending whatever happens to be in the output buffer to the server. The buffer is automatically flushed on every update and after each message.

This function has the same effect as the Flush() function defined for the BView class.

See also: BView::Flush

Frame()

BRect Frame(void) const

Asks the Application Server for the current frame rectangle for the window and returns it. The frame rectangle encloses the content area of the window and is stated in the screen coordinate system. It's first set by the BWindow constructor and is modified as the window is resized and moved.

See also: MoveBy(), ResizeBy(), the BWindow constructor

FrameMoved()

virtual void FrameMoved(BPoint *screenPoint*)

Implemented by derived classes to respond to a notification that the window has moved. The move—which placed the left top corner of the window's content area at *screenPoint* in the screen coordinate system—could be the result of the user dragging the window or of the program calling MoveBy() or MoveTo(). If the user drags the window, `FrameMoved()` is called repeatedly as the window moves. If the program moves the window, it's called just once to report the new location.

The default version of this function does nothing.

See also: `MoveBy()`, "B_WINDOW_MOVED" in Appendix A, *Message Protocols*

FrameResized()

> virtual void **FrameResized**(float *width*, float *height*)

Implemented by derived classes to respond to a notification that the window's content area has been resized to a new *width* and *height*. The resizing could be the result of the program calling `ResizeTo()`, `ResizeBy()`, or `Zoom()`—in which case `FrameResized()` is called just once to report the window's new size. It could also be the result of a user action—in which case it's called repeatedly as the user drags a corner of the window to resize it.

The default version of this function does nothing.

See also: `ResizeBy()`, "B_WINDOW_RESIZED" in Appendix A, *Message Protocols*

GetSizeLimits()   *see SetSizeLimits()*

GetSupportedSuites()

> virtual status_t **GetSupportedSuites**(BMessage **message*)

Adds the name "suite/vnd.Be-window" to the *message*. See "Scripting Support" in the class overview for more information.

See also: `BHandler::GetSupportedSuites()`

Hide(), Show()

> virtual void **Hide**(void)

> virtual void **Show**(void)

These functions hide the window so it won't be visible on-screen, and show it again.

`Hide()` removes the window from the screen. If it happens to be the active window, `Hide()` also deactivates it. Hiding a window hides all the views attached to the window. While the window is hidden, its BViews respond `true` to `IsHidden()` queries.

`Show()` puts the window back on-screen. It places the window in front of other windows and makes it the active window. Since a window is hidden when it's constructed, you must call `Show()` to bring it to life. That first call unlocks the window, spawns the window thread, and begins the message loop.

Calls to `Hide()` and `Show()` can be nested; if `Hide()` is called more than once, you'll need to call `Show()` an equal number of times for the window to become visible again.

A window begins life hidden (as if `Hide()` had been called once); it takes an initial call to `Show()` to display it on-screen.

See also: `IsHidden()`

IsActive()

bool **IsActive**(void) const

Returns `true` if the window is currently the active window, and `false` if it's not.

See also: `Activate()`

IsFront()

bool **IsFront**(void) const

Returns `true` if the window is currently the frontmost window on-screen, and `false` if it's not.

IsHidden()

bool **IsHidden**(void) const

Returns `true` if the window is currently hidden, and `false` if it isn't.

Windows are hidden at the outset. The `Show()` function puts them on-screen, and `Hide()` can be called to hide them again.

If `Show()` has been called to unhide the window, but the window is totally obscured by other windows or occupies coordinates that don't intersect with the physical screen, `IsHidden()` will nevertheless return `false`, even though the window isn't visible.

See also: `Hide()`

KeyMenuBar() *see SetKeyMenuBar()*

MenusBeginning(), MenusEnded()

> virtual void **MenusBeginning**(void)

> virtual void **MenusEnded**(void)

These functions are implemented by derived classes to make sure menus are up-to-date when shown on-screen. `MenusBeginning()` is called just before menus belonging to the window are about to be shown to the user. It gives the BWindow a chance to make any required alterations—for example, disabling or enabling particular items—so that the menus accurately reflect the current state of the window. `MenusEnded()` is called when menus have been put away; the system will call `MenusBeginning()` before they're displayed again.

See also: the BMenu and BMenuItem classes

MessageReceived()

> virtual void **MessageReceived**(BMessage *message*)

Augments the BHandler version of `MessageReceived()` to ensure that `B_KEY_DOWN` messages that find their way to the BWindow object (in the absence of a focus view, for example), are not lost and can contribute to keyboard navigation.

This function also handles scripting messages for the window.

See also: `BHandler::MessageReceived()`

Minimize()

> virtual void **Minimize**(bool *minimize*)

Removes the window from the screen and replaces it with a token representation, if the *minimize* flag is `true`—or restores the window to the screen and removes the token, if *minimize* is `false`.

This function can be called to minimize or unminimize the window. It's also called by the BWindow to respond to `B_MINIMIZE` messages, which are posted automatically when the user double-clicks the window tab to minimize the window, and when the user double-clicks the token to restore the window. It can be reimplemented to provide a different minimal representation for the window.

The token representation is currently an item in the menu of windows associated with the application in the desk bar. The item remains in the menu as long as the BWindow exists, but its icon is dimmed when the window is minimized.

See also: "`B_MINIMIZE`" in the *Message Protocols* appendix, `Zoom()`

MoveBy(), MoveTo()

void **MoveBy**(float *horizontal*, float *vertical*)

void **MoveTo**(BPoint *point*)
void **MoveTo**(float *x*, float *y*)

These functions move the window without resizing it. `MoveBy()` adds *horizontal* coordinate units to the left and right components of the window's frame rectangle and *vertical* units to the frame's top and bottom. If *horizontal* and *vertical* are negative, the window moves upward and to the left. If they're positive, it moves downward and to the right. `MoveTo()` moves the left top corner of the window's content area to *point*—or (*x*, *y*)—in the screen coordinate system; it adjusts all coordinates in the frame rectangle accordingly.

None of the values passed to these functions should specify fractional coordinates; a window must be aligned on screen pixels. Fractional values will be rounded to the closest whole number.

Neither function alters the BWindow's coordinate system or bounds rectangle.

When these functions move a window, a window-moved event is reported to the window. This results in the BWindow's `FrameMoved()` function being called.

See also: `FrameMoved()`

NeedsUpdate()

bool **NeedsUpdate**(void) const

Returns `true` if any of the views within the window need to be updated, and `false` if they're all up-to-date.

See also: `UpdateIfNeeded()`

PreferredHandler()   *see CurrentFocus()*

PulseRate()   *see SetPulseRate()*

Quit(), Close()

virtual void **Quit**(void)

inline void **Close**(void)

`Quit()` gets rid of the window and all its views. This function removes the window from the screen, deletes all the BViews in its view hierarchy, destroys the window thread, removes the window's connection to the Application Server, and, finally, deletes the BWindow object.

Use this function, rather than the `delete` operator, to destroy a window. `Quit()` applies the operator after it empties the BWindow of views and severs its connection to the application and server. It's dangerous to apply `delete` while these connections remain intact.

BWindow's `Quit()` works much like the BLooper function it overrides. When called from the BWindow's thread, it doesn't return. When called from another thread, it returns after all previously posted messages have been responded to and the BWindow and its thread have been destroyed.

`Close()` is a synonym of `Quit()`. It simply calls `Quit()` so if you override `Quit()`, you'll affect how both functions work.

See also: `BLooper::QuitRequested()`, `BLooper::Quit()`, `BApplication::QuitRequested()`

RemoveChild()   *see AddChild()*

RemoveShortcut()   *see AddShortcut()*

ResizeBy(), ResizeTo()

> void **ResizeBy**(float *horizontal*, float *vertical*)

> void **ResizeTo**(float *width*, float *height*)

These functions resize the window, without moving its left and top sides. `ResizeBy()` adds *horizontal* coordinate units to the width of the window and *vertical* units to its height. `ResizeTo()` makes the content area of the window *width* units wide and *height* units high. Both functions adjust the right and bottom components of the frame rectangle accordingly.

Since a BWindow's frame rectangle must line up with screen pixels, only integral values should be passed to these functions. Values with fractional components will be rounded to the nearest whole number.

When a window is resized, either programmatically by these functions or by the user, the BWindow's `FrameResized()` virtual function is called to notify it of the change.

See also: `FrameResized()`

ResolveSpecifier()

virtual BHandler *ResolveSpecifier(BMessage *message, int32 index,
    BMessage *specifier, int32 command, const char *property)

Resolves specifiers for the "Frame", "Title", and "View" properties. See "Scripting Support" in the class overview for more information.

See also: BHandler::ResolveSpecifier()

ScreenChanged()

virtual void ScreenChanged(BRect frame, color_space mode)

Implemented by derived classes to respond to a notification that the screen configuration has changed. This function is called for all affected windows when:

- The number of pixels the screen displays (the size of the pixel grid) is altered.
- The screen changes its location in the screen coordinate system.
- The color mode of the screen changes.

frame is the new frame rectangle of the screen, and mode is its new color space.

(Currently, there can be only one monitor per machine, so the screen can't change where it's located in the screen coordinate system.)

See also: BScreen::Frame(), "B_SCREEN_CHANGED" in Appendix A, Message Protocols

SetDefaultButton(), DefaultButton()

void SetDefaultButton(BButton *button)

BButton *DefaultButton(void) const

SetDefaultButton() makes button the default button for the window—the button that the user can operate by pressing the Enter key even if another BView is the focus view. DefaultButton() returns the button that currently has that status, or NULL if there is no default button.

At any given time, only one button in the window can be the default. SetDefaultButton() may, therefore, affect two buttons: the one that's forced to give up its status as the default button, and the one that acquires that status. Both buttons are redisplayed, so that the user can see which one is currently the default, and both are notified of their change in status through MakeDefault() virtual function calls.

If the argument passed to `SetDefaultButton()` is `NULL`, there will be no default button for the window. The current default button loses its status and is appropriately notified with a `MakeDefault()` function call.

The Enter key can operate the default button only while the window is the active window. However, the BButton doesn't have to be the focus view. Normally, the focus view is notified of key-down messages the window receives. But if the character reported is `B_ENTER`, the default button is notified instead (provided there is a default button).

See also: `BButton::MakeDefault()`

SetKeyMenuBar(), KeyMenuBar()

> void **SetKeyMenuBar**(BMenuBar *menuBar)

> BMenuBar *KeyMenuBar(void) const

`SetKeyMenuBar()` makes the specified BMenuBar object the "key" menu bar for the window—the object that's at the root of the menu hierarchy that users can navigate using the keyboard. `KeyMenuBar()` returns the object with key status, or `NULL` if the window doesn't have a BMenuBar object in its view hierarchy.

If a window contains only one BMenuBar view, it's automatically designated the key menu bar. If there's more than one BMenuBar in the window, the last one added to the window's view hierarchy is considered to be the key one.

If there's a "true" menu bar displayed along the top of the window, its menu hierarchy is the one that users should be able to navigate with the keyboard. `SetKeyMenuBar()` can be called to make sure that the BMenuBar object at the root of that hierarchy is the "key" menu bar.

See also: the BMenuBar class

SetPulseRate(), PulseRate()

> void **SetPulseRate**(bigtime_t *microseconds*)

> bigtime_t **PulseRate**(void)

These functions set and return how often `Pulse()` is called for the BWindow's views (how often `B_PULSE` messages are posted to the window). All BViews attached to the same window share the same pulse rate.

By turning on the `B_PULSE_NEEDED` flag, a BView can request periodic `Pulse()` notifications. By default, `B_PULSE` messages are posted every 500,000 microseconds, as long as no other messages are pending. Each message causes `Pulse()` to be called once for every BView that requested the notification. There are no pulses if no BViews request them.

`SetPulseRate()` permits you to set a different interval. The interval set should not be less than 100,000 microseconds; differences less than 50,000 microseconds may not be noticeable. A finer granularity can't be guaranteed.

Setting the pulse rate to 0 disables pulsing for all views in the window.

See also: `BView::Pulse()`, the BView constructor

SetSizeLimits(), GetSizeLimits(), SetZoomLimits()

> void **SetSizeLimits**(float *minWidth*, float *maxWidth*,
> float *minHeight*, float *maxHeight*)

> void **GetSizeLimits**(float **minWidth*, float **maxWidth*,
> float **minHeight*, float **maxHeight*)

> void **SetZoomLimits**(float *maxWidth*, float *maxHeight*)

These functions set and report limits on the size of the window. The user won't be able to resize the window beyond the limits set by `SetSizeLimits()`—to make it have a width less than *minWidth* or greater than *maxWidth*, nor a height less than *minHeight* or greater than *maxHeight*. By default, the minimums are sufficiently small and the maximums sufficiently large to accommodate any window within reason.

`SetSizeLimits()` constrains the user, not the programmer. It's legal for an application to set a window size that falls outside the permitted range. The limits are imposed only when the user attempts to resize the window; at that time, the window will jump to a size that's within range.

`GetSizeLimits()` writes the current limits to the variables provided.

`SetZoomLimits()` sets the maximum size that the window will zoom to (when the `Zoom()` function is called). The maximums set by `SetSizeLimits()` also apply to zooming; the window will zoom to the screen size or to the smaller of the maximums set by these two functions.

Since the sides of a window must line up on screen pixels, the values passed to both `SetSizeLimits()` and `SetZoomLimits()` should be whole numbers.

See also: the BWindow constructor, `Zoom()`

SetTitle(), Title()

> void **SetTitle**(const char **newTitle*)

> const char ****Title**(void) const

These functions set and return the window's title. `SetTitle()` replaces the current title with *newTitle*. It also renames the window thread in the following format:

`"w>newTitle"`

where as many characters of the *newTitle* are included in the thread name as will fit.

`Title()` returns a pointer to the current title. The returned string is null-terminated. It belongs to the BWindow object, which may alter the string or free the memory where it resides without notice. Applications should ask for the title each time it's needed and make a copy for their own purposes.

A window's title and thread name are originally set by an argument passed to the BWindow constructor.

See also: the BWindow constructor

SetWorkspaces(), Workspaces()

void **SetWorkspaces**(uint32 *workspaces*)

uint32 **Workspaces**(void) const

These functions set and return the set of workspaces where the window can be displayed. The *workspaces* argument passed to `SetWorkspaces()` and the value returned by `Workspaces()` is a bitfield with one bit set for each workspace in which the window can appear. Usually a window appears in just one workspace.

`SetWorkspaces()` can associate a window with workspaces that don't exist yet. The window will appear in those workspaces if and when the user creates them.

You can pass `B_CURRENT_WORKSPACE` as the *workspaces* argument to place the window in the workspace that's currently displayed (the active workspace) and remove it from all others, or `B_ALL_WORKSPACES` to make sure the window shows up in all workspaces, including any new ones that the user might create. `Workspaces()` may return `B_ALL_WORKSPACES`, but will identify the current workspace rather than return `B_CURRENT_WORKSPACE`.

Changing a BWindow's set of workspaces causes it to be notified with a `WorkspacesChanged()` function call.

See also: the BWindow constructor, `WorkspacesChanged()`

SetZoomLimits()   *see SetSizeLimits()*

Show()   *see Hide()*

Title()   *see SetTitle()*

UpdateIfNeeded()

   void **UpdateIfNeeded**(void)

Causes the `Draw()` virtual function to be called immediately for each BView object that needs updating. If no views in the window's hierarchy need to be updated, this function does nothing.

BView's `Invalidate()` function generates an update message that the BWindow receives just as it receives other messages. Although update messages take precedence over other kinds of messages the BWindow receives, the window thread can respond to only one message at a time. It will update the invalidated view as soon as possible, but it must finish responding to the current message before it can get the update message.

This may not be soon enough for a BView that's engaged in a time-consuming response to the current message. `UpdateIfNeeded()` forces an immediate update, without waiting to return the BWindow's message loop. However, it works only if called from within the BWindow's thread.

(Because the message loop expedites the handling of update messages, they're never considered the current message and are never returned by BLooper's `CurrentMessage()` function.)

See also: `BView::Draw()`, `BView::Invalidate()`, `NeedsUpdate()`

WindowActivated()

   virtual void **WindowActivated**(bool *active*)

Implemented by derived classes to make any changes necessary when the window becomes the active window, or when it ceases being the active window. If *active* is `true`, the window has just become the new active window, and if *active* is `false`, it's about to give up that status to another window.

The BWindow receives a `WindowActivated()` notification whenever its status as the active window changes. Each of its BViews is also notified.

See also: `BView::WindowActivated()`

WindowType()

window_type **WindowType**(void) const

Returns what type of window it is. The type is set at construction as one of the following constants:

B_MODAL_WINDOW

B_BORDERED_WINDOW

B_TITLED_WINDOW

B_DOCUMENT_WINDOW

See also: the BWindow constructor

Workspaces()   *see SetWorkspaces()*

WorkspaceActivated()

virtual void **WorkspaceActivated**(int32 *workspace*, bool *active*)

Implemented by derived classes to respond to a notification that the workspace displayed on the screen has changed. All windows in the newly activated workspace as well as those in the one that was just deactivated get this notification.

The *workspace* argument is an index to the workspace in question and the *active* flag conveys its current status. If *active* is `true`, the workspace has just become the active workspace. If *active* is `false`, it has just stopped being the active workspace.

The default (BWindow) version of this function is empty.

See also: "B_WORKSPACE_ACTIVATED" in Appendix A, *Message Protocols*, `activate_workspace()`

WorkspacesChanged()

virtual void **WorkspacesChanged**(uint32 *oldWorkspaces*, uint32 *newWorkspaces*)

Implemented by derived classes to respond to a notification the window has just changed the set of workspaces in which it can be displayed from *oldWorkspaces* to *newWorkspaces*. This typically happens when the user moves a window from one workspace to another, but it may also happen when a programmatic change is made to the set of permitted workspaces. Each workspace is represented by a corresponding bit in the *oldWorkspaces* and *newWorkspaces* masks.

The default (BWindow) version of this function is empty.

See also: "B_WORKSPACES_CHANGED" in Appendix A, *Message Protocols*, SetWorkspaces()

Zoom()

void **Zoom**(void)
virtual void **Zoom**(BPoint *leftTop*, float *width*, float *height*)

Zooms the window to a larger size—or, if already zoomed larger, restores it to its previous size.

The simple version of this function can be called to simulate the user operating the zoom button in the window tab. It resizes the window to the full size of the screen, or to the size previously set by SetSizeLimits() and SetZoomLimits(). However, if the width and height of the window are both within five coordinate units of the fully zoomed size, it restores the window to the size it had before being zoomed.

To actually change the window's size, the simple version of Zoom() calls the virtual version. The virtual version is also called by the system in response to a B_ZOOM system message. The system generates this message when the user clicks the zoom button in the window's title tab.

The arguments to the virtual version propose a *width* and *height* for the window and a location for the left top corner of its content area in the screen coordinate system. It can be overridden to change these dimensions or to resize the window differently.

Zoom() may both move and resize the window, resulting in FrameMoved() and FrameResized() notifications.

See also: SetSizeLimits(), ResizeBy()

Global Functions

Library: libbe.so

This section describes the global (nonmember) functions defined in the Interface Kit. All these functions deal with aspects of the systemwide environment for the user interface—the keyboard and mouse, the screen, workspaces, installed fonts, the list of possible colors, and various user preferences.

With just a few exceptions, the Application Server maintains this environment. Therefore, for a global Interface Kit function to work, your application must be connected to the server. The connection these functions depend on is the one that's established when the BApplication object is constructed. Consequently, none of them should be called before a BApplication object is present in your application.

activate_workspace(), current_workspace()

be/interface/InterfaceDefs.h

void **activate_workspace**(int32 *workspace*)

int32 **current_workspace**(void)

These functions set and return the active workspace, the one that's currently displayed on-screen. For both functions, the workspace is identified by an index. The indices follow the function keys, at least for the first nine workspaces: Command-F1 switches to the workspace at index 0, Command-F2 to the workspace at index 1, and so on.

See also: BWindow::WorkspaceActivated()

count_font_families()   *see get_font_family()*

count_font_styles()   *see get_font_style()*

count_workspaces()   *see set_workspace_count()*

current_workspace()   *see activate_workspaces()*

get_click_speed()   *see set_click_speed()*

get_font_family(), count_font_families(), get_font_style(), count_font_styles()

be/interface/Font.h

status_t **get_font_family**(int32 *index*, font_family **family*,
                uint32 **flags* = NULL)

int32 **count_font_families**(void)

status_t **get_font_style**(font_family *family*, int32 *index*, font_style **style*,
                uint32 **flags* = NULL)

int32 **count_font_styles**(font_family *family*)

These functions are used in combination to get the names of the families and styles of all installed fonts. For example:

```
int32 numFamilies = count_font_families();
for ( int32 i = 0; i < numFamilies; i++ ) {
    font_family family;
    uint32 flags;
    if ( get_font_family(i, &family, &flags) == B_OK ) {
        . . .
        int32 numStyles = count_font_styles(family);
```

```
            for ( int32 j = 0; j < numStyles; j++ ) {
                font_style style;
                if ( get_font_style(family, j, &style, &flags)
                                            == B_OK ) {

                    . . .

                }
            }
        }
}
```

get_font_family() reads one family name from the list of installed fonts, the name at *index*, and copies it into the *family* buffer; count_font_families() returns the number of font families currently installed. Similarly, get_font_style() reads the name of the style at *index* and copies into the *style* buffer. Since each family can have a different set of styles, a *family* name must be passed to get_font_style(); count_font_styles() returns the number of styles for the particular *family*. Family and style names can be up to 64 bytes long including a null terminator. Indices begin at 0.

The names of installed font families and styles are not indexed in any particular order. You might want to alphabetize them before displaying them to the user in a menu or list.

If you pass a *flags* argument to get_font_family() and get_font_style(), they will place a mask with useful information about the particular family or style in the variable that the argument refers to. Currently there are just two flags:

B_IS_FIXED	Indicates that the font is a nonproportional, or fixed-width, font—one for which all characters have the same width.
B_HAS_TUNED_FONT	Indicates that the family or style has versions of the font especially adapted or "tuned" for on-screen display.

If neither flag applies, the variable that *flags* points to will be set to 0.

If you find a family and style that has a tuned font, you can set a BFont object to that family and style, then call the object's GetTunedInfo() function to get details about exactly which combination of font properties (for example, which font sizes) have tuned counterparts. If you set a BFont so it has those properties and make it a BView's current font, the tuned version will be used when the BView draws to the screen.

It's possible for the user to install or remove fonts while the application is running. However, unless update_font_families() has been called to get the updated list, get_font_family() will provide information on the same set of fonts each time it's called. The list isn't automatically updated.

See also: update_font_families(), BView::SetFont(),
BFont::SetFamilyAndStyle()

get_key_info()

be/interface/InterfaceDefs.h

status_t **get_key_info**(key_info *keyInfo*)

Writes information about the state of the keyboard into the `key_info` structure referred to by *keyInfo*. This function permits you to get information about the keyboard in the absence of `B_KEY_DOWN` messages. The `key_info` structure has just two fields:

uint32 **modifiers**

A mask indicating which modifier keys are down and which keyboard locks are on.

uint8 **key_states**[16]

A bit array that records the state of all the keys on the keyboard, and all the keyboard locks. This array works identically to the "states" array passed in a key-down message. See Appendix B, *Keyboard Information*, appendix for information on how to read information from the array.

`get_key_info()` returns `B_OK` if it was able to get the requested information, and `B_ERROR` if the return results are unreliable.

See also: `BView::KeyDown()`; Appendix B, *Keyboard Information*; `modifiers()`

get_key_map()

be/interface/InterfaceDefs.h

void **get_key_map**(key_map **keys*, char **chars*)

Provides a pointer to the system key map—the structure that describes the role of each key on the keyboard. The key map is shared by all applications; you can read from this structure, but should not alter it.

Through the Keymap preferences application, users can configure the keyboard to their liking. The user's preferences are stored in a file (*/system/settings/Key_map*). When the machine reboots, the key map is read from this file. If the file doesn't exist, the original map encoded in the Application Server is used.

The `key_map` structure contains a large number of fields, but it can be broken down into these six parts:

- A version number.
- A series of fields that determine which keys will function as modifier keys—such as Shift, Control, or Num Lock.
- A field that sets the initial state of the keyboard locks in the default key map.

- A series of ordered tables that assign character values to keys. Except for a handful of modifier keys, all keys are mapped to characters, though they may not be mapped for all modifier combinations.

- A series of tables that locate the dead keys for diacritical marks and determine how a combination of a dead key plus another key is mapped to a particular character.

- A set of masks that determine which modifier keys are required for a key to be considered dead.

The following sections describe the parts of the key_map structure.

Version. The first field of the key map is a version number:

uint32 **version**

An internal identifier for the key map.

The version number doesn't change when the user configures the keyboard, and shouldn't be changed programmatically either. You can ignore it.

Modifiers. Modifier keys set states that affect other user actions on the keyboard and mouse. Eight modifier states are defined—Shift, Control, Option, Command, Menu, Caps Lock, Num Lock, and Scroll Lock. These states are discussed under "Modifier Keys" in Appendix B, *Keyboard Information.* They fairly closely match the keys caps found on a Macintosh keyboard, but only partially match those on a standard PC keyboard—which generally has a set of Alt(ernate) keys, rarely Option keys, and only sometimes Command and Menu keys. Because of these differences, the mapping of keys to modifiers is the area of the key map most open to the user's personal judgement and taste, and consequently to changes in the default configuration.

Since two keys, one on the left and one on the right, can be mapped to the Shift, Control, Option, and Command modifiers, the keyboard can have as many as twelve modifier keys. The key_map structure has one field for each key:

uint32 **caps_key**

The key that functions as the Caps Lock key; by default, this is the key labeled "Caps Lock," key 0x3b.

uint32 **scroll_key**

The key that functions as the Scroll Lock key; by default, this is the key labeled "Scroll Lock," key 0x0f.

uint32 **num_key**

The key that functions as the Num Lock key; by default, this is the key labeled "Num Lock," key 0x22.

uint32 **left_shift_key**

A key that functions as a Shift key; by default, this is the key on the left labeled "Shift," key 0x4b.

uint32 **right_shift_key**

Another key that functions as a Shift key; by default, this is the key on the right labeled "Shift," key 0x56.

uint32 **left_command_key**

A key that functions as a Command key; by default, this is key 0x5d, sometimes labeled "Alt."

uint32 **right_command_key**

Another key that functions as a Command key; by default, this is key 0x5f, sometimes labeled "Alt."

uint32 **left_control_key**

A key that functions as a Control key; by default, this is the key labeled "Control" on the left, key 0x5c.

uint32 **right_control_key**

Another key that functions as a Control key; by default on keyboards that have Option keys, this key is the key labeled "Control" on the right, key 0x60. For keyboards that don't have Option keys, this field is unmapped (its value is 0); key 0x60 is used as an Option key.

uint32 **left_option_key**

A key that functions as an Option key; by default, this is key 0x66, which has different labels on different keyboards—"Option," "Command," or a Windows symbol. This key doesn't exist on, and therefore isn't mapped for, a standard 101-key keyboard.

uint32 **right_option_key**

A key that functions as an Option key; by default, this is key 0x67, which has different labels on different keyboards—"Option," "Command," or a Windows symbol. For keyboards without this key, the field is mapped to the key labeled "Control" on the right, key 0x60.

uint32 **menu_key**

A key that initiates keyboard navigation of the menu hierarchy; by default, this is the key labeled with a menu symbol, key 0x68. This key doesn't exist on, and therefore isn't mapped for, a standard 101-key keyboard.

Each field names the key that functions as that modifier. For example, when the user holds down the key whose code is set in the `right_option_key` field, the `B_OPTION_KEY` and `B_RIGHT_OPTION_KEY` bits are turned on in the modifiers mask that the `modifiers()` function returns. When the user then strikes a character key, the `B_OPTION_KEY` state influences the character that's generated.

If a modifier field is set to a value that doesn't correspond to an actual key on the keyboard (including 0), that field is not mapped. No key fills that particular modifier role.

Keyboard locks. One field of the key map sets initial modifier states:

uint32 **lock_settings**

A mask that determines which keyboard locks are turned on when the machine reboots or when the default key map is restored.

The mask can be 0 or may contain any combination of these three constants:

B_CAPS_LOCK

B_SCROLL_LOCK

B_NUM_LOCK

It's 0 by default; there are no initial locks.

Altering the `lock_settings` field has no effect unless the altered key map is made the default (by writing it to a file that replaces */system/settings/Key_map*).

Character maps. The principal job of the key map is to assign character values to keys. This is done in a series of nine tables:

int32 **control_map**[128]

The characters that are produced when a Control key is down but both Command keys are up.

int32 **option_caps_shift_map**[128]

The characters that are produced when Caps Lock is on and both a Shift key and an Option key are down.

int32 **option_caps_map**[128]

The characters that are produced when Caps Lock is on and an Option key is down.

int32 **option_shift_map**[128]

The characters that are produced when both a Shift key and an Option key are down.

int32 **option_map**[128]

The characters that are produced when an Option key is down.

int32 **caps_shift_map**[128]

   The characters that are produced when Caps Lock is on and a Shift key is down.

int32 **caps_map**[128]

   The characters that are produced when Caps Lock is on.

int32 **shift_map**[128]

   The characters that are produced when a Shift key is down.

int32 **normal_map**[128]

   The characters that are produced when none of the other tables apply.

Each of these tables is an array of 128 offsets into another array, the *chars* array of Unicode UTF-8 character encodings. `get_key_map()` provides a pointer to the *chars* array as its second argument.

Key codes are used as indices into the character tables. The offset stored at any particular index maps a character to that key. For example, the code assigned to the *M* key is 0x52; at index 0x52 in the `option_caps_map` is an offset; at that offset in the *chars* array, you'll find the character that's mapped to the *M* key when an Option key is held down and Caps Lock is on.

This indirection—an index to an offset to a character—is required because characters are encoded as Unicode UTF-8 strings. Character values of 127 or less (7-bit ASCII) are just a single byte, but UTF-8 takes two, three, or (rarely) four bytes to encodes values over 127.

The *chars* array represents each character as a Pascal string—the first byte in the string tells how many other bytes the string contains. For example, the string for the trademark symbol (™) looks like this:

`\x03\xE2\x84\xA2`

The first byte (\x03) indicates that Unicode UTF-8 takes 3 bytes to represent the trademark symbol, and those bytes follow (\xE2\x84\xA2). Pascal strings are not null-terminated.

The character map tables are ordered. Values from the first applicable table are used, even if another table might also seem to apply. For example, if Caps Lock is on and a Control key is down (and both Command keys are up), the `control_map` array is used, not `caps_map`. If a Shift key is down and Caps Lock is on, the `caps_shift_map` is used, not `shift_map` or `caps_map`.

Notice that the last eight tables (all except `control_map`) are paired, with a table that names the Shift key (..._shift_map) preceding an equivalent table without Shift:

• `option_caps_shift_map` is paired with `option_caps_map`,
• `option_shift_map` with `option_map`,

- `caps_shift_map` with `caps_map`, and
- `shift_map` with `normal_map`.

These pairings are important for a special rule that applies to keys on the numerical keypad when Num Lock is on:

- If the Shift key is down, the non-Shift table is used.
- However, if the Shift key is *not* down, the Shift table is used.

In other words, Num Lock inverts the Shift and non-Shift tables for keys on the numerical keypad.

Not every key needs to be mapped to a character. If the *chars* array has a 0-length string for a key, the key is not mapped to a character (given the particular modifier states the table represents). Generally, modifier keys are not mapped to characters, but all other keys are, at least for some tables. Key-down events are not generated for unmapped keys.

Dead keys. Next are the tables that map combinations of keys to single characters. The first key in the combination is "dead"—it doesn't produce a key-down event until the user strikes another character key. When the user hits the second key, one of two things will happen: If the second key is one that can be used in combination with the dead key, a single key-down event reports the combination character. If the second key doesn't combine with the dead key, two key-down events occur, one reporting the dead-key character and one reporting the second character.

There are five dead-key tables:

int32 **acute_dead_key**[32]
　　The table for combining an acute accent (´) with other characters.

int32 **grave_dead_key**[32]
　　The table for combining a grave accent (`) with other characters.

int32 **circumflex_dead_key**[32]
　　The table for combining a circumflex (^) with other characters.

int32 **dieresis_dead_key**[32]
　　The table for combining a dieresis (¨) with other characters.

int32 **tilde_dead_key**[32]
　　The table for combining a tilde (~) with other characters

The tables are named after diacritical marks that can be placed on more than one character. However, the name is just a mnemonic; it means nothing. The contents of the table determine what the dead key is and how it combines with other characters. It would be possible, for example, to remap the `tilde_dead_key` table so that it had nothing to do with a tilde.

Each table consists of a series of up to 16 offset pairs—where, as in the case of the character maps, each offset picks a character from the *chars* character array. The first character in the pair is the one that must be typed immediately after the dead key. The second character is the resulting character, the character that's produced by the combination of the dead key plus the first character in the pair. For example, if the first character is "o", the second might be "ô"—meaning that the combination of a dead key plus the character "o" produces a circumflexed "ô".

The character pairs for the default `grave_dead_key` array look something like this:

```
' ', '`',
'A', 'À',
'E', 'È',
'I', 'Ì',
'O', 'Ò',
'U', 'Ù',
'a', 'à',
'e', 'è',
'i', 'ì',
'o', 'ò',
'u', 'ù',
. . .
```

By convention, the first offset in each array is to the `B_SPACE` character and the second is to the dead-key character itself. This pair does double duty: It states that the dead key plus a space yields the dead-key character, and it also names the dead key. The system understands what the dead key is from the second offset in the array.

Character tables for dead keys. As mentioned above, for a key to be dead, it must be mapped to the character picked by the second offset in a dead-key array. However, it's not typical for every key that's mapped to the character to be dead. Usually, there's a requirement that the user must hold down certain modifier keys (often the Option key). In other words, a key is dead only if selected character-map tables map it to the requisite character.

Five additional fields of the `key_map` structure specify what those character-map tables are—which modifiers are required for each of the dead keys:

uint32 **acute_tables**

    The character tables that cause a key to be dead when they map it to the second character in the `acute_dead_key` array.

uint32 **grave_tables**

    The character tables that cause a key to be dead when they map it to the second character in the `grave_dead_key` array.

uint32 **circumflex_tables**

    The character tables that cause a key to be dead when they map it to the second character in the `circumflex_dead_key` array.

uint32 **dieresis_tables**

The character tables that cause a key to be dead when they map it to the second character in the `dieresis_dead_key` array.

uint32 **tilde_tables**

The character tables that cause a key to be dead when they map it to the second character in the `tilde_dead_key` array.

Each of these fields contains a mask formed from the following constants:

B_CONTROL_TABLE	B_CAPS_SHIFT_TABLE
B_OPTION_CAPS_SHIFT_TABLE	B_CAPS_TABLE
B_OPTION_CAPS_TABLE	B_SHIFT_TABLE
B_OPTION_SHIFT_TABLE	B_NORMAL_TABLE
B_OPTION_TABLE	

The mask designates the character-map tables that permit a key to be dead. For example, if the mask for the `grave_tables` field is,

`B_OPTION_TABLE | B_OPTION_CAPS_SHIFT_TABLE`

a key would be dead whenever either of those tables mapped the key to the character of the second offset in the `grave_dead_key` array ("`" in the example above). A key mapped to the same character by another table would not be dead.

See also: `get_key_info()`, `modifiers()`; Appendix B, *Keyboard Information*, `set_modifier_key()`

get_key_repeat_delay()   *see set_key_repeat_rate()*

get_key_repeat_rate()   *see set_key_repeat_rate()*

get_keyboard_id()

`be/interface/InterfaceDefs.h`

status_t **get_keyboard_id**(uint16 *id*)

Obtains the keyboard identifier from the Application Server and device driver and writes it into the variable referred to by *id*. This number reveals what kind of keyboard is currently attached to the computer.

The identifier for the standard 101-key PC keyboard—and for keyboards with a similar set of keys—is 0x83ab.

If unsuccessful for any reason, `get_keyboard_id()` returns B_ERROR. If successful, it returns B_OK.

get_menu_info()   *see set_menu_info()*

get_mouse_map()   *see set_mouse_map()*

get_mouse_speed()   *see set_mouse_map()*

get_mouse_type()   *see set_mouse_map()*

get_scroll_bar_info()   *see set_scroll_bar_info()*

idle_time()

```
be/interface/InterfaceDefs.h
```

bigtime_t **idle_time**(void) const

Returns the number of microseconds since the user last manipulated the mouse or keyboard. This information isn't specific to a particular application; `idle_time()` tells you when the user last directed an action at *any* application, not just yours.

keyboard_navigation_color()

```
be/interface/InterfaceDefs.h
```

rgb_color **keyboard_navigation_color**(void)

Returns the color that should be used to mark the BView that's currently in focus, when the user can change the focus from the keyboard. The keyboard navigation color is typically used to underline the labels of control devices and to outline text fields where the user can type.

See also: the BView class

modifiers()

```
be/interface/InterfaceDefs.h
```

uint32 **modifiers**(void)

Returns a mask that has a bit set for each modifier key the user is holding down and for each keyboard lock that's set. The mask can be tested against these constants:

B_SHIFT_KEY	B_COMMAND_KEY	B_CAPS_LOCK
B_CONTROL_KEY	B_MENU_KEY	B_SCROLL_LOCK
B_OPTION_KEY		B_NUM_LOCK

No bits are set (the mask is 0) if no locks are on and none of the modifiers keys are down.

If it's important to know which physical key the user is holding down, the one on the right or the one on the left, the mask can be further tested against these constants:

B_LEFT_SHIFT_KEY	B_RIGHT_SHIFT_KEY
B_LEFT_CONTROL_KEY	B_RIGHT_CONTROL_KEY
B_LEFT_OPTION_KEY	B_RIGHT_OPTION_KEY
B_LEFT_COMMAND_KEY	B_RIGHT_COMMAND_KEY

By default, the keys closes to the space bar function as Command keys, no matter what their labels on particular keyboards. If a keyboard doesn't have Option keys (for example, a standard 101-key keyboard), the key on the right labeled "Control" functions as the right Option key, and only the left "Control" key is available to function as a Control modifier. However, users can change this configuration with the Keymap application.

See also: "Modifier Keys" in Appendix B, *Keyboard Information;* get_key_map(), get_key_info()

run_add_printer_panel(), run_select_printer_panel()

be/interface/InterfaceDefs.h

void **run_add_printer_panel**(void)

void **run_select_printer_panel**(void)

These two functions have the Print Server place panels on-screen where the user can set up a printer and choose which printer to use. run_add_printer_panel() displays a panel that informs the server about a new printer. run_select_printer_panel() displays a panel that lists all known printers and lets the user select one.

See also: the BPrintJob class

set_click_speed(), get_click_speed()

be/interface/InterfaceDefs.h

status_t **set_click_speed**(bigtime_t *interval*)

status_t **get_click_speed**(bigtime_t **interval*)

These functions set and report the timing for multiple-clicks. For successive mouse-down events to count as a multiple-click, they must occur within the *interval* set by set_click_speed() and provided by get_click_speed(). The interval is measured in microseconds; it's usually set by the user in the Mouse preferences application. The smallest possible interval is 100,000 microseconds (0.1 second).

If successful, these functions return B_OK; if unsuccessful, they return an error code, which may be just B_ERROR.

See also: set_mouse_map()

set_key_repeat_rate(), get_key_repeat_rate(), set_key_repeat_delay(), get_key_repeat_delay()

be/interface/InterfaceDefs.h

status_t **set_key_repeat_rate**(int32 *rate*)

status_t **get_key_repeat_rate**(int32 **rate*)

status_t **set_key_repeat_delay**(bigtime_t *delay*)

status_t **get_key_repeat_delay**(bigtime_t **delay*)

These functions set and report the timing of repeating keys. When the user presses a character key on the keyboard, it produces an immediate B_KEY_DOWN message. If the user continues to hold the key down, it will, after an initial delay, continue to produce messages at regularly spaced intervals—until the user releases the key or presses another key. The delay and the spacing between messages are both preferences the user can set with the Keyboard application.

set_key_repeat_rate() sets the number of messages repeating keys produce per second. For a standard PC keyboard, the *rate* can be as low as 2 and as high as 30; get_key_repeat_rate() writes the current setting into the integer *rate* refers to.

set_key_repeat_delay() sets the length of the initial delay before the key begins repeating. Acceptable values are 250,000, 500,000, 750,000 and 1,000,000 microseconds (.25, .5, .75, and 1.0 second); get_key_repeat_delay() writes the current setting into the variable that *delay* points to.

All four functions return B_OK if they successfully communicate with the Application Server, and B_ERROR if not. It's possible for the set...() functions to communicate with the server but not succeed in setting the *rate* or *delay* (for example, if the *delay* isn't one of the listed four values).

set_keyboard_locks()

be/interface/InterfaceDefs.h

void **set_keyboard_locks**(uint32 *modifiers*)

Turns the keyboard locks—Caps Lock, Num Lock, and Scroll Lock—on and off. The keyboard locks that are listed in the *modifiers* mask passed as an argument are turned on; those not listed are turned off. The mask can be 0 (to turn off all locks) or it can contain any combination of the following constants:

```
B_CAPS_LOCK
B_NUM_LOCK
B_SCROLL_LOCK
```

See also: get_key_map(), modifiers()

set_menu_info(), get_menu_info()

```
be/interface/Menu.h
```

status_t **set_menu_info**(menu_info **info*)

status_t **get_menu_info**(menu_info **info*)

These functions set and get the user's preferences for how menus should look and work. User's express their preferences with the Menu application, which calls set_menu_info(). get_menu_info() writes the current preferences into the **menu_info** structure that into refers to. This structure contains the following fields:

float **font_size**
> The size of the font that will be used to display menu items.

font_name **font**
> The name of the font that's used to display menu items.

rgb_color **background_color**
> The background color of the menu.

int32 **separator**
> The style of horizontal line that separates groups of items in a menu. The value is an index ranging from 0 through 2; there are three possible separators.

bool **click_to_open**
> Whether it's possible to open a menu by clicking in the item that controls it. The default value is true.

bool **triggers_always_shown**
> Whether trigger characters are always marked in menus and menu bars, regardless of whether the menu hierarchy is the target for keyboard actions. The default value is false.

At present, both functions always return B_OK.

See also: the BMenu class

set_modifier_key()

be/interface/InterfaceDefs.h

void **set_modifier_key**(uint32 *modifier*, uint32 *key*)

Maps a *modifier* role to a particular *key* on the keyboard, where *key* is a key identifier and *modifier* is one of the these constants:

B_CAPS_LOCK	B_LEFT_SHIFT_KEY	B_RIGHT_SHIFT_KEY
B_NUM_LOCK	B_LEFT_CONTROL_KEY	B_RIGHT_CONTROL_KEY
B_SCROLL_LOCK	B_LEFT_OPTION_KEY	B_RIGHT_OPTION_KEY
B_MENU_KEY	B_LEFT_COMMAND_KEY	B_RIGHT_COMMAND_KEY

The *key* in question serves as the named modifier key, unmapping any key that previously played that role. The change remains in effect until the default key map is restored. In general, the user's preferences for modifier keys—expressed in the Keymap application—should be respected.

Modifier keys can also be mapped by calling `get_key_map()` and altering the `key_map` structure directly. This function is merely a convenient alternative for accomplishing the same thing. (It's currently not possible to alter the key map; `get_key_map()` looks at a copy.)

See also: `get_key_map()`

set_mouse_map(), get_mouse_map(), set_mouse_type(), get_mouse_type(), set_mouse_speed(), get_mouse_speed()

be/interface/InterfaceDefs.h

status_t **set_mouse_map**(mouse_map **map*)

status_t **get_mouse_map**(mouse_map **map*)

status_t **set_mouse_type**(int32 *numButtons*)

status_t **get_mouse_type**(int32 **numButtons*)

status_t **set_mouse_speed**(int32 *acceleration*)

status_t **get_mouse_speed**(int32 **acceleration*)

These functions configure the mouse and supply information about the current configuration. The configuration should usually be left to the user and the Mouse preferences application.

set_mouse_map() maps the buttons of the mouse to their roles in the user interface, and get_mouse_map() writes the current map into the variable referred to by *map*. The mouse_map structure has a field for each button on a three-button mouse:

uint32 **left**
    The button on the left of the mouse

uint32 **right**
    The button on the right of the mouse

uint32 **middle**
    The button in the middle, between the other two buttons

Each field is set to one of the following constants:

B_PRIMARY_MOUSE_BUTTON

B_SECONDARY_MOUSE_BUTTON

B_TERTIARY_MOUSE_BUTTON

The same role can be assigned to more than one physical button. If all three buttons are set to B_PRIMARY_MOUSE_BUTTON, they all function as the primary button; if two of them are set to B_SECONDARY_MOUSE_BUTTON, they both function as the secondary button; and so on.

set_mouse_type() informs the system of how many buttons the mouse actually has. If it has two buttons, only the left and right fields of the mouse_map are operative. If it has just one button, only the left field is operative. set_mouse_type() writes the current number of buttons into the variable referred to by *numButtons*.

set_mouse_speed() sets the speed of the mouse—the acceleration of the cursor image on-screen relative to the actual speed at which the user moves the mouse on its pad. An *acceleration* value of 0 means no acceleration. The maximum acceleration is 20, though even 10 is too fast for most users. set_mouse_speed() writes the current acceleration into the variable referred to by *acceleration*.

All six functions return B_OK if successful, and an error code, typically B_ERROR, if not.

set_screen_space()

be/interface/InterfaceDefs.h

status_t **set_screen_space**(int32 *index*, uint32 *space*, bool *makeDefault* = true)

Changes the configuration of the screen—its depth and dimensions—to match the values specified in the *space* constant, which can be any of the following:

B_8_BIT_640x400		
B_8_BIT_640x480	B_16_BIT_640x480	B_32_BIT_640x480
B_8_BIT_800x600	B_16_BIT_800x600	B_32_BIT_800x600
B_8_BIT_1024x768	B_16_BIT_1024x768	B_32_BIT_1024x768
B_8_BIT_1152x900	B_16_BIT_1152x900	B_32_BIT_1152x900
B_8_BIT_1280x1024	B_16_BIT_1280x1024	B_32_BIT_1280x1024
B_8_BIT_1600x1200	B_16_BIT_1600x1200	B_32_BIT_1600x1200

The first part of the constant designates the screen depth and color space. B_8_BIT... refers to the B_COLOR_8_BIT color space and B_32_BIT... refers to the B_RGB_32_BIT color space. Although constants are defined for 16-bit depths, the operating system currently doesn't support them. The second part of the constant designates the pixel resolution of the screen. For example, B_32_BIT_1280x1024 means that the frame buffer is 32 bits deep (B_RGB_32_BIT) while the screen grid is 1,280 pixels wide and 1,024 pixels high.

This function affects the screen at *index*. Since the BeOS currently doesn't support more than one screen, the only index that makes sense is 0.

The change to the screen takes effect immediately. If the *makeDefault* flag is true, the new configuration also becomes the default and will be used the next time the machine is turned on. If *makeDefault* is false, the configuration is in effect for the current session only.

Since not all configurations are possible for all graphics cards, set_screen_ space() can fail. It returns B_OK if successful, and B_ERROR if not.

This function is designed for preferences applications—like the Screen application— that permit users to make system-wide choices about the screen. Other applications should respect those choices and refrain from modifying them.

The current screen configuration can be obtained from the BScreen object.

See also: the BScreen class, BWindow::ScreenChanged()

set_scroll_bar_info(), get_scroll_bar_info()

be/interface/InterfaceDefs.h

status_t **set_scroll_bar_info**(scroll_bar_info *info*)

status_t **get_scroll_bar_info**(scroll_bar_info *info*)

These functions set and report preferences that the BScrollBar class uses when it creates a new scroll bar. set_scroll_bar_info() reads the values contained in the scroll_bar_info structure that *info* refers to and sets the system-wide preferences accordingly; `get_scroll_bar_info()` writes the current preferences into the structure provided.

The `scroll_bar_info` structure contains the following fields:

bool **proportional**

> `true` if scroll bars should have a knob that grows and shrinks to show what proportion of the document is currently visible on-screen, and `false` if not. Scroll knobs are proportional by default.

bool **double_arrows**

> `true` if a set of double arrows (for scrolling in both directions) should appear at each end of the scroll bar, or `false` if only single arrows (for scrolling in one direction only) should be used. Double arrows are the default.

int32 **knob**

> An index that picks the pattern for the knob. Only values of 0, 1, and 2 are currently valid. The patterns can be seen in the ScrollBar preferences application. The pattern at index 1 is the default.

int32 **min_knob_size**

> The length of the scroll knob, in pixels. This is the minimum size for a proportional knob and the fixed size for one that's not proportional. The default is 15.

The user can set these preferences with the ScrollBar application. Applications can call `get_scroll_bar_info()` to find out what choices the user made, but should refrain from calling `set_scroll_bar_info()`. That function is designed for utilities, like the ScrollBar application, that enable users to set preferences that are respected system-wide.

If successful, these functions return `B_OK`; if not, they return `B_ERROR`.

See also: the BScrollBar class

set_workspace_count(), count_workspaces()

> be/interface/InterfaceDefs.h

> void **set_workspace_count**(int32 *numWorkspaces*)

> int32 **count_workspaces**(void)

These functions set and return the number of workspaces the user has available. There can be as many as 32 workspaces and as few as 1. The choice of how many there should be is usually left to the user and the Workspaces application.

See also: `activate_workspace()`

system_colors()

```
be/interface/InterfaceDefs.h
```

const color_map *system_colors(void)

Returns a pointer to the system color map. This function duplicates the BScreen `ColorMap()` function, but it permits software that isn't concerned about the on-screen display to get the color map without referring to a particular screen. (Actually it returns the color map for the main screen.)

The `color_map` structure returned by this function belongs to the operating system.

See also: `BScreen::ColorMap()`

update_font_families()

```
be/interface/Font.h
```

bool update_font_families(bool *checkOnly*)

Updates the list of installed fonts, so that it reflects any that have been added or removed since the last time the list was updated. Until the list is updated, `get_font_family()` operates assuming the set of fonts that were installed when the application started up. If the list is unchanged since the last update (or since startup), this function returns `false`; if a font has been installed or an installed font has been removed, it returns `true`.

If the *checkOnly* flag is `true`, `get_font_family()` only reports whether the list has changed; it doesn't modify the current list. If the flag is `false`, it contacts the Application Server to get the updated list, a much more expensive operation.

See also: `get_font_family()`

Global Variables, Constants, and Defined Types

This section lists the various global variables, constants, and types that the Interface Kit defines to support the work done by its principal classes.

Global Variables

System Fonts

```
be/interface/Font.h
```

const BFont *be_plain_font
const BFont *be_bold_font
const BFont *be_fixed_font

These global BFont objects are created when the BApplication object is constructed. They encapsulate the three system fonts—the plain font which is used for labels and small stretches of text in the user interface, the bold font which is used for window and group titles, and the fixed font which is used in Terminal windows and other places where a fixed-width font is required.

These objects are `const` and cannot be modified, nor will they be modified behind your back when the user redefines a system font. The user's changed preferences don't affect applications already running.

See also: the BFont class

Constants

alert_type Constants

> `be/interface/Alert.h`

Constant
B_EMPTY_ALERT
B_INFO_ALERT
B_IDEA_ALERT
B_WARNING_ALERT
B_STOP_ALERT

These constants designate the various types of alert panels that are recognized by the system. The type corresponds to an icon that's displayed in the alert window.

See also: the BAlert constructor

alignment Constants

> `be/interface/InterfaceDefs.h`

Constant
B_ALIGN_LEFT
B_ALIGN_RIGHT
B_ALIGN_CENTER

These constants define the `alignment` data type. They determine how lines of text and labels are aligned by BTextView, BStringView, and BMenuField objects.

See also: `BTextView::SetAlignment()`

button_width Constants

```
be/interface/Alert.h
```

Constant
_____

B_WIDTH_AS_USUAL

B_WIDTH_FROM_LABEL

B_WIDTH_FROM_WIDEST
_____

These constants define the `button_width` type. They determine how the width of the buttons in an alert panel will be set—whether they're set to an standard (minimal) width, a width just sufficient to accommodate the button's own label, or a width sufficient to accommodate the widest label of all the buttons.

See also: the BAlert constructor

border_style Constants

```
be/interface/InterfaceDefs.h
```

Constant
_____

B_PLAIN_BORDER

B_FANCY_BORDER

B_NO_BORDER
_____

These constants define how BBox objects and BScrollViews are bordered.

See also: the BScrollView and BBox classes

Character Constants

```
be/interface/InterfaceDefs.h
```

Constant	Character value
B_BACKSPACE	0x08 (same as "\b")
B_ENTER	0x0a (same as "\n")
B_RETURN	0x0a (synonym for B_ENTER)
B_SPACE	0x20 (same as " ")
B_TAB	0x09 (same as "\t")
B_ESCAPE	0x1b
B_LEFT_ARROW	0x1c
B_RIGHT_ARROW	0x1d
B_UP_ARROW	0x1e

Constant	Character value
B_DOWN_ARROW	0x1f
B_INSERT	0x05
B_DELETE	0x7f
B_HOME	0x01
B_END	0x04
B_PAGE_UP	0x0b
B_PAGE_DOWN	0x0c
B_FUNCTION_KEY	0x10
B_UTF8_ELLIPSIS	"\xE2\x80\xA6"
B_UTF8_OPEN_QUOTE	"\xE2\x80\x9C"
B_UTF8_CLOSE_QUOTE	"\xE2\x80\x9D"
B_UTF8_COPYRIGHT	"\xC2\xA9"
B_UTF8_REGISTERED	"\xC2\xAE"
B_UTF8_TRADEMARK	"\xE2\x84\xA2"
B_UTF8_SMILING_FACE	"\xE2\x98\xBB"
B_UTF8_HIROSHI	"\xE5\xBC\x98"

Constants in the first group stand for the ASCII characters they name. They're defined only for characters that normally don't have visible symbols.

Constants in the second group are Unicode UTF-8 encodings of common characters that have multibyte representations. These constants are strings that can be concatenated with other strings—for example, to set a button label that ends in an ellipsis:

```
myButton->SetLablel("Options"B_UTF_ELLIPSIS);
```

See also: "Function Key Constants" below

color_space Constants

```
be/interface/GraphicDefs.h
```

Constant
B_MONOCHROME_1_BIT
B_GRAYSCALE_8_BIT
B_COLOR_8_BIT
B_RGB_16_BIT
B_RGB_32_BIT
B_BIG_RGB_16_BIT
B_BIG_RGB_32_BIT
B_NO_COLOR_SPACE

These constants define the `color_space` data type. A color space describes three properties of screens and bitmap images:

- How many bits of information there are per pixel (the depth of the image)
- How those bits are to be interpreted (whether as colors or on a grayscale, what the color components are, and so on).
- How are components are arranged

See the "Color Spaces" section in the "Drawing" section of this chapter for a fuller explanation of the color spaces currently defined for this type, particularly `B_RGB_32_BIT`.

See also: "Colors" in the "Drawing" section of this chapter, the BBitmap and BScreen classes

Control Values

`be/interface/Control.h`

Constant	Value
B_CONTROL_ON	1
B_CONTROL_OFF	0

These constants define the bipolar states of a typical control device.

See also: `BControl::SetValue()`

Cursor Transit Constants

`be/interface/View.h`

Constant	Meaning
B_ENTERED_VIEW	The cursor has just entered a view.
B_INSIDE_VIEW	The cursor has moved within the view.
B_EXITED_VIEW	The cursor has left the view.

These constants describe the cursor's transit through a view. Each `MouseMoved()` notification includes one of these constants as an argument, to inform the BView whether the cursor has entered the view, moved while inside the view, or exited the view.

See also: `BView::MouseMoved()`

Dead-Key Mapping

`be/interface/InterfaceDefs.h`

Constant
B_CONTROL_TABLE
B_OPTION_CAPS_SHIFT_TABLE
B_OPTION_CAPS_TABLE
B_OPTION_SHIFT_TABLE
B_OPTION_TABLE
B_CAPS_SHIFT_TABLE
B_CAPS_TABLE
B_SHIFT_TABLE
B_NORMAL_TABLE

These constants determine which combinations of modifiers can cause a key to be the "dead" member of a two-key combination.

See also: `get_key_map()`

drawing_mode Constants

`be/interface/GraphicsDefs.h`

Constant	Constant
B_OP_COPY	B_OP_ADD
B_OP_OVER	B_OP_SUBTRACT
B_OP_ERASE	B_OP_BLEND
B_OP_INVERT	B_OP_MIN
B_OP_SELECT	B_OP_MAX

These constants define the `drawing_mode` data type. The drawing mode is a BView graphics parameter that determines how the image being drawn interacts with the image already in place in the area where it's drawn. The various modes are explained under "Drawing Modes" in the "Drawing" section of this chapter.

See also: "Drawing Modes" in the "Drawing" section of this chapter, `BView::SetDrawingMode()`

font_direction Constants

be/interface/Font.h

Constant
B_FONT_LEFT_TO_RIGHT
B_FONT_RIGHT_TO_LEFT

These constants tell whether a font is used for text that's read left-to-right or right-to-left. Thus is an inherent property of the font.

See also: BFont::Direction()

Font Encodings

be/interface/Font.h

Constant
B_UNICODE_UTF8
B_ISO_8859_1
B_ISO_8859_2
B_ISO_8859_3
B_ISO_8859_4
B_ISO_8859_5
B_ISO_8859_6
B_ISO_8859_7
B_ISO_8859_8
B_ISO_8859_9
B_ISO_8859_10
B_MACINTOSH_ROMAN

The constants name the various character encodings that the BeOS supports. B_UNICODE_UTF8 is the default encoding. It matches ASCII values for 7-bit character codes but uses multiple bytes to encode other values in the Unicode standard.

See also: BFont::SetEncoding(), "Character Encoding" in the "Responding to the User" section of this chapter

Font Flags

be/interface/Font.h

Constant
B_DISABLE_ANTIALIASING
B_IS_FIXED
B_HAS_TUNED_FONT

The first flag, `B_DISABLE_ANTIALIASING`, is passed to a BFont object to turn antialiasing off. Antialiasing should be turned off when printing, but should generally be left on when drawing to the screen.

The other two flags enable `get_font_family()` and `get_font_style()` to give information about a font. `B_IS_FIXED` indicates that the font is nonproportional. `B_HAS_TUNED_FONT` indicates that the family or style has one or more tuned fonts—bitmap fonts that have been adjusted to look good on the screen—for some set of font properties (such as size and shear).

See also: `BFont::SetFlags()`, `get_font_family()`

Font Name Lengths

be/interface/Font.h

Constant	Value
B_FONT_FAMILY_NAME_LENGTH	63
B_FONT_STYLE_NAME_LENGTH	63

These constants define the maximum length of names for font families and styles, exclusive of a null terminator. They're used in the definition of the `font_family` and `font_style` types.

See also: `font_family` under "Defined Types" below

Font Properties

be/interface/View.h

Constant
B_FONT_FAMILY_AND_STYLE
B_FONT_SIZE
B_FONT_SHEAR
B_FONT_ROTATION

Constant
B_FONT_SPACING
B_FONT_ENCODING
B_FONT_FACE
B_FONT_FLAGS
B_FONT_ALL

These constants list the font properties that can be set for a BView individually or in combination. The constants form a mask that's passed, along with a BFont object, to BView's `SetFont()` and BTextView's `SetFontAndColor()` functions. For example:

```
myView->SetFont(theFont, B_FONT_SIZE | B_FONT_ENCODING);
```

`B_FONT_ALL` stands for all properties of the BFont.

See also: `BView::SetFont()`

Font Spacing Modes

> `be/interface/Font.h`

Constant
B_CHAR_SPACING
B_STRING_SPACING
B_BITMAP_SPACING
B_FIXED_SPACING

These constants enumerate the four modes for positioning characters in a line of text.

See also: `BFont::SetSpacing()`

Function Key Constants

> `be/interface/InterfaceDefs.h`

Constant	Constant
B_F1_KEY	B_F9_KEY
B_F2_KEY	B_F10_KEY
B_F3_KEY	B_F11_KEY
B_F4_KEY	B_F12_KEY
B_F5_KEY	B_PRINT_KEY (the "Print Screen" key)
B_F6_KEY	B_SCROLL_KEY (the "Scroll Lock" key)
B_F7_KEY	B_PAUSE_KEY
B_F8_KEY	

These constants stand for the various keys that are mapped to the B_FUNCTION_KEY character. When the B_FUNCTION_KEY character is reported in a key-down event, the application can determine which key produced the character by testing the key code against these constants. (Control-*p* also produces the B_FUNCTION_KEY character.)

See also: "Character Mapping" in Appendix B, *Keyboard Information*

Interface Messages

be/app/AppDefs.h

Constant	Constant
B_ZOOM	B_KEY_DOWN
B_MINIMIZE	B_KEY_UP
B_WINDOW_RESIZED	B_MOUSE_DOWN
B_WINDOW_MOVED	B_MOUSE_UP
B_WINDOW_ACTIVATED	B_MOUSE_MOVED
B_QUIT_REQUESTED	B_VIEW_RESIZED
B_SCREEN_CHANGED	B_VIEW_MOVED
B_WORKSPACE_ACTIVATED	B_VALUE_CHANGED
B_WORKSPACES_CHANGED	B_PULSE

These constants identify interface messages—system messages that are delivered to BWindow objects. Each constant conveys an instruction to do something in particular (B_ZOOM) or names a type of event (B_KEY_DOWN).

See also: "Interface Messages" in the "Responding to the User" section of this chapter

list_view_type Constants

be/interface/ListView.h

Constant
B_SINGLE_SELECTION_LIST
B_MULTIPLE_SELECTION_LIST

These constants distinguish between lists that permit the user to select only one item at a time and those that allow multiple items to be selected.

See also: the BListView class

Main Screen

```
be/interface/Screen.h
```

const screen_id **B_MAIN_SCREEN_ID**

This constant stands for the main screen, the screen that has the origin of the screen coordinate system at its left top corner. (Currently only one screen can be attached to the computer and it is the main screen.)

See also: `screen_id`

menu_bar_border Constants

```
be/interface/MenuBar.h
```

Constant	Meaning
B_BORDER_FRAME	Put a border inside the entire frame rectangle.
B_BORDER_CONTENTS	Put a border around the group of items only.
B_BORDER_EACH_ITEM	Put a border around each item.

These constants can be passed as an argument to BMenuBar's `SetBorder()` function.

See also: `BMenuBar::SetBorder()`

menu_layout Constants

```
be/interface/Menu.h
```

Constant	Meaning
B_ITEMS_IN_ROW	Menu items are arranged horizontally, in a row.
B_ITEMS_IN_COLUMN	Menu items are arranged vertically, in a column.
B_ITEMS_IN_MATRIX	Menu items are arranged in a custom fashion.

These constants define the `menu_layout` data type. They distinguish the ways that items can be arranged in a menu or menu bar—they can be laid out from end to end in a row like a typical menu bar, stacked from top to bottom in a column like a typical menu, or arranged in some custom fashion like a matrix.

See also: the BMenu and BMenuBar constructors

Modifier States

be/interface/InterfaceDef.h

Constant	Constant
B_SHIFT_KEY	B_OPTION_KEY
B_LEFT_SHIFT_KEY	B_LEFT_OPTION_KEY
B_RIGHT_SHIFT_KEY	B_RIGHT_OPTION_KEY
B_CONTROL_KEY	B_COMMAND_KEY
B_LEFT_CONTROL_KEY	B_LEFT_COMMAND_KEY
B_RIGHT_CONTROL_KEY	B_RIGHT_COMMAND_KEY
B_CAPS_LOCK	B_MENU_KEY
B_SCROLL_LOCK	
B_NUM_LOCK	

These constants designate the Shift, Option, Control, Command, and Menu modifier keys and the lock states set by the Caps Lock, Scroll Lock, and Num Lock keys. They're typically used to form a mask that describes the current, or required, modifier states.

For each variety of modifier key, there are constants that distinguish between the keys that appear at the left and right of the keyboard, as well as one that lumps both together. For example, if the user is holding the left Control key down, both B_CONTROL_KEY and B_LEFT_CONTROL_KEY will be set in the mask.

See also: modifiers(), BWindow::AddShortcut(), the BMenu constructor

Mouse Buttons

be/interface/View.h

Constant
B_PRIMARY_MOUSE_BUTTON
B_SECONDARY_MOUSE_BUTTON
B_TERTIARY_MOUSE_BUTTON

These constants name the mouse buttons. Buttons are identified, not by their physical positions on the mouse, but by their roles in the user interface.

See also: BView::GetMouse(), set_mouse_map()

Orientation Constants

`be/interface/InterfaceDef.h`

Constant
_____
B_HORIZONTAL

B_VERTICAL
_____

These constants define the `orientation` data type that distinguishes between the vertical and horizontal orientation of graphic objects. It's currently used only to differentiate scroll bars.

See also: the BScrollBar and BScrollView classes

Pattern Constants

`be/interface/GraphicsDef.h`

const pattern **B_SOLID_HIGH** = { 0xff, 0xff, 0xff, 0xff, 0xff,0xff, 0xff, 0xff }

const pattern **B_SOLID_LOW** = { 0x00, 0x00, 0x00, 0x00, 0x00, 0x00, 0x00, 0x00 }

const pattern **B_MIXED_COLORS**
    = { 0xaa, 0x55, 0xaa, 0x55, 0xaa, 0x55, 0xaa, 0x55 }

These constants name the three standard patterns defined in the Interface Kit.

`B_SOLID_HIGH` is a pattern that consists of the high color only. It's the default pattern for all BView drawing functions that stroke lines and fill shapes.

`B_SOLID_LOW` is a pattern with only the low color. It's used mainly to erase images (to replace them with the background color).

`B_MIXED_COLORS` alternates pixels between the high and low colors in a checkerboard pattern. The result is a halftone midway between the two colors. This pattern can produce fine gradations of color, especially when the high and low colors are set to two colors that are already quite similar.

See also: "Patterns" in the "Drawing" section of this chapter

Resizing Modes

`be/interface/View.h`

Constants
_____
B_FOLLOW_LEFT

B_FOLLOW_RIGHT

B_FOLLOW_LEFT_RIGHT
_____

Constants
_____

B_FOLLOW_H_CENTER

B_FOLLOW_TOP

B_FOLLOW_BOTTOM

B_FOLLOW_TOP_BOTTOM

B_FOLLOW_V_CENTER

B_FOLLOW_ALL

B_FOLLOW_NONE
_____

These constants are used to set the behavior of a view when its parent is resized. They're explained under the BView constructor.

See also: the BView constructor, `BView::SetResizingMode()`

Screen Spaces

    be/interface/GraphicsDef.h

Constant	Constant
B_8_BIT_640x480	B_32_BIT_640x480
B_8_BIT_800x600	B_32_BIT_800x600
B_8_BIT_1024x768	B_32_BIT_1024x768
B_8_BIT_1152x900	B_32_BIT_1152x900
B_8_BIT_1280x1024	B_32_BIT_1280x1024
B_8_BIT_1600x1200	B_32_BIT_1600x1200
B_16_BIT_640x480	B_8_BIT_640x400
B_16_BIT_800x600	
B_16_BIT_1024x768	
B_16_BIT_1152x900	
B_16_BIT_1280x1024	
B_16_BIT_1600x1200	

These constants are currently used to configure the screen—to set its depth and the size of the pixel grid it displays—as well as to report which configurations are possible. However, they may not be supported in the future. 16-bit depths are not currently supported

See also: `set_screen_space()`, `get_screen_info()`

Scroll Bar Constants

be/interface/ScrollBar.h

Constant
B_H_SCROLL_BAR_HEIGHT
B_V_SCROLL_BAR_WIDTH

These constants record the recommended thickness of scroll bars. They should be used to help define the frame rectangles passed to the BScrollBar constructor.

See also: the BScrollBar class

String Truncation Constants

be/interface/Font.h

Constant
B_TRUNCATE_END
B_TRUNCATE_BEGINNING
B_TRUNCATE_MIDDLE
B_TRUNCATE_SMART

These constants instruct a BFont where it should remove characters from a set of strings to shorten them.

See also: BFont::GetTruncatedStrings()

Transparency Constants

be/interface/GraphicsDefs.h

const uint8 **B_TRANSPARENT_8_BIT**

const rgb_color **B_TRANSPARENT_32_BIT**

These constants set transparent pixel values in a bitmap image. B_TRANSPARENT_8_BIT designates a transparent pixel in the B_COLOR_8_BIT color space, and B_TRANSPARENT_32_BIT designates a transparent pixel in the B_RGB_32_BIT color space.

Transparency is explained in the "Drawing Modes" part of the "Drawing" section of this chapter. Drawing modes other than B_OP_COPY preserve the destination image where a source bitmap is transparent.

See also: "Drawing Modes" in the "Drawing" section of this chapter, the BBitmap class, BView::SetViewColor()

View Flags

`be/interface/View.h`

Constant	Meaning
B_FULL_UPDATE_ON_RESIZE	Include the entire view in the clipping region.
B_WILL_DRAW	Allow the BView to draw.
B_PULSE_NEEDED	Report pulse events to the BView.
B_FRAME_EVENTS	Report view-resized and view-moved events.
B_NAVIGABLE	Let users navigate to the view with the Tab key.
B_NAVIGABLE_JUMP	Mark the view for Control-Tab navigation.

These constants can be combined to form a mask that sets the behavior of a BView object. They're explained in more detail under the class constructor. The mask is passed to the constructor, or to the `SetFlags()` function.

See also: the BView constructor, `BView::SetFlags()`

Window Flags

`be/interface/Window.h`

Constant	Constant
B_NOT_MOVABLE	B_NOT_CLOSABLE
B_NOT_H_RESIZABLE	B_NOT_ZOOMABLE
B_NOT_V_RESIZABLE	B_NOT_MINIMIZABLE
B_NOT_RESIZABLE	B_WILL_FLOAT
B_WILL_ACCEPT_FIRST_CLICK	

These constants set the behavior of a window. They can be combined to form a mask that's passed to the BWindow constructor.

See also: the BWindow constructor

window_type Constants

`be/interface/Window.h`

Constant	Meaning
B_MODAL_WINDOW	The window is a modal window.
B_BORDERED_WINDOW	The window has a border but no title tab.

Constant	Meaning
B_TITLED_WINDOW	The window has a border and a title tab.
B_DOCUMENT_WINDOW	The window has a border, tab and resize knob.

These constants describe the various kinds of windows that can be requested from the Application Server.

See also: the BWindow constructor

Workspace Constants

    be/interface/Window.h

Constant
B_CURRENT_WORKSPACE
B_ALL_WORKSPACES

These constants are used—along with designations of specific workspaces—to associate a set of one or more workspaces with a BWindow.

See also: the BWindow constructor, `BWindow::SetWorkspaces()`

Defined Types

alert_type

    be/interface/Alert.h

    typedef enum {. . .} **alert_type**

These constants name the various types of alert panel.

See also: "`alert_type` Constants", the BAlert constructor

alignment

    be/interface/InterfaceDefs.h

    typedef enum {. . .} **alignment**

Alignment constants determine where lines of text are placed in a view.

See also: "`alignment` Constants", `BTextView::SetAlignment()`

button_width

be/interface/Alert.h

typedef enum {. . .} **button_width**

These constants name the methods that can be used to determine how wide to make the buttons in an alert panel.

See also: "**button_width** Constants", the BAlert constructor

color_map

be/interface/GraphicsDefs.h

typedef struct {
    int32 **id**;
    rgb_color **color_list**[256];
    uint8 **inversion_map**[256];
    uint8 **index_map**[32768];
} **color_map**

This structure contains information about the 8-bit color context for a particular screen. All applications that display on the screen share the same color map.

See also: BScreen::ColorMap()

color_space

be/interface/GraphicsDefs.h

typedef enum {. . .} **color_space**

Color space constants determine the depth and interpretation of bitmap images. They're described under "Colors" in the "Drawing" section of this chapter.

See also: "**color_space** Constants"

drawing_mode

be/interface/GraphicsDefs.h

typedef enum {. . .} **drawing_mode**

The drawing mode determines how source and destination images interact.

See also: "Drawing Modes" in the "Drawing" section of this chapter, "**drawing_mode** Constants"

edge_info

be/interface/Font.h

typedef struct {
    float **left**;
    float **right**;
} **edge_info**

This structure records information about the location of a character outline within the horizontal space allotted to the character. Edges separate one character from adjacent characters on the left and right. They're explained under the GetEdges() function in the BFont class.

See also: BFont::GetEscapements()

escapement_delta

be/interface/Font.h

typedef struct {
    float **nonspace**;
    float **space**;
} **escapement_delta**

This structure contains values that should be added to the width of each character in a string when the string is drawn.

See also: BView::DrawString(), BFont::GetEscapements()

font_direction

be/interface/Font.h

typedef enum {...} **font_direction**

This type distinguishes between fonts that are read left-to-right (B_FONT_LEFT_TO_RIGHT) and those that are read right-to-left (B_FONT_RIGHT_TO_LEFT).

See also: BFont::Direction()

font_family

be/interface/InterfaceDefs.h

typedef char **font_family**[B_FONT_FAMILY_LENGTH + 1]

This type defines a string long enough to hold the name of a font family—64 characters including the null terminator.

See also: get_font_family()

font_height

be/interface/Font.h

typedef struct {
    float **ascent**;
    float **descent**;
    float **leading**;
} **font_height**

This type combines the three vertical measurements that determine the height of a line of text.

See also: BFont::GetHeight()

font_style

be/interface/InterfaceDefs.h

typedef char **font_style**[B_FONT_STYLE_LENGTH + 1]

This type defines a string long enough to hold the name of a font style—64 characters including the null terminator.

See also: get_font_style()

key_info

be/interface/View.h

typedef struct {
    uint32 **modifiers**;
    uint8 **key_states**[16];
} **key_info**

This structure is used to get information about the current state of the keyboard in the absence of B_KEY_DOWN messages.

See also: get_key_info()

key_map

be/interface/InterfaceDefs.h

typedef struct {
    uint32 **version**;
    uint32 **caps_key**;
    uint32 **scroll_key**;

```
        uint32 num_key;
        uint32 left_shift_key;
        uint32 right_shift_key;
        uint32 left_command_key;
        uint32 right_command_key;
        uint32 left_control_key;
        uint32 right_control_key;
        uint32 left_option_key;
        uint32 right_option_key;
        uint32 menu_key;
        uint32 lock_settings;
        int32 control_map[128];
        int32 option_caps_shift_map[128];
        int32 option_caps_map[128];
        int32 option_shift_map[128];
        int32 option_map[128];
        int32 caps_shift_map[128];
        int32 caps_map[128];
        int32 shift_map[128];
        int32 normal_map[128];
        int32 acute_dead_key[32];
        int32 grave_dead_key[32];
        int32 circumflex_dead_key[32];
        int32 dieresis_dead_key[32];
        int32 tilde_dead_key[32];
        uint32 acute_tables;
        uint32 grave_tables;
        uint32 circumflex_tables;
        uint32 dieresis_tables;
        uint32 tilde_tables;
    } key_map
```

This structure maps the physical keys on the keyboard to their functions in the user interface. It holds the tables that assign characters to key codes, set up dead keys, and determine which keys function as modifiers. There's just one key map shared by all applications running on the same machine.

See also: `get_key_map()`

menu_bar_border

```
be/interface/MenuBar.h
```

typedef enum {. . .} menu_bar_border

This type enumerates the ways that a menu bar can be bordered.

See also: BMenuBar::SetBorder(), "menu_bar_border Constants" above

menu_info

be/interface/Menu.h

typedef struct {
    float **font_size**;
    font_name **font**;
    rgb_color **background_color**;
    int32 **separator**;
    bool **click_to_open**;
    bool **triggers_always_shown**;
} **menu_info**

This structure records the user's menu preferences.

See also: set_menu_info(), the BMenu class

menu_layout

be/interface/Menu.h

typedef enum {. . .} **menu_layout**

This type distinguishes the various ways that items can arranged in a menu or menu bar.

See also: the BMenu class, "menu_layout Constants" above

mouse_map

be/interface/InterfaceDefs.h

typedef struct {
    uint32 **left**;
    uint32 **right**;
    uint32 **middle**;
} **mouse_map**

This structure maps mouse buttons to their roles as the B_PRIMARY_MOUSE_BUTTON, B_SECONDARY_MOUSE_BUTTON, or B_TERTIARY_MOUSE_BUTTON.

See also: set_mouse_map()

orientation

`be/interface/InterfaceDefs.h`

typedef enum {. . .} **orientation**

This type distinguishes between the `B_VERTICAL` and `B_HORIZONTAL` orientation of scroll bars.

See also: the BScrollBar and BScrollView classes

pattern

`be/interface/GraphicsDefs.h`

typedef struct {
    uchar **data**[8];
} **pattern**

A pattern is a arrangement of two colors—the high color and the low color—in an 8-pixel by 8-pixel square. Pixels are specified in rows, with one byte per row and one bit per pixel. Bits marked 1 designate the high color; those marked 0 designate the low color. An example and an illustration are given under "Patterns" in the "Drawing section of this chapter.

See also: "Pattern Constants" above

print_file_header

`be/interface/PrintJob.h`

typedef struct {
    long **version**;
    long **page_count**;
    long **_reserved_1_**;
    long **_reserved_2_**;
    long **_reserved_3_**;
    long **_reserved_4_**;
    long **_reserved_5_**;
} **print_file_header**

This structure defines the header information for a print job. Although declared publicly, it currently is used only internally by the BPrintJob class.

rgb_color

```
be/interface/GraphicsDefs.h
```

typedef struct {
    uint8 **red**;
    uint8 **green**;
    uint8 **blue**;
    uint8 **alpha**;
} **rgb_color**

This type specifies a full 32-bit color. Each component can have a value ranging from a minimum of 0 to a maximum of 255.

The `alpha` component, which is designed to specify the coverage of the color (how transparent or opaque it is), is currently ignored. However, an `rgb_color` can be made completely transparent by assigning it the special value, `B_TRANSPARENT_32_BIT`.

See also: `BView::SetHighColor()`

screen_id

```
be/interface/Screen.h
```

typedef struct {
    int32 **id**;
} **screen_id**

This type is a unique identifier for a screen. The constant `B_MAIN_SCREEN_ID` is a `screen_id` that identifies the main screen.

See also: the BScreen class

screen_info

```
be/interface/InterfaceDefs.h
```

typedef struct {
    color_space **mode**;
    BRect **frame**;
    uint32 **spaces**;
    float **min_refresh_rate**;
    float **max_refresh_rate**;
    float **refresh_rate**;
    uchar **h_position**;
    uchar **v_position**;

```
        uchar h_size;
        uchar v_size;
    } screen_info
```

This structure holds information about a screen. Its fields are explained under the get_screen_info() global function.

See also: get_screen_info()

scroll_bar_info

be/interface/InterfaceDefs.h

```
typedef struct {
    bool proportional;
    bool double_arrows;
    int32 knob;
    int32 min_knob_size;
} scroll_bar_info
```

This structure captures the user's preferences for how scroll bars should behave and appear.

See also: set_scroll_bar_info(), the BScrollBar class

text_run

be/interface/TextView.h

```
typedef struct {
    int32 offset;
    BFont font;
    rgb_color color;
} text_run
```

The BTextView class uses this structure to keep track of a sequence of characters that are displayed in the same font and color.

See also: BTextView::SetRunArray()

text_run_array

be/interface/TextView.h

```
typedef struct {
    int32 count;
    text_run runs[];
} text_run_array
```

The BTextView class uses this structure to associate character formats with the text it displays.

See also: `BTextView::SetRunArray()`

tuned_font_info

`be/interface/Font.h`

```
typedef struct {
    float size;
    float shear;
    float rotation;
    int32 flags;
    int16 face;
} tuned_font_info
```

This structure lists the properties of a font that has a counterpart that's been tuned to improve its appearance on-screen. The tuned counterpart will be used whenever the font is the BView's current font and `DrawString()` draws to the screen.

See also: `BFont::GetTunedInfo()`, `get_font_family()`

window_type

`be/interface/Window.h`

```
typedef enum {. . .} window_type
```

This type describes the various kinds of windows that can be requested from the Application Server.

See also: the BWindow constructor, "`window_type` Constants"

CHAPTER FIVE

The Kernel Kit

The Kernel Kit

The Kernel Kit is a collection of C functions that let you define and control the contexts in which your application operates. There are five main topics in the Kit:

- "Threads and Teams." A thread is a synchronous computer process. By creating multiple threads, you can make your application perform different tasks at (virtually) the same time. A team is the collection of threads your application creates.

- "Ports." A port can be thought of as a mailbox for threads: A thread can write a message to a port, and some other thread (or, less usefully, the same thread) can then retrieve the message.

- "Semaphores." A semaphore is a system-wide counting variable that can be used as a lock that protects a piece of code. Before a thread is allowed to execute the code, it must acquire the semaphore that guards it. Semaphores can also be used to synchronize the execution of two or more threads.

- "Areas." The area functions let you allocate large chunks of virtual memory. The two primary features of areas are: They can be locked into the CPU's on-chip memory, and the data they hold can be shared between applications.

- "Images." An image is compiled code that can be dynamically linked into a running application. By loading and unloading images you can make run-time decisions about the resources that your application has access to. Images are of particular interest to driver designers.

The rest of the chapter describes these topics in detail. The final sections, "System and Time Information" and "Miscellaneous Functions and Constants," fill in the gaps.

NOTE

The Kernel Kit also includes some straight C file system functions (declared in the *fs_*.h* header files), which are described in Chapter 3, *The Storage Kit*.

Threads and Teams

Declared in: be/kernel/OS.h

Library: libbe.so

Overview

A thread is a synchronous process that executes a series of program instructions. Every application has at least one thread: When you launch an application, an initial thread—the *main thread*—is automatically created (or *spawned*) and told to run. The main thread executes the ubiquitous `main()` function, winds through the functions that are called from `main()`, and is automatically deleted (or *killed*) when `main()` exits.

The Be operating system is *multi-threaded*: From the main thread you can spawn and run additional threads; from each of these threads you can spawn and run more threads, and so on. All the threads in all applications run concurrently and asynchronously with each other.

Threads are independent of each other. Most notably, a given thread doesn't own the other threads it has spawned. For example, if thread A spawns thread B, and thread A dies (for whatever reason), thread B will continue to run. (But before you get carried away with the idea of leap-frogging threads, you should take note of the caveat in "Death and the Main Thread.")

WARNING

Threads and the POSIX fork() function are not compatible. You can't mix calls to `spawn_thread()` (the function that creates a new thread) and `fork()` in the same application: If you call `spawn_thread()` and then try to call `fork()`, the `fork()` call will fail. And vice versa.

Teams

Although threads are independent, they do fall into groups called *teams*. A team consists of a main thread and all other threads that "descend" from it (that are spawned by the main thread directly or by any thread that was spawned by the main thread, and so on). Viewed from a higher level, a team is the group of threads that are created by a single application. You can't "transfer" threads from one team to another. The team is set when the thread is spawned; it remains the same throughout the thread's life.

All the threads in a particular team share the same address space: Global variables that are declared by one thread will be visible to all other threads in that team.

Spawning a Thread

You spawn a thread by calling the `spawn_thread()` function. The function assigns and returns a system-wide `thread_id` number that you use to identify the new thread in subsequent function calls. Valid `thread_id` numbers are positive integers; you can check the success of a spawn thus:

```
thread_id my_thread = spawn_thread(...);

if ((my_thread) < B_NO_ERROR)
   /* failure */
else
   /* success */
```

The arguments to `spawn_thread()`, which are examined throughout this description, supply information such as what the thread is supposed to do, the urgency of its operation, and so on.

Threads and App Images

A conceptual neighbor of spawning a thread is the act of loading an executable (or loading an *app image*). This is performed by calling the `load_image()` function. Loading an image causes a separate program, identified as a file, to be launched by the system. For more information on the `load_image()` function, see "Images."

Telling a Thread to Run

Spawning a thread isn't enough to make it run. To tell a thread to start running, you must pass its `thread_id` number to either the `resume_thread()` or `wait_for_thread()` function:

- `resume_thread()` starts the new thread running and immediately returns. The new thread runs concurrently and asynchronously with the thread in which `resume_thread()` was called.

- `wait_for_thread()` starts the thread running but doesn't return until the thread has finished. (You can also call `wait_for_thread()` on a thread that's already running.)

Of these two functions, `resume_thread()` is the more common means for starting a thread that was created through `spawn_thread()`. `wait_for_thread()` is typically used to start the thread that was created through `load_image()`.

The Thread Function

When you call `spawn_thread()`, you must identify the new thread's *thread function*. This is a global C function (or a static C++ member function) that the new thread will execute when it's told to run. When the thread function exits, the thread is automatically killed.

The `thread_func` type represents a pointer to a thread function:

```
typedef int32 (*thread_func)(void *);
```

- The function accepts a pointer to a buffer of arbitrarily-typed data. What the function does with the data is up to your application. (See "The Thread Function's Argument" for more information and caveats.)

- The return value is a 32-bit integer value that's typically interpreted as an error code. To whom the value is returned is explored in "Thread Function Return Values".

- The function's name isn't prescribed by the protocol; in other words, a thread function doesn't *have* to be named "thread_func".

You specify a thread function by passing a `thread_func` as the first argument to `spawn_thread()`; the last argument to `spawn_thread()` is forwarded as the thread function's *data* argument. Since *data* is delivered as a `void *`, you have to cast the value to the appropriate type within your implementation of the thread function. For example, let's say you define a thread function called `lister()` that takes a pointer to a BList object as an argument:

```
int32 lister(void *data)
{
   /* Cast the argument. */
   BList *listObj = (BList *)data;
   ...
}
```

To create and run a thread that would execute the `lister()` function, you call `spawn_thread()` and `resume_thread()` thus (excluding error checks):

```
BList *listObj = new BList();
thread_id my_thread;

my_thread = spawn_thread(lister, ..., (void *)listObj);
resume_thread(my_thread);
```

The Thread Function's Argument

The `spawn_thread()` function *doesn't* copy the data that *data* points to. It simply passes the pointer through. Because of this, you should never pass a pointer that's allocated locally (on the stack).

The reason for this restriction is that there's no guarantee that the thread function will receive *any* CPU attention before the stack frame from which `spawn_thread()` was called is destroyed. Thus, the thread function won't necessarily have a chance to copy the pointed-to data before the *data* pointer is freed. There are ways around this restriction—for example, you could use a semaphore to ensure that the thread function has copied the data before the calling frame exits. A better solution is to forego the *data* argument and use the `send_data()` function (which *does* copy its data). See "Passing Data to a Thread."

Using a C++ Thread Function

If you're up in C++ territory, you'll probably want to define a class member function that you can use as a thread function. Unfortunately, you can't pass a normal (non-static) member function directly as the thread function argument to `spawn_thread()`—the system won't know which object it's supposed to invoke the function on (it won't have a `this` pointer). To get from here to there, you have to declare two member functions:

- A static member function that is, literally, the thread function.

- A non-static member function that the static function can invoke. This non-static function will perform the intended work of the thread function.

To "connect" the two functions, you pass an object of the appropriate class (through the *data* argument) to the static function, and then allow the static function to invoke the non-static function upon that object. An example is called for:

Here we define a class that contains a static function called `thread_func()`, and a non-static function called `threadFunc()`. By convention, these two are private. In addition, the class declares a public `Go()` function, and a private `thread_id` variable:

```
class MyClass {
public:
    status_t Go(void);

private:
    static int32 thread_func(void *arg);
    int32 threadFunc(void);
    thread_id my_thread;
};
```

`thread_func()` is the literal thread function. It doesn't really do anything—it simply casts its argument as a MyClass object, and then invokes `threadFunc()` on the object:

```
int32 MyClass::thread_func(void *arg)
{
    MyClass *obj = (MyClass *)arg;
    return (obj->threadFunc());
}
```

`threadFunc()` performs the actual work:

```
int32 MyClass::threadFunc(void)
{
    /* do something here */
```

```
   ...
   return (whatever);
}
```

The `Go()` function contains the `spawn_thread()` call that starts the whole thing going:

```
status_t MyClass::Go(void)
{
   my_thread = spawn_thread(thread_func, ..., this);
   return (resume_thread(my_thread));
}
```

If you aren't familiar with static member functions, you should consult a qualified C++ textbook. Briefly, the only thing you need to know for the purposes of the technique shown here, is that a static function's implementation can't call (non-static) member functions nor can it refer to member data. Maintain the form demonstrated above and you'll be rewarded in heaven.

Thread Function Return Values

The thread function's protocol declares that the function should return a `int32` value when it exits. This value can be captured by sitting in a `wait_for_thread()` call until the thread function exits. `wait_for_thread()` takes two arguments:

- The `thread_id` of the thread that you're waiting for.
- A pointer to an `int32` that captures the thread function's return value.

For example:

```
thread_id other_thread;
status_t result;

other_thread = spawn_thread(...);
resume_thread(other_thread);


...
wait_for_thread(other_thread, &result);
```

If the target thread is already dead, `wait_for_thread()` returns immediately (with an error code as described in the function's full description), and the second argument will be set to an invalid value. If you're late for the train, you'll miss the boat.

WARNING

You must pass a valid pointer as the second argument to wait_for_thread(). You mustn't pass NULL even if you're not interested in the return value.

Thread Names

A thread can be given a name which you assign through the second argument to `spawn_thread()`. The name can be 32 characters long (as represented by the `B_OS_NAME_LENGTH` constant) and needn't be unique—more than one thread can have the same name.

You can look for a thread based on its name by passing the name to the `find_thread()` function; the function returns the `thread_id` of the so-named thread. If two or more threads bear the same name, the `find_thread()` function returns the first of these threads that it finds.

You can retrieve the `thread_id` of the calling thread by passing `NULL` to `find_thread()`:

```
thread_id this_thread = find_thread(NULL);
```

To retrieve a thread's name, you must look in the thread's `thread_info` structure. This structure is described in the `get_thread_info()` function description.

Dissatisfied with a thread's name? Use the `rename_thread()` function to change it. Fool your friends.

Thread Priority

In a multi-threaded environment, the CPUs must divide their attention between the candidate threads, executing a few instructions from this thread, then a few from that thread, and so on. But the division of attention isn't always equal: You can assign a higher or lower *priority* to a thread and so declare it to be more or less important than other threads.

You assign a thread's priority (an integer) as the third argument to `spawn_thread()`. There are two categories of priorities: "time-sharing" and "real-time."

- **Time-sharing** (*values from 1 to 99*). A time-sharing thread is executed only if there are no real-time threads in the ready queue. In the absence of real-time threads, a time-sharing thread is elected to run once every "scheduler quantum" (currently, every three milliseconds). The higher the time-sharing thread's priority value, the greater the chance that it will be the next thread to run.

- **Real-time** (*100 and greater*). A real-time thread is executed as soon as it's ready. If more than one real-time thread is ready at the same time, the thread with the highest priority is executed first. The thread is allowed to run without being preempted (except by a real-time thread with a higher priority) until it blocks, snoozes, is suspended, or otherwise gives up its plea for attention.

The Kernel Kit defines seven priority constants. Although you can use other, "in-between" values as the priority argument to `spawn_thread()`, it's suggested that you stick with these:

Time-Sharing Priority	Value
B_LOW_PRIORITY	5
B_NORMAL_PRIORITY	10
B_DISPLAY_PRIORITY	15
B_URGENT_DISPLAY_PRIORITY	20

Real-Time Priority	Value
B_REAL_TIME_DISPLAY_PRIORITY	100
B_URGENT_PRIORITY	110
B_REAL_TIME_PRIORITY	120

Synchronizing Threads

There are times when you may want a particular thread to pause at a designated point until some other (known) thread finishes some task. Here are three ways to effect this sort of synchronization:

- The most general means for synchronizing threads is to use a semaphore. The semaphore mechanism is described in great detail in "Semaphores."

- Synchronization is sometimes a side-effect of sending data between threads. This is explained in "Passing Data to a Thread," and in "Ports."

- Finally, you can tell a thread to wait for some other thread to die by calling `wait_for_thread()`, as described earlier.

Controlling a Thread

There are four ways to control a thread while it's running:

- You can put a thread to sleep for some number of microseconds through the `snooze()` function. After the thread has been asleep for the requested time, it automatically resumes execution with its next instruction. `snooze()` only works on the calling thread: The function doesn't let you identify an arbitrary thread as the subject of its operation. In other words, whichever thread calls `snooze()` is the thread that's put to sleep.

- You can suspend the execution of any thread through the `suspend_thread()` function. The function takes a single `thread_id` argument that identifies the thread you wish to suspend. The thread remains suspended until you "unsuspend" it through a call to `resume_thread()` or `wait_for_thread()`.

- You can send a POSIX "signal" to a thread through the `send_signal()` function. The `SIGCONT` signal tries to unblock a blocked or sleeping thread without killing it; all other signals kill the thread. To override this behavior, you can install your own signal handlers.

- You can kill the calling thread through `exit_thread()`. The function takes a single (`int32`) argument that's used as the thread's exit status (to make `wait_for_thread()` happy). More generally, you can kill any thread by passing its `thread_id` to the `kill_thread()` function. `kill_thread()` *doesn't* let you set the exit status.

Feeling itchy? Try killing an entire team of threads: The `kill_team()` function is more than a system call. It's therapy.

Death and the Main Thread

As mentioned earlier, the control that's imposed upon a particular thread isn't visited upon the "children" that have been spawned from that thread. However, the death of an application's main thread can affect the other threads:

WARNING

When a main thread dies, the game is pretty much over. The main thread takes the team's heap, its statically allocated objects, and other team-wide resources—such as access to standard IO—with it. This may seriously cripple any threads that linger beyond the death of the main thread.

It's possible to create an application in which the main thread sets up one or more other threads, gets them running, and then dies. But such applications should be rare. In general, you should try to keep your main thread around until all other threads in the team are dead.

Passing Data to a Thread

There are three ways to pass data to a thread:

- Through the *data* argument to the thread function, as described in "The Thread Function's Argument."

- By using a port or, at a higher level, by sending a BMessage. Ports are described in the major section "Ports"; BMessages are part of the Application Kit.

- By sending data to the thread's *message cache* through the `send_data()` and `receive_data()` functions, as described below.

The `send_data()` function sends data from one thread to another. With each `send_data()` call, you can send two packets of information:

- A single four-byte value (this is called the *code*)
- An arbitrarily long buffer of arbitrarily-typed data

The function's protocol is shown below:

```
status_t send_data(thread_id thread,
            int32 code,
            void *buffer,
            size_t buffer_size)
```

The arguments are:

- *thread* is the thread that you want to send the data to
- *code* is the four-byte code
- *buffer* is a pointer to the buffer of data
- *buffer_size* is the size of the data buffer, in bytes

In the following example, the main thread spawns a thread, sends it some data, and then tells the thread to run:

```
main()
{
    thread_id other_thread;
    int32 code = 63;
    char *buf = "Hello";

    other_thread = spawn_thread(thread_func, ...);
    send_data(other_thread, code, (void *)buf, strlen(buf));
    resume_thread(other_thread);
    ...
}
```

The `send_data()` call copies the code and the buffer (the second and third arguments) into the target thread's message cache and then (usually) returns immediately. In some cases, the four-byte code is all you need to send; in such cases, the buffer pointer can be `NULL` and the buffer size set to 0.

To retrieve the data that's been sent to it, the target thread (having been told to run) calls `receive_data()`:

```
status_t receive_data(thread_id *sender,
            void *buffer,
            size_t buffer_size)
```

This function returns the four-byte code directly, and copies the data from the message cache into its second argument. It also returns, by reference in its first argument, the `thread_id` of the thread that sent the data:

```
int32 thread_func(void *data)
{
    thread_id sender;
    int32 code;
    char buf[512];
```

```
        code = receive_data(&sender, (void *)buf, sizeof(buf));
        ...
}
```

Keep in mind that the message data is *copied* into the second argument; you must allocate adequate storage for the data, and pass, as the final argument to `receive_data()`, the size of the buffer that you allocated. A slightly annoying aspect of this mechanism is...

WARNING

There isn't any way for the data-receiving thread to determine how much data is in the message cache. It can't tell, before it receives the data, what an "adequate" size for its buffer is. If the buffer isn't big enough to accommodate all the data, the left-over portion is simply thrown away. (But at least you don't get a segmentation fault.)

As shown in the example, `send_data()` is called before the target thread is running. This feature of the system is essential in situations where you want the target thread to receive some data as its first act (as demonstrated above). However, `send_data()` isn't limited to this use—you can also send data to a thread that's already running.

Blocking When Sending and Receiving

A thread's message cache isn't a queue; it can only hold one message at a time. If you call `send_data()` twice with the same target thread, the second call will block until the target reads the first transmission through a call to `receive_data()`. Analogously, `receive_data()` will block if there isn't (yet) any data to receive.

If you want to make sure that you won't block when receiving data, you should call `has_data()` before calling `receive_data()`. `has_data()` takes a `thread_id` argument, and returns `true` if that thread has a message waiting to be read:

```
if (has_data(find_thread(NULL)))
    code = receive_data(...);
```

You can also use `has_data()` to query the target thread before sending it data. This, you hope, will ensure that the `send_data()` call won't block:

```
if (!has_data(target_thread))
    send_data(target_thread, ...);
```

This usually works, but be aware that there's a race condition between the `has_data()` and `send_data()` calls. If yet another thread sends a message to the same target in that time interval, your `send_data()` (might) block.

Thread Functions

exit_thread(), kill_thread(), kill_team()

void **exit_thread**(status_t *return_value*)

status_t **kill_thread**(thread_id *thread*)

status_t **kill_team**(team_id *team*)

These functions command one or more threads to halt execution:

- `exit_thread()` tells the calling thread to exit with a return value as given by the argument. Declaring the return value is only useful if some other thread is sitting in a `wait_for_thread()` call on this thread. `exit_thread()` sends a signal to the thread (after caching the return value in a known place).

- `kill_thread()` kills the thread given by the argument. The value that the thread will return to `wait_for_thread()` is undefined and can't be relied upon. `kill_thread()` is the same as sending a SIGKILLTHR signal to the thread.

- `kill_team()` kills all the threads within the given team. Again, the threads' return values are random. `kill_team()` is the same as sending a SIGKILL signal to any thread in the team. Each of the threads in the team is then handed a SIGKILLTHR signal.

Exiting a thread is a fairly safe thing to do—since a thread can only exit itself, it's assumed that the thread knows what it's doing. Killing some other thread or an entire team is more drastic since the death certificate(s) will be delivered at an indeterminate time. In every case (exiting or killing) the system reclaims the resources that the thread (or team) had claimed. So killing a thread shouldn't cause a memory leak.

NOTE

Keep in mind that threads die automatically (and their resources are reclaimed) if they're allowed to exit naturally. You should only need to kill a thread if something has gone screwy.

Return values:

B_NO_ERROR. The thread or team was successfully killed.
B_BAD_THREAD_ID. Invalid *thread* value.
B_BAD_TEAM_ID. Invalid *team* value.

find_thread()

thread_id **find_thread**(const char **name*)

Finds and returns the thread with the given name. A *name* argument of NULL returns the calling thread.

A thread's name is assigned when the thread is spawned. The name can be changed thereafter through the `rename_thread()` function. Keep in mind that thread names needn't be unique: If two (or more) threads boast the same name, a `find_thread()` call on that name returns the first so-named thread that it finds. There's no way to iterate through identically-named threads.

Return values:

> B_NAME_NOT_FOUND. *name* doesn't identify a valid thread.

get_team_info(), get_next_team_info(), team_info

> status_t **get_team_info**(team_id *team*, team_info **info*)
> status_t **get_next_team_info**(int32 **cookie*, team_info **info*)

> typedef struct {} **team_info**

The functions copy, into the *info* argument, the `team_info` structure for a particular team. The `get_team_info()` function retrieves information for the team identified by *team*.

The `get_next_team_info()` version lets you step through the list of all teams. The *cookie* argument is a placemark; you set it to 0 on your first call, and let the function do the rest. The function returns B_BAD_VALUE when there are no more areas to visit:

```
/* Get the team_info for every team. */
team_info info;
int32 cookie = 0;

while (get_next_team_info(0, &cookie, &info) == B_NO_ERROR)
    ...
```

The `team_info` structure is defined as:

```
typedef struct {
    team_id team;
    int32 thread_count;
    int32 image_count;
    int32 area_count;
    thread_id debugger_nub_thread;
    port_id debugger_nub_port;
    int32 argc;
    char args[64];
    uid_t uid;
    gid_t gid;
} team_info
```

The first field is obvious; the next three reasonably so: They give the number of threads that have been spawned, images that have been loaded, and areas that have been created or cloned within this team.

The debugger fields are used by the, uhm, the...debugger?

The `argc` field is the number of command line arguments that were used to launch the team; `args` is a copy of the first 64 characters from the command line invocation. If this team is an application that was launched through the user interface (by double-clicking, or by accepting a dropped icon), then `argc` is 1 and `args` is the name of the application's executable file.

`uid` and `gid` identify the user and group that "owns" the team. You can use these values to play permission games.

Return values:

B_NO_ERROR. The desired team information was found.

B_BAD_TEAM_ID. *team* doesn't identify an existing team, or there are no more areas to visit.

get_thread_info(), get_next_thread_info(), thread_info

```
status_t get_thread_info(thread_id thread, thread_info *info)
status_t get_next_thread_info(team_id team,
                int32 *cookie,
                thread_info *info)
```

```
typedef struct {} thread_info
```

These functions copy, into the *info* argument, the `thread_info` structure for a particular thread:

The `get_thread_info()` function gets the information for the thread identified by *thread*.

The `get_next_thread_info()` function lets you step through the list of a team's threads through iterated calls. The *team* argument identifies the team you want to look at; a *team* value of 0 means the team of the calling thread. The *cookie* argument is a placemark; you set it to 0 on your first call, and let the function do the rest. The function returns B_BAD_VALUE when there are no more threads to visit:

```
/* Get the thread_info for every thread in this team. */
thread_info info;
int32 cookie = 0;

while (get_next_thread_info(0, &cookie, &info) == B_OK)
    ...
```

The `thread_info` structure is defined as:

```
typedef struct {
    thread_id thread;
    team_id team;
    char name[B_OS_NAME_LENGTH];
    thread_state state;
    int32 priority;
    sem_id sem;
    bigtime_t user_time;
    bigtime_t kernel_time;
    void *stack_base;
    void *stack_end;
} thread_info
```

The fields in the structure are:

- `thread`. The `thread_id` number of the thread.
- `team`. The `team_id` of the thread's team.
- `name`. The name assigned to the thread.
- `state`. What the thread is currently doing (see the thread state constants, below).
- `priority`. The level of attention the thread gets (see the priority constants, below).
- `sem`. If the thread is waiting to acquire a semaphore, this is that semaphore.
- `user_time`. The time, in microseconds, the thread has spent executing user code.
- `kernel_time`. The amount of time the kernel has run on the thread's behalf.
- `stack_base`. A pointer to the first byte in the thread's execution stack.
- `stack_end`. A pointer to the last byte in the thread's execution stack.

The last two fields are only meaningful if you understand the execution stack format. Currently, the stack size is fixed at around 256k.

WARNING

The two stack pointers are currently inverted such that `stack_base` is *less* than `stack_end`. (In a stack-grows-down world, the base should be greater than the end.)

The value of the `state` field is one of following `thread_state` constants:

Constant	Meaning
`B_THREAD_RUNNING`	The thread is currently receiving attention from a CPU.
`B_THREAD_READY`	The thread is waiting for its turn to receive attention.
`B_THREAD_SUSPENDED`	The thread has been suspended or is freshly-spawned and is waiting to start.

Constant	Meaning
B_THREAD_WAITING	The thread is waiting to acquire a semaphore. When in this state, the sem field of the thread_info structure is set to the sem_id number of the semaphore the thread is attempting to acquire. (Note that when a thread is blocked in wait_for_thread(), read_port(), or write_port(), it's actually waiting to acquire a semaphore.)
B_THREAD_RECEIVING	The thread is sitting in a receive_data() function call.
B_THREAD_ASLEEP	The thread is sitting in a snooze() call.

The value of the priority field describes the thread's "urgency"; the higher the value, the more urgent the thread. The more urgent the thread, the more attention it gets from the CPU. Expected priority values fall between 0 and 120. See "Thread Priority" for the full story.

NOTE

Thread info is provided primarily as a debugging aid. None of the values that you find in a thread_info structure are guaranteed to be valid—the thread's state, for example, will almost certainly have changed by the time get_thread_info() returns.

Return values:

B_NO_ERROR. The thread was found; *info* contains valid information.

B_BAD_VALUE. *thread* doesn't identify an existing thread, *team* doesn't identify an existing team, or there are no more threads to visit.

has_data()

bool **has_data**(thread_id *thread*)

Returns true if the given thread has an unread message in its message cache, otherwise returns false. Messages are sent to a thread's message cache through the send_data() call. To retrieve a message, you call receive_data().

kill_team()   *see exit_thread()*

kill_thread()   *see exit_thread()*

receive_data()

int32 **receive_data**(thread_id **sender*,
                void **buffer*,
                size_t *buffer_size*)

Retrieves a message from the thread's message cache. The message will have been placed there through a previous `send_data()` function call. If the cache is empty, `receive_data()` blocks until one shows up—it never returns empty-handed.

The `thread_id` of the thread that called `send_data()` is returned by reference in the *sender* argument. Note that there's no guarantee that the sender will still be alive by the time you get its ID. Also, the value of *sender* going into the function is ignored—you can't ask for a message from a particular sender.

The `send_data()` function copies two pieces of data into a thread's message cache:

• A single four-byte code that's delivered as `receive_data()`'s return value,

• and an arbitrarily long data buffer that's copied into `receive_data()`'s *buffer* argument (you must allocate and free *buffer* yourself). The *buffer_size* argument tells the function how many bytes of data to copy. If you don't need the data buffer—if the code value returned directly by the function is sufficient—you set *buffer* to `NULL` and *buffer_size* to 0.

Unfortunately, there's no way to tell how much data is in the cache before you call `receive_data()`:

• If there's more data than *buffer* can accommodate, the unaccommodated portion is discarded—a second `receive_data()` call will not read the rest of the message.

• Conversely, if `receive_data()` asks for more data than was sent, the function returns with the excess portion of *buffer* unmodified—`receive_data()` doesn't wait for another `send_data()` call to provide more data with which to fill up the buffer.

Each `receive_data()` corresponds to exactly one `send_data()`. Lacking a previous invocation of its mate, `receive_data()` will block until `send_data()` is called. If you don't want to block, you should call `has_data()` before calling `receive_data()` (and proceed to `receive_data()` only if `has_data()` returns true).

Return values:
> If successful, the function returns the message's four-byte code.
> `B_INTERRUPTED`. A blocked `receive_data()` call was interrupted by a signal.

rename_thread()

> status_t **rename_thread**(thread_id *thread*, const char **name*)

Changes the name of the given thread to *name*. Keep in mind that the maximum length of a thread name is `B_OS_NAME_LENGTH` (32 characters).

Return values:
> B_NO_ERROR. The thread was successfully named.
>
> B_BAD_THREAD_ID. *thread* argument isn't a valid `thread_id` number.

resume_thread()

> status_t **resume_thread**(thread_id *thread*)

Tells a new or suspended thread to begin executing instructions.

- If the thread has just been spawned, its execution begins with the thread function (keep in mind that a freshly spawned thread doesn't run until told to do so through this function).

- If the thread was previously suspended (through `suspend_thread()`), it continues from where it was suspended.

This function only works on threads that have a status of B_THREAD_SUSPENDED (newly spawned threads are born with this state). You can't use this function to wake up a sleeping thread (B_THREAD_ASLEEP), or to unblock a thread that's waiting to acquire a semaphore (B_THREAD_WAITING) or waiting in a `receive_data()` call (B_THREAD_RECEIVING).

However, you can unblock a thread by suspending it and *then* resuming it. Blocked threads that are resumed return B_INTERRUPTED.

`resume_thread()` is the same as sending a SIGCONT signal to the thread.

Return values:
> B_NO_ERROR. The thread was successfully resumed.
>
> B_BAD_THREAD_ID. *thread* argument isn't a valid `thread_id` number.
>
> B_BAD_THREAD_STATE. The thread isn't suspended.

send_data()

> status_t **send_data**(thread_id *thread,*
>   int32 *code,*
>   void **buffer,*
>   size_t *buffer_size*)

Copies data into *thread*'s message cache. The target thread can then retrieve the data from the cache by calling `receive_data()`. There are two parts to the data that you send:

- A single four-byte "code" given by the *code* argument.

- An arbitrarily long buffer of data that's pointed to by *buffer.* The length of the buffer, in bytes, is given by *buffer_size.*

If you only need to send the code, you should set *buffer* to NULL and *buffer_size* to 0. After send_data() returns you can free the *buffer* argument.

Normally, send_data() returns immediately—it doesn't wait for the target to call receive_data(). However, send_data() will block if the target has an unread message from a previous send_data()—keep in mind that a thread's message cache is only one message deep. A thread that's blocked in send_data() assumes B_THREAD_WAITING status.

Return values:

> B_NO_ERROR. The data was successfully sent.
> BAD_THREAD_ID. *thread* doesn't identify a valid thread.
> B_NO_MEMORY. The target couldn't allocate enough memory for its copy of *buffer*.
> B_INTERRUPTED. The function blocked, but a signal unblocked it.

set_thread_priority()

> status_t **set_thread_priority**(thread_id *thread*, int32 *new_priority*)

Resets the given thread's priority to *new_priority*.

The value of the *new_priority* can be any positive integer, but it's recommended that you stick with the following constants (the difference between "time-sharing" priorities and "real-time" priorities is explained in "Thread Priority"):

Time-Sharing Priority	Value
B_LOW_PRIORITY	5
B_NORMAL_PRIORITY	10
B_DISPLAY_PRIORITY	15
B_URGENT_DISPLAY_PRIORITY	20

Real-Time Priority	Value
B_REAL_TIME_DISPLAY_PRIORITY	100
B_URGENT_PRIORITY	110
B_REAL_TIME_PRIORITY	120

Return values:

> *Positive integers.* If the function is successful, the previous priority is returned.
> B_BAD_THREAD_ID. *thread* doesn't identify a valid thread.

snooze()

> status_t **snooze**(bigtime_t *microseconds*)

Pauses the calling thread for the given number of microseconds (the function blocks until then). The thread's state is set to B_THREAD_ASLEEP while it's snoozing.

To wake up a thread prematurely, suspend the thread and then resume it:

```
thread_info tinfo;

get_thread_info(thread, &tinfo);
if (tinfo.state == B_THREAD_ASLEEP) {
   suspend_thread(thread);
   /* Just to be sure... */
   snooze(1000);
   resume_thread(thread);
}
```

WARNING

The snooze() in the "controlling" thread is a precaution; if you're pulling this sort of stunt in your own code, you should also snooze for a bit between the suspend and resume—signals are funny that way.

There is, of course, a race condition in this example—the thread could wake up just after the get_thread_info() call. But, as with all signalling operations, the suspend/resume trick is indeterminate and wee bit dangerous. (Actually, the only situation where the race could cause trouble is if the thread wakes up, blocks on a semaphore, is then suspended/resumed AND it doesn't check the acquire_sem() return value.)

Return values:
> B_NO_ERROR. The thread went to sleep and is now awake.
> B_ERROR. Illegal *microseconds* value (less than 0).
> B_INTERRUPTED. The thread received a signal while it was sleeping.

spawn_thread()

> thread_id **spawn_thread**(thread_func *func*,
>   const char **name*,
>   int32 *priority*,
>   void **data*)

Creates a new thread and returns its thread_id identifier (a positive integer). The arguments are:

- *func* is a pointer to a thread function. This is the function that the thread will execute when it's told to run.

- *name* is the name that you wish to give the thread. It can be, at most, B_OS_NAME_LENGTH (32) characters long.

- *priority* is the CPU priority level of the thread. The higher the priority, the more attention the thread gets. The value can be any positive integer, but you should stick with the constants listed about four seconds from now.

- *data* is forwarded as the argument to the thread function.

Time-Sharing Priority	Value
B_LOW_PRIORITY	5
B_NORMAL_PRIORITY	10
B_DISPLAY_PRIORITY	15
B_URGENT_DISPLAY_PRIORITY	20

Real-Time Priority	Value
B_REAL_TIME_DISPLAY_PRIORITY	100
B_URGENT_PRIORITY	110
B_REAL_TIME_PRIORITY	120

For a complete explanation of these constants, see "Thread Priority."

A newly spawned thread is in a suspended state (B_THREAD_SUSPENDED). To tell the thread to run, you pass its thread_id to the resume_thread() function. The thread will continue to run until the thread function exits, or until the thread is explicitly killed (through a signal or a call to exit_thread(), kill_thread(), or kill_team()).

Return values:

    B_NO_MORE_THREADS. All thread_id numbers are currently in use.

    B_NO_MEMORY. Not enough memory to allocate the resources for another thread.

suspend_thread()

status_t **suspend_thread**(thread_id *thread*)

Halts the execution of the given thread, but doesn't kill the thread entirely. The thread remains suspended (suspend_thread() blocks) until it's told to run through the resume_thread() function. Nothing prevents you from suspending your own thread, i.e.:

```
suspend_thread(find_thread(NULL));
```

Of course, this is only smart if you have some other thread that will resume you later.

You can suspend any thread, regardless of its current state. But be careful: If the thread is blocked on a semaphore (for example), the subsequent `resume_thread()` call will "hop over" the semaphore acquisition.

Suspensions don't nest. A single `resume_thread()` unsuspends a thread regardless of the number of `suspend_thread()` calls it has received.

`suspend_thread()` is the same as sending a `SIGSTOP` signal to the thread.

Return values:
> B_NO_ERROR. The thread is now suspended.
> B_BAD_THREAD_ID. *thread* isn't a valid `thread_id` number.

wait_for_thread()

> status_t **wait_for_thread**(thread_id *thread*, status_t **exit_value*)

This function causes the calling thread to wait until *thread* (the "target thread") has died. If *thread* is suspended, the `wait_for_thread()` call will cause it to resume. Thus, you can use `wait_for_thread()` to tell a newly-spawned thread to start running.

When the target thread is dead, the value that was returned by its thread function (or that's imposed by `exit_thread()`, if such was called) is returned by reference in *exit_value*. If the target thread was killed (by `kill_thread()` or `kill_team()`), or if the thread function doesn't return a value, the value returned in *exit_value* is unreliable.

Return values:
> B_NO_ERROR. The target is now dead.
> B_BAD_THREAD_ID. *thread* isn't a valid `thread_id` number.
> B_INTERRUPTED. The target was killed by a signal. This includes `kill_thread()`, `kill_team()`, and `exit_thread()`.

Ports

Declared in: be/kernel/OS.h

Library: libroot.so

Overview

A port is a system-wide message repository into which a thread can copy a buffer of data, and from which some other thread can then retrieve the buffer. This repository is implemented as a first-in/first-out message queue: A port stores its messages in the order in which they're received, and it relinquishes them in the order in which they're stored. Each port has its own message queue.

There are other ways to send data between threads. Most notably, the data-sending and -receiving mechanism provided by the `send_data()` and `receive_data()` functions can also transmit data between threads. But note these differences between using a port and using the `send_data()`/`receive_data()` functions:

- A port can hold more than one message at a time. A thread can only hold one at a time. Because of this, the function that writes data to a port (`write_port()`) rarely blocks. Sending data to a thread will block if the thread has a previous, unread message.

- The messages that are transmitted through a port aren't directed at a specific recipient—they're not addressed to a specific thread. A message that's been written to a port can be read by any thread. `send_data()`, by definition, has a specific thread as its target.

Ports are largely subsumed by the Application Kit's BMessage class (and relatives). The two features of ports that you can't get at the BMessage level are:

- Ports let you set the length of the message queue.
- Ports can be used in C code (as opposed to C++).

For most applications, these are inessential additions.

Creating a Port

A port is represented by a unique, system-wide `port_id` number (a positive 32-bit integer). The `create_port()` function creates a new port and assigns it a `port_id` number. Although ports are accessible to all threads, the `port_id` numbers aren't disseminated by the operating system; if you create a port and want some other thread to be able to write to or read from it, you have to broadcast the `port_id` number to that thread. Typically, ports are used within a single team. The easiest way to broadcast a `port_id` number to the threads in a team is to declare it as a global variable.

A port is owned by the team in which it was created. When a team dies (when all its threads are killed, by whatever hand), the ports that belong to the team are deleted. A team can bestow ownership of its ports to some other team through the `set_port_owner()` function.

If you want to explicitly get rid of a port, you can call `delete_port()`. You can delete any port, not just those that are owned by the team of the calling thread.

The Message Queue: Reading and Writing Port Messages

The length of a port's message queue—the number of messages that it can hold at a time—is set when the port is created. The `B_MAX_PORT_COUNT` constant provides a reasonable queue length.

The functions `write_port()` and `read_port()` manipulate a port's message queue: `write_port()` places a message at the tail of the port's message queue; `read_port()` removes the message at the head of the queue and returns it the caller. `write_port()` blocks if the queue is full; it returns when room is made in the queue by an invocation of `read_port()`. Similarly, if the queue is empty, `read_port()` blocks until `write_port()` is called. When a thread is waiting in a `write_port()` or `read_port()` call, its state is `B_THREAD_SEM_WAIT` (it's waiting to acquire a system-defined, port-specific semaphore).

You can provide a timeout for your port-writing and port-reading operations by using the "full-blown" functions `write_port_etc()` and `read_port_etc()`. By supplying a timeout, you can ensure that your port operations won't block forever.

Although each port has its own message queue, all ports share a global "queue slot" pool—there are only so many message queue slots that can be used by all ports taken cumulatively. If too many port queues are allowed to fill up, the slot pool will drain, which will cause `write_port()` calls on less-than-full ports to block. To avoid this situation, you should make sure that your `write_port()` and `read_port()` calls are reasonably balanced.

The `write_port()` and `read_port()` functions are the only way to traverse a port's message queue. There's no notion of "peeking" at the queue's unread messages, or of erasing messages that are in the queue.

Port Messages

A port message—the data that's sent through a port—consists of a "message code" and a "message buffer." Either of these elements can be used however you like, but they're intended to fit these purposes:

- The message code (a single four-byte value) should be a mask, flag, or other predictable value that gives a general representation of the flavor or import of the message. For this to work, the sender and receiver of the message must agree on the meanings of the values that the code can take.

- The data in the message buffer can elaborate upon the code, identify the sender of the message, or otherwise supply additional information. The length of the buffer isn't restricted. To get the length of the message buffer that's at the head of a port's queue, you call the `port_buffer_size()` function.

The message that you pass to `write_port()` is copied into the port. After `write_port()` returns, you may free the message data without affecting the copy that the port holds.

When you read a port, you have to supply a buffer into which the port mechanism can copy the message. If the buffer that you supply isn't large enough to accommodate the message, the unread portion will be lost—the next call to `read_port()` won't finish reading the message.

You typically allocate the buffer that you pass to `read_port()` by first calling `port_buffer_size()`, as shown below:

```
char *buf = NULL;
ssize_t size;
int32 code;

/* We'll assume that my_port is valid.
 * port_buffer_size() will block until a message shows up.
 */
if ((size = port_buffer_size(my_port)) < B_NO_ERROR)
   /* Handle the error */

if (size > 0)
   buf = (char *)malloc(size);

if (buf) {
   /* Now we can read the buffer. */
   if (read_port(my_port, &code, (void *)buf, size) < B_OK)
   /* Handle the error */
```

Obviously, there's a race condition (in the example) between `port_buffer_size()` and the subsequent `read_port()` call—some other thread could read the port in the interim. If you're going to use `port_buffer_size()` as shown in the example, you shouldn't have more than one thread reading the port at a time.

As stated in the example, `port_buffer_size()` blocks until a message shows up. If you don't want to (potentially) block forever, you should use the `port_buffer_size_etc()` version of the function. As with the other ...etc() functions, `port_buffer_size_etc()` provides a timeout option.

Port Functions

create_port()

port_id **create_port**(int32 *queue_length*, const char **name*)

Creates a new port and returns its `port_id` number. The port's name is set to *name* and the length of its message queue is set to *queue_length*. Neither the name nor the queue length can be changed once they're set. The name shouldn't exceed `B_OS_NAME_LENGTH` (32) characters.

In setting the length of a port's message queue, you're telling it how many messages it can hold at a time. When the queue is filled—when it's holding *queue_length* messages—subsequent invocations of `write_port()` (on that port) block until room is made in the queue (through calls to `read_port()`) for the additional messages. As a convenience, you can use the `B_MAX_PORT_COUNT` constant as the *queue_length* value; this constant represents the (ostensible) maximum port queue length. Once the queue length is set by `create_port()`, it can't be changed.

This function sets the owner of the port to be the team of the calling thread. Ownership can subsequently be transferred through the `set_port_owner()` function. When a port's owner dies (when all the threads in the team are dead), the port is automatically deleted. If you want to delete a port prior to its owner's death, use the `delete_port()` function.

Return values:

B_BAD_VALUE. *queue_length* is too big or less than zero.

B_NO_MORE_PORTS. The system couldn't allocate another port.

delete_port()

status_t **delete_port**(port_id *port*)

Deletes the given port. The port's message queue doesn't have to be empty—you can delete a port that's holding unread messages. Threads that are blocked in `read_port()` or `write_port()` calls on the port are automatically unblocked (and return B_BAD_SEM_ID).

The thread that calls `delete_port()` doesn't have to be a member of the team that owns the port; any thread can delete any port.

Return values:

B_NO_ERROR. The port was deleted.

B_BAD_PORT_ID. *port* isn't a valid port.

find_port()

port_id **find_port**(const char *port_name*)

Returns the `port_id` of the named port. *port_name* should be no longer than 32 characters (B_OS_NAME_LENGTH).

Return values:

B_NAME_NOT_FOUND. *port_name* doesn't name an existing port.

get_port_info(), get_next_port_info(), port_info

status_t **get_port_info**(port_id *port*, port_info **info*)

status_t **get_next_port_info**(team_id *team*,

uint32 **cookie*,

port_info **info*)

struct {} **port_info**

Copies information about a particular port into the `port_info` structure designated by *info*. The first version of the function designates the port directly, by `port_id`.

The `get_next_port_info()` version lets you step through the list of a team's ports through iterated calls on the function. The *team* argument identifies the team you want to look at; a *team* value of 0 means the team of the calling thread. The *cookie* argument is a placemark; you set it to 0 on your first call, and let the function do the rest. The function returns `B_BAD_VALUE` when there are no more ports to visit:

```
/* Get the port_info for every port in this team. */
port_info info;
int32 cookie = 0;

while (get_next_port_info(0, &cookie, &info) == B_OK)
    ...
```

The `port_info` structure is defined as:

```
typedef struct port_info {
    port_id port;
    team_id team;
    char name[B_OS_NAME_LENGTH];
    int32 capacity;
    int32 queue_count;
    int32 total_count;
} port_info
```

The structure's fields are:

- `port`. The `port_id` number of the port.
- `team`. The `team_id` of the port's owner.
- `name`. The name assigned to the port.
- `capacity`. The length of the port's message queue.
- `queue_count`. The number of messages currently in the queue.
- `total_count`. The total number of message that have been read from the port.

Note that the `total_count` number doesn't include the messages that are currently in the queue.

The information in the `port_info` structure is guaranteed to be internally consistent, but the structure as a whole should be considered out-of-date as soon as you receive it. It provides a picture of a port as it exists just before the info-retrieving function returns.

Return values:

B_NO_ERROR. The port was found; *info* contains valid information.

B_BAD_VALUE. *port* doesn't identify an existing port, *team* doesn't identify an existing team, or there are no more ports to visit.

port_buffer_size(), port_buffer_size_etc()

ssize_t **port_buffer_size**(port_id *port*)

ssize_t **port_buffer_size_etc**(port_id *port*,
                uint32 *flags*,
                bigtime_t *timeout*)

These functions return the length (in bytes) of the message buffer that's at the head of *port*'s message queue. You call this function in order to allocate a sufficiently large buffer in which to retrieve the message data.

The `port_buffer_size()` function blocks if the port is currently empty. It unblocks when a `write_port()` call gives this function a buffer to measure (even if the buffer is 0 bytes long), or when the port is deleted.

The `port_buffer_size_etc()` function lets you set a limit on the amount of time the function will wait for a message to show up. To set the limit, you pass B_TIMEOUT as the flags argument, and set *timeout* to the amount of time, in microseconds, that you're willing to wait.

Return values:

B_BAD_PORT_ID. *port* doesn't identify an existing port, or the port was deleted while the function was blocked.

B_TIMED_OUT. The *timeout* limit expired.

B_WOULD_BLOCK. You asked for a *timeout* of 0, but there are no messages in the queue.

See also: `read_port()`

port_count()

int32 **port_count**(port_id *port*)

Returns the number of messages that are currently in *port*'s message queue. This is the number of messages that have been written to the port through calls to write_port() but that haven't yet been picked up through corresponding read_port() calls.

NOTE

This function is provided mostly as a convenience and a semi-accurate debugging tool. The value that it returns is inherently undependable: There's no guarantee that additional read_port() or write_port() calls won't change the count as this function is returning.

Return values:
  B_BAD_PORT_ID. *port* doesn't identify an existing port.

See also: get_port_info()

read_port(), read_port_etc()

```
ssize_t read_port(port_id port,
                  int32 *msg_code,
                  void *msg_buffer,
                  size_t buffer_size)

ssize_t read_port_etc(port_id port,
                      int32 *msg_code,
                      void *msg_buffer,
                      size_t buffer_size,
                      uint32 flags,
                      bigtime_t timeout)
```

These functions remove the message at the head of *port*'s message queue and copy the messages's contents into the *msg_code* and *msg_buffer* arguments. The size of the *msg_buffer* buffer, in bytes, is given by *buffer_size*. It's up to the caller to ensure that the message buffer is large enough to accommodate the message that's being read. If you want a hint about the message's size, you should call port_buffer_size() before calling this function.

If *port*'s message queue is empty when you call read_port(), the function will block. It returns when some other thread writes a message to the port through write_port(). A blocked read is also unblocked if the port is deleted.

The read_port_etc() function lets you set a limit on the amount of time the function will wait for a message to show up. To set the limit, you pass B_TIMEOUT as the flags argument, and set *timeout* to the amount of time, in microseconds, that you're willing to wait.

Return values:

A successful call returns the number of bytes that were written into the *msg_buffer* argument.

B_BAD_PORT_ID. *port* doesn't identify an existing port, or the port was deleted while the function was blocked.

B_TIMED_OUT. The *timeout* limit expired.

B_WOULD_BLOCK. You asked for a *timeout* of 0, but there are no messages in the queue.

See also: `write_port()`, `port_buffer_size()`

set_port_owner()

status_t **set_port_owner**(port_id *port*, team_id *team*)

Transfers ownership of the designated port to *team*. A port can only be owned by one team at a time; by setting a port's owner, you remove it from its current owner.

There are no restrictions on who can own a port, or on who can transfer ownership. In other words, the thread that calls `set_port_owner()` needn't be part of the team that currently owns the port, nor must you only assign ports to the team that owns the calling thread (although these two are the most likely scenarios).

Port ownership is meaningful for one reason: When a team dies (when all its threads are dead), the ports that are owned by that team are freed. Ownership, otherwise, has no significance—it carries no special privileges or obligations.

To discover a port's owner, use the `get_port_info()` function.

Return values:

B_NO_ERROR. Ownership was successfully transferred.

B_BAD_PORT_ID. *port* doesn't identify a valid port.

B_BAD_TEAM_ID. *team* doesn't identify a valid team.

See also: `get_port_info()`

write_port(), write_port_etc()

status_t **write_port**(port_id *port*,
                int32 *msg_code*,
                void **msg_buffer*,
                size_t *buffer_size*)

status_t **write_port_etc**(port_id *port*,
                int32 *msg_code*,
                void **msg_buffer*,

size_t *buffer_size,*

uint32 *flags,*

bigtime_t *timeout*)

These functions place a message at the tail of *port*'s message queue. The message consists of *msg_code* and *msg_buffer.*

- *msg_code* holds the "message code." This is a mask, flag, or other predictable value that gives a general representation of the message.

- *msg_buffer* is a pointer to a buffer that can be used to supply additional information. You pass the length of the buffer, in bytes, as the value of the *buffer_size* argument. The buffer can be arbitrarily long.

If the port's queue is full when you call `write_port()`, the function will block. It returns when a `read_port()` call frees a slot in the queue for the new message. A blocked `write_port()` will also return if the target port is deleted.

The `write_port_etc()` function lets you set a limit on the amount of time the function will wait for a free queue slot. To set the limit, you pass **B_TIMEOUT** as the flags argument, and set *timeout* to the amount of time, in microseconds, that you're willing to wait.

Return values:

B_NO_ERROR. The port was successfully written to.

B_BAD_PORT_ID. *port* doesn't identify an existing port, or the port was deleted while the function was blocked.

B_TIMED_OUT. The *timeout* limit expired.

B_WOULD_BLOCK. You asked for a *timeout* of 0, but there are no free slots in the message queue.

See also: `read_port()`

Semaphores

Declared in: be/kernel/OS.h

Library: libroot.so

Overview

A semaphore is a token that's used to synchronize multiple threads, usually for one of these reasons:

- **Locking**. The most common use of a semaphore is to create a mutually exclusive lock: It ensures that only one thread can execute a "protected" section of code at a time. See "Example 1: Using a Semaphore as a Lock."

- **Execution Oder.** Semaphores can also be used to impose an order in which a series of dependent operations are performed by two or more threads. See "Example 2: Using Semaphores to Impose an Execution Order."

The semaphore concept is simple: To enter into a semaphore-protected "critical section," a thread must first "acquire" the semaphore, through the `acquire_sem()` function. When it passes out of the critical section, the thread "releases" the semaphore through `release_sem()`.

The advantage of the semaphore system is that if a thread can't acquire a semaphore (because the semaphore is yet to be released by the previous acquirer), the thread blocks in the `acquire_sem()` call. While it's blocked, the thread doesn't waste any cycles.

The full story about semaphores is a wee bit more complicated than this quick description, but if all you want to do is create a mutually exclusive lock or impose an execution order, you'll probably learn all you need to know by visiting the examples in the sections referred to above.

The Full Story

A semaphore acts as a key that a thread must acquire in order to continue execution. Any thread that can identify a particular semaphore can attempt to acquire it by passing its `sem_id` identifier—a system-wide number that's assigned when the semaphore is created—to the `acquire_sem()` function. The function blocks until the semaphore is actually acquired.

NOTE

An alternate function, `acquire_sem_etc()` lets you specify the amount of time you're willing to wait for the semaphore to be acquired. Unless otherwise noted, characteristics ascribed to `acquire_sem()` apply to `acquire_sem_etc()` as well.

When a thread acquires a semaphore, that semaphore (typically) becomes unavailable for acquisition by other threads (less typically, more than one thread is allowed to acquire the semaphore at a time; the precise determination of availability is explained in "The Thread Count"). The semaphore remains unavailable until it's passed in a call to the `release_sem()` function.

The code that a semaphore "protects" lies between the calls to `acquire_sem()` and `release_sem()`. The disposition of these functions in your code usually follows this pattern:

```
if (acquire_sem(my_semaphore) == B_NO_ERROR) {
   /* Protected code goes here. */
```

```
    release_sem(my_semaphore);
}
```

Keep in mind that:

- The calls to the acquire and release functions needn't be locally balanced (although this is by far the most common use). A semaphore can be acquired within one function and released in another. Acquisition and release of the same semaphore can even be performed by two different threads.

- Checking the value returned by `acquire_sem()` is *extremely* important. If an acquire-blocked thread is unblocked by a signal (a return of `B_INTERRUPTED`), the thread shouldn't proceed to the critical section.

The Thread Queue

Every semaphore has its own *thread queue*. This is a list that identifies the threads that are waiting to acquire the semaphore. A thread that attempts to acquire an unavailable semaphore is placed at the tail of the semaphore's thread queue where it sits blocked in the `acquire_sem()` call. Each call to `release_sem()` unblocks the thread at the head of that semaphore's queue, thus allowing the thread to return from its call to `acquire_sem()`.

Semaphores don't discriminate between acquisitive threads—they don't prioritize or otherwise reorder the threads in their queues—the oldest waiting thread is always the next to acquire the semaphore.

The Thread Count

To assess availability, a semaphore looks at its *thread count*. This is a counting variable that's initialized when the semaphore is created. Ostensibly, a thread count's initial value (which is passed as the first argument to `create_sem()`) is the number of threads that can acquire the semaphore at a time. (As we'll see later, this isn't the entire story, but it's good enough for now.) For example, a semaphore that's used as a mutually exclusive lock takes an initial thread count of 1—in other words, only one thread can acquire the semaphore at a time.

NOTE

An initial thread count of 1 is by far the most common use; a thread count of 0 is also useful. Other counts are much less common.

Calls to `acquire_sem()` and `release_sem()` alter the semaphore's thread count: `acquire_sem()` decrements the count, and `release_sem()` increments it. When you call `acquire_sem()`, the function looks at the thread count (before decrementing it) to determine if the semaphore is available:

- If the count is greater than zero, the semaphore is available for acquisition, so the function returns immediately.

- If the count is zero or less, the semaphore is unavailable, and the thread is placed in the semaphore's thread queue.

The initial thread count isn't an inviolable limit on the number of threads that can acquire a given semaphore—it's simply the initial value for the sempahore's thread count variable. For example, if you create a semaphore with an initial thread count of 1 and then immediately call `release_sem()` five times, the semaphore's thread count will increase to 6. Furthermore, although you can't initialize the thread count to less-than-zero, an initial value of zero itself is common—it's an integral part of using semaphores to impose an execution order (as demonstrated later).

Summarizing the description above, there are three significant thread count value ranges:

- A positive thread count (n) means that there are no threads in the semaphore's queue, and the next n `acquire_sem()` calls will return without blocking.

- If the count is 0, there are no queued threads, but the next `acquire_sem()` call will block.

- A negative count ($-n$) means there are n threads in the semaphore's thread queue, and the next call to `acquire_sem()` will block.

Although it's possible to retrieve the value of a semaphore's thread count (by looking at a field in the semaphore's `sem_info` structure, as described later), you should only do so for amusement—while you're debugging, for example.

WARNING

You should never predicate your code on the basis of a semaphore's thread count.

Deleting a Semaphore

Every semaphore is owned by a team (the team of the thread that called `create_sem()`). When the last thread in a team dies, it takes the team's semaphores with it.

Prior to the death of a team, you can explicitly delete a semaphore through the `delete_sem()` call. Note, however, that `delete_sem()` must be called from a thread that's a member of the team that owns the semaphore—you can't delete another team's semaphores.

You're allowed to delete a semaphore even if it still has threads in its queue. However, you usually want to avoid this, so deleting a semaphore may require some thought: When you delete a semaphore (or when it dies naturally), all its queued threads are immediately allowed to continue—they all return from `acquire_sem()` at once. You can distinguish between a "normal" acquisition and a "semaphore deleted" acquisition by the value that's returned by `acquire_sem()` (the specific return values are listed in the function descriptions, below).

Broadcasting Semaphores

The `sem_id` number that identifies a semaphore is a system-wide token—the `sem_id` values that you create in your application will identify your semaphores in all other applications as well. It's possible, therefore, to broadcast the `sem_id` numbers of the semaphores that you create and so allow other applications to acquire and release them—but it's not a very good idea.

WARNING

A semaphore is best controlled if it's created, acquired, released, and deleted within the same team.

If you want to provide a protected service or resource to other applications, you should accept messages from other applications and then spawn threads that acquire and release the appropriate semaphores.

Example 1: Using a Semaphore as a Lock

The most typical use of a semaphore is to protect a "critical section": This is a chunk of code that needs to be executed without interruption. The semaphore acts as a lock; `acquire_sem()` locks the code, `release_sem()` releases it. Semaphores that are used as locks are (almost always) created with a thread count of 1.

As a simple example, let's say you keep track of a maximum value like this:

```
/* max_val is a global. */
uint32 max_val = 0;
...

/* bump_max() resets the max value, if necessary. */
void bump_max(uint32 new_value)
{
    if (new_value > max_value)
        max_value = new_value;
}
```

`bump_max()` isn't thread safe; there's a race condition between the comparison and the assignment. So we protect it with a semaphore:

```
sem_id max_sem;
uint32 max_val = 0;


...
/* Initialize the semaphore during a setup routine. */
status_t init()
{
    if ((max_sem = create_sem(1, "max_sem")) < B_NO_ERROR)
        return B_ERROR;
    ...
}
void bump_max(uint32 new_value)
{
    if (acquire_sem(max_sem) != B_NO_ERROR)
        return;
    if (new_value > max_value)
        max_value = new_value;
    release_sem();
}
```

Benaphores

A "benaphore" is a combination of an atomic variable and a semaphore that can improve locking efficiency. If you're using a semaphore as shown in the previous example, you almost certainly want to use the benaphore mechanism instead (if you can).

Here's the example re-written to use a benaphore:

```
sem_id max_sem;
uint32 max_val = 0;
int32 ben_val = 0;

/* Initialize as before */
...

void bump_max(uint32 new_value)
{
    int32 previous = atomic_add(&ben_val, 1);
    if (previous >= 1)
        if (acquire_sem(max_sem) != B_NO_ERROR)
            goto get_out;

    if (new_value > max_value)
        max_value = new_value;

get_out:
    previous = atomic_add(&ben_val, -1);
    if (previous > 1)
        release_sem(max_sem);
}
```

The point here is that `acquire_sem()` is called only if it's known (by checking the previous value of `ben_val`) that some other thread is in the middle of the critical section. On the releasing end, the `release_sem()` is called only if some other thread has since entered the function (and is now blocked in the `acquire_sem()` call).

Example 2: Using Semaphores to Impose an Execution Order

Semaphores can also be used to coordinate threads that are performing separate operations, but that need to perform these operations in a particular order. In the following example, we have a global buffer that's accessed through separate reading and writing functions. Furthermore, we want writes and reads to alternate, with a write going first.

We can lock the entire buffer with a single semaphore, but to enforce alternation we need two semaphores:

```
sem_id write_sem, read_sem;
char buffer[1024];

/* Initialize the semaphores */
status_t init()
{
    if ((write_sem = create_sem(1, "write")) < B_NO_ERROR) {
        return;
    if ((read_sem = create_sem(0, "read")) < B_NO_ERROR) {
        delete_sem(write_sem);
        return;
    }
}

status_t write_buffer(const char *src)
{
    if (acquire_sem(write_sem) != B_NO_ERROR)
        return B_ERROR;

    strncpy(buffer, src, 1024);

    release_sem(read_sem);
}

status_t read_buffer(char *dest, size_t len)
{
    if (acquire_sem(read_sem) != B_NO_ERROR)
        return B_ERROR;

    strncpy(dest, buffer, len);

    release_sem(write_sem);
}
```

The initial thread counts ensure that the buffer will be written to before it's read: If a reader arrives before a writer, the reader will block until the writer releases the read_sem semaphore.

Semaphore Functions

acquire_sem(), acquire_sem_etc()

status_t **acquire_sem**(sem_id *sem*)
status_t **acquire_sem_etc**(sem_id *sem*,
            uint32 *count*,
            uint32 *flags*,
            bigtime_t *timeout*)

These functions attempt to acquire the semaphore identified by the *sem* argument. Except in the case of an error, acquire_sem() doesn't return until the semaphore has actually been acquired.

acquire_sem_etc() is the full-blown acquisition version: It's essentially the same as acquire_sem(), but, in addition, it lets you acquire a semaphore more than once, and also provides a timeout facility:

- The *count* argument lets you specify that you want the semaphore to be acquired *count* times. This means that the semaphore's thread count is decremented by the specified amount. It's illegal to specify a count that's less than 1.

- To enable the timeout, you pass B_TIMEOUT as the *flags* argument, and set *timeout* to the amount of time, in microseconds, that you're willing to wait for the semaphore to be acquired. If the semaphore hasn't been acquired within *timeout* microseconds, the function returns anyway (B_TIMED_OUT). If you specify a *timeout* of 0.0 and the semaphore isn't immediately available, the function immediately returns (B_WOULD_BLOCK).

WARNING

In addition to B_TIMEOUT, the Kernel Kit defines two other semaphore-acquisition flag constants (B_CAN_INTERRUPT and B_CHECK_PERMISSION). These additional flags are used by device drivers—adding these flags into a "normal" (or "user-level") acquisition has no effect. However, you should be aware that the B_CHECK_PERMISSION flag is always added in to user-level semaphore acquisition in order to protect system-defined semaphores.

Other than the timeout and the acquisition count, there's no difference between the two acquisition functions. Specifically, any semaphore can be acquired through either of these functions; you always release a semaphore through release_sem() (or release_sem_etc()) regardless of which function you used to acquire it.

To determine if the semaphore is available, the function looks at the semaphore's thread count (before decrementing it):

- If the thread count is positive, the semaphore is available and the current acquisition succeeds. The `acquire_sem()` (or `acquire_sem_etc()`) function returns immediately upon acquisition.

- If the thread count is zero or less, the calling thread is placed in the semaphore's thread queue where it waits for a corresponding `release_sem()` call to de-queue it (or for the timeout to expire).

Return values:

B_NO_ERROR. The semaphore was successfully acquired.

B_BAD_SEM_ID. The *sem* argument doesn't identify a valid semaphore. It's possible for a semaphore to become invalid while an acquisitive thread is waiting in the semaphore's queue. For example, if your thread calls `acquire_sem()` on a valid (but unavailable) semaphore, and then some other thread deletes the semaphore, your thread will return B_BAD_SEM_ID from its call to `acquire_sem()`.

The other return values apply to `acquire_sem_etc()` only:

- B_BAD_VALUE. Illegal *count* value (less than 1).
- B_WOULD_BLOCK. You specified a *timeout* of 0 and the semaphore isn't available.
- B_TIMED_OUT. The timeout expired (for all values of *timeout* other than 0).

create_sem()

sem_id **create_sem**(uint32 *thread_count*, const char **name*)

Creates a new semaphore and returns a system-wide `sem_id` number that identifies it. The arguments are:

- *thread_count* initializes the semaphore's *thread count*, the counting variable that's decremented and incremented as the semaphore is acquired and released (respectively). You can pass any non-negative number as the count, but you typically pass either 1 or 0, as demonstrated in the examples above.

- *name* is an optional string name that you can assign to the semaphore. The name is meant to be used only for debugging. A semaphore's name needn't be unique—any number of semaphores can have the same name.

Valid `sem_id` numbers are positive integers. You should always check the validity of a new semaphore through a construction such as:

```
if ((my_sem = create_sem(1,"My Semaphore")) < B_NO_ERROR)
    /* If it's less than B_NO_ERROR, my_sem is invalid. */
```

`create_sem()` sets the new semaphore's owner to the team of the calling thread. Ownership may be reassigned through the `set_sem_owner()` function. When the owner dies (when all the threads in the team are dead), the semaphore is automatically deleted. The owner is also significant in a `delete_sem()` call: Only those threads that belong to a semaphore's owner are allowed to delete that semaphore.

Return values:
> B_BAD_VALUE. Invalid *thread_count* value (less than 0).
> B_NO_MEMORY. Not enough memory to allocate the semaphore's name.
> B_NO_MORE_SEMS. All valid `sem_id` numbers are being used.

delete_sem()

status_t **delete_sem**(sem_id *sem*)

Deletes the semaphore identified by the argument. If there are any threads waiting in the semaphore's thread queue, they're immediately unblocked.

WARNING

This function may only be called from a thread that belongs to the semaphore's owner.

Return values:
> B_NO_ERROR. The semaphore was successfully deleted.
> B_BAD_SEM_ID. *sem* is invalid, or the calling thread doesn't belong to the team that owns the semaphore.

get_sem_count()

status_t **get_sem_count**(sem_id *sem*, int32 **thread_count*)

WARNING

For amusement purposes only; never predicate your code on this function.

Returns, by reference in *thread_count*, the value of the semaphore's thread count variable:

- A positive thread count (n) means that there are no threads in the semaphore's queue, and the next n `acquire_sem()` calls will return without blocking.

- If the count is zero, there are no queued threads, but the next `acquire_sem()` call will block.

- A negative count ($-n$) means there are n threads in the semaphore's thread queue and the next call to `acquire_sem()` will block.

By the time this function returns and you get a chance to look at the *thread_count* value, the semaphore's thread count may have changed. Although watching the thread count might help you while you're debugging your program, this function shouldn't be an integral part of the design of your application.

Return values:

> B_NO_ERROR. Success.
>
> B_BAD_SEM_ID. *sem* is invalid (*thread_count* isn't changed).

get_sem_info(), get_next_sem_info(), sem_info

> status_t **get_sem_info**(sem_id *sem*, sem_info **info*)
>
> status_t **get_next_sem_info**(team_id *team*,
>
> > uint32 *cookie,
> >
> > sem_info **info*)
>
> struct {} **sem_info**

Copies information about a particular semaphore into the `sem_info` structure designated by *info*. The first version of the function designates the semaphore directly, by `sem_id`.

The `get_next_sem_info()` version lets you step through the list of a team's semaphores through iterated calls on the function. The *team* argument identifies the team you want to look at; a *team* value of 0 means the team of the calling thread. The *cookie* argument is a placemark; you set it to 0 on your first call, and let the function do the rest. The function returns `B_BAD_VALUE` when there are no more semaphores to visit:

```
/* Get the sem_info for every semaphore in this team. */
sem_info info;
int32 cookie = 0;

while (get_next_sem_info(0, &cookie, &info) == B_OK)
    ...
```

The `sem_info` structure is:

```
typedef struct sem_info {
    sem_id sem;
    team_id team;
    char name[B_OS_NAME_LENGTH];
    int32 count;
    thread_id latest_holder;
} sem_info
```

The structure's fields are:

- `sem`. The `sem_id` number of the semaphore.
- `team`. The `team_id` of the semaphore's owner.
- `name`. The name assigned to the semaphore.
- `count`. The semaphore's thread count.
- `latest_holder`. The thread that most recently acquired the semaphore.

WARNING

The `latest_holder` field is *highly* undependable; in some cases, the kernel doesn't even record the semaphore acquirer. Although you can use this field as a hint while debugging, you shouldn't take it too seriously. Love, Mom.

The information in the `sem_info` structure is guaranteed to be internally consistent, but the structure as a whole should be considered out-of-date as soon as you receive it. It provides a picture of a semaphore as it exists just before the info-retrieving function returns.

Return values:

B_NO_ERROR. Success.

B_BAD_SEM_ID. Invalid *sem* value.

B_BAD_TEAM_ID. Invalid *team* value.

release_sem(), release_sem_etc()

status_t **release_sem**(sem_id *sem*)

status_t **release_sem_etc**(sem_id *sem*, int32 *count*, uint32 *flags*)

The `release_sem()` function de-queues the thread that's waiting at the head of the semaphore's thread queue (if any), and increments the semaphore's thread count. `release_sem_etc()` does the same, but for *count* threads.

Normally, releasing a semaphore automatically invokes the kernel's scheduler. In other words, when your thread calls `release_sem()`, you're pretty much guaranteed that some other thread will be switched in immediately afterwards, even if your thread hasn't gotten its fair share of CPU time. If you want to subvert this automatism, call `release_sem_etc()` with a *flags* value of B_DO_NOT_RESCHEDULE. Preventing the automatic rescheduling is particularly useful if you're releasing a number of different semaphores all in a row: By avoiding the rescheduling you can prevent some unnecessary context switching.

Return values:

B_NO_ERROR. The semaphore was successfully released.

B_BAD_SEM_ID. Invalid *sem* value.

B_BAD_VALUE. Invalid *count* value (less than zero; `release_sem_etc()` only).

See also: `acquire_sem()`

set_sem_owner()

status_t **set_sem_owner**(sem_id *sem*, team_id *team*)

Transfers ownership of the designated semaphore to *team*. A semaphore can only be owned by one team at a time; by setting a semaphore's owner, you remove it from its current owner.

There are no restrictions on who can own a semaphore, or on who can transfer ownership. In practice, however, the only reason you should ever transfer ownership is if you're writing a device driver and you need to bequeath a semaphore to the kernel (the team of which is known, for this purpose, as B_SYSTEM_TEAM).

Semaphore ownership is meaningful for two reason:

- When a team dies (when all its threads are dead), the semaphores that are owned by that team are deleted.

- Threads can only be deleted by threads that belong to a semaphore's owner.

To discover a semaphore's owner, use the `get_sem_info()` function.

Return values:
B_NO_ERROR. Ownership was successfully transferred.
B_BAD_SEM_ID. Invalid *sem* value.
B_BAD_TEAM_ID. Invalid *team* value.

Areas

Declared in: be/kernel/OS.h

Library: libroot.so

Overview

An area is a chunk of virtual memory. As such, it has all the expected properties of virtual memory: It has a starting address, a size, the addresses it comprises are contiguous, and it maps to (possibly non-contiguous) physical memory. The features that an area provides that you *don't* get with "standard" memory are these:

- **Areas can be shared.** Different areas can refer to the same physical memory. Put another way, different virtual memory addresses can map to the same physical locations. Furthermore, the different areas needn't belong to the same application. By creating and "cloning" areas, applications can easily share the same data.

- **Areas can be locked into RAM.** You can specify that the area's physical memory be locked into RAM when it's created, locked on a page-by-page basis as pages are swapped in, or that it be swapped in and out as needed.

- **Areas can be read- and write-protected.**

- **Areas are page-aligned.** Areas always start on a page boundary, and are allocated in integer multiples of the size of a page. (A page is 4096 bytes, as represented by the `B_PAGE_SIZE` constant.)

- **You can specify the starting address of the area's virtual memory.** The specification can require that the area start precisely at a certain address, anywhere above a certain address, or anywhere at all.

Because areas are large—one page, minimum—you don't create them arbitrarily. The two most compelling reasons to create an area are the two first points listed above: To share data among different applications, and to lock memory into RAM.

In all particulars (but one) you treat the memory that an area gives you exactly as you would treat any allocated memory: You can read and write it through pointer manipulation, or through standard functions such as `memcpy()` and `strcpy()`. The one difference is between areas and malloc'd memory is...

- You never `free()` the memory that an area allocates for you. If you want to get rid of an area, use the `delete_area()` function, instead.

Area IDs and Area Names

Each area that you create is tagged with an `area_id` number:

- An `area_id` number is a positive integer that's global and unique within the scope of the computer. They're not unique across the network, nor are they persistent across boots.

- The `area_id` numbers are generated and assigned automatically by the `create_area()` and `clone_area()` functions. The other area functions operate on these `area_id` numbers (they're required as arguments).

- Although they are global, `area_id` numbers have little meaning outside of the address space (application) in which they were created.

- Once assigned, the `area_id` number doesn't change; the number is invalidated when `delete_area()` is called or when the application (team) that created it dies.

- Don't worry about recycled `area_id` numbers. When an area is deleted, it's `area_id` goes with it. (`area_id` values *are* recycled, but the turnover is at 2^31.)

Areas can also be (loosely) identified by name:

- When you create an area (through `create_area()` or `clone_area()`), you get to name it.

- Area names are not unique—any number of areas can be assigned the same name.

- To look up an area by name, use the `FindArea()` function.

Sharing an Area Between Applications

For multiple applications to share a common area, one of the applications has to *create* the area, and the other applications *clone* the area. You clone an area by calling `clone_area()`. The function takes, as its last argument, the `area_id` of the source area and returns a new (unique) `area_id` number. All further references to the cloned area (in the cloning application) must be based on the `area_id` that's returned by `clone_area()`.

So how does a cloner find a source `area_id` in the first place?

- The source application can pass the "original" `area_id` number to the cloners.
- The cloners can find the area by name, by calling `find_area()`.

Keep in mind that area names are not forced to be unique, so the `find_area()` method has some amount of uncertainty. But this can be minimized through clever name creation.

Cloned Memory

The physical memory that lies beneath an area is never implicitly copied—for example, the area mechanism doesn't perform a "copy-on-write." If two areas refer to the same memory because of cloning, a data modification that's affected through one area will be seen by the other area.

Locking an Area

When you're working with moderately large amounts of data, it's often the case that you would prefer that the data remain in RAM, even if the rest of your application needs to be swapped out. An argument to `create_area()` lets you declare, through the use of one of the following constants, the locking scheme that you wish to apply to your area:

Constant	Meaning
B_FULL_LOCK	The area's memory is locked into RAM when the area is created, and won't be swapped out.
B_CONTIGUOUS	Not only is the area's memory locked into RAM, it's also guaranteed to be contiguous. This is particularly—and perhaps exclusively—useful to designers of certain types of device drivers.
B_LAZY_LOCK	Allows individual pages of memory to be brought into RAM through the natural order of things and *then* locks them.
B_NO_LOCK	Pages are never locked, they're swapped in and out as needed.

Keep in mind that locking an area essentially reduces the amount of RAM that can be used by other applications, and so increases the likelihood of swapping. So you shouldn't lock simply because you're greedy. But if the area that you're locking is going to be shared among some number of other applications, or if you're writing a real-time application that processes large chunks of data, then locking can be a justifiable excess.

The locking scheme is set by the `create_area()` function and is thereafter immutable. You can't re-declare the lock when you clone an area.

Area Info

Ultimately, you use an area for the virtual memory that it represents: You create an area because you want some memory to which you can write and from which you can read data. These acts are performed in the usual manner, through references to specific addresses. Setting a pointer to a location within the area, and checking that you haven't exceeded the area's memory bounds as you increment the pointer (while reading or writing) are your own responsibility. To do this properly, you need to know the area's starting address and its extent:

- An area's starting address is maintained as the `address` field in its `area_info` structure; you retrieve the `area_info` for a particular area through the `get_area_info()` function.

- The size of the area (in bytes) is given as the `size` field of its `area_info` structure.

An important point, with regard to `area_info`, is that the `address` field is only valid for the application that created or cloned the area (in other words, the application that created the `area_id` that was passed to `get_area_info()`). Although the memory that underlies an area is global, the address that you get from an `area_info` structure refers to a specific address space.

If there's any question about whether a particular `area_id` is "local" or "foreign," you can compare the `area_info.team` field to your thread's team.

Deleting an Area

When your application quits, the areas (the `area_id` numbers) that it created through `create_area()` or `clone_area()` are automatically rendered invalid. The memory underlying these areas, however, isn't necessarily freed. An area's memory is freed only when (and as soon as) there are no more areas that refer to it.

You can force the invalidation of an `area_id` by passing it to the `delete_area()` function. Again, the underlying memory is only freed if yours is the last area to refer to the memory.

Deleting an area, whether explicitly through `delete_area()`, or because your application quit, never affects the status of other areas that were cloned from it.

Example 1: Creating and Writing into an Area

As a simple example of area creation and usage, here we create a ten-page area and fill half of it (with nonsense) by bumping a pointer:

```
area_id my_area;
char *area_addr, *ptr;

/* Create an area. */
my_area = create_area("my area", /* name you give to the area */
        (void *)&area_addr,    /* returns the starting addr */
        B_ANY_ADDRESS,         /* area can start anywhere */
        B_PAGE_SIZE*10,        /* size in bytes */
        B_NO_LOCK,             /* Lock in RAM?  No. */
        B_READ_AREA | B_WRITE_AREA); /* permissions */

/* All the errors you're likely to see. */
switch(my_area) {
    case B_NO_ERROR:
        break;
    case B_NO_MEMORY:
        printf("Not enough swap space (or RAM if locked).\n");
        return;
    case B_BAD_VALUE:
        printf("Argument to create_area() was invalid.\n");
        return;
    case B_ERROR:
    default:
        printf("Something bad happened\n");
        return;
}

/* Set ptr to the beginning of the area. */
ptr = area_addr;

/* Fill half the area (with random-ish data). */
for (int i; i < B_PAGE_SIZE*5; i++)
    *ptr++ = system_time()%256;
```

You can also `memcpy()` and `strcpy()` into the area:

```
/* Copy the first half of the area into the second half. */
memcpy(ptr, area_addr, B_PAGE_SIZE*5);

/* Overwrite the beginning of the area. */
strcpy(area_addr, "Hey, look where I am.");
```

When we're all done, we delete the area:

```
delete_area(my_area);
```

Example 2: Reading a File into an Area

Here's a function that finds a file, opens it (implicit in the BFile constructor), and copies its contents into RAM:

```
#include <File.h>

area_id file_area;

status_t file_reader(const char *pathname)
{
    status_t err;
    char *area_addr;

    BFile file(pathname, B_READ_ONLY);
    if ((err=file.InitCheck()) != B_NO_ERROR) {
        printf("%s: Can't find or open.\n", pathname);
        return err;
    }

    err = file.GetSize(&file_size);
    if (err != B_NO_ERROR || file_size == 0) {
        printf("%s:  Disappeared?  Empty?\n", pathname);
        return err;
    }

    /* Round the size up to the nearest page. */
    file_size = (((file_size-1)%B_PAGE_SIZE)+1)*B_PAGE_SIZE;

    /* Make sure the size won't overflow a size_t spec. */
    if (file_size >= ((1<<32)-1) ) {
        printf("%s: What'd you do?  Read Montana?\n");
        return B_NO_MEMORY;
    }
    file_area = create_area("File area", (void *)&area_addr,
        B_ANY_ADDRESS, file_size, B_FULL_LOCK,
        B_READ_AREA | B_WRITE_AREA);

    /* Check create_area() errors, as in the last example. */
    ...

    /* Read the file; delete the area if there's an error. */
    if ((err=file.Read(area_addr, file_size)) < B_NO_ERROR) {
        printf("%s: File read error.\n");
        delete_area(file_area);
        return err;
    }

    /* The file is automatically closed when the stack-based
     * BFile is destroyed.
     */
    return B_NO_ERROR;
}
```

Example 3: Accessing a Designated Area

In the previous example, a local variable (`area_addr`) was used to capture the starting address of the newly-created area. If some other function wants to access the area, it must "re-find" the starting address (and the length of the area, for boundary checking). To do this, you call `get_area_info()`.

In the following example, an area is passed in by name; the function, which will write its argument buffer to the area, calls `get_area_info()` to determine the start and extent of the area, and also to make sure that the area is part of this team. If the area was created by some other team, the function could still write to it, but it would have to clone the area first (cloning is demonstrated in the next example).

```
status_t write_to_area(const char *area_name,
               const void *buf,
               size_t len)
{
    area_id area;
    area_info ai;
    thread_id thread;
    thread_info ti;
    status_t err;

    if (!area_name)
        return B_BAD_VALUE;

    area = find_area(area_name);

    /* Did we find it? */
    if (area < B_NO_ERROR) {
        printf("Couldn't find area %s.\n", area_name);
        return err;
    }

    /* Get the info. */
    err = get_area_info(area, &ai);

    if (err < B_NO_ERROR) {
        printf("Couldn't get area info.\n");
        return err;
    }

    /* Get the team of the calling thread; to do this, we have
     * to look in the thread_info structure.
     */
    err = get_thread_info(find_thread(NULL), &ti);

    if (err < B_NO_ERROR) {
        printf("Couldn't get thread info.\n");
        return err;
    }
```

```
    /* Compare this team to the area's team. */
    if (ai.team != ti.team)
        printf("Foreign area.\n");
        return B_NOT_ALLOWED;
    }
    /* Make sure we're not going to overflow the area,
     * and make sure this area can be written to.
     */
    if (len > ai.size) {
        printf("Buffer bigger than area.\n");
        return B_BAD_VALUE;
    }
    if (!(ai.protection & B_WRITE_AREA)) {
        printf("Can't write to this area.\n");
        return B_NOT_ALLOWED;
    }

    /* Now we can write. */
    memcpy(ai.address, buf, len);
    return B_NO_ERROR;
}
```

It's important that you only write to areas that were created or cloned within the calling team. The starting address of a "foreign" area is usually meaningless within your own address space.

You don't *have* to check the area's protection before writing to it (or reading from it). The memory-accessing functions (`memcpy()`, in this example) will simply fail if an invalid read or write is requested.

However, you *do* have to do your own boundary checking. None of the memory-accessing functions know anything about area boundaries: `memcpy()` will gladly write beyond the end of the area (and possibly seg fault) if you that's what you ask for.

Example 4: Cloning and Sharing an Area

In the following example, a server and a client are set up to share a common area. Here's the server:

```
/* Server side */
class AServer
{
    status_t make_shared_area(size_t size);
    area_id the_area;
    char *area_addr;
};

status_t AServer::make_shared_area(size_t size)
{
    /* The size must be rounded to a page. */
```

```
    size = ((size % B_PAGE_SIZE)+1) * B_PAGE_SIZE;
    the_area = create_area("server area", (void *)&area_addr
            B_ANY_ADDRESS, size, B_NO_LOCK,
            B_READ_AREA|B_WRITE_AREA);

    if (the_area < B_NO_ERROR) {
        printf("Couldn't create server area\n");
        return the_area;

    return B_NO_ERROR;
}
```

And here's the client:

```
/* Client side */
class AClient
{
    status_t make_shared_clone();
    area_id the_area;
    char *area_addr;
};

status_t AClient::make_shared_clone()
{
    area_id src_area;

    src_area = find_area("server area");
    if (src_area < B_ERROR) {
        printf("Couldn't find server area.\n");
        return src_area;
    }
    the_area = clone_area("client area",
                (void *)&area_addr,
                B_ANY_ADDRESS,
                B_READ_AREA | B_WRITE_AREA,
                src_area);

    if (the_area < B_NO_ERROR)
        printf("Couldn't create clone area\n");
        return the_area;
    }
    return B_NO_ERROR;
}
```

Notice that the area creator (the server in the example) doesn't have to designate the created area as sharable. All areas are candidates for cloning.

After it creates the cloned area, the client's `area_id` value (`AClient::the_area`) will be different from the server's (`AServer::the_area`). Even though `area_id` numbers are global, the client should only refer to the server's `area_id` number in order to clone it. After the clone, the client talks to the area through its own `area_id` (the value passed backed by `clone_area()`).

Example 5: Cloning Addresses

It's sometimes useful for shared areas (in other words, a "source" and a clone) to begin at the same starting address. For example, if a client's clone area starts at the same address as the server's original area, then the client and server can pass area-accessing pointers back and forth without having to translate the addresses. Here we modify the previous example to do this:

```
status_t AClient::make_shared_clone()
{
   area_id src_area;

   src_area = find_area("server area");

   if (src_area < B_ERROR) {
      printf("Couldn't find server area.\n");
      return B_BAD_VALUE;
   }

   /* This time, we specify the address that we want the
    * clone to start at.  The B_CLONE_ADDRESS constant
    * does this for us.
    */
   area_addr = src_info.address;
   the_area = clone_area("client area",
                (void *)&area_addr,
                B_CLONE_ADDRESS,
                B_READ_AREA | B_WRITE_AREA,
                src_area);

   if (the_area < B_NO_ERROR)
      printf("Couldn't create clone area\n");
      return the_area;
   }
   return B_NO_ERROR;
}
```

Of course, demanding that an area begin at a specific address can be too restrictive; if any of the memory within [area_addr, area_addr + src_info.size] is already allocated, the clone will fail.

Area Functions

area_for()

   area_id **area_for**(void *addr*)

Returns the area that contains the given address (within your own team's address space). The argument needn't be the starting address of an area, nor must it start on a page boundary: If the address lies anywhere within one of your application's areas, the ID of that area is returned.

Since the address is taken to be in the local address space, the area that's returned will also be local—it will have been created or cloned by your application.

Return values:

B_ERROR. The address doesn't lie within an area.

See also: find_area()

clone_area()

area_id **clone_area**(const char *clone_name*,
                void ***clone_addr*,
                uint32 *clone_addr_spec*,
                uint32 *clone_protection*,
                area_id *source_area*)

Creates a new area (the *clone* area) that maps to the same physical memory as an existing area (the *source* area).

- *clone_name* is the name that you wish to assign to the clone area. Area names are, at most, B_OS_NAME_LENGTH characters long.

- *clone_addr* points to a value that gives the address at which you want the clone area to start; the pointed-to value must be a multiple of B_PAGE_SIZE (4096). The function sets the value pointed to by *clone_addr* to the area's actual starting address—it may be different from the one you requested. The constancy of *clone_addr* depends on the value of *clone_addr_spec*, as explained next.

- *clone_addr_spec* is one of four constants that describes how *clone_addr* is to be interpreted. The first three constants, B_EXACT_ADDRESS, B_BASE_ADDRESS, and B_ANY_ADDRESS, have meanings as explained under create_area().

  The fourth constant, B_CLONE_ADDRESS, specifies that the address of the cloned area should be the same as the address of the source area. Cloning the address is convenient if you have two (or more) applications that want to pass pointers to each other—by using cloned addresses, the applications won't have to offset the pointers that they receive. For both the B_ANY_ADDRESS and B_CLONE_ADDRESS specifications, the value that's pointed to by the *clone_addr* argument is ignored.

- *clone_protection* is one or both of B_READ_AREA and B_WRITE_AREA. These have the same meaning as in create_area(); keep in mind, as described there, that a cloned area can have a protection that's different from that of its source.

- *source_area* is the area_id of the area that you wish to clone. You usually supply this value by passing an area name to the find_area() function.

The cloned area inherits the source area's locking scheme (B_FULL_LOCK, B_CONTIGUOUS, B_LAZY_LOCK, or B_NO_LOCK).

Usually, the source area and clone area are in two different applications. It's possible to clone an area from a source that's in the same application, but there's not much reason to do so unless you want the areas to have different protections.

If `clone_area()` clone is successful, the clone's `area_id` is returned. Otherwise, it returns a descriptive error code, listed below.

Return values:

> `B_BAD_VALUE`. Bad argument value; you passed an unrecognized constant for *addr_spec* or *lock*, the *addr* value isn't a multiple of `B_PAGE_SIZE`, you set *addr_spec* to `B_EXACT_ADDRESS` or `B_CLONE_ADDRESS` but the address request couldn't be fulfilled, or *source_area* doesn't identify an existing area.
> `B_NO_MEMORY`. Not enough memory to allocate the system structures that support this area (unlikely).
> `B_ERROR`. Some other system error prevented the area from being created.

See also: `create_area()`

create_area()

> area_id **create_area**(const char **name*,
> 　　　　　　　void **addr,
> 　　　　　　　uint32 *addr_spec*,
> 　　　　　　　uint32 *size*,
> 　　　　　　　uint32 *lock*,
> 　　　　　　　uint32 *protection*)

Creates a new area and returns its `area_id`.

- *name* is the name that you wish to assign to the area. It needn't be unique. Area names are, at most, `B_OS_NAME_LENGTH` (32) characters long.

- *addr* points to the address at which you want the area to start. The value of **addr* must signify a page boundary; in other words, it must be an integer multiple of `B_PAGE_SIZE` (4096). Note that this is a pointer to a pointer: **addr*—not *addr*— should be set to the desired address; you then pass the address of *addr* as the argument, as shown below:

```
/* Set the address to a page boundary. */
char *addr = (char *)(B_PAGE_SIZE * 100);

/* Pass the address of addr as the second argument. */
create_area( "my area", &addr, ...);
```

The function sets the value of **addr* to the area's actual starting address—it may be different from the one you requested. The constancy of **addr* depends on the value of *addr_spec*, as explained next.

- *addr_spec* is a constant that tells the function how the **addr* value should be applied. There are three useful address specification constants, and one that doesn't apply here:

Constant	Meaning
B_EXACT_ADDRESS	You want the value of **addr* to be taken literally and strictly. If the area can't be allocated at that location, the function fails.
B_BASE_ADDRESS	The area can start at a location equal to or greater than **addr*.
B_ANY_ADDRESS	The starting address is determined by the system. In this case, the value that's pointed to by *addr* is ignored (going into the function).
B_CLONE_ADDRESS	This is only meaningful to the clone_area() function.

- *size* is the size, in bytes, of the area. The size must be an integer multiple of B_PAGE_SIZE (4096). The upper limit of *size* depends on the available swap space (or RAM, if the area is to be locked).

- *lock* describes how the physical memory should be treated with regard to swapping. There are four locking constants:

Constant	Meaning
B_FULL_LOCK	The area's memory is locked into RAM when the area is created, and won't be swapped out.
B_CONTIGUOUS	Not only is the area's memory locked into RAM, it's also guaranteed to be contiguous. This is particularly—and perhaps exclusively—useful to designers of certain types of device drivers.
B_LAZY_LOCK	Allows individual pages of memory to be brought into RAM through the natural order of things and *then* locks them.
B_NO_LOCK	Pages are never locked, they're swapped in and out as needed.

- *protection* is a mask that describes whether the memory can be written and read. You form the mask by adding the constants B_READ_AREA (the area can be read) and B_WRITE_AREA (it can be written). The protection you describe applies only to this area. If your area is cloned, the clone can specify a different protection.

If create_area() is successful, the new area_id number is returned. If it's unsuccessful, one of the following error constants is returned.

Return values:

B_BAD_VALUE. Bad argument value. You passed an unrecognized constant for *addr_spec* or *lock*, the *addr* or *size* value isn't a multiple of B_PAGE_SIZE, or you set *addr_spec* to B_EXACT_ADDRESS but the address request couldn't be fulfilled.
B_NO_MEMORY. Not enough memory to allocate the system structures that support this area (unlikely), not enough physical memory to support a locked area, or not enough swap space to allocate virtual memory (in other words, *size* is too big).
B_ERROR. Some other system error prevented the area from being created.

See also: clone_area()

delete_area()

status_t **delete_area**(area_id *area*)

Deletes the designated area. If no one other area maps to the physical memory that this area represents, the memory is freed. After being deleted, the *area* value is invalid as an area identifier.

WARNING

Currently, anybody can delete any area—the act isn't denied if, for example, the `area_id` argument was created by another application. This freedom will be rescinded in a later release. Until then, try to avoid deleting other application's areas.

Return values:

B_NO_ERROR. The area was deleted; *area* is now invalid.

B_ERROR. *area* doesn't designate an actual area.

find_area()

area_id **find_area**(const char **name*)

Returns an area that has a name that matches the argument. Area names needn't be unique—successive calls to this function with the same argument value may not return the same `area_id`.

What you do with the area you've found depends on where it came from:

- If you're finding an area that your own application created or cloned, you can use the returned ID directly.

- If the area was created or cloned by some other application, you should immediately clone the area (unless you're doing something truly innocuous, such as simply examining the area's info structure).

Return values:

B_NAME_NOT_FOUND. The argument doesn't identify an existing area.

See also: `area_for()`

get_area_info(), get_next_area_info(), area_info

status_t **get_area_info**(area_id *area*, area_info **info*)
status_t **get_next_area_info**(team_id *team*, uint32 **cookie*, area_info **info*)

struct {} **area_info**

Copies information about a particular area into the `area_info` structure designated by *info*. The first version of the function designates the area directly, by `area_id`.

The `get_next_area_info()` version lets you step through the list of a team's areas through iterated calls on the function. The *team* argument identifies the team you want to look at; a *team* value of 0 means the team of the calling thread. The *cookie* argument is a placemark; you set it to 0 on your first call, and let the function do the rest. The function returns `B_BAD_VALUE` when there are no more areas to visit:

```
/* Get the area_info for every area in this team. */
area_info info;
int32 cookie = 0;

while (get_next_area_info(0, &cookie, &info) == B_OK)
   ...
```

The `area_info` structure is:

```
typedef struct area_info {
     area_id area;
     char name[B_OS_NAME_LENGTH];
     size_t size;
     uint32 lock;
     uint32 protection;
     team_id team;
     size_t ram_size;
     uint32 copy_count;
     uint32 in_count;
     uint32 out_count;
     void *address;
} area_info;
```

The fields are:

- `area` is the `area_id` that identifies the area.

- `name` is the name that was assigned to the area when it was created or cloned.

- `size` is the (virtual) size of the area, in bytes.

- `lock` is a constant that represents the area's locking scheme. This will be one of `B_FULL_LOCK`, `B_CONTIGUOUS`, `B_LAZY_LOCK`, or `B_NO_LOCK`.

- `protection` specifies whether the area's memory can be read or written. It's a combination of `B_READ_AREA` and `B_WRITE_AREA`.

- `team` is the `team_id` of the team that created or cloned this area.

- `address` is a pointer to the area's starting address. Keep in mind that this address is only meaningful to the team that created (or cloned) the area.

The final four fields give information about the area that's useful in diagnosing system use. The fields are particularly valuable if you're hunting for memory leaks:

- `ram_size` gives the amount of the area, in bytes, that's currently swapped in.

- `copy_count` is a "copy-on-write" count that can be ignored—it doesn't apply to the areas that you create. The system can create copy-on-write areas (it does so when it loads the data section of an executable, for example), but you can't.

- `in_count` is a count of the total number of times any of the pages in the area have been swapped in.

- `out_count` is a count of the total number of times any of the pages in the area have been swapped out.

Return values:
B_NO_ERROR. The area was found; *info* contains valid information.
B_BAD_VALUE. *area* doesn't identify an existing area, *team* doesn't identify an existing team, or there are no more areas to visit.

resize_area()

status_t **resize_area**(area_id *area*, size_t *new_size*)

Sets the size of the designated area to *new_size*, measured in bytes. The *new_size* argument must be a multiple of B_PAGE_SIZE (4096).

Size modifications affect the end of the area's existing memory allocation: If you're increasing the size of the area, the new memory is added to the end of area; if you're shrinking the area, end pages are released and freed. In neither case does the area's starting address change, nor is existing data modified (except, of course, for data that's lost due to shrinkage).

Resizing affects all areas that refer to this area's physical memory. For example, if B is a clone of A, and you resize A, B will be automatically resized (if possible).

Return values:
B_NO_ERROR. The area was successfully resized.
B_BAD_VALUE. *area* doesn't signify a valid area, or *new_size* isn't a multiple of B_PAGE_SIZE.
B_NO_MEMORY. Not enough memory to support the new portion of the area. This should only happen if you're increasing the size of the area.
B_ERROR. Some other system error prevented the area from being created.

set_area_protection()

status_t **set_area_protection**(area_id *area*, uint32 *new_protection*)

Sets the given area's read and write protection. The *new_protection* argument is a mask that specifies one or both of the values `B_READ_AREA` and `B_WRITE_AREA`. The former means that the area can be read; the latter, that it can be written to. An area's protection only applies to access to the underlying memory through that specific area. Different area clones that refer to the same memory may have different protections.

Return values:

> `B_NO_ERROR`. The protection was changed.
>
> `B_BAD_VALUE`. *area* doesn't identify a valid area.

Images

Declared in: be/kernel/image.h

Library: libroot.so

Overview

This isn't about graphics. An *image* is compiled code. There are three types of images:

- An *app image* is an application. Every application has a single app image.
- A *library image* is a dynamically linked library (a "shared library"). Most applications link against the system libraries (*libroot.so*, *libbe.so*, and so on) that Be provides.
- An *add-on image* is an image that you load into your application as it's running. Symbols from the add-on image are linked and references are resolved when the image is loaded. An add-on image provides a sort of "heightened dynamic linking" beyond that of a DLL.

The following sections explain how to load and run an app image, how to create a shared library, and how to create and load an add-on image.

Loading an App Image

Loading an app image is like running a "sub-program." The image that you load is launched in much the same way as had you double-clicked it in the Browser, or launched it from the command line. It runs in its own team—it doesn't share the address space of the application from which it was launched—and, generally, leads its own life.

Any application can be loaded as an app image; you don't need to issue special compile instructions or otherwise manipulate the binary. The one requirement of an app image is that it must have a `main()` function; hardly a restrictive request.

To load an app image, you call the `load_image()` function, the protocol for which is:

```
thread_id load_image(int32 argc,
    const char **argv,
    const char **env)
```

The function's first two arguments identify the app image (file) that you want to launch—we'll return to this in a moment. Having located the file, the function creates a new team, spawns a main thread in that team, and then returns the `thread_id` of that thread to you. The thread that's returned is the executable's main thread. It won't be running: To make it run you pass the `thread_id` to `resume_thread()` or `wait_for_thread()` (as explained in the major section "Threads and Teams").

The *argc*/*argv* argument pair is copied and forwarded to the new thread's `main()` function:

- The first string in the *argv* array must be the name of the image file that you want to launch; `load_image()` uses this string to find the file. You then install any other arguments you want in the array, and terminate the array with a NULL entry. *argc* is set to the number of entries in the *argv* array (not counting the terminating NULL). It's the caller's responsibility to free the *argv* array after `load_image()` returns (remember—the array is copied before it's passed to the new thread).

- *envp* is an array of environment variables that are also passed to `main()`. Typically, you use the global `environ` pointer (which you must declare as an `extern`—see the example, below). You can, of course, create your own environment variable array: As with the *argv* array, the *envp* array should be terminated with a NULL entry, and you must free the array when `load_image()` returns (that is, if you allocated it yourself—don't try to free `environ`).

The following example demonstrates a typical use of `load_image()`. First, we include the appropriate files and declare the necessary variables:

```
#include <image.h>   /* load_executable() */
#include <OS.h>      /* wait_for_thread() */
#include <stdlib.h>  /* malloc() */

/* Declare the environ array. */
extern char **environ;

char **arg_v; /* choose a name that doesn't collide with argv */
int32 arg_c; /* same here vis a vis argc */
thread_id exec_thread;
int32 return_value;
```

Install, in the `arg_v` array, the "command line" arguments. Let's pretend we're launching a program found in */boot/home/apps/adder* that takes two integers, adds them together, and returns the result as `main()`'s exit code. Thus, there are three arguments: The name of the program, and the values of the two addends converted to strings. Since there are three arguments, we allocate `arg_v` to hold four pointers (to accommodate the final NULL). Then we allocate and copy the arguments.

```
arg_c = 3;
arg_v = (char **)malloc(sizeof(char *) * (arg_c + 1));

arg_v[0] = strdup("/boot/home/apps/adder");
arg_v[1] = strdup("5");
arg_v[2] = strdup("3");
arg_v[3] = NULL;
```

Now that everything is properly set up, we call `load_image()`. After the function returns, it's safe to free the allocated `arg_v` array:

```
exec_thread = load_image(arg_c, arg_v, environ);
free(arg_v);
```

At this point, `exec_thread` is suspended (the natural state of a newly-spawned thread). In order to retrieve its return value, we use `wait_for_thread()` to tell the thread to run:

```
wait_for_thread(exec_thread, &return_value);
```

After `wait_for_thread()` returns, the value of `return_value` should be 8 (i.e., 5 + 3).

Creating a Shared Library

The primary documentation for creating a shared library is provided by Metrowerks in their CodeWarrior manual. Beyond the information that you find there, you should be aware of the following amendments and caveats:

- You mustn't export your library's symbols through the `-export all` compiler flag. Instead, you should either use `-export pragma` or `-@export` *filename* (which is the same as `-f` *filename*). See the Metrowerks manual for details on how to use these flags.

- The loader looks for libraries by following the `LIBRARY_PATH` environment variable.

The default library path looks like this:

```
$ echo $LIBRARY_PATH
%A/lib:/boot/home/config/lib:/boot/beos/system/lib
```

where "%A" means the directory that contains the app that the user is launching.

Creating and Using an Add-on Image

An add-on image is indistinguishable from a shared library image. Creating an add-on is exactly like creating a shared library, a topic that we breezed through immediately above. The one difference is where the loader looks for add-ons: The loader follows the trail given by the ADDON_PATH environment variable.

The default ADDON_PATH looks like this:

```
$ echo $ADDON_PATH
%A/add-ons:/boot/home/config/add-ons:/boot/beos/system/add-ons
```

Loading an Add-on Image

To load an add-on into your application, you call the load_add_on() function. The function takes a pathname (absolute or relative to the current working directory) to the add-on file, and returns an image_id number that uniquely identifies the image across the entire system.

For example, let's say you've created an add-on image that's stored in the file /boot/home/add-ons/adder. The code that loads the add-on would look like this:

```
/* For brevity, we won't check errors. */
image_id addon_image;

/* Load the add-on. */
addon_image = load_add_on("/boot/home/add-ons/adder");
```

Unlike loading an executable, loading an add-on doesn't create a separate team, nor does it spawn another thread. The whole point of loading an add-on is to bring the image into your application's address space so you can call the functions and fiddle with the variables that the add-on defines.

Symbols

After you've loaded an add-on into your application, you'll want to examine the symbols (variables and functions) that it has brought with it. To get information about a symbol, you call the get_image_symbol() function:

```
status_t get_image_symbol(image_id image,
    char *symbol_name,
    int32 symbol_type,
    void **location)
```

The function's first three arguments identify the symbol that you want to get:

- The first argument is the image_id of the add-on that owns the symbol.

- The second argument is the symbol's name. This assumes, of course, that you know the name. In general, using an add-on implies just this sort of cooperation.

- The third is a constant that gives the symbol's *symbol type*. The only types you need to care about are B_SYMBOL_TYPE_DATA which you use for variables, and B_SYMBOL_TYPE_TEXT which you use for functions.

The function returns, by reference in its final argument, a pointer to the symbol's address. For example, let's say the adder add-on code looks like this:

```
int32 a1 = 0;
int32 a2 = 0;

int32 adder(void)
{
   return (a1 + a2);
}
```

To examine the variables (addend1 and addend2), you would call get_image_symbol() thus:

```
int32 *var_a1, *var_a2;

get_image_symbol(addon_image, "a1", B_SYMBOL_TYPE_DATA, &var_a1);
get_image_symbol(addon_image, "a2", B_SYMBOL_TYPE_DATA, &var_a2);
```

To get the symbol for the adder() function is a bit more complicated. The compiler mangles a function's name to encode the data types of the function's arguments. The encoding scheme is explained in the next section; to continue with the example, we'll simply accept that the adder() function's symbol is:

```
adder__Fv
```

And so...

```
int32 (*func_add)();
get_image_symbol(addon_image, "adder__Fv", B_SYMBOL_TYPE_TEXT, &func_add);
```

Now that we've retrieved all the symbols, we can set the values of the two addends and call the function:

```
*var_a1 = 5;
*var_a2 = 3;
int32 return_value = (*func_add)();
```

Function Symbol Encoding

The compiler encodes function symbols according to this format:

*function__<Nclass>*F*<arg1><arg2><arg3>*....

function is the name of the function; some C++ names are special:

- Class constructors are always named "__ct".
- Destructors are "__dt".

The *<Nclass>* symbol is used only if the function is a member of a class; *N* is the length (in characters) of the class name and *class* is the name itself.

The optional *<argN>* symbols encode the argument types:

Code	Type
i	int
s	short
l	long
f	float
d	double
c	char
v	void

In addition, if the argument is declared as unsigned, the type code character is preceded by "U". If it's a pointer, the type code (and, potentially, the "U") is preceded by "P"; a pointer to a pointer is preceded by "PP". For example, a function that's declared as

```
void Func(int32, unsigned char **, float *, double);
```

would have the following symbol name:

```
Func__FlUPPcPfd
```

Note that **typedef**'s are translated to their natural types. So, for example, this:

```
void dump_thread(thread_id, bool);
```

becomes

```
dump_thread__FlUc
```

But There's an Easier Way

There's actually an easier, if less elegant, way to find a function's compiler-mangled name: Use **pefdump**.

pefdump the add-on that you want to use, and then copy the function name from the "export symbol table:" section. As an example, let's **pefdump** the Device Kit library, *libdevice.so:*

```
$ cd /system/lib
$ pefdump libdevice.so

/* A LOT of output; and then, at the end... */

  export symbol table:
     class                               name    value
     TVECT                      Close__4BA2DFv   10002260
```

```
TVECT                    Close__9BJoystickFv   10002220
TVECT               __dt__11BSerialPortFv     10002180
TVECT             IsDSR__11BSerialPortFv     100020c0
TVECT                       __ct__4BA2DFv     10002280
TVECT                       __dt__4BA2DFv     10002278
TVECT           Close__12BDigitalPortFv     100021d8
TVECT        ParityMode__11BSerialPortFv     10002110
...
```

So, for example, BSerialPort's `ParityMode()` function is mangled as
"`ParityMode__11BSerialPortFv`".

Image Functions

get_image_info(), get_next_image_info(), image_info

status_t **get_image_info**(image_id *image*, image_info **info*)

status_t **get_next_image_info**(team_id *team*,
                    int32 **cookie*,
                    image_info **info*)

struct {} **image_info**

These functions copy, into the *info* argument, the `image_info` structure for a
particular image. The `get_image_info()` function gets the information for the
image identified by *image*.

The `get_next_image_info()` function lets you step through the list of a team's
images through iterated calls. The *team* argument identifies the team you want to
look at; a *team* value of 0 means the team of the calling thread. The *cookie* argument
is a placemark; you set it to 0 on your first call, and let the function do the rest. The
function returns `B_BAD_VALUE` when there are no more images to visit:

```
/* Get the image_info for every image in this team. */
image_info info;
int32 cookie = 0;

while (get_next_image_info(0, &cookie, &info) == B_OK)
    ...
```

The `image_info` structure is defined as:

```
typedef struct {
    image_id id;
    image_type type;
    int32 sequence;
    int32 init_order;
    B_PFV init_routine;
```

```
        B_PFV term_routine;
        dev_t device;
        ino_t node;
        char name[MAXPATHLEN];
        void *text;
        void *data;
        int32 text_size;
        int32 data_size;
    } image_info
```

The fields are:

- id. The image's image_id number.

- type. A constant (listed below) that tells whether this is an app, library, or add-on image.

- sequence and init_order. These are zero-based ordinal numbers that give the order in which the image was loaded and initialized, compared to all the other images in this team.

- init_routine and term_routine. These are pointers to the functions that are used to initialize and terminate the image (more specifically, the image's main thread). The B_PFV type is a cover for a pointer to a (void*) function.

- device. The device that the image file lives on.

- node. The node number of the image file.

- name. The full pathname of the file whence sprang the image.

- text and text_size. The address and the size (in bytes) of the image's text segment.

- data and data_size. The address and size of the image's data segment.

The self-explanatory image_type constants are:

Constant
B_APP_IMAGE
B_LIBRARY_IMAGE
B_ADD_ON_IMAGE

Return values:

B_NO_ERROR. The image was found; *info* contains valid information.

B_BAD_VALUE. *image* doesn't identify an existing image, *team* doesn't identify an existing team, or there are no more images to visit.

get_image_symbol(), get_nth_image_symbol()

status_t **get_image_symbol**(image_id *image*,
　　　　　char **symbol_name*,
　　　　　int32 *symbol_type*,
　　　　　void ***location*)

status_t **get_nth_image_symbol**(image_id *image*,
　　　　　int32 *n*,
　　　　　char **name*,
　　　　　int32 **name_length*,
　　　　　int32 **symbol_type*,
　　　　　void ***location*)

`get_image_symbol()` returns, in *location*, a pointer to the address of the symbol that's identified by the *image*, *symbol_name*, and *symbol_type* arguments. An example demonstrating the use of this function is given in "Symbols."

`get_nth_image_symbol()` returns information about the *n*th symbol in the given image. The information is returned in the arguments:

- *name* is the name of the symbol. You have to allocate the *name* buffer before you pass it in—the function copies the name into the buffer.

- You point *name_length* to an integer that gives the length of the *name* buffer that you're passing in. The function uses this value to truncate the string that it copies into *name*. The function then resets *name_length* to the full (untruncated) length of the symbol's name (plus one byte to accommodate a terminating NULL). To ensure that you've gotten the symbol's full name, you should compare the in-going value of *name_length* with the value that the function sets it to. If the in-going value is less than the full length, you can then re-invoke `get_nth_image_symbol()` with an adequately lengthened *name* buffer, and an increased *name_length* value.

WARNING

Keep in mind that *name_length* is reset each time you call `get_nth_image_symbol()`. If you're calling the function iteratively (to retrieve all the symbols in an image), you need to reset the *name_length* value between calls.

- The function sets *symbol_type* to B_SYMBOL_TYPE_DATA if the symbol is a variable, or B_SYMBOL_TYPE_TEXT if the symbol is a function. The argument's value going into the function is of no consequence.

- The function sets *location* to point to the symbol's address.

To retrieve `image_id` numbers on which these functions can act, use the `get_next_image_info()` function. Such numbers are also returned directly when you load an add-on image through the `load_add_on()` function.

Return values:

B_NO_ERROR. The symbol was found.

B_BAD_IMAGE_ID. *image* doesn't identify an existing image.

B_BAD_INDEX. *n* is out-of-bounds.

load_add_on(), unload_add_on()

image_id **load_add_on**(const char *pathname)

status_t **unload_add_on**(image_id *image*)

`load_add_on()` loads an add-on image, identified by *pathname*, into your application's address space.

* *pathname* can be absolute or relative; if it's relative, it's reckoned off of the current working directory.

* The function returns an `image_id` (a positive integer) that represents the loaded image. Image ID numbers are unique across the system.

An example that demonstrates the use of `load_add_on()` is given in "Loading an Add-on Image."

You can load the same add-on image twice; each time you load the add-on a new, unique `image_id` is created and returned.

`unload_add_on()` removes the add-on image identified by the argument. The image's symbols are removed, and the memory that they represent is freed. If the argument doesn't identify a valid image, the function returns B_ERROR. Otherwise, it returns B_NO_ERROR.

Return values:

Positive `image_id` value (load) or B_NO_ERROR (unload). Success.

B_ERROR. The image couldn't be loaded (for whatever reason), or *image* isn't a valid image ID.

load_image()

thread_id **load_image**(int *argc,*

                const char **argv,*

                const char **env*)

Loads an app image into the system (it *doesn't* load the image into the caller's address space), creates a separate team for the new application, and spawns and returns the

ID of the team's main thread. The image is identified by the pathname given in *argv*[0].

The arguments are passed to the image's `main()` function (they show up there as the function's similarly named arguments):

- *argc* gives the number of entries that are in the *argv* array.

- The first string in the *argv* array must be the name of the image file. You then install any other arguments you want in the array, and terminate the array with a NULL entry. Note that the value of *argc* shouldn't count *argv*'s terminating NULL.

- *envp* is an array of environment variables that are also passed to `main()`. Typically, you use the global `environ` pointer:

```
extern char **environ;

load_image(..., environ);
```

The *argv* and *envp* arrays are copied into the new thread's address space. If you allocated either of these arrays, it's safe to free them immediately after `load_image()` returns.

The thread that's returned by `load_image()` is in a suspended state. To start the thread running, you pass the `thread_id` to `resume_thread()` or `wait_for_thread()`.

An example that demonstrates the use of `load_image()` is given in "Loading an App Image."

Return values:
  Positive integers. Success.
  B_ERROR. Failure, for whatever reason.

System and Time Information

Declared in: be/kernel/OS.h

Library: libroot.so

The following functions, types, and structures are used to convey basic information about the system, such as the number of CPUs, when the kernel was built, what time it is now, and whether your computer is on fire.

System Info Functions and Structures

get_system_info(), system_info, cpu_info, cpu_type, platform_type

status_t **get_system_info**(system_info *info*)

struct {} **system_info**

struct {} **cpu_info**

enum **cpu_type**

enum **platform_type**

The `get_system_info()` function tells you more than you want to know about the physical capacities and other statistics of your operating system. The function takes a pointer to an allocated `system_info` structure and fills it in.

```
typedef struct {
    machine_id  id;
    bigtime_t  boot_time;
    int32  cpu_count;
    cpu_type  cpu_type;
    int32  cpu_revision;
    cpu_info  cpu_infos[B_MAX_CPU_NUM];
    int64  cpu_clock_speed;
    int64  bus_clock_speed;
    platform_type  platform_type;
    int32  max_pages;
    int32  used_pages;
    int32  page_faults;
    int32  max_sems;
    int32  used_sems;
    int32  max_ports;
    int32  used_ports;
    int32  max_threads;
    int32  used_threads;
    int32  max_teams;
    int32  used_teams;
    char  kernel_name[B_FILE_NAME_LENGTH];
    char  kernel_build_date[B_OS_NAME_LENGTH];
    char  kernel_build_time[B_OS_NAME_LENGTH];
    int64  kernel_version;
} system_info
```

The `system_info` structure holds information about the machine and the state of the kernel. The structure's fields are:

- `id`. The 64-bit number (encoded as two `int32`s) that uniquely identifies this machine.

- `boot_time`. The time at which the computer was last booted, measured in microseconds since January 1st, 1970.

- `cpu_count`. The number of CPUs.

- `cpu_type` and `cpu_revision`. The type constant and revision number of the CPUs.

- `cpu_infos`. An array of `cpu_info` structures, one for each CPU.

- `cpu_clock_speed`. The speed (in Hz) at which the CPUs operate.

- `bus_clock_speed`. The speed (in Hz) at which the bus operates.

- `platform_type`. One of the platform type constants.

- `max_`*resources* and `used_`*resources*. The five pairs of `max`/`used` fields give the total number of RAM pages, semaphores, and so on, that the system can create, and the number that are currently in use.

- `page_faults`. The number of times the system has read a page of memory into RAM due to a page fault.

- `kernel_name`. The (leaf) name of the kernel.

- `kernel_build_date` and `kernel_build_time`. Human-readable strings that tell you when the kernel was built.

- `kernel_version`. A number that identifies the kernel version.

The `cpu_info` structure is:

```
typedef struct {
    bigtime_t active_time;
} cpu_info;
```

- `active_time` is the number of microseconds spent doing useful work since the machine was booted.

Relatedly, `B_MAX_CPU_COUNT` is currently 8.

The `machine_id` type is:

```
typedef int32 machine_id[2];
```

The `cpu_type` constants are:

```
typedef enum {
    B_CPU_PPC_601 = 1,
    B_CPU_PPC_603 = 2,
    B_CPU_PPC_603e = 3,
    B_CPU_PPC_604 = 4,
    B_CPU_PPC_604e = 5,
    B_CPU_PPC_686 = 13,
    B_CPU_AMD_29K,
    B_CPU_X86,
    B_CPU_MC6502,
    B_CPU_Z80,
    B_CPU_ALPHA,
    B_CPU_MIPS,
```

```
    B_CPU_HPPA,
    B_CPU_M68K,
    B_CPU_ARM,
    B_CPU_SH,
    B_CPU_SPARC
} cpu_type;
```

The `platform_type` constants are:

```
typedef enum {
    B_BEBOX_PLATFORM = 0,
    B_MAC_PLATFORM,
    B_AT_CLONE_PLATFORM,
    B_ENIAC_PLATFORM,
    B_APPLE_II_PLATFORM,
    B_CRAY_PLATFORM,
    B_LISA_PLATFORM,
    B_TI_994A_PLATFORM,
    B_TIMEX_SINCLAIR_PLATFORM,
    B_ORAC_1_PLATFORM,
    B_HAL_PLATFORM
} platform_type;
```

I haven't tried it, but I really don't think the BeOS would work at all well on a Timex Sinclair (see `is_computer_on_fire()`).

is_computer_on()

   int32 is_computer_on(void)

Returns 1 if the computer is on. If the computer isn't on, the value returned by this function is undefined.

is_computer_on_fire()

   double is_computer_on_fire(void)

Returns the temperature of the motherboard if the computer is currently on fire. Smoldering doesn't count. If the computer isn't on fire, the function returns some other value.

Time Functions

real_time_clock(), real_time_clock_usecs(), set_real_time_clock()

   uint32 real_time_clock (void)

   bigtime_t real_time_clock_usecs (void)

   void set_real_time_clock (int32 *secs_since_jan1_1970*)

`real_time_clock()` returns the number of seconds that have elapsed since January 1, 1970.

`real_time_clock_usecs()` measures the same time span in microseconds.

`set_real_time_clock()` sets the value that the other two functions refer to.

system_time()

bigtime_t **system_time**(void)

Returns the number of microseconds that have elapsed since the computer was booted.

Miscellaneous Functions and Constants

Miscellaneous Functions

clear_caches()

`be/kernel/image.h`

void **clear_caches**(void *_addr_, size_t _len_, uint32 _flags_)

This function clears or invalidates the instruction and data caches. You should only need this function if you're generating code on the fly, or if you're performing a timing loop and you want to start with fresh caches (to get a "worst case" estimate).

The arguments are:

- _addr_ is the starting address of a section of memory that corresponds to a section of one of the caches.

- _len_ is the length, in bytes, of the instruction or data segment that you want to clear or invalidate.

- _flags_ is one or both of `B_INVALIDATE_ICACHE` and `B_FLUSH_DCACHE`.

By invalidating a section of the instruction cache, you cause the instructions in that section to be reloaded next time they're needed. Flushing the data cache causes the in-memory copy of the data to be written out to the cache.

debugger()

`be/kernel/OS.h`

void **debugger**(const char *_string_)

Throws the calling thread into the debugger. The _string_ argument becomes the debugger's first utterance.

Constants

B_INFINITE_TIMEOUT

be/kernel/OS.h

#define **B_INFINITE_TIMEOUT** (9223372036854775807LL);

The infinite timeout value can be used to specify, to timeout-accepting functions, that you're willing to wait forever.

B_OS_NAME_LENGTH

be/kernel/OS.h

#define **B_OS_NAME_LENGTH** 32

This constant gives the maximum length of the name of a thread, semaphore, port, area, or other operating system bauble.

B_PAGE_SIZE

be/kernel/OS.h

#define **B_PAGE_SIZE** 4096

The `B_PAGE_SIZE` constant gives the size, in bytes, of a page of RAM.

The Support Kit

Support Kit Inheritance Hierarchy

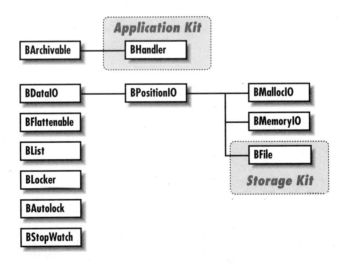

CHAPTER SIX

The Support Kit

The Support Kit contains classes and utilities that any application can take advantage of—regardless of what kind of application it is or what it does. Among other things, it includes:

- The **BArchivable** protocol for objects that can archive themselves and be instantiated from their archives.

- The **BList** class, a container for keeping track of a number of data items, typically object pointers.

- The BLocker and BAutolock classes for implementing locking mechanisms.

- The BDataIO and BPositionIO protocols for objects that can be read and written, and the BMemoryIO and BMallocIO classes that implement the protocols.

- The BFlattenable protocol for objects that can write themselves to a flattened representation.

- Debugging tools, including the BStopWatch class.

- Common defined types and constants, such as `int32` and `int64`.

- The error codes for all the software kits.

- Type codes for identifying data types in messages, attributes, and resources.

- Utility functions such as `atomic_add()`, `write_16_swap()`, and `convert_to_utf8()`.

BArchivable

Derived from: *none*

Declared in: be/support/Archivable.h

Overview

BArchivable is a protocol for *archiving* and *unarchiving* objects. When you archive an object, you copy it to a static form that can be handed to another application, saved to a file, cached in memory, and so on. Unarchiving does the opposite: It takes a static archive and turns it into a functioning object.

Archiving an object entails capturing its current state in a package of some kind. The package that the BeOS uses is a BMessage object. The BMessage can be sent or posted just like any other message, and it can be flattened to a file or other data repository. An object is unarchived by reconstructing it from the values stored in the BMessage archive.

Archiving

To archive an object, you create a BMessage and pass it to the object's `Archive()` function:

```
BMessage message;
theObject->Archive(&message);
```

The message becomes the archive—it will contain all the information necessary to re-create the object.

It's the job of the `Archive()` implementation to write a description of the object into the message. Each class is responsible for archiving the parts of the object that it defines. To incorporate properties archived by its base classes, it should begin its implementation of the function by calling the version of `Archive()` that it inherits from its base class.

The chain of calls to inherited functions ends at the BArchivable root class. Its version of `Archive()` puts the object's class name into the archive under the field named "class". This information is used later when instantiating objects from the archive. It's good practice for derived classes to put their own class names in the "class" array as well, provided that instances of the class can be initialized from the archive. An abstract class should not put its name in the array. (See `validate_instantiation()` for more on this issue.)

If an object doesn't want or need to include inherited archival, it should at least include the BArchivable functionality by putting the name of the object's class in the "class" array:

```
archive->AddString("class", class_name(this));
```

If a class doesn't have any data to add to the BMessage archive, it doesn't need to implement an `Archive()` function; it can rely on the version it inherits. However, it must implement the constructor and static `Instantiate()` function for its objects to be successfully unarchived.

Deep and Shallow Archives

`Archive()`'s second argument, a `bool` flag, indicates whether the archive should be *deep* or *shallow*. By default the flag is `true` (deep).

For a deep archive, a class should include in its archive any other objects that it "owns." For a shallow archive, it should exclude these objects. For example a BView object archives its children for a deep archive, but not for a shallow one.

To perform a deep archive, an object invokes `Archive()` on the objects it owns, and adds the resulting archives to its own archive. For example:

```
status_t TheClass::Archive(BMessage *archive, bool deep)
{
    inherited::Archive(archive, deep);
    archive->AddString("class", "TheClass");
    . . .
    if ( deep ) {
        BMessage cronyArchive;
        if ( crony->Archive(&cronyArchive, deep) == B_OK )
            archive->AddMessage("crony", &cronyArchive);
    }
}
```

Neither a deep nor a shallow archive should include objects that the target object is associated with but doesn't own. For example, a BView doesn't archive its parent or the BWindow to which it's attached.

Names

Name collisions in an archive are not automatically detected and corrected. For example, if both class A and subclass B add fields named "dog", the unarchiving mechanism will get confused.

To try to avoid collisions, all the `Archive()` functions implemented in the Be kits use names beginning with an underbar ("_name"). Use a different convention for naming archived data in the classes you define.

Instantiation

To be unarchivable, a class must implement a constructor that takes a BMessage archive as an argument. The constructor is a counterpart to the `Archive()` function: It begins by calling the constructor for its immediate base class, and then looks in the BMessage for the fields that it knows about (in other words, fields that were added in the `Archive()` function).

But there's a problem: A constructor is named for its class. This forces you to know *at compile time* the class of the object being unarchived. To get around this, every archivable class must implement the static `Instantiate()` function (declared in BArchivable) that doesn't do much more than call the archive-accepting constructor. For example:

```
TheClass *TheClass::Instantiate(BMessage *archive)
{
    if ( validate_instantiation(archive, "TheClass"))
        return new TheClass(archive);
    return NULL;
}
```

(The `validate_instantiation()` function, provided by the Support Kit, is a safety check that makes sure the BMessage object is, in fact, an archive for the named class.)

But we're not through yet: Because the `Instantiate()` function is static, you need an instance of its class to call it. To get around this difficulty, the Support Kit provides the `instantiate_object()` function. When passed a BMessage archive, `instantiate_object()` looks for the first name in the "class" array, finds the `Instantiate()` function for that class, and calls it. Failing that, it picks another name from the "class" array (working up the inheritance hierarchy) and tries again.

`instantiate_object()` returns a BArchivable instance. You then use `cast_as()` to cast the object to a more interesting class. A typical unarchiving session looks something like this:

```
/* archive is the BMessage that we want to turn into an object.
 * In this case, we want to turn it into a BView.
 */
BArchivable *unarchived = instantiate_object(archive);
if ( unarchived ) {
    BView *view = cast_as(unarchived, BView);
    if ( view ) {

        . . .

    }
}
```

Dynamic Loading

As described so far, an application can only unarchive objects that it knows about—it can't unarchive an object that it doesn't have the code to run.

An additional convention gets around this restriction: A BMessage archive can include a `B_STRING_TYPE` field named "add-on" that contains the signature of an add-on that defines the archived object. If `instantiate_object()` fails to unarchive an object on its first try, it will look for the add-on image, load it, and try again.

It's not defined how a host will interact with an unarchived instance of a previously unknown class. It's up to the parties to define entry points and protocols, just as it is for any other add-on module.

Constructor and Destructor

BArchivable()

> BArchivable(void)
> BArchivable(BMessage *archive)

Does nothing.

~BArchivable()

> virtual ~BArchivable(void)

Does nothing.

Static Functions

Instantiate()

> static BArchivable *Instantiate(BMessage *archive)

Returns NULL. You can't create BArchivable instances.

Derived classes should implement Instantiate() to return a new instance of the class constructed from the BMessage *archive*. For example:

```
TheClass *TheClass::Instantiate(BMessage *archive)
{
    if ( !validate_instantiation(archive, "TheClass") )
        return NULL;
    return new TheClass(archive);
}
```

This function depends on a constructor that can initialize the new object from the *archive* BMessage. See the previous section "Instantiation" for more information.

Member Functions

Archive()

   virtual status_t **Archive**(BMessage *archive*, bool *deep* = true) const

The default implementation adds the name of the object's class to *archive*'s "class" field. Derived classes must override `Archive()` to augment this implementation by adding, to the BMessage, data that describes the current state of the object. Each implementation of this function should begin by incorporating the inherited version:

```
/* We'll assume that MyView inherits from BView. */
status_t MyView::Archive(BMessage *archive, bool deep)
{
    BView::Archive(archive, deep);
    . . .
}
```

If the class can be instantiated, it should also add its name to the "class" array:

```
archive->AddString("class", "MyView");
```

The *deep* flag declares whether `Archive()` should include objects that "belong" to the archiving object. For example, a deep BView archive would include archived forms of the view's children. An example is given under "Deep and Shallow Archives" previously in this chapter.

`Archive()` should return `B_OK` if it's successful; otherwise, it should return `B_ERROR` or a more descriptive error code.

BAutolock

Derived from: *none*

Declared in: be/support/Autolock.h

Library: libbe.so

Overview

The BAutolock class provides an easy mechanism for automatically locking and unlocking a BLocker object or, more typically, a BLooper. All you need to do is statically allocate a BAutolock object (put it on the stack) and pass it a target BLocker or BLooper. You may want to make sure the lock is in place before proceeding:

```
BAutolock autolocker(myWindow);
if ( autolocker.IsLocked() ) {
    . . .
}
```

When the BAutolock object is destroyed (when its stack exits), it unlocks the target object.

Constructor and Destructor

BAutolock()

> inline **BAutolock**(BLooper *_looper_)
> inline **BAutolock**(BLocker *_locker_)
> inline **BAutolock**(BLocker &_locker_)

Locks the target _looper_ or _locker_ object.

~BAutolock()

> inline **~BAutolock**(void)

Unlocks the target BLooper or BLocker.

Member Functions

IsLocked()

> inline bool **IsLocked**(void)

Returns `true` if the target BLooper or BLocker is locked, and `false` if not.

BDataIO and BPositionIO

Derived from:	BDataIO: _none_ BPositionIO: public BDataIO
Declared in:	be/support/DataIO.h
Library:	libbe.so

Overview

BDataIO and BPositionIO are abstract classes that define protocols for performing input/output operations. Classes derived from them represent the various kinds of things that can be treated as sources of input data or as repositories for output data. For example, the BFile class, defined in the Storage Kit, represents a file. BMallocIO and BMemoryIO, defined in this kit, represent a dynamically allocated memory buffer.

BDataIO declares only the basic I/O functions `Read()` and `Write()`. BPositionIO declares an additional set of functions (`ReadAt()`, `WriteAt()`, `Seek()`, and `Position()`) for objects that can keep track of the current position in the I/O buffer; it implements `Read()` and `Write()` in terms of these other functions.

Neither class declares any data members, nor do they implement the functions in the protocols they declare. It's up to derived classes to implement them based on the properties of the particular kinds of data sources/repositories they represent.

Constructor and Destructor

BDataIO(), BPositionIO()

```
BDataIO(void)

BPositionIO(void)
```

These constructors have nothing to do. Constructors in derived classes should initialize the object to default values—for example, set the current position to the beginning of the data.

~BDataIO(), ~BPositionIO()

virtual **~BDataIO**(void)

virtual **~BPositionIO**(void)

These destructors do nothing. Destructors in derived classes should free the memory used, if appropriate.

Member Functions

Position()   *see Seek()*

Read(), ReadAt()

BDataIO:
  virtual ssize_t **Read**(void *buffer*, size_t *numBytes*) = 0
BPositionIO:
  virtual ssize_t **Read**(void *buffer*, size_t *numBytes*)

  virtual ssize_t **ReadAt**(off_t *position*, void *buffer*, size_t *numBytes*) = 0

`Read()` is implemented by derived classes to copy *numBytes* bytes of data from the object to the *buffer*. It should return the number of bytes actually read, which may be 0, or an error code if something goes wrong.

Similarly, ReadAt() is implemented by derived classes to read *numBytes* bytes of data beginning at *position* in the data source, and to place them in the *buffer*. Like Read(), it should return the number of bytes actually read, or an error code if something goes wrong.

The BPositionIO class implements Read() in terms of ReadAt(), Seek(), and Position()—so that it will always read starting at the current position and move the current position beyond the data it has read. However, it leaves these latter functions for derived classes to implement.

Seek(), Position()

BPositionIO:

> virtual off_t **Seek**(off_t *position*, int32 *mode*) = 0

> virtual off_t **Position**(void) const = 0

Seek() is implemented by derived classes to modify the current position maintained by the object. The current position is an offset in bytes from the beginning of the object's data. How the *position* argument is interpreted will depend on the *mode* flag. Three possible modes should be supported:

- SEEK_SET. The *position* passed is an offset from the beginning of allocated memory; in other words, the current position should be set to *position*.

- SEEK_CUR. The *position* argument is an offset from the current position; the current position should be incremented by *position*.

- SEEK_END. The *position* argument is an offset from the end of the data; the current position should be the sum of *position* plus the number of bytes in the data.

For the SEEK_SET mode, *position* should be a positive value. The other modes permit negative offsets.

Seek() should return the new current position, as should Position().

SetSize()

BPositionIO:

> virtual status_t **SetSize**(off_t *numBytes*)

Returns B_ERROR to indicate that, in general, BPositionIO objects can't set the amount of memory in the repositories they represent. However, the BMallocIO class in this kit and BFile in the Storage Kit implement SetSize() functions that override this default.

See also: BFile::SetSize(), BMallocIO::SetSize()

Write(), WriteAt()

BDataIO:
    virtual ssize_t **Write**(const void *buffer*, size_t *numBytes*) = 0
BPositionIO:
    virtual ssize_t **Write**(const void *buffer*, size_t *numBytes*)

    virtual ssize_t **WriteAt**(off_t *position*, const void *buffer*, size_t *numBytes*) = 0

`Write()` is implemented by derived classes to copy *numBytes* bytes of data from the *buffer* to the object. It should return the number of bytes actually written, which may be 0, or an error code if the operation fails.

Similarly, `WriteAt()` is implemented by derived classes to copy *numBytes* bytes of data from the *buffer* to the *position* offset in the object's data repository. Like `Write()` it should return the number of bytes it succeeds in writing, or an error code.

The BPositionIO class implements `Write()` in terms of `WriteAt()`, `Seek()`, and `Position()`—so that it always writes to the current position and moves the position marker past the data it has written.

BFlattenable

    Derived from: *none*

    Declared in: be/support/Flattenable.h

    Library: libbe.so

Overview

As its name implies, the BFlattenable class declares a protocol for objects that can be flattened—written to an untyped buffer of bytes—and unflattened from the buffer. By implementing this protocol, a class gives others the ability to manipulate its objects in a flexible manner. Currently, only the BMessage class, through its `AddFlat()` and `FindFlat()` functions, declares an API that can deal with BFlattenable objects. The BPath class in the Storage Kit derives from BFlattenable.

As this class merely declares a protocol for other classes to implement, it doesn't include a constructor or destructor.

Member Functions

AllowsTypeCode()   *see TypeCode()*

Flatten(), Unflatten()

> virtual status_t **Flatten**(void *buffer*, ssize_t *numBytes*) const = 0

> virtual status_t **Unflatten**(type_code *code*, const void *buffer*, ssize_t *numBytes*) = 0

Flatten() is implemented by derived classes to write the object into the *buffer*. There are *numBytes* bytes of memory available at the *buffer* address. If this isn't at least as much memory as the FlattenedSize() function says is necessary, Flatten() should return an error. If successful, it should return B_OK.

Unflatten() is implemented by derived classes to set object values from *numBytes* bytes of data taken from the *buffer*. However, it should read the data only if the type *code* it's passed indicates that the data is a type that it supports—that is, only if its AllowsTypeCode() function returns true for the *code*. If successful in reconstructing the object from the flattened data, Unflatten() should return B_OK. If not, it should return B_ERROR or a more descriptive error code.

FlattenedSize()

> virtual ssize_t **FlattenedSize**(void) const = 0

Implemented by derived classes to return the amount of memory needed to hold the flattened object. This is the minimal amount that must be allocated and passed to Flatten().

IsFixedSize()

> virtual bool **IsFixedSize**(void) const = 0

Implemented by derived classes to return true if all instances of the class take up the same amount of memory when they're flattened, and false if their flattened sizes can differ. The sizes will differ, for example, if a variable-length string is part of the flattened data.

TypeCode(), AllowsTypeCode()

> virtual type_code **TypeCode**(void) const = 0

> virtual bool **AllowsTypeCode**(type_code *code*) const

TypeCode() is implemented by derived classes to return the type code that identifies the class type. The code is used to identify an instance of the class in its flattened state, for example when it's added to a BMessage.

`AllowsType()` returns `true` if the *code* it's passed matches the code returned by `TypeCode()` and `false` if not. If can be modified in derived classes to apply a more liberal standard—to allow more than one type code to identify the object.

See also: `BMessage::AddData()`

Unflatten()   *see Flatten()*

BList

Derived from:	*none*
Declared in:	be/support/List.h
Library:	libbe.so

Overview

A BList object is a compact, ordered list of data pointers. BList objects can contain pointers to any type of data, including—and especially—objects.

An item assigned to a BList is identified by an index to its position in the list. Indices start at 0 and are neither arbitrary nor permanent. If, for example, you insert an item into the middle of a list, the indices of the items at the tail of the list are incremented (by one). Similarly, removing an item decrements the indices of the following items.

A BList stores its items as type `void *`, so it's necessary to cast an item to the correct type when you retrieve it. For example, items retrieved from a list of BBitmap objects must be cast as BBitmap pointers:

```
BBitmap *theImage = (BBitmap *)myList->ItemAt(anIndex);
```

WARNING

There's nothing to prevent you from adding a `NULL` pointer to a BList. However, functions that retrieve items from the list (such as `ItemAt()`) return `NULL` when the requested item can't be found. Thus, you can't distinguish between a valid `NULL` item and an invalid attempt to access an item that isn't there.

Constructor and Destructor

BList()

BList(int32 *count* = 20)
BList(const BList& *anotherList*)

Initializes the BList by allocating enough memory to hold *count* items. As the list grows and shrinks, additional memory is allocated and freed in blocks of the same size.

The copy constructor creates an independent list of data pointers, but it doesn't copy the pointed-to data. For example:

```
BList *newList = new BList(oldList);
```

Here, the contents of *oldList* and *newList*—the actual data pointers—are separate and independent. Adding, removing, or reordering items in *oldList* won't affect the number or order of items in *newList*. But if you modify the data that an item in *oldList* points to, the modification will be seen through the analogous item in *newList*.

The block size of a BList that's created through the copy constructor is the same as that of the original BList.

~BList()

> virtual **~BList**(void)

Frees the list of data pointers, but doesn't free the data that they point to. To destroy the data, you need to free each item in an appropriate manner. For example, objects that were allocated with the **new** operator should be freed with `delete`:

```
void *anItem;
for ( long i = 0; anItem = myList->ItemAt(i); i++ )
    delete anItem;
delete myList;
```

See also: `MakeEmpty()`

Member Functions

AddItem()

> bool **AddItem**(void **item*, int32 *index*)
> bool **AddItem**(void **item*)

Adds an item to the BList at *index*—or, if no index is supplied, at the end of the list. If necessary, additional memory is allocated to accommodate the new item.

Adding an item never removes an item already in the list. If the item is added at an index that's already occupied, items currently in the list are bumped down one slot to make room.

If *index* is out of range (greater than the current item count, or less than zero), the function fails and returns `false`. Otherwise it returns `true`.

AddList()

> bool **AddList**(BList *_list_, int32 _index_)
> bool **AddList**(BList *_list_)

Adds the contents of another BList to this BList. The items from the other BList are inserted at _index_—or, if no index is given, they're appended to the end of the list. If the index is out of range, the function fails and returns `false`. If successful, it returns `true`.

See also: `AddItem()`

CountItems()

> int32 **CountItems**(void) const

Returns the number of items currently in the list.

DoForEach()

> void **DoForEach**(bool (*_func_)(void *))
> void **DoForEach**(bool (*_func_)(void *, void *), void *_arg2_)

Calls the _func_ function once for each item in the BList. Items are visited in order, beginning with the first one in the list (index 0) and ending with the last. If a call to _func_ returns `true`, the iteration is stopped, even if some items have not yet been visited.

func must be a function that takes one or two arguments. The first argument is the currently-considered item from the list; the second argument, if _func_ requires one, is passed to `DoForEach()` as _arg2_.

FirstItem()

> void ***FirstItem**(void) const

Returns the first item in the list, or `NULL` if the list is empty. This function doesn't remove the item from the list.

See also: `LastItem()`, `ItemAt()`

HasItem()

> bool **HasItem**(void *_item_) const

Returns `true` if _item_ is in the list, and `false` if not.

IndexOf()

int32 **IndexOf**(void *item*) const

Returns the index where a particular *item* is located in the list, or a negative number if the *item* isn't in the list. If the item is in the list more than once, the index returned will be the position of its first occurrence.

IsEmpty()

bool **IsEmpty**(void) const

Returns `true` if the list is empty (if it contains no items), and `false` otherwise.

See also: `MakeEmpty()`

ItemAt()

void *****ItemAt**(int32 *index*) const

Returns the item at *index*, or `NULL` if the index is out of range. This function doesn't remove the item from the list.

See also: `Items()`, `FirstItem()`, `LastItem()`

Items()

void *****Items**(void) const

Returns a pointer to the BList's list. You can index directly into the list if you're certain that the index is in range:

```
myType *item = (myType *)Items()[index];
```

Although the practice is discouraged, you can also step through the list of items by incrementing the list pointer that's returned by `Items()`. Be aware that the list isn't null-terminated—you have to detect the end of the list by some other means. The simplest method is to count items:

```
void *ptr = myList->Items();

for ( long i = myList->CountItems(); i > 0; i-- )
{
    . . .
    *ptr++;
}
```

You should *never* use the list pointer to change the number of items in the list.

LastItem()

void *LastItem(void) const

Returns the last item in the list without removing it. If the list is empty, this function returns NULL.

See also: RemoveLastItem(), FirstItem()

MakeEmpty()

void MakeEmpty(void)

Empties the BList of all its items, without freeing the data that they point to.

See also: IsEmpty(), RemoveItem()

RemoveItem(), RemoveItems()

bool RemoveItem(void *item)
void *RemoveItem(int32 index)

bool RemoveItems(int32 index, int32 count)

RemoveItem() removes an item from the list. If passed an *item*, the function looks for the item in the list, removes it, and returns true. If it can't find the item, it returns false. If the item is in the list more than once, this function removes only its first occurrence.

If passed an *index*, RemoveItem() removes the item at that index and returns it. If there's no item at the index, it returns NULL.

RemoveItems() removes a group of *count* items from the list, beginning with the item at *index*. If the index is out of range, it fails and returns false. Otherwise, it removes the items, without checking to be sure that the list actually holds that many items at the index, and returns true.

The list is compacted after an item is removed. Because of this, you mustn't try to empty a list (or a range within a list) by removing items at monotonically increasing indices. You should either start with the highest index and move towards the head of the list, or remove at the same index (the lowest in the range) some number of times. As an example of the latter, the following code removes the first five items in the list:

```
for ( long i = 0; i <= 4; i++ )
    myList->RemoveItem(0);
```

See also: MakeEmpty()

SortItems()

> void *SortItems(int (*compareFunc)(const void *, const void *))

Rearranges the items in the list. The items are sorted using the *compareFunc* comparison function passed as an argument. This function should return a negative number if the first item is ordered before the second, a positive number if the second is ordered before the first, and 0 if the two items are ordered equivalently.

The arguments passed to the comparison function are declared to be `void*`; however, they should be regarded as pointers to the items in the list—in other words, as pointers to pointers.

Operators

= (assignment)

> BList& operator =(const BList&)

Copies the contents of one BList object into another:

```
BList newList = oldList;
```

After the assignment, each object has its own independent copy of list data; destroying one of the objects won't affect the other.

Only the items in the list are copied, not the data they point to.

BLocker

Derived from: *none*

Declared in: be/support/Locker.h

Library: libbe.so

Overview

The BLocker class provides a locking mechanism that can be used to protect a section of critical code. The code that you want to protect should be placed between BLocker's `Lock()` and `Unlock()` calls:

```
BLocker *aLock = new BLocker();
. . .
aLock->Lock();
/* Protected code goes here. */
aLock->Unlock();
```

This guarantees that only one thread at a time will pass through the lock. After a thread has locked the BLocker object, subsequent attempts to lock by other threads are blocked until the first thread calls `Unlock()`.

BLocker keeps track of the locking thread—the thread that's currently between `Lock()` and `Unlock()` calls. It lets the thread make nested calls to `Lock()` without blocking. Because of this, you can wrap a BLocker's lock around a series of functions that might, themselves, lock the same BLocker object.

For example, let's say you have a class called BadDog that's declared thus:

```
class BadDog : public BArchivable
{
public:
    void DoThis();
    void DoThat();
    void DoThisAndThat();

private:
    BLocker lock;
};
```

And let's implement the member functions as follows:

```
void BadDog::DoThis()
{
    lock.Lock();
    /* Do this here. */
    lock.Unlock();
}

void BadDog::DoThat()
{
    lock.Lock();
    /* Do that here. */
    lock.Unlock();
}

void BadDog::DoThisAndThat()
{
    lock.Lock();
    DoThis();
    DoThat();
    lock.Unlock();
}
```

Notice that `DoThisAndThat()` wraps the lock around its calls to `DoThis()` and `DoThat()`, both of which contain locks as well. A thread that gets past the `Lock()` call in `DoThisAndThat()` won't block when it calls the nested `Lock()` calls that it runs into in `DoThis()` and `DoThat()`.

Keep in mind that nested Lock() calls must be balanced by equally-nested Unlock() calls.

See also: the BAutolock class

Constructor and Destructor

BLocker()

BLocker(void)
BLocker(const char *name)

Sets up the object. The optional *name* is purely for diagnostics and debugging.

~BLocker()

virtual ~BLocker(void)

Destroys the lock. If there are any threads blocked waiting to lock the object, they're immediately unblocked.

Member Functions

CountLocks()   *see LockingThread()*

CountLockRequests()   *see LockingThread()*

IsLocked()   *see LockingThread()*

Lock(), LockWithTimeout(), Unlock()

bool Lock(void)

status_t LockWithTimeout(bigtime_t *timeout*)

void Unlock(void)

These functions lock and unlock the BLocker.

Lock() attempts to lock the BLocker. It waits without time limit until it can succeed and return **true**. It returns **false** only under exceptional circumstances—for example, if the BLocker and its lock have been destroyed. While a thread has the BLocker is locked, calls to Lock() by other threads will block. The locking thread, on the other hand, can make additional, nested calls to Lock() without blocking.

LockWithTimeout() is an alternative to Lock() that permits you to limit how long it should block waiting for the lock. The *timeout* is specified in microseconds. If

`LockWithTimeout()` can't acquire the lock before the time limit expires, it returns `B_TIMED_OUT`. If the *timeout* is 0, this function doesn't block but immediately returns `B_OK` (if it locked the BLooper) or `B_ERROR` (if it failed to obtain the lock). If the *timeout* is `B_INFINITE_TIMEOUT`, it blocks without limit, just as `Lock()` does. Note that if `Lock()` returns 0 (`false`), it has failed to lock the BLooper, but if `LockWithTimeout()` returns 0 (`B_OK`), it has succeeded.

`Unlock()` releases one level of nested locks and returns immediately. When the BLocker is completely unlocked—when all nested `Lock()` (or `LockWithTimeout()`) calls have been matched by calls to `Unlock()`—the locking thread is "unset", allowing some other thread to obtain the lock. If there are threads blocked waiting for the lock when the lock is released, the thread that's been waiting the longest acquires the lock.

Although you're not prevented from doing so, it's not good form to call `Unlock()` from a thread that doesn't own the lock. For debugging purposes, you can call `IsLocked()` before calling `Unlock()` to make sure this doesn't happen in your code.

LockingThread(), IsLocked(), CountLocks(), CountLockRequests(), Sem()

thread_id **LockingThread**(void) const

bool **IsLocked**(void) const

int32 **CountLocks**(void) const

int32 **CountLockRequests**(void) const

sem_id **Sem**(void) const

These functions provide information that may be useful for debugging purposes.

`LockingThread()` returns the thread that currently has the BLocker locked, or −1 if the BLocker isn't locked.

`IsLocked()` returns `true` if the calling thread currently has the BLocker locked (if it's the locking thread) and `false` if not (if some other thread is the locking thread or the BLocker isn't locked).

`CountLocks()` returns the number of times the locking thread has locked the BLocker—the number of `Lock()` (or `LockWithTimeout()`) calls that have not yet been balanced by matching `Unlock()` calls.

`CountLockRequests()` returns the number of threads currently trying to lock the BLocker. The count includes the thread that currently has the lock plus all threads currently waiting to acquire it.

`Sem()` returns the `sem_id` for the semaphore that the BLocker uses to implement the locking mechanism.

`LockingThread()` returns the thread that currently has the BLooper locked, or −1 if the BLooper isn't locked.

`IsLocked()` returns `true` if the calling thread has the BLooper locked (if it's the lock owner) and `false` if not (if some other thread is the owner or the BLooper isn't locked).

BMemoryIO and BMallocIO

Derived from:　　public BPositionIO

Declared in:　　be/support/DataIO.h

Library:　　libbe.so

Overview

BMallocIO and BMemoryIO objects represent a buffer of dynamically allocated memory. You assign the buffer to a BMemoryIO object on construction, but a BMallocIO object allocates the buffer when you first call `Write()` or `WriteAt()`. On subsequent calls, it makes sure that enough memory is allocated to hold all the data you intend to write, reallocating it if necessary. Memory is allocated in multiples of a block size that you can set.

Both classes implement the BPositionIO protocol. They inherit the `Read()` and `Write()` functions that BPositionIO implements.

Constructor and Destructor

BMemoryIO(), BMallocIO()

```
BMemoryIO (void *buffer size_t numBytes)
BMemoryIO (const void *buffer size_t numBytes)

BMallocIO (void)
```

The BMemoryIO constructor assigns the object a *buffer* with at least *numBytes* of available memory. If the buffer is declared `const`, the object is read-only; calls to `Write()` and `WriteAt()` will fail. Otherwise, the buffer can be both read and written. In either case, the caller retains responsibility for the buffer; the BMemoryIO object won't free it.

The BMallocIO constructor makes sure that the new object is empty and sets the default block size to 256 bytes. The constructor doesn't allocate any memory; memory is allocated when you first write to the object or when you call `SetSize()` to set the amount of memory.

~BMemoryIO(), ~BMallocIO()

> virtual **~BMemoryIO**(void)

> virtual **~BMallocIO**(void)

The BMemoryIO destructor does nothing; the BMallocIO destructor frees all memory that was allocated by the object.

Member Functions

Buffer(), BufferLength()

BMallocIO:

> const void ***Buffer**(void) const

> size_t **BufferLength**(void) const

`Buffer()` returns a pointer to the memory that the BMallocIO object has allocated, or `NULL` if it hasn't yet had occasion to allocate any memory. `BufferLength()` returns the number of data bytes in the buffer (not necessarily the full number of bytes that were allocated).

Position()   see Seek()

ReadAt()

> virtual ssize_t **ReadAt**(off_t *position*, void **buffer*, size_t *numBytes*)

Copies up to *numBytes* bytes of data from the object to the *buffer* and returns the actual number of bytes placed in the buffer. The data is read beginning at the *position* offset.

This function doesn't read beyond the end of the data. If there are fewer than *numBytes* of data available at the *position* offset, it reads only through the last data byte and returns a smaller number than *numBytes*. If *position* is out of range, it returns 0.

Both classes define essentially the same `ReadAt()` function.

Seek(), Position()

> virtual off_t **Seek**(off_t *position*, int32 *mode*)

> virtual off_t **Position**(void) const

Seek() sets the position in the data buffer where the Read() and Write() functions (inherited from BPositionIO) begin reading and writing. How the *position* argument is understood depends on the *mode* flag. There are three possible modes:

- SEEK_SET. The *position* passed is an offset from the beginning of allocated memory; in other words, the current position is set to *position*. For this mode, *position* should be a positive value.

- SEEK_CUR. The *position* argument is an offset from the current position; the value of the argument is added to the current position.

- SEEK_END. The *position* argument is an offset from the end of the buffer for a BMemoryIO object and an offset from the end of the data for a BMallocIO object (not necessarily from the end of allocated memory). Positive values seek beyond the end of the buffer or data; negative values seek backwards into the data.

For BMallocIO, attempts to seek beyond the end of the data and the end of allocated memory are successful. When Write() is subsequently called, the object updates its conception of where the data ends to bring the current position within range. If necessary, enough memory will be allocated to accommodate any data added at the current position. However, Write() will fail for a BMemoryIO object if the current position is beyond the end of assigned memory.

Both Seek() and Position() return the current position as an offset in bytes from the beginning of allocated memory.

SetBlockSize(), SetSize()

BMallocIO:
> void **SetBlockSize**(size_t *blockSize*)
> virtual status_t **SetSize**(off_t *numBytes*)

SetBlockSize() sets the size of the memory blocks that the BMallocIO object deals with. The object allocates memory in multiples of the block size. The default is 256 bytes.

SetSize() sets the size of allocated memory to *numBytes* (modulo the block size). Shrinking the buffer should always be successful (B_OK); if the buffer can't be grown, B_NO_MEMORY is returned.

WriteAt()

virtual ssize_t **WriteAt**(off_t *position*, const void **buffer, size_t *numBytes*)

Copies *numBytes* bytes of data from *buffer* into allocated memory beginning at *position*, and returns the number of bytes written.

For BMallocIO, a successful `WriteAt()` always return *numBytes*—`WriteAt()` reallocates the buffer (in multiples of the block size) if it needs more room. If the reallocation fails, this function returns `B_NO_MEMORY`.

However, the BMemoryIO version of `WriteAt()` won't write outside the memory buffer. If *position* is beyond the end of the buffer, it returns 0. If the object is read-only, it returns `B_NOT_ALLOWED`.

BStopWatch

Derived from: (nada)

Declared in: be/support/StopWatch.h

Library: libbe.so

Overview

The BStopWatch class is a debugging tool that you can use to time the execution of portions of your code. When a BStopWatch object is constructed, it starts its internal timer. When it's deleted, it stops the timer and prints the elapsed time to standard out in this format:

StopWatch "*name*": *f* usecs.

Where *name* is the name that you gave to the object when you constructed it, and *f* is the elapsed time in microseconds.

Look at all these other things you can do:

- Suspend, resume, and reset the timer (`Suspend()`, `Resume()`, `Reset()`).
- Ask for the current elapsed time without stopping the timer (`ElapsedTime()`).
- Record "lap points" that are printed out at the end of the run (`Lap()`).

Using a BStopWatch is simple; this...

```
BStopWatch *watch = new BStopWatch("Timer 0");
/* The code you want to time goes here. */
delete watch;
...
```

...will produce, on standard out, a message that goes something like this:

```
StopWatch "Timer 0": 492416 usecs.
```

This would indicate that the timed code took about half a second to execute—remember, you're looking at microseconds.

If you want to time an entire function, just toss a StopWatch on the stack:

```
void MyFunc()
{
   BStopWatch watch("Timer 0");
   ...
}
```

When the function returns, the BStopWatch prints its message.

WARNING

BStopWatch objects are useful if you want to get an idea of where your cycles are going. But you shouldn't rely on them for painfully accurate measurements.

There's no run-time toggle to control a BStopWatch. Make sure you remove your BStopWatch objects after you're done debugging your code.

Constructor and Destructor

BStopWatch()

`BStopWatch`(const char *name*, bool *silent* = `false`)

Creates a BStopWatch object, names it, and starts its timer. If *silent* is `false` (the default), the object will print its elapsed time when its destroyed; if it's `true`, the message isn't printed. To get the elapsed time from a silent BStopWatch, call `ElapsedTime()`.

~BStopWatch()

`~BStopWatch`(void)

Stops the object's timer, spits out a timing message to standard out (unless it's running silently), and then destroys the object and everything it believes in. By default the timing message looks like this:

StopWatch "*name*": *f* usecs.

If you've recorded some lap points (through the `Lap()` function), you'll also see the lap times as well:

StopWatch "*name*": *f* usecs.
   [*lap#*: *soFar#thisLap*]   [*lap#*: *soFar#thisLap*]   [*lap#*: *soFar#thisLap*]...

...where *lap#* is the number of the lap, *soFar* is the total elapsed time at that lap, and *thisLap* is the time it took to complete the lap.

Member Functions

ElapsedTime()

bigtime_t ElapsedTime(void) const

Returns the elapsed time, in microseconds, since the object was created or was last Reset(). This function doesn't print the time message, nor does it touch the timer (the timer keeps running—unless it's paused).

```
BStopWatch watch("Timer 0");
...
printf("Elapsed time:  %Ld\n", watch.ElapsedTime());
```

Lap()

bigtime_t Lap()

Records a "lap point" and returns the total elapsed time so far. When the object is destroyed, the lap point times are printed individually. You can record as many as eight lap points; if you ask for a ninth lap point, the lap isn't recorded and this function returns 0. See ~BStopWatch() for a description of what the lap points look like when they're printed.

WARNING

The only way to get the lap times after they've been recorded is by destroying the object. If the object is silent, calling Lap() is effectively the same as calling ElapsedTime().

Name()

const char *Name(void) const

Returns the name of the object, as set in the constructor.

Reset()   *see Suspend()*

Resume()   *see Suspend()*

Suspend(), Resume(), Reset()

void Suspend(void)
void Resume(void)
void Reset(void)

These functions affect the object's timer.

`Suspend()` stops the timer but doesn't reset it.

`Resume()` start the timer running again.

`Reset()` sets the elapsed time to 0, but doesn't stop the timer. You can call `Reset()` at any time, regardless of whether the object is running or suspended.

Functions and Macros

Library: libbe.so

This section lists the Support Kit's general-purpose functions and macros. These functions can be called by programs using any part of the Be operating system.

atomic_add(), atomic_and(), atomic_or()

`be/support/SupportDefs.h`

int32 atomic_add(int32 *atomicVariable*, int32 *addValue*)
int32 atomic_and(int32 *atomicVariable*, int32 *andValue*)
int32 atomic_or(int32 *atomicVariable*, int32 *orValue*)

These functions perform the named operations (addition, bitwise *AND*, or bitwise *OR*) on the 32-bit value found in *atomicVariable*, thus:

```
*atomicVariable += addValue
*atomicVariable &= andValue
*atomicVariable |= orValue
```

Each function returns the previous value of the `int32` variable that *atomicVariable* points to (in other words, they each return the value that was in **atomicVariable* before the operation was performed).

The significance of these functions is that they're guaranteed to be *atomic*: If two threads attempt to access the same atomic variable at the same time (through these functions), one of the two threads will be made to wait until the other thread has completed the operation and updated the *atomicVariable* value.

beep()

`be/support/Beep.h`

status_t **beep**(void)

Produces the system beep. This function engages the Audio Server, but doesn't wait for the sound to play. If it can't contact the server to play the beep, it returns `B_ERROR`. If it can make contact but can't get a satisfactory reply back from the server, it returns `B_BAD_REPLY`. Otherwise, it returns `B_OK`.

See also: `play_sound()` in the Media Kit

cast_as()   *see class_name()*

class_name(), is_instance_of(), is_kind_of(), cast_as()

be/support/ClassInfo.h

const char *class_name(*object*)

bool is_instance_of(*object, class*)

bool is_kind_of(*object, class*)

class *cast_as(*object, class*)

These macros deliver information about an object's type, including the name of its class and its standing in the class hierarchy. In each case, the *object* argument is a pointer to an object; it can be an object of any type (it doesn't have to descend from any particular class). The *class* argument is a class name—*not* a string such as "BApplication", but the type name itself (literally BApplication).

class_name() returns a pointer to the name of *object*'s class.

is_instance_of() returns true if *object* is an instance of *class*, and false otherwise.

is_kind_of() returns true if *object* is an instance of *class* or an instance of any class that inherits from *class*, and false if not.

cast_as() returns a pointer to *object* cast as a pointer to an object of *class*, but only if *object* is a kind of *class*. If not, *object* cannot be safely cast as a pointer to *class*, so cast_as() returns NULL.

For example, given this slice of the inheritance hierarchy from the Interface Kit,

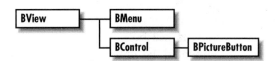

and code like this that creates an instance of the BPictureButton class,

BButton *anObject = new BPictureButton(...);

the first three macros would work as follows:

- The class_name() macro would return a pointer to the string "BPictureButton":

  const char *s = class_name(anObject);

- The is_instance_of() macro would return true only if the *class* passed to it is BPictureButton. In the following example, it would return false, and the message would not be printed. Even though BPictureButton inherits from BView, the object is an instance of the BPictureButton class, not BView:

```
if ( is_instance_of(anObject, BView) )
    printf("The object is an instance of BView.\n");
```

- The is_kind_of() macro would return true if *class* is BPictureButton or any class that BPictureButton inherits from. In the following example, it would return true and the message would be printed. A BPictureButton is a kind of BView:

```
if ( is_kind_of(anObject, BView) )
    printf("The object is a kind of BView.\n");
```

Note that class names are not passed as strings, but class_name() returns the name as a string.

The cast_as() macro is most useful when you want to treat a generic object as an instance of a more specific class. Suppose, for example, that the BPictureButton mentioned above becomes the focus view for a window and you retrieve it by calling the BWindow's CurrentFocus() function:

```
BView *focus = myWindow->CurrentFocus();
```

Since the focus view might be any type of view, CurrentFocus() returns a pointer to an object of the base BView class. Unless you know otherwise, you cannot treat the object as anything more specific than a BView instance. However, you can ask the object if it's a kind of BPictureButton and, if it is, cast it to the BPictureButton type:

```
if ( is_kind_of(focus, BPictureButton) ) {
    BPictureButton *picbutton = (BPictureButton *)focus);
    if ( picbutton->Behavior() == B_TWO_STATE_BUTTON )
        . . .
}
```

The cast_as() macro does the same thing, but more efficiently. It casts the object to the target class if it is safe to do so—if the *object* is an instance of a class that inherits from the target *class* or an instance of the target *class* itself—and returns NULL if not.

```
BPictureButton *picbutton = cast_as(focus, BPictureButton);
if ( picbutton ) {
    if ( picbutton->Behavior() == B_TWO_STATE_BUTTON )
        . . .
}
```

cast_as() is often used in place of the cast operator to assure code safety even where an expected result is anticipated and there's no need for an intermediate variable (like *focus*):

```
BPictureButton *picbutton =
            cast_as(myWindow->CurrentFocus(), BPictureButton);
if ( picbutton ) {
        . . .
}
```

The `cast_as()` and `is_kind_of()` macros work alike; they're both based on the C++ `dynamic_cast` operator and they reflect its behavior. To describe that behavior more precisely, let's adopt the following shorthand terms for an object's type:

- The *real type* of an object is its type on construction. For example, if you construct an instance of the BButton class, as shown above, BButton is its real type.

- The *declared type* of an object is the class label it currently bears. For example, `CurrentFocus()` returns an object whose declared class is BView.

Either of these types can be compared to a *target type*, the type you want to cast the object to or test it against. The target type is the *class* argument passed to the macros.

In the best of all possible worlds, you'd want to ignore the declared type of an object and compare only the real type to the target type. However, the `dynamic_cast` operator—and by extension `cast_as()` and `is_kind_of()`—considers the real type only if it has to. It first compares the object's declared type to the target type. It assumes that the declared type is accurate (that the object is truly the kind of object it's represented to be) and it summarily handles the obvious cases: If the target type is the same as the declared type or if it's a class that the declared type inherits from, the operation will succeed. Consequently, `cast_as()` will cast the object to the target type and `is_kind_of()` will return `true`, regardless of the object's real type. In other words, if the target class is above or at the same level as the declared class in the inheritance hierarchy, the real class is ignored.

However, if the declared type doesn't match or derive from the target type, `dynamic_cast` and the macros look at the real type: If the target class is identical to the real type, or if it's a class that the real type derives from, the operation succeeds. If not, it fails.

Therefore, the `is_kind_of()` and `cast_as()` macros will produce reliable results as long as objects are not arbitrarily cast to types that may not be accurate. For example, you should not cast an object to a target type and then attempt to use `is_kind_of()` to determine if the cast was correct. This code is unreliable:

```
BPictureButton *picbutton =
                    (BPictureButton *)myWindow->CurrentFocus();
if ( is_kind_of(picbutton, BPictureButton) ) {
    . . .
}
```

In this example, `is_kind_of()` will always return `true`, no matter what the class of the current focus view. The general rule is that the declared type of an object must *always* be accurate; an object should be typed only to its own class or to a class that it inherits from. The macros cannot rescue you from an inaccurate cast.

convert_to_utf8(), convert_from_utf8()

```
be/support/UTF8.h
```

status_t **convert_to_utf8**(uint32 *sourceEncoding,*
const char **source,*
int32 **sourceLength,*
char **destination,*
int32 **destinationLength*)

status_t **convert_from_utf8**(uint32 *destinationEncoding,*
const char **source,*
int32 **sourceLength,*
char **destination,*
int32 **destinationLength*)

These functions convert text to and from the Unicode UTF-8 encoding that's standard for the Be operating system and is assumed in most contexts. UTF-8 is described under "Character Encoding" in the section "Responding to the User" of Chapter 4, *The Interface Kit.*

convert_to_utf8() permits you to take text that's encoded according to another standard and convert it to UTF-8 for the BeOS. convert_from_utf8() lets you convert text from UTF-8 to other encodings for other venues (for example, to the encodings commonly used for displaying text on the World Wide Web).

The first argument passed to these functions names the other encoding—the source encoding for convert_to_utf8() and the destination encoding for convert_from_utf8(). It can be any of the following constants:

B_ISO1_CONVERSION

B_ISO2_CONVERSION

B_ISO3_CONVERSION

B_ISO4_CONVERSION

B_ISO5_CONVERSION

B_ISO6_CONVERSION

B_ISO7_CONVERSION

B_ISO8_CONVERSION

B_ISO9_CONVERSION

B_ISO10_CONVERSION

B_MAC_ROMAN_CONVERSION

B_SJIS_CONVERSION

B_EUC_CONVERSION

Most of these constants designate encoding schemes that are supported by the BFont class in the Interface Kit and its `SetEncoding()` function. They parallel the constants that are passed to that function. For example, `B_ISO1_CONVERSION` (for these functions) and `B_ISO_8859_1` (for `SetEncoding()`) both designate the extended ASCII encoding defined in part one of ISO 8859 (Latin 1). Similarly, `B_ISO2_CONVERSION` matches `B_ISO_8859_2`, `B_ISO3_CONVERSION` matches `B_ISO_8859_3`, and so on. `B_MAC_ROMAN_CONVERSION` matches `B_MACINTOSH_ROMAN`. (`B_ISO10_CONVERSION` is not implemented for this release.)

`B_SJIS_CONVERSION` stands for the Shift-JIS (Japanese Industrial Standard) encoding of Japanese and `B_EUC_CONVERSION` stands for the EUC (Extended UNIX Code) encoding of Japanese in packed format.

Both functions convert up to *sourceLength* bytes of text from the *source* buffer. They write up to *destinationLength* bytes of converted text into the *destination* buffer. The amount of text that they actually convert is therefore constrained both by the amount of source text (*sourceLength*) and the capacity of the output buffer (*destinationLength*). Neither function stops at a null terminator ('\0') when reading the input buffer nor adds one to the text in the output buffer; they depend only on *sourceLength* and *destinationLength* for guidance.

When finished, these functions modify the variable that *sourceLength* refers to so that it reports the number of bytes of source text actually converted. They also modify the variable that *destinationLength* refers to so that it reports the number of bytes actually written to the destination buffer. Neither function will stop in the middle of a multibyte source character; they're guaranteed to convert only full characters.

If either function encounters a character in the source that the destination format doesn't allow, it puts a question mark ("?") in its place in the output text. This is much more likely to occur when converting from UTF-8 than when converting to it, since Unicode represents a very large number of characters.

If successful in converting at least one source character, both functions return `B_OK`. If unsuccessful, for example, if they don't recognize the source or destination encoding, they return `B_ERROR`. If there's an error, you should not trust any of the output arguments.

See also: `BFont::SetEncoding()`, "Character Encoding" in the section "Responding to the User" of Chapter 4, *The Interface Kit*

find_instantiation_func()

```
be/support/Archivable.h
```

instantiation_func **find_instantiation_func**(const char *_className_)
instantiation_func **find_instantiation_func**(BMessage *_archive_)

Returns a pointer to the `Instantiate()` function that can create instances of the *className* class, or `NULL` if the function can't be found. If passed a BMessage *archive*, `find_instantiation_func()` gets the name of the class from a `B_STRING_TYPE` field called "class" in the BMessage.

The `instantiation_func` type is defined as follows:

    BArchivable *(*instantiation_func) (BMessage *)

In other words, the function has the same syntax as the `Instantiate()` function declared in the BArchivable class and replicated in derived classes (with class-specific return values).

The function that's returned can be called like any C function; you don't need the class name or another object of the class. For example:

```
instantiation_func func;
if ( func = find_instantiation_func(arhiveMessage) ) {
    BArchivable *object = func(archiveMessage);
}
```

`instantiate_object()` will do this work for you.

See also: `BArchivable::Instantiate()`, `instantiate_object()`

instantiate_object()

    be/support/Archivable.h

BArchivable *__instantiate_object__(BMessage *__archive__)

Creates and returns a new instance of an archived object, or returns `NULL` if the object can't be constructed. The object is created by calling the `Instantiate()` function for the class of the object recorded in the *archive* BMessage.

To find the `Instantiate()` function it should call, `instantiate_object()` gets the class name of the archived object from the BMessage *archive*. It takes the first name it finds in a field called "class". If the class is not part of the loaded image, it looks for a `B_STRING_TYPE` field named "add_on" for the signature of an add-on image it can load. If the signature is found and the file exists, it will load the image and again look for the class definition and `Instantiate()` function in the new code. If it still can't find the function, `instantiate_object()` tries other class names in the "class" array, working its way up the class hierarchy. If, after exhausting the class list, it cannot match the archive to an `Instantiate()` function, it returns `NULL`.

When successful, `instantiate_object()` returns the object that `Instantiate()` created, but typed to the base BArchivable class. The `cast_as()` macro can type it to a more capable class.

```
BArchivable *base = instantiate_object(archive);
if ( base ) {
    TheClass *object = cast_as(base, TheClass);
    if ( object ) {
        . . .
    }
}
```

Because `instantiate_object()` will look for and load the code needed to run the archived object, it's possible to package an object and deliver it to an application that, until the package arrived, knew nothing of the object or its class.

See also: the BArchivable class, `find_instantiation_func()`

is_instance_of()   *see class_name()*

is_kind_of()   *see class_name()*

min(), max(), min_c(), max_c()

be/support/SupportDefs.h

min(*a, b*)
min_c(*a, b*)

max(*a, b*)
max_c(*a, b*)

These macros compare two integers or floating-point numbers. `min()` and `min_c()` return the lesser of the two (or *b* if they're equal); `max()` and `max_c()` return the greater of the two (or *a* if they're equal). `min()` and `max()` are not defined for C++ (that is, if `__cplusplus` is defined), since C++ uses those two names for another purpose. Their identical counterparts, `min_c()` and `max_c()`, are defined for all programs.

read_16_swap(), read_32_swap(), write_16_swap(), write_32_swap()

be/support/SupportDefs.h

int16 `read_16_swap`(int16 *address*)
int32 `read_32_swap`(int32 *address*)

void `write_16_swap`(int16 *address*, int16 *value*)
void `write_32_swap`(int32 *address*, int32 *value*)

The read...() functions read a 16- or 32-bit value from *address*, reverse the order of the bytes in the value, and return the swapped value directly.

The write...() functions swap the bytes in the *value* passed and write the swapped value to *address*.

validate_instantiation()

be/support/Archivable.h

bool **validate_instantiation**(BMessage **archive*, const char **className*)

Returns true if the *archive* BMessage contains data for an object belonging to the *className* class, and false if not. The determination is made by looking for the class name in a "class" array in the *archive*. If the class name appears anywhere in the array, this function returns true. If not, it returns false.

write_16_swap()   *see read_16_swap()*

write_32_swap()   *see read_16_swap()*

Constants and Defined Types

This section lists the constants and types defined by the Support Kit and used throughout the entire Be operating system. Not included here are constants used as status_t values (error codes). They're listed in "Error Codes" on page 846.

Constants

Boolean Constants

be/support/SupportDefs.h

Constant	Value
false	0
true	1

These constants are defined as values for the bool type (described in the next section). The BeOS defines them for C code only. Because they match the boolean symbols that are part of the C++ language, they let you use the same bool type and true and false values when programming in both languages.

See also: bool

Encoding Conversion Constants

`be/support/UTF8.h`

Constant
B_ISO1_CONVERSION
B_ISO2_CONVERSION
B_ISO3_CONVERSION
B_ISO4_CONVERSION
B_ISO5_CONVERSION
B_ISO6_CONVERSION
B_ISO7_CONVERSION
B_ISO8_CONVERSION
B_ISO9_CONVERSION
B_ISO10_CONVERSION
B_MAC_ROMAN_CONVERSION
B_SJIS_CONVERSION
B_EUC_CONVERSION

These constants identify character encodings to the `convert_to_utf8()` and `convert_from_utf8()` functions, which convert text to and from the standard UTF-8 character encoding assumed by the BeOS. They identify the source encoding for a conversion to UTF-8 and the destination encoding for a conversion from UTF-8.

See also: `convert_to_utf8()`, the BFont class in the Interface Kit

Empty String

`be/support/SupportDefs.h`

const char **B_EMPTY_STRING**

This constant provides a global pointer to an empty string ("").

NULL and NIL

`be/support/SupportDefs.h`

Constant	Value
NIL	0
NULL	0

These constants represent "empty" values. They're synonyms that can be used interchangeably.

Type Codes

`be/support/TypeConstants.h`

Constant	Meaning
B_CHAR_TYPE	A single character
B_INT8_TYPE	An 8-bit integer
B_INT16_TYPE	A 16-bit integer
B_INT32_TYPE	A 32-bit integer
B_INT64_TYPE	A 64-bit integer
B_UINT8_TYPE	An unsigned 8-bit integer
B_UINT16_TYPE	An unsigned 16-bit integer
B_UINT32_TYPE	An unsigned 32-bit integer
B_UINT64_TYPE	An unsigned 64-bit integer
B_FLOAT_TYPE	A `float`
B_DOUBLE_TYPE	A `double`
B_BOOL_TYPE	A boolean value (the `bool` type)
B_OFF_T_TYPE	An `off_t` value
B_SIZE_T_TYPE	A `size_t` value
B_SSIZE_T_TYPE	An `ssize_t` value
B_POINTER_TYPE	A pointer of some kind (including `void *`)
B_OBJECT_TYPE	An object pointer (such as BMessage *)
B_MESSAGE_TYPE	A BMessage object (not BMessage *)
B_MESSENGER_TYPE	A BMessenger object
B_POINT_TYPE	A BPoint object
B_RECT_TYPE	A BRect object
B_PATH_TYPE	A BPath object
B_REF_TYPE	An `entry_ref` structure
B_RGB_COLOR_TYPE	An `rgb_color` structure
B_PATTERN_TYPE	A `pattern` structure
B_ASCII_TYPE	Text in ASCII format
B_STRING_TYPE	A null-terminated character string
B_MONOCHROME_1_BIT_TYPE	Raw data for a monochrome bitmap (1 bit/pixel)
B_GRAYSCALE_8_BIT_TYPE	Raw data for a grayscale bitmap (8 bits per pixel)
B_COLOR_8_BIT_TYPE	Raw bitmap data in the `B_COLOR_8_BIT` color space
B_RGB_32_BIT_TYPE	Raw bitmap data in the `B_RGB_32_BIT` color space
B_TIME_TYPE	A representation of the time

Constant	Meaning
B_RAW_TYPE	Raw, untyped data—a stream of bytes
B_MIME_TYPE	The type is specified by a MIME string
B_ANY_TYPE	The type can be any type

These constants describe the types of data held by BMessage objects (the Application Kit) and as resources and file system attributes (the Storage Kit). B_ANY_TYPE refers to all types; it indicates that the exact type doesn't matter. B_MIME_TYPE indicates that the name of the data in the BMessage is a MIME string that specifies its true data type. The other constants refer only to a particular type. The type_code defined type marks where these constants are used in the API.

Applications can define their own type codes for data types not found on this list. All the codes the BeOS defines, or will define in the future, have values formed by concatenating four uppercase letters into a multicharacter constant. For example, B_MESSENGER_TYPE is "MSNG" and B_SIZE_T_TYPE is "SIZT".

To prevent clashes, the type codes you define should use a different convention. For example, you might include at least one lowercase letter in all multicharacter constants or you might choose a range of values that doesn't intersect with the range 0x41414141 through 0x5a5a5a5a.

See also: type_code

Defined Types

bigtime_t

be/support/SupportDefs.h

typedef int64 **bigtime_t**

This type records the time in microseconds as a 64-bit integer. Typically, a bigtime_t variable measures the system time, the number of microseconds since 12:00:00 AM January 1, 1970, UTC (Coordinated Universal Time).

See also: system_time()

bool

be/support/SupportDefs.h

typedef unsigned char **bool**

The C++ language defines bool as its basic boolean type. The BeOs extends the definition to C code, so you can use the same type in both languages. The true and false constants (listed above) are defined as boolean values.

Function Pointers

be/support/SupportDefs.h

typedef int (*B_PFI)()
typedef long (*B_PFL)()
typedef void (*B_PFV)()

These types are pointers to functions that return int, long, and void values respectively.

instantiation_func

be/support/Archivable.h

typedef BArchivable *(*instantiation_func) (BMessage *)

This type is a pointer to a function that can instantiate an object from a BMessage archive and return a pointer to the new object. The member Instantiate() function that's part of the archiving protocol is such a function.

See also: the BArchivable class, find_instantiation_func()

Integer Types

be/support/SupportDefs.h

typedef unsigned char uchar

typedef signed char int8
typedef unsigned char uint8
typedef volatile signed char vint8
typedef volatile unsigned char vuint8

typedef short int16
typedef unsigned short uint16
typedef volatile short vint16
typedef volatile unsigned short vuint16

typedef long int32
typedef unsigned long uint32
typedef volatile long vint32
typedef volatile unsigned long vuint32

typedef long long int64
typedef unsigned long long uint64
typedef volatile long long vint64
typedef volatile unsigned long long vuint64

These type names are defined as shorthands for standard integers of various sizes. They're used in place of int, short, and long throughout the BeOS API.

The number at the end of the type name indicates the size of the integer. For example, a uint32 is an unsigned 32-bit value. The type is guaranteed to be defined to its stated size for all platforms (thus their exact definitions may vary from platform to platform).

Using these types will make the code you write more portable. They'll help avoid problems as the operating system and your application move to other platforms.

status_t

be/support/SupportDefs.h

typedef int32 **status_t**

This type indicates an error code; it's used mainly for function return values.

See also: "Error Codes"

type_code

be/support/SupportDefs.h

typedef uint32 **type_code**

This type is used for the integer codes that indicate a particular data type. The codes—such as B_UINT32_TYPE and B_MIME_TYPE—mark the type of data added to a message or stored as a resource and also appear in other contexts.

See also: the BMessage class in the Application Kit, the BResource class in the Storage Kit

Error Codes

Declared in: be/support/Errors.h

Error codes are returned by various functions to indicate the success or to describe the failure of a requested operation.

All Be error constants except for B_OK (B_NO_ERROR) are negative integers; any function that returns an error code can thus be lazily tested for success or failure by the following:

```
if ( funcCall() < B_NO_ERROR )
   /* failure */
else
   /* success */
```

All constants (except B_NO_ERROR and B_ERROR) are less than or equal to the value of the B_ERRORS_END constant. If you want to define your own negative-valued error codes, you should begin with the value (B_ERRORS_END + 1) and work your way toward 0.

POSIX Errors

The BeOS supports the POSIX error code constants (these constants start with the letter "E", as in EBADF or ENOENT). A number of Be-defined constants are synonyms for the POSIX constants; for example, the Be equivalent for ENOENT is B_ENTRY_NOT_FOUND.

Most of the General Error Codes, and all the File System Error Codes are covers for POSIX errors. The POSIX equivalents are listed where applicable.

The POSIX constants, and the Be synonyms, can be passed to the POSIX strerror() function. The function, defined in *posix/string.h*, returns a human-readable description of the error:

```
char *strerror(int error_code)
```

General Error Codes

Code	POSIX	Description
B_NO_MEMORY	ENOMEM	There's not enough memory for the operation
B_IO_ERROR	EIO	A general input/output error occurred
B_PERMISSION_DENIED	EACCESS	Illegal access
B_BAD_INDEX		The index is out of range
B_BAD_VALUE	EINVAL	An illegal value was passed to the function
B_MISMATCHED_VALUES		Conflicting values were passed to the function
B_BAD_TYPE		An illegal argument type was named or passed
B_NAME_NOT_FOUND		There's no match for the specified name
B_NAME_IN_USE		The requested (unique) name is already used
B_BUSY	EBUSY	A device is busy, or a file is locked
B_NOT_ALLOWED	EPERM	Operation not allowed
B_NO_INIT		An object or structure isn't properly initialized
B_TIMED_OUT	ETIMEDOUT	Time expired before the operation was finished
B_INTERRUPTED	EINTR	A signal interrupted the operation
B_WOULD_BLOCK	EAGAIN	But you don't want to block
B_WOULD_BLOCK	EWOULDBLOCK	Same as the above

Code	POSIX	Description
B_ERROR = -1		A convenient catchall for general errors
B_NO_ERROR = 0		Everything's OK
B_OK		Same as B_NO_ERROR

File System Error Codes

Code	POSIX	Description
B_FILE_ERROR	EBADF	A file error occurred
B_FILE_EXISTS	EEXIST	And you don't want to clobber it
B_ENTRY_NOT_FOUND	ENOENT	The requested entry doesn't exist
B_NAME_TOO_LONG	ENAMETOOLONG	Leaf or pathname too long
B_NO_MORE_FDS	EMFILE	No more file descriptors
B_NOT_A_DIRECTORY	ENOTDIR	When it should have been
B_IS_A_DIRECTORY	EISDIR	When it shouldn't be
B_DIRECTORY_NOT_EMPTY	ENOTEMPTY	Attempt to delete a non-empty directory
B_DEVICE_FULL	ENOSPC	Full disk
B_READ_ONLY_DEVICE	EROFS	Write request on a read-only file system
B_CROSS_DEVICE_LINK	EXDEV	Hard link across devices not allowed
B_LINK_LIMIT	ELOOP	Nested links too deep
B_BUSTED_PIPE	EPIPE	Pipe no longer functional

Application Kit Error Codes

Code	Description
B_DUPLICATE_REPLY	A reply message has already been sent
B_BAD_REPLY	The reply message is inappropriate and can't be sent
B_BAD_HANDLER	The designated message handler isn't valid
B_MESSAGE_TO_SELF	A thread is trying to send a message to itself
B_ALREADY_RUNNING	The application can't be launched again
B_LAUNCH_FAILED	The attempt to launch the application failed
B_AMBIGUOUS_APP_LAUNCH	Odd things happening in app land
B_UNKOWN_MIME_TYPE	Application signature unknown
B_BAD_SCRIPT_SYNTAX	Script syntax malformed

Kernel Kit Error Codes

Code	Description
B_BAD_THREAD_ID	Specified thread identifier (`thread_id`) is invalid
B_BAD_THREAD_STATE	The thread is in the wrong state for the operation
B_NO_MORE_THREADS	All thread identifiers are currently taken
B_BAD_TEAM_ID	Specified team identifier (`team_id`) is invalid
B_NO_MORE_TEAMS	All team identifiers are currently taken
B_BAD_PORT_ID	Specified port identifier (`port_id`) is invalid
B_NO_MORE_PORTS	All port identifiers have been taken
B_BAD_SEM_ID	Semaphore identifier (`sem_id`) is invalid
B_NO_MORE_SEMS	All semaphores are currently taken
B_BAD_IMAGE_ID	Specified image identifier (`image_id`)is invalid
B_NOT_AN_EXECUTABLE	An executable image was expected
B_BAD_ADDRESS	Illegal address

Media Kit Error Codes

Code	Description
B_STREAM_NOT_FOUND	The attempt to locate the stream failed
B_SERVER_NOT_FOUND	The attempt to locate the server failed
B_RESOURCE_NOT_FOUND	The attempt to locate the resource failed
B_RESOURCE_UNAVAILABLE	Permission to access the resource was denied
B_BAD_SUBSCRIBER	The BSubscriber is invalid
B_SUBSCRIBER_NOT_ENTERED	The BSubscriber hasn't entered the stream
B_BUFFER_NOT_AVAILABLE	The attempt to acquire the buffer failed

Mail Errors

Code	Description
B_MAIL_NO_DAEMON	mail_daemon not running
B_MAIL_UNKNOWN_USER	User unknown
B_MAIL_WRONG_PASSWORD	Password doesn't match user
B_MAIL_UNKNOWN_HOST	POP or SMTP host unrecognized
B_MAIL_ACCESS_ERROR	Couldn't access host
B_MAIL_UNKNOWN_FIELD	Unrecognized message field name
B_MAIL_NO_RECIPIENT	Return to sender, address unknown
B_MAIL_INVALID_MAIL	Invalid mail invalid mail invalid

Device Kit Errors

Code
B_DEV_INVALID_IOCTL
B_DEV_NO_MEMORY
B_DEV_BAD_DRIVE_NUM
B_DEV_NO_MEDIA
B_DEV_UNREADABLE
B_DEV_FORMAT_ERROR
B_DEV_TIMEOUT
B_DEV_RECALIBRATE_ERROR
B_DEV_SEEK_ERROR
B_DEV_ID_ERROR
B_DEV_READ_ERROR
B_DEV_WRITE_ERROR
B_DEV_NOT_READY
B_DEV_MEDIA_CHANGED

Message Protocols

This appendix describes the formats for messages that are recognized by Be system software. The list includes every system message and every kind of message that you can deliver to a Be application or a Be-defined class.

For information on the messaging system, see "Messaging" in Chapter 2, *The Application Kit.*

System Messages

Messages that are dispatched and handled in a message-specific manner are known as *system messages.* For the most part, these are messages that the system produces and that applications are expected to respond to (by implementing hook functions matched to the messages), but some are messages that applications must produce themselves. They can be grouped into two categories, based on the scope of the message and the kind of object that's expected to respond:

- *Application messages* are delivered to the BApplication object.
- *Interface messages* are reported to BWindow objects and handled by BWindows and their BView.

Application Messages

Application messages concern the application as a whole, rather than one specific window or thread. They're all received and handled by the BApplication object. See BApplication class description for information on when they're produced and how they should be handled.

B_ABOUT_REQUESTED

This message requests the BApplication object to put a window on-screen with information about the application. Every application should set up an "About..." menu item that will send the message to the BApplication object. The BApplication object dispatches the message by calling its own `AboutRequested()` function.

As defined, this message contains no data. However, since each application must initiate the message on its own and respond to it by implementing `AboutRequested()`, you can add information to it if it suits your purposes.

B_APP_ACTIVATED

This message informs the application that it has become the active application, or that it has relinquished that status to another application. The BApplication object dispatches the message by calling `AppActivated()`.

It contains one data field:

Field	Type code	Description
"active"	B_BOOL_TYPE	**true** if the application has just become the active application, and **false** if it just gave up that status.

B_ARGV_RECEIVED

This message passes the BApplication object command-line strings, typically ones the user typed in a shell. The BApplication object dispatches it by calling `ArgvReceived()`.

The message has the two expected data fields for command-line arguments:

Field	Type code	Description
"argc"	B_INT32_TYPE	The number of items in the "argv" array. This will be the same number that **BMessage::GetInfo()** for "argv" would report.
"argv"	B_STRING_TYPE	The command-line strings. Each argument is stored as an independent item under the "argv" name—that is, there's an array of data items, each of type **char ***, rather than a single item of type **char ****.
"cwd"	B_STRING_TYPE	The full path name of the current working directory of the source of the message.

The path name might be important for interpreting some arguments in the "argv" array. If the message reports what the user typed in a command-line shell, "cwd" is the current working directory of that shell. If the message reports arguments passed to BRoster's Launch() function, "cwd" is the current working directory of the thread in which Launch() was called.

When launching an application, the Tracker sets the current working directory of its main thread to the user's home directory. Spawned threads inherit the current working directory of their parent threads.

B_PULSE

This message contains no data. It's posted at regular intervals as a timing mechanism. The BApplication object dispatches it by calling the Pulse() function declared in the BApplication class.

B_QUIT_REQUESTED

This message asks a BLooper object to quit its message loop and destroy itself. The BLooper dispatches it by calling its own QuitRequested() function. In other words, the dispatching of B_QUIT_REQUESTED messages is defined in the BLooper class.

When it gets the message, the BApplication object interprets it to be a request to shut the entire application down, not just one thread. BApplication's QuitRequested() implementation forwards the message to each of its BWindow objects.

A B_QUIT_REQUESTED message usually contains no data. However, if the source of the message is the Command-*q* shortcut, it will have one data field:

Field	Type code	Description
"shortcut"	B_BOOL_TYPE	true, to indicate that the system produced the message when the user typed Command-*q*. If the message isn't the result of a shortcut, this field will be absent, not false.

B_READY_TO_RUN

This message contains no data fields. It's delivered to the BApplication object to mark the application's readiness to accept message input after being launched. The BApplication object dispatches it by calling ReadyToRun().

B_REFS_RECEIVED

This message passes the application one or more references to entries in the file system. It's typically produced by the Tracker when the user chooses some files for the application to open. The BApplication object dispatches it by calling RefsReceived().

The message has one data field, which might be an array of more than one item:

Field	Type code	Description
"refs"	B_REF_TYPE	One or more entry_ref items referring to files or directories. Typically, they're documents the application is expected to open.

If a B_REFS_RECEIVED message is dropped on a Tracker window, the Tracker will deliver it to the preferred application for the documents in the "refs" array.

Interface Messages

Interface messages inform BWindow objects and their BViews about activity in the user interface. Unlike application messages, most of which consist only of a command constant, almost all interface messages contain data fields describing an event. They're all delivered to a BWindow object, which dispatches some to itself but most to its BViews.

See "Interface Messages" under "Responding to the User" in Chapter 4, *The Interface Kit*, for a discussion of the events these messages report.

B_KEY_DOWN

This message reports that the user pressed a character key on the keyboard. It's dispatched by calling the KeyDown() function of the target BView, generally the window's focus view. However, if a Command key is held down, the message performs a keyboard shortcut and is not dispatched. Most keys produce repeated B_KEY_DOWN messages—as long as the user keeps holding the key down and doesn't press another key.

Each message contains the following data fields:

Field	Type code	Description
"when"	B_INT64_TYPE	When the key went down, given as the number of microseconds since 12:00:00 AM January 1, 1970.
"key"	B_INT32_TYPE	The code for the key that was pressed.
"modifiers"	B_INT32_TYPE	A uint32 mask that identifies which modifier keys the user was holding down and which keyboard locks were on at the time of the event.
"byte"	B_INT8_TYPE	The character that's generated by the combination of the key and modifiers. The character encoding is Unicode UTF-8, which may take from 1 to 3 bytes to represent the character. There's one uint8 item in the "byte" array for each byte in the representation.

Field	Type code	Description
"raw_char"	B_INT32_TYPE	A raw code for the character that's mapped to the key; it equals the ASCII code for the character, minus the effect of the modifier keys.
"states"	B_UINT8_TYPE	A bitfield that records the state of all keys and keyboard locks at the time of the event. Although declared as **B_UINT8_TYPE**, this is actually an array of 16 bytes entered into the message as a single item.

For most applications, the "byte" character is sufficient to distinguish one sort of user action on the keyboard from another. It reflects both the key that was pressed and the effect that the modifiers have on the resulting character. For example, if the Shift key is down when the user presses the *A* key, or if Caps Lock is on, the "byte" produced will be uppercase "A" rather than lowercase "a". If the Control key is down, it will be the B_HOME character. Appendix B discusses the mapping of keys to characters in greater detail.

Although the character is recorded as a UTF-8 array in the B_KEY_DOWN message, it's translated to the encoding of the BView's current font when passed to the KeyDown() function.

The "modifiers" mask explicitly identifies which modifier keys the user is holding down and which keyboard locks are on at the time of the event. The mask is formed from the following constants, which are explained under "Modifier Keys" in Appendix B.

B_SHIFT_KEY	B_COMMAND_KEY	B_SCROLL_LOCK
B_LEFT_SHIFT_KEY	B_LEFT_COMMAND_KEY	B_CAPS_LOCK
B_RIGHT_SHIFT_KEY	B_RIGHT_COMMAND_KEY	B_NUM_LOCK
B_OPTION_KEY	B_CONTROL_KEY	B_MENU_KEY
B_LEFT_OPTION_KEY	B_LEFT_CONTROL_KEY	
B_RIGHT_OPTION_KEY	B_RIGHT_CONTROL_KEY	

The mask is empty if no keyboard locks are on and none of the modifiers keys are being held down.

The "key" code is an arbitrarily assigned number that identifies which character key the user pressed. All keys on the keyboard, including modifier keys, have key codes (but only character keys produce key-down events). The codes for the keys on a standard keyboard are shown in the "Key Codes" section of Appendix B.

The "states" bitfield captures the state of all keys and keyboard locks at the time of the key-down event. (At other times, you can obtain the same information through the Interface Kit's `get_key_info()` function.)

Although it's declared as `B_UINT8_TYPE`, the bitfield is really an array of 16 bytes,

```
uint8 states[16];
```

with one bit standing for each key on the keyboard. For most keys, the bit records whether the key is up or down. However, the bits corresponding to keys that toggle keyboard locks record the current state of the lock. To learn how to read the "states" array, see "Key States" in Appendix B.

B_KEY_UP

This message reports that the user released a key on the keyboard. It's an exact reflection of a `B_KEY_DOWN` message. It has the same data fields as `B_KEY_DOWN` and is dispatched by calling the `KeyUp()` function of the BWindow's focus view. In most cases this will be the same BView that got the `B_KEY_DOWN` message, but not always. See "Handling Keyboard Actions" under "Responding to the User" in Chapter 4 for more detailed information on how both keyboard messages are dispatched.

B_MINIMIZE

This message instructs a BWindow to "minimize" itself—to remove the window from the screen so that it has only a minimal representation as an item in the application's desk bar menu—or to restore the full window to the screen. The message is produced when the user double-clicks the window tab or operates the menu item. It's dispatched by calling the BWindow's `Minimize()` function.

It contains the following data:

Field	Type code	Description
"when"	B_INT64_TYPE	When the user acted, given as the number of microseconds since 12:00:00 AM January 1, 1970.
"minimize"	B_BOOL_TYPE	A flag that's **true** if the window should be removed from the screen, and **false** if it should be restored to the screen from its minimized state.

B_MOUSE_DOWN

This message reports that the user pressed a mouse button while the cursor was over the content area of a window. It's produced only for the first button the user presses—that is, only if no other mouse buttons are down at the time. The BWindow dispatches it by calling the target BView's `MouseDown()` function.

The message contains the following information:

Field	Type code	Description
"when"	B_INT64_TYPE	When the mouse button went down, given as the number of microseconds since 12:00:00 AM January 1, 1970.
"where"	B_POINT_TYPE	Where the cursor was located when the user pressed the mouse button, expressed in the coordinate system of the target BView.
"modifiers"	B_INT32_TYPE	A mask that identifies which modifier keys were down and which keyboard locks were on when the user pressed the mouse button.
"buttons"	B_INT32_TYPE	A mask that identifies which mouse button went down.
"clicks"	B_INT32_TYPE	An integer that counts the sequence of mouse-down events for multiple clicks. It will be 1 for a single-click, 2 for the second of a double-click, 3 for the third of a triple-click, and so on.

The "modifiers" mask is the same as for key-down events and is described under "Modifier Keys" in Appendix B.

The "buttons" mask is one or more of the following constants:

```
B_PRIMARY_MOUSE_BUTTON

B_SECONDARY_MOUSE_BUTTON

B_TERTIARY_MOUSE_BUTTON
```

Because a mouse-down event is reported only for the first button that goes down, the mask will usually contain just one constant.

The "clicks" integer counts clicks. It's incremented each time the user presses the mouse button within a specified interval of the previous mouse-down event, and is reset to 1 if the event falls outside that interval. The interval is a user preference that can be set with the Mouse preferences application.

Note that the only test for a multiple-click is one of timing between mouse-down events. There is no position test—whether the cursor is still in the vicinity of where it was at the time of the previous event. It's left to applications to impose such a test where appropriate.

B_MOUSE_MOVED

This message is produced when the user moves the cursor into, within, or out of a window. Each message captures a small portion of that movement. Messages aren't produced if the cursor isn't over a window or isn't moving. The BWindow dispatches each message by calling the `MouseMoved()` function of every BView the cursor touched in its path from its last reported location.

The message contains the following data fields:

Field	Type code	Description
"when"	B_INT64_TYPE	When the event occurred, given as the number of microseconds since 12:00:00 AM January 1, 1970.
"where"	B_POINT_TYPE	The new location of the cursor, where it has moved to, expressed in window coordinates.
"buttons"	B_INT32_TYPE	Which mouse buttons, if any, are down.

The "buttons" mask is formed from one or more of the following constants:

B_PRIMARY_MOUSE_BUTTON

B_SECONDARY_MOUSE_BUTTON

B_TERTIARY_MOUSE_BUTTON

If no buttons are down, the mask is 0.

B_MOUSE_UP

This message reports that the user released a mouse button. It's produced only for the last button the user releases—that is, only if no other mouse button remains down. The BWindow does not dispatch this message. However, you can look at it from a filter function or, indirectly, by calling BView's `GetMouse()`.

The message contains the following data fields:

Field	Type code	Description
"when"	B_INT64_TYPE	When the mouse button went up again, given as the number of microseconds since 12:00:00 AM January 1, 1970.
"where"	B_POINT_TYPE	Where the cursor was located when the user released the mouse button, expressed in the coordinate system of the target BView.
"modifiers"	B_INT32_TYPE	A mask that identifies which of the modifier keys were down and which keyboard locks were in effect when the user released the mouse button.

The "modifiers" mask is the same as for key-down events and is described under "Modifier Keys" in Appendix B.

B_PULSE

This message serves as a simple timing mechanism. It's posted at regularly spaced intervals and is dispatched by calling the `Pulse()` function of every BView that wants to participate.

The message typically lacks any data fields, but may contain this one:

Field	Type code	Description
"when"	B_INT64_TYPE	When the event occurred, given as the number of microseconds since 12:00:00 AM January 1, 1970.

B_QUIT_REQUESTED

This message is interpreted by a BWindow object as a request to close the window. It's dispatched by calling `QuitRequested()`, which is generally implemented by classes derived from BWindow.

When the Application Server produces the message (for example, when the user clicks the window's close button), it adds the following data field:

Field	Type code	Description
"when"	B_INT64_TYPE	When the event occurred, given as the number of microseconds since 12:00:00 AM January 1, 1970.

However, this information is not crucial to the interpretation of the event. You don't need to add it to B_QUIT_REQUESTED messages that are posted in application code.

B_SCREEN_CHANGED

This message reports that the screen configuration has changed. The BWindow dispatches it by calling its own `ScreenChanged()` function.

The message contains these data fields:

Field	Type code	Description
"when"	B_INT64_TYPE	When the screen changed, given as the number of microseconds since 12:00:00 AM January 1, 1970.
"frame"	B_RECT_TYPE	A rectangle that gives the dimensions of the pixel grid the screen displays.
"mode"	B_INT32_TYPE	The color space of the screen—currently **B_COLOR_8_BIT** or **B_RGB_32_BIT**.

B_VALUE_CHANGED

This message reports that the Application Server changed a value associated with a scroll bar—something that will happen repeatedly as the user drags the scroll knob and presses the scroll buttons. The BWindow dispatches it by calling the BScrollBar object's `ValueChanged()` function.

The message has these data fields:

Field	Type code	Description
"when"	B_INT64_TYPE	When the value changed, given as the number of microseconds since 12:00:00 AM January 1, 1970.
"value"	B_INT32_TYPE	The new value of the object. For a horizontal scroll bar, this is the coordinate value that should be at the left side of the target view's bounds rectangle. For a vertical scroll bar, it's the value that should be at the top of the target's bounds rectangle.

B_VIEW_MOVED

This message reports that a view moved within its parent's coordinate system. Repeated messages may be produced if the view is moving because its parent is being resized as a consequence of the user resizing the window. The BWindow dispatches each message by calling its `FrameMoved()` function.

The message contains the following data:

Field	Type code	Description
"when"	B_INT64_TYPE	When the view moved, given as the number of microseconds since 12:00:00 AM January 1, 1970.
"where"	B_POINT_TYPE	The new location of the left top corner of the view's frame rectangle, expressed in the coordinate system of its parent.

A BView receives B_VIEW_MOVED notifications only if it asks for them with the B_FRAME_EVENTS flag.

B_VIEW_RESIZED

This message reports that a view has been resized. Repeated messages are produced if the resizing is an automatic consequence of the window being resized. The BWindow dispatches each one by calling its `FrameResized()` function.

The message holds the following data:

Field	Type code	Description
"when"	B_INT64_TYPE	When the view was resized, given as the number of microseconds since 12:00:00 AM January 1, 1970.
"width"	B_INT32_TYPE	The new width of the view's frame rectangle.

Field	Type code	Description
"height"	B_INT32_TYPE	The new height of the view's frame rectangle.
"where"	B_POINT_TYPE	The new location of the left top corner of the view's frame rectangle, expressed in the coordinate system of its parent. (The message has a "where" field only if resizing the view also served to move it. The new location of the view would first be reported in a **B_VIEW_MOVED** BMessage.)

A BView receives **B_VIEW_RESIZED** notifications only if it asks for them with the **B_FRAME_EVENTS** flag.

B_WINDOW_ACTIVATED

This message reports that the window has become the active window or has relinquished that status. The BWindow dispatches the message by calling its WindowActivated() function, which notifies every BView with a similar function call.

The message contains two data fields:

Field	Type code	Description
"when"	B_INT64_TYPE	When the window's status changed, given as the number of microseconds since 12:00:00 AM January 1, 1970.
"active"	B_BOOL_TYPE	A flag that records the new status of the window. It's **true** if the window has become the active window, and **false** if it is giving up that status.

B_WINDOW_MOVED

This message reports that the window has been moved in the screen coordinate system. Repeated messages are generated when the user drags a window. The BWindow dispatches each one by calling its WindowMoved() function.

The message has the following fields:

Field	Type code	Description
"when"	B_INT64_TYPE	When the window moved, given as the number of microseconds since 12:00:00 AM January 1, 1970.
"where"	B_POINT_TYPE	The new location of the left top corner of the window's content area, expressed in screen coordinates.

B_WINDOW_RESIZED

This message reports that the window has been resized. It's generated repeatedly as the user moves a window border. The BWindow dispatches each message by calling WindowResized().

The message holds these data fields:

Field	Type code	Description
"when"	B_INT64_TYPE	When the window was resized, given as the number of microseconds since 12:00:00 AM January 1, 1970.
"width"	B_INT32_TYPE	The new width of the window's content area.
"height"	B_INT32_TYPE	The new height of the window's content area.

B_WORKSPACE_ACTIVATED

This message reports that the active workspace has changed. It's delivered to all BWindow objects associated with the workspace that was previously active and with the one just activated. Each BWindow dispatches the message by calling its own WorkspaceActivated() function.

The message contains the following data:

Field	Type code	Description
"when"	B_INT64_TYPE	When the workspace was activated or deactivated, given as the number of microseconds since 12:00:00 AM January 1, 1970.
"workspace"	B_INT32_TYPE	An index to the workspace that's the subject of the message.
"active"	B_BOOL_TYPE	A flag that records the new status of the workspace—**true** if it has become the active workspace, and **false** if it has ceased being the active workspace.

B_WORKSPACES_CHANGED

This message informs a BWindow object that the set of workspaces with which it is associated has changed. The BWindow dispatches the message by calling its own WorkspacesChanged() function.

The message has three data fields:

Field	Type code	Description
"when"	B_INT64_TYPE	When the set of workspaces associated with the window changed, given as the number of microseconds since 12:00:00 AM January 1, 1970.
"old"	B_INT32_TYPE	The set of workspaces where the window could appear before the change.
"new"	B_INT32_TYPE	The set of workspaces where the window can appear after the change.

For this message, each workspace is identified by a bit in a 32-bit mask.

B_ZOOM

This message instructs the BWindow object to zoom the on-screen window to a larger size—or to return it to its normal size. The message is produced when the user operates the zoom button in the window's title tab. The BWindow dispatches it by calling `Zoom()`, declared in the BWindow class.

The message has just one data field:

Field	Type code	Description
"when"	B_INT64_TYPE	When the zoom button was clicked, given as the number of microseconds since 12:00:00 AM January 1, 1970.

Standard Messages

The operating system produces or understands a few standard messages that aren't system messages—that aren't matched to a specific hook function. They fall into several groups:

- Messages that are sent as replies, sometimes automatically, to other messages
- Messages that convey editing instructions
- Messages that act, principally, as data containers
- Messages that control a BStatusBar object
- Messages that report a change in the file system
- Messages that are part of the scripting system
- Messages from a file panel
- Messages from the Node Monitor
- Messages from a live query

Reply Messages

The following three messages are sent as replies to other messages.

B_MESSAGE_NOT_UNDERSTOOD

This message doesn't contain any data. The system sends it as a reply to a message that the receiving thread's chain of BHandlers does not recognize. See `MessageReceived()` and `ResolveSpecifier()` in the BHandler class of the Application Kit.

B_NO_REPLY

This message doesn't contain any data. It's sent as a default reply to another message when the original message is about to be deleted. The default reply is sent only if a synchronous reply is expected and none has been sent. See the `SendReply()` function in the BMessage class of the Application Kit.

B_REPLY

This constant identifies a message as being a reply to a previous message. The data in the reply depends on the circumstances and, particularly, on the original message. For replies to scripting messages, it generally has a "result" field with requested data and an "error" field with an error code reporting the success or failure of the scripted request.

Editing Messages

A handful of messages pass instructions to edit currently selected data or to alter the selection. Because BTextViews are the only kit-defined objects that know how to display editable data, they're the only ones that are set up to respond to these messages.

B_CUT, B_COPY, B_PASTE, and B_SELECT_ALL

A BWindow posts these messages to its focus view (or to itself, if none of its views is currently in focus) when the user presses the Command-x, Command-c, Command-v, and Command-a shortcuts. It puts only one data field in the message:

Field	Type code	Description
"when"	B_INT64_TYPE	When the user pressed the keyboard shortcut, given as the number of microseconds since 12:00:00 AM January 1, 1970.

BTextView objects respond to these messages. See the BTextView class in the Interface Kit for details.

Data Containers

A few constants identify messages as data containers. The system currently uses these constants to mark the containers it constructs for drag-and-drop operations.

B_ARCHIVED_OBJECT

This message constant indicates that the message is an object archive. It contains data that captures the object's state at a particular time and that can be used to reconstruct the object. Among the data fields, there are two that system functions rely on:

Field	Type code	Description
"class"	B_STRING_TYPE	An array of class names, beginning with the name of the archived object's class. This information must be present in every archive.
"add_on"	B_STRING_TYPE	The signature for an add-on executable containing code that defines the class of the archived object. This field is optional.

Note, however, that the `Archive()` functions that produce object archives don't set the `what` constant to `B_ARCHIVED_OBJECT` (or to anything at all). It's up to the caller to identify the archive message as appropriate. For example:

```
BMessage message(B_ARCHIVED_OBJECT);
someObject->Archive(&message);
```

Typically, `B_ARCHIVED_OBJECT` is used when the message might be dragged and dropped. For example, when the BDragger and BShelf classes in the Interface Kit archive an object so that a "replicant" of it can be dragged, they add the `B_ARCHIVED_OBJECT` identifier.

See the `Archive()` function and the BArchivable class in the Support Kit for more information on archiving.

B_MIME_DATA

This message constant indicates that all the data in the message is identified by MIME type names. The type code of every data field is `B_MIME_TYPE` and the name of each field is the MIME type string.

As an example, a BTextView object puts together a `B_MIME_DATA` message for drag-and-drop operations. The message has the text itself in a field named "text/plain"; the `text_run_array` structure that describes the character formats of the text is in a field named "application/x-vnd.Be-text_run_array".

B_SIMPLE_DATA

This message is a package for a single data element. If there are multiple data fields in the message, they present the same data in various formats.

For example, when the user drags selected files and directories from a Tracker window, the Tracker packages `entry_ref` references to them in a `B_SIMPLE_DATA` message. The references are in a "refs" array with a type code of `B_REF_TYPE`. In other words, the message has the same structure as a `B_REFS_RECEIVED` message, but a different `what` constant.

BStatusBar Messages

A BStatusBar object can be controlled synchronously by calling its `Reset()` and `Update()` functions. It can also be controlled asynchronously by sending it messages corresponding to the two functions; the object calls the function when it receives the message. Each message contains fields for the arguments passed to the function.

B_RESET_STATUS_BAR

Field	Type code	Description
"label"	B_STRING_TYPE	A null-terminated string for the label displayed on the left. If this field is omitted, a **NULL** label is passed to `Reset()`.
"trailing label"	B_STRING_TYPE	A null-terminated string for the label displayed on the right. If this field is omitted, a **NULL** trailing label is passed to `Reset()`.

B_UPDATE_STATUS_BAR

Field	Type code	Description
"delta"	B_FLOAT_TYPE	An increment to add to the current value of the object. The current value determines how much of the status bar is filled with the bar color.
"text"	B_STRING_TYPE	A null-terminated string for the text displayed on the left. If this field is omitted, **NULL** is passed to `Update()` for the text.
"trailing_text"	B_STRING_TYPE	A null-terminated string for the text displayed on the right. If this field is omitted, **NULL** is passed to `Update()` for the trailing text.

Node Monitor Messages

The Node Monitor is a mechanism that lets you watch for changes to a particular file or directory (or "node"). You ask the Node Monitor to start or stop watching a given node by calling the `watch_node()` function; you can stop all monitoring through the `stop_watching()` function.

When you call `watch_node()`, you tell the Node Monitor which aspects of the node you want to track—changes to its name, to its size, its attributes, and so on. Each of these "trackable" elements corresponds to a particular type of message (identified by the message's "opcode" field) that's sent back to your application when that element actually changes (when the file is renamed, changes size, gains an attribute, and so on).

All BMessage notifications sent by the Node Monitor look like this:

- The `what` value is always B_NODE_MONITOR.
- The field named "opcode" is an `int32` constant that tells you what happened.
- Additional fields give you information (device, node, name, and so on) about the node (or volume) that it happened to.

There are seven "opcode" constants, as described in separate sections, below. For the full story on the Node Monitor, see "The Node Monitor" in Chapter 3, *The Storage Kit*.

B_ENTRY_CREATED

Field	Type code	Description
"opcode"	B_INT32_TYPE	B_ENTRY_CREATED indicates that a new entry was created.
"name"	B_STRING_TYPE	The name of the new entry.
"directory"	B_INT64_TYPE	The ino_t (node) number for the directory in which the entry was created.
"device"	B_INT32_TYPE	The dev_t number of the device on which the new entry resides.
"node"	B_INT64_TYPE	The ino_t number of the new entry itself. (More accurately, it identifies the node that corresponds to the entry.)

B_ENTRY_REMOVED

Field	Type code	Description
"opcode"	B_INT32_TYPE	B_ENTRY_REMOVED indicates that an entry was removed.
"directory"	B_INT64_TYPE	The ino_t (node) number of the directory from which the entry was removed.
"device"	B_INT32_TYPE	The dev_t number of the device that the removed node used to live on.
"node"	B_INT64_TYPE	The ino_t number of the node that was removed.

B_ENTRY_MOVED

Field	Type code	Description
"opcode"	B_INT32_TYPE	B_ENTRY_MOVED indicates that an existing entry moved from one directory to another.
"name"	B_STRING_TYPE	The name of the entry that moved.
"from directory"	B_INT64_TYPE	The ino_t (node) number of the directory that the node was removed from.
"to directory"	B_INT64_TYPE	The ino_t (node) number of the directory that the node was added to.
"device"	B_INT32_TYPE	The dev_t number of the device that the moved node entry lives on. (You can't move a file between devices, so this value will be apply to the file's old and new locations.)
"node"	B_INT64_TYPE	The ino_t number of the node that was removed.

B_STAT_CHANGED

Field	Type code	Description
"opcode"	B_INT32_TYPE	B_STAT_CHANGED indicates that some statistic of a node (as recorded in its **stat** structure) changed.
"node"	B_INT64_TYPE	The **ino_t** number of the node.
"device"	B_INT32_TYPE	The **dev_t** number of the node's device.

B_ATTR_CHANGED

Field	Type code	Description
"opcode"	B_INT32_TYPE	B_ATTR_CHANGED indicates that some attribute of a node changed.
"node"	B_INT64_TYPE	The **ino_t** number of the node.
"device"	B_INT32_TYPE	The **dev_t** number of the node's device.

B_DEVICE_MOUNTED

Field	Type code	Description
"opcode"	B_INT32_TYPE	B_DEVICE_MOUNTED indicates that a new device (or file system volume) has been mounted.
"new device"	B_INT32_TYPE	The **dev_t** number of the newly-mounted device.
"device"	B_INT32_TYPE	The **dev_t** number of the device that holds the directory of the new device's mount point.
"directory"	B_INT64_TYPE	The **ino_t** (node) number of the directory that acts as the new device's mount point.

B_DEVICE_UNMOUNTED

Field	Type code	Description
"opcode"	B_INT32_TYPE	B_DEVICE_UNMOUNTED indicates that a device has been unmounted.
"new device"	B_INT32_TYPE	The **dev_t** number of the unmounted device.

Live Query Messages

As explained in the BQuery section of the Storage Kit chapter, the query mechanism lets you ask for the set of files that pass certain criteria (or "predicate"). The initial (or "static") winners are retrieved by your application through iterated (synchronous) function calls to BQuery's `GetNextEntry()` function (or its siblings, `GetNextDirent()` and `GetNextRef()`). If you make a "live" query, the mechanism continues to monitor the file system, sending you messages to let you know when a file is admitted into the winner's circle, and when a file drops out.

Except for the `what` field, the form of the BMessage notifications sent from a live query are identical to those from the Node Monitor:

- The `what` value is always `B_QUERY_UPDATE`.
- The field named "opcode" is an `int32` constant that tells you what happened.
- Additional fields give you information (device, node, name, and so on) about the node (or volume) that it happened to.

Live queries messages only use two "opcode" values: `B_ENTRY_CREATED` and `B_ENTRY_REMOVED`. The former indicates that an entry now passes the predicate; the latter tells you that an entry no longer does. For the rest of these messages' fields, see their descriptions in the Node Monitor section, immediately above.

File Panel Messages

The file panel produces three messages: `B_REFS_RECEIVED`, `B_SAVE_REQUESTED`, and `B_CANCEL`. The first of these was discussed under "Application Messages" above. It's produced when the user picks files to open from the panel. The other two messages are described below.

B_SAVE_REQUESTED

The file panel produces this message when the user asks the application to save a document. It has two data fields:

Field	Type code	Description
"directory"	B_REF_TYPE	An `entry_ref` referring to the directory where the document should be saved.
"name"	B_STRING_TYPE	The file name under which the document should be saved.

B_CANCEL

A cancel notification is sent *whenever* a file panel is hidden. This includes the Cancel button being clicked, the panel being closed, and the panel being hidden after an open or a save.

Field	Type code	Description
"old_what"	B_INT32_TYPE	The "previous" `what` value. This is only useful (and dependable) if you supplied the BFilePanel with your own BMessage: The `what` from your message is moved to the "old_what" field. If you didn't supply a BMessage, you should ignore this field (it could contain garbage).
"source"	B_POINTER_TYPE	A pointer to the BFilePanel object.

See the BFilePanel class in Chapter 3 for more information.

Scripting Messages

The scripting system defines four generic messages that can operate on the specific properties of an object and one meta-message that queries an object about the messages it can handle. See "Scripting" in Chapter 2 for a full explanation.

B_SET_PROPERTY, B_GET_PROPERTY, B_CREATE_PROPERTY, and B_DELETE_PROPERTY

These messages—as their names state—target a particular property under the control of the target handler. They have the following data fields:

Field	Type code	Description
"specifiers"	B_MESSAGE_TYPE	An array of one or more BMessages that specify the targeted property. See **AddSpecifier()** in the BMessage class of the Application Kit for details on the contents of a specifier.
"data"	*variable*	For **B_SET_PROPERTY** messages only, the data that should be set. The data type depends on the targeted property.

A class can choose to respond to these messages, in any combination, for any set of self-declared properties.

B_GET_SUPPORTED_SUITES

This message requests the names of all message suites that the receiver supports. It doesn't contain any data, but the message that's sent in reply has one field:

Field	Type code	Description
"suites"	B_STRING_TYPE	An array of suite names.

A suite is a named set of messages and specifiers. A BHandler supports the suite if it can respond to the messages and resolve the specifiers.

Interapplication Messages

The messages that a user drags and drops on a view might have their source in any application, including applications (and objects) that come with the Be operating system. Currently, there are three sources for public, published messages that the user might drop on your application:

- The Tracker puts together **B_SIMPLE_DATA** messages with references to files and directories. See "**B_SIMPLE_DATA**" on page 865.

- The BTextView object puts text in B_MIME_DATA messages. See "**B_MIME_DATA**" on page 865.

- The BDragger and BShelf classes put archived BViews in B_ARCHIVED_OBJECT messages. See "**B_ARCHIVED_OBJECT**" on page 864.

APPENDIX B

Keyboard Information

Applications find out what the user is doing on the keyboard through messages reporting key-down events. An application can usually determine what the user's intent was in pressing a key by looking at the character recorded in the message. But, as discussed under "B_KEY_DOWN" in the *Message Protocols* appendix, the message carries other keyboard information in addition to the character: the key the user pressed, the modifiers that were in effect at the time, and the current state of all keys on the keyboard.

Some of this information can be obtained in the absence of key-down messages through two global functions:

- modifiers() returns the current modifier states
- get_key_info() reports the current state of all the keys, modifiers, and locks

This section discusses the kinds of information that you can get about the keyboard through interface messages and these functions.

Key Codes

To talk about the keys on the keyboard, it's necessary first to have a standard way of identifying them. For this purpose, each key is arbitrarily assigned a numerical code.

The illustrations on the next few pages show the key identifiers for typical keyboards. The codes for the main part of a standard 101-key keyboard are shown in the following figure. Other keyboards differ primarily in having additional keys in the bottom row. These differences are illustrated the next two figures. The codes for the numerical keypad and for the keys between it and the main keyboard are shown in the fourth and fifth figures.

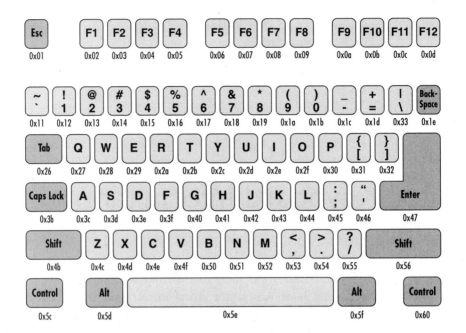

Different keyboards locate keys in slightly different positions. The function keys may be to the left of the main keyboard, for example, rather than along the top. The backslash key (0x33) shows up in various places—sometimes above the Enter key, sometimes next to Shift, and sometimes in the top row (as shown here). No matter where these keys are located, they have the codes indicated in the illustration above.

Some keyboards have additional keys, mainly in the bottom row. The keys at the bottom of a Microsoft natural keyboard are coded as follows:

The keys on the bottom row of a 105-key extended keyboard for the Macintosh have these codes:

The keys on the right of the keyboard are assigned the following codes:

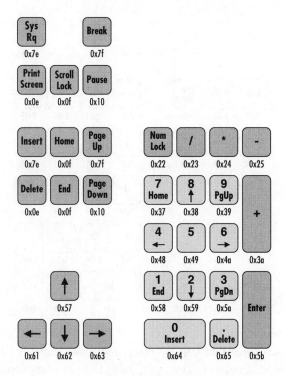

Some of the keys on a Macintosh keyboard have different labels from those shown above, but they have the same key codes. The Macintosh also adds a Power key and an "=" key on the keypad, as shown in the figure on the next page.

The "Euro" key on some European keyboards is coded 0x69.

The BMessage that reports a key-down event contains an field named "key" for the code of the key that was pressed.

Kinds of Keys

Keys on the keyboard can be distinguished by the way they behave and by the kinds of information they provide. A principal distinction is between *character keys* and *modifier keys*:

- *Character keys* are mapped to particular characters; when pressed and released they generate keyboard events (and B_KEY_DOWN and B_KEY_UP messages). Keys not mapped to characters don't generate events.

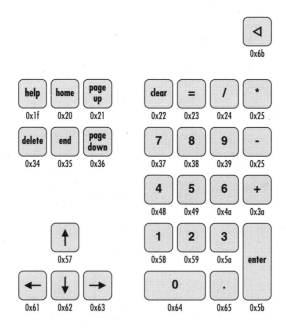

- *Modifier keys* set states that can be discerned independently of keyboard events (through the `modifiers()` and `get_key_info()` functions). Some modifier keys—like Caps Lock and Num Lock—toggle in and out of a locked modifier state. Others—like Shift and Control—set the state only while the key is being held down.

If a key doesn't fall into one of these two categories, there's nothing for it to do; it has no role to play in the interface. For most keys, the categories are mutually exclusive. Modifier keys are typically not mapped to characters, and character keys don't set modifier states. However, the Scroll Lock key is an exception. It both sets a modifier state and generates a character.

Keys can be distinguished on two other grounds as well:

- *Repeating keys* produce a continuous series of key-down events, as long as the user holds the key down and doesn't press another key. After the initial event, there's a slight delay before the key begins repeating, but then events are generated in rapid succession. Each event is reported in a separate `B_KEY_DOWN` message.

All keys are repeating keys except for Pause, Break, and the three that set locks (Caps Lock, Num Lock, and Scroll Lock). Even modifier keys like Shift and Control would repeat if they were mapped to characters.

- *Dead keys* are keys that don't produce characters until the user strikes another key (or the key repeats). If the key the user strikes after the dead key belongs to a particular set, the two keys together produce one character (one key-down event). If not, each produces a separate character. The key-down event for the dead key is delayed until it can be determined whether it will be combined with another key to produce just one event.

Dead keys are dead only when certain prescribed modifiers (by default, just the Option key) are held down. They're most appropriate for situations where the user can imagine a character being composed of two distinguishable parts—such as "a" and "e" combining to form "æ".

The system permits up to five dead keys. By default, they're reserved for combining diacritical marks with other characters. The diacritical marks are the acute (ˊ) and grave (ˋ) accents, dieresis (¨), circumflex (ˆ), and tilde (˜).

The *system key map* determines the role that each key plays—whether it's a character key or a modifier key, which modifier states it sets, which characters it produces, whether it's dead or not, how it combines with other keys, and so on. The map is shared by all applications.

Users can modify the key map with the Keymap utility. Applications can look at it by calling the `get_key_map()` global function. See that function in Chapter 4, *The Interface Kit*, for details on the structure of the map. The discussion here assumes the default key map that comes with the computer.

Modifier Keys

The role of a modifier key is to set a temporary, modal state. There are eight modifier states—eight different kinds of modifier key—defined functionally. Three of them affect the character that's reported in a key-down event:

- The *Shift key* maps alphabetic keys to the uppercase version of the character, and other keys to alternative symbols.

- The *Control key* maps alphabetic keys to Control characters—those with character values below 0x20.

- The *Option key* maps keys to alternative characters, typically characters in an extended set—those with values above 0x7f.

Two modifier keys permit users to give the application instructions from the keyboard:

- When the *Command key* is held down, the character keys perform keyboard shortcuts.

- The *Menu key* initiates keyboard navigation of menus. Command-Esc accomplishes the same thing.

Three modifiers toggle in and out of locked states:

- The *Caps Lock* key reverses the effect of the Shift key for alphabetic characters. With Caps Lock on, the uppercase version of the character is produced without the Shift key, and the lowercase version with the Shift key.

- The *Num Lock* key similarly reverses the effect of the Shift key for keys on the numeric keypad.

- The *Scroll Lock* key temporarily prevents the display from updating. (It's up to applications to implement this behavior.)

There are two things to note about these eight modifier states. First, since applications can read the modifiers directly from the messages that report key-down events and obtain them at other times by calling the `modifiers()` and `get_key_info()` functions, they are free to interpret the modifier states in any way they desire. You're not tied to the narrow interpretation of, say, the Control key given above. Control, Option, and Shift, for example, often modify the meaning of a mouse event or are used to set other temporary modes of behavior.

Second, the set of modifier states listed above doesn't quite match the keys that are marked on a typical keyboard. A standard 101-key keyboard has left and right "Alt(ernate)" keys, but lacks those labeled "Command," "Option," or "Menu."

The key map must, therefore, bend the standard 101-key keyboard to the required modifier states. The default key map does this in three ways:

- Because the "Alt(ernate)" keys are close to the space bar and are easily accessible, the default key map assigns them the role of Command keys.

- It turns the right "Control" key into an Option key. Therefore, there's just one functional Control key (on the left) and one Option key (on the right).

- It leaves the Menu key unmapped. It relies on the Command-Esc combination as an adequate alternative for initiating keyboard navigation of menus.

The illustration below shows the modifier keys on the main keyboard, with labels that match their functional roles. Users can, of course, remap these keys with the Keymap utility. Applications can remap them by calling `set_modifier_key()`.

The extended Macintosh and Microsoft keyboards are mapped to closely match the key caps; all the modifier keys work as you'd expect:

- The keys closest to the space bar are Command modifiers.
- The keys immediately outside the Command keys are Option modifiers.
- The keys on the outside of the bottom row are Control keys.

Current modifier states are reported in a mask that can be tested against these constants:

```
B_SHIFT_KEY

B_COMMAND_KEY

B_CONTROL_KEY

B_MENU_KEY

B_OPTION_KEY

B_NUM_LOCK

B_CAPS_LOCK

B_SCROLL_LOCK
```

The ..._KEY modifiers are set if the user is holding the key down. The ..._LOCK modifiers are set only if the lock is on—regardless of whether the key that sets the lock happens to be up or down at the time.

If it's important to know which physical key the user is holding down, the one on the right or the one on the left, the mask can be more specifically tested against these constants:

```
B_LEFT_SHIFT_KEY      B_RIGHT_SHIFT_KEY

B_LEFT_CONTROL_KEY    B_RIGHT_CONTROL_KEY

B_LEFT_OPTION_KEY     B_RIGHT_OPTION_KEY

B_LEFT_COMMAND_KEY    B_RIGHT_COMMAND_KEY
```

If no keyboard locks are on and the user isn't holding a modifier key down, the modifiers mask will be 0.

The modifiers mask is returned by the modifiers() function and, along with the state of all the keys, by get_key_info(). It's also included as a "modifiers" field in every BMessage that reports a keyboard or mouse event.

Character Mapping

The key map records character values using the UTF-8 encoding of the Unicode Standard, making it possible to map keys to characters in any of the world's scripts. UTF-8 encodes 16-bit Unicode values in a variable number of bytes (from one to four).

A B_KEY_DOWN message holds the character mapped to the key the user pressed as an array of bytes named, simply, "byte". The array is passed as a string to KeyDown() along with a count of the number of bytes in the string:

> virtual void KeyDown (const char *bytes, int32 numBytes)

See "Character Encoding" in the "Responding to the User" section of the Interface Kit for a description of UTF-8 encoding and get_key_map() for an explanation of the key map.

Most keys are mapped to more than one character. The precise character that the key produces depends on which modifier keys are being held down and which lock states the keyboard is in at the time the key is pressed.

A few examples are given in the table below:

Key	No modifiers	Shift alone	Option alone	Shift & Option	Control
0x15	4	$	¢		4
0x18	7	&	¶	§	7
0x26	B_TAB	B_TAB	B_TAB	B_TAB	B_TAB
0x2e	i	I			B_TAB
0x40	g	G	©		0x07
0x43	k	K	‡		B_PAGE_UP
0x51	n	N	ñ	Ñ	0x0e
0x55	/	?	÷	¿	/
0x64	B_INSERT	0	B_INSERT	0	B_INSERT

The mapping follows some fixed rules, including these:

- If a Command key is held down, the Control keys are ignored. Command trumps Control. Otherwise, Command doesn't affect the character that's reported for the key. If only Command is held down, the character that's reported is the same as if no modifiers were down; if Command and Option are held down, the character that's reported is the same as for Option alone; and so on.

- If a Control key is held down (without a Command key), Shift, Option, and all keyboard locks are ignored. Control trumps the other modifiers (except for Command).

- Num Lock applies only to keys on the numerical keypad. While this lock is on, the effect of the Shift key is inverted. Num Lock alone yields the same character that's produced when a Shift key is down (and Num Lock is off). Num Lock plus Shift yields the same character that's produced without either Shift or the lock.

- Menu and Scroll Lock play no role in determining how keys are mapped to characters.

The default key map also follows the conventional rules for Caps Lock and Control:

- Caps Lock applies only to the 26 alphabetic keys on the main keyboard. It serves to map the key to the same character as Shift. Using Shift while the lock is on undoes the effect of the lock; the character that's reported is the same as if neither Shift nor Caps Lock applied. For example, Shift-*G* and Caps Lock-*G* both are mapped to uppercase "G", but Shift-Caps Lock-*G* is mapped to lowercase "g".

  However, if the lock doesn't affect the character, Shift plus the lock is the same as Shift alone. For example, Caps Lock-*7* produces "7" (the lock is ignored) and Shift-*7* produces "&" (Shift has an effect), so Shift-Caps Lock-*7* also produces "&" (only Shift has an effect).

- When Control is used with a key that otherwise produces an alphabetic character, the character that's reported has a value 0x40 less than the value of the uppercase version of the character (0x60 less than the lowercase version of the character). This often results in a character that is produced independently by another key. For example, Control-*I* produces the B_TAB character and Control-*L* produces B_PAGE_DOWN.

  When Control is used with a key that doesn't produce an alphabetic character, the character that's reported is the same as if no modifiers were on. For example, Control-*7* produces a "7".

Character Constants

The Interface Kit defines constants for characters that aren't normally represented by a visible symbol. This includes the usual space and backspace characters, but most invisible characters are produced by the function keys and the navigation keys located between the main keyboard and the numeric keypad. The character values associated with these keys are more or less arbitrary, so you should always use the constant in your code rather than the actual character value. Many of these characters are also produced by alphabetic keys when a Control key is held down.

The table below lists character constants defined in the kit and the keys they're associated with:

Key label	Key code	Character reported
Backspace	0x1e	B_BACKSPACE
Tab	0x26	B_TAB
Enter	0x47	B_ENTER
(space bar)	0x5e	B_SPACE
Escape	0x01	B_ESCAPE
F1 – F12	0x02 through 0x0d	B_FUNCTION_KEY
Print Screen	0x0e	B_FUNCTION_KEY
Scroll Lock	0x0f	B_FUNCTION_KEY
Pause	0x10	B_FUNCTION_KEY
System Request	0x7e	0xc8
Break	0x7f	0xca
Insert	0x1f	B_INSERT
Home	0x20	B_HOME
Page Up	0x21	B_PAGE_UP
Delete	0x34	B_DELETE
End	0x35	B_END
Page Down	0x36	B_PAGE_DOWN
(up arrow)	0x57	B_UP_ARROW
(left arrow)	0x61	B_LEFT_ARROW
(down arrow)	0x62	B_DOWN_ARROW
(right arrow)	0x63	B_RIGHT_ARROW

Several keys are mapped to the B_FUNCTION_KEY character. An application can determine which function key was pressed to produce the character by testing the key code against these constants:

B_F1_KEY	B_F6_KEY	B_F11_KEY
B_F2_KEY	B_F7_KEY	B_F12_KEY
B_F3_KEY	B_F8_KEY	B_PRINT_KEY (the "Print Screen" key)
B_F4_KEY	B_F9_KEY	B_SCROLL_KEY (the "Scroll Lock" key)
B_F5_KEY	B_F10_KEY	B_PAUSE_KEY

Note that key 0x30 (*P*) is also mapped to B_FUNCTION_KEY when the Control key is held down.

Each of the character constants listed above is a one-byte value falling in the range of values where ASCII and Unicode overlap. For convenience, the Interface Kit also defines some constants for common characters that fall outside that range. These characters have multibyte representations in UTF-8, so the constant is defined as a character string. For example:

```
#define B_UTF8_OPEN_QUOTE "\xE2\x80\x9C"
#define B_UTF8_CLOSE_QUOTE "\xE2\x80\x9D"
#define B_UTF8_COPYRIGHT "\xC2\xA9"
```

See "Character Constants" in the "Global Variables, Constants, and Defined Types" section of Chapter 4, *The Interface Kit*, for a full list of these constants.

Key States

You can look at the state of all the keys on the keyboard at a given moment in time. This information is captured and reported in two ways:

- As the "states" field in every B_KEY_DOWN message, and
- As the key_states bitfield reported by get_key_info().

In both cases, the bitfield is an array of 16 bytes,

```
uint8 states[16];
```

with one bit standing for each key on the keyboard. Bits are numbered from left to right, beginning with the first byte in the array, as illustrated below:

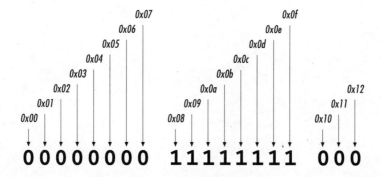

Bit numbers start with 0 and match key codes. For example, bit 0x3c corresponds to the *A* key, 0x3d to the *S* key, 0x3e to the *D* key, and so on. The first bit is 0x00, which doesn't correspond to any key. The first meaningful bit is 0x01, which corresponds to the Escape key.

When a key is down, the bit corresponding to its key code is set to 1. Otherwise, the bit is 0. However, for the three keys that toggle keyboard locks—Caps Lock (key 0x3b), Num Lock (key 0x22), and Scroll Lock (key 0x0f)—the bit is set to 1 if the lock is on and set to 0 if the lock is off, regardless of the state of the key itself.

To test the bitfield against a particular key,

- Select the byte in the `states` array that contains the bit for that key,
- Form a mask for the key that can be compared to that byte, and
- Compare the byte to the mask.

For example:

```
if ( states[keyCode>>3] & (1 << (7 - (keyCode%8))) )
    . . .
```

Here, on the left, the key code is divided by 8 to obtain an index into the `states` array. This selects the byte (the `uint8`) in the array that contains the bit for that key. On the right, the part of the key code that remains after dividing by 8 is used to calculate how far a bit needs to be shifted to the left so that it's in the same position as the bit corresponding to the key. This mask is compared to the `states` byte with the bitwise `&` operator.

Index

More Titles from O'Reilly

Developing Web Content

WebMaster in a Nutshell, Deluxe Edition

By O'Reilly & Associates, Inc.
1st Edition September 1997 (est.)
356 pages (est.), includes CD-ROM
ISBN 1-56592-305-7

The Deluxe Edition of *WebMaster in a Nutshell* is a complete library for web programmers. The main resource is the Web Developer's Library, a CD-ROM, containing the electronic text of five popular O'Reilly titles: *HTML: The Definitive Guide, 2nd Edition*; *JavaScript: The Definitive Guide, 2nd Edition*; *CGI Programming on the World Wide Web*; *Programming Perl, 2nd Edition*—the classic "camel book," written by Larry Wall (the inventor of Perl) with Tom Christiansen and Randal Schwartz; and *WebMaster in a Nutshell*. The Deluxe Edition also includes a printed copy of *WebMaster in a Nutshell*.

WebMaster in a Nutshell, Deluxe Edition, makes it easy to find the information you need with all of the convenience you'd expect from the Web. You'll have access to information webmasters and programmers use most for development—complete with global searching and a master index to all five volumes—all on a single CD-ROM. It's incredibly portable. Just slip it into your laptop case as you commute or take off on your next trip and you'll find everything at your fingertips with no books to carry.

The CD-ROM is readable on all hardware platforms. All files except Java code example files are in 8.3 file format and, therefore, are readable by older systems. A web browser that supports HTML 3.2 (such as Netscape 3.0 or Internet Explorer 3.0) is required to view the text. The browser must support Java if searching is desired.

The Web Developer's Library is also available by subscription on the World Wide Web. See http://www.ora.com/catalog/webrlw for details.

WebMaster in a Nutshell

By Stephen Spainhour & Valerie Quercia
1st Edition October 1996
374 pages, ISBN 1-56592-229-8

Web content providers and administrators have many sources for information, both in print and online. *WebMaster in a Nutshell* puts it all together in one slim volume for easy desktop access. This quick reference covers HTML, CGI, JavaScript, Perl, HTTP, and server configuration.

HTML: The Definitive Guide, 2nd Edition

By Chuck Musciano & Bill Kennedy
2nd Edition May 1997
552 pages, ISBN 1-56592-235-2

This complete guide is chock full of examples, sample code, and practical, hands-on advice to help you create truly effective web pages and master advanced features. Learn how to insert images and other multimedia elements, create useful links and searchable documents, use Netscape extensions, design great forms, and lots more. The second edition covers the most up-to-date version of the HTML standard (HTML version 3.2), Netscape 4.0 and Internet Explorer 3.0, plus all the common extensions.

JavaScript: The Definitive Guide, 2nd Edition

By David Flanagan
2nd Edition January 1997
664 pages, ISBN 1-56592-234-4

This second edition of the definitive reference guide to JavaScript, the HTML extension that gives web pages programming language capabilities, covers JavaScript as it is used in Netscape 3.0 and 2.0 and in Microsoft Internet Explorer 3.0. Learn how JavaScript really works (and when it doesn't). Use JavaScript to control web browser behavior, add dynamically created text to web pages, interact with users through HTML forms, and even control and interact with Java applets and Navigator plugins. By the author of the bestselling *Java in a Nutshell*.

CGI Programming on the World Wide Web

By Shishir Gundavaram
1st Edition March 1996
450 pages, ISBN: 1-56592-168-2

This book offers a comprehensive explanation of CGI and related techniques for people who hold on to the dream of providing their own information servers on the Web. It starts at the beginning, explaining the value of CGI and how it works, then moves swiftly into the subtle details of programming.

O'REILLY™

TO ORDER: **800-998-9938** • *order@oreilly.com* • *http://www.oreilly.com/*
OUR PRODUCTS ARE AVAILABLE AT A BOOKSTORE OR SOFTWARE STORE NEAR YOU.
FOR INFORMATION: **800-998-9938** • **707-829-0515** • *info@oreilly.com*

Developing Web Content *continued*

Information Architecture for the World Wide Web

By Louis Rosenfeld & Peter Morville
1st Edition November 1997 (est.)
200 pages (est.), ISBN 1-56592-282-4

Information Architecture for the World Wide Web is about applying the principles of architecture and library science to web site design. With this book, you learn how to design web sites and intranets that support growth, management, and ease of use. This book is for webmasters, designers, and anyone else involved in building a web site.

Learning VBScript

By Paul Lomax
1st Edition July 1997
616 pages, includes CD-ROM
ISBN 1-56592-247-6

This definitive guide shows web developers how to take full advantage of client-side scripting with the VBScript language. In addition to basic language features, it covers the Internet Explorer object model and discusses techniques for client-side scripting, like adding ActiveX controls to a web page or validating data before sending it to the server. Includes CD-ROM with over 170 code samples.

Web Client Programming with Perl

By Clinton Wong
1st Edition March 1997
228 pages, ISBN 1-56592-214-X

Web Client Programming with Perl shows you how to extend scripting skills to the Web. This book teaches you the basics of how browsers communicate with servers and how to write your own customized web clients to automate common tasks. It is intended for those who are motivated to develop software that offers a more flexible and dynamic response than a standard web browser.

Building Your Own WebSite

By Susan B. Peck & Stephen Arrants
1st Edition July 1996
514 pages, ISBN 1-56592-232-8

This is a hands-on reference for Windows® 95 and Windows NT™ users who want to host a site on the Web or on a corporate intranet. This step-by-step guide will have you creating live web pages in minutes. You'll also learn how to connect your web to information in other Windows applications, such as word processing documents and databases. The book is packed with examples and tutorials on every aspect of web management, and it includes the highly acclaimed WebSite™ 1.1 server software on CD-ROM.

Designing for the Web:
Getting Started in a New Medium

By Jennifer Niederst
with Edie Freedman
1st Edition April 1996
180 pages, ISBN 1-56592-165-8

Designing for the Web gives you the basics you need to hit the ground running. Although geared toward designers, it covers information and techniques useful to anyone who wants to put graphics online. It explains how to work with HTML documents from a designer's point of view, outlines special problems with presenting information online, and walks through incorporating images into web pages, with emphasis on resolution and improving efficienc

How to stay in touch with O'Reilly

1. Visit Our Award-Winning Web Site

http://www.oreilly.com/

★ "Top 100 Sites on the Web" —*PC Magazine*
★ "Top 5% Web sites" —*Point Communications*
★ "3-Star site" —*The McKinley Group*

Our web site contains a library of comprehensiveproduct information (including book excerpts and tables of contents), downloadable software, background articles, interviews with technology leaders, links to relevant sites, book cover art, and more. File us in your Bookmarks or Hotlist!

2. Join Our Email Mailing Lists

New Product Releases

To receive automatic email with brief descriptions of all new O'Reilly products as they are released, send email to: **listproc@online.oreilly.com**
Put the following information in the first line of your message (*not* in the Subject field):
subscribe ora-news "Your Name" of "Your Organization" (for example: subscribe oreilly-news Kris Webber of Fine Enterprises)

O'Reilly Events

If you'd also like us to send information about trade show events, special promotions, and other O'Reilly events, send email to: **listproc@online.oreilly.com**
Put the following information in the first line of your message (*not* in the Subject field):
subscribe ora-events "Your Name" of "Your Organization"

3. Get Examples from Our Books via FTP

There are two ways to access an archive of example files from our books:

Regular FTP

- ftp to:
  ftp.oreilly.com
  (login: anonymous
  password: your email address)
- Point your web browser to:
  ftp://ftp.oreilly.com/

FTPMAIL

- Send an email message to:
  ftpmail@online.oreilly.com
  (Write "help" in the message body)

4. Contact Us via Email

order@oreilly.com
To place a book or software order online. Good for North American and international customers.

subscriptions@oreilly.com
To place an order for any of our newsletters or periodicals.

books@oreilly.com
General questions about any of our books.

software@oreilly.com
For general questions and product information about our software. Check out O'Reilly Software Online at **http://software.oreilly.com/** for software and technical support information. Registered O'Reilly software users send your questions to: **website-support@oreilly.com**

cs@oreilly.com
For answers to problems regarding your order or our products.

booktech@oreilly.com
For book content technical questions or corrections.

proposals@oreilly.com
To submit new book or software proposals to our editors and product managers.

international@oreilly.com
For information about our international distributors or translation queries. For a list of our distributors outside of North America check out:
http://www.oreilly.com/www/order/country.html

O'Reilly & Associates, Inc.
101 Morris Street, Sebastopol, CA 95472 USA
TEL 707-829-0515 or 800-998-9938
  (6am to 5pm PST)
FAX 707-829-0104

Titles from O'Reilly

Please note that upcoming titles are displayed in italic.

WEB PROGRAMMING

Apache: The Definitive Guide
Building Your Own Web Conferences
Building Your Own Website
CGI Programming for the World Wide Web
Designing for the Web
HTML: The Definitive Guide, 2nd Ed.
JavaScript: The Definitive Guide, 2nd Ed.
Learning Perl
Programming Perl, 2nd Ed.
Mastering Regular Expressions
WebMaster in a Nutshell
Web Security & Commerce
Web Client Programming with Perl
World Wide Web Journal

USING THE INTERNET

Smileys
The Future Does Not Compute
The Whole Internet User's Guide & Catalog
The Whole Internet for Win 95
Using Email Effectively
Bandits on the Information Superhighway

JAVA SERIES

Exploring Java
Java AWT Reference
Java Fundamental Classes Reference
Java in a Nutshell
Java Language Reference, 2nd Edition
Java Network Programming
Java Threads
Java Virtual Machine

SOFTWARE

WebSite™ 1.1
WebSite Professional™
Building Your Own Web Conferences
WebBoard™
PolyForm™
Statisphere™

SONGLINE GUIDES

NetActivism   NetResearch
Net Law   NetSuccess
NetLearning   NetTravel
Net Lessons

SYSTEM ADMINISTRATION

Building Internet Firewalls
Computer Crime: A Crimefighter's Handbook
Computer Security Basics
DNS and BIND, 2nd Ed.
Essential System Administration, 2nd Ed.
Getting Connected. The Internet at 56K and Up
Linux Network Administrator's Guide
Managing Internet Information Services
Managing NFS and NIS
Networking Personal Computers with TCP/IP
Practical UNIX & Internet Security, 2nd Ed.
PGP: Pretty Good Privacy
sendmail, 2nd Ed.
sendmail Desktop Reference
System Performance Tuning
TCP/IP Network Administration
termcap & terminfo
Using & Managing UUCP
Volume 8: X Window System Administrator's Guide
Web Security & Commerce

UNIX

Exploring Expect
Learning VBScript
Learning GNU Emacs, 2nd Ed.
Learning the bash Shell
Learning the Korn Shell
Learning the UNIX Operating System
Learning the vi Editor
Linux in a Nutshell
Making TeX Work
Linux Multimedia Guide
Running Linux, 2nd Ed.
SCO UNIX in a Nutshell
sed & awk, 2nd Edition
Tcl/Tk Tools
UNIX in a Nutshell: System V Edition
UNIX Power Tools
Using csh & tsch
When You Can't Find Your UNIX System Administrator
Writing GNU Emacs Extensions

WEB REVIEW STUDIO SERIES

Gif Animation Studio
Shockwave Studio

WINDOWS

Dictionary of PC Hardware and Data Communications Terms
Inside the Windows 95 Registry
Inside the Windows 95 File System
Windows Annoyances
Windows NT File System Internals
Windows NT in a Nutshell

PROGRAMMING

Advanced Oracle PL/SQL Programming
Applying RCS and SCCS
C++: The Core Language
Checking C Programs with lint
DCE Security Programming
Distributing Applications Across DCE & Windows NT
Encyclopedia of Graphics File Formats, 2nd Ed.
Guide to Writing DCE Applications
lex & yacc
Managing Projects with make
Mastering Oracle Power Objects
Oracle Design: The Definitive Guide
Oracle Performance Tuning, 2nd Ed.
Oracle PL/SQL Programming
Porting UNIX Software
POSIX Programmer's Guide
POSIX.4: Programming for the Real World
Power Programming with RPC
Practical C Programming
Practical C++ Programming
Programming Python
Programming with curses
Programming with GNU Software
Pthreads Programming
Software Portability with imake, 2nd Ed.
Understanding DCE
Understanding Japanese Information Processing
UNIX Systems Programming for SVR4

BERKELEY 4.4 SOFTWARE DISTRIBUTION

4.4BSD System Manager's Manual
4.4BSD User's Reference Manual
4.4BSD User's Supplementary Documents
4.4BSD Programmer's Reference Manual
4.4BSD Programmer's Supplementary Documents
X Programming
Vol. 0: X Protocol Reference Manual
Vol. 1: Xlib Programming Manual
Vol. 2: Xlib Reference Manual
Vol. 3M: X Window System User's Guide, Motif Edition
Vol. 4M: X Toolkit Intrinsics Programming Manual, Motif Edition
Vol. 5: X Toolkit Intrinsics Reference Manual
Vol. 6A: Motif Programming Manual
Vol. 6B: Motif Reference Manual
Vol. 6C: Motif Tools
Vol. 8 : X Window System Administrator's Guide
Programmer's Supplement for Release 6
X User Tools
The X Window System in a Nutshell

CAREER & BUSINESS

Building a Successful Software Business
The Computer User's Survival Guide
Love Your Job!
Electronic Publishing on CD-ROM

TRAVEL

Travelers' Tales: Brazil
Travelers' Tales: Food
Travelers' Tales: France
Travelers' Tales: Gutsy Women
Travelers' Tales: India
Travelers' Tales: Mexico
Travelers' Tales: Paris
Travelers' Tales: San Francisco
Travelers' Tales: Spain
Travelers' Tales: Thailand
Travelers' Tales: A Woman's World

O'REILLY™

TO ORDER: **800-998-9938** • *order@oreilly.com* • *http://www.oreilly.com/*
OUR PRODUCTS ARE AVAILABLE AT A BOOKSTORE OR SOFTWARE STORE NEAR YOU.
FOR INFORMATION: **800-998-9938** • **707-829-0515** • *info@oreilly.com*

International Distributors

UK, Europe, Middle East and Northern Africa (except France, Germany, Switzerland, & Austria)

INQUIRIES
International Thomson Publishing Europe
Berkshire House
168-173 High Holborn
London WC1V 7AA, United Kingdom
Telephone: 44-171-497-1422
Fax: 44-171-497-1426
Email: itpint@itps.co.uk

ORDERS
International Thomson Publishing Services, Ltd.
Cheriton House, North Way
Andover, Hampshire SP10 5BE,
United Kingdom
Telephone: 44-264-342-832
 (UK orders)
Telephone: 44-264-342-806
 (outside UK)
Fax: 44-264-364418 (UK orders)
Fax: 44-264-342761 (outside UK)
UK & Eire orders: itpuk@itps.co.uk
International orders: itpint@itps.co.uk

France

Editions Eyrolles
61 bd Saint-Germain
75240 Paris Cedex 05
France
Fax: 33-01-44-41-11-44

FRENCH LANGUAGE BOOKS
All countries except Canada
Phone: 33-01-44-41-46-16
Email: geodif@eyrolles.com

ENGLISH LANGUAGE BOOKS
Phone: 33-01-44-41-11-87
Email: distribution@eyrolles.com

Australia

WoodsLane Pty. Ltd.
7/5 Vuko Place, Warriewood NSW 2102
P.O. Box 935, Mona Vale NSW 2103
Australia
Telephone: 61-2-9970-5111
Fax: 61-2-9970-5002
Email: info@woodslane.com.au

Germany, Switzerland, and Austria

INQUIRIES
O'Reilly Verlag
Balthasarstr. 81
D-50670 Köln
Germany
Telephone: 49-221-97-31-60-0
Fax: 49-221-97-31-60-8
Email: anfragen@oreilly.de

ORDERS
International Thomson Publishing
Königswinterer Straße 418
53227 Bonn, Germany
Telephone: 49-228-97024 0
Fax: 49-228-441342
Email: order@oreilly.de

Asia (except Japan & India)

INQUIRIES
International Thomson Publishing Asia
60 Albert Street #15-01
Albert Complex
Singapore 189969
Telephone: 65-336-6411
Fax: 65-336-7411

ORDERS
Telephone: 65-336-6411
Fax: 65-334-1617
thomson@signet.com.sg

New Zealand

WoodsLane New Zealand Ltd.
21 Cooks Street (P.O. Box 575)
Wanganui, New Zealand
Telephone: 64-6-347-6543
Fax: 64-6-345-4840
Email: info@woodslane.com.au

Japan

O'Reilly Japan, Inc.
Kiyoshige Building 2F
12-Banchi, Sanei-cho
Shinjuku-ku
Tokyo 160 Japan
Telephone: 81-3-3356-5227
Fax: 81-3-3356-5261
Email: kenji@oreilly.com

India

Computer Bookshop (India) PVT. LTD.
190 Dr. D.N. Road, Fort
Bombay 400 001
India
Telephone: 91-22-207-0989
Fax: 91-22-262-3551
Email: cbsbom@giasbm01.vsnl.net.in

The Americas

O'Reilly & Associates, Inc.
101 Morris Street
Sebastopol, CA 95472 U.S.A.
Telephone: 707-829-0515
Telephone: 800-998-9938 (U.S. & Canada)
Fax: 707-829-0104
Email: order@oreilly.com

Southern Africa

International Thomson Publishing
Southern Africa
Building 18, Constantia Park
138 Sixteenth Road
P.O. Box 2459
Halfway House, 1685 South Africa
Telephone: 27-11-805-4819
Fax: 27-11-805-3648

O'REILLY™

O'Reilly & Associates, Inc.
101 Morris Street
Sebastopol, CA 95472-9902
1-800-998-9938

Visit us online at:
http://www.ora.com/
orders@ora.com

O'REILLY WOULD LIKE TO HEAR FROM YOU

Which book did this card come from?

_____

Where did you buy this book?
- ❏ Bookstore
- ❏ Direct from O'Reilly
- ❏ Bundled with hardware/software
- ❏ Other _____
- ❏ Computer Store
- ❏ Class/seminar

What operating system do you use?
- ❏ UNIX
- ❏ Windows NT
- ❏ Other _____
- ❏ Macintosh
- ❏ PC(Windows/DOS)

What is your job description?
- ❏ System Administrator
- ❏ Network Administrator
- ❏ Web Developer
- ❏ Other _____
- ❏ Programmer
- ❏ Educator/Teacher

❏ Please send me O'Reilly's catalog, containing a complete listing of O'Reilly books and software.

Name _____ Company/Organization _____

Address _____

City _____ State _____ Zip/Postal Code _____ Country _____

Telephone _____ Internet or other email address (specify network) _____

Nineteenth century wood engraving
of a bear from the O'Reilly &
Associates Nutshell Handbook®
Using & Managing UUCP.

POST CARD

BUSINESS REPLY MAIL
FIRST CLASS MAIL   PERMIT NO. 80   SEBASTOPOL, CA

Postage will be paid by addressee

O'Reilly & Associates, Inc.
101 Morris Street
Sebastopol, CA 95472-9902